Music Dictionary

Roy Bennett

Published by the Press Syndicate of the University of Cambridge
The Pitt Building, Trumpington Street, Cambridge CB2 1RP
40 West 20th Street, New York, NY 10011-4211, USA
10 Stamford Road, Oakleigh, Melbourne 3166, Australia

First published 1990 by Longman Group UK Limited
First published 1995 by Cambridge University Press, fourth printing

Printed in Great Britain by Bell and Bain Ltd, Glasgow

A catalogue record for this book is available from the British Library

Paperback: ISBN 0 521 569303

Acknowledgements
We are grateful to Wadham Sutton for providing many of the opera and ballet synopses and the articles on opera, ballet, organ, piano and harpsichord.

We are grateful to the following for permission to reproduce photographs: Bibliothèque Municipale de Laon, page 205 left; Pierpont Morgan Library, New York, M 653, f. 1 *detail* page 205 right.

Illustrations by Jones Sewell & Associates.

A Abbreviation standing for *alto. **A** [Italian] and **à** [French] have various meanings, such as: at, by, for, in, in the manner of, on, to, with. (For *a 2*, see **A due*. For *a 3*, see under **Tre*; *a 4*, see under **Quattro*.)

Ab [German] Off. As in *Dämpfer ab*, (take the) mute off.

A B A A 'formula' used by musicians to describe the plan of a piece of music designed in *ternary (three-part) form.

A battuta See *Battuta 2.

Abbandono [Italian] Abandonment. **Abbandonamente** or **con abbandono**, with abandonment, wildly.

Abbreviations For the commonest abbreviations used by composers for words indicating expression, dynamics, and so on, see individual alphabetical entries throughout the dictionary. See also: *Repeat signs, and *Octave signs. Many musical abbreviations in the form of signs and symbols will be found in Table 3 on page 388. For notational abbreviations indicating the repetition of notes or bars, see Table 11 on pages 392–393. *Ornaments, too, are a form of musical abbreviation. For abbreviations of names of instruments most often used in scores, see Table 15 on pages 396–397.

Abduction from the Seraglio, The (*Die Entführung aus dem Serail*; in Italian: *Il seraglio*) Opera in three acts by Mozart, first produced in Vienna in 1782 (libretto by Stephanie after various models). The setting is Turkey. Belmonte (tenor) finds that his beloved, Constanze (soprano), and her maid Blonde, along with Pedrillo (who is Blonde's lover and Belmonte's servant), have been taken captive by the Pasha, Selim. Hoping to rescue them he hurries to the palace, but is impeded by Osmin (bass), the Pasha's overseer, who, knowing him to be a friend of Pedrillo's, is suspicious of him. Pedrillo (tenor) introduces Belmonte to the Pasha as an architect, and despite Osmin's protests he is made welcome. Osmin is rebuffed by Blonde (soprano), whom he is busily wooing, while Selim (spoken role) makes advances to Constanze, who rejects him; but Belmonte makes Osmin drunk and releases the ladies and Pedrillo. As they try to escape from the palace they are caught by Osmin and some slaves and taken before the Pasha. Selim discovers that Belmonte is the son of a sworn enemy, but he decides to show mercy and pardons all four of them. The opera, which is an outstanding example of the *Singspiel, has been given in an Italian translation in London and other places, including, of course, Italy.

Abegg Variations Set of variations for piano, Opus 1, composed by Schumann in 1829–30. He dedicated the music to his friend, Meta Abegg, and the opening notes of the theme spell out the letters of her name: A–B♭–E–G–G. (B♭ is called B in German; B♮ is called H.)

Abendlied [German] Evening song. **Abendmusik**, evening music.

Aber [German] But.

Abridged sonata form As the name implies, this is a shortened version of *sonata form – in fact, sonata form without a development section. Instead, after the exposition, a *link* leads back to the tonic key for the recapitulation section. This link may be a few bars long, or it may consist of just a single chord – a dominant seventh immediately followed by the recapitulation section in the tonic key. The plan of a piece or a movement in abridged sonata form is therefore:

Exposition: First subject (in the tonic key)
Bridge passage (changing key)
Second subject (in a new, but related, key)
Link – joining exposition to recapitulation
Recapitulation: First subject (in the tonic key as before)
Bridge passage – altered, to lead to:
Second subject (now *also* in the tonic key)
Coda – to round off

Because of its compactness, abridged sonata form has been used for operatic overtures (e.g. Mozart: Overture to *The Marriage of Figaro*; Beethoven: 'Prometheus' Overture; Rossini: Overture to *The Thievish Magpie*), and for slow movements of works such as sonatas, symphonies, string quartets, and so on, where, due to the speed of the music, a full sonata form might take too long to unfold. (Abridged sonata form is also sometimes called 'modified sonata form'.)

Absolute music (abstract music) Instrumental or orchestral music that is composed to be listened to for its own sake, purely as music – i.e. the music is not based in any way upon any background story or *programme*, is not illustrative in any way, and is not intended to conjure up any visual images in the mind or imagination of the listener. [See: *Programme music]

Absolute pitch The gift, or acquired ability, of immediately recognizing and naming the pitch of any note sounded, or of singing any note mentioned by name without any help being given. On the other hand, **relative pitch** means that a note is recognized and named or produced by working out its interval or pitch-distance from another note which is heard.

Abstract music The same as *Absolute music.

Academic Festival Overture A concert overture, Opus 80, by Brahms. It was composed in 1880 after he had received from the University of Breslau an honorary degree of Doctor of Philosophy, and it was first performed at the university the following year. The overture is based on four German student songs, and ends with a rousing presentation of *Gaudeamus igitur* (Let us rejoice therefore).

A cappella (sometimes, *alla cappella*) [Italian] A term, really meaning 'in the style of the chapel', used to describe choral music performed without instrumental accompaniment.

A capriccio [Italian] According to the caprice or fancy of the performer. [See also: *Capriccio]

Accelerando (abbrev.: **accel.**) [Italian] Accelerating; becoming gradually faster.

Accent Stress or emphasis on certain notes. This may occur naturally in the music – e.g. in $\frac{4}{4}$ time or metre, a main accent normally occurs on the first beat of a bar, with a secondary accent on the third. This is called **metrical accent**. However, there are other ways in which an effect of extra stress or emphasis may be created, such as:
(a) **dynamic accent**, sudden emphasis or extra loudness on a note in any part of a bar, usually marked with a sign such as $<$ or $>$ or with the letters *fz* (*forzato*), *sf* or *sfz* (*sforzando*), *fp* (*forte-piano*), *sfp* (*sforzando-piano*), *rf* or *rfz* (*rinforzando*) [see separate alphabetical entries for precise meanings of these];
(b) **expressive** (or **agogic**) **accent**, a lingering pressure on certain notes, especially those which form a dissonance against the accompanying harmony;
(c) **rhythmical accent**, such as occurs, for example, when a note is stressed after a rest placed on a strong beat. [See also: *Syncopation]

Accentato [Italian] Accented, stressed.

Acciaccatura See *Ornaments.

Accidentals Notation signs used during the course of a piece of music to indicate the raising or lowering of the pitch of a note, and also to cancel any such alteration:

♯	sharp	raises the pitch of the note by one semitone
♭	flat	lowers the pitch of the note by one semitone
♮	natural	lowers a sharpened note, or raises a flattened note, by one semitone (so that, on the piano, it becomes a 'white' note)
𝄪 or ♯♯	double sharp	raises a note by two semitones (= one whole tone)
♭♭	double flat	lowers a note by two semitones (= one whole tone)

After a double sharp or a double flat, ♮♯ or ♮♭ (*or* simply ♯ or ♭) restores the pitch to that of a single sharp or flat. After a double sharp or a double flat, the sign ♮ (sometimes given as ♮♮) restores the note to its natural ('white-note') pitch.

Usually it is understood that any accidental, unless it is cancelled (contradicted), also affects all other notes of the same pitch which follow in the same bar. If an accidental appears before a note tied across the bar-line, it affects both notes joined by the tie.

Accompagnamento [Italian] Accompaniment. **Accompagnato**, accompanied. [See also under *Recitative]

Accompanied canon See under *Canon.

Accompaniment (abbrev.: **Accomp.**) The musical support or background provided for one or more principal parts in the musical texture. For example, in a piano piece, chords for the left hand supporting a melody played by the right hand. Similarly, music for solo voices or instruments may have an accompaniment for piano or for orchestra. (However, in many songs – especially *Lieder – and also sonatas, the piano part is given equal importance rather than being treated as a mere accompaniment.)

Accordion (piano accordion) A small portable reed organ, invented in Germany in 1822. The sounds are made by free reeds (thin metal tongues) being forced to vibrate by air from a bellows pulled and pushed by the player. Tunes are played with the fingers of the right hand on a piano-like keyboard, while the fingers of the left hand press buttons, called basses, which produce single bass-notes and full chords. The treble and bass registers change the timbre (or tone-quality) of the notes being played.

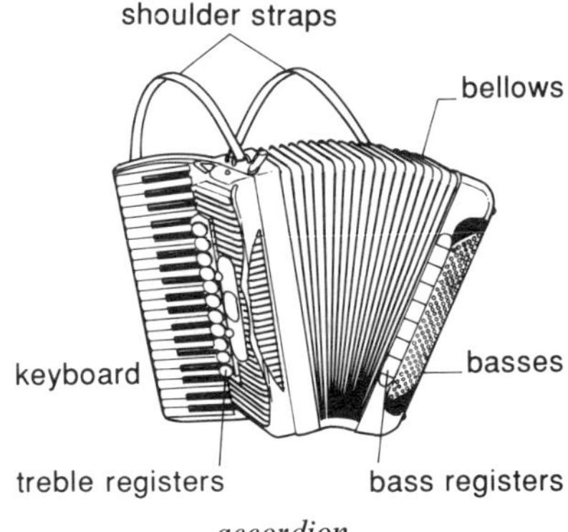

accordion

Achtel [German: 'eighth'] A quaver, eighth-note.

Acid rock See under *Rock.

Acoustics **1** The science of sound, the investigation of the nature of sound, its properties and characteristics. The four main characteristics of a sound are its pitch, volume (or intensity), timbre (tone-colour, tone-quality), and duration (the length of time for which it continues). **2** The acoustics of a concert hall, opera house, theatre, church, and so on, are the special characteristics in its design, construction, fabric, and decoration which enhance sounds and enable them to be heard with clarity.

Act tune (curtain tune, curtain music) Terms used in the 17th and 18th centuries for music played between the acts of a play while the curtain was down. [See also: *Entr'acte; *Intermezzo; *Interlude]

Adagietto [Italian] Fairly slow, but not as slow as *Adagio. Also used as a title for a shortish piece in *adagio* tempo.

Adagio [Italian: really *ad agio*, 'at ease'] Slow and leisurely. Also used as a title for a slow piece or movement – for example, Barber's **Adagio for Strings*.

Adagio for Strings A piece for string orchestra, Opus 11, by the American composer, Samuel Barber. It is his own arrangement of the slow movement from his String Quartet, composed in 1936.

Adagissimo [Italian] Very slow.

Added sixth chord A *chord consisting of a triad (made up of root, 3rd, and 5th) with the 6th added.

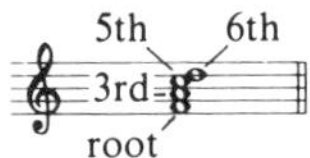

Additional accompaniment Parts for extra instruments in addition to those originally included in the composer's score (for example, Mozart's arrangement of Handel's **Messiah*).

À demi-voix [French] With half the power of the voice.

Adieux, Les Title by which Beethoven's Piano Sonata No. 26 in E flat (Op. 81a; 1809–10) is usually known. Beethoven originally entitled the three movements *Das Lebewohl*, *Abwesenheit*, and *Wiedersehen* (Farewell, Absence, and Return), and dedicated the music to Archduke Rudolph of Austria who left Vienna for nine months during the French occupation. Beethoven's publisher, however, decided to change the titles into French: *Les Adieux, L'Absence, et Le Retour*.

Ad libitum (abbrev.: **ad lib.**) [Latin: 'at will'] An indication giving the performer the freedom to vary from the strict rhythm or tempo; to include or omit (sometimes repeat) a note or a passage of music so marked; to improvise, or add ornamentation; to include a *cadenza at the moment indicated; to include or omit at will the music for a voice or instrument whose part is so marked.

A due (*a 2*) [Italian: 'in twos', or 'by twos'] This term has two (opposite) meanings. **1** For two instruments whose music is written on the same stave in a score (e.g. oboes I and II, trumpets I and II, etc.) *a due* or *a 2* (or, in German scores, *zu 2*) means that both instruments are to play the same note(s) in unison (whereas *1* or *Solo* indicates that only the first instrument plays). **2** In choral music or orchestral string music (*divisi*) *a 2* is (less frequently) used to mean that voices or instruments in that section should divide into two groups, taking one note each.

Aeolian mode See *Church modes.

Aerophone A term used to describe any musical instrument whose sound is principally produced by the movement and vibration of air. The main group of aerophones includes woodwind and brass instruments. [See also: *Idiophone; *Membranophone; *Chordophone; *Electrophone]

Affanato [Italian] Breathless; agitated; hurried and excited.

Affections (Doctrine of Affections) A theory maintained during the Baroque period, especially in Germany, that different 'affections' (moods, feelings, emotions) can be expressed through different kinds of music. Simple examples are: sorrow expressed through slowish music in a minor key; joy through swifter, more lilting music in a major key. It was held that a single 'affection' [German: *Affekt*] should persist throughout an entire piece or movement.

Affetto [Italian] Affection, tenderness. **Affettuoso**, affectionate, with warmth and tenderness. **Affettuosamente**, affectionately.

Affrettando [Italian] Hurrying, hastening. **Affrettato**, hurried.

Agevole [Italian] Lightly.

Agilità [Italian]; **Agilité** [French] Agility, nimbleness.

Agitato [Italian]; **Agité** [French] Agitated, excited. **Agitatamente** [Italian], agitatedly.

Agnus Dei See *Mass.

Agrémens; **Agréments** [French] Ornaments, grace notes.

Aida Opera in four acts by Verdi, first produced in Cairo in 1871 (libretto by Ghislanzoni based on the French of du Locle). Contrary to popular belief this work was not written for the opening of either the Suez Canal or the Cairo Opera House. The action takes place in ancient Egypt. Radamès, an army captain (tenor), is in love with Aida (soprano), a slave to the Pharaoh's daughter, Amneris. He is made a general, given command of the Egyptian armies, and departs to lead them against the Ethiopians. But Amneris (mezzo-soprano) is also in love with Radamès, and suspecting that Aida may be a rival, she tricks her into revealing the fact and swears vengeance. At length Radamès returns victorious with, among his captives, Amonasro, the Ethiopian king (baritone). Aida recognizes Amonasro as her father, but he swears her to secrecy, convinces his captors that the king is dead, and secures the release of his followers. Amonasro is held to ransom and the Pharaoh gives Radamès Amneris's hand in betrothal. Radamès, his heart set on Aida, is horrified. Urged by Amonasro, Aida tricks Radamès into telling her his military plan. But he is overheard by Amneris, arrested as a traitor and condemned to be buried alive. Amneris alone can save him, but will do so only if he abandons Aida. He refuses. Aida joins him in the tomb, and they die together while the frustrated Amneris prays for Radamès' soul.

Air **1** Song. **2** Also sometimes used to mean a simple melody or tune. **3** Occasionally used as a title for a melodious movement in a Baroque *suite which is song-like rather than dance-like. [See also: *Aria; *Ayre; *Variations]

Ais [German] The note A sharp. **Aisis**, the note A double sharp.

Al [Italian] At the; to the; as far as the. [See also: *All', alla]

Alberti bass A type of accompaniment pattern (first extensively used by the Italian composer, Domenico Alberti) often found in piano music by Classical composers such as Haydn and Mozart. It consists of chords broken up into patterns played by the left hand, keeping the music moving while outlining harmonies to support a melody in the right hand. For example:

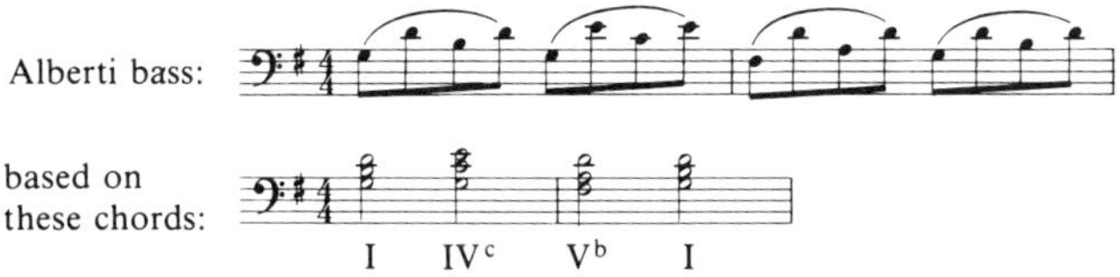

Alborada [Spanish: 'dawn'] Morning music, or morning song. The fourth piece from Ravel's **Miroirs* is called *Alborada del gracioso* (The jester's morning song) and Rimsky-Korsakov begins his **Spanish Caprice* with a lively *alborada* (repeated as the third movement). In north-western Spain, an *alborada* is often played on bagpipes or a rustic oboe accompanied by a small drum. [See also: *Aubade]

Albumblatt [German] Albumleaf – a name for a short piece originally copied by the composer into someone's autograph album. Later, the title became popular among 19th-century composers for short piano pieces.

Alceste Opera in three acts by Gluck, first produced in Vienna in 1767 (text by Calzabigi loosely based on the tragedy by Euripides). A crowd laments the illness of the Greek king Admetus (tenor). Led by his wife Alceste (soprano) and her two children, they offer sacrifices to the gods, but the Oracle reveals that, unless a willing substitute can be found, the king will die. Alceste offers herself in his place and he recovers, but when he learns what she has done he is overcome with horror. Alceste dies and Admetus follows her. Meanwhile Hercules (baritone) has returned to Greece and has learnt from Evander (tenor) of the king's death. At the gates of Hell, Admetus reminds Alceste of her duty to her children. Thanatos (baritone) reveals that only one of them is to die. He gives Alceste the choice, and, to Admetus's grief, she again offers herself. But Hercules has vowed to restore both king and queen to Greece. He appears on the scene, and he and Admetus fight the forces of the Underworld. Apollo (baritone) secures for Hercules a place among the gods, and Alceste and Admetus return together in triumph to Greece. In the preface to the manuscript score Gluck explained his much-quoted operatic 'reforms' (see under *Opera).

Alcuna; **Alcuno** [Italian] Certain, some. For example: *con alcuna licenza*, with some licence, with a certain freedom.

Aleatoric A word sometimes (misguidedly) used to mean *Aleatory.

Aleatory music ('chance-choice' music) [from Latin, *alea*: 'a dice'] 'Aleatory' is a word used since about 1950 to describe music which involves elements of chance or choice – either in the way it is composed, or performed, or both. A composer may take decisions about which notes to use and how to use them by throwing a dice. A performer may be asked to choose between several alternatives, such as selecting which notes or which sections of music to perform, perhaps also making decisions about speed, dynamics, and expression. The pitch of notes may be indicated but not their duration, or vice versa. The performer may be asked to provide some notes of his or her own choice by improvising. In some aleatory pieces the composer may provide no notes at all – merely a collection of symbols, a diagram, a drawing, or just a basic idea, to be freely and imaginatively interpreted. 'Chance-choice' elements such as these in the music mean that no two performances of the piece can be exactly alike.

Two notable composers who have explored the possibilities of aleatory music are Karlheinz Stockhausen, e.g. in **Zyklus* and *Piano Piece XI* (see under *open form), and the American composer John Cage, whose *Concert* (1957–8) may be performed as a solo, ensemble piece, symphony, aria (with soprano), or piano concerto. Each player chooses, in any order, any number of pages from his or her part. [See also: *Indeterminacy; *Graphic score; *Open form]

Al fine [Italian] To the end.

All'; **Alla** [Italian] At the, to the, in the style of, in the manner of. For example: *All' ongarese*, in Hungarian style; *Alla marcia*, in the manner of a march; *Alla zingarese*, in the style of gypsy music. [See also: *Alla breve; Alla *francese; Alla *tedesca; Alla *turca; Alla *zoppa. For *All' 8va* (short for *All' ottava*) see *Octave signs]

Alla breve [Italian] A tempo marking indicating a relatively brisk speed, with each beat as a minim – in other words, $\frac{2}{2}$ or 𝄵 (two minim beats to each bar) instead of $\frac{4}{4}$ (four crotchet beats). See, for example, the music printed under *Bourrée and under *Branle.

Allargando [Italian] Broadening – slowing down, and usually implying that the music also becomes louder and more dignified.

Allegramente [Italian] Brightly, gaily; fairly fast.

Allegretto [Italian] Fairly fast – but not as fast as *Allegro.

Allegrezza [Italian] Cheerfulness.

Allegrissimo [Italian: 'very cheerful'] Very quick. [See also: *Allegro]

Allegro [Italian] Really meaning 'lively' or 'cheerful', but used to indicate a fairly quick speed, regardless of the actual mood of the music.

Allein [German] Alone.

Alleluia [Latin form of the Hebrew *Hallelu Jah*, 'Praise ye the Lord'] The third item of the Proper of the *Mass. The Alleluia is an expression of joy and praise, and is sung immediately after the Gradual. [See also: *Jubilus]

Allemande [French for 'German', or 'German dance'] **1** The first dance movement in a Baroque keyboard *suite. Moderate in speed, and usually in $\frac{4}{4}$ time, beginning with an *anacrusis of a quaver or a semiquaver. An allemande often has an intricate musical texture, with running semiquaver figures passed from one part to another.

English composers of the 16th and 17th centuries used other spellings of allemande, such as **alman**, **almand**, **almain**, and **almayne**.

2 In the late 18th and early 19th centuries, *Allemande* was the name given to a swift, waltz-like dance in triple time (for example, Beethoven's Bagatelle Op. 119 No. 3 is marked 'à l'Allemande').

Allentando [Italian] Slowing down.

Allmählich [German] Gradually; by degrees.

All'ottava; **All'8va** See *Octave signs.

All'unisono [Italian] In unison; at the unison.

Almain; **Alman**; **Almand**; **Almayne** See *Allemande.

Al rovescio [Italian: 'back to front'] A term which may refer either to *inversion of a melody (as in the *Trio al rovescio* from Mozart's Serenade in C minor, K388) or to *retrograde motion (as in the *Menuetto al rovescio* from Haydn's Piano Sonata No. 26 or Symphony No. 47 in G).

Al segno (abbrev.: **A.S.**) [Italian: 'to the sign'] An indication, when a section of music is to be repeated, to continue only as far as the sign (usually printed as 𝄋). [See also: *Dal segno]

Also sprach Zarathustra (Thus spake Zarathustra) A lengthy symphonic poem, Opus 30, by Richard Strauss, composed in 1895–6, and based on the prose-poem of the same title by the German philosopher, Nietzsche. Strauss scores the music for very large orchestra which includes: 3 flutes and 2 piccolos, 3 oboes and cor anglais, 2 clarinets, E♭ clarinet and bass clarinet, 3 bassoons and double bassoon; 6 horns, 4 trumpets, 3 trombones and 2 bass tubas; kettle drums, bass drum, triangle, cymbals, glockenspiel, a low bell in E; 2 harps, organ, and a large string section. [See also: *Ein *Heldenleben*]

Alt **1** German for alto or contralto, or for 'old'. **2** Italian term (meaning 'high') for the notes immediately above the treble stave from G to the F above, each of which may be described as being 'in alt'. Notes of the next octave (from the next G upwards) are said to be 'in altissimo' ('very high').

Altered chord Same as Chromatic chord (see under *Chromatic).

Alternativo [Italian]; **Alternativement** [French] A term indicating that one section of a piece is to alternate with another. For example (from Bach's English Suite No. 2): *Bourreé I (alternativement)*, *Bourrée II*, means that these two dances are to be performed in 'sandwich' fashion:

Bourrée I	Bourrée II	**Bourrée I**

[See also: *Minuet and Trio form]

Altflöte [German] Alto flute.
Altissimo See *Alt 2.
Alto [Italian: 'high'] **1** The highest adult male *voice (produced in *falsetto), much used in English church music and early vocal music. **2** The lowest, unbroken, boy's voice. **3** Abbreviation for contralto, the lowest female voice. **4** [French] Viola.
Alto clef See *Clef.
Alto flute See under *Flute.
Alto Rhapsody Composition by Brahms (Op. 53; 1869) for solo contralto, chorus of male voices, and orchestra, setting words from Goethe's poem *Harzreise im Winter* (Winter journey in the Harz Mountains).
Alzati [Italian: 'lifted'] Indication, in music for bowed string instruments, that mutes should be removed (*sordini alzati*).
Amabile [Italian] Lovable, amiable. **Con amabilità**, with love; tenderly.
Amarevole [Italian] Bitterly. **Amarezza**, bitterness.
'Amen' cadence See *Cadences.
American in Paris, An A programmatic orchestral piece by George Gershwin, composed in 1928. The music is scored for a large orchestra including, in the percussion section, four Parisian taxi horns.
'American' Quartet Nickname of Dvořák's String Quartet No. 12 in F, Op. 96, composed in 1893 when he was resident in the USA. Several of the themes have characteristics of Negro melodies. There are four movements: 1 *Allegro ma non troppo* (in sonata form); 2 *Lento*; 3 *Molto vivace* (a scherzo and trio); 4 *Vivace ma non troppo* (in sonata-rondo form).
Amid Nature See **Carnival Overture*.
Amor brujo, El (Love, the magician) Ballet in one act, composed by Manuel de Falla, first produced in Madrid in 1915 (choreography by Imperio). The story concerns the gypsy girl Candélas, whose romance with the handsome Carmelo is hindered by the ghost of her former lover. There are several versions. In one, Carmelo rids Candélas of her hallucinations by impersonating the ghost; in another, Candélas's friend Lucia acts as a decoy, leaving Candélas and Carmelo free to wed. Unusually, there is a singing role for a solo soprano. The score also includes the colourful and exhilarating *Ritual Fire Dance*.
Amore [Italian]; **Amour** [French] Love, affection. In the names of old instruments (e.g. *oboe d'amore, *viola d'amore) the word indicates a sweeter tone-quality and, often, a deeper pitch than normal.
Amoroso [Italian] Loving, affectionate.
Anacrusis One or more unstressed notes appearing before the first strong beat (downbeat) of a musical phrase – particularly at the beginning of a piece or of a movement:

Chopin: Prelude Op. 28 No. 7

Mozart: *Eine kleine Nachtmusik*

Anche [French] **1** Reed. **2** Reed instrument.

Ancora [Italian] Again (same as French: *encore*). It also means 'yet' or 'still', as in **ancora forte**, still loud; **ancora più lento**, yet more slowly, slower still.

Andante [Italian: 'going'] A tempo marking indicating that the music should be 'moving along', 'at an easy walking pace', 'flowing along at a moderate speed'. Most composers tend to think of *andante* as a slowish (but not slow) pace; and so **più** (more) **andante** generally means slower than normal *andante*; whereas **meno** (less) **andante** and **andante con moto** are both generally slightly faster than *andante*. **Andante** is also used as a title for a piece or movement in a moderately slow yet flowing tempo. [See: *Andantino]

Andantino [Italian: diminutive of *andante*] Tempo marking which usually indicates a speed slightly faster than *Andante. Also used as a title for a shortish piece in *andante* tempo.

An die ferne Geliebte (To the distant beloved) *Song-cycle by Beethoven (Op. 98; 1816) consisting of six songs for voice and piano to words by A. Jeitteles.

Anfang [German] Beginning. **Anfangs**, at first. **Wie am Anfang**, as at the beginning, as at first. **Vom Anfang**, from the beginning (same meaning as the Italian term **da capo*).

Anglaise [French for 'English', or 'English dance'] A lively dance of the 17th and 18th centuries, in swift duple time. However, composers often used this title for any dance thought to be English in origin or character (e.g. a hornpipe, or a country dance).

Anima [Italian] Soul. **Con anima**, with soul (and therefore emotion). *Anima* also means the soundpost of a string instrument which connects the back and the belly and enriches the tone-quality – and therefore may be thought of as the 'soul' of the instrument.

Animando [Italian] Becoming more lively (and therefore faster). **Animato**, enlivened, lively, animated.

Animé [French] Animated, lively, brisk.

Animo [Italian] Spirit, courage, boldness. **Con animo**, with spirit, with boldness. **Animoso**, bold, spirited.

Années de pèlerinage (Years of pilgrimage) Three volumes of descriptive piano pieces by Liszt. Volume 1, entitled *Suisse* (Switzerland), 1848–54, includes *Au lac de Wallenstadt* (By the lake of Wallenstadt), *Au bord d'une source* (Beside a spring) and *Eglogue*. Volume 2, *Italie* (Italy), 1837–49, includes the three *Petrarch Sonnets* and the *Dante Sonata*. The third volume (without title), 1867–77, includes *Les jeux d'eau à la Villa d'Este* (The fountains at the Villa d'Este).

Answer See under *Fugue.

Antarctic Symphony See **Sinfonia antartica*.

Antecedent The name given to the leading voice in a *canon, or to the subject of a fugue.

Anthem A short, sacred choral piece sung during a Protestant church service (the counterpart of a *motet, but sung in English not Latin). A **full anthem** is sung by the choir throughout, usually **a cappella*. In a **verse anthem**, verses sung by one or more soloists with instrumental accompaniment alternate with sections where the whole choir joins in. Examples are: full anthem – *Sing joyfully* by Byrd, and Tallis's anthems *If ye love me* and *Heare the Voyce and Prayer*; verse anthem – Gibbons's anthems *This is the Record of John* and *Behold, Thou hast made my days*, and Purcell's *Rejoice in the Lord Alway* (also known as the *'Bell' Anthem).

Anticipation The effect of one or more notes of a chord being sounded before the rest of the chord, creating a dissonance against the preceding chord.

Antiphon A short text, usually from the Scriptures, set to a fairly simple melody with mainly one note to each syllable, and usually sung before and after a psalm or canticle in Roman Catholic church services. Some antiphons, however, are composed to be sung as separate complete pieces.

Antiphonal [From a Greek word, meaning 'counter-sound', or 'sound-against-sound'] In antiphonal singing, one choir or group of voices (perhaps situated on the left) is heard in alternation with another group (on the right) – the one answering the other (the kind of effect which nowadays might be described as 'stereophonic'). The effect of **antiphony** can also, of course, be created by alternating contrasting groups of instruments or sections of the orchestra.

Antique cymbals See under *Cymbals.

Aperto [Italian] Open. In horn music, an instruction to return to normal playing after playing stopped notes (*chiuso*) (see *Stopping, 2). In string music, an instruction to play an open note, i.e. using an open (unstopped) string.

A piacere [Italian] 'At pleasure' – indicating a passage of music to be freely performed (especially with regard to speed) according to the will or feelings of the performer. [See also: *Ad libitum]

Appalachian Spring A ballet composed by Aaron Copland in 1943–4 for the dancer and choreographer, Martha Graham. The story, which takes place in the hills of Pennsylvania during the early 19th century, tells of a group of settlers who hold a celebration in springtime around a newly-built farmhouse. The two main characters are a young farmer and the girl who shortly becomes his bride. Copland originally scored the ballet for thirteen instruments. He selected some of the music from the ballet to make a suite in eight movements, the seventh piece consisting of five variations on the well-known Shaker melody called 'Simple Gifts'. In 1945 he scored both the suite and the entire ballet score for full orchestra. [See also: **Billy the Kid*; **Rodeo*]

'Appassionata' Sonata (*Sonata appassionata*) Nickname of Beethoven's Piano Sonata No. 23 in F Minor, Op. 57, composed in 1804–5. It is in three movements: 1 *Allegro assai* (in sonata form); 2 *Andante con moto* (theme and variations, in D♭ major); 3 *Allegro ma non troppo* (in sonata form).

Appassionato [Italian] Impassioned, passionate.

Appena [Italian] Scarcely, hardly.

Appoggiatura See *Ornaments.

Apprenti sorcier, L' See *The *Sorcerer's Apprentice.*

Après-midi d'un faune, L' See **Prélude à 'L'Après-midi d'un faune'.*

Arabesque [French; German: *Arabeske*] Really referring to the florid ornamentation found in Arabic art and architecture, and so the word is used in music to describe a passage, or a whole composition, whose melody is flowing and highly decorated or includes intricate figuration. Examples include Debussy's two *Arabesques* for piano; Schumann's *Arabeske*, Op. 18, for piano; and *An Arabesk* for baritone, chorus, and orchestra by Delius.

Arab instruments See: *Daff; *Darabukka; *Kamancha; *Nāy; *Qānūn; *Rabāb; *Ṭār; *'Ūd.

Aragonesa [Spanish]; **Aragonaise** [French] Names for dances from the region of Aragon in north-eastern Spain. [See also: *Jota]

Arcato [Italian] Bowed.

'Archduke' Trio Nickname of Beethoven's Piano Trio in B flat, Op. 97, composed in 1810–11 and dedicated to Archduke Rudolph of Austria. It is the greatest of Beethoven's piano trios, and is in four movements: 1 *Allegro moderato* (in sonata form); 2 Scherzo: *Allegro*; 3 *Andante cantabile* (variations); 4 *Allegro moderato* (sonata-rondo).

Archet [French] A bow (of a string instrument).

Arch form A term used to describe the form or structure of a piece of music which is symmetrical, and so the basic plan of the music implies an arch. At its simplest, arch form is ternary: **A B A**. By extension it becomes **A B C B A**, or even **A B C D C B A**. One composer in particular who was fond of structuring compositions in arch form was Bartók (a well-known example is the fourth movement, 'Interrupted Intermezzo', of the Concerto for Orchestra).

Archi [Italian] Bows; therefore used to refer to any group of string instruments played with a bow.

Archlute [Italian: *arcileuto* or *arciliuto*] A large bass lute which had two sets of pegs, one set to tune strings to be stopped with the fingers and the other set to tune a number of independent bass strings which were unstopped (i.e. played as open strings). It was developed in the 16th century, and during the Baroque period (1600–1750) was used in solo music and also as a *continuo instrument. The term 'archlute' was also used generally to describe any bass plucked instrument with two sets of pegs (e.g. the theorbo and the chitarrone).

Arco [Italian] Bow. The term **arco**, or **col arco**, is used after a **pizzicato* passage to mean 'go back to using the bow'. [See also: *Archi]

Ardito [Italian] Bold. **Con arditezza**, with boldness.

Aria [Italian; German: *Arie*] An air, a song, a melody. Generally, the word refers to a quite lengthy and elaborate vocal solo (occasionally duet) with instrumental accompaniment, forming part of a work such as an opera, oratorio or cantata, particularly of the 17th and 18th centuries. An aria is often preceded by a *recitative. [See also: *Da capo aria; *Opera seria]

In instrumental music, *Aria* may be used as a title for a song-like piece, or a piece in a light dance style, or a theme suitable for variations.

Arie [German] *Aria.

Arietta [Italian] A short, simple aria (usually without a middle section). Sometimes also used as a title for a short, song-like instrumental piece (e.g. Grieg's *Arietta* from *Lyric Pieces*, Op. 12, for piano).

Arioso [Italian] **1** A short *aria. **2** A special type of recitative which is particularly expressive and melodious, often of an emotional or dramatic nature, and with a fully worked out accompaniment. Its style lies midway between declamatory recitative and lyrical aria which has a steady rhythm. **3** An instrumental piece in a similar style.

Arlésienne, L' (The girl from Arles) Incidental music by Bizet, composed in 1872 for Alphonse Daudet's play which is set in Provence. Bizet later arranged some of the music as an orchestral suite in four movements: Prelude, Minuet, Adagietto, and Carillon. After Bizet's death, his friend Giraud arranged a further four pieces to make a second suite: Pastorale, Intermezzo, Minuet, Farandole.

Armonica See *Musical glasses.

Arpa (plural: *arpe*) [Italian] Harp.

Arpège [French] Same as the Italian word *arpeggio.

Arpeggio [from Italian, *arpeggiare*: 'to play the harp'] The sounding of a chord in such a way that its notes are spread out one after another 'in harp fashion'. **Arpeggiando** and **arpeggiato** mean the same thing.

Arraché [French: 'torn away'] In string music, a term indicating a particularly forceful, violent *pizzicato*.

Arrangement (transcription) An adaptation or reworking of a piece for an instrument or combination of instruments other than that originally chosen by the composer. For example, a song or an orchestral piece arranged for piano solo, an organ piece arranged for brass band, and so on. An arrangement may be a more elaborate version of the original piece – or it may be a simpler version (e.g. a difficult piano piece arranged in such a way that a less able performer may play it and enjoy it).

Arrival of the Queen of Sheba, The Popular name for the lively *Sinfonia* for two oboes and strings which opens Part 3 of Handel's oratorio *Solomon*, composed in 1749.

Ars Antiqua A term meaning 'The Old Art', used to distinguish music of the late 12th and 13th centuries from music of the 14th century (called *Ars Nova). At the beginning of the Ars Antiqua period, Paris became the main centre of musical activity when the construction of Notre Dame Cathedral was begun in 1163. Of the composers connected with music there (called 'The Notre Dame School') only two are known to us by name: Léonin, who was possibly the first choir-master of the cathedral; and Pérotin, who worked there from about 1180 to 1225.

The main musical achievements of the Ars Antiqua period were the development of early polyphonic forms (*organum, the *clausula, the early *motet), and the *conductus. Also, the first use of strictly measured rhythm ('mensural music') with notes now given precise time-values in relation to each other by being based on strict rhythm patterns called 'rhythmic modes', all in triple time and in fact borrowed from poetry. Alongside these developments there was an important flowering of monophonic songs. [See: *Troubadours; *Trouvères; *Minnesinger; *Minstrels; *Cantiga; *Lauda. See also the time-chart of composers on pages 398–413]

Ars Nova [Latin: 'the new music', 'the new art'] The name given to medieval music composed during the 14th century, e.g. by such composers as the Frenchman Guillaume de Machaut (*c*1300–1377) and the blind Italian composer Francesco Landini (*c*1325–1397). Musicians then began to refer to the style of the previous century as *Ars Antiqua. By comparison, Ars Nova style was rather more polished and expressive. Rhythms became more flexible, more adventurous; and the counterpoint (or polyphony) began to weave more freely.

The main types of composition by French Ars Nova composers include the *ballade, *rondeau, *virelai, and *motet; by Italian Ars Nova composers: the *ballata, *caccia, and early *madrigal. [See also: *Hocket; *Isorhythm; *Messe de Notre Dame; The *New Music. Also, the time-chart of composers on pages 398–413]

Articulé [French]; **Articuliert** [German]; **Articolato** [Italian] Clearly; well articulated.

Art of Fugue, The (*Die Kunst der Fuge*) A work by J. S. Bach, composed *c*1745–50, consisting of a series of *fugues and four *canons, all based on a single theme (see overleaf) and ingeniously demonstrating every possible kind of imitative counterpoint and fugal device – including *augmentation, *diminution, *inversion, *stretto, *canon, *double fugue, *triple fugue, *mirror fugue. The final fugue remains incomplete; Bach planned this as a *quadruple fugue, with *B–A–C–H as one of its four subjects. Bach did not specify which instruments he intended should play *The Art of Fugue*, but several editions have been published for keyboard (harpsichord, organ or piano), string quartet, strings and woodwind, and orchestra.

A.S. Abbreviation of **Al segno.*

As [German] The note A flat. **Ases**, the note A double flat.

Assai [Italian] Very. (For example: *Allegro assai*, very quick.)

Assez [French] Enough, rather, fairly, quite. (For example: *Assez lent*, rather slow; *Assez vite*, fairly fast.) [But see also: *Assai]

A tempo [Italian: 'In time'] After a change of speed (such as *ritenuto, più lento, accelerando*) *a tempo* indicates a return to the original speed.

Athematic [from Greek, meaning 'without themes'] A term used to describe music which, rather than making use of recognizable themes or melodies, explores instead other musical ingredients such as changing textures, dynamics, 'blocks' of harmony, isolated pitches, timbres, and so on.

Atonality (atonal music) Atonality means total absence of tonality, or *key. Atonal music avoids any key or mode by making free use of the notes of the chromatic scale – considering all twelve notes to be of *equal* importance. There can therefore be no pull towards any particular tonic note – and so in atonal music there is no sense of tonality, or key, whatsoever.

Atonality is in fact the logical outcome of a trend which began during the Romantic period. Some composers (Wagner in particular) had freely used chromatic discords – bringing in notes from outside the key to 'colour' the harmonies. In time, so many chromaticisms were included, together with abrupt, adventurous modulations, that there were occasions when the listener became uncertain which key the music was in. Gradually, tonality – the major-minor key system which had ruled Western music for almost 300 years – weakened, and began to crumble. The next logical step was towards atonality.

The first composer seriously to explore the possibilities of atonality was Arnold Schoenberg; for example: in the last movement of his Second String Quartet (1908); Three Piano Pieces, Op. 11 (1909); and **Pierrot lunaire* (1912). [See also: *Expressionism; *Twelve-note technique; *Polytonality; *Pointillism]

Attacca [Italian] Attack, begin. A direction meaning 'go straight on immediately without a pause'.

Aubade [From French, *aube*: 'dawn'] Morning music, or morning song. Prokofiev, in Act 3 of his ballet *Romeo and Juliet*, included an atmospheric *Aubade* (in the original version, featuring mandolins and solo violin), and Poulenc composed an *Aubade* for piano and a chamber orchestra of eighteen instruments. [See also: *Alborada]

Auf [German] In, on, at, up, to.

Auflösungszeichen [German] The natural sign (♮).

Augmentation Lengthening the original values of the notes in a theme – usually doubling their value so that, for instance, a quaver becomes a crotchet, a crotchet becomes a minim, and so on. Music example (b), below, is (a) in augmentation:

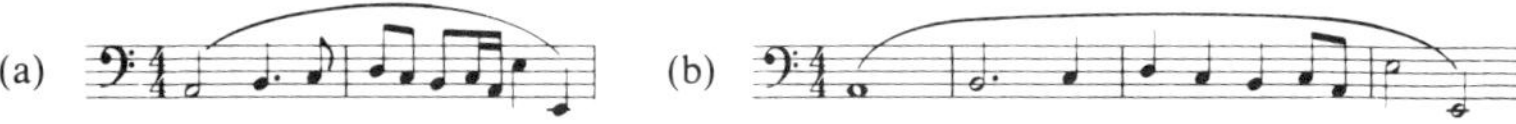

[See also: *Diminution, which is the reverse process]

Augmented interval See under *Intervals.

Augmented sixth chords These are chords built upon either the flattened supertonic (second degree) or, more frequently, the flattened submediant (sixth degree) of the scale. In either case, the chord includes the *interval of an augmented 6th from the bass. There are three varieties of augmented sixth chord, commonly referred to as Italian sixth, French sixth, German sixth.

The **Italian sixth** consists of major 3rd and augmented 6th above the bass. The **French sixth** consists of major 3rd, augmented 4th, and augmented 6th above the bass. The **German sixth** consists of major 3rd, perfect 5th, and augmented 6th above the bass. Here are each of these three types, shown in C major, and built upon the flattened submediant:

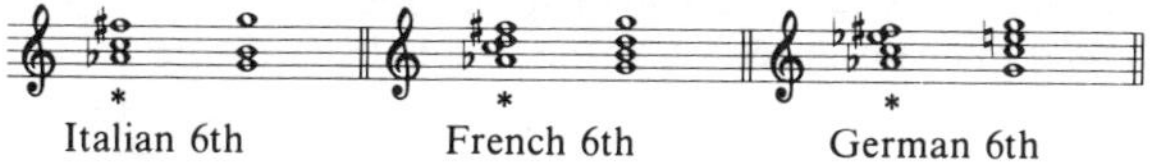

Augmented triad See *Triad.

Augmenter [French] Increase, in tone and volume.

Ausdruck [German] Expression. **Ausdrucksvoll**, expressively.

Äusserst [German] Extreme, utmost; extremely.

Auszug [German] *Arrangement.

Authentic cadence See under *Cadences.

Autoharp A type of simple, easily-played zither, which the player strums with the fingers or a plectrum. Ready-made chords are selected by pressing down damper bars. Each bar damps all the strings except those sounding the notes of its own particular chord.

Auxiliary note A kind of passing note which, rather than passing on to a new note, passes back to the note sounded before it. The auxiliary note may be a tone or a semitone above or below the 'main' note. For example:

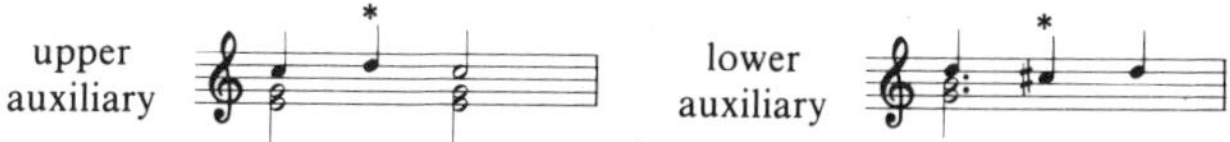

Avant garde A term (really meaning 'advance guard') applied to particularly 'modernistic' or experimental composers and also to the music they compose.

Avec [French] With.

Ayre Air, or song. During the late 16th century, an ayre was considered to be one of the three main kinds of English *madrigal (along with the madrigal 'proper' and the *ballett). Like a ballett, an ayre was usually strophic, meaning that the same music was repeated for each verse of the poem (as in a hymn).

The music of an ayre was often printed with the parts facing in three directions so that performers, seated around a table, might share the same copy. The upper voice-part was printed on the left-hand page, with the lower parts on the right. Beneath the upper part was a version of the lower parts which could be played on a lute. This meant the ayre might be performed in one of several ways – for example: (1) solo voice with lute accompaniment; (2) solo voice with other instruments (such as viols) playing the other parts; (3) with all the parts sung – with, or without, instrumental accompaniment.

The most famous composer of ayres was the English composer and lute player, John Dowland. Examples, from the many ayres he composed, are: *Awake, sweet love*; *Come again, sweet love doth now invite*; *Fine knacks for ladies*; *Flow my teares*; *Sleep, wayward thoughts*; *What if I never speed?*

During the 17th and 18th centuries, composers continued to use the word 'ayre' to mean solo song.

B **1** The German equivalent to our note B *flat*. For the note B natural (B♮) Germans use the letter H. **2** Abbreviation standing either for Bass, or for Basso.

B–A–C–H The letters of Bach's name which, according to German note-names (see the entries for *B and *H) make this four-note theme:

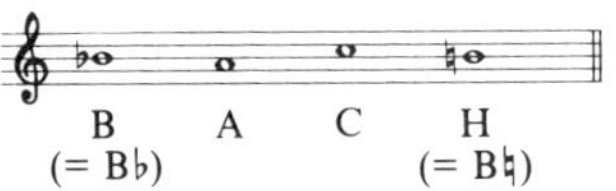

Countless composers have at times woven this theme into their music, including Bach himself (in his **Art of Fugue*).

Bachianas brasileiras Nine suite-like compositions by the Brazilian composer, Heitor Villa-Lobos, in which he attempted to combine Brazilian folk melodies and rhythms with contrapuntal aspects of the style of J. S. Bach. (Villa-Lobos's title might be translated as 'Brazilian Bach-Music'.) Of the nine compositions, for various combinations of instruments and/or voices, the most popular are No. 2 (1930) for small orchestra, ending with a vivid piece describing the journey of 'The Little Train of the Caipira' (*caipira* means 'peasant'), and No. 5 (1938–45) for solo soprano and eight cellos, in two movements, the first of which is a haunting and lyrical *vocalise.

Backing Colloquial term sometimes used to mean the accompaniment in a piece of music or to describe whatever sounds are forming a background or support to the main, more important events in the music.

Badinerie (*badinage*) [French] A lively and light-hearted or playful piece. An example is the *Badinerie* from Bach's Orchestral Suite No. 2 in B minor for flute, strings, and continuo.

Bagatelle [French, also German] A 'trifle'; a short piece, usually in light-hearted mood. Beethoven composed three sets of *Bagatellen* for piano, Opp. 33, 119, and 126. Dvořák composed a suite of five *Bagatelles* for a chamber ensemble of two violins, cello, and harmonium (composed specially to be played at the home of a friend who possessed a harmonium).

Bagpipe An ancient wind instrument. In the simplest form of bagpipe, air is blown through the blowpipe (which has a non-return valve) into the bag. The player compresses the bag with his or her arm – forcing the wind into the pipes, which have single or double reeds. The melody is played on the chanter, which has finger-holes, while the fixed-pitch dronepipe sounds a drone – a single continuous note. In Medieval times, the bagpipe was a popular instrument to accompany dancing.

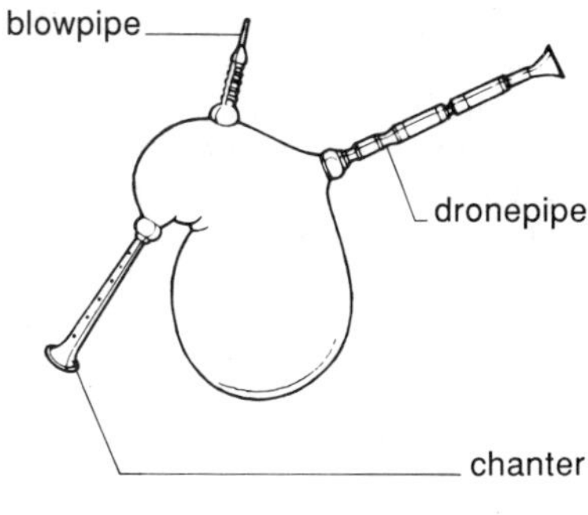

bagpipe

Baguette [French] Drumstick; *baguettes de bois*, wooden-headed drumsticks; *baguettes d'éponge*, sponge-headed drumsticks.

Baile [Spanish] Dance, dancing.

Balalaika A type of Russian guitar, made in several sizes. It has a triangular-shaped body, long neck with frets, and there are usually three strings made of gut.

Ballabile [from Italian, *ballare*: to dance] In a dancing manner; suitable for dancing.

Ballad A word which has changed in meaning over the centuries. Originally, a ballad was a dance-song. From the 16th century to the 19th, it came to mean a narrative poem (a poem telling a story) set to music. The music for a popular ballad was often improvised. During the 19th century, 'ballad' came to mean a simple, tuneful, and often sentimental song (also called 'drawing-room ballad'). Nowadays, pop musicians often refer to a particularly tuneful song, simple in style and sentimental in mood, as a 'ballad'. [See also: *Ballade; *Ballad opera; *Broadside ballad]

Ballade **1** One of the three main forms of medieval poetry and music (together with the *virelai and the *rondeau) used by French composers from the 13th century to the 15th (e.g. Guillaume de Machaut, *c*1300–1377). The plan of the music was **A A B** – the first phrase or section (**A**) being repeated, then followed by a refrain (**B**). This same music would then be repeated for any further stanzas, or verses, in the poem. An example of a simple *monophonic ballade is *Ja nun hons pris* by Richard Coeur-de-Lion (Richard I, King of England). **2** The word 'ballade' was used by 19th-century German Romantic composers to describe a fairly lengthy narrative song, *through-composed, and usually powerfully dramatic. Schubert's *Erlkönig* (The Erlking) is a good example. **3** The word 'ballade' has also been used as a title by some composers (e.g. Chopin, Liszt, Brahms) for dramatic piano pieces which seem to tell a story or resemble a *ballad.

Ballad opera An 18th-century English type of opera in which simple songs, mostly using well-known tunes of the day but with new words, alternated with spoken dialogue which carried the story forward. The first ballad opera was *The *Beggar's Opera* by John Gay; it was produced with enormous success in London in 1728. Later ballad operas made use of freshly invented tunes, though they were still composed in simple ballad style. [See also: *Ballad; *The *Threepenny Opera*]

Ballata One of the three main forms of poetry and music (along with the *madrigal and the *caccia) used by 14th-century Italian *Ars Nova composers (Francesco Landini in particular). A ballata was constructed in the same way as a French *virelai (but was quite different from a French *ballade). An example is Landini's ballata, *Ecco la primavera.*

Ballet A type of staged entertainment originating in Italy in the 15th century. It consists of dance and mime, and is usually accompanied by instruments and acted in costume. A story may be implied, or a mood evoked. In France, in 1581, Beaujoyeux, a dance arranger, assembled an entertainment called *Le Balet comique de la Royne*, initiating the form known as *ballet de cour*. The royal family and the nobility took part in these 'court ballets', which often marked festive occasions. The story was spoken or sung by a narrator, the gestures had symbolic meaning, and the costumes were voluminous and heavy. In the reign of Louis XIV the ballet master Beauchamp and the composer Lully produced stylized ballets, often based on mythological stories and containing formal dances like the minuet and the gavotte. In Paris, the Académie Royale de Danse (founded 1661) and the Académie Royale de Musique (1669) began to train professional dancers; the first ballet to employ them was Beauchamp and Lully's *Le Triomphe de l'amour* (1681).

The early 18th century saw the birth of the *ballet d'action*, which was entirely wordless. The ballerina Camargo initiated an energetic style of dancing in which high jumps were prominent; and the choreographers Noverre and Angiolini worked with composers like Rameau (*Les Indes galantes*, 1735) and Gluck (*Don Juan*, 1761) to establish the *opéra-ballet* form, in which singing and dancing were of more or less equal importance. A five-act format was normal.

Perhaps unexpectedly, the Romantic style in ballet came before the Classical. Around 1814 the technique of dancing on the tips of the toes (pointes) was introduced, and was used to great effect by the ballerina Taglioni. Costumes were shorter (and included the skin-tight maillot), and the ballerina became all-important, stealing the limelight from the male dancers. From about the 1840s a greater realism pervaded ballet, with topical stories and spectacular effects. The music was frequently melodious and memorable (**Giselle*, 1841; **Coppélia*, 1870; **Sylvia*, 1876), and dance also became a central component of the opera. In France the love of ballet was almost a mania. Rossini and Donizetti included dance sequences in some of their operas staged in Paris, and even Verdi (who disliked ballet) felt bound to conform – writing a dance scene for the Paris première of (of all things) **Otello*. Some French impresarios even injected ballet into operas which lacked it (for instance, dances from Bizet's *L'Arlésienne* found their way into **Carmen*), and Wagner added ballet music to **Tannhäuser* for use in Paris in 1861.

In 1801 Didelot, a pupil of Noverre, had emigrated to St Petersburg (now Leningrad), carrying the French influence to Russia (though royal schools of ballet already existed in both St Petersburg and Moscow). The *nationalism which soon pervaded Russian music also affected the ballet, which found its greatest choreographer in Marius Petipa and its most distinguished composer in Tchaikovsky (**Swan Lake*, 1875/6; *The *Sleeping Beauty*, 1890; *The *Nutcracker*, 1892). Petipa took the ballet d'action form, interspersed additional fantasy dances, often irrelevant to the plot, and forged the style which led to the Classical ballet (*The Sleeping Beauty* is a notable example).

Early in the 20th century the American dancer Isadora Duncan, and the choreographer Fokine, strove to achieve a greater freedom in ballet. In 1909, the impresario Diaghilev set up a Russian ballet (Ballets Russes) in Paris, commissioning original scores from composers like Ravel (**Daphnis and Chloë*, 1912) and Stravinsky (**Firebird*, 1910; **Petrushka*, 1911; *The *Rite of Spring*, 1913) and engaging world-famous dancers like Nijinsky and Pavlova. It was Diaghilev who established the short, one-act ballet (e.g. *Jeux*, to music by Debussy) and he often used music originally written for concert use (e.g. *Les *Sylphides*). Bakst and Picasso designed scenery for him, and Stravinsky, apart from writing original music, reworked older scores, using music by Pergolesi (and others) for his **Pulcinella* and themes by Tchaikovsky for *Le Baiser de la fée* (The Fairy's Kiss). Prokofiev was another famous composer who wrote for Diaghilev (e.g. *Chout*), and his works for the Bolshoi Ballet (*Romeo and Juliet*; *Cinderella*) are masterpieces. The choreographers Lifar, Massine, and Balanchine came from Diaghilev's company. Massine favoured detailed individual gestures (in, e.g., *La *Boutique fantasque*; *The *Three-Cornered Hat*). Balanchine worked extensively in the United States, choreographing ballets such as *The Four Temperaments* (music by Hindemith), *Serenade*, *Jewels*, and Stravinsky's **Orpheus*, as well as Broadway musicals such as *On Your Toes* and *The Boys from Syracuse*. Ballet of this type is usually referred to as Modern Dance.

The year 1926 saw the formation in London of the Academy of Choreographic Art. This laid the foundations for the Vic-Wells Ballet (1931), which became the Sadler's Wells Ballet in 1940. Six years later, the company moved its base to Covent Garden, and a second group (The Sadler's Wells Theatre Ballet) was formed to dance in the operas staged at Sadler's Wells. From 1956, both companies called themselves the Royal Ballet, and, on their return to Sadler's Wells in 1977, they became the Sadler's Wells Royal Ballet. In September 1990 they moved their base to the Hippodrome Theatre, Birmingham, and adopted the title of The Birmingham Royal Ballet. Ninette de Valois and Lilian Baylis were prominent figures in the administration of 20th-century ballet in Britain, with Frederick Ashton and Marie Rambert (who founded the Ballet Rambert company in 1926). Fonteyn and Nureyev are among the greatest dancers to appear in Britain. European companies have included the now-defunct Ballets Suédois and Ballets Jooss. The German Mary Wigman and the American Martha Graham have been inspired dancers teachers, and choreographers. Famous Russian companies include the Kirov and the Bolshoi.

The avant-garde also has been represented in modern dance. The collaboration between the American choreographer Merce Cunningham and the composer John Cage has produced ballets in which music and dance steps are actually at variance with each other. Electronic, and even aleatory, music have also found a place; and jazz, and ethnic music, have been used.

Ballett One of the three main kinds of madrigal (along with the *madrigal 'proper' and the *ayre) popular in England during the 16th century. A ballett was a lighter kind of madrigal, copied from the Italian *balletto*, originally danced as well as sung. So an Elizabethan ballett has a clear-cut dance-like rhythm, and the texture is mainly *homophonic. Whereas a madrigal proper is through-composed, a ballett is strophic – two or more verses set to the same music (as in a hymn). The most noticeable feature of a ballett is the 'fa-la-la' refrain which is heard at section endings. Examples of Elizabethan balletts are: *Now is the month of maying* and *Sing we and chant it* by Thomas Morley, *Sing we at pleasure* by Thomas Weelkes, and *Come away, sweet love, and play thee* by Thomas Greaves.

Balletto [Italian] **1** Ballet. **2** An Italian vocal composition of the late 15th and early 16th centuries, with dance-like rhythms, and often with a '*fa-la-la*' refrain after each verse. [See also: *Ballett]

Ballo [Italian] Ball, dance. **Da ballo**, in the style of a dance. **Tempo di ballo**, at a dance-like speed (very often that of a fairly swift waltz).

Band A name which may be given to any fairly large combination of instrumentalists, but often referring in particular to a group which consists mainly of wind players – such as a *brass band, a *military band, or a *symphonic band. The word 'band' may also be applied to particular groups of instruments, such as accordion band, *steel band, percussion band, and so on. The word has also been widely used in jazz and popular music (e.g. jazz band, dance band, big band).

Bandora (pandora) A low-sounding plucked string instrument, invented in England around 1560. The strings were of metal, and arranged in pairs. It was used to accompany vocal music, and was included in the 'broken *consort' – as in Thomas Morley's **First Booke of Consort Lessons* (1599).

bandora

Banjo A plucked string instrument, originating with the American Negroes in the 19th century, and much used in popular and folk music, and also in early jazz. The body of the banjo is in the form of a shallow drum, covered with parchment on the upper side and left open below. The long neck has frets and the strings, which vary in number from five to nine, are plucked with the fingers or with a plectrum.

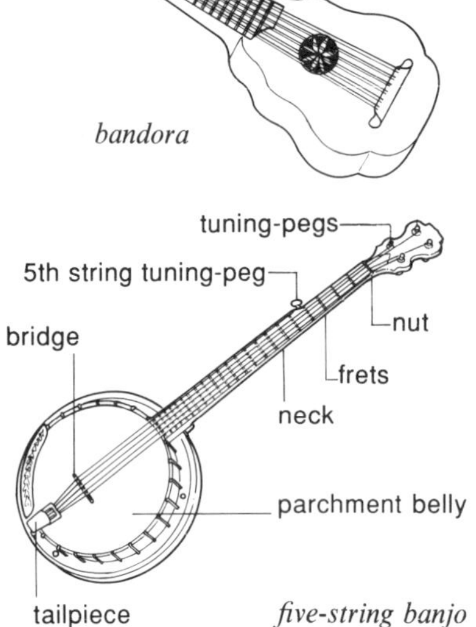

five-string banjo

Bar (measure) The amount of music contained (or 'measured') between two *bar-lines.

Barbaro [Italian] Barbarous, wild.

Barber of Seville, The (*Il barbiere di Siviglia*) Comic opera in two acts by Rossini, first produced in Rome in 1816 (libretto by Sterbini after a comedy by Beaumarchais). Count Almaviva (tenor) has fallen in love with Rosina, the ward of old Dr Bartolo (bass), and is pursuing her under the assumed name of Lindor. He is aided in his romance by the barber Figaro (baritone). But Bartolo himself hopes to marry his ward, and he plans to start a scandal and drive his rival out of town. Posing as a drunken soldier, Almaviva forces his way into Bartolo's house, but is recognized and arrested. Undaunted, he tries again, pretending to be a stand-in for Rosina's singing teacher, Don Basilio (bass), who, he says, is ill. While Rosina (soprano) is having her lesson the real Don Basilio arrives and is hurriedly bundled out of the room. With Figaro's help the lovers plot to elope, but they are overheard by Bartolo, who decides to forestall them by marrying Rosina quickly himself. To his horror, the lawyer he summons weds Rosina to Almaviva instead, and Bartolo has to be satisfied with the dowry.

To prevent confusion with Paisiello's *Il barbiere di Siviglia*, Rossini's opera was originally entitled *Almaviva, ossia L'inutile precauzione* (Almaviva, or The useless precaution). The overture, not specially composed, had already been used for two previous operas.

Barcarola [Italian]; **Barcarolle** [French] A boating song (as sung by Venetian gondoliers) and hence a title for a piece which imitates the rocking, lilting movement of a boat. (For example: Chopin's *Barcarolle* in F sharp, and the *Barcarolle* from the opera *The Tales of Hoffmann* by Offenbach.)

Barform [German] A very old musical form or design, on the plan of **A A B**, found in many of the songs of the *troubadours, *trouvères, *Meistersinger and *Minnesinger. In German, the two **A** sections are called *Stollen* (literally, 'posts' or 'props') and the **B** section is called the *Abgesang* ('after-song').

Baritone **1** A type of male *voice whose range lies between that of a bass and a tenor. **2** Short for baritone horn, a valved brass instrument with bell pointing upwards, and built in the key of B♭. Its range is the same as that of the rather similar euphonium, but it has a narrower bore. (In American publications of band music, 'baritone' denotes euphonium.)

Bar-lines The vertical lines drawn down through the stave to divide the music into metrical units (two beats to a bar, three beats to a bar, and so on). A **double bar** (which is really a 'double bar-line') consists of a pair of vertical lines (often one thin, one thick) drawn down through the stave to mark the end of a piece or of a section of music. [See also: *Repeat signs]

Baroque music The word 'Baroque' comes from the Portuguese *barroco*, meaning an irregularly-shaped pearl or piece of jewellery. The word was originally used derogatively to describe the very ornate style of architecture and art of the 17th century. It was taken up by musicians to describe the period in the *history of Western music extending from the birth of *opera and *oratorio to the death of J. S. Bach – that is, from around 1600 to 1750. The beginning of the Baroque period is marked by the emergence of the new *monody or monodic style (see also *Le *Nuove Musiche*).

Besides opera and oratorio, new forms and types of music which came into being and were developed during the Baroque period include: *cantata, *aria (see also *da capo aria), and *recitative; *fugue, *chaconne and passacaglia, the *chorale prelude, dance *suite, *sonata (solo sonata, trio sonata), *overture, and *concerto (concerto grosso, solo concerto; see also *ritornello form). Forms used by Renaissance composers which were retained and developed by Baroque composers include the *toccata, *fantasia, and *variations (see also *double).

The *violin family gradually replaced the *viols. And the *orchestra began to take shape, with a strong section of strings as its basis – though the other three sections were as yet not standardized. The system of church modes gave way to the major-minor key system upon which harmony was based for the next two and a half centuries or more.

The main distinguishing features of most Baroque music are the inclusion of the *basso *continuo* or figured bass – often providing a purposeful bass-line which causes the music to press steadily forward (see also *walking bass), and the use of contrasts – particularly of dynamics (*'terraced' dynamics), of instrumental timbres, and also between the separate movements of works such as the suite, sonata, and concerto. [See also: *Affections; *Gallant style]

The most important Baroque composers include: Monteverdi, Corelli, Alessandro Scarlatti, Vivaldi, and Domenico Scarlatti in Italy; Lully, Couperin, and Rameau in France; Schütz and J. S. Bach in Germany; and Purcell and Handel in England. [See the time-chart of composers on pages 398–413]

Bartered Bride, The Opera in three acts by Smetana, first produced in Prague in 1866 (text by Sabina). (Four earlier versions, some in two acts, were completed). The peasant girl Mařenka (soprano) is in love with Jeník (tenor), but her parents have chosen as her husband the 'son of Mícha', whom she has never met, and who turns out to be the stuttering simpleton Vašek (tenor). The marriage broker Kecal (bass) attempts to seal the union, but Mařenka sends Vašek off after another woman, and he falls for a circus dancer. Kecal offers Jeník 300 crowns to abandon Mařenka, and Jeník accepts the bribe on the condition that she genuinely weds Mícha's son. In spite, Mařenka decides to marry Vašek after all, but in the nick of time it is revealed that Jeník himself is Vašek's elder half-brother, and therefore is the 'son of Mícha'. He and Mařenka marry and also, quite justifiably, keep the 300 crowns. The opera is sometimes staged in a German translation (*Die verkaufte Braut*). A *suite (usually consisting of the *Overture*, *Polka*, *Furiant*, and *Dance of the Comedians*) is played from time to time at orchestral concerts.

Baryton A type of bass viol of the 18th century. It had six strings played with the bow, and a great many sympathetic strings (see under *sympathetic vibrations). Haydn wrote almost 200 compositions for the baryton since his patron, Prince Nikolaus Esterházy, played the instrument.

Bas; **Basse** [French] Low.

Bass **1** The lowest male *voice. **2** The lowest-sounding note in a chord. **3** The succession of notes making up the lowest part or voice in a passage or piece of music. **4** Short for *double bass. **5** Describing instruments of low range – the largest instrument in a family, or (if a contrabass exists) the second largest. **6** Familiar term, in brass and military bands, for bombardon (bass tuba and contrabass tuba).

Bassa [Italian] Low. **Ottava bassa**, an octave lower (see under *Octave signs).

Bassa danza See *Basse danse.

Bass clarinet A single-reed woodwind instrument, twice the length of the B♭ *clarinet, and pitched an octave lower. The lower part of the instrument curves upwards in a flared metal bell; the top part curves backwards to the player's mouth. The bass clarinet is a *transposing instrument, and its music is usually written one octave and a tone higher than it actually sounds.

bass clarinet

The sound of the bass clarinet is rich and resonant, but with a hollow, 'woody' quality. It can be heard in Act 2 Scene 3 of Wagner's opera *Tristan and Isolde*, in the middle section of *Khadra's Dance* from *Belshazzar's Feast* by Sibelius, in the *Dance of the Sugar-Plum Fairy* (together with celesta) from Tchaikovsky's ballet *The Nutcracker*, at the beginning of the slow movement of Khatchaturian's Piano Concerto, in Delius's Prelude to *Irmelin* (brief solos at the beginning and end), and in Janáček's **Mládí* (especially the fourth movement) usually playing the lowest notes of the ensemble. Shostakovich gives the bass clarinet a lengthy solo about three-quarters way through the second movement of his Seventh Symphony (*'Leningrad'); and the Czech composer Alois Hába has written a Suite for solo bass clarinet.

Bass clef See *Clef.

Bass drum A percussion instrument consisting of a large cylindrical wooden shell with one or both sides covered with stretched hide or plastic. Normally, a large padded stick is used to play single strokes, and kettle drum sticks are used to play a roll. The sound is low and 'booming', and of indefinite pitch. For special effects, the bass drum may be struck with hard sticks; or beaten with a *rute* – a bundle of birch rods or a thin split cane – either on the body-shell or on the drum-skin. The bass drum can be clearly heard in the *Storm* section of Rossini's *William Tell Overture*, in the *Hungarian March* (*Rákóczi March*) from *The *Damnation of Faust* by Berlioz, and in the *Dies irae* section of Verdi's Requiem. It is heard being beaten with a rute in the third movement of Mahler's Second Symphony ('The *Resurrection') and also in his song 'St Anthony of Padua's Sermon to the Fishes' (on which this movement is based).

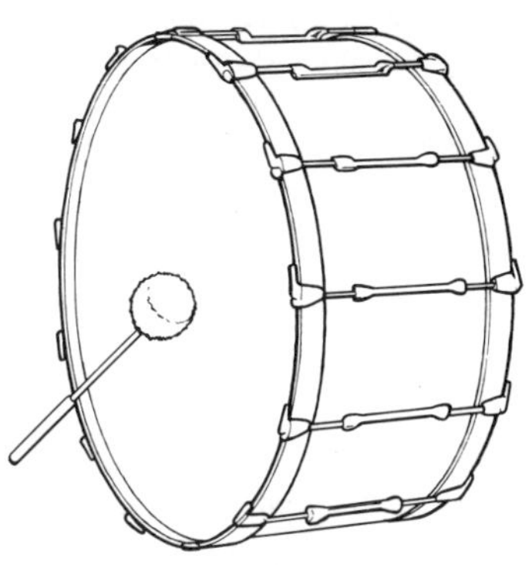
bass drum

Basse [French] Bass.

Basse danse [French; Italian: *bassa danza*] A slow, stately dance (sometimes in triple time, sometimes in duple), very popular during the late 15th and 16th centuries. The feet glided along, barely leaving the ground – hence the name *basse danse* ('low dance') compared with other dances which included jumps, skips, and leaps. During the 15th century, music for a basse danse was often based on a traditional tune (used as a tenor) played in long notes on a sackbut, trumpet, or bowed string instrument, while above it, one or two shawm players would play rhythmic running phrases – often improvised on the spur of the moment. A basse danse would often be paired with a succeeding faster dance which was more agile (e.g. a *tordion). The first movement of Warlock's **Capriol Suite* is based on a 16th-century basse danse:

Basset-horn A tenor clarinet, usually pitched in F. It is included in scores by Mozart (e.g. the Requiem, and the Serenade in B♭ for thirteen wind instruments) and also in scores by Richard Strauss (e.g. his opera *Elektra*).

Bass flute See under *Flute.

Bassklarinette [German] Bass clarinet.

Bass-line The lowest-sounding notes, in succession, in a passage or piece of music.

Basso [Italian] **1** Bass; *col basso*, with (play the same notes as) the bass. **2** Low.

Basso continuo See *Continuo.

Basson [French] Bassoon.

Bassoon A double-reed *woodwind instrument; the bass member of the oboe family, and the lowest-sounding of the four main orchestral woodwinds (the other three being the flute, oboe, and clarinet). The bassoon's tube is conical, and because of its length (about 2.5 metres) it is doubled back upon itself, with the bell pointing upwards. (The Italian name for the instrument, *fagotto*, means 'a bundle of sticks'.) The double reed – rather like the oboe's, but shorter and broader – is fixed into the end of a metal 'crook' which curves backwards and down to the player's lips. Cut into the tube of the bassoon are a number of finger-holes, some of them controlled by keys and levers. As the player blows, different pitches are obtained by opening and closing holes, using fingers and thumbs.

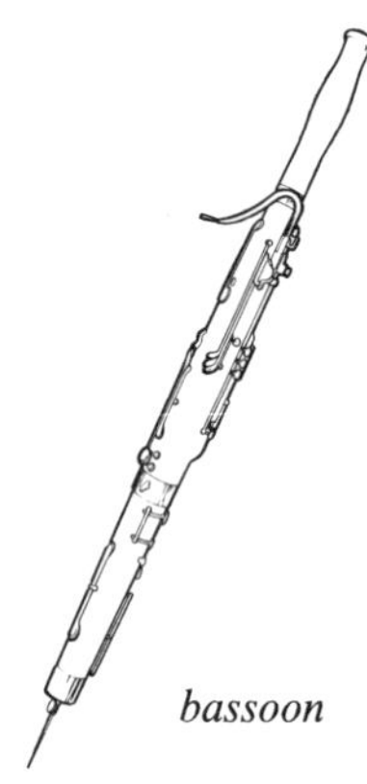
bassoon

The range of the bassoon lies two octaves below that of the oboe. Lower notes are written in the bass clef, higher notes in the tenor clef.

Range: 

When played *legato*, the bassoon sounds dignified, if rather plaintive; played *staccato*, the tone is dryish, even comic. The bassoon joined the orchestra early in the 17th century. It is almost always included in *chamber music for wind ensemble, and is a regular member of the military band and the symphonic band.

Orchestral solos for bassoon include *In the Hall of the Mountain King* from Grieg's music for *Peer Gynt*, *The Sorcerer's Apprentice* by Dukas, the opening of Tchaikovsky's *Pathétique Symphony*, Rimsky-Korsakov's **Sheherazade* (just after the beginning of the second movement), the opening of Stravinsky's *The Rite of Spring* (very high register), and the *Prélude* to Act 2 of Bizet's opera *Carmen* (two bassoons). Compositions for solo bassoon and orchestra include several concertos by Vivaldi, Mozart's Bassoon Concerto in B♭, Weber's Bassoon Concerto in F, the *Allegro spiritoso* by Senaillé, and Elgar's *Romance*.

[See also: *Double bassoon]

Basso ostinato [Italian, meaning 'obstinately repeating bass'] Same, in meaning, as *ground bass.

Bassposaune [German] Bass trombone.

Bat, The See *Die *Fledermaus.*

Baton [French] The stick used by a conductor to beat time.

Batteria [Italian]; **Batterie** [French] 'Battery' – and therefore, the percussion section of the orchestra. The French word is also used with other meanings: (1) a drum-roll; (2) a technique in guitar-playing in which the player strikes the strings instead of plucking them; (3) an indication in early music for keyboard or harp that chords are to be played in arpeggio fashion or in broken-chord figuration.

Battuta [Italian] **1** Bar or measure. **2** Beat. *A battuta* (similar to *a tempo*) means 'return to the strict beat'. In a quick tempo, *battuta* (plural: *battute*) may refer to the strong beat at the beginning of each bar. In the Scherzo of his Ninth Symphony, Beethoven writes *ritmo di tre battute* to mean that one-in-a-bar beats should be grouped into three-bar phrases.

Battuto [Italian] Hit, tapped, beaten, struck.

Bāyā See *Tablā.

B.c. Abbreviation of *basso *continuo.*

Be [German] The flat sign (♭).

Beam See under *Note.

Bearbeitung [German] Arrangement. **Bearbeitet**, arranged, edited.

'Bear' Symphony (*L'Ours*) Nickname of Haydn's Symphony No. 82 in C (1786). The last movement begins with music which sounds like a bear growling as it dances to the accompaniment of bagpipes – a sight which would have been fairly common in Haydn's time. [See also: *'Paris' Symphonies]

Beat The basic *unit* of time used in a composition (e.g. quaver, crotchet, dotted crotchet, minim) decided upon by the composer and indicated in the time signature. [See also: *Pulse]

Beautiful Maid of the Mill, The See *Die *Schöne Müllerin.*

Bebop See *Bop.

Bebung [German: 'trembling'] A vibrato effect used in *clavichord-playing.

Bécarre [French] The natural sign (♮).

Becken [German] Cymbals. **Becken frei** or **hängendes Becken**, suspended cymbal.

'Bee's Wedding, The' See *'*Spinning Song*'.

Beggar's Opera, The Ballad opera in three acts to music arranged and composed by Pepusch, first produced in London in 1728 (text by John Gay). Captain Macheath (tenor), leader of a band of highwaymen and a chaser of women, secretly marries Polly (soprano), the daughter of Peachum, a receiver of stolen goods. Discovering this, Peachum (bass) and his wife plot to bring Macheath to justice, believing that when he is hanged his ill-gotten wealth will pass to Polly, and that they will benefit. But Macheath has also promised marriage to Lucy Lockit (soprano), the daughter of the gaoler of Newgate, and when he is committed to that gaol and she confronts him, he vigorously denies that Polly is his wife. To his embarrassment the two girls meet, and his deception is discovered. In spite of this, Lucy helps him to escape, but he is recaptured. Eventually the Beggar (spoken role) arrives and provides a happy ending in which Macheath is pardoned and released.

The opera is a satire on politicians (Macheath is a take-off of Walpole, the Prime Minister) and famous singers of the day. There are several modern versions, but the one by Britten is so extensively rewritten that it amounts to an original composition. [See also: *Ballad opera; *The *Threepenny Opera*]

Begleitung [German] Accompaniment.

Bei [German] By, near, at, with.

Bel See *Decibel.

Bel canto [Italian: 'beautiful song', 'beautiful singing'] The Italian style and technique of singing developed during the 18th century (admired and adopted by singers of other countries) which emphasizes beauty and clarity of tone and articulation, flexibility, extremely smooth phrasing, and carefully graded dynamics. The art of *bel canto* reached its peak during the 19th century.

Opera singers consider *bel canto* to be a basic vocal technique, essential especially in performing operas by Italian composers such as Rossini, Bellini, Donizetti, and Verdi, and also the operas of Mozart.

Bell The name given to the flaring end of the tube of a brass instrument, farthest away from the mouthpiece. The word is also used in connection with some woodwind instruments (e.g. clarinet, cor anglais, shawm).

'Bell' Anthem Nickname given to Purcell's verse anthem *Rejoice in the Lord alway*, for alto, tenor, and bass soloists, chorus, strings, and continuo. The descending scale passages of the instrumental introduction suggest the pealing of bells.

Bell-lyra See under *Glockenspiel.

Belly The front (or top surface) of the main body or soundbox of a string instrument, over which the strings are stretched. Also called the **table**.

Belshazzar's Feast **1** Oratorio (1930–31) by William Walton, to words selected from the Old Testament by Osbert Sitwell. The music – which is extremely colourful, imaginative, and full of powerful contrasts – is scored for mixed choir, solo baritone, large orchestra with particularly varied percussion section, piano, organ, and two brass bands. **2** Suite of incidental music by Sibelius, composed in 1906 for a play by a friend of his named Hjalmar Procopé.

Bémol [French]; **Bemolle** [Italian] Flat (♭). For example, *Si bémol* or *Si bemolle* = B flat.

Ben; **Bene** [Italian] Well, very. For example, *ben marcato*, well marked, or well accented.

Benedictus See *Mass.

Bequadro [Italian] The natural sign (♮).

Berceuse [French] A lullaby or cradle-song. Sometimes used as a title for an instrumental piece (usually in lilting $\frac{6}{8}$ time) which imitates the gentle rocking of a cradle (e.g. Chopin's *Berceuse* in D flat, Op. 57, and the opening piece in Fauré's *'Dolly' Suite*).

Bes [German] The note B double flat. (Also called *Heses*.)

Bestimmt [German] Decided.

Betont [German] Accented, emphasized, stressed.

Bewegt [German] Moved (either in speed, or emotion). **Bewegter**, quicker, more agitated.

Bewegung [German] **1** Speed, or movement. **2** Emotion.

Bianca [Italian: 'white'] A minim ('white' note).

Bien [French] Well; very.

Big band See under *Swing.

Big drum *Bass drum.

Billy the Kid A 'cowboy' ballet, composed by Aaron Copland in 1938, about the life and death of the Wild West cattle rustler and gunman, Henry McCarty – alias 'Billy the Kid'. Copland's score evokes the atmosphere of the wide open spaces of the prairie lands in the Southwest of America, and includes the tunes of several traditional cowboy songs. Copland later arranged some of the music from the ballet to make an orchestral suite in seven sections. [See also: **Rodeo*; **Appalachian Spring*]

Binary form A basic musical *form or structure in which the music is built up in *two* sections (*bi*-nary meaning 'two' – as in *bi*cycle, *bi*sect). Section **A** makes a musical statement which sounds incomplete on its own. This is answered, and balanced, by the music of section **B**. Usually, both sections are marked to be repeated:

Section A :‖: Section B :‖

In most binary pieces, the music modulates towards the end of **A** so that this section ends in a new key. If the tonic is a major key, then usually this modulation will be to the dominant key; if the tonic is a minor key, the modulation will very likely be to the *relative major. During section **B**, the music returns to the tonic key.

In a binary piece both sections, **A** and **B**, usually share the same musical ideas. The tune which begins **A** is likely to be repeated at the beginning of **B** – though it may be presented in *inversion, or put down into the bass. In the binary piece below, the four bars which begin **A** form a *sequence. This same musical idea is then presented in inversion at the beginning of **B**.

Purcell: Minuet from Harpsichord Suite No. 1 in G

In this binary piece, **A** and **B** are equal in length (eight bars each). In many binary pieces, however, **B** is longer than **A**, and the composer may take the music of **B** through several *related keys before making for 'home' and closing in the tonic key:

A	tonic key ⟶	to a related key	:‖:	**B**	through other related keys ⟶	closing in tonic key	:‖

A may end with a distinctive musical idea which reappears at the end of **B** – so that the endings of the two sections are similar, except for key.

Binary form was used extensively during the 17th and 18th centuries, and was the standard musical form for the individual movements of the Baroque *suite. Since then, binary form has rarely been used except for short piano pieces or themes for *variations.

Bind A word sometimes used to mean a *tie.

'Bird' Quartet (*Vogelquartett*) Nickname of Haydn's String Quartet in C, Op. 33 No. 3, so called because some parts of the music suggest birdsong – for example, the second subject of the first movement, the trio section of the second (*Scherzando*) movement, and much of the final rondo. [See: *'Russian' Quartets]

Birds, The (*Gli uccelli*) Suite for small orchestra composed by Respighi in 1927. The five movements, all based on bird pieces for lute and harpsichord by 17th- and 18th-century composers, are entitled: 1 Prelude (also introducing themes to be heard in the succeeding movements); 2 The Dove; 3 The Hen (based on a well-known harpsichord piece by Rameau, called *La *Poule*); 4 The Nightingale; and 5 The Cuckoo.

Bis [Latin] Twice (meaning, repeat the note or passage so marked).

Bis [German] Up to; as far as; until.

Bisbigliando [Italian] Whispering.

Bitonality See *Polytonality.

Biwa A Japanese plucked lute (originally brought to Japan from China in the 7th century). It is pear-shaped, and has four or five silk strings, which are plucked with a plectrum. [See also: *P'i-p'a]

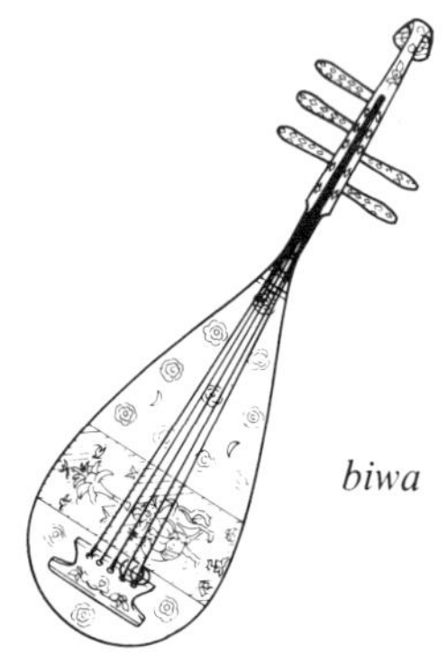

biwa

'Black Key' Study Nickname of Chopin's Study (Étude) No. 5 in G♭ major (1830) from his first set of Twelve Studies for piano, Op. 10. Throughout the piece, the pianist's right hand is confined to the black keys – with the exception of the note F in bar 66 (in some editions this note is one of four printed with stems up in the left-hand part, but is more naturally taken by the right hand).

Blanche [French: 'white'] A minim ('white' note).

Blaník See **Má vlast*.

Blasend [German] Blown. **Stark blasend**, same as the French term **cuivré*.
Bläser [German: 'blowers'] Wind players; also wind instruments.
Bläserquintett [German] *Wind quintet.
Blasinstrumente [German] Wind instruments.
Blasmusik [German: 'blow-music'] Music for wind instruments.
Blech [German] Brass; the brass section of the orchestra. **Blechbläser**, brass players. **Blechblasinstrumente** or **Blechinstrumente**, brass instruments.
Blechmusik [German: 'brass music'] Music for brass instruments, or for a brass band.
Bleiben [German] To stay, remain (in use). **Bleibt**, remains in use.
Blockflöte [German: 'block flute'] *Recorder.
Block harmony Term describing a musical texture in which the lower parts, keeping rhythmically in step with each other, move in a series of chords forming 'blocks' below the melody (as, for example, in many hymn-tunes).
Blue Danube, The (*An der schönen blauen Donau*) One of the most famous concert waltzes by Johann Strauss the Younger, composed in 1867 as his Opus 314. Originally, Strauss also included parts for chorus.
Bluegrass See under *Country music.
'Blue' notes In *blues and jazz (and in music influenced by, or imitating, those styles) the slight flattening or lowering of certain notes of the major scale, especially the 3rd and the 7th – for example, in C major, the notes E and B. The effect is of a wavering between major key and minor key. Taking the note E as an example, the true 'blue' note will sound flatter than E♮, but usually not so flat as E♭ – the sound lies somewhere between the two. On the piano, of course, this is impossible, since the true blue notes lie 'in the cracks' between the notes on the keyboard. And so a pianist aims for the effect of a blue note in the melody (marked * in the music below) by playing it fully flattened, but also simultaneously includes the same note, but unaltered, in the accompanying harmony or by sounding it as a minor second against the melody note.

Blues 1 A style of music which originated as a type of black American folk-music, with roots partly in spirituals and work-songs, and which later developed alongside, and became an important ingredient in, American jazz. Early examples were often improvised and were for solo voice with instrumental accompaniment, the words expressing melancholy ('feeling blue'), yearning, disappointment and misfortune, but often with a touch of sardonic humour.

The blues is in $\frac{4}{4}$ time, usually (but not always) slow to moderate in speed, and is most often patterned on a 12-bar structure (though 8-bar and 16-bar structures also exist). Each verse in a typical 12-bar blues structure has three lines of 4 bars each – the second line repeating the words of the first. The accompanying chords (harmonies) frequently follow the scheme shown overleaf, or some variant or elaboration of it. Throughout the blues this 12-bar chord scheme is repeated for each verse (rather in the manner of a chaconne or ground bass).

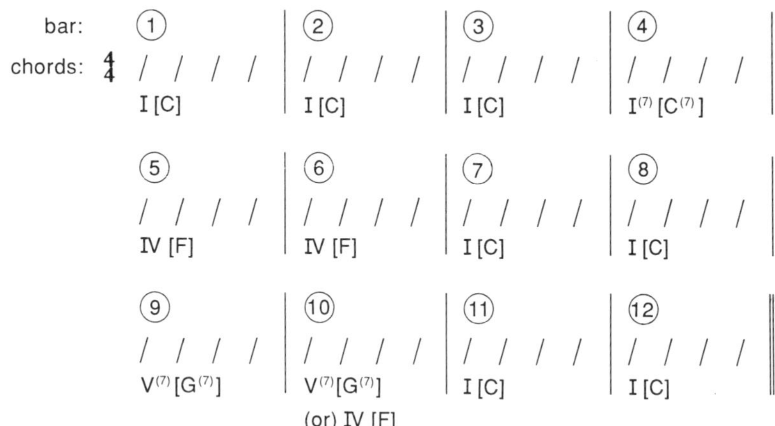

Other characteristic features of the blues are a syncopated melody line which frequently includes *'blue' notes and, at the end of lines where the melody does not fill up the four bars, a short improvised 'break' played by the accompanying instrument(s).

Among important blues singers were Huddie 'Leadbelly' Ledbetter, Gertrude 'Ma' Rainey, Blind Lemon Jefferson, and Bessie Smith (the 'Empress of the Blues'). Characteristic features of the blues became important in the development of jazz and, later, of *rhythm and blues, and *rock.

2 The word 'Blues' may be used as a title, or part of the title, of a piece aiming to evoke the typical mood and style of the blues – which may or may not include specific characteristics of the blues such as the 12-bar structure, 'blue' notes, breaks.

B minor Mass A setting of the Latin text of the Roman Catholic Mass by J. S. Bach, for five soloists (two sopranos, alto, tenor, bass), choir, and orchestra. It consists of the usual five items of the Ordinary of the *Mass (Kyrie, Gloria, Credo, Sanctus, and Agnus Dei). However, Bach splits up the Latin text into twenty-four sections, which he sets as separate arias, duets, and choruses. For some of these he adapted music from various cantatas he had written earlier (e.g. the great *Crucifixus*, structured on a ground bass, originates from Cantata No. 12, *Weinen, Klagen*). Bach took several years to complete the Mass in B minor. The original version of the Sanctus was composed for Christmas 1724. In 1733 Bach composed the Kyrie and Gloria, dedicating them to the new Elector of Saxony, Frederick Augustus III. It is believed he composed the remaining items, and revised the Sanctus, over the next five years.

Bocca [Italian] Mouth. **Bocca chiusa**, 'closed mouth' – instruction sometimes found in vocal music, indicating wordless humming.

Boehm system An improved key mechanism for the flute, invented and developed during the 1830s by the German flautist and goldsmith, Theobald Boehm. The holes are still cut in the correct acoustical positions along the tube of the instrument, but Boehm's system of metal keys and levers ensures that they are all within comfortable control of the player's fingers. The system has also been adapted to the oboe, clarinet, and bassoon.

Bogen [German] A bow (of a string instrument).

Bohème, La (The Bohemian girl) Opera in four acts by Puccini, first produced in Turin in 1896 (libretto by Giacosa and Illica, based on a novel by Henri Murger). Four friends, Rodolfo (a poet), Marcello (a painter), Colline (a philosopher), and Schaunard (a musician), share a meagre attic. They are hard up, and when Benoit, the landlord (bass), calls for the rent, they make him drunk and he leaves without the money. Rodolfo (tenor) is alone, when there is a knock at the door. It is Mimi (soprano), seeking a light for her candle. She drops her key, and as the two of them grope for it their fingers meet, and they fall in love. Marcello (baritone) wins back his former sweetheart, Musetta, from Alcindoro (bass), an old gentleman hanging on to the pleasures of youth. But tragedy strikes. Rodolfo, imagining that Mimi has other lovers, becomes jealous; though he repents when he realizes she is desperately ill. Musetta (soprano) flirts with a stranger, and she and Marcello quarrel. The four friends try to forget their sorrows in a mad frolic in the attic, but this is interrupted by Musetta, who brings in Mimi, now too weak to climb the stairs unaided. The men lift Mimi onto the bed, but she is beyond help, and, as they frantically try to save her, she dies.

Leoncavallo's *La Bohème* is based on the same novel. Balfe's *The Bohemian Girl* is a lightweight treatment of a much slighter story.

Bois [French] Wood. **Les bois**, the woodwind instruments of the orchestra. **Baguette de bois**, wooden-headed drumstick.

Bolero A Spanish dance in moderate triple time. A true bolero is performed by a couple or by a single dancer to the accompaniment of singing, hand-claps, and the clicking of castanets. The bolero has occasionally been used by composers – for example: Chopin's *Bolero*, Op. 1; the *Danse espagnole* (Spanish Dance) from Tchaikovsky's ballet *Swan Lake*; and, most famous of all, Ravel's *Bolero* for orchestra, composed for the dancer Ida Rubinstein. In this piece, which lasts for about eighteen minutes, a single theme – accompanied by a persistent snare drum rhythm – is repeated again and again in a gradual *crescendo*, beginning *pp* with only a few instruments and ending *ff* on the entire orchestra (see *Ostinato).

Bombard Medieval name for a large *shawm. Later, however, 'bombard' became interchangeable with 'pommer' to mean any size of shawm.

Bombardon In brass bands and military bands, a term used for the bass tuba and contrabass (double-bass) tuba.

Bongos Small single-headed drums with conical or cylindrical hardwood shells. They are usually of the same height but of different diameter and joined together as a pair. Each drum is tuned to give a clear, high-sounding note – the two notes being at least a 4th apart. Bongos, which are Cuban in origin, are usually played with the bare hands.

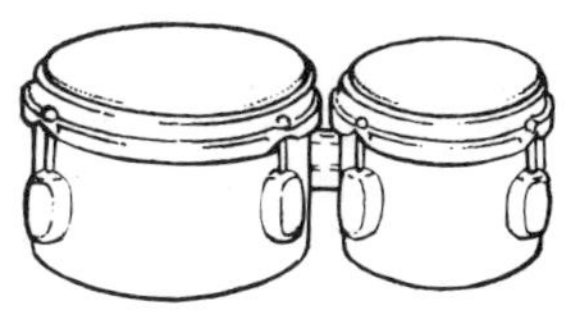

bongos

Boogie-woogie A *jazz style, originating in the USA in the 1920s as a special type of piano *blues. Boogie-woogie (or simply **boogie**) is characterized by a rhythmic repetitive bass pattern (*ostinato) forcefully played by the left hand, above which the right hand improvises a syncopated melodic line, often producing dissonant harmonies. Like the blues, the music is often built up in

12-bar sections. Important performers of boogie-woogie included Clarence 'Pine Top' Smith, and Meade 'Lux' Lewis.

Two typical boogie-woogie bass patterns are:

Bop (bebop, rebop) A *jazz style originating in the USA around 1945, named after the nonsense syllables sometimes sung by its performers. The music was swift-moving, and characterized by complicated melodic lines improvised against dissonant harmonies and complex rhythms. Important performers of bop included the saxophonist Charlie 'Bird' Parker, trumpeters Dizzy Gillespie and Miles Davis, and drummer Max Roach.

Bore The inside width or diameter of the tube of a wind instrument – for example: wide bore, narrow bore, conical bore (cone-shaped, gradually expanding), cylindrical bore (the diameter remaining the same for much or all of the tube-length).

Boree; **Borry** [English] *Bourrée.

Boris Godunov Opera in a prologue and four acts by Musorgsky, first produced (complete) at St Petersburg in 1874, later twice revised by Rimsky-Korsakov (libretto by Musorgsky after a play by Pushkin). The Tsar of Russia has died. Boris Godunov (bass), having engineered the murder of the boy Dmitri, rightful heir to the throne, has become Tsar in his place; but he is torn with guilt and has a premonition of evil. A young monk, Grigory (tenor), seeking to bring Boris to justice, poses as Dmitri and makes for Lithuania, meaning to start a revolt. On the way he meets two vagabond monks, Varlaam (bass) and Missail (tenor), and is questioned on suspicion of being a wanted man, but he escapes. In Moscow, Boris's daughter Xenia (soprano) is mourning the death of her fiancé, Ivan, when Boris himself enters. Prince Shuisky (tenor) brings him news of 'a pretender to the throne, who claims to be Dmitri', and Boris is overcome with fear. Shuisky reassures him that the real Dmitri is dead. Outside St Basil's Cathedral the crowd begins to believe in the false Dmitri's right to the throne, and when he arrives, on horseback, they hail him as Tsar. In the Council the boyars decree that the pretender must be caught and burnt to death. Suddenly Boris, crazed by visions of the murdered boy, staggers in. The monk Pimen (bass) appears and tells of the young Dmitri, now numbered among the saints of God. It is too much for the demented Boris, who falls dead.

Bouché [French] Short for *sons bouchés* – stopped notes on the horn. The instruction is cancelled by the French word *ouvert*. [See: *Stopping 2]

Bourrée A dance of French origin, popular during the 17th and 18th centuries and often found as one of the movements in a Baroque *suite. A bourrée is usually in a fast tempo, and in $\frac{2}{2}$ time (occasionally $\frac{4}{4}$) beginning on the last quarter of the bar. One well-known Bourrée is that from Handel's Suite: *The Water Music*; another is heard during his *Music for the Royal Fireworks*:

Boutique fantasque, La (The Fantastic Toyshop) Ballet in one act to music by Rossini adapted by Respighi, first produced in London in 1919 (story by Massine based on Hassreiter's *The Fairy Doll*; original choreography by Massine). A toyshop owner and his assistant demonstrate their dolls and mechanical toys to some potential customers. Two families (one American, one Russian) each reserve a doll, to be collected next day, and the proprietor shuts up shop for the night. No sooner has he done so than all the dolls come to life and dance, and the reserved ones depart into the outside world. Next day, when the customers return, they find their purchases missing. Thinking that the shopman has cheated them they set about him with sticks, but he is saved by the remaining dolls, who come to life and protect him.

Bow The wooden stick with horse-hair stretched tightly along it, used to play certain string instruments (e.g. the violin); so called because originally the stick curved slightly outwards, resembling the shape of an archery bow. The modern bow, designed around 1780 by François Tourte, has the stick curving slightly inwards.

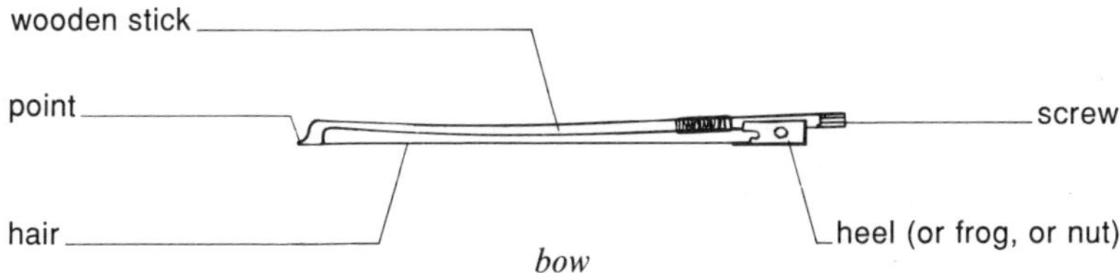

bow

A screw mechanism adjusts the tension of the hair, which stretches in a flat 'ribbon' from point to heel. Before using the bow, the player rubs resin (usually pronounced 'rosin') onto the hair to produce friction when the bow is drawn across the strings of the instrument, so causing them to vibrate.

Bowing The particular way in which the *bow is used on a string instrument. The two basic strokes or movements of the bow are called **up-bow**, in which the bow moves from point to heel across the string, and **down-bow**, moving from heel to point. Signs sometimes printed in the music are ∨ for up-bow, ⊓ for down-bow.

The most commonly used bowing-stroke is called *legato* [Italian: 'smoothly'] using up-bows and down-bows in such a way that each note – one, or more, to each stroke – is followed smoothly by the next. [See also: *Détaché; *Flautando; *Martelé; *Ricochet; *Saltando; *Punta d'arco; *Tallone; Col *legno; Sul *ponticello; Sul *tasto; *Tremolo]

Brace A bracket connecting two or more staves of music.

Brandenburg Concertos Six concertos by Bach, composed between 1711 and 1721 and dedicated to Christian Ludwig, Margrave of Brandenburg. Bach departed from the usual way of composing a concerto grosso and scored the six concertos for unusual combinations of instruments:

1 in F	oboe, 2 horns, *violino piccolo* (a small-sized violin), accompanied by 2 oboes, bassoon, strings, and *continuo;
2 in F	trumpet, recorder, oboe, violin, with strings and continuo;
3 in G	three groups of strings (each consisting of violin, viola, cello), with double bass and continuo;
4 in G	violin, 2 recorders, accompanied by strings and continuo;
5 in D	flute, violin, and harpsichord, with strings and continuo;
6 in B♭	2 violas, 2 violas da gamba, cello, with double bass and continuo.

Branle (or **Bransle**) [from French: 'to swing'] A lively 16th-century French country dance, performed in a circle or a line with a sideways step. It later became popular at court. In England, sometimes called a **brawl**. The example below is the first of two 16th-century French bransles on which Warlock bases the fourth movement of his **Capriol Suite*.

Brass band A band consisting of brass instruments plus percussion (as distinct from a *military band, which also includes woodwind instruments). The instruments of a typical brass band include: 1 soprano cornet in E♭, 8 or 10 cornets in B♭, 1 flugelhorn in B♭, 3 tenor horns (E♭ horns), 2 baritones in B♭, 2 tenor trombones and 1 bass trombone, 2 euphoniums in B♭, 2 basses (bombardons, bass tubas) in E♭ and 2 in low B♭; also drums and other percussion as needed. (Occasionally, saxophones – not strictly brass instruments – are also included.) In the score of a piece for brass band, all the instruments except bass trombone and percussion have their music notated in the treble clef and are treated as *transposing instruments.

Brass instruments The name given to a large group of *wind instruments, formerly made of brass (though nowadays other metals may be used), in which the air column inside the instrument is set in vibration by the player's lips vibrating against a metal mouthpiece. (The group does not include reed-mouthpiece instruments made of metal, e.g. saxophones, or blow-hole instruments which may be made of metal, e.g. flute; these are counted as *woodwind instruments.)

The mouthpiece of a brass instrument may be funnel-shaped, as that of the *horn; or cup-shaped, as that of the *trumpet, *trombone, and *tuba. At the other end, the tube flares (to a greater or lesser degree) into the 'bell'. The bore (inside width or diameter) of the tube may be wide or narrow, mainly conical (cone-shaped, gradually expanding) as in the horn and tuba, or mainly cylindrical, as in the trumpet and trombone. The type of mouthpiece, the nature of the bore of the tube, and the degree

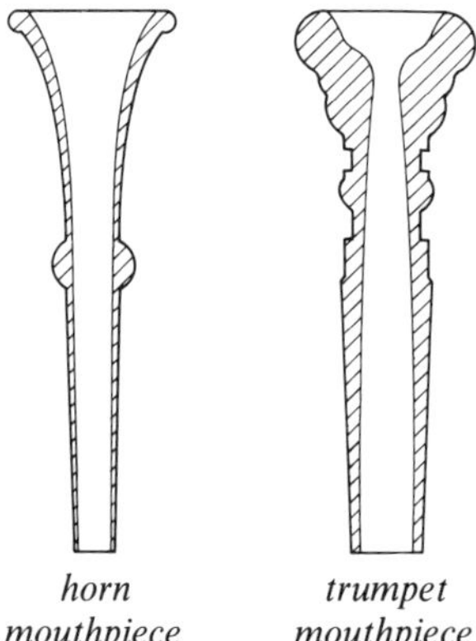

horn mouthpiece *trumpet mouthpiece*

of flare of the bell, are all main factors determining the individual timbre or tone-quality of a brass instrument.

A 'natural' brass instrument ('natural' horn, 'natural' trumpet) consists of a simple tube – with no extra mechanism of any kind. Such an instrument is able to produce only the notes of its own *harmonic series – successively higher notes of the series being produced as the player gradually increases lip tension. But to sound notes not included in that particular harmonic series, the length of the air column must be changed in order to provide a new fundamental and therefore a different harmonic series. To do this, early horn and trumpet players were provided with a set of *crooks – extra pieces of tubing, of differing lengths, each of which could be fixed into the instrument temporarily to change the overall length of the tube. But time was needed during the music to change from one crook to another, and each crook provided only those notes of the harmonic series of the new total length of tube. (Players of the *trombone, of course, had always been able to lengthen or shorten the instrument's tube-length instantly by means of the slide mechanism.)

An attempt was made during the 1790s to provide the trumpet with more notes by introducing a 'keyed trumpet' (for which Haydn composed his Trumpet Concerto). This trumpet had side-holes, with keys, bored into the tube – but the result was unpopular due to a decrease in brilliance of tone. Another attempt was the 'slide trumpet', provided with a slide mechanism similar to that of the trombone, but this made the trumpet decidedly less agile. However, around 1815, all these problems were solved by the invention of the *valve system – which is like having a complete set of crooks permanently fixed into a brass instrument and enabling it to be fully chromatic (able to sound all semitones throughout its pitch-range).

The number and type of instruments required in the **brass section** of the orchestra vary from one composition to another, but a typical symphony orchestra brass section includes: 4 horns, 3 trumpets; 2 tenor trombones and 1 bass trombone, 1 tuba.

Other brass instruments include the cornet, flugelhorn, euphonium, baritone horn, sousaphone, and various sizes of saxhorn. Among older brass instruments are the bugle, posthorn, clarino, clarion, buisine, and sackbut. The cornett and the serpent are also counted as brass instruments.

Bratsche (plural: *Bratschen*) [German] Viola.

Bravura [Italian: 'bravery', 'skill'] The brilliant (and usually extremely difficult) 'display' element in certain pieces which challenges the performer's technique and musical capability.

Brawl See *Branle.

Break In jazz, a short cadenza-like passage, coming at the end of a phrase, during which one (or more than one) soloist improvises, usually without accompaniment from the rhythm section.

Breit [German] Broad (and therefore slow). **Breiter**, broader.

Breve [from Latin, *brevis*: 'short', 'brief'] A note, introduced in the early 13th century, which was originally a short note – half the value of the note which was called a **long**. However, as even shorter notes were introduced, the breve became relatively longer. It is rarely used in modern notation. A breve has the time-value of two semibreves, or four minims, or eight crotchets. It may be written as 𝅜 or 𝅜 or 𝅜 and the equivalent *rest is shown as 𝄺 (The American name for a breve is double whole note.) [See also: *Alla breve]

Bridge The piece of wood on a string instrument across which the strings are stretched. Besides supporting the strings it also carries their vibrations down to the body of the instrument so that the sounds are amplified (made louder).

Bridge passage A term which may be used to describe any passage of music which serves as a link, leading from one theme to another. However, the term is used especially in *sonata form, where the purpose of the bridge passage is to connect the first subject-group to the second subject-group, and also to modulate to the key of the second subject-group. (The term *transition is sometimes used to mean the same thing.)

Brigg Fair **1** An 'English Rhapsody' for orchestra composed in 1907 by Delius, which is a set of variations on the Lincolnshire folk-song 'Brigg Fair', introduced to Delius by the Australian composer, Percy Grainger. **2** Setting of the same folk-song made in 1906 (revised 1911) by Percy Grainger for unaccompanied voices, consisting of solo tenor and four-part choir (sopranos, altos, tenors, basses).

Brillant [French]; **Brillante** [Italian] Brilliant.

Brindisi [Italian: 'a toast'] A drinking song, especially in operas. A famous example is 'Libiamo' ('Let us drink') in Act I of Verdi's opera *La *Traviata.*

Brio [Italian] Vigour, spirit, energy, fire. **Con brio**, vigorously, with spirit.

Brioso [Italian] Lively, spirited, vivacious.

Broadside ballad A *ballad printed on one side of a single long sheet of paper (called by printers a 'broadside'). In England, from the 16th century to the 19th, ballad singers sang, and sold, broadside ballads in the streets. These ballads often served the same purpose as newspapers and television today by relating recent interesting events (e.g. a hanging, a murder, the exploits of a notorious highwayman, and so on).

Broken chord A chord 'broken up' so that its notes are sounded one after another (instead of simultaneously) and perhaps in a repeating pattern. The *Alberti bass is an example; a more musically imaginative use of broken-chord patterns can be found, for example, in many of Chopin's piano pieces. (Sometimes also called an arpeggio.)

Broken consort See *Consort.

Buffa; **Buffo** [Italian] Comic. **Opera buffa**, a comic opera. Can also describe a comic role played by a singer in an opera – for example, **basso buffo**, a comic role sung and acted by a bass singer (such as Doctor Bartolo in Rossini's *The *Barber of Seville*).

Buff stop Another name for harp stop (see under *Harpsichord).

Bugle A brass instrument with a wide bore; it is a 'natural' instrument (without valves) capable of producing notes from one harmonic series only.

Buisine Name for the long medieval straight trumpet or herald's trumpet (over six feet long), the shorter type being called *clarion.

Burden A refrain, or chorus, in which the same music and words recur at the end of each verse in a song or a *carol.

Burla; **Burlesca** [Italian]; **Burleske** [German]; **Burlesque** [French] A piece in playful, joking mood.

'Butterfly' Study Nickname of Chopin's Study (Étude) No. 9 in G♭ major (1834) from his second set of Twelve Studies for piano, Op. 25. The music (marked *leggiero*; later, *leggierissimo*) suggests the delicate flitting of a butterfly.

Buxheimer Orgelbuch (Buxheim Organ Book) A large and important collection (*c*1470) of organ compositions, notated in tablature. The manuscript was originally kept at the monastery of Buxheim near Munich. Besides sacred pieces, there are settings of German songs and French chansons, and a number of basse danses.

BWV Letters standing for *Bach-Werke-Verzeichnis* – a catalogue of Bach's works prepared by the German music librarian, Wolfgang Schmieder. Linked to the title of any piece by Bach, **BWV** followed by a number indicates that piece's numbered entry in the catalogue. Sometimes, instead of BWV, an initial letter **S**, is used, standing for 'Schmieder catalogue number'. For example, Bach's famous Toccata and Fugue in D minor for organ may be identified either as BWV565 or as S565.

C **1** Abbreviation of contralto. **2** Two decorated versions of the letter C (**C** and **₵**) are used as *time signatures (though, originally, this sign was in fact a broken, or imperfect, circle). [See also the table of Time signatures on page 389]

c Abbreviation of the Latin word **circa.*

c.a. Abbreviation of *col *arco.*

Cabaletta [Italian] Originally, a *cabaletta* was a brief aria (found, for example, in the operas of Rossini) which was simple in style and uniform in rhythm, and with a repeat which invited the singer to improvise ornamentation. Later (for example, in the operas of Bellini and Verdi) the word came to mean the concluding section – usually swift in speed and mounting in excitement – of a longish aria or duet.

Cabinet organ See *Positive organ.

Caccia [Italian] **1** Chase, hunt (**alla caccia**, in hunting style). **2** One of the three main types of secular vocal music (together with the *madrigal and the *ballata) used by Italian 14th-century *Ars Nova composers (such as Francesco Landini and Jacopo da Bologna). For a caccia the composer took a lively text, vividly describing hunting or fishing, and set it for two voices in *canon (one chasing the other, as in a hunt). Sometimes an instrumental part was also included. An example is Francesco Landini's *Così pensoso* (which may also be described as a *pesca*, a fishing song).

Cachucha [Spanish] A graceful Spanish dance, in triple time, from the region of Andalusia. It is similar to the bolero, but swifter and more energetic.

Cadences [from Latin, *cadere*: 'fall'] Cadences in a piece of music are 'resting-points', marking the endings of phrases and sections. They are important in establishing or confirming the tonality, and also serve as 'musical punctuation' (the musical equivalents of commas, full stops, and, in some instances, exclamation marks). Essentially, a cadence consists of the progression of two chords. Many terms are used to describe the four basic types of conventional cadence (as found in the music of 18th- and 19th-century composers) – but it must be emphasized that these terms are by no means standard. (For example, American musicians use some of these terms with different meaning, or use other terms altogether.)

(1) A **perfect cadence** (or **full cadence** or **full close**) consists of the dominant chord followed by the tonic chord (as in Example 1, opposite). A perfect cadence gives the music a sense of completion, of finality.

(2) A **plagal cadence** consists of the subdominant chord followed by the tonic chord (Example 2). It may also be called an **'Amen' cadence** since it is often used to harmonize this word at the end of hymns.

(3) An **imperfect cadence (half cadence, half close)** causes the music at the point where it is used to sound incomplete, unfinished (as its name implies). An imperfect cadence normally consists of the dominant chord preceded by almost any other chord – but most often either the tonic or the subdominant (Example 3).
(4) An **interrupted cadence (surprise cadence, deceptive cadence, false close)** deceives the listener into expecting a perfect cadence (the progression V–I) – but this is 'interrupted'. Instead of the dominant chord being followed by the expected tonic, the ear is surprised by another chord instead. This is very often the submediant chord (as in Example 4a) though an even more startling chord may be used if the composer wishes to emphasize the surprise element (Example 4b).

Any of these four main types of cadence may be decorated by the addition of other notes (e.g. the addition of the 7th to the dominant chord) or extended in some way.

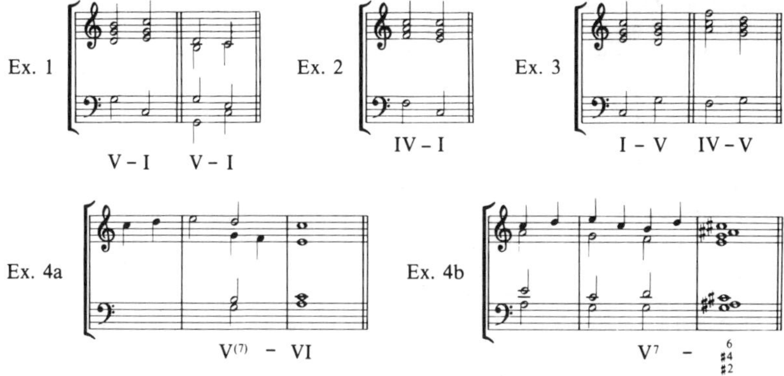

Other terms sometimes used in connection with cadences include the following (again, not all meanings are standard):
authentic cadence – (1) same meaning as perfect cadence, (2) a perfect cadence whose last chord has the tonic note in the top part as well as in the bass, (3) a perfect cadence which has both chords in root position; **inverted cadence** – any cadence which has either or both chords inverted; **feminine cadence** – describing any cadence in which the two chords move from a strong beat to a weak beat, whereas in a **masculine cadence** (which is more usual) they move from weak beat to strong beat; **mixed cadence** – an imperfect cadence consisting of subdominant chord followed by dominant chord.

[See also: *Tierce de Picardie; *Phrygian cadence]

Cadenza [Italian: 'cadence'] A showy passage intended to display the brilliance of a performer's technical ability. The term was first used in connection with 18th-century operatic arias, the custom being for a singer to introduce a brilliant improvisation before the final cadence. Similarly, in the first movement of a Classical *concerto, at the end of the recapitulation section, the orchestra played a second inversion of the tonic chord, then paused while the soloist performed a cadenza. Originally, a soloist was expected to improvise a cadenza on the spot – and besides impressing the audience with dazzling playing, to make reference to themes heard earlier in the movement. Later on, composers provided soloists with written-out cadenzas (Beethoven was first to take away the soloist's option of improvising by incorporating a written-out cadenza into the first movement of his *'Emperor' Concerto.) A cadenza usually ends with a trill over dominant seventh harmony – a signal to the orchestra to re-enter to play the coda. A cadenza might also occur in either of the two remaining movements of a concerto.

Caisse [French] Drum. **Caisse claire**, snare (side) drum. **Caisse roulante**, tenor drum. **Grosse caisse**, bass drum.

Calando [Italian] Waning – becoming slower, or softer, or both.

Calcando [Italian] Pressing forward.

Calinda, La Orchestral piece by Delius – originally a wedding dance for orchestra and voices performed during Act 3 of his opera *Koanga* (1895–7), the story of which takes place in the Deep South of the USA. A still earlier version of the music formed the second half of the opening movement of his orchestral suite, *Florida* (1886).

Call-and-response A term describing a simple musical pattern or design in which a soloist (leader) is answered, or responded to, by a group. Examples include certain medieval songs and carols, also *work-songs, and instances in church services where the congregation responds to the officiant (e.g. 'O Lord, open Thou our lips'; [response:] 'And our mouths shall show forth Thy praise.').

Calmato [Italian] Calmed.

Calore [Italian] Warmth.

Calypso A type of popular song, with syncopated rhythm and repetitious melody, originating from the Caribbean islands (Trinidad in particular). The words, which are often improvised, usually pass satirical comment on politics or current events, or poke fun at some emminent personality of the time.

Cambia; **Cambiano**; **Cambiare** [Italian: 'it changes'; 'they change'; 'to change'] Directions occasionally found in orchestral scores and parts for a woodwind player to change instruments (e.g. from flute to piccolo), a brass player to change crooks, or for the timpanist to change the tuning of kettle drums. However, more commonly the Italian word **muta* is used.

Camera [Italian] Chamber, room (as opposed to hall, church, theatre, opera house). The Italian phrase *da camera* indicates that the music is intended for domestic or private performance, rather than for public or church performance (e.g. cantata da camera).

Camerata A group of writers and composers who frequented the salon of Count Giovanni de' Bardi in Florence, Italy, during the last quarter of the 16th century. Among the members of the group were the composers Giulio Caccini and Vincenzo Galilei (father of the scientist Galileo). The Camerata set out to recreate the way in which the ancient Greeks had performed their dramas. They believed that these had been sung throughout; it was this mistaken idea which gave birth to opera. [See also: **Dafne; *Euridice; Le *Nuove Musiche*]

Campana [Italian] Bell.

Campane [Italian] Tubular bells.

Campanella, La [Italian: 'Little bell'] The title of the third of Liszt's six *Études d'exécution d'après Paganini* (Transcendental Studies after Paganini), composed in 1838 and revised in 1851. Liszt bases the music upon the theme of the last movement of Paganini's Violin Concerto No. 2 in B minor in which a small bell is used in the accompaniment.

Campanelle [Italian] Tubular bells.

Campanelli; **Campanette** [Italian] Glockenspiel.

Cancan High-kicking 19th-century Parisian dance with two fast beats to a bar. Boisterously performed, with gaiety, abandon, and (very often) a certain amount of vulgarity. The most famous *Cancan* is from Offenbach's opera, *Orpheus in the Underworld.*

Canción [Spanish] Song.

Cancrizans [Latin: 'crab-like'] A term indicating that a part or a melody is to be performed backwards (or in *retrograde motion), beginning with the last note and ending with the first. [See also under *Canon]

Canon [Greek: 'rule' or 'law'] A contrapuntal piece, or a section of a piece, which essentially relies upon **imitation.* One vocal or instrumental part leads off with a melody, and then, shortly afterwards, a second part begins to perform the same melody. And so the 'rule' is that the second part imitates, note for note, the melody being given out by the leading part. The imitating part may follow at a distance of half a bar, one bar, two bars, or at any other distance, according to the composer's choice. Other parts may also enter, successively, with the same melody.

The leading part may be called the *antecedent* or *dux* [Latin for 'leader']; an imitating part may be called *consequent* or *comes* [Latin, 'follower' or 'companion'].

There are several varieties of canon – depending upon the method of imitation. The second part may imitate the melody at the same pitch as the first (described as **canon at the unison**), or an octave higher or lower (**canon at the octave**), a fifth higher or lower (**canon at the fifth**), or at any other interval – again, according to the composer's choice. In a **double canon**, *two* melodies are given out simultaneously by two parts, and imitated by another two parts – two canons, on two different melodies, going on at once.

The following example (from the *Farandole* from Bizet's *L'Arlésienne Suite* No. 2) shows a canon at the octave, the second (imitating) part entering a half-bar after the first (leading) part:

Other varieties of canon include:

(a) **canon by inversion**, or **contrary motion** (*per arsin et thesin, per motum contrarium*): in this type of canon, the imitating part presents the melody in inversion ('turned upside down') – intervals originally rising in pitch, now fall by the same amount (and vice versa);

(b) **canon by augmentation**: the imitating part gives out the melody in longer note-values (usually doubled);

(c) **canon by diminution**: the imitating part gives out the melody in shorter note-values (usually halved); here, the imitating part must start off rather late or it (the 'follower') will overtake the 'leader';
(d) **crab canon** (*canon cancrizans*) or **retrograde canon** (*recte et retro*): the imitating part gives out the melody backwards – beginning with the last note and ending with the first;
(e) **mirror canon** – this has two meanings: (1) a crab canon (see above), or (2) a canon in which the imitating part presents the melody in retrograde (backwards) *and* in inversion (upside down) at the same time;
(f) **infinite canon** or **perpetual canon** (*canon perpetuus*): in this kind of canon, as each part reaches the end of the melody it goes back to the beginning and starts all over again; a **round** (such as *Frère Jacques*) is a simple type of infinite canon at the unison;
(g) **accompanied canon**: a canon accompanied by one or more other independent parts which do not take part in imitating the melody.

A canon may consist of a combination of some of the above – for example: (a) and (b) combined, or (a) and (c). A canon may be *strict* or *free*. In a **strict canon**, each *interval is imitated exactly, in both number and quality; in a **free canon**, although each interval may be imitated in number (numerical size), the quality may vary – for example, a minor 3rd in the original melody may be imitated as a major 3rd, and so on.

A canon may also be described in figures. The first figure refers to the number of parts; the second to the number of melodies being imitated. For example, **canon 2 in 1** means a single melody, given out by one part, is imitated by one other part. **Canon 3 in 1**, a single melody is imitated first by one part, then by another. **Canon 4 in 2** is the same as *double canon* (see page 41).

[See also: *Puzzle canon: **Sumer is icumen in; The *Musical Offering; The *Art of Fugue;* *'Goldberg' Variations; *'Mourning' Symphony]

Canone [Italian] *Canon.

Canonic In the style of a canon.

Cantabile; **Cantando** [Italian] In a singing style.

Cantata [Italian: 'sung'] Originally, a title for a piece that is sung – as opposed to *sonata*, a piece that is played. The earliest cantatas, by 17th-century Italian composers, were settings of secular words for one or two solo voices and continuo or a small group of instruments, and consisted of the alternation of recitatives and contrasting arias or duets. The idea was taken up by composers of other countries – particularly German composers, who favoured the church cantata to a sacred text rather than the secular cantata. The cantata now became more elaborate, including chorus and orchestra and several solo voices.

The most notable composer of cantatas was J. S. Bach. He composed about twenty-five secular cantatas (including the **Peasant Cantata* and the **Coffee Cantata*); and five complete cycles of church cantatas for the ecclesiastical year, of which 200 have survived. In many of these, Bach included a *chorale. A typical Bach cantata opens with an extended chorus (often fugal), continues with recitatives, arias, and duets for the soloists, then closes with a harmonized chorale in which the congregation would be expected to join.

The term **chorale cantata** is used to describe a cantata in which the words of the chosen chorale, and usually the melody as well, are used in other movements besides the final one. In Bach's Cantata No. 4, **Christ lag in Todesbanden*, the chorale is used in each movement; in his Cantata No. 140, **Wachet auf*, the chorale appears in three of the seven movements.

Since the time of Bach, the title *cantata* implies a choral work, sacred or secular, for soloists, chorus, and orchestra. It differs from an oratorio by being on a smaller scale, and by setting a text which is less narrative, less continuous. More recent examples include Vaughan Williams's *Dona nobis pacem*, Bartók's *Cantata profana*, Stravinsky's *Cantata* (setting anonymous English lyrics), Orff's **Carmina burana*, and Britten's *Cantata academica* and *Cantata misericordium*.

Cantate [German] *Cantata.

Cante [Spanish] Song, singing.

Cantiga A type of Spanish monophonic song of the 13th century, similar in structure to the French *virelai. A large, finely illustrated collection of cantigas was made by King Alfonso the Wise (ruled 1252–84), some of them probably his own compositions. Many of the cantigas are written in praise of the Virgin Mary, but a few deal with secular subjects.

Cantilena Name given to a lyrical song, or a flowing instrumental passage in a similar sustained style.

Canto [Italian] Chant; song; melody.

Canto fermo [Italian] *Cantus firmus.

Cantor **1** In the Jewish and early Christian Church, the person leading the singing. **2** In the Lutheran Church in Germany, the Cantor (sometimes spelt *Kantor*) was the director of music (e.g. Bach was cantor at St Thomas's Church, Leipzig, from 1723 until his death in 1750).

Cantoris [Latin] The section of the choir occupying the stalls on the north side of a church or cathedral (the cantor's or precentor's side).

Cantus [Latin] Melody, song.

Cantus firmus [Latin: 'fixed song', 'firm melody'; Italian: *canto fermo*] A pre-existing melody which a composer takes as a 'fixed song' or 'foundation tune' upon which he structures his music by weaving one or more parts for other voices and/or instruments above and below it. Until 1300 almost all polyphonic compositions were built up in this way – in each case, the cantus firmus was a melody borrowed from plainsong, very often with the notes drawn out in very long values in the tenor part (see *Tenor, 3). Forms structured on a cantus firmus included *organum and the *clausula and, in the 13th and 14th centuries, motets and Mass movements. (An exception was the *conductus, which was freely composed, i.e. not based on a cantus firmus.) Sometimes a composer chose a secular tune as the cantus firmus for a motet, rather than a plainchant, and this became a common feature of Masses composed during the 15th century (see *L'*Homme armé*). Towards the end of the 15th century, the practice of using a cantus firmus began to decline; in the 16th century, a Mass or motet which was so based was considered to be old-fashioned. But the practice survived in certain types of composition, e.g. the English *In nomine of the 16th and 17th centuries, and the Baroque *chorale prelude.

Canzona (*canzon, canzone*; plural: *canzoni*) [Italian: 'song'] **1** Name used during the 16th century for an instrumental arrangement of a French *chanson* (song) and so sometimes called a **canzona francese**. **2** A type of instrumental music which developed from the above, often given the title *canzona per sonare* (a 'song to be sounded on instruments'). A canzona might be written in fugal style for keyboard (e.g. an organ canzona); or for instrumental ensemble with the music built up in several sections, contrasted in speed, rhythm, metre, and texture. Eventually, the contrasting sections became longer, and finally developed into the separate movements of the Baroque *sonata. **3** Canzona was sometimes used as a title for a movement of a Baroque sonata, denoting that the music was written in fugal style. **4** A lyrical song, simple in style, may be entitled *Canzona* (especially in Italian operas).

Canzonet; **Canzonetta** [Italian: 'little song', or small *canzona] A short polyphonic song, tuneful and often dance-like, popular in Italy and England during the 16th and 17th centuries.

Capella A misspelling of the Italian word **Cappella.*

Capelle See *Kapelle.

Capellmeister See *Kapellmeister.

Capo [Italian: 'head'] Beginning (of a piece or movement). [See: *Da capo]

Cappella The Italian word for 'chapel' – used in a special sense in the term **a cappella.* [See also: *Maestro di cappella]

Capriccio [Italian: 'caprice'] Title for a piece which is capricious, fanciful, or humorous in character, or free and unconventional in form or style, or perhaps includes some surprising or original effects. Brahms used the title for some of his later piano pieces (conventional in form but capricious in character); the 20th-century Czech composer, Janáček, wrote a *Capriccio* for piano (the pianist using the left hand only) with a wind ensemble made up of flute, piccolo, two trumpets, and four trombones.

Capriccio espagnol See **Spanish Caprice.*

Capriccio italien See **Italian Caprice.*

Caprice [French; also English] Same as the Italian term **capriccio.*

Capriol Suite Suite of dances for string orchestra, composed in 1926 by Peter Warlock. The six dances are based on old French dance-tunes from a book published by Arbeau in 1589 called *Orchésographie* (the study of dancing). The rhythms and steps of popular 16th-century dances are discussed by Arbeau and a lawyer named Capriol. The six dances in Warlock's *Capriol Suite* are: 1 *Basse-danse*; 2 *Pavane*; 3 *Tordion*; 4 *Bransles*; 5 *Pieds-en-l'air*; 6 *Mattachins.*

Carillon **1** A set of bells – particularly those hung in towers and on which tunes can be played by means of a keyboard. **2** The word is also used in French orchestral scores to mean *glockenspiel.

Carmans Whistle, The Title of a set of variations by William Byrd, included in the *Fitzwilliam Virginal Book as item number 58. Byrd borrowed the tune which the carman whistles from a ballad printed in 1592. ('Carman' is the Elizabethan word for a carter.)

Carmen Opera in four acts by Bizet, first produced in Paris in 1875 (libretto by Meilhac and Halévy after the novel by Mérimée). The story is set in the year 1820. Micaela (soprano) arrives in a square in Seville, seeking her lover Don José (tenor), a corporal of the guard. José, however, has become attracted to the gypsy Carmen (mezzo-soprano), who is employed in the local cigarette factory. During a quarrel at work Carmen stabs another girl and is arrested by José's superior officer, Captain Zuniga (bass). José helps her to escape, and is himself arrested as a result. Meanwhile, Carmen arrives at an inn used by smugglers. There she falls in love with Escamillo, a handsome toreador (baritone), but her first concern is for José, and she persuades him to flee to safety with her and some smugglers from the inn. Escamillo pursues them and fights with José, and when Zuniga intervenes José draws his sword on him. Quickly realizing his folly in attacking a superior officer, he escapes with Carmen to the smugglers' retreat in the hills. But Carmen's fondness for Escamillo grows and she promises herself to him if he wins a forthcoming fight in the bullring. By now José is mad with jealousy, and he begs Carmen to love him. She rebuffs him and he stabs her. Escamillo emerges, victorious, from the bullring as José gives himself up to justice.

Carmina burana (Songs from Beuron) A 'scenic cantata', with optional mimed action, composed by Carl Orff in 1937; for soprano, tenor, and two baritone soloists, boys' choir, mixed chorus, and orchestra. It consists of settings of twenty-four 13th-century poems in Latin, old French, and old German, describing life and love in the Middle Ages. The poems, written by wandering scholars and vagrant monks, are from a collection found in the Benedictine monastery of Beuron in Bavaria. [See also: *Goliard songs]

Carnaval (Carnival) A suite of twenty-one piano pieces, Opus 9, composed by Schumann between 1833 and 1835. It has the subtitle 'Scènes mignonnes sur quatre notes' (miniature scenes on four notes). The four notes are *A–S–C–H* which, taking S as standing for *Es*, are the German names for the notes A–E♭–C–B. These are the four 'musical' letters included in Schumann's name; they also spell the name Asch, the home town of the girl he was in love with at the time. Several of the pieces open with these four notes; some of the others begin with the three-note 'motto' *As–C–H* (German names for A♭–C–B).

The descriptive titles Schumann gives to the pieces suggest he is imagining himself at a masked ball. It is attended by several of his friends, including Chopin, Paganini, Estrella (the girl from Asch), and Chiarina (Schumann's future wife, Clara Wieck). Also present are characters from the *commedia dell'arte*, such as Pierrot, Harlequin, and Pantalon and Columbine. Schumann portrays himself in two of the pieces: *Eusebius, and Florestan. [See also: *'Character' piece]

Carnaval romain, Le (Roman Carnival) A concert overture, Opus 9, by Berlioz, composed in 1844 and based on musical ideas from his unsuccessful opera, *Benvenuto Cellini.*

Carnival of Animals, The (*Le Carnaval des animaux*) A 'grand zoological fantasy' by Saint-Saëns, for two pianos, flute, clarinet, glockenspiel, xylophone, two violins, viola, cello, and double bass (the string parts are often played by a full string section). There are fourteen short pieces: 1 Introduction and royal march of the lions; 2 Hens and cockerels; 3 Wild asses; 4 Tortoises; 5 The elephant (double bass solo); 6 Kangaroos; 7 The aquarium; 8 Persons with long ears; 9 The cuckoo in the depths of the wood; 10 The aviary; 11 Pianists; 12 Fossils; 13 The swan (cello solo); 14 Finale.

Saint-Saëns composed the music in 1886 as a musical joke to amuse his closest friends, and would not allow public performance during his lifetime. In several of the pieces, he makes fun of well-known tunes – for example: in *Fossils*, a tune from his own **Danse macabre*; and in *Tortoises*, the galop from Offenbach's *Orpheus in the Underworld.*

Carnival Overture (*Karneval*) Orchestral work, Opus 92, composed by Dvořák in 1891. It is the second of three concert overtures which he intended should be played as a group, with the overall title 'Nature, Life, and Love'. The first of them is called *In nature's realm* (or *Amid nature*), and the third is *Othello.*

Carol A song, not only associated with the joy and cheer of Christmas, but in fact celebrating any religious festival, or season of the year (such as spring or harvest), or any important occasion or event (e.g. the Agincourt Carol which was composed to celebrate the English victory at the battle of Agincourt in 1415). Early carols (13th–15th centuries) were often danced as well as sung – probably as *round dances. The verses were sung by one or more soloists, alternating with the *burden* (or refrain) which was sung by everyone.

Carole A medieval French name for a *round dance.

Cassa [Italian] Drum. **Cassa rullante**, tenor drum. **Gran cassa** or **cassa grande**, bass drum.

Cassation [Italian: *cassazione*] An 18th-century composition in several movements, for small orchestra (similar to a *divertimento or a *serenade), and often intended for outdoor performance. Mozart wrote two cassations: in G major (K63) and in B♭ (K99), both composed in 1769.

Casse-noisette See *The *Nutcracker*.

Castanets [from Spanish, *castaña*: 'chestnut'] A percussion instrument consisting of two tiny saucers of hard wood. True Spanish castanets are joined together by a cord, wound around the dancer's thumb and finger and clicked together with crisp, rhythmic precision. However, when castanets are used in the orchestra or a band, for convenience they are usually hinged on a stick; they can be shaken, or the player can tap one against the other with the finger, or against the knee. The castanets can be heard in the *Spanish Dance* from Tchaikovsky's ballet *Swan Lake*, in *Castillane* from Massenet's *Le Cid*, and in *Noche espagnole* from Walton's *Façade Suite* No. 2.

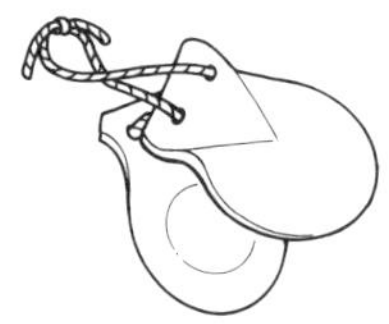

Spanish castanets

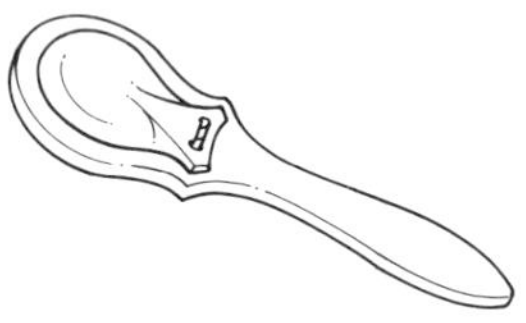

orchestral castanets

Castrato (plural: *castrati*) During the 17th and 18th centuries, an adult male singer, castrated before puberty. This prevented his voice from 'breaking' or deepening, and so preserved the pitch-range and youthful tone-quality of his treble or alto voice, eventually combined with the lung capacity and vocal power of a man. Composers of **opera seria* often included parts for castrati. Nowadays, these parts are either transposed down an octave (for tenor or baritone), or taken by a female soprano or mezzo-soprano wearing male costume.

Catch Name used in England during the 17th and 18th centuries for a short *round for three or more unaccompanied voices. The words of a catch were often humorous, occasionally bawdy.

Catena di trilli [Italian] A 'chain', or series, of trills.

Catgut Tough cord sometimes used for strings on violins, etc. It is made from intestines of certain animals, particularly sheep (but *not*, as might be suggested by the name, cats).

Cathédrale engloutie, La (The submerged cathedral) The tenth of Debussy's piano preludes, Book 1, composed in 1910. It is a musical impression of an old legend from the coast of Brittany: on certain moonlit nights, or clear mornings as a chilly dawn is breaking, the cathedral of Ys – long submerged centuries ago beneath the sea – rises again from the waters. Debussy's music suggests rocking waves, the ghostly tolling of bells, and long-dead priests chanting organum.

Cavalleria rusticana (Rustic chivalry) Opera in one act (but two scenes) by Mascagni, first produced in Rome in 1890 (libretto by Menasci and Targioni-

Tozzetti after a story by Verga). Turiddu (tenor), a soldier returned from the wars, finds his former love, Lola, married to the wagoner Alfio (baritone). He makes Santuzza (soprano) his mistress and she becomes pregnant by him, but unknown to Alfio he loses his heart again to Lola (mezzo-soprano). Santuzza begs him to remain faithful, but her plea is of no avail and in a fit of rage she tells Alfio of the association between his wife and Turiddu. The two men fight a duel and Turiddu is killed. The action takes place in Sicily on Easter morning, and the scenes are separated by the famous orchestral Intermezzo. Frequently the opera shares a programme with Leoncavallo's **Pagliacci*. [See also: *Verismo]

Cavatina **1** A short, simple song or aria in operas of the 18th and 19th centuries, lacking elaborate repetition of words or music. **2** Sometimes used as a title for a tuneful and song-like instrumental piece.

C.b. Abbreviation standing for: **1** *col basso* [Italian], with (play the same notes as) the bass; or **2** *contrabasso* [Italian], double bass.

C clef See *Clef.

C.d. Abbreviation for *colla destra*, with the right hand.

Cebell; **Cibell** A type of *gavotte.

Cecilia, Saint The patron saint of music, believed to have been martyred in Sicily in AD 230. Her association with music, however, does not seem to have begun until the 15th century, when Italian painters often depicted her with harp, organ, and other musical instruments. Her saint day (St Cecilia's Day), 22 November, is widely celebrated. [See also: *Ode]

Cédez [French: 'yield', 'give way'] Indication that the music becomes slower (and usually also softer).

Celere [Italian] Quick, swift. **Celerità**, rapidity, speed.

Celesta A keyboard percussion instrument, invented in 1886 by Auguste Mustel. In appearance it resembles a small upright piano. Pressing down the keys operates a piano-like action inside the instrument, causing felt-covered hammers to strike steel plates, graded in size and therefore in pitch. Beneath each plate is a resonator which helps to enrich and sustain the sound. There is a damper pedal, enabling the player to damp the sound when required. The tone is silvery and clear, with a bell-like chiming quality. The first composer to use the celesta was Tchaikovsky, who featured it in the *Dance of the Sugar-Plum Fairy* in his ballet *The Nutcracker*. Another work in which the instrument has an important part is Bartók's **Music for Strings, Percussion, and Celesta*.

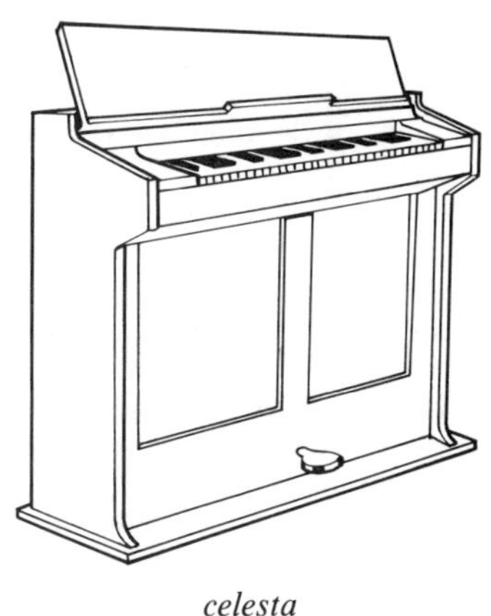

celesta

Music for celesta is written an octave lower than it actually sounds, and on two bracketed staves (like music for piano).

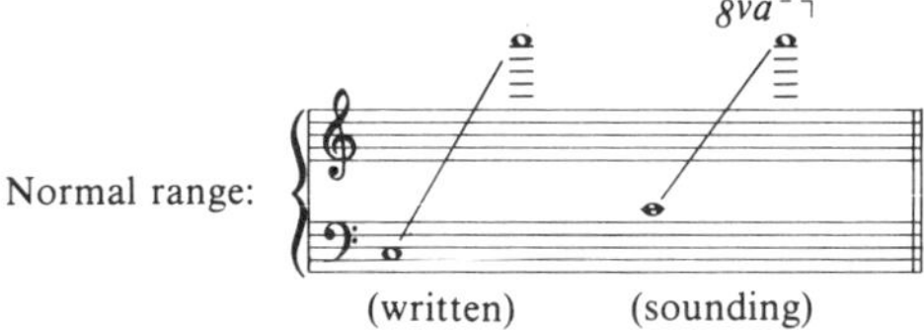

Five-octave celestas are sometimes found, in which the range is extended downwards for a further octave.

Céleste [French] Celesta.

Cello A bowed string instrument which is the third largest member of the *violin family. The full name of this instrument is *violoncello* [Italian, meaning 'little big-violin'] but the abbreviation *cello* has now become standard. Its shape is very similar to that of the violin, and it is about twice as big (1.23 m). It is held lightly between the knees as it is played, resting on the ground on an adjustable spike or 'end-pin'.

cello

The four strings of the cello are tuned in 5ths, one octave lower than the viola.

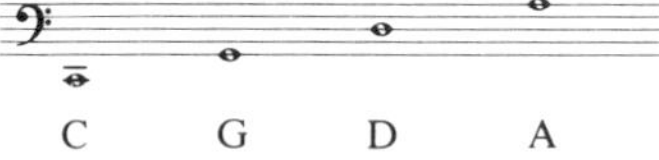

The range of the cello covers almost four octaves.

Lower notes are written in the bass clef; higher notes are written in the tenor clef, or even the treble clef.

The sound of the cello can be full and penetrating, the tone-quality warm and rich. It has a wide range of expression, and the largest dynamic range of all the string instruments. The cello is a standard member of the string quartet (along with first violin, second violin, and viola); the orchestra includes a section of cellos (often ten or more). Famous melodies for the cello section occur in the third movement of Brahms's Third Symphony, the second movement of Tchaikovsky's *Pathétique Symphony*, and the first movement (the second subject) of Schubert's 'Unfinished' Symphony. Concertos for cello and orchestra include those by Haydn, Schumann, Saint-Saëns, Dvořák, Elgar, Walton, Shostakovich, and Lutosławski; also, Britten's Cello Symphony. Brahms's 'Double' Concerto in A minor is for violin, cello, and orchestra.

One of the best-known pieces for solo cello is *The Swan* from *The *Carnival* *of Animals* by Saint-Saëns. Notable cello sonatas include those by Beethoven (5), Brahms (2), Fauré (2), and Debussy (1). Among works for unaccompanied cello are the six Suites by Bach, two Suites by Britten, Kodály's Sonata Op. 8, and *Nomos alpha* by Xenakis. The first of Villa-Lobos's *Bachianas brasileiras* is for 'at least eight cellos'; the fifth is for solo soprano and eight cellos.

The cello is included in many chamber works, besides the string quartet (e.g. string trio, piano trio, piano quintet, etc.; see under *Chamber music). During the 17th and 18th centuries, the cello was much used as a *continuo instrument, together with harpsichord, organ, or lute.

Cembalo Short for *clavicembalo* (Italian for harpsichord).

Cencerro [Spanish: 'cattle bell'] A Latin-American percussion instrument – a Cuban cowbell which is struck with a drumstick.

cencerro

Ceremony of Carols, A A work by Benjamin Britten (Op. 28; 1942) setting various carols for treble voices accompanied by harp. There are eleven movements of which the seventh is an Interlude for solo harp, and the work begins and ends with the plainchant *Hodie Christus natus est* (On this day Christ is born).

Ces [German] The note C flat. **Ceses**, C double flat.

Ceterone A bass *cittern.

C.f. Abbreviation of **cantus firmus* or *canto fermo*.

Chaconne and **Passacaglia** Two terms about which there has often been confusion among musicians (including composers). Originally, the chaconne was a slow, stately dance in triple time; passacaglia was the name given to the ritornello of a certain type of song. During the Baroque period, each of these became a type of continuous variations based on an ostinato ('obstinately repeating') idea. The distinction between them became blurred. But basically, a passacaglia is variations upon an ostinato theme which is usually found in the bass (*ground bass) – though it may be transferred to an upper part; a chaconne is variations on an ostinato idea which is really a harmonic progression, a chain of harmonies, rather than an actual tune or melody.

Chacony Old English term for *chaconne. For example: Purcell's *Chacony* in G minor for strings.

Chalumeau [French, from Latin *calamus*: 'reed'] **1** A rustic reed-pipe. **2** The chanter of a bagpipe. **3** A single-reed woodwind instrument introduced in the 17th century, considered to be an ancestor of the clarinet. **4** The term *chalumeau* is now used to describe the clarinet's lower register with its distinctive hollow and velvety tone-quality.

Chamber music Music intended for performance in a room, or chamber, rather than in a large hall. It is performed by a small group of solo musicians, with only one performer per part (whereas in orchestral music, two or more players may be sharing the same part). Essentially involved is the pleasure of shared music-making on the part of two or more solo performers – with, or without, an audience being present.

In its broadest sense, chamber music covers a wide variety of music of all periods – including for example, Medieval instrumental *hockets, Renaissance songs and madrigals, Elizabethan consort pieces, Baroque trio sonatas and 'solo' sonatas.

However, many musicians use the term **chamber music** in a narrower sense – limiting it in time from around 1750 (the beginning of the Classical period) to the present day, and applying it to works for instruments only, played by two or more performers. This excludes vocal works, and also works for solo performer (e.g. piano sonatas). But it does include duet sonatas for two performers (such as sonatas for violin and piano, cello and piano, and so on).

The main types of chamber work are described below. (Examples of the various types of duet sonata – violin sonata, cello sonata, etc. – are given in the list at the end of the article on *sonata; for examples of the other types of chamber work, see individual articles, e.g. *string trio, *piano trio, *string quartet, etc.)

Duet sonata (two players): *violin sonata* – violin and piano; *cello sonata* – cello and piano (similarly, clarinet sonata, horn sonata, etc.)
Trio (three players): **string trio* – violin, viola, cello; **piano trio* – piano, violin, cello.
Quartet (four players): **string quartet* – 2 violins, viola, cello; **piano quartet* – piano + string trio (and similarly, *flute quartet, *oboe quartet, etc.)
Quintet (five players): **string quintet* – an extra viola, or cello, or a double bass, added to the string quartet; **piano quintet* – usually, piano + string quartet; **clarinet quintet* – clarinet + string quartet (and so, similarly, *oboe quintet, *horn quintet); **wind quintet* – most often: flute, oboe, clarinet, horn, bassoon.
Sextet (six players): **string sextet* – 2 violins, 2 violas, 2 cellos; **wind sextet* – most likely: 2 oboes, 2 horns, 2 bassoons; or, 2 clarinets, 2 horns, 2 bassoons.

Next, come: ***Septet** (seven players), ***Octet** (eight), and ***Nonet** (nine). These types of chamber work, for a large number of solo players, offer the composer a wide choice of instruments – and it is usually impossible to tell from the title-word alone which particular combination of instruments has been chosen.

Whatever the combination of instruments involved, a chamber work is essentially a *sonata*, and is often similarly planned in four movements:

1 a fairly fast movement; almost always structured in *sonata form.
2 a lyrical slow movement; in ternary form, theme and variations, or sonata form again – perhaps *abridged sonata form.
3 a Minuet, or a brisk *Scherzo (either of these being built up in *minuet and trio form.
4 a quick finale, often light-hearted in mood; in simple rondo form, sonata form, a mixture of both (sonata-rondo form), or variations.

In some works, the Minuet (or Scherzo) precedes the slow movement.

Chamber orchestra A 20th-century term implying an orchestra of modest size consisting, for example, of a small body of strings together with a selection of wind instruments, either singly or in pairs (though trombones and tuba are normally excluded). Such an orchestra is ideal for performing 18th-century works such as the symphonies of Haydn and Mozart, and also 20th-century works specifically written for a small orchestra rather than a full symphony orchestra.

Chamber organ See *Positive organ.

Chamber sonata See under *Sonata.

Champêtre [French] Rustic. **Danse champêtre**, a peasant dance performed in the open air.

Chance-choice music See *Aleatory music.

Chandos Anthems A series of anthems by Handel, for solo voices, chorus, and orchestra. He composed them in 1717–18 when he was resident composer at Cannons (near Edgware in Middlesex) for James Brydges, Earl of Caernarvon, created Duke of Chandos in 1719.

Changing notes These are a kind of passing note, used as melodic decoration. Here are some examples:

As each example shows, there is always an interval of a third between the two changing notes, and they are pitched a step above and a step below the harmony note which immediately follows them (marked *).

Chanson In French, *chanson* simply means 'a song', but the word is used with special significance to refer to (1) the monophonic songs of the troubadours and trouvères of the 12th and 13th centuries; (2) the instrumentally accompanied songs by composers of the 14th and 15th centuries such as Machaut, Dufay, and Binchois (see *ballade, *rondeau, *virelai); and particularly (3) the 16th-century polyphonic chanson, for four or five voices. (The modern French word referring specifically to a song for solo voice with piano accompaniment is *mélodie*.)

Chanter See under *Bagpipe.

Chanterelle [French] Name given to the highest string on a violin or a lute, and meaning 'the singing one'.

Chanty See *Shanty.

'Character' piece A general term used to describe various types of instrumental piece (usually for solo piano) by 19th-century composers, each usually intended to portray a certain mood or character. Examples include pieces with titles such as Nocturne, Prelude, Impromptu, Étude, Moment musical, Song without Words, Ballade, Romance, Capriccio, Rhapsody, Intermezzo, Fantasiestück (fantasy piece). Many character pieces are designed in ternary form, presenting two contrasted moods. Sometimes, several such pieces, linked to the same background idea, are intended to be played in sequence as a suite (e.g. Schumann's **Carnaval* and **Kreisleriana*).

Chasseur maudit, Le (The accursed huntsman) A *symphonic poem by César Franck, composed in 1882. It is based on a ballad by Gottfried Bürger, telling of a count who goes hunting on a Sunday rather than attending church. As a punishment, he is relentlessly pursued by demons and must 'flee ever faster – over abysses by day, through the sky by night'.

Cheng A Chinese half-tube zither, with usually sixteen metal strings, each stretched over a movable bridge, and plucked with the fingernails of the right hand.

Chest of viols A name used in England in the 16th and 17th centuries for a set of *viols (usually six: two trebles, two tenors, two basses) which, when not in use, were stored in a chest lined with green baize 'to keepe the instruments from being injured bye the weather'. [See: *Consort]

Chest voice The lowest register of a singer's range, the sounds appearing to resonate in the chest. The other two registers are middle (or medium) voice, and *head voice.

Chevalet [French] Bridge (of string instruments such as the violin). **Au chevalet, sur le chevalet**, indications to bow very close to the bridge, producing a rather eerie tone-quality, especially when combined with bowed *tremolo.

Chiaro [Italian] Distinct, clear; clearly.

Chicago style (Chicago jazz) Terms used to describe the adaptation and development by white jazz musicians, in the 1920s, of the New Orleans style (see *New Orleans jazz).

Chiesa [Italian] Church; the term *da chiesa* is used to indicate that a composition was originally intended for use in church (e.g. sonata da chiesa).

Childhood of Christ, The See *L'*Enfance du Christ.*

Child of Our Time, A An oratorio by Michael Tippett, for soprano, alto, tenor, and bass soloists, chorus, and orchestra, setting words written by Tippett himself. It was composed between 1939 and 1941, but not heard till 1943. The event which inspired this work was the shooting of a German diplomat by a seventeen-year-old Polish Jew, in a desperate reply to the Nazi persecution of his parents. As in a Handel oratorio, there are recitatives, arias, and dramatic choruses. At key points, Tippett brings in settings of Negro spirituals – in the same way that Bach uses chorales in a setting of the Passion – to intensify the most solemn and deeply-moving moments.

Children's Corner A suite for piano composed by Debussy between 1906 and 1908 and dedicated to his four-year-old daughter. Debussy gave the six pieces English rather than French titles: 1 Doctor Gradus ad Parnassum; 2 Jimbo's lullaby; 3 Serenade of the doll; 4 The snow is dancing; 5 The little shepherd; 6 *Golliwogg's cakewalk. (By 'Jimbo' Debussy means 'Jumbo'; 'golliwogg' is his own spelling of 'golliwog'.)

Children's Games See **Jeux d'enfants.*

Chime bells A set of bells, without tongues, much used in Medieval times. They were graded in size, and therefore in pitch, suspended from a frame and hit with small hammers or beaters.

Chimes American name for *tubular bells.

Ch'in (chyn, qin) A Chinese plucked string instrument which has been in use for over 3,000 years. It is a long zither with seven silk strings of equal length and varying thicknesses; there are no bridges. Stopping positions for the strings are marked out by thirteen discs of ivory or mother-of-pearl which are inlaid along the soundboard. The strings are plucked with the fingers; a plectrum is not used.

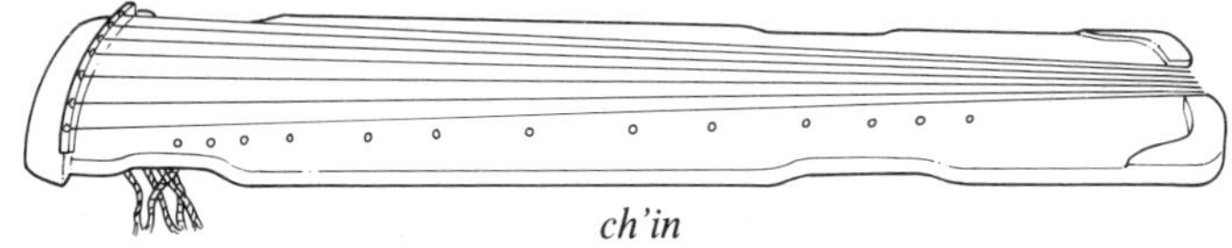

ch'in

Chinese block See *Woodblocks.

Chinese instruments See: *Cheng; *Ch'in; *Ch'ing; *Hu-ch'in; *P'i-p'a; *San-hsien; *Sheng; *Yüeh-ch'in; *Yün-lo.

Chinese pavilion See under *Janissary music.

Chinese temple block See *Woodblocks.

Ch'ing Chinese stone chimes, consisting of sonorous stones of different sizes, each shaped roughly like a letter L, hung from a frame and struck with a stick.

Ching-hu See *Hu-ch'in.

Chitarrone [Italian] A type of large bass lute.

Chiuso [Italian] Closed. In horn music, an instruction to the player that the note(s) should be fully stopped with the hand. The instruction is cancelled by the Italian word *aperto*. [See: *Stopping, 2]

Choeur [French] Choir, chorus.

Choir **1** A group of singers in which there are several performers per part. **2** Short for choir organ (see under *organ).

C-holes See *Soundholes.

Chor [German] Choir, chorus.

Choral **1** [English] Describing music for, or involving, a chorus or choir. **2** [German; pronounced ko-*rahl*] A hymn-tune of the German Protestant Church (see *chorale); also, the German word for plainchant.

Chorale [from German: *Choral*] A congregational hymn-tune of the German Protestant Church, founded by Martin Luther (1483–1546). It had been one of Luther's aims that the congregation should take more part in the church service, and so the words were always in German, rather than Latin. Some chorales were specially composed, many were based on plainsong Latin hymns of the Roman Catholic Church, and others were adapted from the melodies of secular songs. Well-known chorale melodies include *Wachet auf* ('Sleepers, wake' – included in most hymnbooks to the words 'Wake, O wake for night is flying'), *Ein' feste Burg* ('A safe stronghold' or 'A mighty fortress') and *Nun danket alle Gott* ('Now thank we all our God'). Bach includes settings of chorales in his Passions (see *Passion music and *'Passion Chorale') and also in his *cantatas (see, for example, **Wachet auf,* **Christ lag in Todesbanden,* **Jesu, joy of man's desiring*). The following shows the opening bars of Bach's four-part harmonization of *Ein' feste Burg*, a chorale originally adapted by Martin Luther from a plainsong melody. [See also: *Chorale prelude]

Chorale cantata See under *Cantata.

Chorale fantasia An organ composition (usually quite lengthy) in which the melody of a *chorale is treated freely, in the style and manner of a *fantasia. An example is *Ein' feste Burg* (BWV720) by Bach.

Chorale motet A composition for voices or organ in which the melody of a *chorale is treated in the style of a motet. The lines of the chorale melody are treated in turn to form a succession of sections, each based on *imitational entries. Examples are the first movement of Bach's Cantata No. 60, *O Ewigkeit, du Donnerwort*, and his organ chorale prelude *Nun komm' der Heiden Heiland* (BWV661) with the chorale melody sounding on the pedals.

Chorale partita A set of variations for organ, based upon the melody of a *chorale. Examples are Bach's chorale partitas on *Sei gegrüsset, Jesu gütig* (BWV768) and *Von Himmel hoch* (BWV769).

Chorale prelude A composition for organ, based in some way upon the melody of a *chorale, and intended to be played during the church service before the chorale is sung by the congregation. There are several ways in which the composer might treat the chosen melody. For example, he might treat it in fugal style, or compose variations on it, or weave one or more other melodic lines around it. The melody might appear in the top part of the musical texture, perhaps elaborated with ornaments and other extra notes; or it might be drawn out in long notes in the tenor or bass, accompanied by imitational figures in quicker notes in other parts of the texture.

Outstanding among composers of chorale preludes is J. S. Bach, who wrote about 140 examples, of all types (see **Orgelbüchlein*, *Schübler Chorales, and also **Clavierübung*).

'Choral' Symphony Beethoven's Symphony No. 9 in D minor, Op. 125, composed between 1822 and 1824 and originally entitled 'Symphony with final chorus'. There are four lengthy movements. The first (*Allegro, ma non troppo, un poco maestoso*) is in sonata form. The second movement is a Scherzo (*Molto vivace*) and Trio (*Presto*), the slow movement (*Adagio molto e cantabile*) being placed third. The Finale begins with quotations from the previous three movements; then follows a lengthy set of variations (beginning *Allegro assai*) in which the orchestra is joined by soprano, alto, tenor and baritone soloists and mixed chorus singing settings of verses from Schiller's *An die Freude* (Ode to Joy).

Other symphonies which use voices (soloists and/or chorus) include: Liszt's **Faust Symphony*; Symphonies 2 (*'Resurrection'), 3, 4, and 8 (*'Symphony of a Thousand') by Mahler; *A *Sea Symphony*, **Pastoral Symphony*, and **Sinfonia antartica* by Vaughan Williams; and *A *Spring Symphony* by Benjamin Britten.

Chord A combination of two or more notes sounding at the same time. (If two notes, only, are sounded, then the ear usually accepts that a third note is 'implied'.)

The basic, simplest type of chord is the **triad** – a chord of three notes, built upon a main note called the **root**, together with the notes forming a 3rd and a 5th above it (see *triad). Here are the four different kinds of triad built on G as the root:

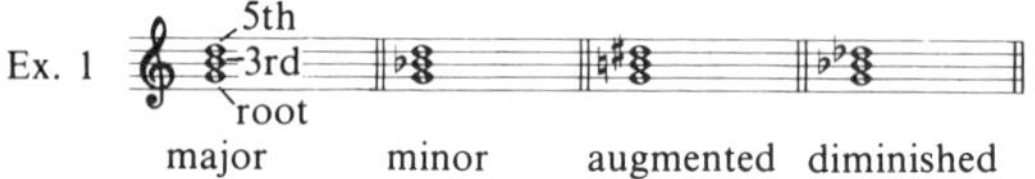

The three notes of a triad may be used to build up a fuller-sounding chord by doubling (duplicating) one or more of the notes at another octave. For example, these chords are all built from just the three notes of the G major triad:

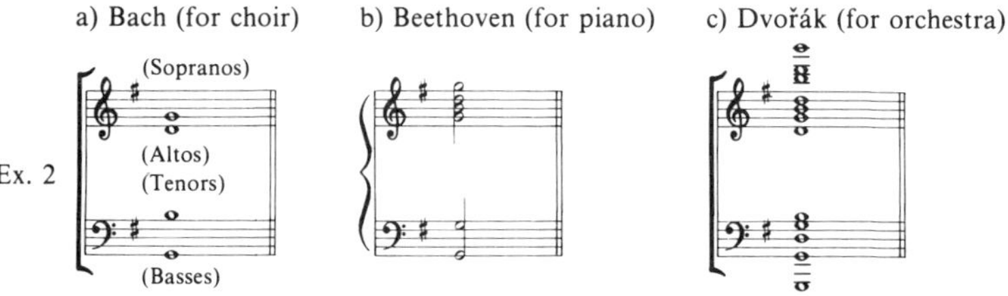

Each of the four types of triad (as shown in Example 1) consists of two 3rds stacked one above the other. For instance, the G major triad consists of a major 3rd (G–B) plus a minor 3rd (B–D). Adding another note, a 3rd higher, produces a **seventh chord** (or **chord of the seventh**) – so called because it includes an interval of a 7th above the root (Example 3). The seventh chord built upon the dominant (fifth degree) of any major or minor scale is called a **dominant seventh**; Example 3 shows the dominant seventh (V^7) of C major. Example 4 shows chords produced when other notes are added, a 3rd higher each time.

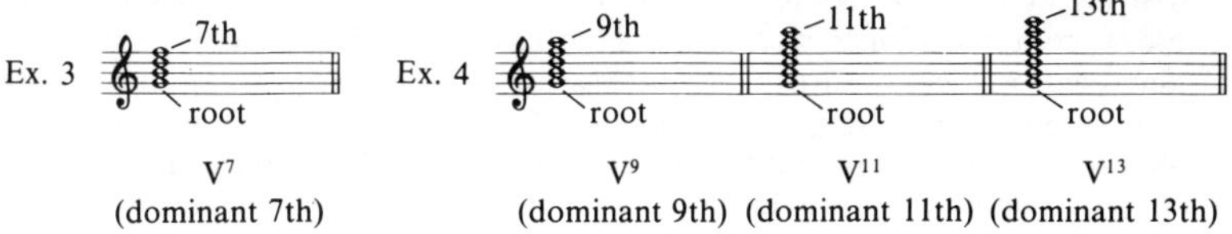

Triads and seventh chords are the basic components, or building-blocks, of 'traditional' harmony. Any major or minor triad is a **concord**; all other chords are, technically, counted as **discords**.

If the lowest-sounding note (bass-note) of a chord is also its root (as in all the examples above) then the chord is said to be in **root position**. If the notes are arranged in any position in which the root is not in the bass, then the chord is said to be in **inversion**. Example 5 shows the C major triad, with its two inversions. Example 6 shows a seventh chord (four notes: G–B–D–F) with its three inversions.

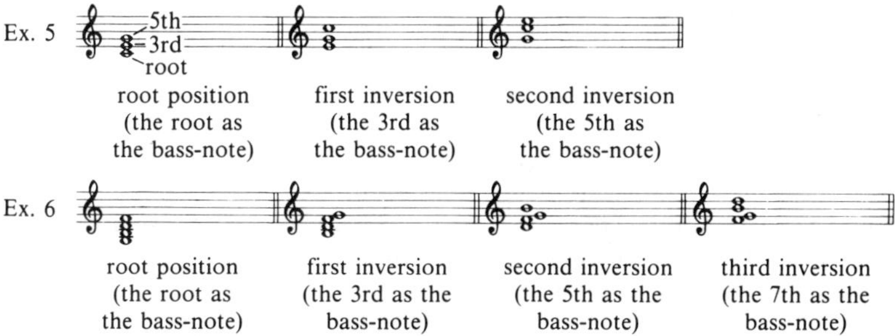

[For further information and other types of chord see: *Concords and discords; *Ninth chord; *Eleventh chord; *Thirteenth chord; *Six-three chord; *Six-four chord; *Added sixth chord; *Augmented sixth chords; *Diminished seventh chord; *Neapolitan sixth chord; *Fourth chord; *Note-cluster. See also under *Chromatic]

Chordal style A term describing the kind of musical texture where all the parts, in forming a series of chords, tend to keep rhythmically in step with each other – therefore lacking the rhythmic independence of the various parts in a *polyphonic, or contrapuntal, texture. [See also: *Block harmony; *Homophonic]

Chordophone A term used to describe any musical instrument whose sound is produced by the vibration of stretched strings being plucked, bowed, or struck (see *string instruments). [See also: *Idiophone; *Membranophone; *Aerophone; *Electrophone]

Chord stream See *Parallel chords.

Choreography [from Greek, *choreia*: 'dancing' + *graphē*: 'writing'] The art of planning a ballet and of devising, arranging, and linking together the various steps and movements of the dancers, sometimes by noting these down in detail by means of graphic symbols. Someone who so devises the steps and movements for a dance or a ballet is called a **choreographer**.

Chorus **1** A group of singers with several performers per part (as opposed to soloists) in a vocal work such as an opera or an oratorio. **2** Music composed for such a group. **3** The refrain of a song.

Christe eleison See *Kyrie eleison.

Christ lag in Todesbanden (Christ Lay in Death's Bonds) J. S. Bach's Cantata No. 4, composed for Easter, probably in 1707 or 1708; for soprano, alto, tenor, and bass soloists, chorus, and orchestra. It is a 'chorale cantata' in seven movements, each based on the following Lutheran chorale (based on an earlier melody, which was probably, in turn, based on a plainsong melody):

Bach also used this chorale as a basis for two chorale preludes for organ. One of them (BWV625) is No. 27 of *Das *Orgelbüchlein*; the other (BWV718) is in part three of **Clavierübung*.

'Christmas Concerto' Corelli's Concerto Grosso in G minor, Op. 6 No. 8, for strings and continuo, published in 1714. Corelli added the title *Fatto per la notte di Natale* ('composed for Christmas night'). The concerto is in six movements, the last being a *pastorale. Other composers who wrote similar concertos include Torelli (Op. 8 No. 6 in G minor; published in 1709) and Manfredini (Op. 3 No. 12 in C; published in 1718).

Christmas Oratorio (*Weihnachts Oratorium*) A choral work by Bach for solo singers, chorus, and orchestra; composed in 1734–5. It in fact consists of six cantatas, telling the story of Christ's nativity.

Chromatic [from Greek, *chrōmatikos*; 'coloured'] A **chromatic note** (or chromatically altered note) is one which does not belong to the scale of the key prevailing at the time. Similarly, a **chromatic chord** is one which includes one or more such notes (examples are *diminished seventh chords, *augmented sixth chords). **Chromatic harmony** describes harmony which makes extensive use of chromatic chords. A **chromatic *scale** is one which proceeds entirely by semitones, so dividing the octave into twelve equal steps of one semitone each.

Chromatic Fantasy (Fantasia) **and Fugue in D minor** A work for harpsichord (or clavichord) composed by Bach around the year 1720. The Fantasy makes much use of chromatic harmony; and chromatic notes are included in the subject of the Fugue:

Chromatic semitone A *semitone consisting of two notes with the same letter-name, and therefore with one or both of them affected by an accidental. For example: C–C♯; B♭–B♮. (A chromatic semitone is in fact the interval of an augmented unison.)

Church cantata See *Cantata.

Church modes (ecclesiastical modes) The medieval system of scales on which Western music of all types (i.e. not church music alone) was based until around 1600. You can play a mode on the piano by starting on a white note (say, D) and playing upwards step by step – but keeping to white notes only. Playing other modes, beginning on other notes, will show that no two modes share the same arrangement of tones and semitones. It is mainly the particular order of tones and semitones which gives each mode its special character or 'flavour'.

Originally, eight church modes were recognized. The main four, described as *authentic* modes, were called **Dorian** (D to D), **Phrygian** (E to E), **Lydian** (F to F), and **Mixolydian** (G to G). The note on which each of these modes began and ended was called the *final* (shown as a white note on the chart below). To each of these authentic modes was coupled another mode, described as *plagal*, whose range lay a 4th lower; since it shared the same final, it took the name of the authentic mode – but with the prefix 'hypo' (meaning 'under'). And so the four plagal modes were named **Hypodorian, Hypophrygian, Hypolydian**, and **Hypomixolydian**. Therefore the particular mode in which a melody is written is identified (1) by its *final* (the note on which the melody ends), but also (2) by the general *range* of the melody – the lowest note to the highest. For example: final note D, general range of melody D to D – Dorian mode; final note D, but general range of melody A to A – Hypodorian mode.

Later, four other modes became accepted into the system of church modes (even though composers had already made frequent use of them). These were the **Aeolian** (A to A) and the **Ionian** (C to C) together with their plagal forms, **Hypoaeolian** and **Hypoionian** (see overleaf), so making twelve modes altogether. (The Ionian mode is essentially the same as the major mode or major scale of the later major-minor key system; in Medieval times it had been called the 'wanton' mode and considered suitable only for secular music.)

In each mode, one note was called the *dominant* (shown by a letter *d* on the chart). Modes may also be referred to by number (indicated by the roman numerals on the chart). A mode may be transposed to another pitch – but to keep its particular identity (character, or 'flavour') the same arrangement of tones and semitones needs to be retained. [See: *Musica ficta]

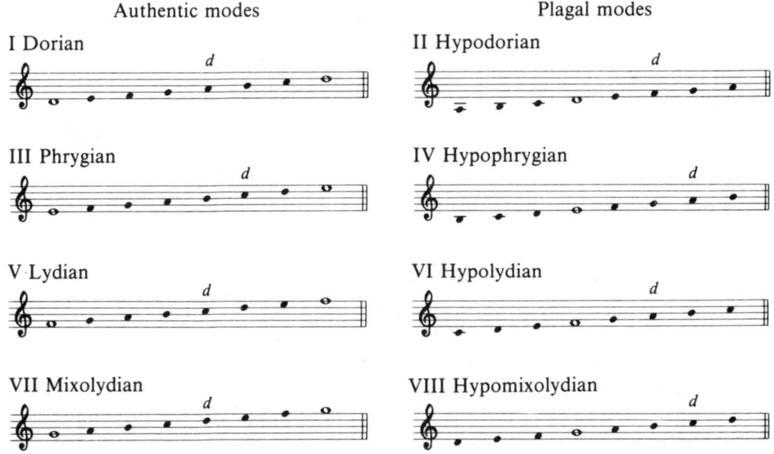

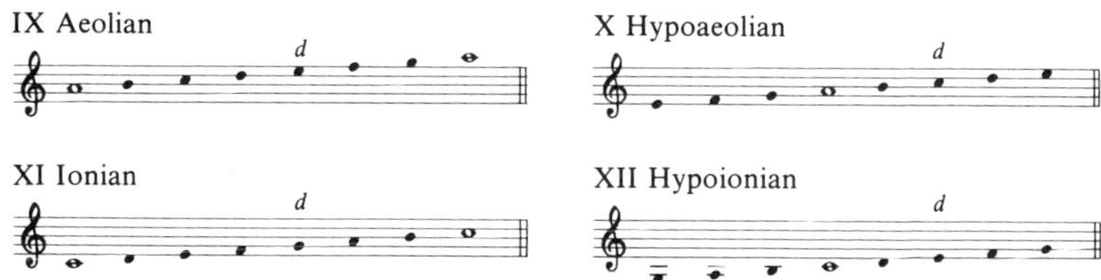

Church sonata See under *Sonata.

Chyn See *Ch'in.

Ciaccona [Italian] *Chaconne.

Cid, Le Opera in four acts by Massenet, first produced in Paris in 1885 (libretto by d'Ennery, Blau, and Gallet, based on the play by Corneille). The opera is set in 11th-century Spain, and tells of the famous knight and warrior called *El Cid.* A sequence of colourfully orchestrated dances, from Act II, is often played at concerts. They are: 1 *Castillane*; 2 *Andalouse*; 3 *Aragonaise*; 4 *Aubade*; 5 *Catalane*; 6 *Madrilène*; 7 *Navarraise.*

Cimbalom A type of dulcimer used in Hungary. The strings, divided by bridges into different tuned lengths, are beaten by hammers held one in each hand. In country districts in Hungary, a small kind of cimbalom is used to supply a background to fiddles and bass by playing chords, flourishes, and *tremolos* – two notes swiftly repeated in alternation. The concert version is provided with legs, and a damper pedal. [See also: **Háry János*]

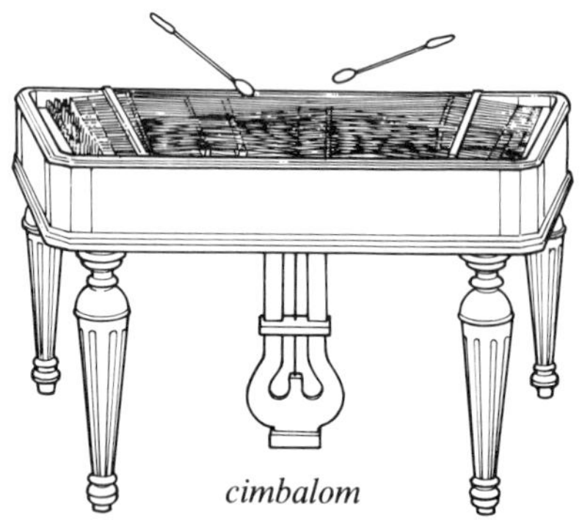
cimbalom

Cinelli [Italian] Cymbals.

Circa (often abbreviated simply to: *c*) A Latin word meaning 'about'. When linked to a year (e.g. Thomas Tallis: born *c*1505, died 1585) it indicates a date which is likely, though not known with absolute certainty.

Cis [German] The note C sharp. **Cisis**, C double sharp.

Citole A medieval plucked string instrument with four brass strings.

Cittern A plucked string instrument, pear-shaped and with a flat back, popular during the 16th and 17th centuries. The metal strings, arranged in pairs, were plucked either with the fingers or with a plectrum. The cittern was sometimes used as a melody instrument; it also played an important part in filling in the chords in music for 'broken *consort' (see **First Booke of Consort Lessons*). As the cittern was easier to play than the lute, it was very popular with amateur musicians (a cittern would be found in most barbers' shops so that waiting customers might

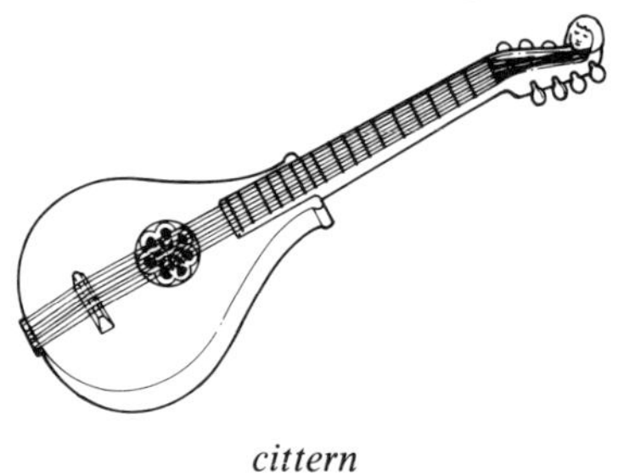
cittern

amuse themselves by strumming and picking out tunes). A larger, bass version of the cittern was called a **ceterone**.

Clair de lune (Moonlight) The third piece in Debussy's **Suite bergamasque* for piano, composed in 1890.

Claque A group of hired applauders, paid to clap and cheer the efforts of a performer (usually an opera-singer) regardless of the standard of his or her technique or musicianship. Often, members of a claque were paid according to a fixed scale of charges related to the volume, extent, and enthusiasm of their applause.

Claquebois [French: 'clack-wood' or 'bang-wood'] Xylophone.

Clarinet A single-reed *woodwind instrument which, together with the flute, oboe, and bassoon, is one of the four main orchestral woodwinds. The clarinet was the last of these to join the orchestra, not gaining a regular place until the last quarter of the 18th century – though it had been invented around 1690 by Johann Denner, a Nuremberg woodwind maker. The instrument he produced was an improvement and development of the 17th-century *chalumeau.

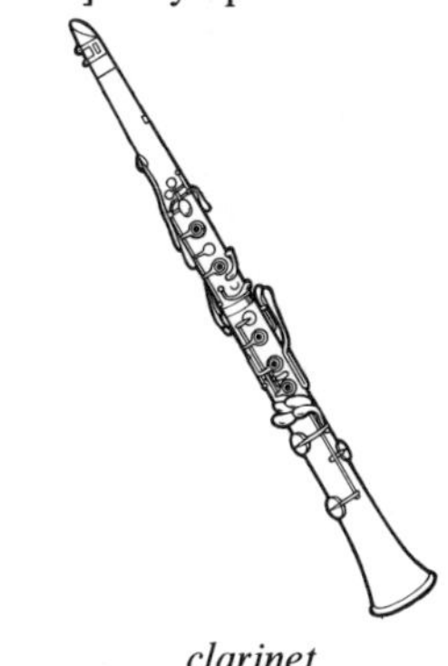

clarinet

The clarinet's tube is mainly cylindrical, ending in a flared bell. The single reed consists of a shaped flat piece of cane, delicately shaved thin at one end. This fits over an oblong hole in the beak mouthpiece, and is held in place by a metal clamp called a ligature. As the player blows, the reed vibrates, causing the air column inside the clarinet to vibrate also, and so sound a note. Different pitches are obtained by opening and closing holes, cut into the side of the clarinet, by means of a system of keys and levers (see *Boehm system).

Originally, clarinets were made in three sizes, pitched in C, in B♭, and in A. Those most commonly used today are the B♭ clarinet (66.7 cm long) and the A clarinet (69.8 cm long). Both are *transposing instruments. Music for B♭ clarinet is written a tone higher than it actually sounds; music for A clarinet is written a minor 3rd higher than it actually sounds.

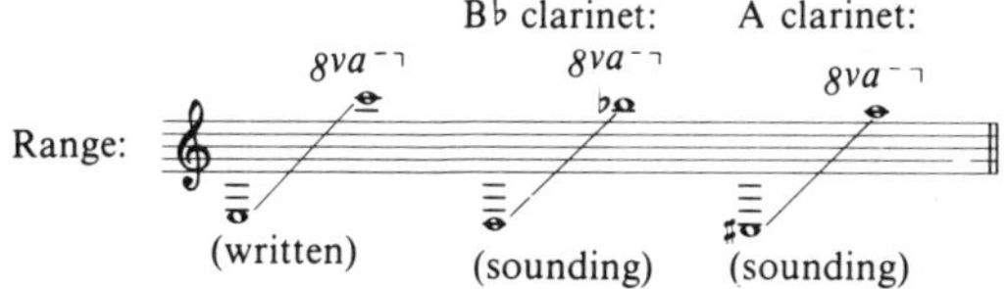

The clarinet is very agile, and is capable of a wide range of dynamics and expression. The lowest octave of its range of notes is called the *chalumeau* register; these notes sound dark, rather hollow, yet rich and velvety. Notes in the middle register are rather clearer and brighter, and increase in brilliance as they go into the upper register where, played louder, the sounds can be quite piercing, even strident.

Most orchestral music since the late 18th century includes parts for clarinet.

It is also used in *chamber music, frequently in music for wind ensemble, is a regular member of the symphonic band, and a staple member of the *military band (in which clarinets play much the same role as violins in the orchestra). The clarinet is also much used in jazz, notable jazz clarinettists including Johnny Dodds, Benny Goodman, Artie Shaw, and Woody Herman.

Orchestral solos for clarinet include *The Pines of the Janiculum* from Respighi's *The Pines of Rome*, the opening of Sibelius's First Symphony, the second movement of Brahms's Third Symphony, the music of the Cat in Prokofiev's *Peter and the Wolf*, the opening of Gershwin's *Rhapsody in Blue*, the opening of Tchaikovsky's Fifth Symphony (two clarinets, in the low register), the Trio of the third movement of Mozart's Symphony No. 39 (two clarinets, one low, one high), and *Dawn* from *Four Sea Interludes* from Britten's opera *Peter Grimes*. Among works for solo clarinet and orchestra are the concertos by Mozart, Weber, Nielsen, and Copland, Debussy's *Rapsodie*, and Stravinsky's **Ebony Concerto*. Stravinsky also composed Three Pieces for solo (unaccompanied) clarinet. Chamber works with clarinet include Beethoven's Trio in B♭ and Brahms's Trio in A minor (each for clarinet, cello, and piano), the clarinet quintets of Mozart, Brahms, Reger, and Bliss, Bartók's *Contrasts* for violin, clarinet, and piano, and Poulenc's Clarinet Sonata.

Other types and sizes of clarinet include: the alto clarinet in F (which is really a modern version of the *basset-horn), the *bass clarinet, the *contrabass clarinet, and the high-pitched small clarinets in D and in E♭. There is a part for the small clarinet in D in Strauss's *Till Eulenspiegel*, and the small clarinet in E♭ can be heard soon after the beginning of the last movement of Berlioz's **Symphonie fantastique*.

Clarinet quintet *Chamber music for clarinet plus string quartet (two violins, viola, cello). Fine examples are Mozart's Clarinet Quintet in A major (K581; 1789), Brahms's Clarinet Quintet in B minor (Op. 115; 1891), and Bliss's Clarinet Quintet (Op. 50; 1931).

Clarinette [French]; **Clarinetto** (plural: *clarinetti*) [Italian] Clarinet.

Clarinette basse [French]; **Clarinetto basso** [Italian] Bass clarinet.

Clarino **1** In Medieval times and the Renaissance, a type of trumpet. **2** From around 1600, the word came to describe the high register (*clarino* register) of the trumpet. Trumpeters were specially trained in the art and skill of clarino-playing – producing the higher notes in the *harmonic series where the pitches fall closer together and offer an ungapped scale. **3** From 1750, in Italy, *clarino* meant clarinet (the normal term now being *clarinetto*).

Clarion Name for the shorter medieval straight trumpet (two or three feet long), the longer type being called *buisine.

Clarone [Italian] Bass clarinet.

Classical music **1** Used in its precise and musical sense, this term is applied to music composed from around 1750 to around 1810 – that is, the fairly short period in the *history of Western music which followed the Baroque period and preceded 19th-century Romanticism. The Classical period therefore includes the works of Haydn and Mozart, and the earlier works of Beethoven. Some musicians would set the second date later – perhaps at 1827, the year of the death of Beethoven; others, however, maintain that Beethoven's later works, and most of the works of Schubert, are expressive of the style of Romantic music, rather than Classical.

Characteristics of music of the Classical period include: placing an importance on balance and proportion, order and control, clarity and simplicity; also, grace and beauty of line (melody, consisting of fairly short and clear-cut phrases) and perfection of shape (form, design, the structure of the music). Most important of all, Classical music strikes a perfect balance between expressiveness and formal structure; emotion is often present – but always in moderation, and under control.

During the Classical period, the harpsichord was replaced by the piano, and the Baroque sonata ('solo' sonata, trio sonata) gave way to the Classical sonata (see under *sonata) and to various types of *chamber music composition such as the trio, the quintet, and, especially, the string quartet. The period also saw the development of the *symphony (which stemmed mainly from the 'Italian overture') and of the Classical concerto (see under *concerto). Composers also wrote other, lighter works, mainly for entertainment, such as the serenade (see *serenade, 2) and the *divertimento.

The most important single musical form or structure, established and developed during the Classical period, was that of sonata form – based on the presentation and development of two 'subjects' (themes, or groups of themes or musical ideas) contrasted in key and usually also in mood or character. (See *sonata form.)

Compared with the often elaborate and contrapuntal Baroque style, the style of Classical music, while still making use of counterpoint at times, tends more often to be *homophonic (basically, 'melody-plus-accompaniment') and the musical texture is lighter, clearer, less complicated. There is more variety and contrast, within a piece, of tunes, rhythms, keys, and dynamics (now including *crescendo, diminuendo,* and *sforzando*), together with frequent changes of timbre (tone-colour) and also of mood.

Towards the end of the 18th century, the orchestra became more standardized (see under *orchestra). There was now a self-contained woodwind section, and the keyboard *continuo fell out of use.

Although during the Classical period instrumental music was predominant, fine vocal works were composed in the form of *opera (especially by Mozart), *oratorio (Haydn), and the *Mass.

[See also: *Viennese School; *Pre-Classical; *Mannheim School; *Gallant style; *Alberti bass; and also the time-chart of composers on pages 398–413]

2 In a very much looser way, 'classical music' is often used as a general term when dividing music into two very broad catagories: 'classical music' and 'popular music'.

Classical Symphony The title given by Prokofiev to his Symphony No. 1 in D major (1916–17) which is in *Neoclassical style. The orchestra is of exactly the same size as that used by Haydn in his last symphonies (2 flutes, 2 oboes, 2 clarinets, 2 bassoons; 2 horns, 2 trumpets; 2 kettle drums; and strings). And Prokofiev said he composed the music 'as Haydn might have written it if he had lived in our day'. The rhythms have a similar grace and elegance, but harmonies are frequently dissonant, and tunes are often given sudden 'twists' which send them off into unexpected keys, giving the music a definite 20th-century flavour. The third of the four movements, rather than being a minuet, is a dignified gavotte, with a *musette as a contrasting trio section.

Clausula (plural: *clausulae*) [Latin] The name given to a section within an *organum of the late 12th and early 13th centuries where the plainchant which the composer had chosen as his *tenor* offered a melisma – a melodious succession of notes sung to a single syllable. The text sung would therefore consist of a single word, or just a syllable – e.g. '*Do*' from 'Benedicamus *Domino*', or '*No-strum*' from 'Alleluia: Pascha *nostrum*' (see music B at the end of the article on *Organum). During the clausula, the tenor would also move in rhythm, the notes arranged according to a short rhythmic pattern repeated throughout. Clausulae were also composed separately – either to be substituted for those found in earlier organa, or to be performed as self-contained pieces. Eventually, it became the practice to add full texts to the upper voice-parts of clausulae – and this gave rise to the important form known as the *motet (from French *mots,* 'words').

Clavecin [French] Harpsichord.

Claveciniste A French word referring to **1** a player of the *clavecin* (harpsichord), and also **2** any 17th- or 18th-century French composer who particularly wrote for harpsichord (e.g. Couperin, Rameau, Daquin).

Claves [Spanish] Latin-American percussion instrument consisting of two hardwood sticks. One stick, resting in the cupped palm of one hand, is struck with the second stick held by the other hand. The light, clicking sound of claves can be heard at various times during Gershwin's *Cuban Overture* (e.g. about half a minute from the start; again at around two minutes), in Walton's *Johannesburg Festival Overture* (about three and a half minutes from the start), and in many Latin-American pieces played by dance bands.

claves

Clavicembalo [Italian] Harpsichord.

Clavichord [French: *clavicorde, manicorde;* German: *Clavichord, Klavichord;* Italian: *clavicordo, manicordo*] One of the oldest *keyboard instruments, possibly dating from the 14th century. It is rectangular in shape, with the *keyboard set into one of the long sides. The strings run parallel to the keyboard (i.e. at right angles to the keys themselves). They are anchored to hitch-pins at the left-hand end of the instrument, and pass over a *bridge* and the *soundboard* (which acts as a resonator) to the tuning-pins on the right. The clavichord is a quieter instrument than the *harpsichord, and well suited to intimate music-making.

clavichord

The later instruments (known as *unfretted* or *fret-free* clavichords) have two strings to each note. When a key is pressed down, a brass *tangent* at its far end strikes its pair of strings, effectively dividing them into two parts. Only one part vibrates, the other being damped by the *listing cloth*. The length of the vibrating part determines the actual pitch of the note. The tangent remains in contact with the strings until the key is released, enabling the player, by wiggling the finger, to achieve an effect known as *Bebung* [German: 'trembling']. This is a *vibrato* – a wavering in the pitch of the note caused by swift variations in the string-tension as the player varies the pressure of the finger on the key.

In the earlier (*fretted*) clavichords, each pair of strings was shared by two or more different keys (easily arranged, as the strings were parallel to the keyboard). The tangents struck the strings at different points in their length, producing notes of different pitches. Obviously, notes produced by the same string could not be sounded simultaneously, so the keys sharing the string were a tone or semitone apart, and unlikely, in the clavichord era, to be required in combination. The range of the instrument varies between four and five octaves.

In the 18th century, some unfretted clavichords had a second set of strings tuned to 4-foot pitch (an octave higher than the written notes); a few even had a pedal-board like that of an *organ. The clavichord, like the harpsichord, fell out of favour as the *piano gained ground in the early 19th century, but was revived later. The action of the clavichord is shown in the diagram below. [See also: *Short octave]

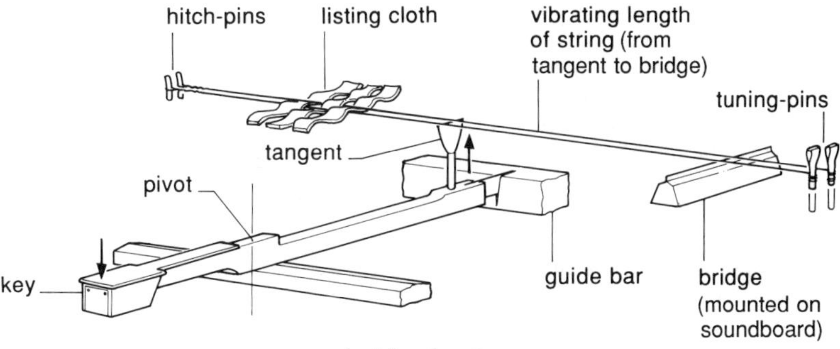

clavichord action

Clavier [French] Keyboard. The same word was borrowed by German composers to mean any kind of instrument with a keyboard (though in the 19th century, when it came to refer mainly to the piano, it was spelled *Klavier*).

Clavierübung (*Klavierübung*) [German: 'keyboard practice'] Collection, in four parts, of keyboard music, some for harpsichord and some for organ, by J. S. Bach. Part 1 (1731) contains the six Partitas. Part 2 (1735) has the *Italian Concerto and the French Overture (Partita in B minor). Part 3 (1739) includes twenty-one chorale preludes, the organ Prelude in E♭ and the Fugue in E♭ ('St Anne'), and four *duetti* for harpsichord. Part 4 (1741–2) consists of the *'Goldberg' Variations.

Clef [from Latin, *clavis*: 'a key'] A sign placed at the beginning of a stave, fixing the pitch of one of the lines and so giving the 'key', or clue, to the other lines and spaces. The three clefs now in use (which are decorated or ornamental forms of the letters G, F, and C) are:

(1) The treble clef, or G clef – circling around the second line of the stave, and fixing this line as G above middle C.

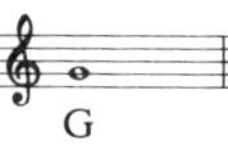

(2) The bass clef, or F clef – whose two dots are placed one each side of the fourth line of the stave, fixing this line as F below middle C.

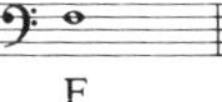

(3) The C clef – which always fixes middle C. This clef may be centred on the middle line, in which case it is usually called the viola clef or alto clef (it was formerly used in music for alto voice and alto trombone but is now used only in music for viola).

Or it may be centred on the fourth line, in which case it is called the tenor clef (and used for the upper notes of cellos, bassoons, and tenor trombones).

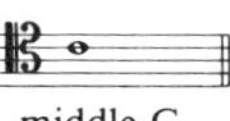

Strangely, music for tenor voice does not use the tenor clef; instead, the treble clef is generally used – on the understanding that all the sounds will be one octave lower than the printed notes. To make this implication clear, the treble clef may be modified in some way (as in the three examples on the right).

In scores of older music, staves for soprano voice may use the 'soprano clef', which is the C clef centred on the lowest line, but this is now obsolete. [See also: *Great stave]

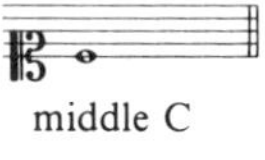

Cloche [French] Bell. **Cloches**, tubular bells.

'Clock' Symphony (*Die Uhr*) Nickname given to Haydn's Symphony No. 101 in D major, composed 1793–4 (one of his *'London' Symphonies). The slow movement begins with a theme whose accompaniment, played by *pizzicato* violins and *staccato* bassoons, suggests the tick-tock of a clock. The four movements of the symphony are: 1 *Adagio* leading to *Presto* (in sonata form); 2 *Andante*; 3 Menuetto: *Allegretto*; 4 Finale: *Vivace* (in rondo form).

Clog box See *Woodblocks.

Clos See under *Estampie.

Close A word sometimes used to mean *cadence.

Close position See *Spacing.

Cockaigne A concert overture, Opus 4, subtitled 'In London Town', composed by Elgar in 1900–1901. The music, which evokes the mood and spirit of Edwardian London, pictures a pair of lovers strolling through a London park, listening to bands playing, entering a quiet church, then going out into the street again to mingle with the bustling crowds.

Elgar's title, *Cockaigne*, refers to a mythical land of idleness and luxurious living from which the word 'Cockney' is said to derive.

Coda [Italian: 'tail', 'end'] A passage or section which rounds off a piece or a movement, bringing it to a satisfactory conclusion with an air of finality. A coda may be of any length. It may be based on one or more ideas previously presented and/or it may introduce new material. [See also: *Codetta; and under *Sonata form]

Codetta [Italian: 'little tail', 'small coda'] **1** A *coda of small dimensions, rounding off a composition. **2** In *sonata form, the name given to the material (the final part of the second subject-group) which closes the exposition section. **3** Codetta has a special meaning in *fugue, where it refers to any passage, however brief, during the exposition section which links an entry of the subject to the succeeding entry of the answer (or vice versa).

Coffee Cantata The nickname of Bach's secular cantata: *Schweigt stille, plaudert nicht* ('Be quiet, do not chatter'), composed around 1732; for soprano, tenor, and bass voices, flute, strings, and continuo. It is (unusually for Bach) a comic work, poking fun at the growing popularity of coffee at the time. It tells of a girl, Lieschen, who will not give up her excessive coffee-drinking until her father provides her with a husband. But when he complies, Lieschen still intends to continue her habit, and vows there will be a clause to that effect in the marriage contract.

Col; **Coll'**; **Colla** Italian for 'with the', and used in such expressions as: *col *arco; col *basso; col *legno; coll' 8va and coll' ottava* (see under *Octave signs); *colla *destra* and *colla *sinistra; colla *parte* and *colla *voce.*

Color See under *Isorhythm.

Coloratura [Italian: 'colouring'] A term describing florid, virtuoso passages, involving swift scales, runs, arpeggios, ornaments, and trills. It is particularly used in connection with vocal music. A **coloratura soprano** is one who has been trained to execute such passages with ease and verve.

Come [Italian] As, like. **Come prima,** as at first.

Comes See *Dux.

Come, ye Sons of Art, Away A cantata for four solo voices (soprano, two male altos or countertenors, bass), chorus, and orchestra, composed by Purcell in 1694 as a birthday *ode for Queen Mary. There are nine movements, of which the first is a French *overture (Purcell used the same music a year later as the overture to his opera *The Indian Queen*). The fourth movement is the famous 'Sound the Trumpet', a duet for two male altos (or countertenors) and continuo accompaniment, the music being structured on a *ground bass.

Comme [French] As, like.

Commodo See *Comodo.

Common chord Any major, or minor, *triad.

Common time Four crotchet beats to a bar, indicated by a *time signature shown either as $\frac{4}{4}$ or as **C**.

Communion The last item in the Proper of the *Mass.

Comodo (*commodo*) [Italian] Comfortable, easy, convenient. (For example: *Tempo comodo*, at a comfortable speed – neither rushed nor dragging.)

Compass The range of notes, extending from low to high, which a particular voice or instrument is capable of producing. [See Table 13 on page 394]

Compositional devices See *Devices.

Compound binary form Term sometimes used to mean *sonata form – indicating its origin in binary form.

Compound interval An *interval larger than an octave.

Compound time See under *Time, and also the table of Time signatures on page 389.

Con [Italian] With. (For example: *con espressione,* with expression.)

con 8 See *Octave signs.

Concert Performance, before an audience, of a programme of music (but not a stage performance or religious service) given by a fairly large body of musicians. (A performance by one or two musicians is usually called a *recital.)

Concertante [Italian] A term used during the second half of the 18th century to describe a symphonic work in which two or more instruments have important solo parts. Examples are: Mozart's *Sinfonia Concertante* in E♭, K364, for violin, viola, and orchestra; Haydn's *Sinfonia Concertante* in B♭ for oboe, bassoon, violin, cello, and orchestra; and Dittersdorf's *Sinfonia Concertante* in D for viola, double bass, and orchestra.

Concert band See *Symphonic band.

Concertino [Italian] **1** A short or small-scale *concerto. **2** The group of soloists in a concerto grosso (see under *Concerto).

Concertmaster American term meaning the leader (principal violinist) of an orchestra, who sits at the front on the conductor's left.

Concerto [Italian; French: *concert*; German: *Konzert*] An instrumental composition, most often in three movements, and featuring a soloist (or small group of soloists) contrasted against an orchestra.

The word *concerto* may come from a Latin word meaning 'to strive', or from an Italian word meaning 'get together'. Late 16th-century composers used it as a title for pieces for one or more voices with instrumental accompaniment, and also for pieces written for two (or more) opposing groups, providing contrasts of various kinds, e.g. in pitch, volume, and timbre (tone-colour).

Baroque concertos This basic idea of contrast led to the Baroque **concerto grosso**, popular during the first half of the 18th century. In this, the composer contrasted two instrumental groups – a group of soloists, often two violins and cello, called the *concertino* ('little ensemble') against a string orchestra called either the *ripieno* ('filling'), *concerto grosso* ('large ensemble'), or *tutti* ('all', 'everyone'). Sometimes the concertino instruments played alone; sometimes they were heard in combination with the ripieno group. And there was also a **continuo* part for harpsichord or organ – the player continuing throughout the piece to fill in the harmonies and decorate the textures.

A concerto grosso was structured in several movements (often four or five). One of these might be in the style of a fugue; other forms used were binary and ternary, and – especially for quick movements – *ritornello form. A concerto, like a Baroque sonata, might be styled *concerto da camera* (chamber concerto), or *concerto da chiesa* (church concerto) in which case the music was written in a generally more serious style.

From the concerto grosso grew the **solo concerto**. In this, a single solo instrument was pitted against the orchestra – one against many – and the element of contrast became stronger. A solo concerto was usually structured in three movements (quick – slow – quick) with the quick movements built up in ritornello form.

The Classical concerto (Mozart and Beethoven) The Classical concerto, most often featuring solo piano in competition with the orchestra, developed from the Baroque solo concerto. In structure it followed the same plan as the Classical sonata (see under *sonata) but with three important differences. (1) There are three movements only (the minuet or scherzo being omitted). (2) The first movement is in *sonata form – but with a *twofold* exposition. *Exposition I* is played by the orchestra only – presenting a sequence of themes, usually all in the tonic key. (This is variously described as the 'orchestral statement', 'orchestral exposition', 'opening tutti', 'opening ritornello'.) *Exposition II* begins (still in the tonic key) with the entry of the soloist. Themes are now restated, with the soloist joining in. However, all, or only some, of the themes already presented by the orchestra may now be restated – one or more may be omitted, to reappear only in the recapitulation; and it is likely that the composer will have held back at least one important theme – to be introduced as the soloist's 'own' theme. Only now does the composer make clear his grouping of themes into first subject and second subject by basing the second subject-group in a new key. (3) At the end of the recapitulation section in the first movement, the orchestra pauses while the soloist plays an unaccompanied **cadenza*. This usually ends with a trill, as a signal to the orchestra to re-enter to play the coda. A cadenza might also occur in either of the two remaining movements.

The Romantic (19th-century) concerto Romantic composers made changes to the structure and character of the concerto. Normally, there were still three movements. But in the first, it became more usual to do away with the twofold exposition and, instead, to have a *single* exposition, with the themes shared between soloist and orchestra right from the beginning. The cadenza might now occur at the end of the development section, rather than immediately before the coda. (The first composer to make both these innovations was Mendelssohn, a fine example being the first movement of his Violin Concerto in E minor.)

Rapid advancement in performing technique (particularly among pianists and violinists) encouraged composers to make solo parts increasingly more brilliant and difficult, and to oppose the soloist with a much larger orchestra. The elements of contrast and display were even more sharply emphasized, and a concerto could prove to be an exciting and dramatic contest – the power of the full orchestra challenged by the artistry and technical brilliance of the soloist. The most famous example of this style of concerto is Tchaikovsky's Piano Concerto in B♭ minor (which he himself described as 'a duel rather than a duet').

Of all the large-scale musical forms it is possibly the concerto which fascinates audiences the most. 20th-century composers have continued to write concertos of all types – often using the style of the 19th-century 'display' concerto, but sometimes returning to the 'polite competition' of the Classical concerto, or even reviving the principles of the Baroque concerto grosso.

The following list includes some notable concertos, of various kinds, from the Baroque period to the present day. (For dates of composers, see the time-chart on pages 398–413.)

Baroque concertos CORELLI: twelve Concerti Grossi, Op. 6 (No. 8 being the *'Christmas Concerto'). BACH: six *Brandenburg Concertos; Violin Concertos in A minor and E major; Double Concerto in D minor for two violins and strings; Harpsichord Concertos in D minor and F minor. HANDEL: six Concerti Grossi, Op. 3; twelve Concerti Grossi, Op. 6; Oboe Concerto in G minor;

twenty-one Organ Concertos. VIVALDI: more than 400 concertos, among the best known of which are *The *Four Seasons* (four solo concertos for violin and strings), Concerto in D for lute or guitar, Flute Concerto in D ('The Goldfinch'), Bassoon Concerto in B♭ ('Night'), Concerto in C for two trumpets and strings.

Classical concertos HAYDN: Trumpet Concerto in E♭; Piano Concerto in D; Violin Concerto in G; Cello Concerto in D; Sinfonia Concertante in B♭ for oboe, bassoon, violin, cello, and orchestra. MOZART: twenty-seven Piano Concertos – Nos. 1 to 4 are arrangements of works by other composers, but the rest include such masterpieces as Piano Concerto No. 17 in G (K453), No. 20 in D minor (K466), No. 21 in C (K467), No. 23 in A (K488), No. 24 in C minor (K491), No. 27 in B♭ (K595); Bassoon Concerto in B♭; Clarinet Concerto in A; four Horn Concertos; Flute and Harp Concerto; Sinfonia Concertante in E♭ for violin, viola, and orchestra. BEETHOVEN: Piano Concerto No. 1 in C, No. 2 in B♭, No. 3 in C minor, No. 4 in G, No. 5 in E♭ ('The *Emperor'); Violin Concerto in D; Triple Concerto in C for piano, violin, cello, and orchestra.

Romantic (19th-century) concertos PAGANINI: Violin Concerto No. 1 in D. MENDELSSOHN: Piano Concerto No. 1 in G minor; Violin Concerto in E minor. SCHUMANN: Piano Concerto in A minor; Cello Concerto in A minor. CHOPIN: Piano Concerto No. 1 in E minor, and No. 2 in F minor. LISZT: Piano Concerto No. 1 in E♭, and No. 2 in A (in one movement, the contrasting sections unified by *thematic transformation). BRAHMS: Piano Concerto No. 1 in D minor, and No. 2 in B♭ (in four movements – the second being, unusually, a scherzo); Violin Concerto in D; Double Concerto in A minor, for violin, cello, and orchestra. BRUCH: Violin Concerto No. 1 in G minor. TCHAIKOVSKY: Piano Concerto No. 1 in B♭ minor, and No. 2 in G; Violin Concerto in D. DVOŘÁK: Cello Concerto in B minor. GRIEG: Piano Concerto in A minor.

20th-century concertos ELGAR: Violin Concerto in B minor, Cello Concerto in E minor. SIBELIUS: Violin Concerto in D minor. GLIÈRE: Harp Concerto; Concerto for *coloratura soprano and orchestra. VAUGHAN WILLIAMS: Oboe Concerto; Tuba Concerto. RACHMANINOV: Piano Concerto No. 2 in C minor, and No. 3 in D minor. SCHOENBERG: Violin Concerto; Piano Concerto. RAVEL: Piano Concerto in G; Piano Concerto for the left hand. BLOCH: Concerto Grosso No. 2 for strings and piano. BARTÓK: Violin Concerto No. 2; Concerto for Orchestra; Piano Concerto No. 3. STRAVINSKY: Concerto for piano and wind; *'Dumbarton Oaks' Concerto; **Ebony Concerto* for clarinet and jazz ensemble. BERG: Chamber Concerto for piano, violin, and thirteen winds; Violin Concerto. PROKOFIEV: Piano Concerto No. 3; Violin Concerto No. 1. POULENC: *Concert champêtre* for harpsichord and orchestra; Organ Concerto. RODRIGO: *Concierto de Aranjuez* for guitar and orchestra. WALTON: Viola Concerto. TIPPETT: Concerto for double string orchestra; Concerto for Orchestra; Triple Concerto, for violin, viola, cello, and orchestra. SHOSTAKOVICH: Piano Concerto No. 2; Cello Concerto No. 1. LUTOSŁAWSKI: Concerto for Orchestra.

[See also: *Double concerto; *Triple concerto; *Concerto for orchestra]

Concerto for orchestra The term *concerto* normally describes a work in which one or more soloists are pitted against an orchestra. A 'concerto for orchestra', however, spotlights the orchestral members themselves, who at various times serve as soloists – either singly, or in groups – and are continually given brilliant and difficult passages to play. Bartók, Tippett, and Lutosławski have each written a Concerto for Orchestra.

Concerto grosso See under *Concerto.

Concert overture See under *Overture.

Concertstück Another spelling of **Konzertstück*.

Concierto de Aranjuez Title of Rodrigo's concerto for guitar and orchestra, composed in 1939.

Concords and **Discords** A concord is a chord in which all the notes seem to 'agree' with each other. This kind of chord sounds 'at rest', and is complete within itself. In a discord, certain notes disagree, or clash, producing an effect of tension or restlessness. Any discord sounds incomplete by itself, as if it needs to be followed by a concord in which the tension will be relaxed (the correct musical term is 'resolved'). Those chords which are built simply from the three notes of a major or a minor triad are the only concords. Technically, all other chords are discords. Until the end of the 19th century, music was built mainly from concords, but spiced with discords to add tension to a greater or lesser degree. 20th-century music, however, makes far greater use of discords which, rather than resolving onto concords, merge into further discords. In some compositions, in fact, concords are deliberately avoided altogether.

[See also under *Intervals; also *Preparation and *Resolution]

Conducting The musical art and technique of directing and controlling an orchestra, band, choir, or ensemble (of instrumentalists, singers, or both) in rehearsal and then in performance, by means of hand gestures (with or without a baton), movements of the head and body, and facial expressions – the eyes being of paramount importance.

The first responsibility of the conductor is to know and understand the *score of the music in every minute detail. The conductor must formulate clear ideas as to how the music should sound from beginning to end, and these ideas – the conductor's *interpretation* of the score – must then be clearly communicated to the performers. It is of the greatest importance, however, that this interpretation is as true to the composer's wishes and intentions as possible.

In rehearsal and performance, the main function of the conductor is to indicate the beats – to beat time. The diagrams below show the basic movements of a conductor's right hand (with or without the use of a baton) when beating 2, 3, 4, or 6 in a bar. According to the character of the music, the movements may be large (suggesting loudness) or small (quietness), smooth and flowing, or angular and urgently dramatic.

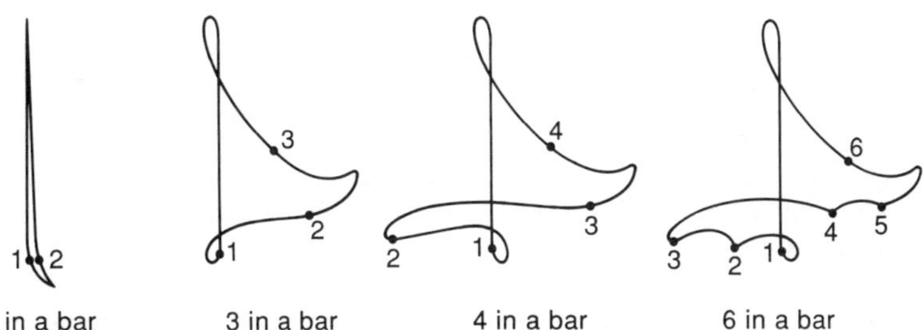

The conductor must control the tempo (speed) of the music – maintaining a steady speed when necessary, indicating any change of speed and holding the ensemble perfectly together in, for example, an accelerando, rallentando, or ritenuto. Another important responsibility is to control the overall *balance* of the sound, ensuring that no instruments or voices are too loud or too soft in relation to others.

The conductor also, normally with the left hand, indicates entries (bringing in instruments or voices at exactly the right moment); controls expression, *accent, dynamics, and the shading of dynamics; indicates changes of mood; and moulds and shapes the *phrasing of the music while making clear its underlying basic structure.

Conductus [Latin] A type of vocal composition of the 12th and 13th centuries, written in *note-against-note style for between one and four voices. The words, which might be sacred or secular, were in Latin. For example:

School of Worcester, c1300
(etc.)
Be - a - ta vi - sce - ra Ma - ri - ae vir - gi - nis,
[Blessed womb of the Virgin Mary]

Congas (conga drums) Latin-American (Afro-Cuban) long drums – which may be either conical or barrel-shaped – each with a single skin, played with the fingers and palm of the hand rather than with sticks.

Conjunct 'Connected'. Moving by step, rather than by leap. [See: *Motion]

Consecutive fifths and octaves See *Parallel fifths and octaves.

Consequent The name given to the imitating (following) part or parts in a *canon.

Conservatoire; **Conservatory** A school of music, or college of music. For example, the Paris Conservatoire, founded in 1795.

Console Those parts of an *organ which are under the direct control of an organist, i.e. the manuals (keyboards), pedals, stops, and so on.

Consonance The sounding together of two or more notes which 'agree' with each other and so produce a *concord.

Consort A term used in England, from about 1570 to about 1700, referring to a small ensemble of instruments playing together (possibly originating from the French word *concert*). If all the instruments taking part came from one family only – viols, for instance, or recorders – then it was called a *whole consort*. Today, the description *broken consort* (or *mixed consort*) is used if instruments of different types are mixed together – for example, viols, recorders and lutes – since the sameness of sound is then 'broken'. However, the term 'broken consort' does not seem to have been used until 1661 when Matthew Locke published 'The Broken Consort, First Part, 24 pieces in 6 suites'. The term consort may also be applied to an ensemble of voices, with or without accompaniment. [See also: *Chest of viols; **First Booke of Consort Lessons*]

Contes d'Hoffmann, Les See *The *Tales of Hoffmann.*

Continuo Abbreviation for *basso continuo* [Italian: 'continuous bass']. An essential feature of almost every kind of music of the Baroque period (1600–1750). A continuo part consisted of a bass-line only (the *basso continuo*) to be played on an instrument such as cello, viola da gamba, double bass, or bassoon. However, the composer expected another continuo player on a chord-playing instrument such as harpsichord, organ, or lute to fill in the harmonies by building up chords on the bass-line. Very often, composers wrote figures beneath the bass-line to indicate which chords were expected – and so such a bass-line is called a **figured bass*. In music for orchestra, performances were often directed from the keyboard, and so the continuo player, besides filling out the harmonies and decorating the texture of the music, was also responsible for holding the performance together.

Contrabass [German]; **Contrabasso** (or **Contrabbasso**) [Italian]; **Contrebasse** [French] Double bass.

Contrabass clarinet A single-reed woodwind instrument, usually built in B♭ and pitched one octave below the bass clarinet, two octaves below the normal clarinet. It is sometimes called 'double-bass clarinet' or 'pedal clarinet'. Music for contrabass clarinet is written one octave and a tone higher than it actually sounds.

Contrabassoon The same as *Double bassoon.

Contrafagotto (properly, *controfagotto*) [Italian] Double bassoon.

Contralto The lowest, deepest type of female *voice.

Contrapuntal Describing a musical *texture in which two or more parts or melodic lines weave along together in *counterpoint. (Another term, with much the same meaning, is *polyphonic.)

Contrary motion See *Motion.

Contrast See under *Form.

Contrebasse [French] Double bass.

Contrebasson [French] Double bassoon.

Contredanse [French; German: *Contratanz, Kontratanz*; Italian: *contradanza*] A lively dance which became popular in Germany and especially France in the 18th century, and which originated from the English *country dance (of which the French name is a mispronunciation). Haydn, Mozart, and Beethoven composed sets of *contredanses*.

Controfagotto [Italian] Double bassoon.

Cool jazz A jazz style of the 1950s, lighter and quieter, more relaxed and restrained ('cool') in sound and mood than the *bop which preceded it. Melodies and also harmonies (now more complex) showed influences from 'classical' music, and rhythms were more subtle and flexible (e.g. based upon five or seven beats to a bar, rather than the standard four). Among notable exponents of the cool jazz style were trumpeter Miles Davis and pianist and composer Dave Brubeck.

Coperto; Coperti [Italian] Covered. To a percussion player, an indication that the drum(s) should be muted, or muffled, either by having a piece of cloth draped over the skin or by placing a folded cloth (duster) on the skin, opposite the striking point.

Coppélia, or **La Fille aux yeux d'émail** (The girl with enamel eyes) Ballet in three acts, composed by Delibes, first produced in Paris in 1870 (scenario by Nuitter and Saint-Léon, based on Hoffmann's *Der Sandmann*; original choreography by Saint-Léon). Franz is in love with Swanilda, but when Dr Coppélius, an elderly doll-maker, fulfils his ambition to create a doll with a soul (the 'Coppélia' of the title) Franz mistakenly believes her to be alive and transfers his affection to her. Eventually he realizes she is only a doll, and he and Swanilda are reconciled. The ballet has been staged in many different versions, and various selections from the music (usually including the Prelude, Waltz, and Csárdás) are played at orchestral concerts.

Cor [French] Horn.

Cor anglais The French name means (and this instrument is often called) 'English horn' – but it is not English in origin, nor is it a horn. It is in fact a type of tenor oboe, pitched a 5th below the normal *oboe. It is possible that *anglais* was originally a misspelling of the French word *anglé*, meaning 'angled', and referring to the way the crook (into which the double reed is fixed) is bent backwards to the player's mouth. The tube of the cor anglais is 80 centimetres long and ends in a distinctive pear-shaped bell (whereas the bell of the oboe is slightly flared). This makes the tone-quality of the cor anglais rather softer, richer, and mellower, and even more plaintive, than that of the oboe. The cor anglais is a *transposing instrument, and its music is written a 5th higher than it actually sounds.

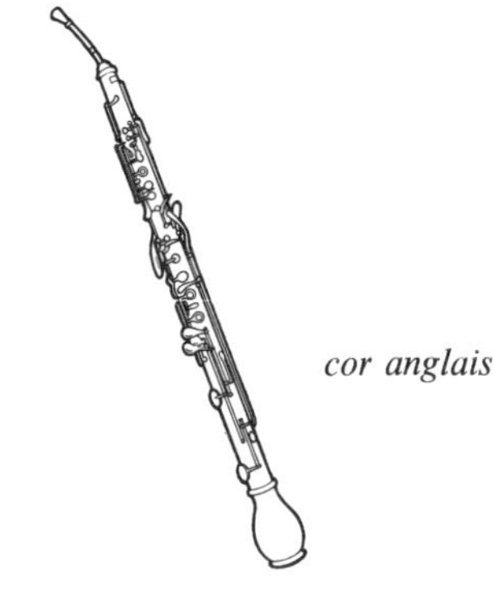
cor anglais

Normal range:

Famous solos for cor anglais occur in the second movement of Dvořák's Ninth Symphony (**From the New World*), the second movement of Franck's Symphony in D minor, and the second movement of Rodrigo's *Concierto de Aranjuez* for guitar and orchestra. The cor anglais is featured in Sibelius's *The Swan of Tuonela* and in William Alwyn's *Autumn Legend.*

Corant; **Coranto** *Courante.

Cor à pistons [French] Valve horn.

Corda [Italian] String. **Corde**, strings. **Strumenti a corde**, string instruments.

Corde [French] String. **Cordes**, strings, also snares. **Instruments à cordes**, string instruments.

Coriolan (*Coriolanus*) Overture, Opus 62, by Beethoven, composed in 1807 for a performance of the play *Coriolan* by Heinrich Joseph von Collins (not for Shakespeare's *Coriolanus*, as is sometimes thought).

Cori spezzati See under *Polychoral.

Cornamusa; **Cornemuse** A type of bagpipe. Also the name of an instrument in use around 1600, of which no example has survived; it was possibly a kind of shawm but with a cap enclosing the reed, giving a softer and sweeter tone.

Cornemuse French name for bagpipe. [See also: *Cornamusa]

Cornet A brass instrument of wide bore (partly cylindrical, partly conical), with three valves, and a cup-shaped mouthpiece. The cornet is normally built in B♭, and is similar to the B♭ trumpet in size and range, though squatter in shape. The tone-quality is less brilliant, more mellow, than that of the

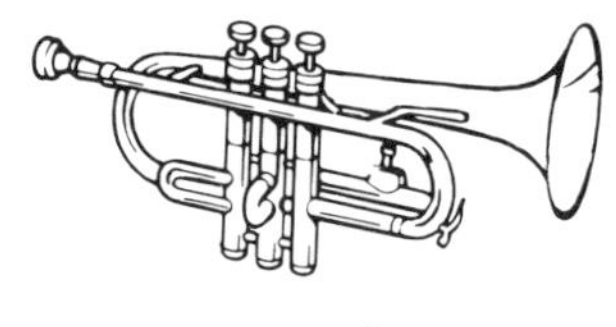
cornet

trumpet. Due to its wide bore, the cornet has great flexibility. Music for B♭ cornet (like that for B♭ trumpet) is written one tone higher than it actually sounds.

Normal range of B♭ cornet: (written) (sounding)

Cornets are much used in brass bands and military bands, and sometimes in the orchestra – many scores by French composers (e.g. Berlioz, Bizet, Franck) include a pair of cornets in addition to a pair of trumpets. Orchestral solos for cornet occur in Prokofiev's **Lieutenant Kijé*, e.g. in the first movement (at the beginning and again, muted, at the end) and in the third movement. The cornet was also much used in jazz until the 1920s (when the fashion changed to using trumpet instead), its most notable player being Louis Armstrong ('Satchmo', or 'Satchelmouth').

Cornet à pistons [French] Cornet (the modern valved cornet).

Cornett A wind instrument (completely different from the modern cornet), mainly in use from the end of the 15th century to the end of the 17th. The cornett was made of wood, sometimes bound round with leather. It had finger-holes, like a recorder; and a cup-shaped mouthpiece, like a trumpet. A wide range of expression was available to sensitive players. Cornetts were made in three main sizes, and in ensemble music were often combined with *sackbuts.

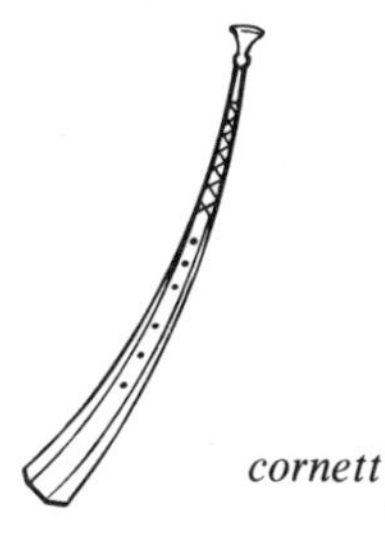
cornett

Even though made of wood, the cornett is classed as a 'brass' instrument, due to its cup-shaped mouthpiece. [See also: *Serpent]

Cornetto (plural: *cornetti*) [Italian] *Cornet, or *cornett.

Corno (plural: *corni*) [Italian] Horn. (*Corno cromatico, a macchina, a pistoni, ventile,* all refer to the modern valve horn.) **Corno di bassetto,** basset-horn; **corno da caccia,** hunting horn. **Corno inglese,** English horn or *cor anglais.

Coro [Italian: 'chorus', 'choir'] A term sometimes used by composers, in scores, to refer to a group or ensemble which may consist of voices, or instruments, or both.

Coronation Anthems Four anthems by Handel, composed in 1727 for the coronation of George II. They are: 1 *Zadok the Priest; 2 The King shall rejoice; 3 My heart is inditing; and 4 Let thy hand be strengthened. The words of 'My heart is inditing'; had previously been set by Purcell as an anthem for the coronation of James II in 1685.

Corrente *Courante.

Cortège [French] Procession.

Così fan tutte (Women are like that) Opera in two acts by Mozart, first produced in Vienna in 1790 (text by da Ponte). Two officers, Ferrando (tenor) and Guglielmo (baritone), believe that if they were to go away their respective sweethearts, Fiordiligi and Dorabella (sopranos), would remain faithful to them. A cynical old bachelor, Don Alfonso (baritone), bets them that this is not so, and devises a plot to prove it. He announces their departure on active service, but they return, heavily disguised as 'foreigners', and each tries to woo the other's lover. Unsuccessful, they pretend to take poison, to the horror of the women, but the ladies' maid, Despina (soprano), who is in the plot, disguises herself as a doctor and 'cures' them by magic. They renew their endeavours and both Dorabella and Fiordiligi gradually surrender. A lawyer (again Despina in disguise) arrives with a marriage contract, but before they can sign it Don Alfonso announces that Ferrando and Guglielmo have returned and are fast approaching. The 'foreigners' flee in panic – and return in their true identities. Alfonso reveals the plot and the lovers are happily reconciled.

Cotillion (cotillon) A lively 19th-century ballroom dance in which the leading couple performed a variety of steps and movements, imitated by all the other couples. It was usually the final dance of the evening.

Counter-exposition See under *Fugue.

Counterpoint [from Latin, *punctus contra punctum*: 'note against note'; and so, by extension, 'melody against melody'] **1** The combining of two or more melodic lines, or parts, of equal importance and independence.

Bach: Two-part *Invention No. 13

The musical *texture created in this way, as the individual melodic strands weave along together, is described as *contrapuntal.* Another word, with much the same meaning, is *polyphonic. [See also: *Invertible counterpoint]

2 When a contrapuntal part is added to another part, each is then called the counterpoint of the other. [See: *Part, 2]

Counter-subject See under *Fugue.

Countertenor An adult male *voice, higher than a tenor, with strong and pure tone, and produced by resonances mainly in the head. It was very popular until the end of the 18th century, and has recently become fashionable again with the increased interest in 'early music'.

Country dance The name given to a whole group of English figure dances, originally and traditionally performed by country-folk on the village green. These dances became popular at the court of Elizabeth I, and many were later described in detail by John Playford in his book *The English Dancing Master,* published in 1651. [See also: *Contredanse]

Country music; **Country and Western** The name used, in general, for white American folk-music, with roots lying mainly in British folk-music (folk-songs, ballads, dances) brought over by English and Scottish settlers. Until around 1940, when it became commercial, it was known as 'hillbilly music' ('hillbilly' being a derogative term for someone living in the backwoods of the southern USA).

Several types and styles of country music developed, including 'bluegrass' music (originating in the Blue Ridge Hills of Virginia), Western (cowboy) songs, and various types of religious songs and work-songs. Country music became influenced by black American styles such as spirituals, blues, and jazz. It first became widely popular after 1925 when the radio station WSM in Nashville, Tennessee, began to broadcast a weekly country music programme called *The Grand Ole Opry* ('opry' from the musical term 'opera'). The instruments used to accompany the voice(s) in country music are usually string instruments. Originally, these were fiddle, banjo, and guitar. After 1900, double bass and mandolin were added; and in the 1930s, drums, piano, and Hawaiian guitar. Nowadays, the electric guitar is often included.

Coupler See under *Organ, and under *Harpsichord.

Couplet **1** Another name for a *duplet. **2** In rondos by French composers of the 17th and 18th centuries, the episodes separating appearances of the rondo theme are often called *couplets.*

Courante [French: 'running', 'flowing'; Italian: *corrente*; English: corant, coranto] A lively French 'running' dance of the 16th century. In the 17th century it became the second of the four standard dance movements of the Baroque keyboard *suite. Two different styles were possible: a French *courante,* or an Italian *corrente.* The courante was in $\frac{3}{2}$ or $\frac{6}{4}$ time, frequently shifting from one to the other (especially at cadences) and giving the effect of *hemiola. The corrente was generally swifter, in $\frac{3}{4}$ or $\frac{3}{8}$ time, and the musical texture was usually simpler. Bach, in each of his six *English Suites, uses a courante; in his six *French Suites he uses a courante in the first and third suites, but a corrente in each of the remaining four (even though the title 'Courante' is still used).

Course A term used in connection with the strings of plucked instruments, particularly the lute. A course is a 'set' of strings – often consisting of a pair of strings (called a double course) which may be tuned in unison, i.e. to the same pitch; or a thinner string of a pair may be tuned an octave higher (then called an octave course). A course may consist of three strings (triple course), or it may consist of a single string only (single course). A typical 'six-course' *lute has eleven strings arranged in six courses – ten of the strings arranged in pairs, or double courses, plus a single top string (known as the **chanterelle*).

Crab canon See under *Canon.

Cracoviak; **Cracovienne** See *Krakowiak.

Creation, The (*Die Schöpfung*) An oratorio by Haydn for soprano, tenor, and bass soloists, chorus, and orchestra; composed between 1796 and 1798. Haydn set a German text by Baron Gottfried von Swieten, translated from an English text (by an unknown author) based on Milton's poem *Paradise Lost*. One of the best-known items is the chorus: 'The heavens are telling the glory of God'.

Création du monde, La (The Creation of the World) A ballet in one act by Darius Milhaud (see *Les *Six*). When Milhaud visited New York in 1922 he became so fascinated with the jazz he heard in Harlem, performed by black musicians, that he eagerly looked forward to writing a work which would include some of the ingredients of jazz blended with characteristics of his own musical style (which often made use of *polytonality). The chance came the following year when he was asked to write music for a ballet depicting the creation of the world, as portrayed in African folk legends. *La Création du monde* is scored for seventeen soloists. This orchestra (an expansion of the jazz groups Milhaud heard in Harlem) consists of 2 flutes, oboe, 2 clarinets, saxophone and bassoon; horn, 2 trumpets and trombone; 2 violins, cello, and double bass; piano and percussion. The ballet is in six sections, played without a break.

Creatures of Prometheus, The *(Die Geschöpfe des Prometheus)* Ballet in two acts, composed by Beethoven, and first produced in Vienna in 1801 (choreography by Salvatore Vigano). The music consists of an overture (often called 'Prometheus Overture'), an introduction, and sixteen numbers. Beethoven used one of the themes from the finale in three later works: No. 7 of *12 Contredanses*; as the theme of the *'Eroica' Variations for piano (sometimes called the 'Prometheus' Variations); and in the finale of the **Eroica Symphony*.

Crécelle [French] Ratchet.

Credo See *Mass.

Crescendo [Italian: 'growing'] Becoming gradually louder. Often abbreviated to **cresc.**, or indicated by a 'hairpin' sign [See also: *Decrescendo; *Diminuendo]

Croche [French] A quaver. (The word for crotchet is *noire*.)

Croma [Italian] A quaver.

Cromorne [French] Crumhorn.

Crook An extra piece of tubing fixed into 'natural' (valveless) brass instruments such as horns and trumpets temporarily to increase the overall length of the tube. This provided a different set of notes – those available from the *harmonic series of the new total length of tube. Until the introduction of the *valve system, players needed a set of crooks of different lengths in order to play in a variety of keys. [See also under *Transposing instruments]

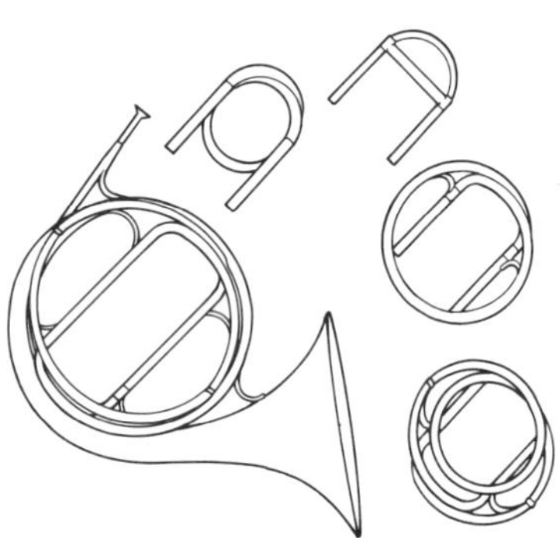

early 19th-century 'natural' horn with crooks

Cross relation See *False relation.

Cross rhythm A term used by some musicians to describe the effect of two conflicting rhythm patterns proceeding simultaneously (e.g. two notes against three, as in the music printed below), and by others to describe the effect which occurs when the accents of a passage conflict with those indicated by the time signature (e.g. the division of $\frac{4}{4}$ time into 3 + 3 + 2 quavers).

from Mozart: Sonata in F, K332

cresc.

Crot See *Crwth.

Crotales See under *Cymbals.

Crotchet The note which is half the value of a minim, twice the value of a quaver, and a quarter of the value of a semibreve. (The American name for a crotchet is a quarter-note.) A crotchet is written: ♩ and a crotchet *rest is shown either as 𝄽 or 𝄾 [See also Tables 1 and 2 on page 387]

Crowd See *Crwth.

Crown Imperial A march for orchestra by Walton, composed for the coronation of George VI in 1937. [See also: **Orb and Sceptre*]

Cruit See *Crwth.

Crumhorn [from German, *Krummhorn*: 'curved horn'] A woodwind instrument which was developed around 1500; in shape, like an inverted walking-stick. A wooden cap enclosed a double reed to give a rather soft, but reedy tone. Crumhorns were made in different sizes, to form a family.

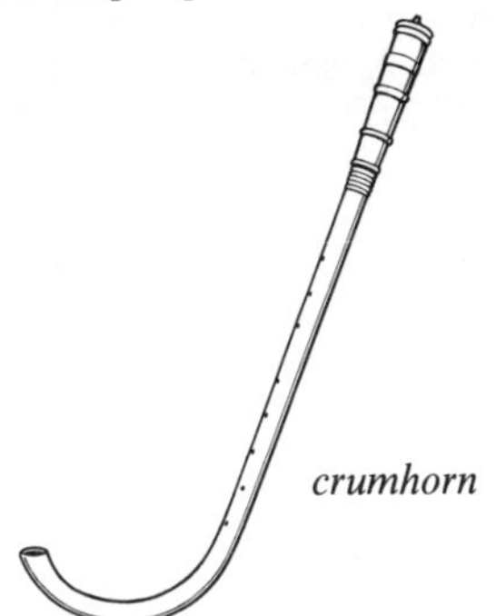
crumhorn

Crushed note English name for an acciaccatura. [See under *Ornaments and grace notes]

Crwth [Welsh; Irish: *crot, cruit*; English: *crowd*] An ancient Celtic bowed string instrument (a bowed lyre), roughly rectangular in shape, and with usually six strings – four melody strings and two drone strings (which might be bowed, or plucked with the left thumb).

C.s. Abbreviation for *colla sinistra,* with the left hand.

Csárdás [from Hungarian: 'country tavern'] A Hungarian dance in duple time, usually built up in two contrasting sections: a slow introduction (*lassan* or *lassu*) followed by a swift, wild dance (*friska* or *friss*). Liszt wrote Nos. 2, 13, and 19 of his *Hungarian Rhapsodies* in this form. Tchaikovsky included a csárdás in his ballet **Swan Lake*; another occurs in Delibes' ballet **Coppélia.*

Cuivre [French] Copper, brass. **Les cuivres**, the brass instruments of the orchestra.

Cuivré [French: 'brassed'] Instruction to a brass player (especially of the horn) to blow the note(s) with attack and slight tensing of the lips, producing a particularly 'brassy', blaring tone-quality.

Curtain tune; **Curtain music** See *Act tune.

Curved line (in notation) See *Slur.

Cyclic A composition in several movements is said to be 'cyclic', or in '**cyclic form**', if one or more themes from one movement reappear in any of the later movements. Usually, when a theme recurs in a later movement, it is modified or changed in mood and character. Examples of works in cyclic form are Beethoven's Piano Sonata No. 28 in A (Op. 101), Berlioz's **Symphonie fantastique*, César Franck's Symphony in D minor, and Dvořák's Symphony No. 9 in E minor (**From the New World*). [See: *Thematic transformation]

Cymbales [French] Cymbals. **Cymbale suspendue,** suspended cymbal. **Cymbales antiques**: see under *Cymbals.

Cymbals Percussion instruments, of ancient origin, and consisting of convex plates of metal. A pair of cymbals, equal in size, may be held by their leather straps and clashed together, or gently brushed together, or agitated against each other to produce a 'two-plate roll'. A single cymbal may be suspended and struck in a variety of ways – with a hard or soft-headed drumstick, wire brush, triangle beater; or a roll may be played on it using two sticks. Normal cymbals produce sounds which can be immensely varied in tone and volume, but the sounds are of indefinite pitch. However, there are much smaller, thicker cymbals (originally used like castanets by dancers in ancient Egypt, Greece, and Rome) which produce a sound of definite pitch. In orchestral scores they may be referred to as **antique cymbals** or *cymbales antiques* (e.g. Debussy) or as **crotales** (e.g. Ravel, Stravinsky). These may be in pairs, with one of a pair struck lightly against the other; or they may be mounted on a stand or suspended from a frame, and struck individually with a beater.

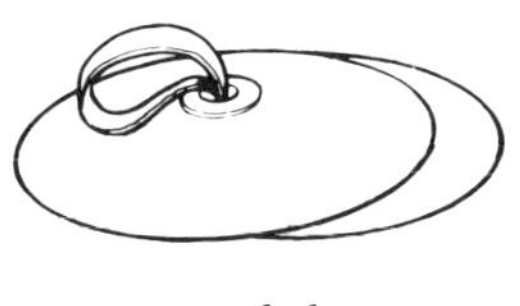

cymbals

Dvořák features clashed cymbals in his first and eighth Slavonic Dances. A suspended cymbal struck forcefully with a hard drumstick adds excitement to the *Hoe-Down* from Copland's *Rodeo*. And a variety of sounds and effects on cymbals can be heard in Bartók's Sonata for two pianos and percussion. The silvery, high-pitched sounds of antique cymbals (sounding the notes E and B) are heard during the last two minutes or so of Debussy's *Prélude à 'L'Après-midi d'un faune'*.

[See also: *Hi-hat]

Czárdás See *Csárdás.

D Abbreviation standing for: **1** dominant; **2** *destra* [Italian] or *droite* [French] meaning 'right' and referring to the right hand; **3** Deutsch (Otto Erich Deutsch) who in 1951 published a thematic catalogue of the works of Schubert. Linked to the title of any composition by Schubert, the letter **D** followed by a number indicates that piece's numbered entry in Deutsch's catalogue (e.g. Piano Quintet in A major, 'The Trout', D667).

Da [Italian] For, from, of, by.

Da capo (abbrev.: **D.C.**) [Italian] Indication that the music is to be repeated from the beginning. **Da capo al Fine**, repeat from the beginning, ending at the word *Fine*. **Da capo al segno**, repeat from the beginning to the sign 𝄋.

Da capo aria An *aria in *ternary form (**A¹ B A²**) but with only the first two sections of music actually written out. As the music of the third section was the same as the first, the composer wrote **Da capo* (or simply *D.C.*) at the end of the contrasting second section (**B**). When repeating the first section, the singer was expected to add his or her own vocal ornaments and decorations to the printed melody. And it became customary to improvise a *cadenza*, a florid passage displaying the brilliance of the singer's technique, just before the final cadence of either **B** or **A²**.

Da capo aria form was first extensively used by Alessandro Scarlatti (father of Domenico Scarlatti); it became one of the standard forms of the *Baroque period, and was a particular feature of **opera seria*. Examples of da capo aria include: 'Rejoice greatly' and 'Why do the nations so furiously rage together?' from Handel's *Messiah*, the arias *V'adoro pupille* and *Piangerò la sorte mia* from Handel's opera **Giulio Cesare*, and the aria *Dove sei* (often sung in the translation 'Art thou troubled') from his opera *Rodelinda*, and 'Grief for sin' and 'Break in grief' (numbers 10 and 12) from Bach's *St Matthew Passion*.

Da-daiko A huge type of Japanese double-headed drum. It is suspended in a frame, and struck with lacquered beaters.

Daff (duff) In Arab music of the Near East and north Africa, the general term for a frame *drum – which may be circular, rectangular, or octagonal. Some have snares; others have metal jingles set into the frame (as the tambourine). [See: *Ṭār]

Dafne Title of the first known opera, produced in Florence in 1597. The libretto, based on an old Greek legend, was by Rinuccini. The music was by Jacopo Peri and Jacopo Corsi, but unfortunately only a few fragments still survive. [See also: **Euridice*]

Dal segno (abbrev.: **D.S.**) [Italian] Indication to repeat the music from the point where the sign 𝄋 is printed. **Dal segno al Fine**, repeat from the sign, ending at the word *Fine*.

Damnation of Faust, The A cantata by Berlioz (Op. 24; 1845–6) for mezzo-soprano, tenor, baritone, and bass soloists, chorus, and orchestra; based on a French translation of Goethe's *Faust*. Berlioz described the work as a 'dramatic legend', and it is occasionally staged as an opera. The best-known items from the score are the Hungarian March (**Rákóczi March*) and two dance-pieces: Dance of the Sylphs and Minuet of the Will-o'-the-wisps. [See also: **Faust*]

Damper pedal Another name for the sustaining pedal (the right pedal) on the *piano.

Dampers The pieces of wood covered with felt which 'damp' the strings of the *piano (i.e. stop them vibrating). In the *harpsichord there is a damper of cloth or felt at the top of each jack; when the key is at rest, the damper prevents the string from vibrating.

Dämpfer [German] Mute or mutes; referring to: **1** the *dampers of the piano; **2** the *mutes of brass instruments and bowed string instruments. **Mit Dämpfer(n)**, with mute(s); **ohne Dämpfer**, without mute(s); **Dämpfer ab**, remove the mute(s). **Dämpfung**, muting, or use of the soft pedal in piano playing. **Gedämpft**, muted.

Dance [French: *danse*; German: *Tanz*; Italian, also Spanish: *danza*] An instrumental composition, either written specifically as an accompaniment to dancing, or written in the style of a particular dance but intended to be played and listened to, rather than danced (as, for example, the stylized dance pieces of the Baroque *suite). Since dancing – either for ritualistic purposes or simply for enjoyment – is an activity which has been practised by people of all cultures from the earliest times, it is most probable that dance music was the earliest type of purely instrumental music. However the earliest examples which have survived, in the form of the *estampie, date from the 13th century.

For details of individual dances of various types, styles, and periods, see: *Allemande; *Anglaise; *Aragonesa; *Basse danse; *Bolero; *Bourrée; *Branle; *Cancan; *Carol; *Carole; *Cebell; *Chaconne and Passacaglia; *Contredanse; *Cotillion; *Country dance; *Courante; *Csárdás; *Deutscher Tanz; *Écossaise; *Estampie; *Fandango; *Farandole; *Flamenco; *Folía; *Forlana; *Foxtrot; *Furiant; *Galliard; *Galop; *Gavotte; *Gigue; *Gopak; *Habanera; *Halling; *Hey; *Hoe-down; *Hornpipe; *Jota; *Krakowiak; *Ländler; *Lezghinka; *Loure; *Malagueña; *Matachin; *Mazurka; *Minuet; *Moresca; *Morris; *Musette; *Nachtanz; *Padoana; *Passamezzo; *Passepied; *Pavan; *Piva; *Polka; *Polonaise; *Quadrille; *Quickstep 2; *Ragtime; *Reel; *Rigaudon; *Round dance; *Rumba; *Saltarello; *Samba; *Sarabande; *Schottische; *Seguidilla; *Siciliana; *Springdans; *Square dance; *Tambourin 3; *Tango; *Tarantella; *Tedesca; *Tordion; *Trepak; *Volta 2; *Waltz; *Zapateado. [See also: *Ballet; and *Suite]

Danse macabre (Dance of Death) A symphonic poem by Saint-Saëns (Op. 40; 1874) for solo violin and orchestra. The music is based on a poem by Henri Cazalis, describing the gruesome happenings in a churchyard on Hallowe'en. As the clock strikes midnight, the cloaked figure of Death appears and summons skeletons from their graves to dance to tunes he plays on a violin. The clattering of the skeletons' bones is vividly suggested by the sound of the xylophone. Eventually, as cock-crow (solo oboe) heralds the first light of dawn, the skeletons vanish back into their graves; then Death, too, disappears.

Danserye A collection of dances for four-part instrumental ensemble, published in 1551 by Tylman Susato at his printing works and music shop called *In de Kromhoorn* (meaning 'At the Sign of the Crumhorn') in Antwerp. Susato gives no indication exactly which instruments are to take part, but simply describes the music as 'pleasing and suitable to be played on all kinds of instruments'.

Danza [Italian; also Spanish] Dance; dance music.

Daphnis and Chloë (*Daphnis et Chloé*) Ballet in three scenes, by Ravel, first produced in Paris in 1912 (choreography by Fokine; décor by Bakst). The ballet is based on an ancient Greek story by Longus which tells of the love of Daphnis, a shepherd, for Chloë. She is captured by pirates, but the god Pan intervenes and restores Chloë to Daphnis. Ravel scores the music for a large orchestra, and also wordless chorus. Two suites from the ballet, arranged by Ravel himself, are frequently played at concerts.

Darabukka (darbukka) In Arab music of the Middle East and north Africa, a single-headed goblet-shaped *drum made of wood, metal, or pottery. It is held under the arm, or rested on the leg, and played with both hands.

dB Abbreviation of *Decibel.

D.C. Abbreviation of **Da capo*.

Death and the Maiden **1** Song (*Der Tod und das Mädchen*) composed by Schubert in 1817. **2** Nickname of Schubert's String Quartet No. 14 in D minor (D810) composed in 1824. For the slow second movement, he wrote a series of variations on his earlier song.

Decani [Latin] The section of the choir occupying the stalls on the south side of a cathedral – the side on which the Dean sits.

Deceptive cadence Same as an interrupted cadence. [See under *Cadences]

Decibel (Often abbreviated to **dB**) A **bel** (from Alexander Graham Bell, the Scottish inventor) is a unit for measuring the volume or loudness of sound. A **decibel** (= one tenth of a bel) represents the smallest degree of difference in loudness that the human ear can detect. A violin played softly rates about 25 dB; while a large orchestra playing at full volume rates about 100 dB. Around 125 dB, sounds approach the 'threshold of pain' of human hearing.

Décidé [French]; **Deciso** [Italian] Decisively, with decision.

Declamato [Italian] In a declamatory manner; declaimed; in the manner of 'impassioned speech'.

Decoration Method of varying the repetition of a melody, a phrase, or a whole section of a piece, in such a way that it is 'decorated' by the addition of ornaments or other extra notes:

Decrescendo [Italian] Decreasing in volume; becoming gradually softer. Often abbreviated to **decresc**. [See also: *Crescendo; *Diminuendo]

Definite pitch See under *Percussion instruments.

Degree Any note of a major or minor scale or key in relation to the other notes.

The degrees, or steps, of a scale may be referred to by their technical names, by number (using Roman numerals), or by sol-fa names:

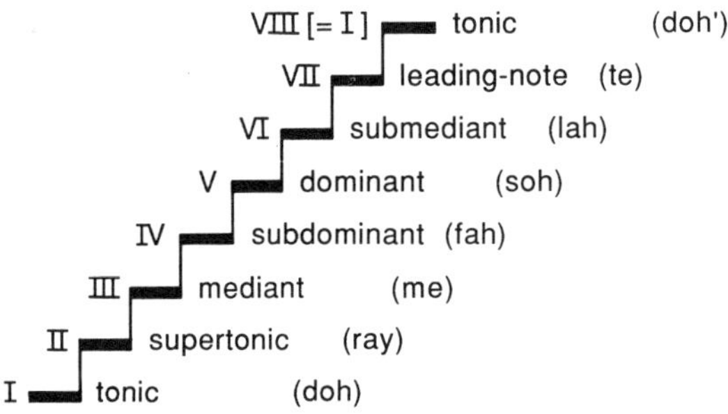

Delicato [Italian] Delicate. **Delicatissimo**, very delicate. **Delicatamente**, delicately. **Delicatezza**, delicacy.

Delirando [Italian] Delirious; frenzied.

Demi [French] Half.

Demisemiquaver The note which is half the value of a semiquaver and twice the value of a hemidemisemiquaver. Eight demisemiquavers are equal to one crotchet; thirty-two demisemiquavers equal one semibreve. (The American name for a demisemiquaver is a thirty-second note.) The examples below show (a) a single demisemiquaver (three hooks to the stem); (b) a group of four demisemiquavers; and (c) a demisemiquaver *rest. [See also Tables 1 and 2 on page 387]

(a) 𝅘𝅥𝅰 (b) ♬ (c) 𝅀

Des [German] The note D flat. **Deses**, D double flat.

Descant **1** Originally, the name for the highest voice (treble, or soprano) in part-music; and so used to describe certain high-pitched instruments (e.g. descant recorder). **2** In hymn-singing, a counter-melody sung by trebles or sopranos above the main hymn-tune. **3** The same in meaning as *discant.

Descriptive music See *Programme music; also, *Word-painting.

Desiderio [Italian] Desire, longing.

Desk The music-stand shared by two orchestral players. The same word is sometimes used to refer to the players themselves.

Desolato [Italian] Desolate; forlorn.

Desto [Italian] 'Wide-awake'; in an exuberant, sprightly manner.

Destra; **Destro** [Italian] Right. **Mano destra**, right hand. **Colla destra**, with the right (hand).

Détaché [French: 'detached'] A type of *bowing stroke on string instruments in which each note is played with a separate bow-stroke.

Deutlich [German] Distinct, clear.

Deutscher Tanz (plural: *deutsche Tänze*) [German] German dance. [See also under *Ländler]

Deutsches Requiem, Ein See *A *German Requiem*.

Deux [French] Two. **À deux** (or **à 2**) carries the same meanings as **A due* in Italian. **Deuxième**, second.

Development **1** The treatment of thematic ideas in a composition – bringing them under musical 'discussion' by exploring their melodic, rhythmic, or harmonic possibilities in various ways (described below). **2** The central section ('development section') of a piece or movement structured in *sonata form.

There are many ways in which a composer may develop, explore, or 'work out' the musical possibilities of themes or ideas presented previously. The following list includes the most important methods of development (which may be employed singly, or in combination; treating one idea at a time, or two or more simultaneously).

(a) change(s) of key; perhaps also of mode (a change from major to minor or vice versa);
(b) changing or varying the original harmonies (perhaps adding harmonies to a passage previously presented unharmonized);
(c) altering or varying the *dynamics;
(d) changing the register (e.g. putting a theme down into the bass);
(e) altering the intervals of a melody so that its contour (possibly also its character) is changed;
(f) changing or varying the rhythm, or the metre; altering the rhythmic accents of a theme (perhaps using *syncopation);
(g) varying the normal phrase-lengths, by extending or contracting them;
(h) adding a different kind or style of accompaniment;
(i) breaking down a theme into smaller figures or fragments, perhaps developing these 'component parts' individually, or in combination, or regrouping them to form new phrases;
(j) building up a passage by working a phrase (or perhaps just a figure or fragment of a previous theme) in *sequence;
(k) treating ideas by contrapuntal devices such as *imitation, *inversion, *augmentation, *diminution, *invertible counterpoint;
(l) using an idea or a fragment as an *ostinato;
(m) using a theme or a distinctive fragment to build up a *fugato;
(n) changing or varying the timbre or tone-colour in a noticeable way (e.g. if the music is for orchestra, re-presenting a theme with a marked change of orchestration).

A development section often ends with a *pedal point – usually a 'dominant pedal' emphasizing the return to (the re-establishment of) the tonic key at the beginning of the recapitulation section.

Devices For various musical, compositional, melodic, and rhythmic devices and techniques used by composers, see: *Decoration; *Sequence; *Imitation; *Inversion; *Retrograde and Retrograde inversion; *Augmentation; *Diminution; *Dynamics; *Antiphony; *Echo effects; *Heterophony; *Ostinato; *Riff; *Ground bass; *Pedal point; *Syncopation; *Hemiola; *Polymetre; *Polyrhythm; *Thematic transformation; *Klangfarbenmelodie; *Voice-exchange; *Hocket; *Cantus firmus; *Isorhythm; *Fugato; *Invertible counterpoint. See also under *Variations; *Development; *Fugue; *Canon. For Repetition and Contrast, see under *Form. [See also: *Orchestral devices]

'Devil's Trill' Sonata Tartini's Sonata in G minor for violin and continuo which he is said to have composed upon waking from a dream in which the Devil visited him and played his violin. During the final movement of the sonata the accompaniment ceases, and the violin weaves a web of double-stoppings and trills of fiendish difficulty.

'Diabelli' Variations Beethoven's set of variations for piano, Opus 120, composed between 1819 and 1823. The publisher Antonio Diabelli sent a simple waltz he had composed to fifty composers – including Beethoven, Schubert, and Liszt (then only eleven years old) – asking them to write one variation each. Beethoven, however, responded with thirty-three variations, comprising one of the finest sets of variations ever composed.

Diabolus in musica [Latin: 'The Devil in music'] Medieval name for the **tritone** – the *interval of an augmented 4th which spans three whole tones (e.g. F to B). As a melodic interval it is very difficult to sing in tune, and was therefore forbidden by medieval theorists.

Diatonic A word describing any note belonging to the scale (major or minor) of the key in which the music is written at any given moment. And so the word *diatonic* may also be used to describe intervals, melodies, chords, and harmonies confined to such notes, to the exclusion of *chromatic notes. (In minor keys, the sharpened sixth and seventh notes, as and when they occur, are also regarded as being diatonic.)

Diatonic scale Any major or minor *scale may be referred to as a diatonic scale (as opposed to the chromatic scale).

Di chiaro [Italian] Clearly.

Dichterliebe (Poet's Love) A *song-cycle, Opus 48, for voice and piano, composed by Schumann in 1840, setting sixteen poems by Heine. The titles of the songs are: 1 *Im wunderschönen Monat Mai* (In the lovely month of May); 2 *Aus meinen Tränen* (From my tears); 3 *Die Rose, die Lilie* (The rose, the lily); 4 *Wenn ich in deine Augen seh'* (When I gaze into your eyes); 5 *Ich will meine Seele tauchen* (I want to sink my soul); 6 *Im Rhein, im heiligen Strome* (In the Rhine, in the holy river); 7 *Ich grolle nicht* (I do not complain); 8 *Und wüssten's die Blumen* (If only the flowers knew); 9 *Das ist ein Flöten und Geigen* (There is a fluting and fiddling); 10 *Hör ich das Liedchen klingen* (I hear a song ringing out); 11 *Ein Jüngling liebt ein Mädchen* (A youth loved a girl); 12 *Am leuchtenden Sommermorgen* (On a shining summer morning); 13 *Ich hab' im Traum geweinet* (I have wept in my dreams); 14 *Allnächtlich im Traume seh' ich dich* (Each night I see you in my dreams); 15 *Aus alten Märchen* (From old tales); 16 *Die alten, bösen Lieder* (The old, bad songs).

Dido and Aeneas Purcell's only true opera (his other stage-works being classed as *semi-operas); in three acts, setting a text by Nahum Tate based on Book IV of Virgil's *Aeneid.* Dido, Queen of Carthage, falls deeply in love with Aeneas, a Trojan prince who has arrived at her court after being shipwrecked during a violent storm. Aeneas, however, is tricked by witchcraft into deserting Dido. As she is dying, her heart broken, she sings the famous lament, 'When I am laid in earth' (see *Ground bass). Purcell's opera was first performed in 1689 at Josias Priest's School for Young Gentlewomen in Chelsea, London, with all the parts – except those of Aeneas and the male members of the chorus – sung by girls of the school.

Dièse [French]; **Diesis** [Italian] Sharp (♯). For example, *Fa-dièse* or *Fa diesis* = F sharp.

Dies irae [Latin: 'Day of Wrath'] A poem by Thomas of Celano (died *c*1250) which forms part of the *Requiem Mass. Its plainsong melody (see the music example) is sometimes quoted in compositions by 19th- and 20th-century composers to bring into the listener's mind not only the symbol of death, or horrifying thoughts of the Day of Judgement, but also fear of the supernatural. For example: Berlioz in the final movement ('The Witches' Sabbath') of his *Symphonie fantastique*; Liszt in *Totentanz* (Dance of Death); Rachmaninov in

The Isle of the Dead and *Rhapsody on a Theme of Paganini* (Variations 7 and 24).

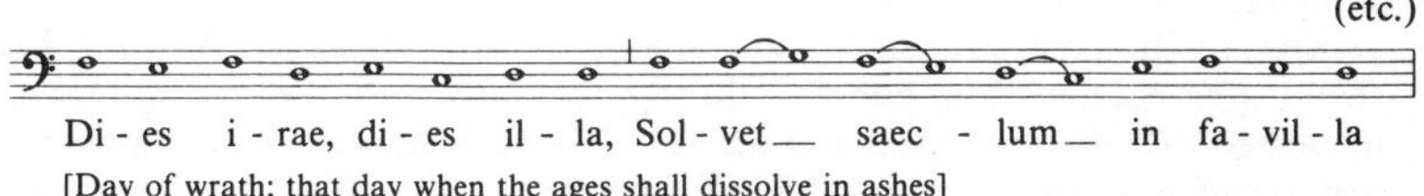
(etc.)
Di - es i - rae, di - es il - la, Sol - vet saec - lum in fa - vil - la
[Day of wrath; that day when the ages shall dissolve in ashes]

Diferencias A 16th-century Spanish term meaning 'variations'.
Dim.; **dimin.** Abbreviations of **diminuendo.*
Diminished interval See under *Intervals.
Diminished seventh chord A chord which consists of three minor 3rds stacked one above another, so that the interval between the root and the seventh is a diminished 7th. It is an extremely useful chord for *modulation to distant keys since it can pivot onto any degree of the chromatic scale. In the examples below the initial chords are identical in sound, though one or more notes may be 'spelt' in a different way.

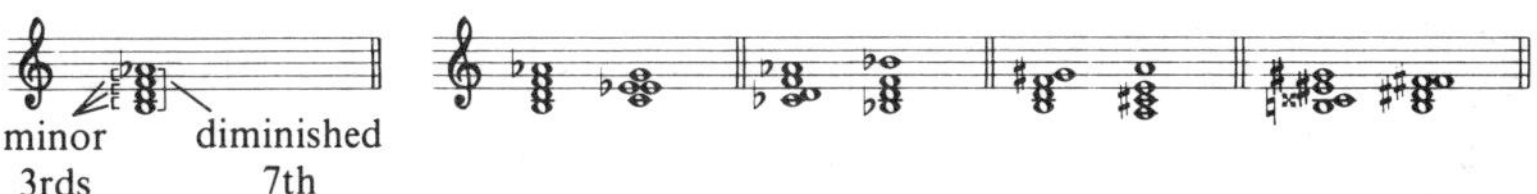
minor
3rds
diminished
7th

Diminished triad See *Triad.
Diminuendo [Italian] Diminishing in volume; becoming gradually softer. Often abbreviated to **dim.** or **dimin.**, or indicated by a 'hairpin' sign ⟩ [See also: *Crescendo; *Decrescendo]
Diminution Shortening the original values of the notes in a theme – usually halving their value so that, for instance, a minim becomes a crotchet, a crotchet a quaver, and so on. Music example (b), below, is (a) in diminution:

(a)
(b)

[See also: *Augmentation, which is the reverse process]
Di molto [Italian] Extremely. (For example: *Adagio di molto*, extremely slow.)
Di nuovo [Italian] Anew, again, once more.
Directing (an ensemble, choir, or orchestra) See *Conducting.
Dirigent [German] Conductor.
Dis [German] D sharp (but, until the early 19th century, often standing for E flat).
Discant A style in 13th-century compositions such as clausulae, motets, and conductus in which all the voice-parts moved in rhythm, mainly in *note-against-note style.
Discord The opposite of concord. [See: *Concords and Discords]
Disis [German] D double sharp.
Disjunct 'Disconnected'. Moving by leap rather than by step. [See: *Motion]
Dissonance The sounding together of two or more notes which 'disagree' and so produce a discord. [See: *Concords and Discords]
'Dissonance' Quartet Nickname for Mozart's String Quartet No. 19 in C (K465) composed in Vienna in 1765. The slow introduction contains some unusual dissonances which would have sounded surprisingly harsh to 18th-century listeners. [See also: *'Haydn' Quartets]

Dissonant Having the effect of dissonance or discord. [See: *Concords and Discords]

Distinto [Italian] Distinct, clear.

Divertimento [Italian: 'diversion', 'enjoyment', 'entertainment'] A type of instrumental composition popular during the late 18th century, in several movements (from three to eight or more). The music was usually composed for performance by an ensemble of solo instruments, and was light and entertaining in style. A divertimento combines features of the symphony and the suite. Other similar compositions, related to the divertimento, include the *serenade, *cassation, and *notturno.

Divertissement [French] **1** Same in meaning as **divertimento.* **2** An *entr'acte* – music performed between acts. **3** In French operas of the 17th and 18th centuries, a sequence of solos, *ensembles, and dances, usually (though not always) diverting from the main thread of the plot. **4** A sequence of dances in a ballet, forming a diversion from the main story; also, a selection of dances from a ballet, arranged and performed within a concert programme of dances. **5** A composition in popular style based on melodies from another source (e.g. from an opera).

Divisés [French]; **Divisi** [Italian] (often abbreviated to **div.**) 'Divided'. An indication, applied particularly to the string section of the orchestra, that the players of a part (e.g. first violins) are to divide into two or more groups, each group now playing a separate part. The instruction is cancelled by *unis* or *unisono*, indicating a return to playing in unison.

Division A 17th-century term for a type of variation in which a simple melodic line is elaborated with ornamentation and swift figuration. 'Divisions on a ground' were variations on a *ground bass, and were often improvised by the soloist (e.g. on flute or viol, accompanied by harpsichord).

Dixieland A term which may be used with various meanings: (1) *Traditional (trad.) jazz, or (2) *New Orleans jazz, or (3) the music of certain white jazzmen working in or originating from New Orleans (e.g. the Original Dixieland Jazz Band, who made the first jazz recordings in 1917 in New York).

Dmpf; **Dpf** Abbreviations of either **Dämpfer* or *Dämpfern.*

Do [Italian] The note C.

Doch [German] But, yet, though, nevertheless.

Dodecaphonic [from Greek, meaning 'twelve-sound'] A term used **1** to mean the same as 'atonal' [see *atonality], or **2** to describe music written in *twelve-note technique.

'Dog' Waltz See under *'Minute' Waltz.

Dolce (abbrev.: **dol.**) [Italian] Sweet, soft, gentle. **Dolcissimo** (abbrev. **dolciss.**), very sweet. **Dolcemente**, sweetly. **Dolcezza**, sweetness.

Dolente [Italian] Sorrowful, mournful.

Dolly A suite of six pieces for piano duet, composed by Fauré between 1894 and 1897, and dedicated to a very young friend of his, Hélène ('Dolly') Bardac – the daughter of Emma Bardac who later became Debussy's second wife. The six pieces are: 1 *Berceuse* (Lullaby); 2 *Mi-a-ow* (Dolly's pronunciation of her brother Raoul's name); 3 *Le jardin de Dolly* (Dolly's garden); 4 *Kitty-Valse* (Kitty was in fact the name of Raoul's bitch-puppy); 5 *Tendresse* (Tenderness, or fondness); 6 *Le pas espagnol* (Spanish dance). The music was orchestrated as a ballet in 1906 by Henri Rabaud.

Dolore [Italian] Sorrow, grief, regret.

Doloroso [Italian] Sad, sorrowful, mournful, grief-laden.

Dominant The fifth step or *degree of a major or minor scale; next in importance to the *tonic. For example: in the scale of C major and C minor, C is the tonic and G, a 5th higher, is the dominant; the **dominant chord**, which has the dominant as its root, is built from the notes G–B–D; and the **dominant seventh chord** adds the seventh note above the root: G–B–D–F. [See also under *Chord; also *Ninth chord; *Eleventh chord; *Thirteenth chord]

Dompe (dump) Title given to several instrumental pieces by English composers of the 16th and 17th centuries. Although the exact meaning is uncertain, it has been suggested that a *dompe* or *dump* may originally have been a kind of lament or sorrowful song. An example is *My Lady Careys Dompe* by an anonymous composer; and this is one of the three earliest pieces (in a manuscript of *c*1530) which are known to have been specially written for the virginals.

Don Giovanni Opera buffa in two acts by Mozart, first produced in Prague in 1787 (libretto by da Ponte based on the Don Juan legend). Don Giovanni (baritone), a noted woman-chaser, is helped in his escapades by his servant Leporello. Disguised, he visits the house of Donna Anna (soprano), the daughter of the Commendatore, but she and her father chase him out; the two men fight and the Commendatore (bass) is slain. Anna and her fiancé, Don Ottavio (tenor), swear vengeance. Giovanni's former sweetheart Donna Elvira (soprana) appears, and Leporello (bass) reads her a long list of his master's lovers. Two peasants, Zerlina (soprano) and Masetto (bass), arrive with their wedding party, and Giovanni contrives to get Zerlina on her own and pay court to her, but he is interrupted by Elvira, who hotly denounces him. Anna and Ottavio appear, and Anna recognizes Giovanni as her father's killer. At a masked ball in Giovanni's palace Anna, Ottavio, and Elvira reveal that they know all, but characteristically Giovanni gives them the slip. He now turns his attention to Elvira's maid, but fearing a beating from the enraged peasants he disguises himself as Leporello. Meanwhile the real Leporello, mistaken for Giovanni, takes refuge in a churchyard beside a statue of the dead Commendatore. He is joined there by Giovanni, who is also making good his escape. Mockingly, Giovanni invites the statue to supper. To his horror it accepts, and arrives to drag him down to Hell.

Don Juan Symphonic poem, Opus 20, composed by Richard Strauss in 1888, and based upon passages from a lengthy poem of the same title by Nikolaus Lenau. The legendary character of Don Juan – a Spanish aristocrat and infamous woman-chaser – has been made the subject of several musical works, the most famous being Mozart's opera **Don Giovanni*. [See also: *Ein *Heldenleben*]

Don Quixote Symphonic poem, Opus 35, composed by Richard Strauss in 1896–7, describing characters and events from the novel of the same title by Cervantes. Strauss described the music as 'Fantastic variations upon a theme of knightly character'. The work is scored for a large orchestra – including important solo parts for viola and cello – and also requires the use of a *wind machine. [See also: *Ein *Heldenleben*]

Dopo [Italian] After, then.

Doppel [German] Double.

Doppio [Italian] Double. **Doppio movimento** or **Doppio tempo**: double the speed of the preceding passage (therefore: twice as fast). **Doppio bemolle**, double flat (𝄫). **Doppio diesis**, double sharp (𝄪).

Dorian mode See *Church modes.

Dot **1** A dot after a note or a rest makes it half as long again. For example:

𝅗𝅥. = 𝅗𝅥 ♩   ♩. = ♩ ♪   𝄽. = 𝄽 𝄾

If there is a **double dot**, the second dot adds on half the value of the first:

𝅗𝅥.. = 𝅗𝅥 ♩ ♪   ♩.. = ♩ ♪ 𝅘𝅥𝅯   𝄽.. = 𝄽 𝄾 𝄿

2 A dot placed above or below a note indicates that it is to be played **staccato*. [For dots placed vertically alongside a double bar ('double bar-line') see *Repeat signs. For the Baroque custom of 'double-dotting', see under *Overture]

Dotted notes See *Dot.

Double [French] A term used during the first half of the 18th century (the time of Bach and Handel) to mean a type of variation in which quite elaborate ornamentation was added to the original melody. (And so *double* is similar in meaning to the English **division*.) For example, Bach writes a double after the Sarabande in his sixth English Suite.

Double bar; **Double bar-line** See *Bar-lines.

Double bass (contrabass, string bass, bass) The largest and lowest-pitched bowed string instrument in common use. In the orchestra, there are often eight or more double basses whose deep, resonant sound provides the foundation of the string section, and of the orchestra as a whole. The double bass is 1.85 metres high, and so rests on the ground as it is played, the performer either standing or perching on a high stool.

double bass

The double bass differs slightly in shape from the violin, viola, and cello. The shoulders slope more, and the back is flatter. (These are characteristics of the viol family; the double bass is a descendant of the double-bass viol or *violone.) Originally, double basses had only three strings. Now they have four, tuned in 4ths – and sometimes a fifth string, tuned to low C, so that the range then lies exactly an octave below that of the cello.

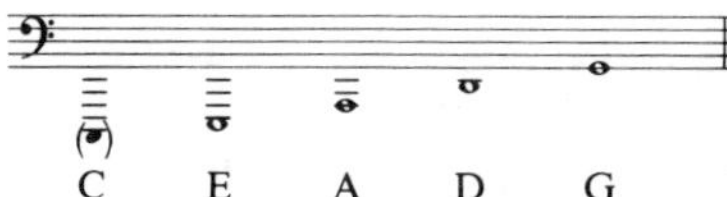

Music for double bass is written one octave higher than it actually sounds, so avoiding too many leger lines below the stave. The highest notes in the range may be written in the treble clef.

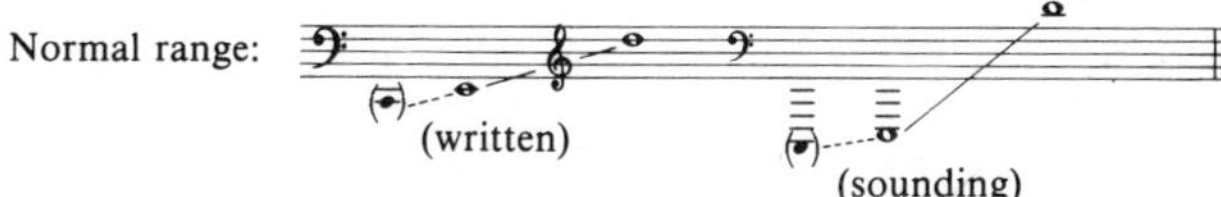

The thick strings of the double bass produce a rather dry, gruff, 'buzzy' tone-quality when played with the bow; played *pizzicato*, however, the sound is splendidly rich, round, and resonant. Solos for double bass include *The Elephant* from *The *Carnival of Animals* by Saint-Saëns, the third movement of Mahler's First Symphony, the *Romance* from Prokofiev's **Lieutenant Kijé*, and the *Vivo* (a humorous duet with trombone) from Stravinsky's *Pulcinella.* Among chamber works including double bass are Beethoven's *Septet, Schubert's *Octet and *'Trout' Quintet, Dvořák's *String Quintet in G (Op. 77), and Saint-Saëns' Septet for piano, trumpet, string quartet, and double bass. There are double bass concertos by Dittersdorf (who also wrote a Sinfonia Concertante for viola, double bass, and orchestra), and also by Dragonetti, Bottesini, and Koussevitzky (these last three being famous double bass players). The double bass is also much used (almost always played *pizzicato*) in dance bands and jazz ensembles, one of the finest jazz bass players being Charles Mingus.

Double-bass clarinet See *Contrabass clarinet.

Double bassoon (contrabassoon) A double-reed woodwind instrument, pitched an octave lower than the normal *bassoon. The double bassoon is the largest and deepest-sounding of the orchestral woodwinds; its lengthy tube, which doubles back on itself four times, is 5.6 metres long – double the length of the ordinary bassoon. Music for double bassoon (like that for double bass) is written one octave higher than it actually sounds.

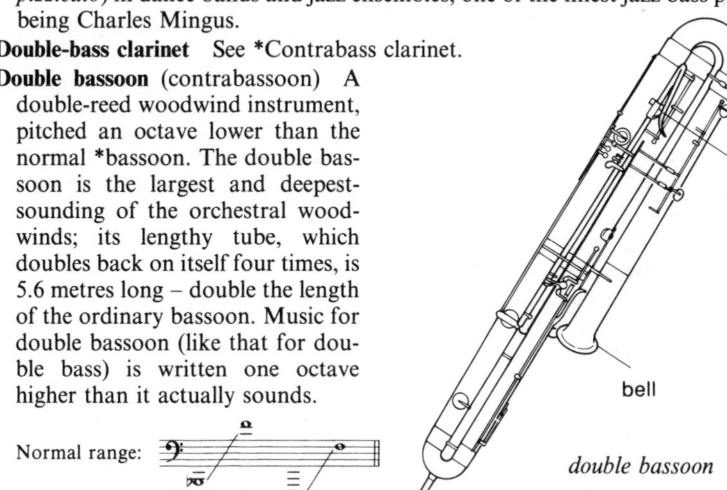

double bassoon

Ravel features the sound of the double bassoon in *Beauty and the Beast* from his *'*Mother Goose' Suite*, and also at the beginning of his Piano Concerto for the left hand. It is also heard in Variation 4 (in duet with a piccolo) from Dohnányi's **Variations on a Nursery Tune*.

Double bémol [French] The double flat sign (♭♭).

Double canon See under *Canon.

Double chorus A chorus, in a work such as an oratorio, written for two choirs and usually involving *antiphonal singing. Fine examples are 'He gave them hailstones', No. 7 from Handel's oratorio **Israel in Egypt*; and the Osanna from Bach's *B minor Mass.

Double concerto A *concerto which features two solo instruments pitted against an orchestra. Examples include: Bach's Concerto in D minor for two violins and string orchestra; Hummel's Concerto in G major for piano, violin, and orchestra; Brahms's Concerto in A minor for violin, cello, and orchestra; and Hans Werner Henze's Double Concerto (1966) for oboe, harp, and string orchestra.

Double counterpoint See *Invertible counterpoint.

Double dièse [French] The double sharp sign (𝄪).

Double dot See *Dot.

Double flat See *Accidentals.

Double fugue A *fugue based on two subjects. They may either be treated simultaneously; or treated first separately and then in combination. Fugues which treat three or four subjects in a similar way are called triple and quadruple fugues respectively.

Double pedal **1** In organ-playing, using both feet simultaneously to play two notes or two *parts. **2** A *pedal point which involves two notes simultaneously (most often the tonic and dominant).

Double reed See *Reed.

Double sharp See *Accidentals.

Double stop; **Double stopping** See *Stopping 1.

Double string orchestra A composition for 'double string orchestra' is in fact written for two string orchestras – either equal in size, or one consisting of fewer players than the other. Often, the composer will make use of *antiphonal effects between the two orchestras, or perhaps create *echo effects, also joining the two orchestras together to produce a richer, fuller sound, often with a more elaborate, complicated texture. Examples include the Concerto for Double String Orchestra by Tippett and **Fantasia on a Theme by Thomas Tallis* by Vaughan Williams.

Double tonguing See *Tonguing.

Double woodwind See under *Woodwind instruments.

Douce; **Doux** [French] Sweet, gentle. **Doucement**, sweetly, gently.

Douloureux [French] Sad, mournful.

Downbeat The strong first beat of a bar of music (as would be marked by the downward movement of the conductor's baton).

Down-bow See *Bowing.

Drag See under *Snare drum.

Dramma per musica [Italian: 'play for music'] A term often used to mean the earliest Italian operas (e.g. those of Monteverdi), though the term was in fact used by 17th-century Italian poets and dramatists to mean a play written specially to be set to music.

Drammatico [Italian] Dramatic; in a dramatic style.

Drängend [German] Hurrying, pressing forward.

Dream of Gerontius, The A choral work (Op. 38; 1899–1900) by Elgar, for mezzo-soprano, tenor, and bass soloists, chorus, and orchestra. It is a setting of a religious poem of the same title by Cardinal Newman, and is often described as an oratorio, though Elgar himself did not approve of the description.

Drei [German] Three. **Dreifach**, threefold, in three instrumental parts or voice-parts.

Dreigroschenoper, Die See *The *Threepenny Opera.*

Dringend [German] Rushing, pressing forward.

Drone **1** One (sometimes more than one) note, often in the bass, and sustained or persistently repeated throughout a piece or part of a piece; often called a **drone bass**. **2** The low-pitched pipes of a bagpipe which sound as an accompaniment to the melody.

Drone strings On certain string instruments, strings which, bowed or plucked, each sound a single pitch only, and so produce an accompanying *drone. Examples of instruments with drone strings are *hurdy-gurdy, *medieval fiddle, *sarod, *sitar, and *vīṇā.

Drum A percussion instrument consisting of a frame or some kind of hollow vessel (the body-shell) over which is stretched a membrane of skin or plastic. A drum is usually sounded by striking the membrane with the bare hands or with one or two hard-headed sticks or padded beaters. The skin vibrates, and its vibrations are amplified by the hollow body-shell.

Drums are counted among the very oldest musical instruments, and they exist in a wide variety of shapes and sizes in all parts of the world. According to shape of body-shell, drums divide into three groups: (1) frame drums, (2) bowl-shaped or kettle drums, (3) tubular drums. The third group, tubular drums, includes shapes such as: cylindrical, conical, barrel, waisted or hour-glass, and goblet.

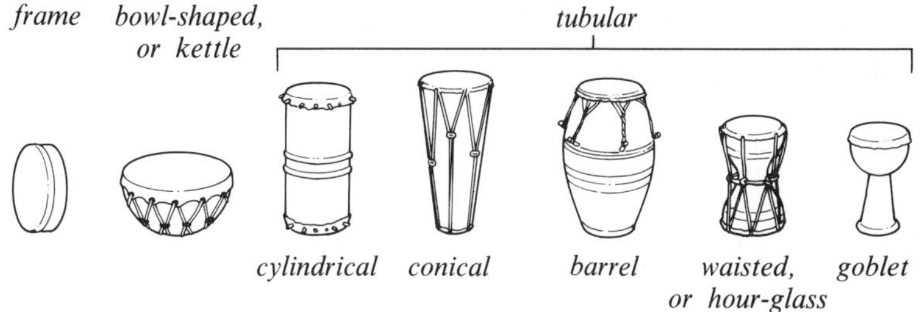

A tubular drum may be single-headed (a single skin stretched over one end of the tube, the other end being left open or closed), or double-headed (skin stretched over each end of the tube).

[For types of drum regularly used in orchestras and bands, see: *Kettle drum (timpani); *Snare drum (side drum); *Bass drum; *Tenor drum; *Tambourine. See also: *Membranophone; *Bongos; *Congas (conga drums); *Daff; *Darabukka; *Drum kit; *Mṛdaṅgam; *Nakers; *Tablā; *Tabor; *Ṭār; *Tom-toms]

Drum kit (drum set) The set of percussion instruments (often referred to simply as '**drums**') played by one person in a jazz band, swing band, pop or rock group, etc., and arranged around the player in such a way that all are within easy reach and control of the player. The basic components of the drum kit are: bass drum (not as large as the orchestral bass drum) worked by a foot-pedal with the right foot; one or more *tom-toms, fixed above the bass drum; large tom-tom (floor tom-tom) or tenor drum; snare drum (side drum); suspended cymbals ('crash', 'ride', 'sizzle') fixed to drums or on individual stands; and *hi-hat. The instruments are played with drum-sticks or wire brushes. There may also be other types of drums and cymbals, and extras such as Chinese block and temple blocks (see *wood-blocks) and cowbell (or *cencerro).

drum kit

'Drum Roll' Symphony (*'Paukenwirbel' Symphonie*) Haydn's Symphony No. 103 in E♭, composed in 1795 (one of his *'London' Symphonies). The nickname refers to the solo kettle drum roll which opens the symphony. There are four movements: 1 *Adagio* (a lengthy slow introduction) leading to *Allegro con spirito* (in sonata form); 2 *Andante* (a set of variations on two themes alternately); 3 Menuetto; 4 Finale: *Allegro con spirito* (in simple rondo form, but based on a single theme).

Drum set See *Drum kit.

Dry recitative See under *Recitative.

D.S. Abbreviation of **Dal segno*.

Due [Italian] Two.

Duet [German: *Duett*; Italian: *duetto*] A piece for two voices or instruments, with or without accompaniment; or a piece for two performers on a single instrument (e.g. a piano duet). [See also: *Duo]

Duet sonata A term sometimes used to describe a sonata for two instrumentalists – for example, violin and piano (violin sonata), clarinet and piano (clarinet sonata), a sonata for violin and cello, or for flute and oboe, and so on.

Duettino [Italian] A small or short *duet.

Duetto [Italian] *Duet.

Duff See *Daff.

Dulcian Name commonly used for the early type of bassoon, made in a single piece rather than in joints or sections like the modern bassoon.

Dulcimer A medieval struck string instrument. It is basically a *psaltery but the strings, rather than being plucked, were hit with sticks or hammers, one held in each hand.

'Dumbarton Oaks' Concerto in E♭ for fifteen instruments, composed by Stravinsky in 1938. It was commissioned by Mrs R. W. Bliss and first performed at her villa, Dumbarton Oaks, near Washington. The Concerto is in three movements, and is scored for a chamber orchestra consisting of flute, clarinet, bassoon, 2 horns, 3 violins, 3 violas, 2 cellos, and 2 double basses. Stravinsky said he modelled the work on Bach's *Brandenburg Concertos. [See: *Neoclassicism]

Dumka (plural: *dumky*) A type of Slavonic folk-ballad whose music continually alternates between two sharply contrasting moods: darkly sorrowful and wildly joyful. Dvořák wrote several instrumental pieces in the style of a *dumka* – for example: his Slavonic Dance No. 2 in E minor; the second movement of his Piano Quintet in A major, Op. 81; and the set of six *dumky* which make up his 'Dumky' Trio in E minor, Op. 90, for violin, cello, and piano.

'Dumky' Trio See under *Dumka.

Dump See *Dompe.

Duo **1** Title sometimes given to an instrumental (rather than a vocal) *duet. **2** Two players (e.g. a pianist and violinist) who regularly perform together may refer to themselves as a duo.

Duplet (couplet) A group of two notes played or sung evenly in the time taken by three notes of the same kind. (The reverse of *triplet.)

Duple time (duple metre) Any kind of *time (or metre) which has two beats to each bar. The beat may be a plain note (such as ♩ or 𝅗𝅥) or it may be a dotted note (such as ♩. or 𝅗𝅥.). [See the articles on *Time and *Time signature, and also the table of Time signatures on page 389]

Duplum [Latin: 'twofold', 'double'] The second voice-part – that added next above the tenor *cantus firmus* (see *Tenor, 3) – in an *organum or *clausula written by a composer of the Notre Dame School (see under *Ars Antiqua). If the composer added a third, and possibly a fourth, voice-part he called these *triplum* and *quadruplum* respectively. These words were also used as adjectives; for example, an *organum duplum* was a twofold organum – an organum in two voice-parts.

In the 13th-century *motet, when words were provided for the duplum voice-part, it then became known as the *motetus* (from French *mots*, 'words').

Dur [German] Major, meaning 'major key'. (For example: *C-dur*, C major.) [See also: *Moll]

Durchaus [German] Throughout.

Durchkomponiert [German] Through-composed. [See under: *Strophic]

Dux and **comes** [Latin: 'leader', and 'follower' or 'companion'] The names given, respectively, to the leading and imitating (or following) parts in a *canon.

Dynamic markings (marks) Markings added to the music (usually by the composer but sometimes by an editor) to indicate varying degrees, or changes, of volume or loudness. They may be words, abbreviations, letters, or signs. For example: *pp*, *forte*, *crescendo*, *dim.* < > [See the table of Dynamic markings on page 390]

Dynamics The varying degrees of loudness or softness which a composer calls for in the performance of a piece. [See: *Dynamic markings; also *'Terraced' dynamics]

E; **Ed** [Italian] And.

Early music The term popularly used to describe music composed during Medieval times and the Renaissance. In recent years, a keen interest has developed in the music of these periods, and many ensembles have been formed whose aim is to give performances which are as authentic as possible. Unfortunately, relatively few original instruments have survived. But modern copies are made, often based on information found in treatises, poems, and chronicles of the time, together with help from illustrations in old manuscripts, paintings, sculptures, wood-carvings, tapestries, and stained-glass windows.

Ebony Concerto A concerto by Stravinsky for clarinet (which in jazz slang is an 'ebony stick') and jazz band. The work, which includes jazz ingredients, was composed for the jazz clarinettist Woody Herman, who gave its first performance with his band in New York in 1946.

Ecclesiastical modes Same as *Church modes.

Echo effects Various methods used by composers, in both instrumental and vocal music, to imitate the effect of natural echo by the soft repetition of a phrase or part of a phrase. Besides being quieter, the effect may be further enhanced in various ways. For example: by giving the repeated (echo) portions to a smaller group of performers (see *semichorus; also *double string orchestra); by spatially separating the groups (e.g. placing the echoing group to the side of the main group, or behind it so that the echoes come from a distance); or by also bringing in a change of timbre or tone-colour (as on a two-manual harpsichord, or using contrasting stops on the organ, or having full orchestra softly echoed by, say, horns only).

Echoklavier [German] The echo organ. [See under *Organ]

Echo organ See under *Organ.

Éclatant [French] Brilliant, sparkling; piercing.

Eclogue A pastoral song, or short instrumental piece in a similar style.

Écossaise [French for 'Scottish', or 'Scottish dance'] A swift dance in $\frac{2}{4}$ time, popular in England and France during the late 18th and early 19th centuries. In spite of the name, it was not Scottish in origin. Among composers who wrote pieces with this title are Beethoven, Schubert, and Chopin.

E flat horn See *Tenor horn.

Egmont Overture and incidental music, Opus 84, composed by Beethoven in 1809–10 to accompany a performance of Goethe's play. The famous overture is frequently played separately as a concert piece.

Eguale [Italian] Equal; even. **Egualmente**, equally, evenly, alike.

Eighteen-Twelve (*1812*) A 'festival overture', Opus 49, composed by Tchaikovsky in 1880. It commemorates the retreat from Moscow, in 1812, of

Napoleon and his Grande Armée. Tchaikovsky brings in the French national anthem (*La Marseillaise*) and the Tsarist national anthem, and a number of Russian folk-tunes. He originally intended that the music should be performed out-of-doors in a Moscow square; and that at the climax, the sound of the orchestra should be augmented by military band, cannon fire, and the pealing of cathedral bells.

Eight-foot See *Foot.

Eighth-note *Quaver.

Eilend [German] Hastening, hurrying, accelerating. **Nicht eilen**, do not hurry.

Einfach [German] Simple; in a simple way or manner.

Einleitung [German] An introduction, or prelude.

Eis [German] The note E sharp. **Eisis**, E double sharp.

Élargissant [French] Broadening. (Same as Italian: *allargando*.)

Electric guitar See under *Guitar.

Electronic music Originating in Germany in the 1950s, electronic music makes use of any sounds picked up by a microphone (as in *Musique concrète) and also any sounds produced from electronic sound-generators, amplified through loudspeakers, and usually (but not always) recorded onto magnetic tape. The basic sound-producing component is an oscillator. Sounds produced may be as 'pure' (meaning free from harmonics or overtones) or as 'impure' as required. A sine-tone, for example, is a single 'pure' sound, such as accompanies a TV test card. Another kind of sound is 'white noise' – a rushing sound made up of all possible frequencies (heard, for example, if you say 'Shhhh ... ').

In constructing an electronic composition, sounds may be electronically modified in various ways, including adjustment of volume, change of pitch, filtering (cutting out unwanted frequencies), or adding vibrato ('wavering'), adding reverberation ('delay' added so that sounds die away gradually, blending together – as if in a huge cathedral), or adding echo (the sound is actually repeated over and over as it dies away).

Sounds may be mixed together, superimposed, or 'chopped' into separate fragments. Individual sounds may be recorded onto separate pieces of tape which are then spliced together in sequence, or a tape 'loop' may be made so that sounds can be repeated as an *ostinato effect. Also, the basic techniques of *musique concrète* play an important part, such as reversing sounds (often producing a crescendo ending with abrupt 'cut-off') and altering the pitch – though by electronic means, the pitch may be changed gradually to produce a *glissando effect. Attack and/or decay of sounds may be deleted by tape-editing.

An electronic composition may consist solely of electronically generated sounds, either pre-recorded on tape or manipulated 'live' before an audience. Or a composer may choose to combine electronic sounds with instruments or voices, sounding naturally or transformed by electronic means, in 'live' performance or pre-recorded on tape.

Among the many composers who have explored the exciting possibilities of electronic music are Karlheinz Stockhausen (see **Gesang der Jünglinge*; **Kontakte*), Edgard Varèse (see **Poème électronique*), John Cage, Pierre Boulez, Luigi Nono, and Luciano Berio (see **Visage*).

Electrophone A term used to describe any musical instrument whose sound is produced by electronic means – from electrically-generated vibrations (e.g. electronic organ; *ondes Martenot). [See also: *Idiophone; *Membranophone; *Chordophone; *Aerophone]

Elegiaco [Italian] Elegiac, plaintive, mournful.

Elegy [Italian: *elegia*; French: *élégie*] A song-like piece, usually rather slow, which is plaintive or mournful in mood.

Elements of music See *Ingredients of music.

Eleventh See under *Intervals.

Eleventh chord (chord of the eleventh) A chord consisting of root, 3rd, 5th, 7th, 9th, and 11th – making five 3rds stacked one above another. It most often occurs as a **dominant eleventh** (being then built upon the *dominant of the scale).

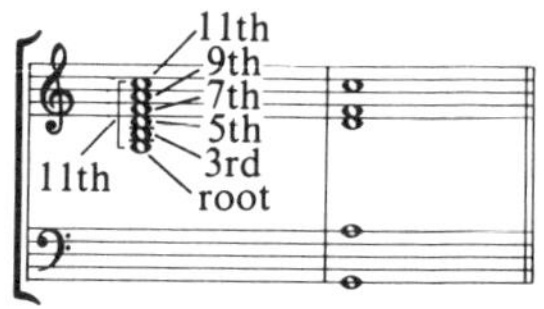

Elijah Oratorio in two parts by Mendelssohn, for soprano, contralto, tenor, bass, and treble soloists, boys' choir, chorus, and orchestra, first performed at the Birmingham Festival in 1846 (text by Schrubring based on the Old Testament story). The chorus has a dramatic role. Among the best-known numbers are the contralto aria 'O rest in the Lord'; the bass aria 'It is enough'; the chorus 'He, watching over Israel'; and the dramatic 'Baal' choruses, interspersed with recitatives for Elijah.

Embellishments Ornaments, decorations.

Embouchure **1** The mouthpiece of a wind instrument. **2** The shaping and position of the lips in the playing of wind instruments. Correct embouchure is extremely important, since it is the basis of control of sound. It varies according to which wind instrument is being played.

'Emperor' Concerto Nickname of Beethoven's last piano concerto: No. 5 in E flat, Op. 73, composed in 1809. In structure, it differs from earlier piano concertos. The first movement (*Allegro*) begins with a written-out cadenza for the soloist, punctuated by *fortissimo* chords for the orchestra; the slow second movement (*Adagio un poco mosso*) is linked to the final rondo (*Allegro*).

'Emperor' Quartet (*Kaiserquartett*) Nickname of Haydn's String Quartet in C, Op. 76 No. 3, composed in about 1797. The slow second movement is a set of variations on the **Emperor's Hymn*, each instrument in turn playing the melody: first violin (theme), second violin (variation 1), cello (var. 2), viola (var. 3), first violin (var. 4).

Emperor's Hymn (*Kaiserlied*) A four-part patriotic chorus composed by Haydn in 1797. It became the national anthem of Austria, later of Germany; and the music is often used in Britain as a hymn-tune, particularly to the words 'Glorious things of Thee are spoken'. [See also: *'Emperor' Quartet]

Empfindung [German] Feeling, emotion.

En animant [French] Becoming animated, livelier.

Enchaînez [French: 'link up'] A term instructing the performer to go straight on to the next section or movement, without a pause.

Encore [French] Again; still; yet. An 'encore' is: **1** a repeat of part or all of a composition, or **2** an additional short piece, performed at the end of a programme, in response to enthusiastic applause from the audience.

En dehors [French] Standing out, emphasized, made prominent.

Energico [Italian] Energetic, vigorous, powerful.

Enfance du Christ, L' (The Childhood of Christ) An oratorio, Opus 25, by Berlioz, composed between 1850 and 1854. The music, setting a text written by Berlioz himself, is scored for seven solo voices (soprano, two tenors, baritone, and three basses), choir, and orchestra. Particularly well known is the chorus

'Thou must leave Thy lowly dwelling' (the shepherd's farewell to the Holy Family).

Englisches Horn [German] English horn or *cor anglais.

English flute Older name for the recorder – to distinguish it from the transverse flute (which was called the 'German flute').

English horn *Cor anglais.

English Suites Six suites for harpsichord, composed by Bach around the year 1715. The name was not given to these suites by Bach himself, but a manuscript of the music which belonged to his son Johann Christian is headed with the words 'fait pour les Anglais' ('composed for the English'). Each suite begins with a lengthy prelude, followed by a group of dances, including allemande, courante, sarabande, and gigue. Between sarabande and gigue there is a pair of extra dances: Suites 1 and 2, two bourrées; 3, two gavottes; 4, two menuets; 5, two passepieds; 6, two gavottes. [See also: *French Suites]

Enharmonic Notes are said to be enharmonic when they have different names but share the same key on the piano *keyboard and therefore have the same sound. For example: C♯ = D♭; D♯ = E♭ = F♭♭. In fact, in relation to the piano keyboard, all sounds can have three names except one: G♯/A♭. Intervals, chords, and keys can also be described as enharmonic (e.g. C♯ major = D♭ major). An **enharmonic change** is a change of name without a change of sound. The example below shows five bars from Chopin's Polonaise in A♭ major, Op. 53. The original tonic, A♭ (end of bar 79), is now thought of as G♯ (bar 80) – to become the mediant of the new key: E major.

'Enigma' Variations (*Variations on an Original Theme: 'Enigma'*) Set of orchestral variations by Elgar, composed in 1898–9. The enigma (or puzzle) is to do with the theme on which the variations are based. Elgar mysteriously remarked that right through the music 'another, larger, theme "goes" – but is not played'. What this other, unheard, tune actually is, no one has ever discovered.

Elgar dedicated the work 'to my friends pictured within', and each variation is in fact a musical portrait, identified by initials or a nickname. They are: 1 C.A.E. (Caroline Alice Elgar, the composer's wife); 2 H.D.S.-P. (Hew David Steuart-Powell, a pianist); 3 R.B.T. (Richard Baxter Townshend, an 'amiable eccentric' with a high-pitched voice); 4 W.M.B. (William Meath Baker, an impetuous country squire); 5 R.P.A. (Richard Penrose Arnold – son of the poet Matthew Arnold, and a keen music-lover); 6 Ysobel (Isabel Fitton, a viola player); 7 Troyte (Arthur Troyte Griffith, an architect friend of Elgar's); 8 W.N. (Winifred Norbury, a pianist); 9 Nimrod (A. J. Jaeger, a friend connected with music publishing; Nimrod is the 'mighty hunter' in the Bible, *Jaeger* is German for 'hunter'); 10 Dorabella (Dora Penny, who spoke with a slight stutter); 11 G.R.S. (George Robertson Sinclair, organist of Hereford Cathedral – though the music is more concerned with his boisterous bulldog named Dan); 12 B.G.N. (Basil G. Nevinson, a cellist); 13 *** (Lady Mary Lygon); 14 E.D.U. (representing Elgar himself – 'Edoo' being his wife's nickname for him, a shortened version of the French name for Edward: Éduard).

En saga ('A saga', or 'A tale that is told') A symphonic poem, Opus 9, by Sibelius; composed in 1892, and revised in 1902. The music does not express a specific story, but evokes the characteristic atmosphere of old Scandinavian sagas.

Ensemble [French: 'together'] **1** A group of singers or players, usually one per part (e.g. vocal ensemble, wind ensemble). **2** In an opera, an ensemble is a piece for two or more soloists (i.e. a duet, trio, quartet, and so on), or for soloists and chorus. Mozart, for instance, often makes the final scene of an act an elaborate ensemble, all the characters singing at once but each voicing his or her own reactions to the situation which has come about. **3** The word 'ensemble' is also used when describing the performance of a group of players ('good ensemble', 'untidy ensemble') indicating whether or not they keep in perfect time with each other and maintain precision of attack and balance of tone. [See also: *Conducting]

En serrant [French] Pressing forward, hurrying, quickening.

Entführung aus dem Serail, Die See *The *Abduction from the Seraglio.*

Entr'acte [French: 'between acts'] A piece played between the acts or scenes of an opera or play. [See also: *Intermezzo; *Interlude; *Act tune]

Entry The 'entrance' or 'appearance' of a theme in any part of the musical texture during a piece (particularly a *fugue), not just at the beginning but on later occasions as well. [See also: *Imitational entries]

Enunciation *Exposition.

Epilogue Title sometimes given by a composer to a concluding movement or section of a composition.

Episode **1** A section of music within a composition (usually a piece in *ternary form or *rondo form) which is sandwiched between two appearances of the same musical material. The episode presents a contrast in key and/or character. For example, in ternary form (**A B A**) section **B** forms an episode. **2** For another use of the word 'episode', see *Fugue.

Episodical form A term sometimes used to describe the form of a piece which is essentially *minuet and trio form – but rather than being in clear-cut divisions with repeats, each section merges smoothly into the next. (The word *episodical* is used because the middle section – the 'trio' – is an *episode.)

Equale; **Equali** [Italian] Title for a composition for *equal voices, or instruments (i.e. of the same kind) – for example, Beethoven's three *Equali* (1812) for four trombones.

Equal temperament See *Temperament.

Equal voices Strictly speaking, music for 'equal voices' is written for voices of the same type – for example: three groups of sopranos, two solo tenors, etc. (It does not refer to unison singing.) Sometimes, however, 'for equal voices' is used loosely to mean (a) music for men's voices only, or for female voices only; or (b) music for two voices of comparable *compass – for example: soprano and tenor.

Erlking, The (*Erlkönig*) Song by Schubert, composed in 1815 (when he was 18). It is a setting of a ballad by Goethe. Both the voice part and the piano accompaniment are fiendishly difficult. Not only must the singer become a narrator, telling the story, but he must also change his voice to present three different characters: the terrified boy, his father who is trying to comfort him, and the dreaded Erlking – the demon who haunts the forest through which they are riding. The pianist, from beginning to end, plays thundering octaves and chords in groups of three, striking an atmosphere of terror.

Eroica [Italian] Heroic.

Eroica Symphony Beethoven's Symphony No. 3 in E♭, Op. 55, composed in 1803. He originally intended to dedicate this symphony to Napoleon, but changed his mind when Napoleon declared himself Emperor of France, thereby betraying the principles of freedom which Beethoven held so dearly. When the symphony was completed, Beethoven wrote on the title page: 'Heroic Symphony, composed to celebrate the memory of a great man'. The movements of the symphony are: 1 *Allegro con brio* (in sonata form); 2 *Marcia funebre: Adagio assai*; 3 Scherzo: *Allegro vivace*; 4 Finale: *Allegro molto* (a set of variations incorporating a theme which Beethoven borrows from his ballet *The *Creatures of Prometheus*).

'Eroica' Variations Nickname of Beethoven's Piano Variations in E♭, Op. 35, composed in 1802. A year later, Beethoven used the same theme (again for variations) in the finale of his **Eroica Symphony*. He took the theme from his ballet *The *Creatures of Prometheus* and for this reason the variations are sometimes called 'Prometheus' Variations.

Erst; **Erste**; **Erster**; **Erstes**; **Ersten** [German] First.

Es [German] The note E flat. **Eses**, E double flat.

Esercizio [Italian] An exercise, or study. (*Esercizio* was the title originally given by Domenico Scarlatti to each of his keyboard sonatas.)

Espagne [French] Spain. **Espagnol** is French for 'Spanish'; **à l'espagnol**, in the Spanish manner, in Spanish style.

España (Spain) A lively and colourful rhapsody for orchestra by the French composer Chabrier, based on folk-tunes he collected on a visit to Spain in 1882–3.

Espressione (abbrev.: **espr**. or **espress**.) [Italian] Expression. **Con espressione**, with expression, expressively.

Espressivo (abbrev.: **espr**. or **espress**.) [Italian] Expressive.

Essential note Same as *Harmony note.

Estampes ('Prints', or 'Engravings') Three descriptive piano pieces composed by Debussy in 1903. Their titles are: 1 *Pagodes* (Pagodas); 2 *La soirée dans Grenade* (Evening in Granada); 3 *Jardins sous la pluie* (Gardens in the rain).

Estampie [French; Provençal: *estampida*; Italian: *istampita*; Latin: *stantipes*] A medieval instrumental and dance form, popular during the 13th and 14th centuries. As a dance, it was possibly a 'stamping dance', most likely a round dance with the dancers holding hands and moving round in a circle. The music for an estampie is built up in several sections (each one called a *punctus*, plural: *puncta*). Each section is played twice – the first time with an 'open' ending (*ouvert*), the second time with a 'closed' ending (*clos*). The same two endings are used for all the sections. Here are the first two of the four *puncta* which make up *La quinte estampie Real* (The Fifth Royal Estampie):

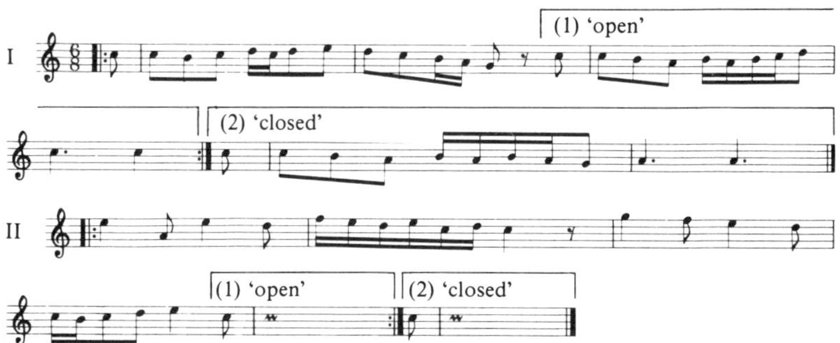

Estatico [Italian] Ecstatic, enraptured, entranced.

Estinguendo [Italian: 'extinguishing'] Dying away.

Estinto [Italian: 'extinguished'] As soft as possible.

Estremamente [Italian] Extremely.

Et [French] And.

Étouffé [French: 'stifled'] A direction that the sound produced on an instrument (e.g. harp, kettle drum) should be immediately damped or deadened.

Étude [French]; **Etüde** [German] *Study.

Etwas [German] Somewhat, rather.

Euphonium A valved brass instrument which, basically, is a tenor *tuba. It is an important instrument in *brass bands and *military bands.

Euridice The first opera whose music has survived complete. The libretto, based on the Greek legend of Orpheus and Eurydice, was by Ottavio Rinuccini; the music was by Jacopo Peri, with some arias and choruses by Giulio Caccini. It was first produced in Florence in 1600. [See also: **Dafne*; and **Orpheus*]

Eusebius and **Florestan** Two pseudonyms sometimes used by Schumann, signifying what he considered to be two sides of his character and personality – Eusebius the poetic, sensitive dreamer, and Florestan the fiery, romantic extrovert. (Pieces 5 and 6 of **Carnaval* are entitled 'Eusebius' and 'Florestan' respectively.)

Exposed fifths and octaves These result when the *outer parts move by similar *motion to a fifth or an octave, especially when the upper part moves by leap. The effect is generally considered to sound unmusical.

Exposition The first section of a *fugue, or of a movement or piece in *sonata form, in which the composer first presents or 'exposes' the main material on which the music is going to be based.

Expressif [French] Expressive.

Expressionism (Expressionist style) A term borrowed from painting, originally describing the style of the 'Expressionists', a group of artists working in Vienna in the early 20th century. In their vivid, disturbing paintings, they aimed to express their innermost feelings, thoughts, and imaginings: dark, secret fears and fantastic visions of the subconscious mind – sometimes suggestive of mental breakdown.

Musicians borrowed the word 'Expressionism' to describe a style which at first was really an exaggeration – distortion even – of late Romanticism, in which composers poured the most intense emotional expressiveness into their music. In its early stages, Expressionist music relied on harmonies which became increasingly *chromatic. And this soon led to *atonality – total rejection of key or tonality.

Expressionist music in atonal style is characterized by extremely *dissonant harmonies; frenzied melodies with wild, jagged leaps; and violent, explosive contrasts with instruments often played harshly and at the extremes of their ranges.

The leading Expressionist composers were Arnold Schoenberg (1874–1951), who was also a painter, and two of his pupils: Alban Berg (1885–1935) and Anton Webern (1883–1945). These three became known as 'The Second Viennese School' ('The First Viennese School' referring to earlier composers who had worked in Vienna, such as Haydn, Mozart, Beethoven, and Schubert).

Compositions in Expressionist style include: Schoenberg's *Five Pieces for Orchestra*, Op. 16 (1909) and **Pierrot lunaire* (1912); Berg's *Three Pieces for Orchestra*, Op. 6 (1915) and his opera **Wozzeck* (1922); and Webern's *Five Pieces for Orchestra*, Op. 10 (1913).

Expression markings (expression marks) Instructions added to the music (usually by the composer but sometimes by an editor) to indicate the manner of performance. They fall into three main categories: (1) *tempo markings (indicating speed); (2) mood or style markings (e.g. **appassionato*, **cantabile*, **maestoso*, *alla* **marcia*, etc.); and (3) *dynamic markings.

Extemporization Same as *Improvisation.

Extrêmement [French] Extremely.

Extreme parts Same as *Outer parts.

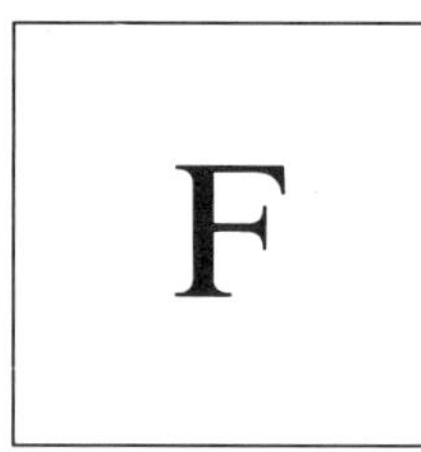

F; *f* Abbreviation standing for **forte*.

Fa [French and Italian] The note F.

Faburden See *Fauxbourdon.

Façade A work by William Walton, composed in 1920–21, and then revised several times. He described it as 'an entertainment with poems by Edith Sitwell, for speaking-voice and six instrumentalists' (flute doubling piccolo, clarinet doubling bass clarinet, saxophone, trumpet, cello, and percussion). Walton later arranged the work (but without the poems) as two suites for full orchestra – the first containing five pieces, the second containing six. These have sometimes been used as the basis for a ballet with the same title.

Facile [Italian; also French] Easy.

Fagott (plural: *Fagotte*) [German]; **Fagotto** (plural: *fagotti*) [Italian] Bassoon.

Fair Maid of the Mill, The See *Die *Schöne Müllerin.*

Fairy Queen, The A *semi-opera by Purcell, first performed in 1692 at Dorset Garden, London. The plot is an adaptation of Shakespeare's play *A Midsummer Night's Dream.*

False cadence; **false close** Same as Interrupted cadence. [See: *Cadences]

False relation (cross relation) A 'clashing' effect which occurs when two vocal or instrumental parts are given notes of the same letter-name, but one of the notes is chromatically altered – for example: F♮ and F♯, or B♮ and B♭. The clash results from the two notes being heard in quick succession in the two different parts – as in music (a) below; or even sounded simultaneously – as in music (b). The effect of false relation is especially characteristic of English composers of the 16th and 17th centuries.

Falsetto High notes in the treble range produced by an adult male singer whose range would normally be tenor, baritone, or bass. The notes are 'falsely', or artificially, produced by making the vocal cords vibrate in a length shorter than usual.

Falstaff **1** Opera in three acts by Verdi, first produced at Milan in 1893 (libretto by Boito based on Shakespeare's *The Merry Wives of Windsor* and *Henry IV*). The wives, Alice Ford (soprano) and Meg Page (mezzo-soprano), receive identical love-letters from the fat knight Falstaff, and plan to teach him a lesson. Aided by Mistress Quickly (mezzo-soprano), they lure him to Alice's house when her husband, Ford (baritone), is out. Ford, however, has been forewarned, and posing as a 'Master Fontana' he tricks Falstaff (baritone), into betraying his secret. The Fords' daughter, Nannetta (soprano), is distraught at her father's plan to wed her not to her sweetheart Fenton (tenor), but to the elderly dullard Dr Caius. Falstaff is pressing his attentions on Alice when Ford bursts in, forcing him to hide in a laundry basket, from which he is dumped unceremoniously in a river. Alice then invites him to meet her in Windsor Park, where the whole company, dressed as fairy-folk, scare him into mending his ways. Ford decides to complete the festivities by marrying Nannetta to Dr Caius (tenor), but confused by the disguises, he weds her to Fenton by mistake. The opera ends happily, with Falstaff leading the company in a rousing fugue.

2 A symphonic poem for large orchestra by Elgar (Op. 68; 1913). Elgar described the work as a 'symphonic study'. The music portrays the character and deeds of Falstaff, 'a knight, a gentleman, and a soldier', as he is depicted in Shakespeare's plays *Henry IV* and *Henry V*.

Fancy (fantasy, plus many other spellings such as 'fancie', 'fantazy', 'fantazie', etc.) Titles used by 17th-century English composers for an instrumental piece (for keyboard, lute, or *consort – most often viols) which corresponded to the Italian **fantasia*. Such a piece was usually contrapuntal in style, with much use of *imitation, and often the music was built up in contrasting sections.

Fandango A lively Spanish dance in triple time and moderately quick tempo, accompanied by castanets. Rimsky-Korsakov ends his **Spanish Caprice* with an exciting 'Fandango Asturiano'.

Fanfare A call or flourish played on trumpets and/or other brass instruments, often to signal the arrival of an important person or to introduce a ceremony or important event. A fanfare often consists of only the notes of a simple chord.

Fantasia [Italian; German: *Fantasie*, *Phantasie*; French: *fantaisie*; also many variations in the spelling of these] A term, dating from the Renaissance, for an instrumental composition in which the composer's imagination (or 'fantasy' or 'fancy') was given free rein and not restricted to any particular musical form or design. Such titles have been given to a variety of types of composition: including pieces of a free, improvisatory character; compositions in contrapuntal style, strict or free, often built up in sections contrasting in mood and style; even compositions in which existing tunes (perhaps folk-tunes, or melodies from an opera) are linked together in sequence. [See also: *Fancy]

Fantasia on a Theme by Thomas Tallis A work composed by Vaughan Williams in 1910 (revised in 1913 and 1919) for *double string orchestra (the second orchestra containing fewer instruments than the first) and string quartet. The theme Vaughan Williams used is the third of nine psalm tunes which Tallis composed in 1567 for the psalter of Matthew Parker, Archbishop of Canterbury.

Fantasia on 'Greensleeves' An arrangement by Ralph Greaves, for two flutes, harp, and string orchestra, of an interlude from Vaughan Williams's opera *Sir John in Love* (1924–8). 'Greensleeves', the main melody on which the music is based, is a traditional English tune which dates back at least as far as the 16th century (it is twice mentioned by Shakespeare in his play *The Merry Wives of Windsor*). In the central section of the piece, Vaughan Williams introduces another English folk-tune called 'Lovely Joan'.

Fantasiestücke [German] Fantasy pieces.

Fantastico [Italian]; **Fantasque** [French] Fantastic, fanciful, strange.

Fantastic Symphony See **Symphonie fantastique*.

Fantastic Toyshop, The See *La *Boutique fantasque*.

Fantasy See *Fancy.

Farandole A chain dance from Provence in southern France, performed with the dancers holding hands in a long winding line and usually accompanied by music played on pipe and tabor. An exciting orchestral Farandole provides the conclusion to the second suite from Bizet's *L'Arlésienne*:

'Farewell' Sonata See *Les *Adieux*.

'Farewell' Symphony (*Abschiedssymphonie*) Nickname of Haydn's Symphony No. 45 in F sharp minor (1772). Haydn composed this symphony as a hint to his employer, Prince Nicholas Esterházy, to bring to an end his lengthy stay at his summer residence at Esterháza so that his musicians could at last return home to their families. The symphony is in five movements – the usual four, followed by an extra *adagio*. Haydn constructed this last movement in such a way that the musicians ceased playing in turn. As each player came to the end of his music, he blew out the candle on his music desk and quietly left – until only two violinists (one of them Haydn himself) remained playing. Then they too left, leaving the hall in darkness. Prince Nicholas took the hint – and the following day, everyone bade farewell to Esterháza.

The 'Farewell' Symphony is scored for 2 oboes, bassoon, 2 horns, and strings (2 first violins, 2 second violins, viola, cello, and double bass). The order in which the instruments cease playing in the final *adagio* is: oboe 1 and horn 2 (bar 31), bassoon (47), oboe 2 (54), horn 1 (55), double bass (67), cello (77), violins 3 and 4 (85), viola (93), leaving only violins 1 and 2 playing for the remaining fourteen bars.

Fassung [German] Version.

Fastoso [Italian] Proud, stately.

Faust Opera in five acts by Gounod, first produced in Paris in 1859 (libretto by Barbier and Carré, based on Goethe). Faust (tenor) is bemoaning his old age. The Devil, Méphistophélès (bass) appears, and promises to restore Faust's lost youth and to give him the beautiful Marguérite (soprano) in return for the sacrifice of his soul. Faust agrees, and is young again. Marguérite's brother, Valentine (baritone), off to the wars, entrusts her to the care of Siebel (mezzo-soprano), a humble youth who loves her. But Faust takes advantage of Valentine's absence and seduces Marguérite. The soldiers return, and Valentine learns of his sister's disgrace, challenges Faust to a duel, and is himself killed. Stricken with grief, Marguérite enters a church and tries to pray, but the evil power of Méphistophélès (which pervades the whole opera) obstructs her. She kills her child, the fruit of her association with Faust, and is cast into prison to await execution. But Méphistophélès has kept his side of the bargain, and he again enters, to claim Faust's soul. Horrified, Marguérite recognizes him and prays to the Angels for salvation. As the Devil drags Faust away to Hell, we see Marguérite's soul rise to Heaven.

(Other works based on the Faust legend include Wagner's *Faust Overture*, Liszt's **Faust Symphony* and *Mephisto Waltzes*, and Berlioz's *La *Damnation de Faust*.)

Faust Symphony, A (*Eine Faust-Symphonie*) A symphony by Liszt for tenor soloist, male voices, and orchestra, composed between 1854 and 1857, and based upon Goethe's poem *Faust*. The symphony is subtitled 'in three character studies' and during its three movements – 'Faust', 'Gretchen' (= Marguérite), and 'Mephistopheles' – Liszt makes use of the technique of *thematic transformation.

Fauxbourdon (faburden) A 15th-century term for music written for two voice-parts, proceeding in 6ths with an occasional octave, while a third voice copied the higher part at a distance of a 4th below. This largely resulted in chains of 'six-three' chords (triads in first inversion), with 6ths between lower and higher voices and 3rds between lower and middle voices:

F clef See *Clef.

Feierlich [German] Solemn; festive.

Feldmusik; Feldpartita [German; *Feld* meaning 'field'] Titles for compositions in the form of a suite or a divertimento, intended to be played in the open air by wind instruments or a military band.

Feminine cadence See under *Cadences.

Feminine ending A phrase of music is said to have a 'feminine' ending if it closes on a weak or unstressed beat.

Fermata [Italian: 'stop'; German: *Fermate*] *Pause, often indicated by the sign 𝄐 above or below a note or rest.

Fern [German] Distant, far off. **Ferne**, distance. **Wie aus der Ferne**, as if from the distance.

Feroce [Italian] Fierce, wild, ferocious. **Ferocità**, ferocity.

Fes [German] The note F flat. **Feses**, F double flat.

Feste romane See **Roman Festivals*.

Festlich [German] Festive; solemn.

Fêtes See **Nocturnes*.

Feuille d'album [French] Albumleaf. [See: *Albumblatt]

Feurig [German] Fiery, with fire; impetuously.

FF; *ff* Abbreviation standing for **fortissimo*.

***f*-holes** See *Soundholes.

Fiato [Italian] Breath. **Fiati**, or **strumenti a fiato**, wind instruments.

Fiddle **1** Familar name for the violin, and for instruments closely resembling it, especially when used in folk-music. **2** In Medieval times, a general name for all bowed string instruments, but particularly the type nowadays referred to as the *medieval fiddle.

Fidelio Opera in two acts by Beethoven, first produced in its present form in Vienna in 1814 (libretto based on a German version of Bouilly's *Léonore, ou L'amour conjugal*). Pizarro (bass-baritone), a cruel prison governor, unjustly holds in a dungeon a Spanish nobleman called Florestan (tenor). Florestan's wife, Leonore (soprano), disguised as a boy and calling herself Fidelio, arrives at the prison hoping to free him. Rocco, the genial gaoler (bass), engages Fidelio as an assistant, but Rocco's daughter Marzelline (soprano), not realizing that Fidelio is a girl, falls in love with him, to the dismay of her true lover Jaquino (tenor). At this point the Minister, Don Fernando, resolves to inspect the prison, and, anxious that Florestan's presence should not be discovered, Pizarro decides to have him killed. He tries to bribe Rocco to commit the murder, but Rocco refuses, and he and Fidelio are sent to dig the grave. Pizarro himself will do the grisly deed. But as he prepares to stab Florestan, 'Fidelio' draws a pistol and reveals that she is the prisoner's wife. Heralded by a trumpet fanfare the Minister arrives, and Pizarro hurries off to meet him. As he enters the prison Don Fernando (bass) recognizes Florestan, a friend he had thought dead. Pizarro is arrested, and the prisoners are released – Leonore herself removing her husband's chains. [See also: *Leonora Overtures]

Fife A small type of transverse flute, with a very narrow tube producing shrill, high-pitched sounds.

Fifteenth See under *Intervals.

Fifth See *Intervals.

'Fifths' Quartet (*Quintenquartett*) Nickname of Haydn's String Quartet in D minor, Op. 76 No. 2, composed in 1797. The first subject of the opening movement begins with two downward leaps of a 5th (A–D, E–A). The third movement is sometimes called the 'Witches' Minuet'. The main minuet section is a canon between the two violins and the other two instruments.

Figuration The persistent use, in building up the texture of a piece or a section of a piece, of a distinctive musical *figure – particularly in variations on a theme, and also in an accompaniment.

Figure A brief melodic idea, usually with rhythmic character, which may be repeated or used along with other such ideas to build up a theme or subject. A figure may also be featured, repetitively, as a significant idea in the texture of an accompaniment (see *Figuration).

Figured bass A system of musical shorthand used during the Baroque period (1600–1750) in which music for a *continuo player (on harpsichord, organ, or perhaps lute) consisted merely of a bass-line, but with figures printed beneath the notes. The figures indicated the intervals of the chords the player was expected to build up on the printed bass-notes. For example, a figure 6 meant play the note a 6th above the printed note, a figure 4 meant play the note a 4th above, and so on. The choice of octave at which to sound a note was left to the player. The example below shows two bars of figured bass, first as presented to the player, then in a simple 'realization'.

Certain points were taken for granted. For example: a note with no figure meant 'play the 3rd and 5th notes above the printed note'; if 3 or 4 were printed alone, 5 was to be played as well; 6 or 7 alone implied 3 also. An accidental might be printed next to a figure, or indicated by a stroke through a figure; if printed without a figure (as in the music example) it referred to the 3rd of the chord. Much, too, depended upon the skill and imagination of the player who was expected to breathe life into the music and, as and when suitable, to decorate the texture by adding ornaments and decorations, runs and passing notes – using the suggested chord-scheme merely as a framework.

Fin [French] End. [But see also under *Fino]

Final See *Modes.

Finale [Italian] The final movement of a composition in several movements (such as a sonata, symphony, or concerto), or the concluding section of an act in an opera, usually an ensemble. Also sometimes used to mean the final item in a musical programme.

Fine [Italian] End, close, conclusion. *Da capo al Fine* means 'repeat from the beginning, ending at the word *Fine*'. [But see also: *Fino]

Fingal's Cave See *The *Hebrides.*

Fingerboard On string instruments, the long strip of wood fixed to the neck, above which the strings are stretched. The fingers of the left hand press the strings against the fingerboard, 'stopping' them to produce the different notes.

Finger-holes See under *Woodwind instruments.

Fingering The methodical use of the fingers (both for ease and efficiency) in the playing of a musical instrument. Sometimes small numbers are printed above or below notes to suggest the most comfortable and efficient fingering. In piano-playing, for example, 1 indicates the use of the thumb (which, for a pianist, is counted as a 'finger'), 2 indicates the index finger, and so on up to 5 for little finger. For a string player: O indicates open string; 1 to 4, index finger to little finger.

Finlandia A symphonic poem, Opus 26, by Sibelius, composed in 1899 and revised in 1900. Although all the themes are of Sibelius's own invention, they have the spirit and flavour of Finnish folk-tunes. Finns look upon the broad and hymn-like main melody (played first by woodwind, then by strings) as a second national anthem.

Fino (sometimes shortened to **Fin**) [Italian] As far as, until, up to. And so **Fino al segno** means 'as far as the sign' (printed as 𝄋). (*Fino* should not be confused with *Fine.*)

Fipple flute (whistle flute) Any instrument of the flute family whose sound is produced by the breath being directed through a channel against a sharp edge or 'lip' (e.g. the recorder), as opposed to any kind of flute where the breath is directed across a mouth-hole or 'embouchure' (e.g. the modern orchestral flute). The 'fipple' is the plug which stops the playing end of the instrument, shaped to form a mouthpiece.

Firebird, The (L'Oiseau de feu) Ballet in one act and three scenes, composed by Stravinsky, first produced in Paris in 1910 (story by Fokine based on Russian fairy tales; choreography by Fokine). Prince Ivan strays into the enchanted garden of the ogre Kastchei. There he captures the resplendent Firebird, but frees her in return for a magic feather which will protect him from evil. Thirteen bewitched princesses arrive to dance and play with golden apples, among them the beautiful Tsarevna, with whom Ivan falls in love. He vows to set her free, but Kastchei appears and tries to turn him to stone. Waving the feather he summons the Firebird, who shows him an egg containing Kastchei's soul. Ivan smashes the egg, the princesses are released from the spell, and he and the Tsarevna wed.

In 1911 Stravinsky made a *suite from the ballet for concert use. A second suite, for smaller orchestra, appeared in 1919 and a third (combining music from the first two) in 1945. The most frequently played (1919) suite consists of: 1 Introduction and Dance of the Firebird (*Introduction – L'oiseau de feu et sa danse*); 2 Round Dance of the Princesses (*Ronde des princesses*); 3 Infernal Dance of King Kastchei (*Danse infernale du roi Kastchei*); 4 Lullaby and Finale (*Berceuse – Final*).

Fireworks Music (*Music for the Royal Fireworks*) An instrumental suite composed by Handel to accompany a firework display in Green Park, London, in 1749 to celebrate the Peace of Aix-la-Chapelle. Handel originally scored the music for huge wind band and percussion (24 oboes, 12 bassoons, 9 trumpets, 9 horns, 3 pairs of kettle drums, and side drums). Later, for indoor performance, he reduced the number of players, and added string parts.

The movements of the Suite are: 1 Overture; 2 Bourrée; 3 Siciliano: La Paix (The peace); 4 La Réjouissance (The rejoicing); 5 Minuets I and II. Four of these movements (in the order: Overture, La Paix, Bourrée, Minuets) are often played in an orchestral arrangement by Sir Hamilton Harty.

First In music for voices, 'first' indicates the higher-pitched of two parts for the same type of voice – for example, first soprano, or first tenor. In orchestral music, 'first' indicates the higher-pitched (and generally the more important) of two or more parts for the same type of instrument – for example, first clarinet, first horn, first trumpet. The violins of the orchestra are divided into two groups: first violins and second violins – the first violins usually playing higher than the seconds. (Similarly, in chamber music, first violin and second violin.)

First Booke of Consort Lessons A collection of pieces for 'broken' *consort, published by Thomas Morley in 1599; important because it was the first of its kind to state clearly exactly which instruments are to play the music. Morley's broken consort consists of six instruments of three different types:

(a) two bowed string instruments: treble and bass *viol;
(b) three plucked string instruments: *lute, *cittern, and *bandora;
(c) one woodwind instrument: either a flute or a recorder.

The flute (or recorder) and treble viol serve as melody instruments, the bass viol providing the bass-line. Of the three plucked instruments, the lute (gut strings) is frequently given brilliant solo passages to play, while the function of the other two (which have metal strings) is to fill in the harmonies – the cittern at the top of the texture and the larger bandora in the bass.

First movement form Another name for *Sonata form.

Fis [German] The note F sharp. **Fisis**, F double sharp.

Fitzwilliam Virginal Book The largest collection we know of Tudor keyboard music. It is named after its last private owner, but it should really be called 'Francis Tregian's Virginal Book', for that is the name of the man who actually copied all the pieces into the book. Tregian was a Cornishman who was imprisoned for his religious beliefs. Many of the 297 pieces were copied when he was kept in the Fleet Prison in London. The three main composers represented in the collection are William Byrd (1543–1623), John Bull (1563–1628), and Giles Farnaby (*c*1563–*c*1640). [See also: *Parthenia]

Five, The In the 1860s in St Petersburg, the Russian composer Balakirev gave four other amateur musicians lessons in composition. The group eventually became known as 'The Mighty Handful' [Russian: *moguchaya kuchka*], 'The Russian Five', or simply 'The Five'. Their aim was to write music which was truly Russian in flavour, and not influenced by the great German composers of the time (see *Nationalism). All five had originally followed other careers: Balakirev (1837–1910) was a mathematician; Rimsky-Korsakov (1844–1908) a sailor; Borodin (1833–1877) a chemist; Musorgsky (1839–1881) a soldier; and Cui (1835–1918) also a soldier. Among their best works, those which show the Russian nationalist spirit most strongly are Balakirev's symphonic poems *Russia* and **Tamara*; Rimsky-Korsakov's **Russian Easter Festival Overture* and his operas *The Snow Maiden* and *The Golden Cockerel*; Borodin's opera **Prince Igor* (which includes the 'Polovtsian Dances'); Musorgsky's symphonic poem **Night on the Bare Mountain*, and his opera **Boris Godunov*.

Five-three chord The common triad in root position – which, when indicated in figured bass, is denoted by the figures $\substack{5\\3}$, referring to the 3rd and 5th to be sounded above the written root (for example: C–E–G).

Flag See under *Note.

Flageolet A type of small end-blown flute, very popular in the 17th century. It had six holes – four in front, and two thumb-holes at the back.

Flageolet-notes Harmonics on string instruments (see *Harmonic 2).

Flam See under *Snare drum.

Flamenco Dance and dance-music of Spanish gypsy origin, mainly from Andalusia in southern Spain. Typically, flamenco involves dance (*baile*) and song (*cante*) accompanied by castanets, solo guitar music (*toque*), stamping and tapping steps (*zapateado*), and hand-claps (*palmada*).

Flat **1** The sign ♭ which lowers the pitch of a note by a semitone. [See also: *Accidentals; *Key signature] **2** Describing any musical sound which is lower in pitch than it should be.

Flatten To lower the pitch of a note by a semitone – but not *necessarily* by means of a flat sign (♭). For example, if the note B is flattened it becomes B flat; but if F sharp is flattened, it becomes F natural. [See: *Keyboard, diagram 2]

Flatterzunge [German] *Flutter-tonguing.

Flautando (*flautato*) [Italian] Flute-like. A term used, for example, to instruct a violinist either to use the bow lightly across the strings over the end of the fingerboard to produce a flute-like tone-quality, or to use harmonics (see *Harmonic 2).

Flauto (plural: *flauti*) [Italian] Flute. **Flauto piccolo**, piccolo. **Flauto dolce** ('gentle flute'), recorder. In Baroque scores, however (e.g. those of Bach and Handel) *flauto* always refers to the recorder (*flauto piccolo* then meaning a small recorder, not piccolo) and the flute is indicated by *traversa* or *flauto traverso* ('transverse flute'). **Flauto contralto** or **flautone**, alto flute.

Flebile [Italian] Mournful, plaintive.

Fledermaus, Die (The bat) Opera in three acts by Johann Strauss the Younger, first produced in Vienna in 1874 (text by Haffner and Genée after a comedy by Meilhac and Halévy). Alfred (tenor) is serenading Roselinde (soprano), whose husband, Eisenstein, having insulted a tax inspector, is about to go to gaol. Eisenstein's friend, the notary Falke (baritone), invites him to a masked ball at the home of Prince Orlovsky (mezzo-soprano or tenor), persuading him to attend it without telling his wife. However, he also invites Roselinde herself, as well as the governor of the gaol, Frank (bass). Roselinde arrives disguised as a

Hungarian countess, and Eisenstein (tenor), failing to recognize her as his wife, flirts with her appallingly. To add to the confusion Eisenstein's maid, Adele (soprano), turns up in one of Roselinde's dresses. The following morning, rather the worse for wear, they all arrive at the prison, where, in true operatic fashion, the situation is resolved to everyone's satisfaction.

Fliegende Holländer, Der See *The *Flying Dutchman.*

Fliessend [German] Flowing.

Flight of the Bumble Bee, The A descriptive orchestral interlude from Rimsky-Korsakov's opera *The Tale of Tsar Saltan* (1899–1900) in which the Prince is transformed into a bumble bee and stings his scheming aunts. The piece has become popular in arrangements for various solo instruments (e.g. flute, trumpet, violin, cello, piano, harpsichord).

Florestan See *Eusebius.

Flöte (plural: *Flöten*) [German] Flute; also sometimes called *grosse Flöte*, in distinction to *kleine Flöte* meaning piccolo.

Flue pipe See under *Organ.

Flugelhorn A brass instrument, similar in design to a cornet but with a wider bore and bell, producing a fuller tone-quality.

Flute A general name for a very large and varied family of wind instruments, each consisting of a hollow body, and sounded by 'edge-tone' – the player blows, and directs a stream of air against the sharp edge of an opening. Flutes of various kinds, shapes and sizes have existed since ancient times, and are found in every continent. The two main types of flute are (1) 'end-blown' flutes – those which are held upright and blown through the end (e.g. *recorder, *fipple flute, *shakuhachi, *nāy), and (2) 'transverse' or 'side-blown' flutes – those which are held horizontally, the player blowing across a hole cut in the side near one end. The modern orchestral flute is of this second type.

flute

The modern orchestral flute – usually referred to simply as 'the flute' – is one of the four main orchestral woodwinds (the others being the oboe, clarinet, and bassoon). It is still classified as a *woodwind instrument even though it may nowadays be made of metal (often silver) rather than wood. The tube, which is cylindrical and 68 cm long, is closed at one end. There is no reed. The player holds the flute horizontally, and to the right, and blows a stream of air across an oval-shaped blow-hole (mouth-hole, or *embouchure*) cut into the instrument, near its closed end. The farther edge of the hole splits the stream of air, causing the air column inside the flute to vibrate, and so sound a note. Different pitches are obtained by opening and closing holes, cut into the side of the flute, by means of a system of keys operated by the fingers (see *Boehm system).

The range of the flute covers three octaves.

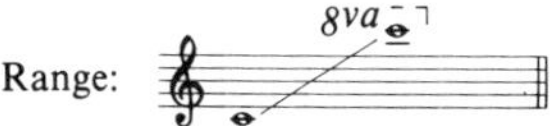

Notes in the lower part of the range have a soft, warm, rich, and haunting tone-quality. Higher notes are clear, cool, silvery, and penetrating.

The flute found a regular place in the orchestra around the middle of the

17th century. It is also used in *chamber music, and is a standard member of the military band and the symphonic band.

Orchestral solos for flute occur at the beginning of Debussy's *Prélude à 'L'Après-midi d'un faune'*, Delius's *Brigg Fair* and Fauré's *Pavane*, in the *Minuet* of Bizet's *L'Arlésienne Suite* No. 2 and the Prélude to Act 3 of his opera *Carmen*, and in the *Dance of the Flutes* (three flutes) from Tchaikovsky's ballet *The Nutcracker*. Works for solo (unaccompanied) flute include Debussy's *Syrinx*, *Density 21.5* by Varèse, and Berio's *Sequenza 1*. Among compositions featuring solo flute with orchestra are Bach's Orchestral Suite No. 2, Mozart's two flute concertos and the Flute and Harp Concerto, Nielsen's Flute Concerto, Griffes's *Poem*, and Martin's *Ballade*. Chamber works with flute include flute sonatas by Bach, Handel, Prokofiev, and Poulenc; also Mozart's Flute Quartets and Debussy's Sonata for flute, viola, and harp.

In addition to the normal orchestral flute, there is the *piccolo, pitched one octave higher, and also the alto flute and bass flute. The alto flute is pitched in G, a 4th lower than the normal flute; its music is written a 4th higher than it actually sounds. It can be heard during 'Dance of the Youths and Maidens' (at figure 27 of the score) of Stravinsky's *The Rite of Spring*, and in Ravel's *Daphnis and Chloë Suite* No. 2 (just over halfway through, 1 bar after figure 187). It can also be heard in *Le Marteau sans maître* by Boulez. The bass flute is pitched one octave below the normal flute. It rarely appears on the concert platform, but is sometimes used in pop music, and music for films and television. In the first movement of Ligeti's Double Concerto (flute, oboe, and orchestra; 1972) the flautist plays first on alto flute, then on bass flute. (Confusingly, in Britain, the alto flute is sometimes referred to as bass flute, and the bass flute as contrabass flute.)

[See also: *German flute; *Traversa; *Flauto]

Flûte (**Grande flûte**) [French] Flute. **Petite flûte**, piccolo. In Baroque scores, though, *flûte* (and also *flûte à bec*, 'beak flute', and *flûte douce*, 'gentle flute') refer to the recorder, and the ordinary flute is indicated by *traversière* or *flûte traversière* ('transverse flute'). **Flûte en sol** ('flute in G'), the alto flute.

Flute quartet *Chamber music for flute plus string trio (violin, viola, cello). Examples are Mozart's Flute Quartets in D major (K285; 1777) and A major (K298; 1786–7).

Flutter-tonguing [German: *Flatterzunge*] A method of *tonguing in which the player rolls the letter 'r'; it is especially effective on the flute, but is also used on other wind instruments.

Flying Dutchman, The (*Der fliegende Holländer*) Opera in three acts by Wagner, first produced in Dresden in 1843 (libretto by the composer based on a legend recounted by Heine). Vanderdecken (baritone), the accursed Flying Dutchman, has been condemned by the Devil to sail the seas aimlessly for ever. He may, however, come ashore once every seven years and seek the faithful woman whose love will save him. Driven to the coast of Norway by a raging storm he meets the sea captain Daland (bass) and offers him treasures if he will shelter him for the night and grant him the hand of his daughter, Senta. Long fascinated by the legend of the Dutchman, Senta (soprano) vows that she will free him from the curse. To the horror of her fiancé Erik (tenor) she falls for the Dutchman and they agree to wed. Daland's sailors and some local girls carry food and drink to the Dutch vessel, but its eerie stillness oppresses them and ghostly happenings put them to flight. Senta rejects Erik's passionate bid to win her back, but the Dutchman, seeing them together, thinks that he himself has been abandoned. He summons his crew and weighs anchor. Frantic, Senta avows her love and leaps into the sea. Her loyalty has saved him. The ship sinks, and the lovers are seen together ascending to a higher bliss.

Fois [French] Time.

Folía (*follia*, or *folies d'Espagne*) Originally the name for a Portuguese dance, very wild in character (*folía* means 'folly' or 'madness'), dating from the early 16th century. One folía dance-tune, with accompanying *basso ostinato*, became particularly famous as it was used by many composers as a basis for *variations – for example, Handel: *Sarabande from Keyboard Suite XI, Corelli: Violin Sonata Op. 5 No. 12, Liszt: *Rhapsodie espagnole* (1863), Rachmaninov: *Variations on a Theme of Corelli* (1932).

La Folía

Folk rock See under *Rock.

Folk-tunes (folk-songs, folk-dances) Tunes, the world over, made up over the years by ordinary folk, rather than by trained composers, and passed on orally from one generation to the next, so that tunes (and words) are inevitably changed and reshaped here and there. [See also: *Nationalism]

Follia See *Folía.

Fontane di Roma See *The *Fountains of Rome*.

Foot In organ building, a measure of pitch of an organ stop, based on the length of the lowest (longest) pipe in the rank. Some ranks of pipes sound at 'normal' pitch, i.e. the pitch corresponding exactly with their keys on the keyboard. Other ranks of pipes sound at one or more octaves higher or lower than the pitch indicated by their keys. 'Normal' pitch is called 8-foot pitch (or 8′ pitch) since the lowest pipe, sounding C below the bass stave, is approximately 8 feet (2.44 metres) long. A 16-foot stop (lowest pipe 16 feet long) sounds an octave lower than normal pitch – and therefore an octave lower than the written notes. A 4-foot stop sounds an octave higher. There are also stops of 2-foot (two octaves higher), 1-foot (three octaves higher), 32-foot (two octaves lower) and, on some organs, 64-foot (three octaves lower than normal pitch). The same terminology may also be used in connection with harpsichords which have two or more sets of strings of different range, e.g. one set at 8-foot pitch (normal pitch), a shorter set at 4-foot pitch (sounding an octave higher) and perhaps another, longer, set at 16-foot pitch (sounding an octave lower).

Forlana (*furlana*) [Italian]; **Forlane** [French] Originally a lively Italian folk-dance in $\frac{6}{4}$ or $\frac{6}{8}$ time. It later became an aristocratic French court dance, rather similar to the *gigue. Bach includes a *forlane* in his Orchestral Suite No. 1 in C (see music example (a) below), and Ravel includes one (b) in his suite *Le *Tombeau de Couperin*.

(a) Bach

Form A term used to describe the basic plan or structure of a composition – the way the music is 'put together' and built up to form a complete and satisfactory whole. No matter how simple or complex a composition may be, the composer must plan the music with the same care as an architect designing a building. In both cases, the finished work must have shape and continuity, proportion and balance. The composer, however, is at the same time both architect *and* builder – first designing and planning the work, then shaping, building up, extending and developing his musical material to create a balanced structure in *time*.

A composer may decide to invent a musical form or structure if this seems necessary to the composition he or she is planning – or, instead, may choose from several set musical forms which have become established over the years. These fall into two categories:

1 Basic musical forms These include *strophic form, *binary form, *ternary form, *rondo (simple rondo, sonata-rondo), *variations (including *ground bass), *minuet and trio form, *ritornello form, *sonata form, and *abridged sonata form.

2 Large-scale musical forms These larger structures may be divided into two groups:

A *Instrumental works*, with titles such as *suite, *sonata, *symphony, *concerto, *overture, and *symphonic poem, and *chamber music works (with titles such as trio, quartet, quintet, etc.);

B *Vocal works*, with titles such as *Mass, *opera, *oratorio, *cantata, and *Passion.

Every one of these various types of musical form depends upon a balance of two essential ingredients – repetition, and contrast. A certain amount of **repetition** of musical ideas is necessary during the course of a composition – to bring *unity* to the piece. Otherwise, the music will appear to wander aimlessly, be shapeless, and lack form and balance. Repetition may be *exact* – as, for example, in the recurrence (repeat) of a whole section of music; or it may occur as *varied* repetition – as, for example, in a theme and *variations. Repetition also occurs when a composer makes use of musical devices such as *imitation, *sequence, and *ostinato.

However, too *much* repetition of the same musical ideas will eventually lead to monotony. And so, to keep the listener's (and the performer's) interest, the composer must introduce *variety* by bringing in a certain amount of musical **contrast**. There are many ways in which this can be achieved. Most effective of all is to introduce a completely different tune or idea. Also important, in most compositions, is the contrast of different, but *related keys – often also involving a contrast of major and minor. Other ways of achieving contrast include changes of mood, speed, rhythm, time (or metre), dynamics, pitch, texture, and timbre (or tone-colour).

Of the works mentioned in group A above, most overtures and all symphonic poems are single pieces. The other works are invariably built up from several individual pieces called *movements, which contrast with each other in mood and character, and also in speed. Each movement may be built up in one of the basic musical forms – which are thus used as main components in building up the overall structure of the complete work.

Of the works mentioned in group B, a Mass is usually structured in five large sections or 'items' (Kyrie, Gloria, Credo, Sanctus, and Agnus Dei) though these, too, may be referred to as 'movements'. The remaining works are frequently structured in individual, self-contained pieces referred to as 'numbers' – so called because they are often separately numbered throughout the score. Any of these *may* be built up in one of the basic musical forms (e.g. an aria from an opera may be in ternary form, a chorus from an oratorio may be in ritornello form). However, an important factor concerning all vocal works is that, in many instances, the shape and structure of the music is determined by the structure of the text or (especially in operas) the various changes of dramatic situation.

[See also *Da capo aria; *Chaconne and Passacaglia; *Canon; *Fugue; *Cyclic form; *Arch form; *Open form; *Lied; *Motet; *Canzona; *Fantasia; *Divertimento; *Serenade 2; *Cantus firmus; *Isorhythm; *Motive; *Phrase; *Sentence; *Development]

Forte (abbrev.: **For.**, **F**, ***f***) [Italian] Loud, strong. [See also: *Fortissimo]

Fortepiano See under *Piano.

Forte-piano (dynamic marking) See *Fp.

Fortissimo (abbrev.: **fortiss.**, **FF**, ***ff***) [Italian] Very loud. **FFF** or ***fff*** means 'extremely loud'. (Some 19th- and 20th-century composers occasionally increase the number of 'F's to ***ffff*** or even ***fffff***.) [See the table of Dynamic markings on page 390]

Forty-Eight, The ('The 48') See *The *Well-Tempered Clavier*.

Forza [Italian] Force. **Con forza**, with force. **Con tutta forza**, with all (possible) force.

Forzando; **Forzato** (both usually abbreviated to ***fz***) [Italian] Forcing, forced – indicating that a note or chord is to be accented or strongly emphasized. *Sforzando* and *sforzato* (both abbreviated to ***sfz***) mean exactly the same.

Fouet [French] Whip.

Foundation stops See under *Organ.

Fountains of Rome, The (*Fontane di Roma*) Symphonic poem by Respighi, composed between 1914 and 1916. The work is in four sections, each offering a musical impression of one of Rome's famous fountains at a certain time of day: 1 The fountain of the Valle Giulia at dawn; 2 The Triton fountain in the morning; 3 The Trevi fountain at midday; 4 The fountain of the Villa Medici at sunset. [See also: *The *Pines of Rome*; **Roman Festivals*]

Four-foot See *Foot.

Four Last Songs See **Vier letzte Lieder*.

Four Seasons, The (*Le quattro stagione*) Four concertos for solo violin, strings, and continuo by Vivaldi, published in about 1725. The music is *programmatic, each concerto depicting scenes from a certain season of the year: 1 Spring (in E major); 2 Summer (G minor); 3 Autumn (F major); 4 Winter (F minor). The score of each concerto is prefaced by a descriptive poem (possibly by Vivaldi himself) on which the music is based. These concertos are the first four of a set of twelve, to which Vivaldi gave the overall title *Il cimento dell'armonia e dell'inventione* (The trial between harmony and invention).

Four Serious Songs See **Vier ernste Gesänge*.

Fourteenth See under *Intervals.

Fourth See *Intervals.

Fourth chord A chord consisting of intervals of a 4th, or mainly of 4ths but combined with other intervals:

Such chords are an important style ingredient in certain works of some 20th-century composers (e.g. Scriabin, Hindemith, Bartók) where this superimposing of 4ths replaces the more traditional method of building up chords by superimposing 3rds (*triads, *seventh chords, *ninth chords, *eleventh chords, *thirteenth chords).

Foxtrot A ballroom dance which first became popular in the USA around 1912, originally in duple time and with a syncopated rhythm derived from *ragtime. There were two types of step: a gliding walk at two beats to each step, and a quick trot at one beat to each step. Later, however, many variants of the dance appeared.

Fp; ***fp*** Abbreviation of *forte-piano* [Italian: 'loud-soft'], a dynamic marking meaning 'attack the note loudly, then immediately reduce the volume to soft'.

Francesca da Rimini ('Symphonic fantasia after Dante') A symphonic poem, Opus 32, by Tchaikovsky, composed in 1876, based on part of Canto V of Dante's *Inferno*. Dante meets Francesca in the Second Circle of the infernal regions; she relates to him the story of her adulterous love for the young and handsome brother of her elderly husband. Tchaikovsky's symphonic poem begins and ends with music vividly descriptive of the gloom and terror of the Second Circle of Hell.

Francese The Italian word for 'French'. **Alla francese**, in the French style, in the French manner.

Frauenlieben und -leben (Woman's Love and Life) A song-cycle, Opus 42, for female voice and piano, composed by Schumann in 1840. It consists of eight songs, setting poems by Adalbert von Chamisso.

Free fantasia Name sometimes given to the development section of a piece designed in *sonata form.

Free jazz (free-form jazz) A *jazz style which originated in the USA in the 1960s, involving elaborate collective improvisation on a theme, against complex harmonies which often crossed over the border into *atonality. Important exponents included Ornette Coleman and John Coltrane.

Free reed See *Reed.

Frei [German] Free, freely.

Freischütz, Der (The marksman) Opera in three acts by Weber, first produced in Berlin in 1821 (libretto by F. Kind). A forester, Max (tenor), hopes by winning a shooting competition to gain both promotion and the hand of Agathe (soprano), the chief huntsman's daughter. Kaspar (bass), another forester, offers to show him how to forge magic bullets which never miss their target. They arrange to meet at midnight in the ghostly Wolf's Glen. On his arrival there, Max finds Kaspar with Zamiel (speaking role), who is actually the Devil, and to whom Kaspar has sold his soul. They cast seven bullets, but, unknown to Max, the seventh is under Zamiel's control. The contest is almost over when Max aims the fateful bullet at a dove, but the wicked Zamiel has earmarked it for Agathe. The timely intervention of a Hermit (bass) diverts it to the branches of a tree, and it kills instead Kaspar, who happens to be hiding there. Prince Ottokar (baritone) orders Max to abandon Agathe and leave the country, but the Hermit persuades him that Kaspar was the victim of his own evil ways. He relents and all ends happily.

French horn The name by which the orchestral *horn is often known.

French overture See under *Overture.

French sixth See *Augmented sixth chords.

French Suites A set of six keyboard suites (for harpsichord or clavichord) by Bach, composed around 1720. The reason for the title (not, in fact, used by Bach) is unclear, since the French element is no greater than in other keyboard suites by Bach. Although there are no opening preludes (as there are in the six *English Suites) each French Suite contains the four standard dance movements – allemande, courante, sarabande, gigue – with other dances inserted between sarabande and gigue. Suite No. 1 has two menuets; No. 2, an air and a menuet; No. 3, a menuet and trio, and an anglaise; No. 4, a gavotte, a menuet, and an air; No. 5, a gavotte, a bourrée, and a loure; No. 6, a gavotte, a polonaise, a bourrée, and a menuet.

Frequency The rate or speed of vibration. The pitch of a note depends upon the frequency, or number, of vibrations per second. The higher the frequency the higher the pitch of the note, and vice versa.

Frets Strips of gut, wood, or metal on the fingerboard of certain string instruments (e.g. viol, lute, guitar, p'i-p'a, sitar) indicating where to place the fingers to obtain the different notes.

Frisch [German] Brisk, lively, fresh.

Friska; **Friss** See *Csárdás.

Frog The same as *Heel.

'Frog' Quartet (*Froschquartett*) Haydn's String Quartet in D, Op. 50 No. 6, composed in 1787. The nickname refers to the 'croaking' main theme of the final movement – the effect produced by quickly repeated notes played alternately on an open string and a stopped string. This string quartet is the last in a set of six known as Haydn's *'Prussian' Quartets.

Fröhlich [German] Cheerful, happy, joyous.

From Bohemia's Meadows and Forests See **Má vlast*.

From my Life (*Z mého života*) Smetana's title for each of his string quartets – No. 1 in E minor (1876) and No. 2 in D minor (1882–3) – both of which are autobiographical. However, the title is now usually applied only to the first quartet. This describes the happy years of his youth and early manhood, but towards the end of the fourth movement the first violin plays a sustained high E, representing the high-pitched whistling in Smetana's ear which marked the onset of his deafness.

From the New World (*Z nového světa*) Title given by Dvořák to his Ninth Symphony in E minor, Op. 95, composed in 1893 when he was resident in the United States. Dvořák said he tried to write the music 'in the spirit of American Negro folk-melodies', though none are actually quoted. In fact, many critics maintain that the music is typically Czech in flavour. The four movements are: 1 *Adagio* (a dramatic slow introduction) leading to *Allegro molto* (in sonata form); 2 *Largo* (including the famous melody for cor anglais); 3 Scherzo: *Molto vivace*; 4 *Allegro con fuoco* (in sonata form). The symphony is structured in *cyclic form, several of the themes being used in more than one movement.

Frosch [German: 'frog'] The heel (or frog or nut) of the *bow used by string players; *am Frosch* ('at the frog') is a direction to use that part of the hair nearest the heel.

Frottola A type of song for three or four voices, very light in style and often humorous, popular in Italy during the 15th and 16th centuries. The music was usually composed in a simple *chordal style. An example is *El grillo* (The cricket) by Josquin des Prez.

Frühlingslied [German] Spring song.

Frusta [Italian] Whip.

Ft. Abbreviation of *Foot.

Fuga [Italian]; **Fuge** [German] *Fugue.

Fugal In the style of a *fugue.

Fugato [Italian: 'fugued'; 'fugue-like'] A term describing a passage of music which is based on *imitational entries of a theme and so sets off in the manner of a *fugue, yet is less strict or less complete than a true fugue. A fugato may be used to build a climax within a movement of a work such as a sonata, symphony, string quartet, etc.

Fughetta [Italian: 'little fugue'] A short *fugue.

Fugue [from Latin, meaning 'flight'] A fugue is a contrapuntal piece, essentially based upon the idea of **imitation*. The texture is woven from separate strands of melody (usually three or four) called **parts** or **voices** (whether the fugue is vocal *or* instrumental). These are usually referred to as soprano, alto, tenor, bass. A fugue is structured in three main sections, called **exposition**, **middle section**, and **final section**. But these sections are by no means as clear-cut as in musical forms such as ternary or rondo. In fact, some musicians do not count fugue as a musical *form*; instead, they define it as a 'texture' or 'procedure' or *style* of composing.

No two fugues are exactly alike in structural details, but here is an outline of the basic characteristics of a four-part fugue:

Exposition The entire fugue grows mainly from a fairly brief but distinctive tune called the **subject**. The exposition begins with the subject presented in the tonic key in one voice, unaccompanied. A second voice then answers, a 5th higher or a 4th lower in the dominant key, with the same tune – but it is now referred to as the **answer** (see the diagram overleaf). If it is an *exact* imitation of the subject, it is called a *real* answer; if any intervals are at all modified, it is a *tonal* answer.

The third voice follows with the subject (in the tonic), and the fourth voice replies with the answer (in the dominant). The voices may enter in any order – according to the composer's choice.

Each voice, having stated either subject or answer, goes on with another tune in counterpoint. If each voice in turn presents the *same* tune, it is called the **counter-subject**; but should a voice continue with a tune which does not recur regularly, it is called a **free part**. After the fourth voice has completed the answer, the first voice may be given an 'extra' entry of the subject – called a **redundant entry** – so that the fourth voice may also have a chance of stating the counter-subject. The counter-subject must be written in *invertible counterpoint since it must sound equally well above *or* below either subject or answer.

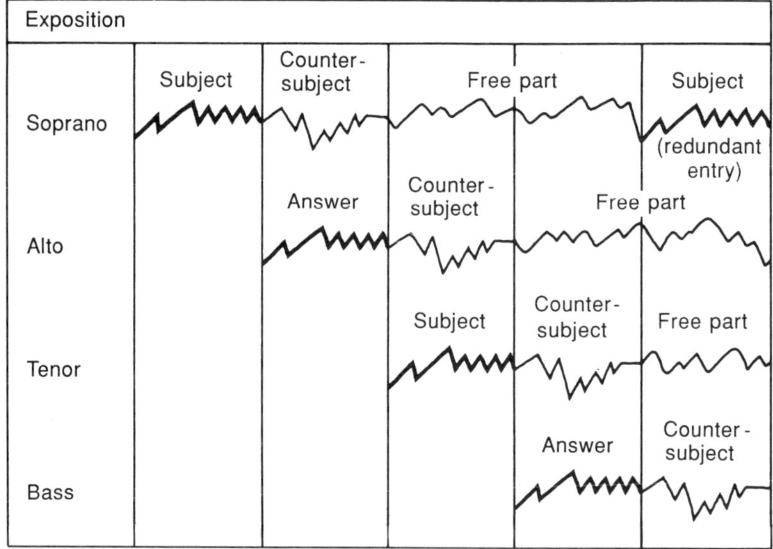

Sometimes a composer delays a succeeding entry of subject or answer for a moment or so. The intervening linking music, however brief, is called a **codetta** (a quite different meaning from *codetta* in *sonata form).

(In some fugues, the exposition is followed by a *counter-exposition*, a 'second exposition', in which those voices which took the subject now take the answer, and vice versa.)

Middle section In this section entries of the subject, called **middle entries**, occur in *related keys (usually avoiding the tonic key). These middle entries may appear singly, or in groups – as subject and answer. Other passages of music occur called **episodes**. These serve as 'modulating links', and also offer relief from entries of the subject. But whereas in musical forms such as ternary and rondo an episode is a complete contrast, an episode in fugue is frequently based on a fragment taken from the subject, or perhaps the counter-subject.

Final section This begins when the subject returns in the tonic key once more. The subject may occur in one voice only, or in several voices in turn. Any music after the end of the last complete entry is called the **coda**.

During the middle section and/or the final section, the composer may build up tension and excitement by using certain 'devices', either singly or in combination. For example: treating the subject by *inversion, *augmentation, or *diminution; or by using a *pedal point. In the final section, to bring the fugue to a climax, a special fugal device may be used called **stretto** [Italian: 'squeezed together', 'drawn together'] in which entries of subject and answer follow closely one after another so that they overlap. In a **close stretto** the overlapping is considerable, so that voices enter very swiftly indeed one after another. In a **stretto maestrale** ('masterly stretto') all voices take part, each presenting subject or answer absolutely complete and unmodified.

[See also: *Fugato; *Fughetta; *Ricercare; *Canzona; *Double fugue;

*Triple fugue; *Quadruple fugue; *Mirror fugue; *The *Art of Fugue*; *The *Well-Tempered Clavier*]

Full anthem See *Anthem.

Full close Another name for Perfect cadence. [See: *Cadences]

Full organ A direction to an organist to play the organ at full strength – using all the loud stops and with the great organ and the swell organ coupled together (and perhaps another manual as well).

Full score See *Score.

Fundamental The lowest sound in a *harmonic series.

Funebre [Italian]; **Funèbre** [French] Funeral, funereal, mournful. And so: **marcia funebre** or **marche funèbre**, funeral march.

Fuoco [Italian] Fire.

Für [German] For.

Für Elise (For Elise) A bagatelle in A minor for piano, composed by Beethoven around the year 1809. It is now thought that 'Elise' may have been a music copyist's mistake for 'Therese' (Therese von Brunswick) with whom Beethoven was in love at the time.

Furiant [Czech] A vigorous Bohemian folk-dance. The music is written in $\frac{3}{4}$ time, but accented in such a way that it seems to alternate between $\frac{2}{4}$ and $\frac{3}{4}$ – as in the Furiant from Smetana's opera *The Bartered Bride*, or in this Slavonic Dance by Dvořák (No. 8 in G minor):

Furioso [Italian] Furiously (but implying enthusiasm and energy rather than anger).

Furlana See *Forlana.

Furore [Italian] Fury.

Fz; ***fz*** Abbreviation of **forzando* or *forzato* (***sf*** and ***sfz***, standing for *sforzando* and *sforzato*, mean exactly the same).

G Abbreviation of *gauche* [French: 'left'], referring to the left hand.

Gagliarda [Italian]; **Gaillard** [French] *Galliard.

Gai [French] Gay, cheerful. **Gaiement**, gaily.

Gaiamente (*gajamente*) [Italian] Gaily.

Galant See *Gallant style.

Galanterien [German; French and English: *galanteries*] Optional extra movements (e.g. Minuet, Bourrée, Gavotte, Passepied) any of which a Baroque composer might include in a *suite in addition to the four standard dance movements (Allemande, Courante, Sarabande, Gigue). They were usually placed between the Sarabande and the Gigue.

Gallant style [German: *galanter Stil*; French: *style galant*] A term used to describe the 'courtly style' of much early Classical music. The style emerged in the early 18th century, during the latter part of the Baroque period. In contrast to the often serious, elaborately contrapuntal Baroque style, music composed in the gallant style aimed to please and entertain; it was basically homophonic, often highly ornamented, light and lacking in depth, yet polished and extremely elegant. The gallant style is apparent in the music of Couperin, Telemann, and Domenico Scarlatti, in the music of Bach's sons, Carl Philipp Emanuel and Johann Christian, and in many early compositions of Haydn and Mozart (particularly keyboard compositions). [See also: *Rococo; and the time-chart of composers on pages 398–413]

Galliard [Italian: *gagliarda*; French: *gaillarde*] A lively and spirited 16th-century court dance (the Italian name means 'vigorous', 'energetic'). A galliard was often performed immediately after a *pavan; although its music was not much quicker than that of the pavan, the steps themselves were much swifter and more intricate – involving exaggerated leaps, and requiring some very nimble footwork. The music of a galliard was usually in triple or compound duple time – the composer often making use of *hemiola. The example below is the beginning of Byrd's 'Galiardo, Mistress Marye Brownlo' (the fifth piece from *Parthenia).

Galop A swift and lively round dance in $\frac{2}{4}$ time. Together with the waltz and the polka, it became one of the most popular 19th-century ballroom dances.

Gamba See *Viola da gamba.

Gamelan The general name for an Indonesian orchestra or instrumental ensemble (e.g. from Bali or Java) consisting mainly of instruments similar in sound to xylophones and marimbas, metallophones similar in sound to glockenspiel and celesta, together with sets of gongs graded in size (gong-chimes), various kinds of single tuned gongs of bronze, bamboo chimes, and various drums. There may also be cymbals, flute, two-stringed rabāb, and zither-like (plucked string) instruments.

A gamelan is often made up of fifteen to twenty players; there is no conductor. The music is based on the principle of *heterophony. There is a main, fixed melody – known in Java as the *balungan* (meaning 'skeleton', and therefore the 'skeleton tune'). This melody is played in long notes on lower-sounding instruments, and punctuated by the large gongs. Above and around this, other instruments weave decorated versions of the same melody, building up a complicated, continuously changing web of sound made up of interlocking patterns. In general, the higher the pitch of an instrument, the more notes it contributes to the musical texture.

reyong (gong-chime)

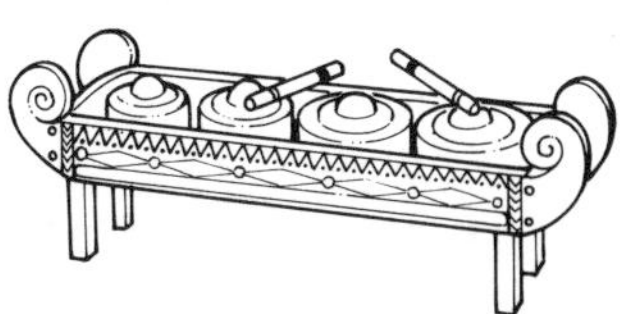

kendang (double-headed drum)

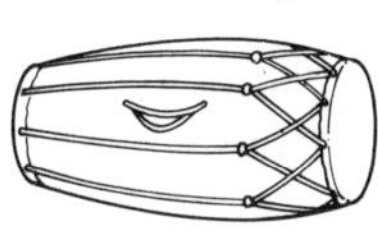

saron (metallophone)

three of the instruments used in Balinese gamelan music

Gamut Originally this was the name of a single note: *gamma ut*, the G on the lowest line of the bass clef. Later, it came to imply the complete *range* of musical sounds, from the lowest to the highest.

Ganze; **Ganzenote**; **Ganze Taktnote** [German] Semibreve, whole note.

Gapped scale Any scale which includes one or more intervals larger than a whole tone and which contains less than seven notes (e.g. the *pentatonic scale).

Garden of Fand, The Tone poem by Arnold Bax, composed 1913–16. The music depicts a story from Celtic mythology. Fand – daughter of Manannan, lord of the ocean – lures mortals onto her enchanted island. There is feasting and revelry. Fand sings her 'song of immortal love' and then the revels begin again, until suddenly, vast waves overwhelm the island, imprisoning the mortals for ever in Fand's garden – the sea.

Gaspard de la Nuit A set of three piano pieces by Ravel, composed in 1908 and inspired by a set of poems of the same title by Aloysius Bertrand. The titles of the pieces are: 1 *Ondine* (a water-sprite who lures sailors to their death); 2 *Le Gibet* (the gallows); 3 *Scarbo* (the name of the clown in a Punch and Judy show). Gaspard de la Nuit (Caspar of the Night) is another name for Satan.

'Gastein' Symphony See under **Grand Duo*.

Gavotte [French; Italian: *gavotta*] A dance of French origin, popular during the 17th and 18th centuries, and often found as one of the movements in a Baroque *suite. It was rather dignified in character, though not slow in speed; in $\frac{2}{2}$ or $\frac{4}{4}$ time, usually with each phrase beginning halfway through a bar:

Gavotte: 'La Bourbonnoise', by Couperin

[See also: *Musette]

Gayaneh A ballet in four acts, composed by Khatchaturian, and first performed in 1942 (choreography by Anisimova). The story takes place on a large farm in Armenia and tells how the lovely Gayaneh, a cotton-picker, is cruelly treated by her husband, Giko. He tries to murder her by setting fire to the farm-house, but Gayaneh is rescued and Giko thrown into gaol. Several of the items in the score are often performed in the concert hall, including Dance of the Rose Maidens, Awakening and Dance of Ayshe, Lullaby, Lezghinka, and the popular and colourfully orchestrated Sabre Dance.

Gazza ladra, La See *The *Thievish Magpie.*

G clef See *Clef.

Gedämpft [German] Muted.

Gehalten [German] Sustained, steady.

Gehend [German] 'Going'; moving at a moderate, reasonable speed.

Geige [German] Violin; fiddle.

Geistertrio See *'Ghost' Trio.

Geistlich [German] Sacred, religious, spiritual.

Gemütlich [German] Expressive.

Generalbass A German term meaning the same as thorough bass or *basso *continuo.*

Generalpause [German] General pause (abbreviated to **G.P.**) indicating a (usually unexpected) rest during which the entire orchestra or ensemble is silent.

German flute Older name for the transverse flute (i.e. the ordinary flute) to distinguish it from the recorder, which was called the 'English flute'.

German Requiem, A (*Ein deutsches Requiem*) A choral work in seven movements, Opus 45, by Brahms, for soprano and baritone soloists, chorus, and orchestra. It was composed between 1857 and 1868. Instead of using the traditional text of the *Requiem Mass, Brahms set his own selection of passages from Luther's translation of the Bible.

German sixth See *Augmented sixth chords.

Ges [German] The note G flat. **Geses**, G double flat.

Gesang [German] Song. **Geistlicher Gesang**, sacred song or hymn.

Gesang der Jünglinge (Song of the Youths) An *electronic work by Stockhausen, composed in 1955–6. The voice of a boy, speaking and singing the *Benedicite*, is electronically transformed and combined with electronic sounds as a setting for the story of the burning fiery furnace from the Book of Daniel.

Gesangvoll [German] Song-like; in a singing style.

Geschöpfe des Prometheus, Die See *The *Creatures of Prometheus.*

Geschwind [German] Swift, rapid.

Geses [German] The note G double flat.

Gestopft [German] Stopped; referring to stopped notes on the horn. The instruction is cancelled by the German word *offen*. [See: *Stopping 2]

Geteilt (abbrev.: **get.**) [German] Divided. [See: *Divisés, Divisi; and also *Zusammen]

Getragen [German: 'carried'] Sustained.

Gewidmet [German] Dedicated (as, for example, when a composer has 'dedicated' a composition to a friend or to an influential person).

'Ghost' Trio Nickname of Beethoven's Piano Trio in D, Op. 70 No. 1, composed in 1808; so called because of the mysterious ghost-like atmosphere conjured up during the slow movement.

Gigue [French; Italian: *giga*] A lively dance with skipping rhythms, forming the final movement of a Baroque *suite; usually in compound duple time ($\frac{6}{8}$) or compound quadruple (e.g. $\frac{12}{8}$ or $\frac{12}{16}$). It originated from the **jig**, a swift and lively dance popular in England, Ireland, and Scotland during the 16th century.

Handel: Keyboard Suite No. 7

Gigue

(etc.)

Giocoso [From an Italian word meaning 'game'] Playful, merry.

Gioioso (*giojoso*) [Italian] Joyous, joyful, cheerful, merry.

Gioviale [Italian] Jovial, cheerful.

Gis [German] The note G sharp. **Gisis**, G double sharp.

Giselle, or **Les Wilis** Ballet in two acts, composed by Adolphe Adam, first produced in Paris in 1841 (story based on Heine; choreography by Coralli and Perrot). A peasant girl, Giselle, is in love with Albert (known in some versions as Albrecht), and her love is returned. She does not realize that Albert is a Count, or that he is already engaged to Bathilde, the daughter of the Duke of Courland. The jealous Hilarion, a gamekeeper whose love for Giselle is rebuffed, discloses Albert's identity, and as a result Giselle becomes insane and dies. At midnight the Wilis (spirits of brides-to-be who died before their wedding day) appear, and having driven Hilarion into a lake they turn their attention to Albert. But Giselle knows that the Wilis must return to their graves at dawn, and she saves Albert by dancing with him until day breaks. This is widely regarded as the pre-eminent example of true romantic ballet. The music was written within a week.

Gitana, Alla [Italian] In the gypsy style.

Giulio Cesare (Julius Caesar) Opera seria in three acts by Handel, first produced in London in 1724 (libretto by Haym). It is set in Alexandria and tells of the love affair between Caesar and Cleopatra, and of the struggle between Cleopatra and her brother, Ptolemy, for the right to the throne of Egypt. Especially well known are Cleopatra's aria *V'adoro pupille* ('I love you, eyes') and her lament *Piangerò la sorte mia* ('I shall weep for my fate'), both of which are da capo arias. [See: *Opera seria; *Da capo aria]

Giusto [Italian] Just, exact, strict, proper. **Tempo giusto** can mean 'in strict time', or 'at the proper (appropriate) speed'.

Glass harmonica See *Musical glasses.

Glee A type of *partsong, exclusively English, intended for unaccompanied male voices. It was very popular in the 18th and early 19th centuries. The Glee Club (the first of many English glee clubs) was formed in London in 1787 and lasted until 1857.

Gli altri [Italian] The others, the remainder.

'Gli Scherzi' See *'Russian' Quartets.

Glissando (abbrev.: **gliss.**) This is in fact a made-up word, taken to mean 'sliding', or 'a slide' – from one pitch to another some distance away, taking in all the pitches in between. A glissando can be played, for example, on the trombone, a bowed string instrument, the harp (by sweeping the strings with the fingertips), the piano (by sliding along the keys using the nail of the middle finger or the thumb), or on a pedal-tuned *kettle drum. [See also: *Portamento]

Glocken [German] Tubular bells.

Glockenspiel [German: 'play of bells'] A high-pitched percussion instrument with a series of oblong plates of metal (usually steel) set out in an arrangement similar to that of a piano keyboard. The plates are graded in length, and therefore in pitch. The player strikes them with light mallets, the heads of which may be of wood, hard or soft rubber, plastic, or metal. The tone of the glockenspiel is silvery, bell-like, and penetrating. Another form of glockenspiel, sometimes used in the orchestra, is fitted with a small piano keyboard; as keys are depressed, metal hammers strike the plates from below. A portable form of glockenspiel used by marching bands is called a bell-lyra or lyra-glockenspiel since its U-shaped frame resembles that of a Greek lyre. Music for glockenspiel is written two octaves lower than it actually sounds.

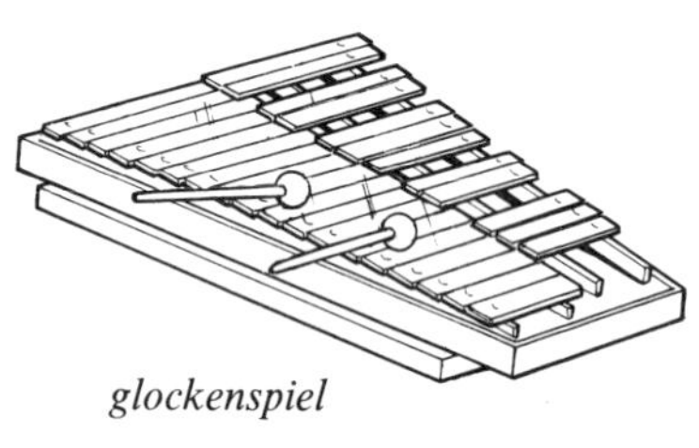

glockenspiel

Normal range of orchestral glockenspiel:

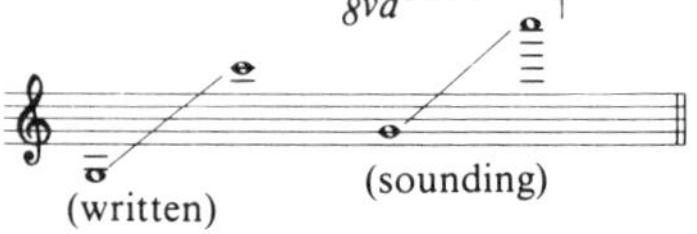

The sound of the glockenspiel can be clearly heard in the *Chinese Dance* from Tchaikovsky's ballet *The Nutcracker* and in the *Lullaby* from Khatchaturian's ballet *Gayaneh*.

Glogauer Liederbuch A manuscript collection (*c*1480) of 294 polyphonic pieces. Most of them are for voices, but also included are instrumental canons and dance pieces.

Gloria [Latin] The second movement of the Ordinary of the *Mass. *Gloria in excelsis Deo* means 'Glory to God in the Highest'.

'Goldberg' Variations Set of thirty variations for harpsichord composed by Bach around 1741–2 and published as the fourth part of the **Clavierübung*. It is believed that they were composed for the harpsichordist, Johann Gottlieb Goldberg, who played the harpsichord each night for a count who suffered from insomnia. The variations are written for double-manual harpsichord, and often demand the highest level of technical ability on the part of the player.

Every third variation (numbers 3, 6, 9, and so on) is a *canon. The final variation is a *quodlibet, after which Bach presents the theme in exactly the same way as when it was first heard.

'Golden' Sonata Nickname of Purcell's Sonata No. 9 in F for two violins, *bassus* (cello, or some other low string instrument), and continuo, from the set of 'Ten Sonatas of Four Parts' published in 1697, two years after his death. It is, in fact, a trio sonata – the 'figured bass' is printed as a separate part for the keyboard player (accounting for the 'fourth part' implied by the title) but only occasionally does it differ from the bassus part.

Goliard songs Songs and Latin poems written by the goliards – wandering students and young clerics of the 10th to 13th centuries. The most famous collection is called the *Carmina burana* ('songs from Beuron') named after the Benedictine monastery where the manuscript was kept. Many of the poems are provided with melodies notated in *neumes. The 20th-century German composer, Carl Orff, selected some of these poems for his cantata **Carmina burana*, though the musical settings are his own.

Golliwogg's Cakewalk The sixth and most popular piece from Debussy's piano suite **Children's Corner* (1906–8). Debussy deliberately imitates the style of *ragtime piano pieces, many of which copied the rhythms of the 'cakewalk' – a dance popular at the time.

Gondellied [German]; **Gondoliera** [Italian] A gondola song, or *barcarolle.

Gong A percussion instrument, of Eastern origin, made in various sizes and consisting of a circular metal plate, usually with the edge bent over. The gongs used in the orchestra may be of definite pitch, or of indefinite pitch. One larger type of gong, of indefinite pitch, is called the **tam-tam**. Most often, the player uses a soft-padded beater (though other types of beater may be used for special effects). Single strokes or a roll (tremolo) played softly sound mysterious; forceful strokes or a roll played in a gradual crescendo can be intensely dramatic, even terrifying.

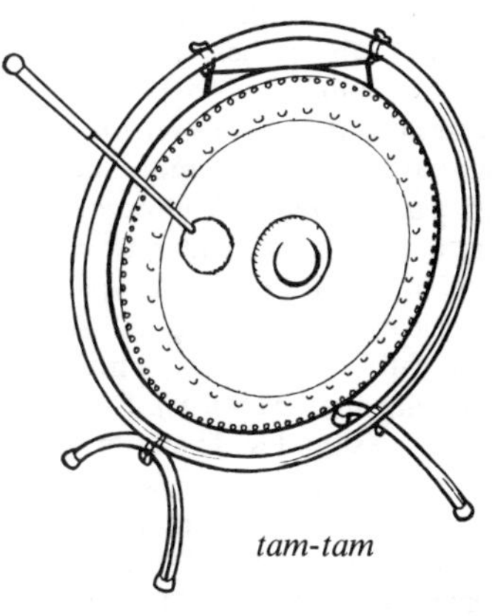

tam-tam

In the last movement of his Eighth Symphony, Vaughan Williams uses three tuned gongs. The score of Puccini's opera *Madama Butterfly* includes a set of eleven tuned gongs. The sound of the tam-tam can be heard at the beginning of the fourth section of Respighi's *The *Pines of Rome* (a single stroke played *ppp*) and also in the final bars (rolls and forceful strokes played *fff*); at the beginning (a 39-bar roll, ending *cresc. fff*) and near the end of *Mars* from Holst's Suite *The *Planets*; and in Copland's *Fanfare for the Common Man*. The sound of one particular tam-tam is familiar to millions – that of the genuine Chinese tam-tam which was recorded to be used at the beginning of each J. Arthur Rank film. [See also: *Yün-lo; *Gamelan]

Gopak (hopak) A fast, lively Russian dance (from the Ukraine) in duple time.

Gospel (gospel music) Terms used to describe the fervent, emotional style of black spiritual and other religious singing, which was often rhythmically accompanied by hand-clapping and foot-stamping. The style was one of the important elements in the emergence of jazz.

Götterdämmerung (Twilight of the Gods) See *Der *Ring des Nibelungen.*

G.P. Initials standing for **Generalpause.*

Grace notes Notes, usually printed in small music type, which 'grace' (ornament or decorate) a melody. [See: *Ornaments]

Gracieux [French] Graceful. **Gracieusement**, gracefully.

Gradual **1** The second item in the Proper of the *Mass, consisting of verses and responses. **2** The liturgical book of the Roman Catholic Church which contains all the plainchants for the Mass, both Proper and Ordinary.

Gran [Italian] Large, great. **Gran cassa**, bass drum.

Grand See under *Piano.

Grand; **Grande** [French] Large, great.

Grand choeur [French] *Full organ.

Grand Duo Schubert's Sonata in C major for piano duet (D812) composed in 1824. Some people think it is an arrangement of his lost 'Gastein' Symphony supposed to have been composed at Gastein in 1825, the manuscript of which has never been discovered.

Grande flûte [French] The normal orchestral flute.

Grande Messe des Morts A setting of the *Requiem Mass, Op. 5, by Berlioz. It is scored for solo tenor, boys' choir, chorus, and a huge orchestra including eight pairs of kettle drums and four extra brass groups positioned at the four corners of the orchestra. Berlioz composed the work in 1837, and revised it in 1852 and 1867.

Grandezza [Italian] Grandeur.

Grandioso [Italian] Grandly, nobly, stately, majestic.

Grand jeu [French] *Full organ.

Grand opera A particular type of opera on a huge scale which originated in Paris in the late 1820s. A typical *grand opera* is based on a tragic story (often historical), the costumes and stage-settings are colourful and extravagant, and there will be a ballet sequence and spectacular scenes (especially crowd scenes involving a large chorus). Rossini's *William Tell*, Gounod's *Faust*, and Verdi's *Aida* are examples. The term 'grand opera' is, however, often used in a looser sense to mean any serious opera which employs music throughout (i.e. without any spoken dialogue interspersed).

Grand orgue [French] The great organ (see under *Organ).

Graphic score A score in which a 20th-century composer indicates his or her intentions visually to the performer(s) by means of symbols, a drawing, shapes, lines, patterns, and so on. Normally notated notes may or may not be included; if so, the pitches of sounds may be indicated (precisely, or merely vaguely) but not their duration, or vice versa. The composer may provide certain verbal instructions or suggestions. Most graphic scores rely heavily upon the musical creativity of the performer(s), and the resulting music will necessarily be *aleatory since no two performances of such a score will be exactly alike.

A graphic score may also be made of a composition which may already exist in normal notation to indicate (by symbols, lines, dots, shapes, etc.) important aspects of the music such as pitch, rhythm, duration, dynamics, textures, timbres.

Grave [Italian; also French] Heavy, serious – and so usually taken to mean 'very slow and solemn'. **Con gravità**, with seriousness, with solemnity. (The

French *grave* can also mean 'low-pitched', 'low-sounding' – as, for example, in *tam-tam grave*.)

Gravicembalo Italian 17th-century name for the harpsichord.

Grazia [Italian] Grace, charm. **Grazioso**, graceful, charming. **Graziosamente**, gracefully.

'Great' C major Symphony Schubert's last completed symphony, No. 9 in C major (D944). The nickname is used to distinguish it from his shorter Symphony No. 6, also in C major. The four movements of the lengthy symphony are: 1 *Andante* leading to *Allegro ma non troppo*; 2 *Andante con moto*; 3 Scherzo: *Allegro vivace*; 4 Finale: *Allegro vivace*.

'Great Fugue' See **Grosse Fuge*.

Great organ See under *Organ.

'Great' Quartets See *'Sun' Quartets.

Great stave A large (but in fact imaginary) stave consisting of eleven lines and ten spaces – as if treble and bass staves were brought closer together and linked by a line representing middle C. The 'great stave' has no practical use, but makes a useful diagram to show the relative positions of the various clefs:

The soprano and mezzo-soprano clefs are normally only found in older music; the other clefs are still in common use. [See: *Clef]

Greensleeves See under **Fantasia on 'Greensleeves'*.

Gregorian chant See *Plainsong.

Grelots [French] *Sleigh bells or jingles.

Gretchen am Spinnrade (Gretchen at the spinning-wheel) A **lied*, setting words from Goethe's *Faust*, composed by Schubert in 1814 when he was seventeen. It was his first setting of a poem by Goethe – and it was also his first masterpiece. Gretchen, suffering the torments of first love, voices her troubled thoughts as she sits spinning. Essentially, the song is *durchkomponiert* (through-composed) – though the music of the first verse recurs as a refrain, and the opening two lines are very effectively repeated yet again at the close. The song is further unified by a continuous figure in the accompaniment, representing the whirring of the spinning-wheel. This breaks off, however, as Gretchen, imagining her lover's kiss, suddenly ceases to work the treadle. There is a silence. Then, hesitantly, she starts the wheel again, and resumes her spinning. The song has been described as one of the miracles of music. Its spontaneity suggests that Schubert, as he read Goethe's poem, conceived the entire song – its mood and structure, melody and accompaniment – in a single flash of inspiration.

Griffbrett [German] The fingerboard of a string instrument. **Am Griffbrett**, indication to the player to bow the string(s) near, or over, the end of the fingerboard, producing a flute-like tone-quality.

Gross; **Grosse** [German] Large, great. **Grosse Flöte**, flute (see under *Flöte). **Grosses Orchester**, full orchestra. **Grosse Trommel**, bass drum.

Grosse caisse [French] Bass drum.

Grosse Fuge (Great Fugue) Beethoven's Fugue in B flat, Op. 133, for string quartet (1825–6) – lengthy, complex, and extremely difficult to play. He had intended it to be the final (sixth) movement of his String Quartet No. 13 in B flat, Op. 130; but later he decided to compose a new final movement for the quartet, and published the *Grosse Fuge* as a separate work. [See also: *'Late quartets']

Grossen Quartette, Die See under *'Sun' Quartets.

Ground bass (ground) A type of *variation writing, very popular during the 16th and 17th centuries, in which a theme (the 'ground') is repeated over and over again in the bass, while above, the composer weaves a continuous, varying texture of melody and harmonies. In some pieces the divisions of the ground are overlapped by the melody above, binding the whole texture firmly together. And the composer may make the upper parts gradually more complicated, so that tension increases as the music progresses. A ground bass is also sometimes called a *basso ostinato*.

The ground bass was particularly popular with Henry Purcell. He composed four Grounds for keyboard, and there are many examples in his vocal music – the most famous being *Dido's Lament* from the opera, **Dido and Aeneas*:

Other fine examples of ground bass include several by William Byrd (such as *Hugh Aston's ground, My Ladye Nevells ground*); the duet 'Sound the Trumpet'

from Purcell's **Come, ye Sons of Art, Away*; and the *Crucifixus* from Bach's B minor Mass, and his *Passacaglia* in C minor for organ. [See also: *Division; *Chaconne and Passacaglia. For 16th-century bass patterns used as ground bass or basso ostinato, see: *Folía; *Romanesca; *Ruggiero; *Passamezzo]

Gruppetto [Italian] Turn. [See: *Ornaments]

Guglielmo Tell; Guillaume Tell Italian and French titles of Rossini's **William Tell.*

Güiro A Cuban percussion instrument, usually consisting of a notched gourd scraped with a stick, producing a dry, penetrating sound. It is often used in Latin-American dance music, and can also be heard in Stravinsky's *The *Rite of Spring*, during the 'Procession of the Sage' (at figure 70 in the score), and in Villa-Lobos's piece 'The Little Train of the Caipira' from **Bachianas brasileiras* No. 2.

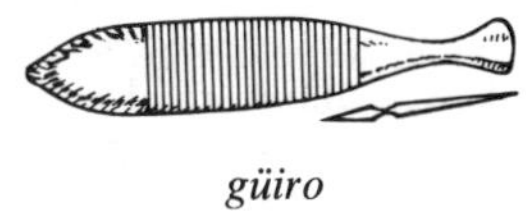

güiro

Guitar [French: *guitare*; German: *Gitarre*; Italian: *chitarra*; Spanish: *guitarra*] A plucked string instrument, dating back at least to the 14th century, and existing in many forms. The present-day guitar may also be called the classical guitar, the Spanish guitar, or the acoustic guitar (to distinguish it from the electric guitar). It has a flat front and back, and the sides curve inwards, giving the hollow body its characteristic shape of a figure 8. The fingerboard has metal *frets, and the six strings, plucked with the fingers or with a plectrum, are tuned to the notes E, A, D, G, B, E (the highest-sounding string being nearest the ground as the player holds the guitar in the playing position).

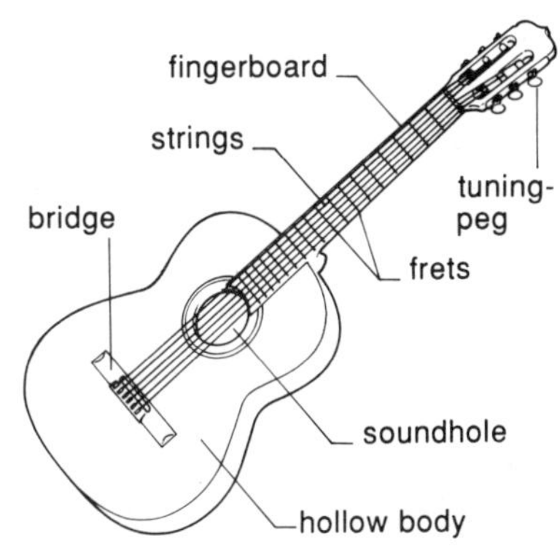

Spanish guitar

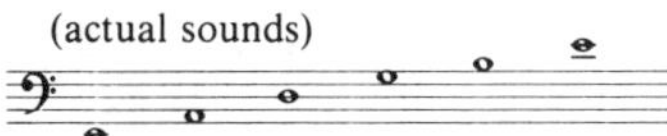

Music for guitar is written in the treble clef, one octave higher than it actually sounds. The guitar is widely used in folk-music, pop music and jazz. It is also played as a classical instrument; many 20th-century composers have written music for solo guitar, and included the instrument in chamber works. Concertos for guitar and orchestra include those by Castelnuovo-Tedesco, Malcolm Arnold, and Richard Rodney Bennett, and several by the Spanish composer, Joaquín Rodrigo, e.g. *Concierto de Aranjuez*, and *Concierto Andaluz* (four guitars and orchestra).

Electric guitar There are two main types of electric guitar. The first type (called 'semi-acoustic' guitar) has a hollow body and six strings, and can be played with, or without, an amplifier. The second type of electric guitar has a solid wood body. Beneath the strings are one to four *pickups* – microphones which 'pick up' the vibrations of the guitar strings and convert them into electrical impulses. These impulses are fed through a pre-amplifier (where both loudness and tone-quality can be controlled) and then through an amplifier before being converted back into sounds through one or more loudspeakers. [See also: *Hawaiian guitar]

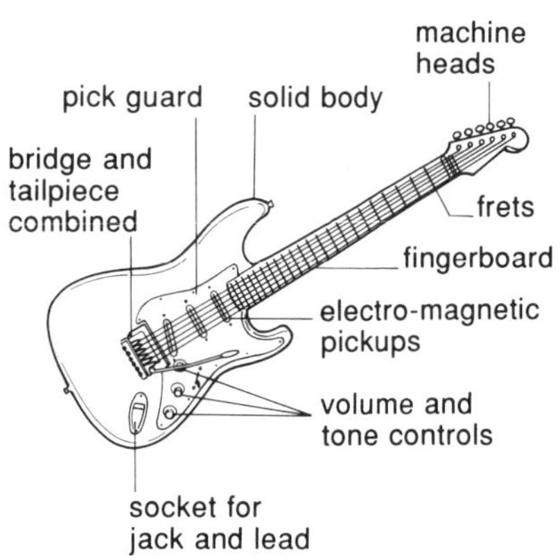

electric guitar

Gurrelieder (Songs of Gurra) A large-scale work (a mixture of song-cycle and cantata) by Schoenberg, begun in 1900 and finally completed in 1911. It is a setting of German translations of Danish poems by Jens Peter Jacobsen which tell of the medieval legend of King Waldemar and his beloved Tove. Gurra is the hunting castle where they enjoy blissful happiness and passionate love until Tove is poisoned by the jealous Queen Helvig. Waldemar, agonized at his loss, curses God – and is condemned for ever to hunt nightly, with ghostly and grisly companions, in the woods of Gurra.

Gurrelieder, which takes two hours or more to perform, is one of the finest and most notable examples of late Romantic style – yet by the time Schoenberg had finally completed its orchestration he had already struck out, in other works, in a very different direction (see under *Atonality). *Gurrelieder* is scored for solo voices, choruses, and a huge orchestra, including: soprano, mezzo-soprano, 2 tenors, bass, and speaker (using *Sprechgesang); 3 four-part male choruses and eight-part mixed chorus; 8 flutes and 4 piccolos, 3 oboes and 2 cors anglais, 2 E♭ clarinets, 3 clarinets in A or B♭ and 2 bass clarinets, 3 bassoons and 2 double bassoons; 10 horns, 6 trumpets and 1 bass trumpet, 1 alto trombone, 4 tenor-bass trombones and 1 contrabass trombone, 4 Wagner tubas and 1 contrabass tuba; 6 kettle drums, bass drum, cymbals, triangle, glockenspiel, snare drum, tenor drum, xylophone, ratchet, several large iron chains, tam-tam, and celesta; 4 harps; and a huge string section.

Gusto [Italian] Taste. **Gustoso**, tastefully. **Con gusto**, with taste, with style, with zest and exuberance.

Gymel [from Latin: *cantus gemellus*, 'twin song'] A medieval term for music in two parts proceeding mainly in parallel 3rds.

H **1** Germans use the letter H to mean our note B natural (B♮). For our note B flat (B♭) they simply use the letter B. **2** See: *Hob.

Habanera A Spanish-Cuban dance and song (taking its name from the capital, Havana) in duple time, moderate to slow in speed. A habanera often combines a rhythmic accompaniment (music example (a)) with *triplets in the melody (b). A famous example is heard in Act I of Bizet's opera, *Carmen*.

(a) $\frac{2}{4}$ | or |

(b) $\frac{2}{4}$ 3 | or | 3 3 |

'Haffner' Serenade Mozart's Serenade No. 7 in D (K250) in eight movements, composed, together with a March (K249), in 1776 for the wedding of Elizabeth Haffner, daughter of the burgomaster of Salzburg. The movements are: 1 *Allegro maestoso* leading to *Allegro molto*; 2 *Andante*; 3 *Menuetto*; 4 *Rondo: Allegro*; 5 *Menuetto galante*; 6 *Andante*; 7 *Menuetto* (with two trios); 8 *Adagio* leading to *Allegro assai*. Movements 2–4 feature solo violin and are, in effect, a violin concerto within the serenade.

'Haffner' Symphony Nickname of Mozart's Symphony No. 35 in D (K385), composed in 1782 for the Haffner family of Salzburg. The four movements are: 1 *Allegro con spirito*; 2 *Andante*; 3 *Menuetto*; 4 *Presto*.

Hairpins Term used by musicians for signs (< and >) indicating *crescendo and *diminuendo.

Halb; Halbe [German] Half. **Halbe, Halbenote**, or **Halbe Taktnote**, minim, half-note.

Half close Another name for Imperfect cadence. [See: *Cadences]

Half-note *Minim.

Half-step; Half-tone A semitone.

Hälfte [German] Half.

Hallelujah Chorus The famous chorus which is sung at the end of Part Two of Handel's **Messiah*, and which includes many repetitions of the Hebrew word *Hallelujah* meaning 'Praise ye the Lord'. King George II was present at the first London performance of *Messiah* in 1743. During the singing of this chorus, the King was so impressed by Handel's music that he rose to his feet. This caused the entire audience to stand as well – so setting a tradition still followed to this day.

Halling A lively Norwegian dance, usually in $\frac{2}{4}$ time, taking its name from Hallingdal, between Oslo and Bergen. Grieg wrote several pieces in this style, e.g. the fourth of his *Lyric Pieces* for piano, Op. 38, and the fourth of his Op. 47 set; and the main theme of the final movement of his Piano Concerto in A minor is also in the style of a *halling* (towards the end of the movement, though, transformed into three beats to a bar and presented in the style of a **springdans*).

Hamlet Several composers have written works connected with Shakespeare's tragedy *Hamlet*. They include: **1** Symphonic poem by Liszt, composed in 1858; **2** Fantasy-Overture by Tchaikovsky, composed in 1888; **3** Opera in three acts by Ambroise Thomas (libretto by Jules Barbier and Michel Carré) first performed in 1868; **4** Incidental music composed by Walton in 1947 for Sir Laurence Olivier's film version of *Hamlet*.

Hammerklavier [German: 'hammer keyboard'] An early 19th-century German name for the piano.

'Hammerklavier' Sonata Name by which Beethoven's Piano Sonata No. 29 in B flat (Op. 106; 1817–18) is known. Although Beethoven used the subtitle 'for the Hammerklavier' for other piano sonatas, this is the only one popularly known by that name. It is in four movements: 1 *Allegro* (in sonata form); 2 Scherzo: *Assai vivace*; 3 *Adagio sostenuto* (also in sonata form); 4 Introduction: *Largo*, leading to *Allegro risoluto* – a massive and elaborate three-part *fugue.

Hand [German] Hand. **Hände**, hands.

Hängendes Becken [German] Suspended cymbal.

Hard rock See under *Rock.

Harfe (plural: *Harfen*) [German] Harp.

Harmonic **1** See *Harmonic series. **2** A high-pitched sound, with a soft and flute-like tone-quality, produced on a string instrument by lightly touching a string at a certain point (rather than pressing it down to the fingerboard). There are two kinds of harmonics – 'natural', and 'artificial'. *Natural harmonics* are played on an open string. On the violin, for example, two of the natural harmonics which can be sounded on the G string are shown below in Example (a). (The black notes show the points where the string should be lightly touched as it is bowed.) Natural harmonics are notated either by a small circle above the sound (harmonic) to be produced, or by a diamond-shaped note indicating the point on the string where it is to be lightly touched. *Artificial harmonics* are produced from a stopped string – the player stops the string with one finger and lightly touches it with another. This is indicated, as in Example (b), by a normally-printed note to be stopped, with a diamond-shaped note above it showing where the string should be lightly touched. The harmonic sounded is two octaves higher than the lower note shown.

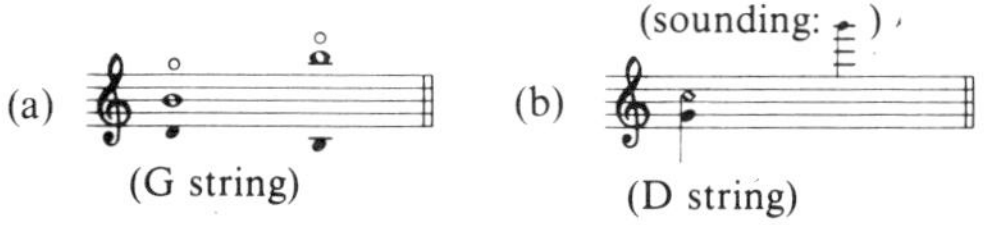

In harp-playing, harmonics may be sounded by placing the base of the hand lightly against the middle of the string, and plucking the top half only. This is indicated in the music by a small circle above or below a normal printed note, showing which string to use; the sound (harmonic) produced is one octave higher.

Harmonica **1** Another name for *Mouth organ. **2** See *Musical glasses.

Harmonic minor scale See *Scale.

Harmonic sequence See under *Sequence.

Harmonic series When a length of stretched string or the air in a length of tube is made to vibrate, it not only vibrates as a whole, but also in two halves, three thirds, four quarters, and so on, simultaneously. The human ear picks up most strongly the vibrations of the whole, and thus determines the pitch of the note being sounded. But this main note is in fact only the lowest, or **fundamental**, in a whole series of pitches, called the *harmonic series*. The vibrations of the halves, thirds, quarters, and so on are at the same time producing higher, fainter pitches which 'colour' the tone of the main note. These are called **harmonics**, or **overtones**, or **upper partials**. If the stretched string, or tube, is of such a length that the main note (i.e. the fundamental) being sounded is C below the bass clef, then the first sixteen notes of the harmonic series will be as shown below. The main note (the fundamental) is counted as the first harmonic; the second note shown is counted as the second harmonic or first overtone or first upper partial; and so on. (The four notes marked with a cross are not in tune with any normal scale in use.)

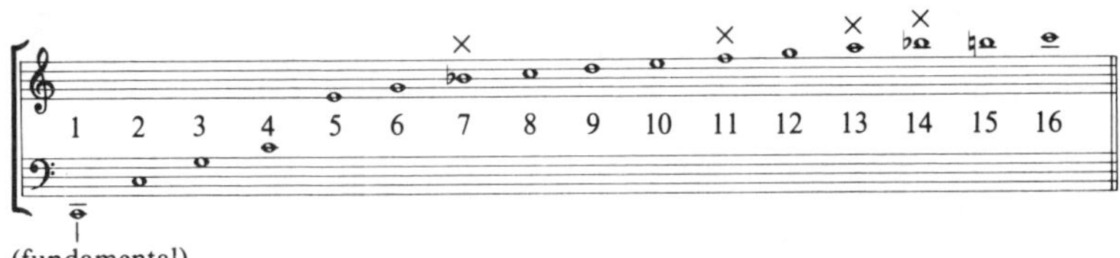

A different fundamental would of course offer another series of pitches, but the notes would still be in exactly the same proportion to each other – i.e. the second harmonic is always an octave above the first harmonic (or fundamental), the third harmonic is always a 5th higher still, the fourth is a 4th above that, and so on.

[See also: *Timbre]

Harmonie [French, also German] **1** Harmony. **2** Wind band (consisting of woodwind, brass, and percussion).

'Harmonious Blacksmith, The' Nickname given to the final movement – an Air with variations – of Handel's Fifth Keyboard Suite (1720). Apparently, a young man who was once a blacksmith opened a music-shop in the city of Bath. He was always singing – and often it was this Air of Handel's. Due to his previous occupation he became known as the 'Harmonious Blacksmith', the nickname eventually becoming transferred from the man to the tune itself.

Harmonium A small organ whose sounds are produced by the vibration of free reeds (thin metal tongues). The vibrations are caused by air from a bellows worked by the player's feet. A number of stops offer the player a choice of tone-colours.

Harmonize To add parts or chords to an existing part (e.g. to a melody, or above a bass-line) to produce satisfying harmony.

Harmony The sounding-together of musical sounds (pitches) to produce chords (which may be *concords or discords). The word harmony is also used to describe the particular choice of notes which make up a chord; and also, in a broader sense, to describe the overall flow or progression of chords throughout a composition, and their relationship, one to another. [See also: *Ingredients of music]

Harmony note (essential note) A note which, at any given point, forms part of the harmony and is an actual note of the chord being sounded (as distinct from a passing note, appoggiatura, suspension, and so on, which are called non-harmonic notes, or unessential notes).

Harold in Italy A *programme symphony, Opus 16, by Berlioz, based on scenes from Byron's poem *Childe Harold.* Berlioz composed this symphony, which includes an important part for solo viola, in 1834 at the request of Paganini who wanted a work which would demonstrate the exceptionally fine sound of a Stradivarius viola he had acquired. When presented with the music, however, Paganini refused to perform it as he found the solo part to be insufficiently 'showy'. *Harold in Italy* is in four movements, with descriptive titles: 1 Harold in the mountains: scenes of melancholy, happiness and joy; 2 March of the pilgrims singing the Evening Hymn; 3 Serenade of an Abruzzi mountaineer to his beloved; 4 Orgy of the brigands – reminiscences of earlier scenes.

Harp A plucked string instrument which, in its earliest forms, is one of the oldest of all musical instruments. It consists of a set of strings, graded in length, stretched over an open frame which is basically triangular. The strings rise from the soundboard (which slopes up at an angle) and they are plucked by the player's thumbs and fingers – except the little finger of each hand. The modern orchestral harp (*double-pedal harp* or *double-action harp*) is about 1.83 metres high, and usually has forty-seven strings, covering the following range:

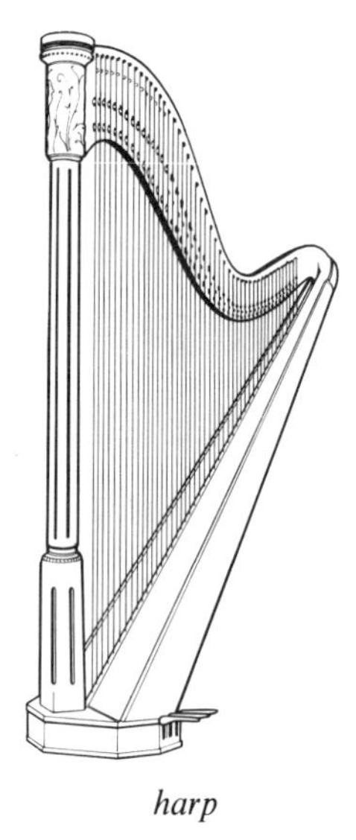

harp

At the base of the harp there are seven pedals, one for each note of the octave – one pedal controlling all the C strings, another controlling all the D strings, and so on. For each pedal there are three positions. Taking the C pedal as an example: when the pedal is in the 'up' position, all the C strings sound the note C♭ at their respective octaves. Pressing the pedal down a notch shortens all the C strings slightly, so that they now sound a semitone higher – the note C♮. Pressing the pedal down into the lowest notch shortens them further so that they now sound a semitone higher still – the note C♯. And so by using the pedals in various combinations it is possible to play in any key.

A harpist may pluck single notes, or play a melody and/or accompaniment. Chords may be sounded – either with the notes plucked together, or, more characteristically, with the notes spread out one after another in *arpeggio* style [from *arpa*, the Italian word for harp]. Another typical harp effect is the *glissando*, in which the player sweeps a finger or fingernail across the strings. Other, special, effects include: *sons étouffés* [French: 'stifled sounds'] in which the string, as soon as it is plucked, is immediately damped; *près de la table* [French] indicating that the string(s) should be plucked near the soundboard, producing a thinner, rather metallic tone-quality; and also *harmonics* (indicated by a small circle above or below a note) which are made by placing the base of the hand lightly against the mid-point of the string and plucking the top half only – the resulting, haunting sound being one octave higher than the written note.

Orchestral pieces in which the harp can be heard include *Waltz of the Flowers* from Tchaikovsky's ballet *The Nutcracker*, the *Prélude* to Act 3 of Bizet's opera *Carmen* and the second *Minuet* from his music for *L'Arlésienne*, the second movement of Franck's Symphony in D minor, and the second movement (including two harps) of Berlioz's *Symphonie fantastique*. Among chamber works including harp are Ravel's *Introduction and Allegro*, Debussy's Sonata for flute, viola, and harp, and Bax's Quintet for harp and strings. Concertos for harp include Handel's Concerto in B♭ (Op. 4 No. 6), Mozart's Flute and Harp Concerto, Glière's Harp Concerto, Frank Martin's *Petite symphonie concertante* for harp, harpsichord, piano, and two string orchestras, and William Alwyn's *Lyra angelica*.

Harpsichord [French: *clavecin*; German: *Cembalo*; Italian: *cembalo*, *clavicembalo*] The main *keyboard instrument pre-dating the *piano. (The earliest mention of the harpsichord dates from 1397.) Not unlike the grand piano in shape, it was popular between about 1550 and 1800, being, for much of that period, a regular member of the orchestra and the favourite keyboard instrument for the *continuo. Early in the 19th century the piano superseded it, but in 1882 Érard of Paris made an updated model, sparking off a revival. These late harpsichords embodied features unavailable in the old instruments, but from about 1945 there has been a return to classical principles of design.

When a key is pressed down it raises a vertical strip of wood called a *jack*, which has a *plectrum* fixed to its upper end. The plectrum rises slightly, plucking a string. When the key is released, the plectrum returns, a pivoted tongue preventing it from plucking the string a second time. A **damper*, also

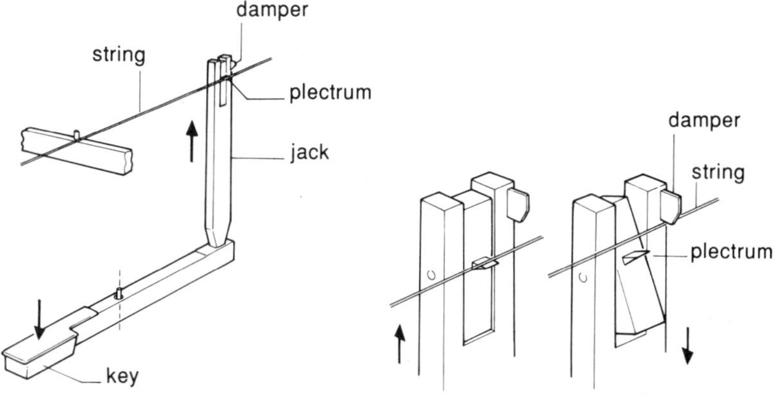

harpsichord action

attached to the jack, then terminates the sound. The vibrations of the strings travel along *bridges* to the *soundboard*, which acts as a resonator.

By 1600, harpsichords were widespread in Europe, with manufacturers in Italy, Flanders, France, Germany, and England. The early Italian models were of simple design, with one manual (*keyboard), a single set of strings at right angles to the keyboard, and a range of four octaves. Later, one-manual instruments were made, in Italy and elsewhere, with two sets of strings (*registers*), one at 8-foot pitch (sounding the notes as written), the other at 4-foot pitch (sounding an octave higher than the written notes). Some instruments had, instead, two 8-foot registers, to which a third, at 4-foot pitch, was sometimes added. Plectrums of varying grades of hardness and softness were used, not all of them plucking the strings at the same place. They were controlled by handstops which determined the strings and the plectrums to be used. The *lute stop* governed plectrums which plucked near the ends of the strings, producing a thin, reedy sound. The *harp* (or *buff*) *stop* brought pads in contact with the strings, giving a muted *pizzicato* effect. The choosing of stops was called *registration*. The harpsichord is more responsive to the player's touch than is sometimes suggested, but variations of dynamics are possible only by varying the stops used.

a double-manual harpsichord

In the early 18th century the range grew to five octaves. Double-manual harpsichords were built, with 8-foot and 4-foot registers on the upper manual, and 8-foot and 16-foot (the latter sounding an octave below the written notes) on the lower. *Couplers* (also activated by handstops) brought the resources of one manual through to the other. This gave greater tonal variety by enabling the player to mix freely sounds obtainable anywhere on the instrument. (J. S. Bach exploited the contrast of two manuals in his *Italian Concerto for solo harpsichord.)

Later there were even three-manual harpsichords (with multiple sets of strings and jacks), and harpsichords with a pedal-board like that of an *organ. From 1765, *'machine' stops* were introduced (pedals for changing stop combinations quickly), and some instruments had *swell mechanisms* (also operated by a pedal), by which part of the lid was raised and lowered, or the slatted side of an inner box opened and closed, to give *crescendo* and *diminuendo* effects.

The *spinet is a type of one-manual harpsichord; the name is sometimes wrongly used to describe a square *piano.

[See also: *Virginal]

Harp stop See under *Harpsichord.

'Harp' Study Nickname of Chopin's Study (Étude) No. 1 in A♭ major (1836) from his second set of Twelve Studies for piano, Op. 25. Throughout, the texture of the music is spun from harp-like arpeggios and broken-chord figures in both hands.

Háry János An opera by Kodály, first performed in 1926 in Budapest. The hero, Háry János (John Háry), was a soldier who became famous throughout Hungary for telling fabulous stories about his imaginary exploits.

In 1927, Kodály arranged an orchestral suite of six pieces from the opera: 1 Prelude (The fairy tale begins); 2 The Viennese musical clock; 3 Song; 4 The battle and defeat of Napoleon; 5 Intermezzo; 6 Entrance of the Emperor and his court. (Pieces 3 and 5 feature the colourful sounds of the Hungarian instrument called the *cimbalom.)

Hassan Incidental music by Delius, composed in 1920 for James Elroy Flecker's play *Hassan*. The two best-known pieces are the Intermezzo and the Serenade.

Hastig [German] Hasty, hurried.

Haupt [German] Principal, main. **Hauptsatz**, the first subject-group of a composition in sonata form. **Hauptstimme**, a term introduced by Schoenberg for the principal voice or *part in a complicated musical texture, and indicated at the appropriate points throughout the score by the symbol H⌐ (see also **Nebenstimme*). **Hauptthema**, the main theme of a composition. **Hauptwerk**, Great organ (see under *Organ).

Haut; **Haute** [French] High.

Hautbois [French] Oboe.

Hautboy (hoboy) Old English name for oboe (from French: *hautbois*).

Havanaise French for **habanera*.

Hawaiian guitar (steel guitar) An instrument which combines certain characteristics of the guitar and the zither. It is often oblong in shape, and played across the knees or resting on a table. The player uses the left hand to stop the metal strings with a 'steel' (a steel bar, or steel tube, or the neck of a bottle) and strums the strings with the fingers of the right hand. By gliding the 'steel' along the strings, the player produces special effects such as *glissando* and exaggerated *vibrato*. Most often, the instrument is now used with electronic amplification.

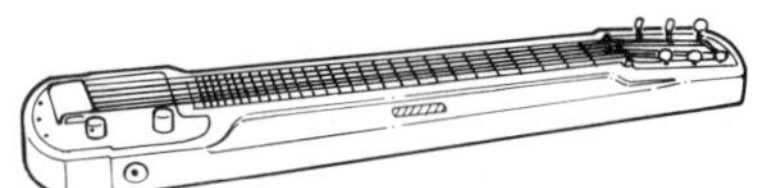

electric Hawaiian guitar

A **pedal steel guitar** is mounted on a stand, and has one to four knee-levers and as many as eight foot-pedals. The player uses these to change string tunings and to select different ready-made chords.

Hay See *Hey.

'Haydn' Quartets Six of Mozart's twenty-three string quartets. He composed them between 1782 and 1785, and dedicated them to Haydn. They include: No. 14 in G (K387), No. 15 in D minor (K421), No. 16 in E flat (K428), No. 17 in B flat (K458) nicknamed 'The *Hunt', No. 18 in A (K464), and No. 19 in C (K465) nicknamed *'Dissonance' Quartet. At performances of these six quartets in Mozart's house, Haydn played first violin and Mozart played viola.

Head voice The highest register of a singer's range, the sounds resonating mainly in the head. The other two registers are middle (or medium) voice, and *chest voice.

Heavy metal See under *Rock.

Heavy rock See under *Rock.

Hebrides, The (*Fingal's Cave*) A programmatic concert overture, Opus 26, by Mendelssohn; inspired by a visit to Fingal's Cave in the Hebrides in 1829. In its original version, composed in the same year, the overture was called 'The Lonely Island'. Mendelssohn revised it, giving it its present title, in 1832.

Heckelphone A baritone oboe, invented in 1904 by the German firm of Heckel. It is pitched one octave below the oboe.

Heel (frog, nut) The part of the *bow of a string instrument, at the end where the player holds the bow, which secures the hair.

Heftig [German] Fierce, forcible, violent.

Heldenleben, Ein (A hero's life) A lengthy symphonic poem, Opus 40, composed by Richard Strauss in 1897–8. The hero of the title is Strauss himself, portrayed as a composer struggling to achieve recognition and success. *Ein Heldenleben* is scored for a large orchestra, consisting of 3 flutes and piccolo, 4 oboes and cor anglais, 2 clarinets, E♭ clarinet and bass clarinet, 3 bassoons and double bassoon; 8 horns, 5 trumpets, 3 trombones, and tenor and bass tubas; kettle drums, bass drum, cymbals, snare drum, tenor drum, tam-tam and triangle; 2 harps, and a large string section. The work is in six sections – the fifth bringing in musical quotations from earlier works by Strauss, including **Don Juan*, **Also sprach Zarathustra*, **Till Eulenspiegel*, and **Don Quixote*.

Heldentenor [German: 'heroic tenor'] A type of voice which has considerable strength, brilliance of tone, and dramatic power (such as is necessary, for instance, for certain tenor roles in operas by Wagner, e.g. Siegfried).

Helicon Name given to the tuba when made in a circular form to make it more convenient for carrying and playing in a marching band.

Hemidemisemiquaver The note which is half the value of a demisemiquaver. Sixteen hemidemisemiquavers are equal to one crotchet; and sixty-four hemidemisemiquavers equal one semibreve. (The American name for a hemidemisemiquaver is a sixty-fourth note.) The examples below show (a) a single hemidemisemiquaver (four hooks to the stem); (b) a group of four hemidemisemiquavers; and (c) a hemidemisemiquaver *rest.

(a) (b) (c)

[See also: *Semihemidemisemiquaver; and Tables 1 and 2 on page 387]

Hemiola (or **Hemiolia**) [from Greek, implying a ratio of 3:2] Hemiola is most often found in music as a rhythmic device which gives the impression of changing triple time into duple, and vice versa. For instance, in a courante, a Baroque composer would often mix bars of $\frac{6}{4}$ (duple time) with bars of $\frac{3}{2}$ (triple). Similarly in triple time (say, $\frac{3}{4}$) a composer might, towards the end of a phrase, make two bars of three beats sound like three bars of two beats:

Handel: Minuet from Royal Fireworks Music

Certain 19th-century composers, too, were fond of the effect of hemiola, particularly Schumann and Brahms:

'Hen' Symphony (*La Poule*) Haydn's Symphony No. 83 in G minor, the second of his *'Paris' Symphonies, composed in 1785. It acquired this nickname during the 19th century because of the 'clucking' effect of the second subject of the opening movement.

'Heroic' Polonaise Nickname by which Chopin's Polonaise in A flat for piano, Op. 53 (1843), is sometimes known.

Hero's Life, A See *Ein *Heldenleben.*

Hertz (abbrev.: **Hz**) The unit of *frequency. Named after the German physicist Heinrich Hertz who, in 1887, discovered radio waves. A loudspeaker, for example, may have the specification of being capable of reproducing sounds ranging from 50 Hz to 20 kHz (20 kilohertz or 20,000 hertz).

Hervortretend [German: 'coming forward'] Emphasized; made prominent.

Herzlich [German] Heartily, or heartfelt.

Heses See *Bes.

Heterophony [from Greek, meaning 'difference of sounds'] The simultaneous performance of different versions of the same melody. For instance, one voice or instrument performs a simple melody while at the same time another presents a more elaborate, decorated version of it.

Other voices or instruments may also join in, adding yet more versions of the melody – decorating it, varying it, even simplifying it (picking out just a few important notes). This style of performance (described as **heterophonic** style) is often found, for instance, in African music, in the folk-music of certain European countries, and in the music of China, Japan, Bali and Java (see *Gamelan).

Hexachord [Greek: 'six strings'] A sequence of six notes proceeding by steps a tone at a time, except between the third and fourth notes where there is a step of a semitone.

For example:  or:

When the term hexachord is used in connection with 20th-century music composed in *twelve-note technique, it refers to groups of six notes resulting from dividing the note row into two halves.

Hey A type of country dance performed with the dancers forming a long winding line, then eventually making a circle. (One of Percy Grainger's best-known pieces has the title *Shepherd's Hey*.)

Hichiriki A small Japanese double-reed instrument, made of bamboo, and with seven finger-holes and two thumb-holes.

Hi-hat Name used by jazz and pop drummers for a pair of cymbals which are fixed one above the other on a stand. They are clashed together by means of a foot-operated pedal – the lower cymbal remains stationary, the upper one rises and falls to clash against it.

His [German] The note B sharp. **Hisis**, B double sharp.

Histoire du soldat, L' (The Soldier's Tale) A stage-work by Stravinsky (with French text by C. F. Ramuz, based on a Russian tale) intended 'to be read, played, and danced'. Three actors take part (the Narrator, the Soldier, and the Devil) and a dancer (the Princess). The music is scored for clarinet, bassoon, cornet, trombone, percussion, violin, and double bass. (Stravinsky said he wanted to include 'the most representative instruments, in treble and bass, of the instrumental families'.) The work was first performed in 1918. Later that year, Stravinsky arranged several pieces from the score as a separate concert suite, of which the movements are: 1 The soldier's march; 2 Music to Scene I; 3 Music to Scene II; 4 The royal march; 5 The little concert; 6 Three dances (Tango, Waltz, Ragtime); 7 The Devil's dance; 8 The great chorale; 9 Triumphal march of the Devil.

History of Western music For convenience of investigation, study, and background understanding, the history of Western music is divided into separate periods of time – each of which, broadly speaking, may be identified by certain aspects and characteristics of musical style or general musical outlook. The change of style from one period to another is, of course, a gradual rather than sudden process, and styles may overlap. The following is one possible way of dividing the history of Western music into six main periods (though musicians sometimes disagree about the dates singled out to mark the beginning and end of periods, or about the names used to describe them, and may subdivide one or more of the periods):

*Medieval music	*c*500–*c*1450
*Renaissance music	1450–1600
*Baroque music	1600–1750
*Classical music	1750–1810
19th-century *Romanticism	1810–1910
*20th-century music	1900 onwards

[See also: The *New Music; and the time-chart of composers on pages 398–413]

Hob. (or simply **H.**) Abbreviation standing for Hoboken (Anthony van Hoboken, a Dutch bibliographer) who spent more than thirty years compiling a thematic catalogue of the works of Haydn. Linked to any composition by Haydn, **Hob.** (or **H.**) followed by a number indicates that work's numbered entry within the relevant section of Hoboken's catalogue (e.g. Piano Sonata in E♭, Hob. XVI: 52).

Hoboe (plural: *Hoboen*) [German] Oboe.

Hoboy See *Hautboy.

Hoch [German] High. **Hochzeit**, wedding.

Hocket (hoquet; hoquetus, etc.) [from a Latin word meaning 'hiccup'] A medieval technique, popular during the 13th and 14th centuries, in which a melodic line is broken up into fragments, even separate notes, with rests in between. Hocket is usually shared between two vocal or instrumental parts, their sounds and silences 'staggered' in such a way that a lively, 'hiccuping', syncopated dialogue results:

Seven three-part instrumental hockets are included in the 13th-century manuscript called the Bamberg Codex. These represent the earliest-known medieval instrumental pieces, aside from dance-tunes.

Hoe-down A term describing certain types of folk-dance, especially square dances, performed in the USA and Britain; also, a party at which such dances are performed.

Holberg Suite ('From Holberg's Time') A suite, Opus 40, composed by Grieg in 1884 – originally for piano, then in the same year made into a version for string orchestra, and, one year later, arranged for full orchestra. The music was written to celebrate the bicentenary of the birth of Ludvig Holberg (1684–1754) who was a Norwegian playwright. The suite is in five movements, incorporating typical dances 'from Holberg's time': 1 Prelude; 2 Sarabande; 3 Gavotte and Musette; 4 Air; 5 Rigaudon.

Holz [German] Wood; also woodwind. **Holzbläser**, woodwind players. **Holzblasinstrumente**, woodwind instruments. **Holzschlegel**, wooden drumstick.

Holzharmonika [German: 'wood-harmonica'] Xylophone.

Holzklapper [German] Whip.

Homme armé, L' [French: 'The armed man'] A 15th-century French chanson which was frequently used by composers, from the 15th century to the 17th, as a *cantus firmus for Masses (e.g. Dufay, Ockeghem, Josquin, Obrecht, Palestrina, Carissimi):

Recent research suggests the song may have been named after a tavern.

Homophonic [Greek: 'like-sounding'] A term describing a musical *texture which focuses attention on a single melody with accompanying harmonies (i.e. 'melody-plus-accompaniment'); or a texture in which all the parts tend to keep rhythmically in step with each other (sometimes also called chordal style) as distinct from *polyphonic or contrapuntal style. The music below, the opening of Thomas Morley's ballett *Now is the month of maying*, shows an example of homophonic musical texture.

Hook See under *Note.

Hopak See *Gopak.

Horn The modern orchestral horn is a valved *brass instrument, with a deep funnel-shaped mouthpiece, and (mainly) conical tube which is intricately coiled and expands very gradually into a widely-flared bell. It is sometimes called the French horn since its first development took place in France, in the 1660s, when it appeared as an improved form of circular hunting horn.

This early type of horn was a 'natural' instrument – consisting of a simple tube, with no extra mechanism of any kind – and so was only able to produce the 'natural' notes of the *harmonic series corresponding to the length of its tube. The introduction, early in the 18th century, of insertable crooks – extra lengths of tubing – offered players of the 'natural' horn, or 'hand-horn', a wider choice of range (see *crook, and also under *brass instruments). But

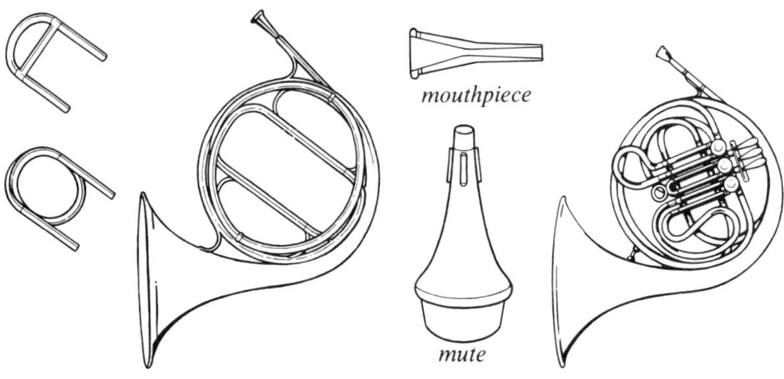

'natural' horn, with crooks *'modern' horn (valve horn)*

each crook basically provided only those notes of the harmonic series of the new total length of tube. Horn players found that extra notes could be produced by adjusting the position of the right hand inside the bell; but these 'faked' notes, or 'stopped' notes, had a noticeably different tone from other notes.

The problems were solved, around 1815, by the invention of the *valve system. This is the same as having a whole set of crooks permanently fixed into the instrument, any one of which can instantly be brought into action. The modern horn has three or four valves (sometimes five, occasionally six) and these make it fully chromatic throughout its range, which covers about three and a half octaves. The valves, which are usually of the rotary type, are controlled by the player's left hand, while the right hand rests (normally) lightly inside the bell.

The horn is a *transposing instrument. After the introduction of valves, it became usual to write all horn parts for 'horn in F', with all the notes written a 5th higher than they actually sound. Usually, no key signature is used – instead, sharps, flats, and naturals are written in as they occur in the music. The treble clef is used mainly, changing to the bass clef if the pitch of the notes is low enough to require it. (In earlier scores the custom was to write any notes in the bass clef one octave lower than was demanded; nowadays they are written a 5th higher than they actually sound.)

Range: 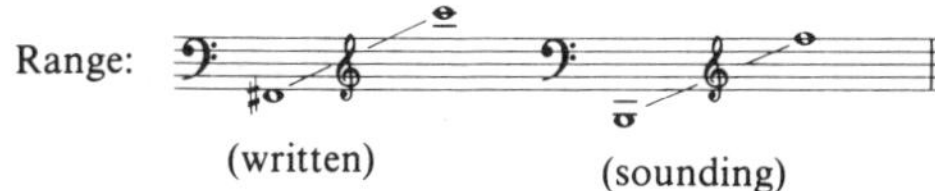

Most orchestral horn players now use the 'double horn' in F/B♭. This has an extra amount of tubing, and is in fact two horns in one. An extra, fourth, valve (controlled by the left thumb) instantly switches the instrument from a horn in F to a horn in B♭, a 4th higher.

The normal tone-quality of the horn is rich and round, warm, and rather dark. However, the player can use special techniques to alter the sound. The most important of these is *stopping*, which may be indicated in the music by the sign +, by the word 'stopped', or by a foreign term such as *chiuso* [Italian], *bouché* or *sons bouchés* [French], or *gestopft* [German]. To play a stopped note, the player inserts the right hand further into the bell. The resulting note is a semitone higher in pitch, and sounds muffled or muted – metallic and rather sinister if blown loudly, or echo-like, as if coming from a distance, if blown softly. The terms *con sordino* [Italian], *sourdine* [French] and *Dämpfer* or *gedämpft* [German] indicate that a pear-shaped or cone-shaped mute of wood, metal, cardboard, or plastic should be used. Again, the resulting sound is muffled or veiled, but the mute does not alter the pitch.

From around 1650, the horn was used at times in theatre orchestras. By the early 18th century, it was being used regularly in the orchestra. Classical composers, such as Haydn and Mozart, normally used two horns in their symphonies. Early 19th-century composers began to include four horns in their scores, and this has remained the standard number required in the symphony orchestra – though certain composers (e.g. Wagner, Mahler, Richard Strauss) have sometimes asked for eight horns. The horn is also used in *chamber music, especially in wind ensemble music, and is a standard member of the military band (but not the brass band, where the term 'horn' denotes E♭ tenor horn, a type of saxhorn).

Among the many passages featuring the horn in orchestral works are: the *Nocturne* from Mendelssohn's incidental music to *A Midsummer Night's Dream*, the slow movement of Tchaikovsky's Fifth Symphony, Ravel's **Pavane pour une infante défunte*, Bach's Brandenburg Concerto No. 1 (three horns), the Trio of Beethoven's Fifth Symphony (three horns), the opening of the Overture to Weber's opera *Der Freischütz* (four horns), and the opening of the second movement (Variations) of Rimsky-Korsakov's *Spanish Caprice* (four horns) – during the second variation of which, the effect can be heard of open notes followed by stopped notes. Passages for muted horn occur at the end of Beethoven's Sixth Symphony (*Pastoral*), at the end of Debussy's *Prélude à 'L'Après-midi d'un faune'*, and at the end of the second verse of *Nocturne* from Britten's *Serenade* for tenor, horn, and strings.

Compositions for solo horn and orchestra include the two concertos by Haydn, four by Mozart, two by Richard Strauss, and one concerto each by Hindemith and Thea Musgrave. Vivaldi wrote two concertos for two horns, and Schumann composed a *Konzertstück* for four horns and orchestra. Among chamber works including horn are Mozart's Quintet in E♭ (K407) for horn and string quartet, Beethoven's Sonata in F, Op. 17, for horn and piano (composed for the famous horn player, Giovanni Punto), Brahms's Trio in E♭ for violin, horn, and piano, Poulenc's Sonata for horn, trumpet, and trombone, and Hindemith's Sonata for horn and piano; Hindemith and Tippett each composed a Sonata for four horns. Poulenc's *Élégie* for horn and piano was composed in memory of the great English horn player, Dennis Brain.

Hörner [German] Horns.

Hornpipe Originally, a 'hornpipe' was a single-reed woodwind instrument (also called a *pibcorn*) found in certain parts of the British Isles, used to provide music for a lively dance which came to be associated chiefly with sailors. Later on, 'hornpipe' came to describe the dance itself.

'Hornpipe' Quartet See under *'Lark' Quartet.

Horn quintet *Chamber music for horn plus string quartet (two violins, viola, cello); e.g. Mozart's Horn Quintet in E♭, K407, composed in 1782.

'Hornsignal' Symphony Haydn's Symphony No. 31 in D major, composed in 1765. It includes a fanfare and an ancient hunting call ('signal'), sounded by four horns during the first movement. The fanfare is heard again at the end of the Finale, which is a set of variations giving solos to various instruments, the extremely difficult fourth variation featuring the four horns. It was Haydn himself who gave this symphony the subtitle 'With the Horn Signal'.

Horn Trio Brahms's Trio in E♭, Op. 40, for horn, violin, and piano, composed in 1865.

'Horseman' Quartet See *'Rider' Quartet.

HPSCHD See under *Multimedia.

Hu-ch'in A general name for several varieties of Chinese bowed lutes – but referring mainly to one in particular: the *ching-hu*. This is a spike fiddle, the lower part of the spike piercing the small resonator and the upper part forming the neck. There are two silk strings, and the hair of the bow is permanently caught between them.

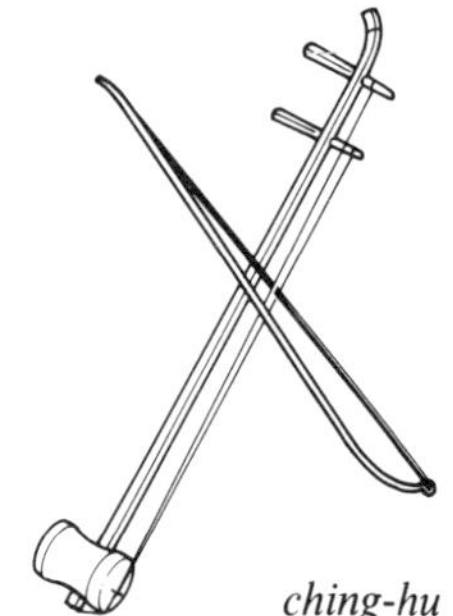

ching-hu

Humor [German] Humour.

Humoreske [German; French: *humoresque*] A 'good-humoured' piece – usually very tuneful and with well-marked rhythm (e.g. Dvořák's *Humoreske* in G flat).

Hungarian Dances Twenty-one dances for piano duet by Brahms, composed between 1852 and 1869, and published in four volumes. Many of the melodies are genuine Hungarian gypsy tunes; others are of Brahms's own invention. All the dances exist in versions for full orchestra, but only three of them (Nos. 1 in G minor, 3 in F, and 10 in F) were orchestrated by Brahms himself.

Hungarian Fantasia (*Hungarian Fantasy*) See under **Hungarian Rhapsodies.*

Hungarian Rhapsodies Nineteen works for solo piano by Liszt, published between 1848 and 1886. Some imitate the form of the Hungarian dance called the **csárdás*. Rhapsody No. 2 in C sharp minor is particularly well known; No. 15 is a version of the **Rákóczi March*; and Liszt used No. 14 as a basis for his *Hungarian Fantasia* for piano and orchestra. Orchestral versions exist of several of the Rhapsodies, some by Liszt in collaboration with Franz Döppler. However, confusion arises since these are sometimes referred to according to a new scheme of numbers, and sometimes identified according to Liszt's original numbering of the solo piano versions. (For example, the famous Rhapsody No. 2 for solo piano became No. 4 for orchestra – yet it is still, in its orchestral version, often referred to as 'No. 2'.)

'Hunt' Quartet Mozart's String Quartet No. 17 in B flat (K458) composed in 1784 (one of his set of six known as the *'Haydn' Quartets). It has acquired this nickname because the first subject of the opening movement, in six-eight time, suggests hunting calls.

Hurdy-gurdy A string instrument, dating from Medieval times, in which the strings were made to vibrate, not by a bow, but by a rotating wheel turned by a handle. The melody strings were 'stopped' by wooden sliders pressed down by the fingers, while other strings sounded a continuous drone. The tone was rather nasal in quality.

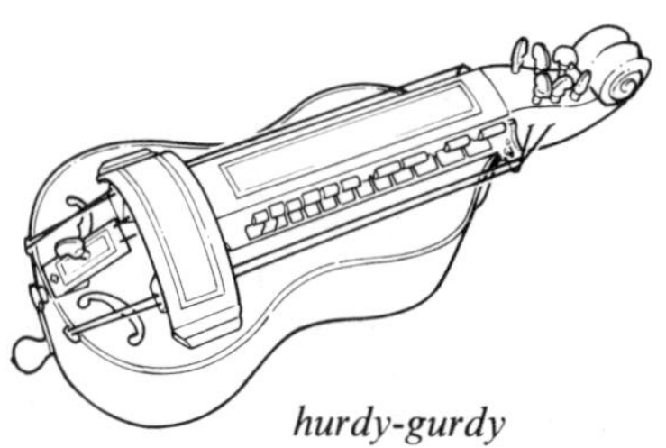

hurdy-gurdy

Hydraulis See under *Organ.

Hypoaeolian; **Hypodorian; Hypolydian** (etc.) See *Church modes.

I

Iberia A set of thirteen piano pieces (in four volumes) by Albéniz, composed between 1906 and 1908 (the year in which he died). Iberia is the old Latin name for Spain, and the pieces present thirteen musical pictures of different parts of Spain. The titles are: 1 *Evocación*, 2 *El puerto*, 3 *El Corpus en Seville*; 4 *Rondeña*, 5 *Almería*, 6 *Triana*; 7 *El Albaicín*, 8 *El polo*, 9 *Lavapiés*; 10 *Málaga*, 11 *Jerez*, 12 *Eritaña*; 13 *Navarra* (completed by de Séverac). Several of the pieces were later orchestrated by the Spanish conductor, Fernandez Arbós, who had been a friend of Albéniz. [For Debussy's *Ibéria*, see: **Images*]

Idée fixe [French: 'fixed idea'] Berlioz's term for the main theme of his **Symphonie fantastique*, which recurs in different guises during the symphony's five movements. [See also: *Leading-motive; *Thematic transformation]

Idiophone A term used to describe any musical instrument whose sound is produced solely by the vibration of the substance of the instrument itself. It may be by percussion (being beaten or struck), e.g. triangle; by concussion (clashed together, struck together), e.g. a pair of cymbals, castanets; by being shaken, e.g. sleigh bells; by being plucked, e.g. jew's harp; by being scraped, e.g. güiro; by means of friction (being rubbed), e.g. musical saw. Drums are not counted as idiophones, but as membranophones. [See: *Membranophone; *Chordophone; *Aerophone; *Electrophone]

Idyll A piece intended to express a mood of contentment, often connected in some way with nature or country life.

Illuminations, Les A *song-cycle, Opus 18, for soprano or tenor and string orchestra, composed by Benjamin Britten in 1939. Britten sets nine prose poems by the French symbolist poet, Arthur Rimbaud (1854–91).

Illustrative music See *Programme music; also, *Word-painting.

Im [German] In the.

Images (Pictures) **1** An orchestral work in *Impressionist style by Debussy, composed between 1905 and 1912. It is in three parts, entitled: 1 *Gigues* (Jigs); 2 *Ibéria* (the old Latin name for Spain); 3 *Rondes de printemps* (Round dances of Spring). The second part (*Ibéria*) is in fact made up of three pieces, called *Par les rues et par les chemins* (Through streets and byways), *Les parfums de la nuit* (Fragrances of the night), and *Le matin d'un jour de fête* (The morning of a festival day).

2 Six piano pieces in Impressionist style by Debussy, grouped into two sets. The first set (1905) consists of: 1 *Reflets dans l'eau* (Reflections in the water); 2 *Hommage à Rameau*; 3 *Mouvement*. The second set (1907) consists of: 1 *Cloches à travers les feuilles* (Bells heard through the leaves); 2 *Et la lune descend sur la temple qui fût* (And the moon descends over the ruined temple); 3 *Poissons d'or* (Goldfish).

Imitation A very common musical device in which an idea presented in one part of the musical texture is immediately imitated, or copied, in another part (see the music printed below). The imitation may be **strict** (an exact copy) or **free** (recognizably similar). Or it may involve some special treatment of the basic musical idea such as *inversion, *augmentation, or *diminution. Any *canon, *round, or *fugue is essentially built upon the principle of imitation. [See also: *Imitational entries; *Point]

Handel – Chorus: 'Glory to God' from *Messiah*

Imitational entries Various entries (or appearances) of a melodic idea closely following one another in *imitation in different parts of the musical texture. (See the music printed above, which includes eight imitational entries, occurring in the order: basses, tenors, altos, sopranos, altos, basses, tenors, sopranos.)

Immer [German] Always; still; continually.

Imperfect cadence See *Cadences.

Impeto [Italian] Impetus, impetuosity, impulse, dash. **Impetuoso**, impetuous, violent, dashing.

Impressionism (Impressionist style) A term borrowed from the style of painting of a French group of artists, working during the last quarter of the 19th century, who became known as the 'Impressionists'. Rather than making their paintings look 'real' as in a photograph, these artists aimed to give an *impression* of what the eye might take in at a single glance – an impression of vague, hazy outlines, and the play of shimmering light and movement.

It was during the early 1890s that the French composer, Claude Debussy, determined to break away from the heavy Romantic style of German composers (especially Wagner) who had for some time strongly influenced the music of other countries. His means of achieving this was compared to the techniques of the Impressionist painters. As they treated colour and light, so Debussy treated harmonies and tone-colours. For instance, he frequently uses chords for their expressive 'colour' effects, trusting his musical instinct rather than obeying any musical rules, so that *discords merge into further discords; or similar chords (often ninth chords or thirteenth chords) flow in 'chord streams' moving in parallel motion (see *Parallel chords). This brings a vague, fluid, shifting effect to Debussy's music, heightened by his use of unusual scales – modal scales based on a mode rather than a major or minor scale (see *Church modes), the five-note *pentatonic scale, or the *whole-tone scale.

In his orchestral pieces in Impressionist style, Debussy explores fresh combinations of tone-colours, fluid rhythms, shimmering textures, new effects of light and shade: avoiding hard, clear-cut outlines – *suggesting* rather than stating.

Debussy's finest orchestral works in Impressionist style include; **Prélude à 'L'Après-midi d'un faune', La *Mer, *Nocturnes*, and **Images*. Compositions in Impressionistic style by other composers include **Nights in the Gardens of Spain* by Falla, and *The *Pines of Rome* by Respighi.

Impromptu 19th-century title for a piano piece in a spontaneous style suggesting a free and inspired improvisation – as if the music occurred to the composer in a flash of inspiration and he dashed it off 'on the spur of the moment'. Fine impromptus were written by Schubert, Chopin (including the *Fantaisie-Impromptu*), and Fauré.

Improvisation The creation of music 'on the spot', *as* it is being performed – making up the music as one goes along. A section or passage within a composition may be improvised (as, originally, in the case of a *cadenza), or a complete piece. An improvisation may be entirely of the performer's own creation, or it may be based on one or more given themes. It may consist of varying or decorating a section of music when it is repeated (e.g. in a *da capo aria), or perhaps of adding harmonies to a melody and bass-line, as in the interpretation of a figured bass by a player on harpsichord, organ, or lute (see *continuo). In the 20th century, improvisation has been an important element in *jazz, and also in the performance of *aleatory music. [See also: *Division; *Voluntary]

In alt; **In altissimo** See *Alt.

Incalzando [Italian: 'chasing', 'urging forward'] Indicating an increase in speed (and often also in volume).

Incidental music Music specially composed to be heard at certain points during the performance of a play. It may set the mood for the act or scene which is to follow; entertain the audience while scenery is being changed between acts or scenes; serve as an accompaniment to the action in certain scenes, or as background music while characters are speaking. It may also include songs and dances performed during the course of the play.

A composer may collect together several of the pieces of incidental music he has written for a play to make a *suite for performance on the concert platform. Well-known examples include: Mendelssohn's music for Shakespeare's *A *Midsummer Night's Dream*; Bizet's music for Daudet's play *L'*Arlésienne*; and Grieg's music for Ibsen's **Peer Gynt*.

[See also: *Entr'acte; *Intermezzo; *Interlude; *Overture; *Prelude]

Inciso [Italian: 'incised'] Incisive in rhythm and attack.

Indeciso [Italian] Undecided, hesitant; wavering in speed.

Indefinite pitch See under *Percussion instruments.

Indeterminacy A term first used in the 1950s by the American composer John Cage (born 1912) to describe *aleatory music which is not written down in fixed conventional notation (traditional note-symbols such as crotchets and quavers, etc., which determine the pitches and durations of musical sounds) but instead uses newly invented symbols, or a diagram or drawing, or just a basic idea to be freely interpreted. The number and kind of sounds which will result in a performance of the piece are therefore left undetermined by the composer – and, of course, no two performances of such a piece can be exactly alike. The term 'indeterminacy' (or **indeterminate music**) may be especially applied to aleatory compositions which rely upon choices and decisions being made by the performer(s), rather than depending upon elements of chance.

Indian instruments See: *Mṛdaṅgam; *Nāgasvaram; *Sāraṅgī; *Sarod; *Shahnāī; *Sitar; *Tablā; *Tamburā; *Vīṇā.

Infinite canon (perpetual canon) A *canon composed in such a way that each of the *parts, upon coming to the end of the printed music, goes straight back to the beginning again, so that the music may be repeated any number of times. Examples are *Tallis's Canon* ('Glory to Thee my God this night') and **Sumer is icumen in*. A simple type of infinite canon is also called a 'round' (e.g. *Frère Jacques*).

Inglese The Italian word for 'English' (e.g. *corno inglese*, English horn).

Ingredients of music (elements of music) The basic musical materials available to a composer, and with which he or she works when building up a piece of music – combining and balancing them to produce a desired total effect. The basic ingredients of a musical composition include *melody, *rhythm, *harmony, *timbre (tone-colour, tone-quality), *texture, and musical *form (design, structure) – though not all of these ingredients may be present in every composition. (Other factors which may contribute to the overall effect include tempo, dynamics, and expression.)

In modo di [Italian] In the manner of.

In Nature's Realm See **Carnival Overture*.

Inner part Any *part in the music, vocal or instrumental, which lies between the highest part (treble) and the lowest (bass). [See also: *Outer parts]

Innig [German] Heartfelt, sincere. **Mit innigster Empfindung**, 'with inmost heartfelt emotion'. **Innigkeit**, sincerity, inmost feeling.

In nomine A special type of contrapuntal composition (for keyboard, lute, or viols) written only by 16th- and 17th-century English composers, and based upon the plainchant *Gloria tibi Trinitas* as it was used by John Taverner (*c*1490–1545) in the Benedictus of his mass of the same name. The words of the Benedictus are: *Benedictus qui venit in nomine Domini* (Blessed is he who comes in the name of the Lord), and the plainchant (see overleaf) is heard complete, sung by the altos, at the words *in nomine*. Someone, possibly Taverner himself, made a keyboard arrangement of this section of his Benedictus, calling it *In nomine*. This set a fashion, and *In nomines* – all written in contrapuntal style

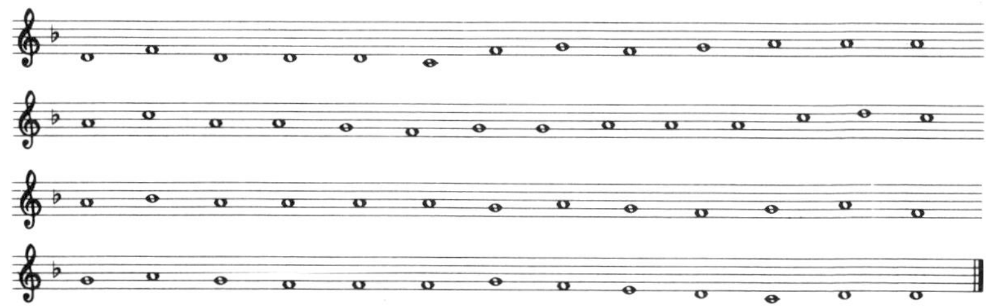

with the plainchant *cantus firmus threading through the texture in long note-values – were written by many composers, including Byrd, Bull, Gibbons, and Purcell. [See also the music example given under *Polyphonic]

Inquieto [Italian] Unquiet, restless, troubled.

Insieme [Italian] Together.

Instrumental devices; **Instrumental effects** See *Orchestral devices.

Instrumental music Music composed solely for one or more instruments (solo, instrumental duet or duo, chamber music group, instrumental ensemble, orchestra), and not including any voices. [Compare: *Vocal music]

Instrumentation **1** In a strict sense: the study of instruments, their characteristic sounds and playing techniques. But the term may also be used to mean **2** the art and technique of using (writing and scoring for) instruments in a musical composition (i.e. the same meaning as *orchestration), or **3** the particular choice or combination of instruments being used.

Instruments All objects and contrivances devised and/or used to produce what the ear accepts as musical sounds. (The human singing *voice is also regarded by some as a musical instrument.) The instruments of Western music may be grouped according to the following categories: (1) *string instruments, (2) *wind instruments – which include *woodwind instruments and *brass instruments, (3) *percussion instruments, (4) *keyboard instruments. Another way of classifying instruments, so that non-Western instruments are included, is (1) *idiophones, (2) *membranophones, (3) *chordophones, (4) *aerophones, (5) *electrophones. [Several non-Western instruments are listed under: *Arab instruments; *Chinese instruments; *Indian instruments; *Japanese instruments. See also: *Gamelan]

Intensity The volume, or loudness, of a sound. [See also the table of Dynamic markings (markings of intensity) on page 390]

Interlude [from Latin, meaning 'played between'] Music played or sung between the sections or the movements of a composition; or, more commonly, between the acts or scenes of an opera or play (and therefore the same as an *entr'acte* or *intermezzo*).

Intermezzo (plural: *intermezzi*) [Italian] There are several meanings, including: **1** A piece played between the acts or scenes of an opera or play (the same as *entr'acte*); **2** A short comic opera of the early 18th century whose two scenes were performed between the acts of a full-length *opera seria. The most famous example is *La *Serva padrona* by Pergolesi (1710–1736). By the middle of the 18th century, intermezzi were performed as separate one-act operas; **3** A title given by certain 19th-century composers (e.g. Schumann and Brahms) to some of their piano pieces.

Internal pedal A *pedal point sounding at middle pitch within the musical texture, rather than in the bass. Sometimes also called 'middle pedal'.

Interrupted cadence See *Cadences.

Intervals An interval is the distance, or difference, in pitch between two notes. The notes may be sounded simultaneously, making a *harmonic interval*; or they may be sounded one after another, as in a melody, making a *melodic interval*.

Number and quality An interval is identified by *number* – the number of letter-names it covers. And so C–E is a 3rd, since it covers three letter-names (C, D, E); C–G is a 5th (C, D, E, F, G). Top *and* bottom notes are included in the count:

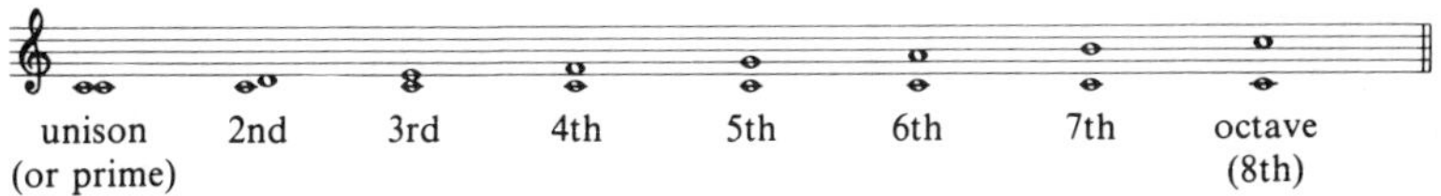

An interval is identified, more precisely, also by *quality*. Five descriptions are used, according to the number of semitones the interval contains: perfect, major, minor, augmented, diminished.

Perfect intervals are: unison, 4th, 5th, and octave.

2nds, 3rds, 6ths, and 7ths may be *major* or *minor*.

The intervals in the above example are all shown as steps of the *major scale* – which is used as a standard for measuring all intervals. (In most of the examples given here, the scale in question is C major, but *any* major scale might have been used.) The lower note of the interval is taken to be the tonic (or *doh*) of a major scale. The quality of the interval then depends upon whether the upper note occurs in that scale (in which case the interval will be either perfect or major) or whether it has been lowered or raised. If major intervals are reduced by a semitone, they become *minor*:

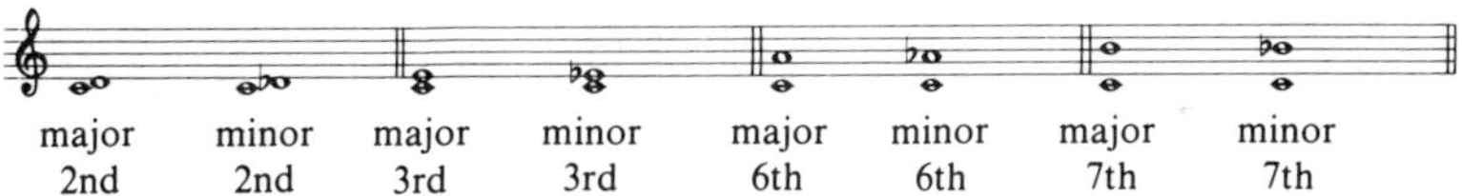

If perfect or major intervals are increased by a semitone, they become *augmented* ('made larger'). For example:

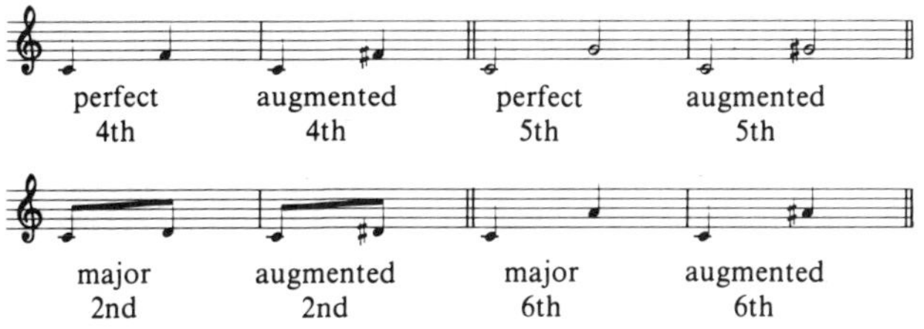

If perfect or minor intervals are reduced by a semitone, they become *diminished* ('made smaller'). For example:

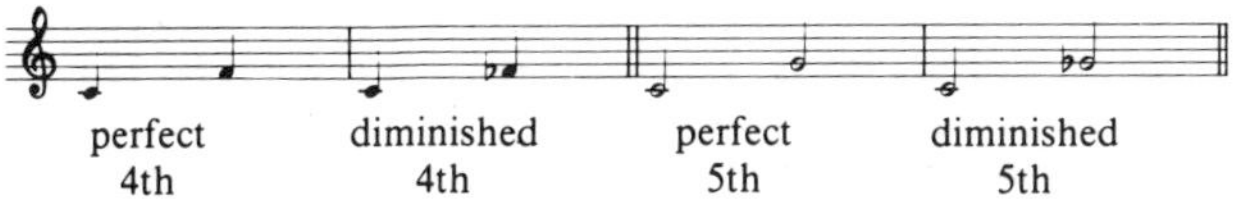

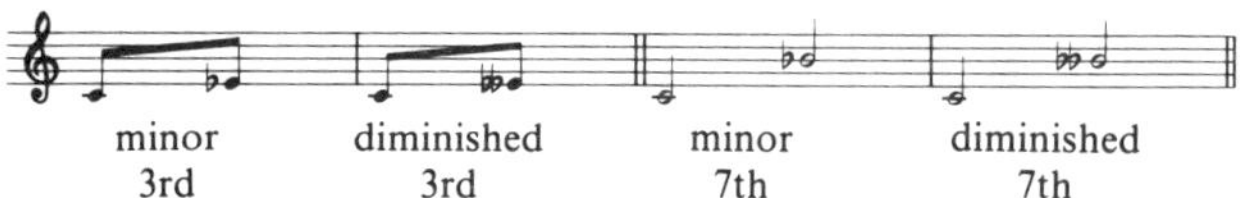

Compound intervals Intervals greater than an octave are sometimes described as *compound* intervals. And so, for instance, a 10th is also a compound 3rd (an octave + a 3rd) – but it is quite usual to refer to C–E simply as a 3rd, regardless of how many octaves may intervene.

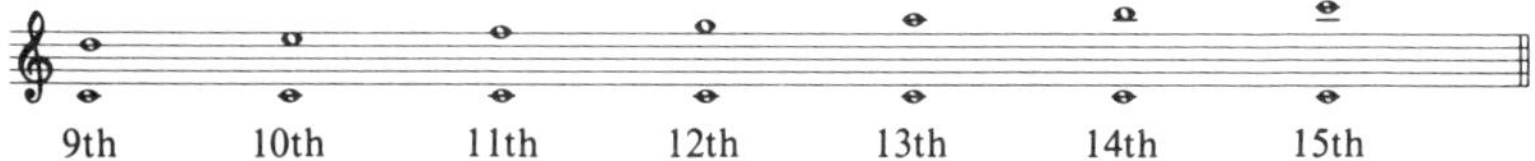

Inversion of intervals If the notes of an interval change position, the interval is said to be **inverted**. This will give a new *number* – found by subtracting the original number from 9 (and so a 2nd becomes a 7th; a 3rd becomes a 6th; a 4th becomes a 5th). This is what happens to the *quality* of an interval when it becomes inverted:

major becomes minor; minor becomes major;
augmented becomes diminished; diminished becomes augmented;
but perfect always remains perfect.

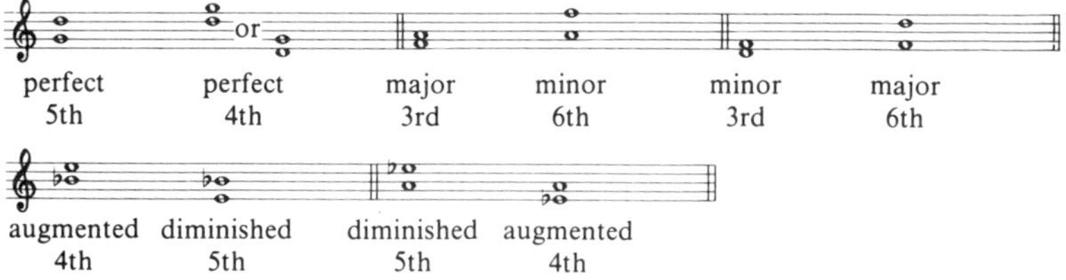

Concords and discords Intervals are also classed as *concords or discords. There are two kinds of concord: perfect, and imperfect. The perfect concords are the perfect unison, 4th, 5th, octave. The imperfect concords are the major 3rd, minor 3rd, major 6th, minor 6th. All other intervals (2nds and 7ths of any kind, and all augmented or diminished intervals) are classed as discords.

[See also Table 12 on page 393]

In the South A descriptive concert overture, Opus 50, composed by Elgar in 1903–4. He also called it *Alassio* after the name of the town in southern Italy where he was staying when he first sketched the music.

In the Steppes of Central Asia A tone poem composed by Borodin in 1880. He described it as an 'orchestral picture' depicting the gradual approach and passing of an Oriental caravan as it crosses the Russian plain, safely protected by Russian arms. The two themes – a Russian song and an Oriental, or Asiatic, melody – are first presented separately, then later combined together.

Intime [French]; **Intimo** [Italian] Intimate, inmost, inward.

Intonation **1** The degree to which a singer or a player, such as a violinist, is in tune (good intonation) or out-of-tune (poor intonation). **2** The opening notes of a Gregorian chant. [See also: *Just intonation]

Intrada [Italian, from Spanish *entrada*: 'entrance'] A title used by 16th- and 17th-century composers for a piece (usually of a bright, march-like character) announcing or accompanying an entrance in a play, opera, or ballet, or at a festive event; or a piece serving as an introduction to a *suite for instrumental ensemble. Later composers have sometimes used this title for a short overture.

Introduction [Italian: *introduzione*] A section of music (often slow in tempo) placed at the beginning of a movement or a work, preparing the listener for what is to follow (e.g. at the beginning of the first movement of a symphony). It may be several bars long (e.g. Beethoven: Piano Sonata No. 8, *Pathétique*), or just a couple of chords (Beethoven: Symphony No. 3, *Eroica*); or even a separate piece, complete in itself, placed at the beginning of a collection of pieces such as a suite (e.g. the opening piece in Stravinsky's suite from his ballet *The Firebird*).

Introit [from Latin, *introitus*] **1** The first item in the Proper of the *Mass. **2** In other church services, a short introductory anthem.

Inventions Name given to two sets of keyboard pieces, fifteen in two-part texture and fifteen in three-part texture, composed by Bach in 1720 for his son, Wilhelm Friedemann. Each piece is a study in imitative counterpoint. The first set has become known as the 'Two-part Inventions', and the second set (which Bach called 'Sinfonias') as the 'Three-part Inventions'.

Inversion; Inverted These two words are used in music with several meanings, all in some way connected with 'turning upside down', or substituting higher pitches for lower pitches (and vice versa):

(1) **Inversion of a melody** If a melody is presented in inversion it is 'turned upside down', so that notes rising in pitch in the original now fall, and vice versa:

from Bach: *The Art of Fugue*

(2) **Inversion of parts** If two or more simultaneous melodies (i.e. the melodic lines, or individual strands, in a contrapuntal texture) are inverted, they exchange places – so that the higher part now becomes the lower, and so on. [See: *Invertible counterpoint]

(3) **Inversion of intervals** If an interval is inverted, the lowest note is raised an octave, or the highest note is lowered an octave. [See under *Intervals]

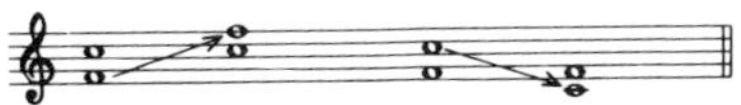

(4) **Inversion of a chord** If a chord is inverted, its notes are arranged in any position in which the root is not in the bass. [See under *Chord]

(5) **Inverted cadence** Any *cadence which has one or both chords inverted.

Inverted mordent Same as upper mordent (see under *Ornaments).

Inverted pedal (upper pedal) A *pedal point sounding in an upper part, rather than in the bass or the middle of the musical texture.

Inverted turn See *Ornaments.

Invertible counterpoint Counterpoint composed in such a way that the parts (melodic lines, or individual strands, in the musical texture) may change places with each other and still produce a musically satisfactory result. For example, the treble may interchange with the bass (as in the music overleaf). If only two parts are involved, this may also be termed **double counterpoint**; if three, **triple counterpoint**; and if four, **quadruple counterpoint**.

Bach: Two-part *Invention No. 6

Invitation to the Dance (*Aufforderung zum Tanze*) A *rondo brillante* for piano, composed by Weber in 1819, which pictures a scene in a ballroom. It begins with an introduction (the 'invitation'); then follows the dance, which is a brilliant waltz. The music is often heard in a version for orchestra made by Berlioz in 1841, now used for the ballet called *Le Spectre de la rose*.

Ionian mode See *Church modes.

Ionisation A work by Edgard Varèse, composed between 1929 and 1931, for thirteen percussion players in charge of forty-two instruments plus two sirens. An 'ion' is an atom or group of atoms, electrically charged. *Ionisation* means 'converting into atoms' – suggesting, in this case, continuous bursts of particles of sound released into space.

Irato [Italian] Irate, angry.

Isorhythm [from Greek: 'equal rhythm', 'same rhythm'] A technique used to structure a composition, first employed by 14th-century Medieval composers (e.g. Machaut). First the composer chooses a plainchant melody which becomes the tenor *cantus firmus. He then arranges the notes of the melody according to a rhythmic pattern of his own devising; this pattern is repeated again and again throughout the piece. The melody itself is called *color*. Each statement of the rhythmic pattern is called a *talea*. The music of the other voice-parts is then woven above and below this tenor cantus firmus. The example below shows the first four *taleae* (or taleas) of the tenor on which Machaut builds the **isorhythmic** Kyrie of his **Messe de Notre Dame*.

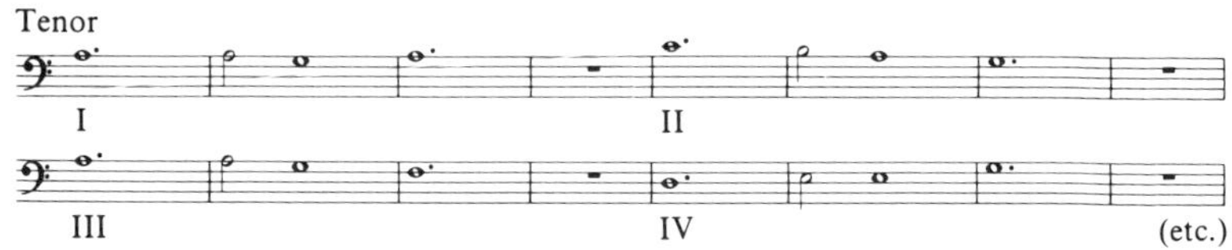

Israel in Egypt Oratorio in two parts by Handel, for six soloists (there are duets for sopranos and basses), chorus, and orchestra, first performed in London in 1739 (text from the Old Testament, probably selected by Handel). Predominantly choral, the work is notable for its *double choruses and for Handel's many unacknowledged 'borrowings', from himself and from other composers, including Kerll.

Istampita [Italian] *Estampie.

Istesso [Italian] Same. **L'istesso tempo**, the same speed (as before) – also indicating that although the metre changes (e.g. from $\frac{4}{4}$ to $\frac{3}{4}$) the speed of the *beat* remains precisely the same. (So in a change from $\frac{2}{4}$ to $\frac{6}{8}$, the dotted crotchet beat of $\frac{6}{8}$ takes the same time as the plain crotchet beat of the preceding $\frac{2}{4}$)

Italian Caprice Orchestral piece, Opus 45, by Tchaikovsky. He composed it during a visit to Italy in 1879, and several of the tunes included are based on Italian folk-songs which he heard there. The piece is also known by the title *Capriccio italien.*

Italian Concerto A work for solo harpsichord by Bach, published in 1735 in part two of the **Clavierübung*. Although no orchestra is involved, the music is written in the form and style of a solo *concerto by an Italian composer, such as Vivaldi. Contrasts of *solo* and *tutti* are imitated by contrasts of dynamics (*piano* and *forte*) as available on a double-manual *harpsichord. There are three movements, the first and last being in *ritornello form.

Italian overture See under *Overture.

Italian Serenade Piece for string quartet, composed by Hugo Wolf in 1887. Five years later, he made an arrangement of the music for small orchestra.

Italian sixth See *Augmented sixth chords.

Italian Symphony Mendelssohn's title for his Symphony No. 4 in A major, Op. 90. The music was begun during a visit to Italy in 1831, and shows influence of sights and sounds which Mendelssohn experienced there. The four movements are: 1 *Allegro vivace*; 2 *Andante con moto*; 3 *Con moto moderato*; 4 Saltarello: *Presto*. The slow second movement, with its steady rhythm, is sometimes called 'The Pilgrims' March'; the fourth movement includes melodic and rhythmic characteristics of the old Italian dance called the *saltarello. The Italian Symphony was completed in 1833, but was not published until 1847. [See also: **Scottish Symphony*]

Ite, missa est See *Mass.

Jack See under *Harpsichord.

Jagd [German] Hunt. **Jagdhorn**, hunting horn. **Jagdlied**, hunting song.

Jahreszeiten, Die See *The *Seasons.*

Jam To a jazz musician, 'jam' means 'improvise'; and so at a **jam session** (usually an informal get-together) a group of musicians select a tune familiar to them and improvise on it and around it, both in ensemble and as soloists.

Janissary music The Janissaries were the military bodyguard of the Turkish sultans. Their music strongly featured percussion instruments such as kettle drums, side drums, cymbals, triangles, tambourines, and the Turkish crescent (or 'Jingling Johnny' or Chinese pavilion). This was a long pole topped by a crescent, and with cross-bars from which many tiny bells and brass plates were suspended, making jingling sounds as the pole was shaken or pushed up and down. 18th- and 19th-century composers occasionally imitated the noisy but fascinating sounds of this Turkish music – for example, Haydn in his *'Military' Symphony; Mozart in his opera *The *Abduction from the Seraglio*, and in the last movement (*Alla turca*) of his Piano Sonata in A, K331; and Beethoven in *The Ruins of Athens*, and the march-like 'Turkish interlude' in the finale of his Ninth Symphony (the 'Choral').

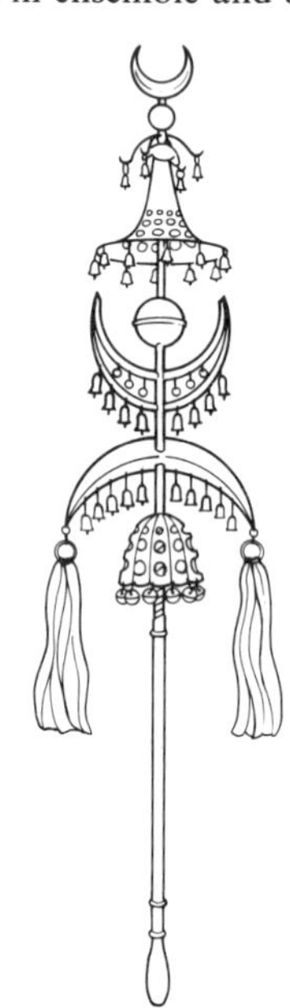

Turkish crescent

Japanese instruments See: *Biwa; *Da-daiko; *Hichiriki; *Kakko; *Koto; *Shakuhachi; *Shamisen; *Shō; *Tsuridaiko.

Jazz An important type of popular music (and, also, a skill and art of performance) originating in the southern states of the USA towards the end of the 19th century, and – by the inspiration and musicianship of countless musicians, both black and white – developing through various styles at various times. Among the many ingredients which eventually blended together to become jazz were elements of European popular music, West African rhythms, *work-songs, *gospel music, *spirituals, *blues, *ragtime, the music of marching bands, and the music of the late 19th-century minstrel shows (which was in fact the white man's version of the music performed by the black slaves).

Typically, early jazz was played by a small band made up of a melody section, consisting of one or two cornets (or trumpets), clarinet, trombone (and, later, saxophone); and a rhythm section, consisting of piano, drum kit, bass, and guitar or banjo.

Early jazz musicians played by ear (few could read music), exuberantly improvising together, on and around a chosen melody, over a repeating scheme of harmonies. Characteristically, they used the melodic style of the blues (including the use of *'blue' notes) together with the syncopated rhythms of ragtime above a strong and steady beat in $\frac{4}{4}$ time. (The improvisations on the chosen melody were really variations on a theme; and the repetitions of the harmonic scheme, underlying these variations, gave the music a structure similar to that of a chaconne.)

Later on, a common plan for a jazz item might be: (1) one or two choruses (i.e. playings of the melody) by the ensemble in collective improvisation; followed by (2) two or more choruses, each featuring one of the melody instruments in solo improvisation, decorating or changing the melody in various ways; ending with (3) final chorus, ensemble in collective improvisation.

It is generally accepted that jazz originally took shape mainly in New Orleans – in particular, in the notorious Storyville district with its many brothels and gambling joints. Many early jazz bands played in bars there. But when, in 1917, the illegal entertainments of Storyville were closed down, many New Orleans jazzmen moved north, up river, to Chicago and New York. Jazz, by its vitality, spontaneity, and emotional impact, became increasingly popular, and soon began to spread internationally.

For some of the many further developments in jazz and various jazz styles and terms, see *New Orleans jazz; *Traditional (trad.) jazz; *Dixieland; *Chicago style; *Boogie-woogie; *Swing; *Bop; *Modern jazz; *Progressive jazz; *Cool jazz; *Mainstream; *Third stream; *Free jazz; *Break; *Riff; *Jam.

From its beginnings, jazz has interested and influenced certain composers of so-called 'serious' or 'classical' music who have deliberately emphasized jazz ingredients in some of their compositions. Among them are Ravel, Stravinsky (e.g. in *Ragtime* for eleven instruments, and the **Ebony Concerto*), Milhaud (see *La *Création du monde*), Copland, and Kurt Weill.

Jesu, joy of man's desiring The concluding *chorale for choir, strings, and continuo, with oboe *obbligato, from Bach's Cantata No. 147, *Herz und Mund und Tat und Leben*. The chorale is presented in eight phrases, spaced out so that as the voices rest after each phrase, the oboe continues to weave its flowing melody in triplets. This music is also sometimes heard in an arrangement for solo piano by the pianist, Myra Hess.

Jesus Christ Superstar Rock opera by Andrew Lloyd Webber (libretto by Tim Rice), issued on records (1970), staged (New York, 1971), and filmed (1973). The work employs solo singers, adult chorus, children's choir, and orchestra, with pianos, electric piano, organ, synthesizers, electric and acoustic guitars, tenor sax, and drums. The text, written in a racy modern style, tells of Mary Magdalene's ministrations to Jesus at Bethany, Caiaphas's plot to have him killed, his dismissal of the money-lenders from the Temple, his betrayal by

Judas and denial by Peter, Pilate's weak evasiveness, and the resultant Crucifixion.

Jeté See *Ricochet.

Jeu [French: 'play'] Organ stop. **Jeux de fonds**, foundation stops. **Jeux d'anches**, reed stops. **Jeux à bouche**, flue stops.

Jeu de clochettes; Jeu de timbres [French] Glockenspiel.

Jeux d'enfants (Children's games) A set of twelve pieces for piano duet by Bizet, composed in 1871. Bizet later arranged five of the pieces, including the March and Galop, as an orchestral suite.

Jew's harp A small instrument, usually of metal and consisting of a thin flexible blade, fixed to a surrounding frame and projecting beyond the 'arms'. The player holds the rounded part of the frame in the left hand and, taking the arms of the frame loosely between the teeth, twangs the free end of the blade with the right hand. The player's mouth acts as a resonator. By making various movements of the tongue, cheeks, and larynx to change the shape of the mouth (and therefore the volume of the air cavity) the player is able to produce notes of different pitch. The jew's harp has no particular connection with the Jewish people, and the origin of the name has never been satisfactorily explained (though it has been suggested that it is a corruption of 'jaw's harp').

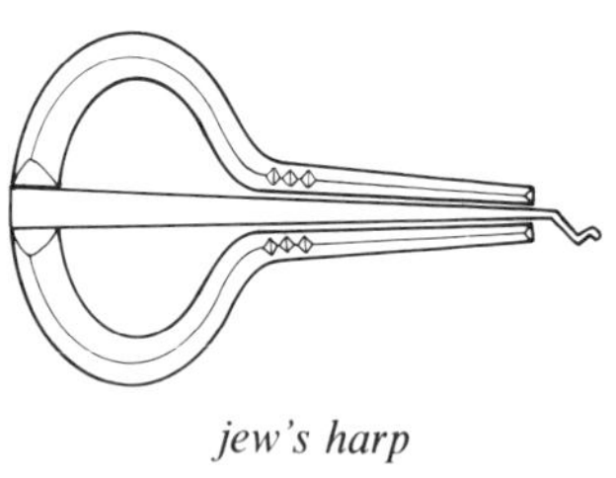

jew's harp

Jig See *Gigue.

Jingles; Jingle bells See *Sleigh bells.

Jingling Johnny See under *Janissary music.

Jodel (jodelling) A type of singing or 'calling', typical of Alpine regions such as Switzerland and Austria. It is produced by rapid alternation of vocal register, between low chest voice and high falsetto.

'Joke' Quartet Nickname of Haydn's String Quartet in E flat, Op. 33 No. 2, composed in 1781 – the second of the set of six known as the *'Russian' Quartets. It is known as the 'Joke' because of many humorous touches which Haydn brings into the music, e.g. in the Minuet (placed second rather than third, and marked *Scherzando: Allegretto*) and, particularly, in the final rondo – the main joke being that it is impossible to tell when the music has in fact come to an end.

Jongleur [French] A French minstrel of the 12th and 13th centuries, tending to remain 'free-lance' rather than seeking to gain a permanent position in a household.

Joseph and the Amazing Technicolor Dreamcoat Musical by Andrew Lloyd Webber (libretto by Tim Rice based on the story in Genesis). First performed in London in 1968 as a 20-minute school cantata, the work gradually developed into a full-length stage show, receiving its première, also in London, in 1973. It employs solo singers, adult chorus, and children's choir supported by an instrumental group including keyboards (piano, harpsichord, and organ) and an array of percussion.

Jota A couple-dance from Aragon (a province in north-eastern Spain) in swift triple time, and accompanied by guitars, castanets, tambourine. The *Final Dance* of Falla's ballet *The Three-Cornered Hat* is a jota. A famous jota tune is the *jota aragonesa*; this was used by Liszt in his **Rhapsodie espagnole*, and also by Glinka in his orchestral *Capriccio brillante on the jota aragonesa*:

Joyeux [French] Joyous, joyful, cheerful. **Joyeusement**, joyfully, cheerfully.

Jubilus In plainsong, the lengthy, flowing *melisma sung to the final vowel of the *Alleluia.

Judas Maccabaeus Oratorio in three parts by Handel, for soprano, mezzo-soprano, tenor, and bass soloists, chorus, and orchestra, first performed in London in 1747 (text by the Revd Thomas Morell based on an Old Testament story). Written to celebrate the return of the Duke of Cumberland from his victory over the Young Pretender at Culloden, it includes the popular chorus 'See, the conquering hero comes'.

Julius Caesar See **Giulio Cesare*.

'Jungfern' Quartets See *'Russian' Quartets.

'Jupiter' Symphony Nickname given to Mozart's final symphony, No. 41 in C major (K551), probably due to the dignified and majestic opening of the first movement. Mozart's three last and greatest symphonies – No. 39 in E flat (K543), No. 40 in G minor (K550), and No. 41, 'The Jupiter' – were all composed in the short time of six weeks during the summer of 1788, yet each is very different from the other two in mood and character. The four movements of the 'Jupiter' Symphony are: 1 *Allegro vivace* (in sonata form); 2 *Andante* (in sonata form); 3 Menuetto: *Allegretto*; 4 Finale: *Molto allegro* (in sonata form combined with all kinds of contrapuntal treatment of the various themes).

Jusque [French] As far as, until, up to. **Jusqu'à la fin**, until the end.

Just intonation (pure intonation) A system of tuning in which all the intervals of the scale are tuned in precise accordance with acoustical theory. It is based on the 'pure' 5th and 3rd, and all other intervals are derived from these. [See also: *Temperament]

K **1** Abbreviation standing for **Köchel** (Ludwig von Köchel), an Austrian botanist and mineralogist, who in 1862 published a *thematic catalogue of the works of Mozart, arranging them in order according to date of composition. Linked to the title of any work by Mozart, **K** followed by a number (the 'Köchel number') indicates that composition's place in the catalogue (e.g. Symphony No. 40 in G minor, K550). Occasionally the letters **KV** standing for *Köchel-Verzeichnis* (Köchel Catalogue) are used instead. (The catalogue has been revised several times.)

2 Also an abbreviation standing for Kirkpatrick (Ralph Kirkpatrick), an American keyboard player, who prepared a catalogue in 1953 of the works of Domenico Scarlatti. In connection with any piece by Scarlatti, **K** followed by a number identifies that particular piece in Kirkpatrick's catalogue. Sometimes, to avoid any possible confusion with Köchel, the prefix **Kk** is used. [See also: *L, 2]

Kadenz [German] **1** *Cadence. **2** *Cadenza.

Kaiserquartett See *'Emperor' Quartet.

Kakko A Japanese double-headed barrel *drum. It lies horizontally on a stand, and both heads are struck with thin, hard sticks.

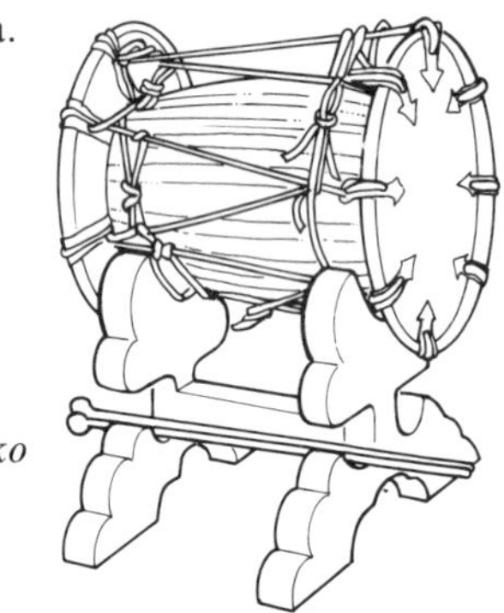

kakko

Kalevala The Finns' national epic poem, consisting of a collection of legends telling of the adventures of gods and heroes from Finnish mythology. Several of the compositions of Sibelius (1865–1957) are based upon legends from the Kalevala, including his 'Kullervo' Symphony (1892), and his symphonic poems *The *Swan of Tuonela* and *Pohjola's Daughter*.

Kamancha Kamānja) In Arab music, a bowed string instrument, usually a spike fiddle, and with one to four strings, tuned in 5ths.

Kammer [German] Chamber, room. **Kammermusik**, *chamber music.

Kanon [German] *Canon.

Kantate [German] *Cantata.

Kanun See *Qānūn.

Kapelle [German: 'chapel'] Name used during the 17th and 18th centuries for the musical establishment of a chapel, or of a court.

Kapellmeister (*Capellmeister*) [German] Originally, the director of music in the chapel of a German court. Later, the title was used more broadly to mean the musician responsible for all the various types of music at a court. Haydn, for instance, as Kapellmeister to the Hungarian family named Esterházy, was in charge of orchestra, choir, and many solo musicians, and was expected to compose, rehearse, and conduct orchestral and chamber works for the palace concert room, operas for the Esterházy private theatre, and religious music for services in the chapel.

Karelia An overture (Opus 10) and an orchestral suite (Opus 11) composed in 1893 by Sibelius. The suite contains three movements: *Intermezzo, Ballad, Alla marcia*. Karelia is a province in southern Finland, where Sibelius was living at the time.

Kastagnetten [German] Castanets.

Kaum [German] Hardly, barely. **Kaum hörbar**, barely audible.

Kettle drums [Italian: *timpani*] The most important of all orchestral *percussion instruments; the only type of *drum regularly used in the orchestra capable of producing notes of definite pitch.

A kettle drum consists of a large bowl-shaped body-shell, usually of copper, over the top of which is stretched a single membrane of calfskin or plastic. To tune the drum to a specific note, tension on the drum-skin is adjusted by turning T-shaped screws around the rim. Tightening the skin raises the pitch; slackening it lowers the pitch. Many players now use the more modern pedal-tuned (or 'chromatic' or 'machine') kettle drums in which the pitch can be swiftly changed by a foot-pedal, instead of by hand.

kettle drums

Kettle drums are played with two sticks, normally headed with felt, though sticks headed with another material (e.g. leather, sponge, cork, wood) may be used for special effects. The softness or hardness of the heads, and the place at which the drum-skin is struck, affect attack, volume, and tone-quality.

pedal-tuned kettle drum

The kettle drum player (timpanist) may play single strokes or rhythms on two or more kettle drums in combination, strike two drums simultaneously to produce two notes at the same time, or play a *roll on a single kettle drum. On a pedal-tuned kettle drum, a *glissando is also possible, sliding up or down in pitch.

Up to and including Beethoven, the orchestra included only two kettle drums (one slightly larger than the other) most often tuned to the tonic and dominant of the key. Many scores of the later 19th century and the 20th century require three kettle drums, sometimes more.

Approximate diameters and ranges of kettle drums are:

Pieces in which kettle drums are particularly featured include: Variation 7 ('Troyte') from Elgar's *'Enigma' Variations; the Scherzo of Sibelius's First Symphony; the Finale of Nielsen's Fourth Symphony (two sets of kettle drums); the first movement of Janáček's *Sinfonietta*; and the *Tuba mirum* from Berlioz's *Requiem* (sixteen kettle drums, needing ten players!). Pedal-tuned kettle drums are featured in the third movement of Bartók's **Music for Strings, Percussion, and Celesta.*

[See also: *Membranophone; *Coperto, coperti; *Nakers]

Key 1 A term used in connection with tonality. Any piece or passage of music in which the composer constructs melodies and harmonies which are firmly based on the notes of a major or minor *scale, is said to be 'in a *key*'. And according to which of these two types of scale is forming the basis for the music, the key is similarly described as being *major* or *minor*. So a piece or a passage of music may be said to be 'in the key of' (for instance) C major, or D major, or A minor. All major keys are exactly alike except for the difference of pitch. And the same is true for all minor keys.

Whatever the key, certain notes will assume greater importance than others. In music written in the key of C major, for instance, the ear will sense a strong 'pull' towards the most important note of that particular key: the *tonic* note, or *key-note*, C – which is also the first (lowest) note and last (highest) note of the scale of C major. In the following tune, the ear senses that C is the most important note. C is the key-note, and the tune is in the key of C major.

If the music modulates (changes key) to, say, G major, it will then be based on the notes of the scale of G major, and the ear will sense that the 'pull' is now towards the new key-note, G:

There may be further modulations, to other keys, but almost certainly the composer will end the piece in the key in which it began, and (if the melody is harmonized) usually with the key-note as the last note in the bass part.

A key is sometimes mentioned in the title of a composition. In single pieces and movements, this refers to the main key (the tonic key) of the music, the key in which it begins and ends – though in between, there may be many modulations to other keys. In compositions made up of several movements (e.g. Symphony in F major, Piano Concerto in D minor) it means that this is the main key of the first movement (and usually of the last movement as well).

[See also: *Key signature, and the table of Key signatures on page 389; *Related keys; *Relative keys; *Polytonality; *Atonality]

2 On instruments such as the piano, organ, harpsichord, and clavichord, a key is one of a series of balanced, black or white levers which the player presses down to produce the sound. (See *Keyboard). On *woodwind instruments, keys are metal levers (with pads in metal cups) which are controlled by the player's fingers to uncover or cover one or more air-holes. [See also: *Boehm system]

Keyboard The horizontal series or set of black and white levers, called keys, found on keyboard instruments, such as the piano, organ, harpsichord, clavichord. Each key is a balanced, pivoted lever, whose movement is similar to that of a see-saw. As the player presses down the nearer end of a key, its further end (extending into the instrument) rises. This initiates the *action*, or 'sound-producing mechanism', of the instrument, causing the note to sound. The diagram below shows the familiar design of the keyboard: two rows of keys, arranged according to a set pattern – adjacent white keys, and shorter, raised, black keys in alternate groups of two and three. (The actual number of keys varies from one instrument to another; and on many old instruments the 'colours' of the keys – white and black – are reversed.)

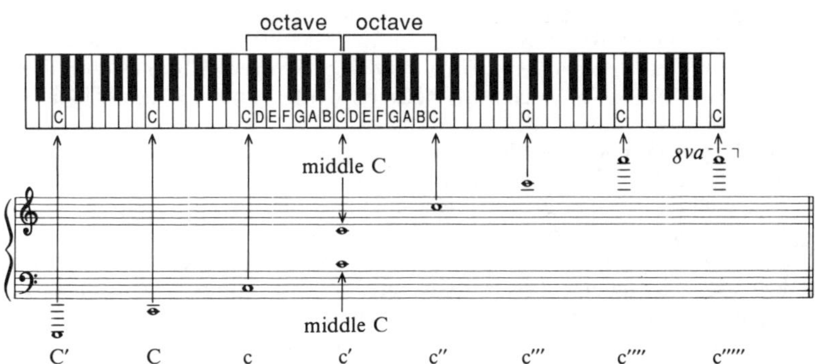

The earliest keyboards included only what we would call the 'white' keys. During the 12th century, a shorter, raised, black key was added (B♭) by cutting away a section of the white keys A and B. Early in the 14th century, two other black keys, F♯ and G♯, were added; then before long, the remaining two: C♯ and E♭. As the diagram on the right shows, the black keys take their names from their neighbouring white keys; and accordingly, each has two names.

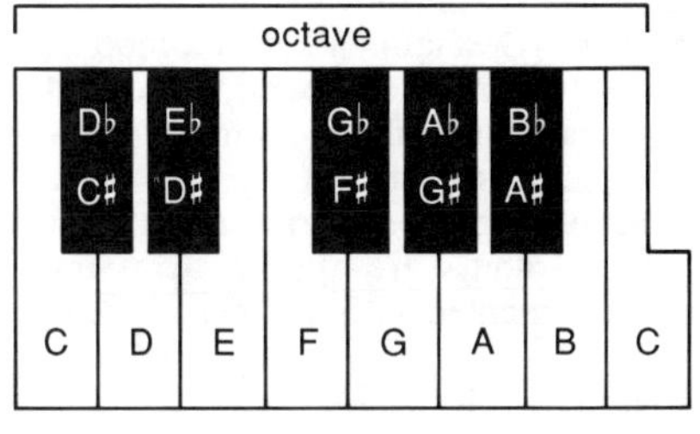

[See also: *Manual; *Pedal-keyboard; *Short octave]

Keyboard instruments Instruments whose sounds are initiated by pressing down levers (keys) on a *keyboard. This group of instruments includes the *piano, various types of *organ (including *portative, *positive, and *regal), the *clavichord, *harpsichord, *spinet, and *virginals. (Although certain other instruments – such as the celesta and accordion – also have a keyboard, they are not usually counted as members of the group.)

Keyboard music A general term for all music written for keyboard instruments; but especially music up to the time of Bach and Handel, a great deal of which was not intended for any one keyboard instrument in particular, but might be played on either organ, harpsichord (or virginals), or clavichord.

Key-centre See *Related keys.

Key-chord The chord or triad built upon the *key-note of a scale.

Key-note The same as *tonic – the first note of the scale of a key (major or minor) which gives its name to the key. For example, the note C is the key-note of the keys C major and C minor.

Key signature The sharps or flats which are printed at the beginning of each stave, straight after the clef, which 'signify' the key of the piece. However, (1) each key signature is shared by two keys – a major key, and its relative minor, whose scale begins three semitones lower (see *relative keys); and (2) the key signature for C major and A minor, needing neither sharps nor flats, is a 'blank'. [See the table of Key signatures on page 389]

Kinderscenen (Scenes from Childhood) Thirteen short piano pieces, Opus 15, composed by Schumann in 1838. Each piece has a descriptive title, the seventh being the well-known *Träumerei* (Dreaming, or Reverie).

Kindertotenlieder (Songs upon the death of children) A *song-cycle for voice and orchestra (or piano) composed by Mahler between 1901 and 1904. The five songs are settings of poems by Rückert, written after the death of his two children.

'King of Prussia' Quartets See *'Prussian' Quartets 2.

King's Hunt, The Title of a set of variations by John Bull, included in the *Fitzwilliam Virginal Book as item number 135. The music is programmatic (see *programme music), vividly conjuring up the sights and sounds of the hunt: jingling harnesses, galloping hooves, and hunting calls. Bull gradually increases the excitement by introducing more decorations, repeated notes, and rapid runs passing from one hand to the other.

Kirche [German] Church. **Kirchenkantate**, church cantata.

Kit A miniature type of violin once used by dancing-masters, and small enough to be carried in the tail-pocket of a frock coat. The French name is *pochette* ('little pocket').

Kk See *K 2.

Klagend [German] Plaintive, mournful.

Klang [German] **1** Sound, or sonority. **2** Also used to mean 'chord'.

Klangfarbe [German] Tone-colour, timbre, tone-quality.

Klangfarbenmelodie [German: 'tone-colour-melody'] A term invented by Schoenberg to describe a device in composing in which constantly varying tone-colours are applied to a single pitch, or to different pitches. He had experimented with this idea in the third of his *Five Pieces for Orchestra*, Op. 19 (1909).

Klarinette (plural: *Klarinetten*) [German] Clarinet.

Klavichord [German] Clavichord.

Klavier (*Clavier*) A German word (borrowed from French) used to mean **1** keyboard; or **2** the piano – though before the 19th century it could refer to other keyboard instruments with strings, such as the harpsichord and the clavichord.

Klavierauszug [German] Piano arrangement.

Klaviermusik [German] Music for keyboard instrument (especially the piano) but excluding the organ.

Klavierstück (plural: *Klavierstücke*) [German] Piano piece.

Klavierübung See **Clavierübung*.

Klein; **Kleine** [German] Small, little. **Kleine Flöte**, piccolo. **Kleine Trommel**, snare (side) drum.

Kleine Nachtmusik, Eine (A little night-music) Title of one of the most famous of all Mozart's works – his Serenade No. 13 in G major (K525; 1787) for string orchestra, or for string quartet plus double bass. There are four movements: 1 *Allegro* (in sonata form); 2 *Romanze: Andante;* 3 Minuet: *Allegretto*; 4 Rondo: *Allegro*. [See also the music printed under *Sonata form, and under *Minuet and Trio form]

Klingen [German] To sound. **Klingend**, sounding, resonating. **Klingen lassen**, allow to continue to sound or resonate (e.g. a cymbal clash, a stroke on a gong, a piano chord).

Knaben Wunderhorn, Des (Youth's magic horn) A group of twelve songs for voice and orchestra or voice and piano, composed during the 1890s by Mahler, with words based on German folk-poems from a collection with the same title. Mahler also made separate settings of three further poems from the collection. He incorporated some of the songs, or quotations from their music, in his second, third, and fourth symphonies. [See: *'Resurrection' Symphony]

Knarre [German] Ratchet.

Köchel; **Köchel-Verzeichnis** See *K 1.

Kontakte (Contacts) An *electronic work by Stockhausen, composed in 1959–60, and existing in two versions. The first is for four-track tape alone. The second combines electronic sounds on four-track tape with live performance by a percussion player, managing a great variety of instruments, and a pianist, who must play eight percussion instruments in addition to the piano. Stockhausen's aim in composing *Kontakte* in its second version was to seek 'contact' between electronic sounds and instrumental sounds, pitched notes and noises, familiar sounds and unfamiliar sounds – and contact between composer and listener by way of the live performers and the pre-recorded tape.

Kontrabass (plural: *Kontrabässe*) [German] Double bass.

Kontrafagott [German] Double bassoon.

Konzert [German] **1** Concert. **2** *Concerto.

Konzertstück (*Concertstück*) [German] Concert-piece – usually for one (but occasionally for more than one) solo instrument featured against an orchestra – for example, Weber's *Konzertstück* in F minor for piano and orchestra, and Schumann's *Concertstück* in F for four horns and orchestra.

Koppel (*Koppelung*) [German] Coupler on the *organ or the *harpsichord.

Korean temple block See *Woodblocks.

Koto A Japanese plucked string instrument – a long zither with thirteen silk or

koto

nylon strings, equal in length, thickness, and tension, and each of them stretched over a movable bridge. They are plucked with ivory plectrums worn on the thumb, forefinger, and middle finger of the right hand. The player uses the left hand to press down on the strings, behind the bridges, altering the tuning, adding ornaments, and also achieving effects such as vibrato and slides. According to Japanese legend, the shape of the koto symbolizes a crouching dragon.

Kraft [German] Energy, vigour, power. **Kräftig**, energetically, vigorously.

Krakowiak [Polish; French: *cracovienne*] A Polish dance in swift duple time, often with syncopated rhythms, named after the Kraków region of Poland. Chopin composed a *Krakowiak*, Op. 14, for piano and orchestra.

Kreisleriana A suite of eight contrasted piano pieces (Op. 16; 1838) by Schumann, named after a character called Kapellmeister Kreisler invented by the German novelist, E. T. A. Hoffmann. Schumann dedicated the pieces to Chopin. [See also: *'Character' piece]

'Kreutzer' Sonata Nickname of Beethoven's Violin Sonata No. 9 in A major, Op. 47, composed in 1802–3. Beethoven dedicated it to the French violinist, Rodolphe Kreutzer, but it is believed that he never played the work. The first performance was given by the English violinist, George Bridgetower, with Beethoven at the piano. The sonata, which Beethoven described as being 'in a very concerto-like style', is in three movements: 1 *Adagio sostenuto* leading to *Presto* (in sonata form); 2 *Andante* (variations); 3 Finale: *Presto* (in sonata form).

Kreuz [German] The sharp sign (♯).

Krummhorn [German] Crumhorn.

Kuchka See The *Five.

Kunst der Fuge, Die See *The *Art of Fugue.*

Kurz [German] Short, abrupt.

KV See *K 1.

Kyrie eleison [Greek] The opening item of the Ordinary of the *Mass. The complete text consists of three invocations: *Kyrie eleison; Christe eleison; Kyrie eleison* (Lord, have mercy; Christ, have mercy; Lord, have mercy). In a 'ninefold Kyrie', each invocation is sung three times over.

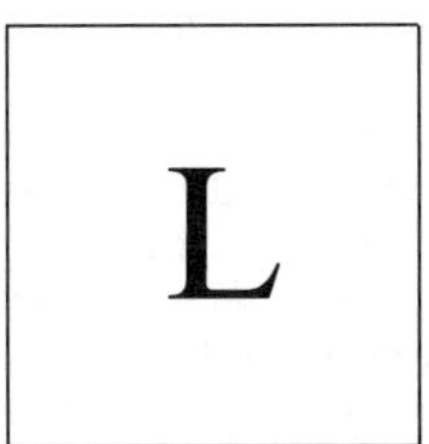

L

L **1** Abbreviation, in piano music, for 'left hand'. **2** Also an abbreviation standing for Longo (Alessandro Longo, Italian pianist and composer) who between 1906 and 1910 published an edition of 544 keyboard sonatas by Domenico Scarlatti. Linked to any of these sonatas, the letter **L** followed by a number identifies that particular sonata in Longo's Edition. [See also: *K 2]

La [French and Italian] The note A.

Lac des cygnes, Le See **Swan Lake.*

Lacrimosa; **Lacrimoso; Lagrimosa; Lagrimoso** [Italian] Tearful, mournful.

Lai (*lay*) [French] A form of narrative poetry and music used by the *trouvères in northern France during the 13th century. Sometimes a *lai* might consist of sixty or more lines, divided into verses of variable length.

Laisser [French] Leave, let, allow. [See also: *Vibrer]

Lamentabile; **Lamentoso** [Italian] Lamenting, sorrowful.

Lamento [Italian] A lament, or dirge.

Landini cadence A cadence in which the leading-note, instead of rising directly to the tonic, passes by way of the submediant (the sixth degree of the scale). Named after the blind Italian Ars Nova composer, Francesco Landini (*c*1325–1397).

Ländler An Austrian and Bavarian country dance with three beats to a bar – rather like a slow waltz, but more heavy-footed. It was originally an outdoor dance but later became a fashionable dance in the ballrooms of Vienna, and sometimes called *deutscher Tanz* ('German Dance'). Mozart, Beethoven, and Schubert each wrote collections of Ländler.

Schubert: Ländler in A major

Land of Hope and Glory See **Pomp and Circumstance.*

Lang; **Lange** [German] Long.

Langsam [German] Slow. **Langsamer**, slower.
Langueur [French] Languor.
Languido [Italian] Languid, languidly.
Largamente [Italian] Broadly; often also implying a more majestic or stately manner of performance and/or a slowing down of the tempo.
Largando [Italian] Broadening, and therefore becoming slower.
Large [French] Broad. **Largement**, broadly.
Larghetto [Italian] Rather broadly (but in speed, not as slow as *Largo). Also used as a title for a (usually fairly short) piece which has a broad, dignified character.
Larghezza [Italian] Breadth, spaciousness.
Larghissimo [Italian] Very broad. [See *Largo]
Largo [Italian] Broad, slow. (Usually indicates a very slow, stately tempo – slower than *Adagio.)
Lark Ascending, The A romance for solo violin and orchestra composed by Vaughan Williams in 1914 (revised in 1920). The music was inspired by a poem of the same title by George Meredith.
'Lark' Quartet (*Lerchenquartett*) Nickname of Haydn's String Quartet in D, Op. 64 No. 5 (1790), so called because of the soaring theme played by the first violin at the beginning. This is the eleventh of the *'Tost' Quartets. It is also occasionally called the 'Hornpipe' Quartet, due to the character of the final movement.
Lassan; **Lassu** See *Csárdás.
'Late quartets' A popular label used in reference to the last five of Beethoven's sixteen string quartets. They are: No. 12 in E♭, Op. 127 (1823–4), in four movements; No. 13 in B♭, Op. 130 (1825–6), in six movements; No. 14 in C♯ minor, Op. 131 (1826), in seven movements; No. 15 in A minor, Op. 132 (1825), in five movements; No. 16 in F, Op. 135 (1826), in four movements. [See also: *Grosse Fuge]
Lauda [laude] **spirituale** (plural: *laude* [*laudi*] *spirituali*) [Italian: 'spiritual praise'] Italian songs of praise and devotion, originally associated with the followers of St Francis of Assisi (*c*1182–1226). The earliest *laude* (from 1250–1400) were *monophonic, and consisted of a series of verses each with a brief refrain. During the 16th and 17th centuries, many *laude* were composed in *polyphonic style. The use of *laude* in 16th-century plays formed the seeds from which *oratorio later grew.
Laute [German]; **Lauto** [Italian] Lute.
Lavolta English name for the Italian dance called the *volta.
Lay See *Lai.
Leader The principal first violinist of an orchestra; also the principal member of a chamber ensemble, such as a string quartet. (In the USA however, an orchestral leader is called a 'concertmaster', and the word 'leader' is often used to mean 'conductor'.)
Leading-motive (leitmotif) [from German: *Leitmotiv*; plural, *Leitmotive*] A distinctive theme or musical idea, recurring throughout a work, and representing a person, an object, an idea or emotion, an event, or a place. The first composer to use leading-motives intensively was Wagner, and nowhere more so than in his cycle of four operas *Der *Ring des Nibelungen* which includes more than a hundred leading-motives. Throughout, Wagner continually develops these symbolic musical ideas in various ways – changing and transforming them, also combining them, according to the changing situation

on stage and the psychological development of the characters. Sometimes leading-motives are heard in the voice-parts. More often, they are woven into the orchestral parts – providing a musical commentary on the drama, and sometimes offering vital information about the characters, revealing their hidden thoughts, memories, emotions, and intentions, which are *not* expressed in the actual words being sung. The following leading-motives from Wagner's *Der Ring des Nibelungen* are: (1) the Gold motive; (2) the Ring motive (absolute power); (3) the Sword motive; (4) Siegfried's horn-call – together with two of its many transformations (4b as it is heard during the funeral march played after his death).

Wagner was not the first to use the principle of the leading-motive. For example, in opera it had occasionally been used by Mozart, and Weber (e.g. his use, in *Der *Freischütz*, of a diminished 7th chord to signify the evil presence of Zamiel); also, in orchestral music, by Berlioz (who called it **idée fixe*), and by Liszt (who used the term *thematic transformation).

Leading-note The seventh step or degree of a major or minor scale. It is a semitone below the tonic, and gives a strong impression of needing to rise, or 'lead', to the tonic. [See: *Degree]

Leap Any melodic *interval greater than a 2nd.

Lebendig [German] Lively, vivacious.

Lebewohl, Das See *Les *Adieux*.

Lebhaft [German] Lively, brisk. **Lebhafter,** brisker. **Lebhaftigkeit,** liveliness, sprightliness.

Ledger lines See *Leger lines.

Legato [Italian: 'bound'] Smooth. A style of playing or singing in which each note flows smoothly into the next without any break. **Legatissimo,** very smooth. [See also: *Staccato; *Bowing]

Legend [German: *Legende*; French: *légende*] Title sometimes used by 19th- and 20th-century composers for a piece whose music is based upon, or merely suggests the mood and character of, a legend. Examples are: Liszt's *Deux Légendes* (1863) for piano solo (St Francis of Assisi preaching to the birds, St François de Paule walking on the water); Dvořák's ten *Legends*, Op. 59, for piano duet (which he also arranged for full orchestra); Bax's *Winter Legends* for piano and orchestra (1930); and Ireland's *Legend* for piano and orchestra (1933).

Leger lines (ledger lines) Extra short lines drawn above or below the stave to accommodate notes whose pitches lie higher or lower than those shown by the stave itself. For example:

Léger; **Légère** [French] Light. **Légèrement**, lightly, nimbly.

Leggero; **Leggiero** [Italian] Light. **Leggerezza**, lightness, nimbleness. **Leggerissimo**, very light, very nimble. **Leggermente, Leggiermente** (but occasionally misspelt *leggeramente* or *leggieramente*), lightly, nimbly.

Leggiadro [Italian] Graceful, charming. **Leggiadramente**, gracefully.

Legni See under *Legno.

Legno [Italian] Wood. **Col legno** ('with the wood'), instruction to players of bowed string instruments to turn the *bow over and use the wooden part on the strings instead of the horse-hair; **legno battuto**, beat the strings with the wood of the bow. **Strumenti di legno** (or simply **legni**), woodwind instruments. **Bacchetta di legno**, wooden-headed drumstick.

Leicht [German] **1** Light. **2** Easy.

Leid [German] Sorrow.

Leis; **Leise** [German] Soft, gentle.

Leitmotif; **Leitmotiv** See *Leading-motive.

Leningrad Symphony Shostakovich's title for his Symphony No. 7 in C, Op. 60, composed in 1941 during the German siege of Leningrad. Shostakovich had been warned to leave Leningrad as the Germans were advancing, but remained through the siege as a fire-fighter. The symphony is in four movements, the first including a lengthy section in which a march-tune, accompanied by a persistent snare drum rhythm, is repeated over and over with changing orchestration. (It was this tune that Bartók parodied in the fourth movement of his Concerto for Orchestra.)

Lent; **Lente** [French] Slow. **Lentement**, slowly. **Lenteur**, slowness.

Lentamente [Italian] Slowly. **Lentando**, becoming gradually slower.

Lento [Italian] Slow. **Lentissimo** (also **Lento di molto**), extremely slow.

Leonora (Leonore) **Overtures** Three overtures which Beethoven composed for his opera **Fidelio* (which he originally intended to call *Leonore*, after its heroine). *Leonora No. 2* was played at the first performance of the opera in 1805. Beethoven composed *Leonora No. 3* to be performed with his first revision of the opera in 1806. *Leonora No. 1* was composed in 1806–7, but never performed with the opera. In 1814 Beethoven again revised the opera, and composed yet another version of the overture, now known as the *Fidelio Overture*. The three Leonora Overtures are performed nowadays as separate concert overtures. The second and third both include a fanfare played by an off-stage trumpet.

Lesson From the late 16th century to the 18th, a name for an instrumental piece (usually for harpsichord or organ). Some 17th-century composers used the title *lesson* to mean *suite. Purcell's *A Choice Collection of Lessons for the Harpsichord or Spinet* includes eight suites and five separate pieces.

Let's Make an Opera Children's entertainment in two parts by Britten, first produced at the Aldeburgh Festival, Suffolk, in 1949 (text by Eric Crozier). There are roles for children and adults. The first part is a spoken play in which the writing of an opera is discussed and some of it, including four audience songs, rehearsed. The second part is the opera itself, *The Little Sweep*, in which the cruel sweep-master Black Bob (bass) and Clem (tenor) send their 8-year-old apprentice, Sammy, up the narrow nursery chimney of Iken Hall, from which he is rescued by some other children and hidden in the toy cupboard. He is given a bath (though not on stage!) by the nursery maid Rowan (soprano) and almost discovered in hiding by the bossy housekeeper Miss Baggott (contralto). Eventually some children departing for home smuggle him away in a trunk and restore him to his family.

Leuto [Italian] Lute.

Lezghinka An energetic dance of the Mohammedan tribe known as the Lezghians on the borders of the USSR and Iran (Persia). An exciting example, featuring a persistent snare drum rhythm, occurs in Khatchaturian's ballet *Gayaneh*.

L.H.; **l.h.** Abbreviation standing for 'left hand', and also for *linke Hand* [German] which has the same meaning.

Liberamente [Italian]; **Librement** [French] Freely.

Libitum [Latin] Will; pleasure. [See: *Ad libitum]

Librettist One who provides a composer with the *libretto for a work such as an opera or oratorio.

Libretto [Italian: 'booklet'] The text (words) of a composition such as an opera, oratorio, or cantata. Famous partnerships between librettist and composer include: Lorenzo da Ponte and Mozart (*The *Marriage of Figaro; *Don Giovanni*), Arrigo Boito and Verdi (**Otello; *Falstaff*), and of course Gilbert and Sullivan (e.g. *The *Mikado, The *Pirates of Penzance*). Some composers – notably, Wagner – have written their own librettos.

Licenza [Italian] Licence, freedom.

Liebeslieder-Walzer (Love-song waltzes) A set of eighteen songs by Brahms (Op. 52; 1868–9) for soprano, alto, tenor, and bass soloists with accompaniment for piano duet. In 1874 he composed another set of fifteen songs (Op. 65) for the same forces, with the title *Neue Liebeslieder-Walzer* (New love-song waltzes). Both sets were later published (as Op. 52a and Op. 65a) in versions for piano duet alone.

Liebesträume (Dreams of love) Three nocturnes by Liszt which are piano transcriptions he made of three of his songs. *Liebestraum* No. 3, in A flat, is the one which is played most often.

Lied (plural: *Lieder*) In German, the word *Lieder* simply means 'songs' – for example, the songs of the German minnesingers of Medieval times, or the polyphonic *Lied* (often in four voice-parts, and with the melody in the tenor part) which was developed by German Renaissance composers.

However, musicians often use the word 'lieder' with special significance – to refer only to songs by 19th-century German and Austrian Romantic composers, usually for solo voice and piano. The musical structure of a lied most often depends upon the poem being set. A large number of lieder are in **strophic** form ('verse-repeating') in which the same music is basically repeated for each verse of the poem (as in a hymn). If, for one verse, the composer makes a noticeable change (e.g. changing the mode from major to minor, or vice versa) then the lied is described as being in **modified strophic** form. Some lieder are in **ternary** form, A^1 B A^2, in which the middle section (B) provides a definite musical contrast, and A^2 uses the same music as A^1. Many of the finest lieder, however, are **durchkomponiert** (German, 'through-composed'). In this kind of lied there will be little or no musical repetition. The composer allows the words to determine the structure of the music. Throughout, each line of words is set to fresh music, so that the voice-part can more faithfully match the changing mood and dramatic events in the poem.

The first important composer of German lieder was Schubert. He composed more than 600 lieder, touching on every possible mood and emotion, and ranging from strophic songs in a fairly simple style such as *Heidenröslein* (Rose among the heather) and *An die Musik* (To music), to through-composed dramatic songs such as *Erlkönig* (The *Erlking) and *Der Doppelgänger* (The ghostly double). Schubert was one of the first composers to make the piano part really important – rather than serving as a mere support for the voice. In many of his lieder, voice and piano are treated as equal partners. The piano immediately establishes the mood of the song, and may even conjure up vivid pictorial detail: a rippling brook, a moonlit night, a whirring spinning-wheel.

After Schubert, other notable composers of German lieder include Schumann, Brahms, Wolf, Richard Strauss, and Mahler (these last two also composing several lieder with orchestral accompaniment). [See also: **Gretchen am Spinnrade*; *Song-cycle; **Vier ernste Gesänge; *Vier letzte Lieder*]

Liederbuch [German] Songbook.

Lieder eines fahrenden Gesellen (Songs of a wayfaring fellow) A *song-cycle for mezzo-soprano or baritone and orchestra (or piano), composed between 1833 and 1835 by Mahler. The four songs in the cycle, to poems written by Mahler himself, are thematically linked to his Symphony No. 1 in D major.

Liederkreis [German: 'song-circle'] A *song-cycle.

Lieder ohne Worte See **Songs without Words.*

Lied von der Erde, Das (The Song of the Earth) A *song-cycle (or song-symphony) composed by Mahler in 1908–9, for two solo voices (tenor, and either alto or baritone) and orchestra. The six songs are settings of German translations of 8th-century Chinese poems. The titles of the songs are: 1 *Das Trinklied von Jammer der Erde* (The drinking-song of Earth's sorrow); 2 *Der Einsame im Herbst* (The lonely one in Autumn); 3 *Von der Jugend* (A song of youth); 4 *Von der Schönheit* (A song of beauty); 5 *Der Trunkene im Frühling* (The drunken one in Spring); 6 *Der Abschied* (The farewell).

Lieto [Italian] Joyous.

Lieutenant Kijé An orchestral suite, Opus 60, composed by Prokofiev in 1934, and based on music he had written the previous year for a film of the same title. There are five movements: 1 The birth of Kijé; 2 Romance; 3 The wedding of Kijé; 4 Troika (a sleigh ride); 5 The burial of Kijé. The second and fourth movements include an optional part for solo baritone.

Linear counterpoint Term used to describe modern (20th-century) dissonant counterpoint (e.g. by Stravinsky, Bartók, Hindemith) in which two or more melodic lines are woven together in such a way that they spark off clashing dissonances, so that the separate strands in the counterpoint are thrown into sharp relief.

Link A passage of music, usually not more than a few bars long, which is used to smoothly join together two important sections of a piece or a movement, perhaps also changing key.

Linke [German] Left. **Linke Hand** (in piano music), left hand.

'Linz' Symphony Nickname of Mozart's Symphony No. 36 in C (K425), composed and performed during his stay at the home of Count Thun in Linz, Austria, during the autumn of 1783. The symphony is in four movements (all, except the third, in sonata form): 1 *Adagio* leading to *Allegro spiritoso*; 2 *Poco adagio*; 3 Minuet and Trio; 4 *Presto*.

Lira A bowed string instrument of the 15th and 16th centuries, made in two sizes: (1) the **lira da braccio** [Italian, *braccio*: 'arm'] which was held 'on the arm' (against the shoulder or under the chin) and had seven strings – five melody strings plus two drone strings; (2) the larger **lira da gamba** [*gamba*: 'leg'] or **lirone** which was held 'on the leg' (on or between the knees) and had nine to fourteen melody strings plus two drone strings. The lira da braccio is counted as one of the important ancestors of the violin.

Lirico [Italian] Lyric, lyrical.

L'istesso tempo See *Istesso.

Litany A sequence of brief supplications sung or recited by a priest or minister, each one followed by a fixed response from the congregation.

Liturgy The officially authorized rites and services of a Christian church. Music belonging to the liturgy is called **liturgical music**.

Liuto [Italian] Lute.

Lochamer (Locheimer) **Liederbuch** A manuscript (*c*1452–1460) forming the most important source of early German folk-song. Some of the pieces in the collection are monophonic, some are three-part compositions.

Loco [Italian: 'place'] A word immediately following a passage of music affected by an octave sign, warning the performer to return to the normal pitch of the printed notes.

Lohengrin Opera in three acts by Wagner, first produced at Weimar in 1850 (text by the composer after an old epic). The action takes place in the 10th century. In a meadow near Antwerp, by the River Scheldt, Henry the Fowler, King of Germany (bass), learns that Godfrey, heir to the duchy of Brabant, has vanished; also that Godfrey's sister Elsa (soprano) has been accused by their guardian, Frederick of Telramund, of his murder. For this the King orders that Frederick (baritone) must fight a duel with any knight gallant enough to represent Elsa. A boat appears on the river, drawn by a swan and bearing a mysterious stranger. It is Lohengrin (tenor). He pledges himself to fight for Elsa on the understanding that if the victory is his she shall be his bride; but she must never ask him who he is or whence he comes. He wins the fight, and Frederick's wife, Ortrud (mezzo-soprano), plans her revenge. She warns Elsa that her rescuer is a magician concealing his identity for wicked ends. The wedding takes place, but Elsa, sorely troubled, breaks her promise and asks Lohengrin who he is. He tells her. He is the son of Parsifal and comes from Montsalvat, where they keep the Holy Grail. But he is sad, for having revealed his secret he must leave her. The boat returns, but as they watch, the swan is transformed into Godfrey, whom Ortrud has bewitched. As the white dove of the Holy Grail leads Lohengrin away, Elsa sinks lifeless into Godfrey's arms.

Lointain [French] Distant; as if from the distance.

Lombard rhythm (Lombardic rhythm, Lombardy rhythm) A 'reversed' dotted rhythm in which an accented short note is followed by a weaker dotted note. Also called a **Scotch snap** since it is a feature of many Scottish folk-tunes.

Comin' thro' the Rye

London Overture, A A concert overture composed in 1936 by John Ireland. (An earlier version, called *A Comedy Overture*, was written for brass band.) The music is an impression of some of the sights and sounds of London. Ireland said that a bus conductor calling out 'Piccadilly!' had given him the idea for the melody and rhythm of the main theme.

'London' Symphonies Haydn's last twelve symphonies, Nos. 93 to 104, which he composed between 1791 and 1795 for the London impresario, Johann Peter Salomon. They were first performed during Haydn's two visits to London in 1791–2 and 1794–5. They are also known as the 'Salomon' Symphonies. Six of them have individual nicknames: No. 94 in G major, *'Surprise'; No. 96 in D, *'Miracle'; No. 100 in G, *'Military'; No. 101 in D, *'Clock'; No. 103 in E flat, *'Drum Roll'; and, taking its nickname from that of the complete set – No. 104 in D, the *'London' Symphony.

'London' Symphony Haydn's last symphony: No. 104 in D major (see under *'London' Symphonies). It was composed in 1795, and is in four movements: 1 *Adagio* leading to *Allegro* (in sonata form); 2 *Andante* (in a combination of episodical form and variation form); 3 Menuetto: *Allegro*; 4 Finale: *Spiritoso* (in sonata form).

London Symphony, A Title given by Vaughan Williams to his Second Symphony, composed in 1912–13 (revised in 1920, and again in 1933). The music evokes the spirit and atmosphere of London, and includes references such as the Westminster chimes (the chimes of Big Ben), the jingle of hansom cabs, and the street cry of a lavender-seller. The symphony is in four movements: 1 *Lento* leading to *Allegro risoluto*; 2 *Lento*; 3 Scherzo (Nocturne): *Allegro vivace*; 4 *Andante con moto – Maestoso alla marcia – Allegro – Lento* – Epilogue (*Andante sostenuto*).

Long; **Longue** [French] Long.

Lontano [Italian] Distant, remote; as if coming from the distance.

Loud and soft signs See *Dynamic markings; also Table 6 on page 390.

Loud pedal The name sometimes used (but incorrectly) for the sustaining pedal on the *piano.

Lourd [French] Heavy, weighty. **Lourdement**, heavily, weightily.

Loure **1** French name for a type of bagpipe, found particularly in Normandy. **2** A French dance, popular during the late 17th and early 18th centuries. It was in slow $\frac{6}{4}$ time and rather like a slow gigue, but made a feature of dotted rhythms. Bach includes a Loure (incorrectly titled 'Bourrée II' in some editions) in his fifth French Suite:

Bach: Loure, from French Suite No. 5 in G

(etc.)

Love, the Magician See *El* **Amor brujo*.

Lower mordent See *Ornaments.

Lt. Kijé See **Lieutenant Kijé*.

Lucia di Lammermoor Opera in three acts by Donizetti, first produced in Naples in 1835 (text by Cammarano based on Scott's *The Bride of Lammermoor*). The setting is Scotland in about 1700. An age-old feud divides the Ashton and Ravenswood families. To his horror Sir Henry Ashton (baritone) learns that his sister Lucy (the 'Lucia' of the title) is in love with Edgar of Ravenswood. Edgar (tenor) leaves for France on a diplomatic mission, and hoping to marry off Lucy (soprano) to the wealthy Laird of Bucklaw and at the same time to ruin Edgar, Sir Henry forges a letter to Lucy, purportedly from Edgar, breaking off the relationship. Bucklaw (tenor) arrives, and Lucy grudgingly agrees to marry him, but Edgar, back from France, appears dramatically and denounces them all. In a raging storm outside Ravenswood Castle, Edgar foresees his fate. Sir Henry gloatingly informs him that Lucy has become Bucklaw's bride, but the wedding festivities are interrupted by the discovery that she has gone mad and murdered her bridegroom. She appears, the famous 'Mad Scene' takes place, and she herself dies. In the final act Edgar, standing amid his ancestors' tombs, sees Lucy's funeral procession pass and, tormented with grief, stabs himself.

Lugubre [Italian] Lugubrious.

Lungo; **Lunga** [Italian] Long, lengthy. **Lunga pausa**, 'long rest', and so indicating a lengthy pause.

Lusingando [Italian: 'flattering'] In a tender, coaxing manner.

Lustig [German] Merry, cheerful.

Lute (from Arabic, *'ūd*, meaning 'wood') [French: *luth*; German: *Laute*; Italian: *lauto, leuto, liuto*] A plucked string instrument (originating in the East) extensively used throughout Europe from Medieval times to the 18th century. The lute became particularly popular during the 16th century. It was used to accompany the voice, and was often included in consort music. Also, a great deal of solo music was written for the lute – both original compositions, such as fantasias, variations, and dances, and also arrangements for lute of vocal pieces such as motets, madrigals, and chansons.

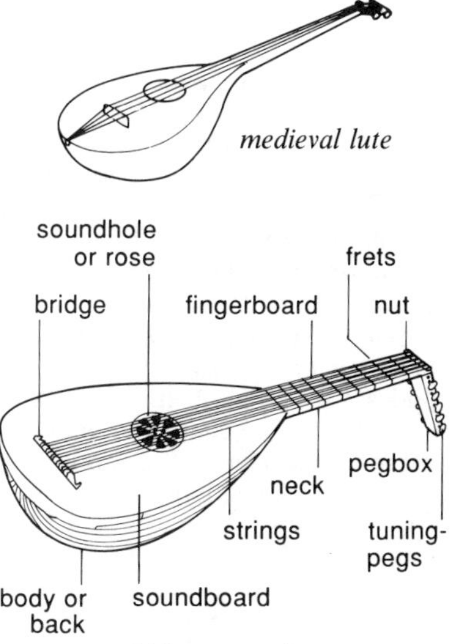

medieval lute

16th-century lute

The typical 16th-century lute had a rounded back, and was shaped like half a pear. The pegbox was bent back at an angle, and the fingerboard had *frets. Lutes were made in several sizes. The strings were always of gut, and though the number varied there were often eleven – ten tuned in pairs, or double *courses, plus a single top string known as the *chanterelle* (meaning 'the singing one'). A typical tuning was: G, C, F, A, D, G (the lowest string being G on the lowest line of the bass clef). Music for lute was usually written in *tablature.

[See also: *Archlute; *Theorbo; *Mandolin. Also: *Biwa; *P'i-p'a; *San-hsien; *Sarod; *Shamisen; *Sitar; *Tamburā; *'Ūd; *Vīṇā; *Yüeh-ch'in]

Lute stop See under *Harpsichord.

Luth [French] Lute.

Lydian mode See *Church modes.

Lyra-glockenspiel See under *Glockenspiel.

Lyra viol A type of small bass *viol.

Lyre An ancient string instrument, existing in many forms (the earliest known example dating from around 3,000 BC), the strings usually plucked, though in some cases played with a bow. A lyre consists of a soundbox with two projecting arms, the strings stretched from the soundbox to a 'yoke' or crossbar.

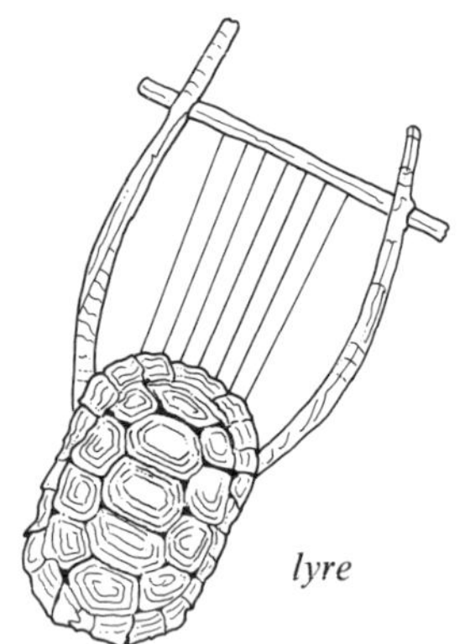

lyre

Lyric Piece A shortish instrumental piece, expressive and tuneful in style. (Grieg composed ten books of *Lyric Pieces* for piano solo.)

Lyric Pieces Ten books of piano pieces by Grieg, composed between 1884 and 1901. Each piece has a descriptive title – for example: *Night Watchman's Song* (Book 1); *Butterfly, The Lonely Wanderer,* and *To the Spring* (Book 3); *Wedding Day at Troldhaugen* (Book 8). This last piece was later arranged for piano duet by Grieg, and for orchestra by Huppertz.

Lyrics The text, or words, of a 20th-century pop song or musical show.

Lyric Suite **1** A suite for orchestra (1904) which is Grieg's arrangement of four of his six Lyric Pieces for piano (Book 5), Op. 54. The titles are: Shepherd Boy; Norwegian March; Nocturne; March of the Dwarfs.

2 A work for string quartet, composed by Alban Berg in 1925–6. There are six movements, alternately quick and slow, and planned in such a way that the quick movements get quicker and the slow movements get slower: 1 *Allegretto gioviale*; 2 *Andante amoroso*; 3 *Allegro misterioso*, with *Trio estatico*; 4 *Adagio appassionato*; 5 *Presto delirando . . . Tenebroso*; 6 *Largo desolato*. Movements 2 and 4 are atonal; 1 and 6, the *Allegro misterioso* of 3, and the *Tenebroso* sections of 5 are composed in *twelve-note or serial technique. In 1928, Berg arranged movements 2, 3, and 4 for string orchestra.

Lyrische [German] Lyric.

M; m Abbreviation standing for: **1** manual (keyboard); **2** metronome; **3** *main* [French] or *mano* [Italian], hand; **4** *menuetto* or *minuetto*, as in M.D.C. standing for *Minuetto da capo*; **5** *mezza* or *mezzo* [Italian], half; **6** minor (e.g. Gm = G minor).

Ma [Italian] But.

Madama Butterfly Opera by Puccini, originally in two acts (though later revised), first produced in Milan in 1904 (libretto by Giacosa and Illica after the drama by David Belasco). Pinkerton (tenor), an American naval officer serving in Japan, falls in love with a dancer, Cio-Cio-San (soprano), who is also known as Butterfly. In spite of warnings from the American consul Sharpless (baritone) and opposition from the girl's uncle, the couple wed. Pinkerton, recalled to America, assures Butterfly that he will return. Eagerly she awaits him with the infant son born shortly after his departure. But Pinkerton does not regard the Japanese wedding ceremony as binding, and three years later, when he does return, he brings with him a new American wife. Butterfly is devastated, and Pinkerton, overcome with shame, offers to adopt the child. Unemotionally Butterfly agrees: if he will leave her for half an hour he may then take the boy away. Pinkerton withdraws. Left on her own, Butterfly embraces the child. Then, taking down her father's sword from the wall, she falls on it and dies.

Madrigal This word has two meanings. **1** In the 14th century, the madrigal was one of the three main forms of poetry and music (along with the *ballata and the *caccia) used by Italian *Ars Nova composers, such as Jacopo da Bologna and Francesco Landini. The music was composed in two (sometimes three) voice-parts, the upper in a very decorative and florid style in quickish note-values, and the lower one in a simpler style in notes of longer value. The poem consisted of two or three stanzas (verses) of three lines each, set to identical music, followed by a final stanza of two lines, set to different music. Examples are the madrigals *Una colomba candida* (A gentle white dove) by Francesco Landini, and *Non suo amante* (Never did Diana please her lover so much) by Jacopo da Bologna.

2 More commonly, the word 'madrigal' refers to a type of secular vocal composition which originated in Italy in the 16th century. It had no musical connection with the early madrigal (described above) but in fact descended from the *frottola. The music, setting a poem which was most often pastoral or amorous, was written for three to six solo voices, usually unaccompanied. The first examples were mainly homophonic, but composers were soon using a polyphonic style (similar to that of the 16th-century motet).

In 1588, a collection of Italian madrigals with English words was published in England. This book caused much interest and English composers were soon writing their own madrigals which were performed, usually with one singer per part, in the homes of keen music-lovers everywhere (it was a time when Elizabethan England was described as 'a neste of syngynge byrdes'). There came to be three main kinds of English madrigal: the *ballett, the *ayre (particularly when all the parts were sung), and the madrigal proper.

A 'madrigal proper' is composed for three to six unaccompanied solo voices, each given an interesting melodic line to sing. The composer makes much use of *imitation (see also *point). In this way, all the voices are given equal importance, often weaving in and out and following their own independent rhythms to create a springy, contrapuntal musical texture. This kind of madrigal is 'through-composed' – meaning that throughout there will be little or no musical repetition, each line of words being set to fresh music (though there will often be a good deal of repetition within the words themselves). Words and music are closely matched, and the composer seizes every chance to introduce *word-painting – vivid musical illustrations to bring out the special meaning of certain words in the poem.

The following are a few typical examples from the huge repertory of 16th-century madrigals. [*Italian*] Arcadelt: *Il bianco e dolce cigno* (The sweet white swan) for 4 voices; Marenzio: *Occhi lucenti e belle* (Beautiful sparkling eyes), 5 voices; Monteverdi: *O Primavera* (O Spring), 5 voices; Gesualdo: *Mille volti il di moro* (A thousand times a day I die), 5 voices. [*English*] Byrd: *This sweet and merry month of May*, 6 voices; Morley: *April is in my mistress' face*, 4 voices; Bennet: *All creatures now are merry-minded*, 5 voices; Weelkes: *As Vesta was from Latmos Hill descending*, 6 voices; Wilbye: *Sweet honey-sucking bees*, 5 voices; Vautor: *Sweet Suffolk owl*, 5 voices.

[See also: *Ballett; *Ayre; *The *Triumphes of Oriana*]

Maelzel See under *Metronome.

Maestà [Italian] Majesty, dignity, grandeur. **Maestoso**, Majestic, stately.

Maestrale [Italian] Masterly.

Maestro [Italian] Master.

Maestro di capella [Italian] The musical director of a chapel. [See also: *Kapellmeister]

Maggiore [Italian] Major (key). Also used as a heading (e.g. in variations, or for the middle section of a piece in ternary form) to indicate a sudden switch from minor to major. [See also: *Minore]

Magic Flute, The (*Die Zauberflöte*) A *Singspiel, in two acts, by Mozart, first produced in Vienna in 1791 (libretto by Schikaneder based on an Oriental fairy tale). Tamino (tenor) is saved from a huge snake by three ladies-in-waiting to the Queen of Night. He mistakenly imagines the bird-catcher Papageno to have been his rescuer, and for encouraging this belief Papageno (baritone) is punished by having his mouth padlocked. Tamino is shown a portrait of the Queen's daughter Pamina, and learns that she has been carried off by the evil Sarastro and is captive in his castle, guarded by Monostatos (tenor), a wicked Moor. Falling in love with the portrait, Tamino vows that he and Papageno will save Pamina, and for protection they are given a magic flute and a chime of bells. Sarastro (bass) turns out to be not an ogre but a wise priest, holding Pamina (soprano) to protect her from the real villain, the Queen herself. When she has acquired wisdom he will free her. Tamino and Papageno undergo initiation ordeals, and a vow of silence which almost drives Pamina to suicide. Papageno longs for a wife, and an old woman turns into the beautiful

Papagena (soprano). They meet, and she is immediately snatched away. Eventually, protected by the magic flute, Tamino and Pamina pass through fire and water and are welcomed to Sarastro's temple. Papagena is restored, the lovers reunited, and the opera ends with a chorus of rejoicing.

Magnificat The hymn or canticle of the Virgin Mary, beginning 'My soul doth magnify the Lord' (Luke 1: 46–55). It is sung at Vespers in the Roman Catholic Church, at Evensong in the Anglican Church. Notable settings of the Magnificat include those by Palestrina, Schütz, and Bach (Magnificat in D, for two sopranos, alto, tenor, and bass, chorus, and orchestra).

Mailloche [French] The heavy, two-headed drumstick occasionally used to play the bass drum.

Main [French] Hand. **Main droite** (or **m.d.**), right hand; **main gauche** (or **m.g.**), left hand; **à deux mains**, for two hands; **à quatre mains**, for four hands.

Mainstream A *jazz term introduced in the late 1950s to describe the 'central' type of jazz whose style fell between the two extremes of *traditional jazz and *modern jazz. Used to describe the jazz of such musicians as Count Basie, Duke Ellington, Coleman Hawkins, Humphrey Lyttelton.

Mais [French] But.

Majeur [French] Major (key).

Major A word meaning 'greater'. **Major intervals** are those lying between the tonic and 2nd, 3rd, 6th, or 7th degrees of any major scale. In C major, for instance, C–E is a major 3rd (see *intervals). A **major triad** is one which has a major 3rd and perfect 5th above the root (see *triad). A **major scale** is one in which there is a semitone between the 3rd and 4th, and the 7th and 8th degrees, elsewhere the degrees being separated by a tone (see *scale). The main characteristic of a major scale is that the 3rd degree lies a major 3rd above the tonic. A **major key** is the key based on the scale of the same name. [See also: *Minor; *Mode, 2]

Mal [German] Time. **Einmal**, once; **zweimal**, twice; **das erste Mal**, the first time; **das zweite Mal**, the second time; **noch einmal**, once more, over again.

Malagueña A dance from the provinces of Málaga and Murcia in southern Spain. It is in fact a variety of *fandango. Examples include the well-known *Malagueña* by the Cuban composer Ernesto Lecuona, and *Málaga* from **Iberia* by Albéniz.

Malinconia [Italian] Melancholy, sadness. **Malinconico**, melancholy, sad.

Ma mère l'oye See *'*Mother Goose' Suite*.

Mancando [Italian] Fading away; waning or decreasing in volume.

Mandolin (mandoline) A small instrument of the *lute family, originating in Italy probably in the 15th century. The body is shaped like half a pear, and the neck is slightly bent back. There are usually eight wire strings, arranged in pairs and tuned to the same pitches as a violin (G, D, A, E). The strings, plucked with a plectrum, may be played with single strokes (as on a guitar), or in *tremolando* ('trembling') style in which notes are sustained by a swiftly-repeated vi-

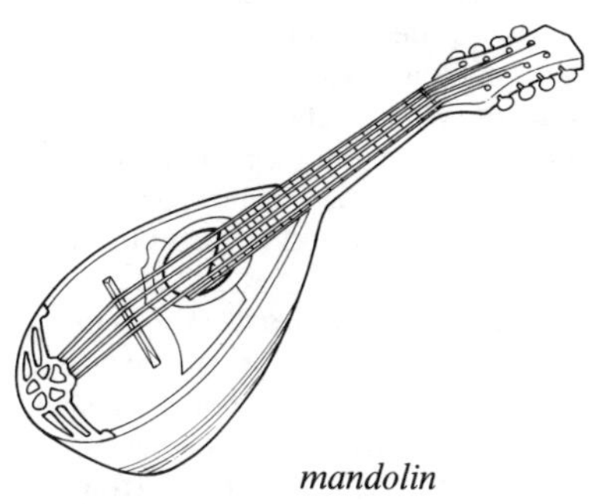
mandolin

brating movement of the plectrum. Vivaldi and Hummel each wrote concertos for the mandolin; the instrument is also included in Schoenberg's *Serenade*, Op. 24, and in the last three of Webern's *Five Pieces for Orchestra*, Op. 10.

Manfred **1** Incidental music (Op. 115; 1848–9) by Schumann to Byron's verse drama of the same title. **2** A programme symphony (unnumbered) by Tchaikovsky, based on Byron's verse drama. It is in four movements, each with a detailed descriptive heading, and was composed in 1885.

Mani [Italian] Hands. [See also: *Mano]

Manicorde [French]; **Manicordo** [Italian] Clavichord.

Maniera [Italian] Manner, fashion, style.

Mannheim School The name given to a group of composers working at the Court of Mannheim in Germany around the middle of the 18th century. These composers played an important part in shaping and developing the early symphony, before Haydn and Mozart. Most notable among them were Johann Stamitz (1717–57), Franz Xaver Richter (1709–89), and Christian Cannabich (1731–98).

In 1750, Stamitz was appointed Director of instrumental music, and under his training and direction the **Mannheim Court Orchestra** became famous throughout Europe for its excellent performing technique – the fire and drive of its playing, its polished phrasing, unanimity of bowing, and precise ensemble. The orchestra, and the Mannheim composers who wrote for it, also became notorious for certain sonic 'effects'. These included the so-called 'Mannheim steamroller' – a long-drawn *crescendo* usually above repeated notes in the bass, the 'Mannheim sky-rocket' – an arpeggio theme surging swiftly upwards, and the 'Mannheim birdies' – trills, and other bird-like figurations. There were also frequent *tremolo* passages, contrasts of timbre, and abrupt changes of dynamics: sudden *fortes*, swift *diminuendos*, *forte* immediately followed by *piano*.

Mano [Italian] Hand. **Mano destra** (or **m.d.**), right hand; **mano sinistra** (or **m.s.**), left hand; **a due mani**, for two hands; **a quattro mani**, for four hands.

Manual [from Latin, *manus*: 'hand'] The name given to a keyboard of an organ or a harpsichord.

'Manzoni' Requiem The name sometimes given to Verdi's Requiem, composed in 1874 in memory of Alessandro Manzoni, an Italian poet and novelist.

Maracas Latin-American percussion instruments consisting, in their original form (invented by South American Indians), of hollow dried gourds inside which seeds rattle when shaken. Modern imitations, made of wood, plastic, or some other material, may be filled with beads or lead-shot. Maracas are usually played in pairs, one held in each hand.

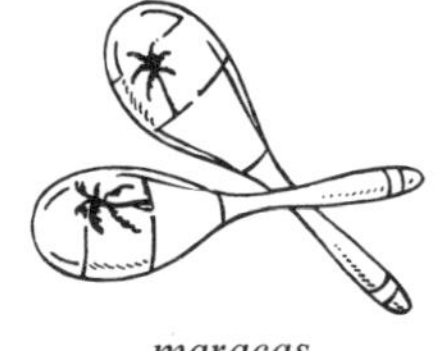
maracas

Maracas can be heard, alternating with tambourine (see music example), in *Dance of the Antilles Girls* (sometimes called *Dance of the Maidens with the Lilies*) from Prokofiev's *Romeo and Juliet*; and,

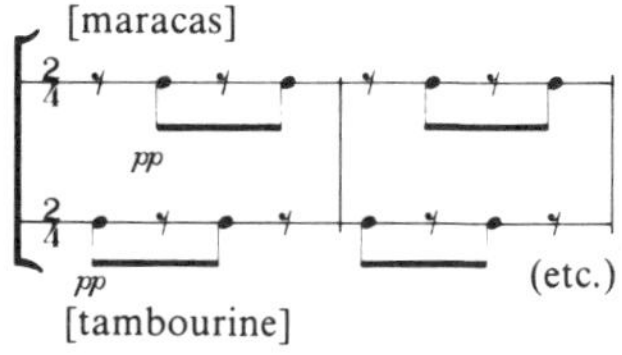

played vigorously, in Walton's *St Johannesburg Festival Overture* (at around three and a half minutes from the start). They can also be heard in many pieces by the Cuban composer, Lecuona (e.g. *Danza lucumí*) and in most pieces played by Latin-American dance bands.

Marcato [Italian] Marked, emphasized, accented; also used to indicate that a melody, bass-line, or inner part should be strongly brought out. Also: **ben marcato**, well marked; **marcatissimo**, extremely marked or emphasized.

Marcellus Mass See **Missa Papae Marcelli.*

March A composition intended to accompany the marching or ceremonial progression of a group of people, soldiers in particular. Typically, a march is in strongly-marked duple or quadruple time (e.g. $\frac{2}{4}$ or $\frac{4}{4}$, sometimes $\frac{6}{8}$ for a quick march). In structure, the music often consists of the alternation of a main section with a contrasting trio section. Examples of famous marches include the *Wedding March* from Mendelssohn's incidental music to *A *Midsummer Night's Dream*, the **Rákóczi March*, Strauss's **Radetzky March*, the *Grand March* from Verdi's opera *Aida*, *Siegfried's Funeral March* from *Götterdämmerung* by Wagner, Elgar's **Pomp and Circumstance Marches*, and marches by John Philip Sousa such as *Semper Fidelis*, *The Washington Post*, and *The Stars and Stripes Forever*.

Marche [French] March.

Marche Slave A 'Slavonic march' composed by Tchaikovsky in 1876 for a concert given in aid of Serbian soldiers who had been wounded in the war against Turkey. It includes several traditional tunes, both Serbian and Slavonic, as well as the Russian national anthem.

Marcia [Italian] March. **Alla marcia**, in the style or manner of a march. **Tempo di marcia**, in march time.

Marimba A Latin-American percussion instrument of African origin. It is similar to the xylophone but larger, and with a bulb-shaped tuned resonator below each wooden bar. It is pitched one octave below the xylophone, and the tone is more mellow. The **marimbaphone** is similar, but the bars are of metal instead of wood.

Markiert [German]; **Marqué** [French] Marked. (Same as Italian: **marcato*.)

Marriage of Figaro, The (*Le nozze di Figaro*) Opera in four acts by Mozart, first produced in Vienna in 1786 (libretto by da Ponte after Beaumarchais's comedy). The action takes place within a single day. Figaro (baritone), valet to Count Almaviva, is to marry Susanna (soprano), the Countess's maid, but he has rashly promised himself also to Dr Bartolo's elderly housekeeper Marcellina (mezzo-soprano). The Count too is pursuing Susanna, while Cherubino (soprano), a page-boy, is flirting so outrageously that he is ordered off to join the army. The Count (baritone) arranges a rendezvous with Susanna, but the resourceful Figaro devises a plan to send Cherubino, suitably diguised, to keep the date instead. As he tries on Susanna's clothes Cherubino is almost caught by the Count, but he escapes by jumping from a window. Figaro is saved from marrying Marcellina by the discovery that he is her long-lost son, Bartolo being the father. She gives him a dowry and embraces him, to the dismay of Susanna who, entering quickly, misunderstands the situation. The Countess (soprano), tired of her husband's flirtations with other women, resolves to confront him. She dictates to Susanna a letter, purporting to be from the maid herself, inviting the Count to meet her in the garden at night. The two women then switch dresses, to the confusion of both the Count (who finds that he is making advances to his own wife) and Figaro (who takes her to be Susanna). The opera ends happily, with all the couples united.

Marsch [German] March.

Martelé [French]; **Martellato** [Italian] Hammered. Used mainly as a direction to players of bowed string instruments (the violin, etc.) to bow the notes separately with heavy, short, vigorous up-and-down strokes. Usually, the point of the bow is used; *martelé au talon* indicates that the heel of the bow should be used. **Martellato** is also sometimes used in 20th-century piano music, directing the player to use extreme force (often involving use of the hands in swift alternation, acting like hammers).

Martenot See *Ondes Martenot.

Marziale [Italian] Martial, war-like – as for example in *Allegro marziale*.

Masculine cadence See under *Cadences.

Mask; **Maske** See *Masque.

Masque (mask, maske) A type of court entertainment of the 16th and 17th centuries, combining poetry and dancing with vocal and instrumental music, acted out in costume, with scenery and often elaborate scenic effects. The masque originated in Italy and France; it was introduced into England in the 16th century and remained popular till after the Restoration. Examples are Thomas Campion's *Lord Hayes Masque* (1607) and James Shirley's *The Triumph of Peace* (1634).

Mass The central and most solemn service of the Roman Catholic Church, commemorating the Last Supper and Christ's Crucifixion and Resurrection. The musical items of the mass, sung in Latin, fall into two categories: (i) the **Proper** – those items whose texts vary according to (are 'proper' to) the day or season, and these are the Introit, Gradual, Alleluia, Offertory, and Communion; and (ii) the **Ordinary** – those items whose texts are invariable, regardless of day or season, and these consist of:

1 **Kyrie** (Lord, have mercy; Christ, have mercy)
2 **Gloria** (Glory to God in the highest)
3 **Credo** (I believe in one God)
4 **Sanctus** (Holy, holy, holy), **Osanna** (Hosanna), and **Benedictus** (Blessed is he that cometh in the name of the Lord)
5 **Agnus Dei** (Lamb of God)

At the end of the service are sung the words *Ite missa est* (Go, ye are sent forth), and it is from this Latin word *missa* that the Mass originally took its name. In musical terms, the title 'Mass' implies a setting of the five items of the Ordinary, possibly with the addition of *Ite missa est*.

The earliest settings of the Mass were in plainsong. In the 12th century, composers began to make polyphonic settings of the items of the Mass, basing the music on one of the original plainchants as a *cantus firmus. The earliest known complete polyphonic setting of the Ordinary of the Mass by a single composer is the **Messe de Notre Dame* by the French composer, Guillaume de Machaut (*c*1300–1377). Numerous 15th- and 16th-century composers made settings of the Mass – among the more notable being Dufay, Josquin, Palestrina (105 settings), Lassus (about 100), Byrd, and Victoria. Later composers include Bach, Haydn, Mozart, Beethoven, Schubert, and Bruckner; and, among 20th-century composers, Vaughan Williams, Kodály, Stravinsky, and Britten. [See also: *L'*Homme armé*; **Missa Papae Marcelli*; **B minor Mass*; *Parody mass; *Requiem]

Mässig [German] Moderate; moderately. **Mässig bewegt**, moderately moved (i.e. not very quick).

Master of the King's (Queen's) **Music** (Musick) A post dating back at least to the first half of the 17th century, when Charles I had a band of musicians in charge of which he appointed a Master. Charles II maintained a sizeable group of musicians, the 'King's Music', including a string orchestra of twenty-four players – in imitation of the *Vingt-quatre Violons* of Louis XIV, the 'Sun King' of France. Nowadays, the duties of the Master only involve the composing of certain pieces (such as fanfares, marches) for state and royal occasions. Composers who have held the post of Master include: Nicholas Lanier (from 1625–49 and 1660–66), William Boyce (from 1755–79), Edward Elgar (from 1924–34), Arnold Bax (from 1942–53), Arthur Bliss (from 1953–75), Malcolm Williamson (from 1975).

Mastersingers See *Meistersinger.

Mastersingers of Nuremberg, The See *Die *Meistersinger von Nürnberg.*

Master stretto; **Masterly stretto** See under *Fugue.

Matachin (mattachins) A sword dance, of ancient origin, performed by men in silvered or gilded armour. It is also known as 'Les bouffons'. An example occurs in Warlock's **Capriol Suite*:

Mathis der Maler (Matthias the painter) **1** An opera by Hindemith, composed between 1933 and 1935, and based on the life of Matthias Grünewald (*c*1480–1528) and the nine scenes he painted for the altar of St Anthony's Church at Isenheim in Germany. **2** A symphony by Hindemith, composed in 1934, based on music from his opera. The three movements are entitled: 1 *Engelkonzert* (Concert of the Angels); 2 *Grablegung* (The Entombment of Christ); 3 *Versuchung des heiligen Antonius* (The Temptation of St Anthony).

Matin, Le; Le Midi; Le Soir (Morning; Midday; Evening) Titles of three symphonies composed by Haydn in 1761 – No. 6 in D; No. 7 in C; and No. 8 in G, the last movement of which is entitled *La tempesta* (The storm). During these three symphonies, Haydn often selects different members of the orchestra to play interesting solos.

Matins The first of the eight services of the day (the Divine *Office, Canonical Hours, Daily Hours) of the Roman Catholic Church, often taking place around 3 o'clock in the morning. [See also: *Te Deum]

Má vlast (My Country) A cycle of six symphonic poems composed by Smetana between 1872 and 1879, inspired by Czech scenes, legends, and history. They are: 1 *Vyšehrad* (The High Castle); 2 *Vltava* (the river, also known as the Moldau, which flows through Prague); 3 *Šárka* (the ruthless female warrior of Czech folk history); 4 *From Bohemia's Meadows and Forests*; 5 *Tábor* (an ancient Czech fortress city, stronghold of the Hussites); 6 *Blaník* (a mountain near Prague within which, according to legend, the Hussite heroes lie sleeping until required to defend their country should freedom be threatened).

Mazurka [from Polish: *mazur*] A Polish country dance named after the Mazurs who inhabited the plains around Warsaw. A mazurka is in triple time, moderate to quick in speed, and is characterized by dotted rhythms, often with an accent occurring on the second or third beat of the bar. Chopin composed over fifty mazurkas for solo piano.

Chopin: Mazurka in A minor, Op. 33 No. 3

M.D.; **m.d.** Abbreviation of *mano destra* [Italian] or *main droite* [French], right hand.

Mean-tone temperament See *Temperament.

Measure **1** A *bar. **2** Old English name for any kind of dance-tune.

Mediant [from a Latin word meaning 'middle'] The third step or degree of a major or minor scale, so called because of its intermediate, or midway, position between the two most important notes: the tonic (or key-note) and the dominant. The mediant determines whether a scale is major or minor; e.g. the mediant of C major is E; the mediant of C minor is E♭. [See: *Degree]

Medieval bells See *Chime bells.

Medieval fiddle (fidel, fiedel, fithele, fidula, vielle, etc.) A bowed string instrument (slightly larger than the modern viola) popular from the 12th century to the 15th. The body was shaped rather like a figure eight, and there were usually five strings, the lowest often used as a drone. The bridge was fairly flat, so that three or more strings could easily be bowed at once. The medieval fiddle was one of the important ancestors of the violin.

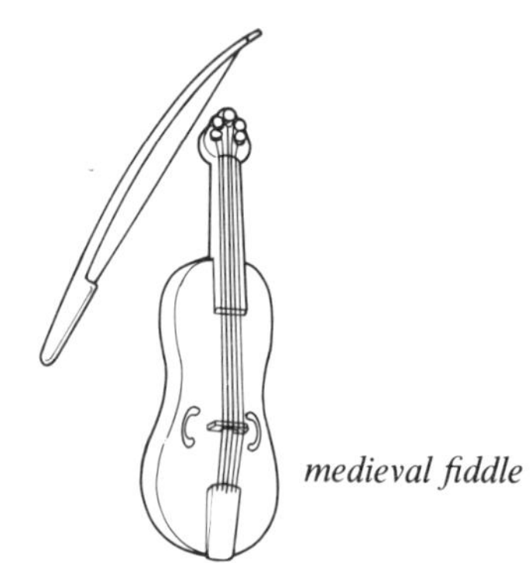
medieval fiddle

Medieval music Music 'of the Middle Ages' – in the *history of Western music, the period from about 500 to around 1450. Few very early examples of secular (non-sacred) music, such as songs and dances, have come down to us, since this kind of music was rarely written down. And so most of the music which has survived from before the 12th century is that which was composed for the various services of the Church.

This music, known as *plainsong or plainchant, was monophonic – consisting of a single melodic line. The voices sang in unison, with no supporting chords or harmonies. The melodies were built from scales called modes (see *church modes). From the 9th to the 13th centuries, additions were made to the chants in the form of *tropes.

The earliest experiments in composing *polyphonic music (music in more than one voice-part) began in the 9th century and continued with further elaboration until the early part of the 13th. These early examples of polyphony are called *organum (see also *cantus firmus).

Music composed during the late 12th and 13th centuries is known as *Ars Antiqua. Besides organum, other forms of music composed at this time included the polyphonic *conductus, *clausula, and early *motet. There was also an important flowering of monophonic songs composed by the *troubadours, *trouvères, and *minnesingers (see also *minstrels and *jongleurs).

An important turning-point in the history of Western music occurred around 1300, and music composed at the beginning of the 14th century is described as *Ars Nova (see also: The *New Music). Musical style became more expressive, more rhythmically flexible, and counterpoint (polyphony) now began to weave more freely. Polyphony was now used in secular music, as well as sacred. The main types of composition by French Ars Nova composers (e.g. Guillaume de Machaut) were the *ballade, *rondeau, *virelai, and *motet; the Italians (e.g. Francesco Landini) favoured the *ballata, *caccia, and early *madrigal.

Generally, Medieval composers tended to sharply contrast the separate strands in their music, one against another. Very often, compositions were built up by adding successive layers of melody and words, one above another. When adding a third layer or voice-part, a composer would make sure it fitted with one of the previous two, but not necessarily both – resulting in frequent discordant clashes and sharp contrasts.

During the first half of the 15th century, the English composer John Dunstable was leader in a trend towards a fuller, less discordant musical style which looked forward to the smoother, more blended texture of Renaissance style. Dunstable used gracefully-curving melodies and supple rhythms. But most impressive of all was his blending of the voice-parts in smooth, flowing harmonies – often consisting of chains of 'six-three' chords (see *fauxbourdon). Dunstable's style was much admired, and copied, by other composers, such as Guillaume Dufay and Gilles Binchois. Composers were also now turning their attention to an important polyphonic form of church music – complete settings of the Ordinary of the *Mass.

Many of the instrumental pieces which have survived from Medieval times are dances (see *estampie, and *saltarello). Most of them are monophonic, but a few are polyphonic. Other types of instrumental piece include variations, instrumental motets, and instrumental arrangements of vocal pieces.

The following lists many of the instruments used during Medieval times:

Strings (bowed)
medieval fiddle
rebec
crwth
hurdy-gurdy

Strings (plucked)
medieval long-necked lute
guitar
psaltery
medieval lyre
medieval (minstrel's) harp
citole

Strings (hammered)
dulcimer

Wind
bagpipe
pipe (and tabor)
recorders
medieval flute
early shawm
long straight trumpet

Percussion
chime bells
nakers
tabor
timbrel (tambourine)
cymbals
triangle

Keyboard
early church organ
portative organ
positive organ
clavichord

[See also: *Early music; and the time-chart of composers on pages 398–413]

Mehr [German] More.

Meistersinger [German: 'mastersingers'] Members of literary and musical guilds of craftsmen, flourishing in certain German cities in the 15th and 16th centuries. Their songs – entirely monophonic, and often florid – were composed according to a rigid system of rules. Members graduated through various ranks, from apprentice to master. The most famous mastersinger was Hans Sachs of Nuremberg (1494–1576). [See: *Die *Meistersinger von Nürnberg*; also, *Barform]

Meistersinger von Nürnberg, Die (The Mastersingers of Nuremberg) Opera in three acts by Wagner, first produced at Munich in 1868 (text by the composer). The action takes place in the 16th century. Walther (tenor) falls in love with Eva (soprano), whose father, the goldsmith Pogner, has promised her to the winner of a song contest to be held by the Guild of Mastersingers. He decides to compete and sings a trial song to the Masters, but the marker, Beckmesser (baritone), himself in love with Eva, declares it a failure. However, the kindly shoemaker Hans Sachs (high bass) is haunted by its melody. Beckmesser arrives to serenade Eva, but Sachs hammers away and drowns the singing, and his apprentice, David (tenor), thinking his own lover, Magdalena, is being serenaded, sets about Beckmesser with a cudgel. Alone with Sachs, Walther sings a new song, and the shoemaker, impressed, writes it down. Beckmesser finds the copy, and believing it to be Sachs's own work he steals it and sings it at the contest. His performance is a disaster. It is Walther who gives the song a perfect rendering, is admitted by Pogner (bass) to the Guild, and proudly claims Eva as his bride. The overture is a contrapuntal triumph with, at one point, three of the main themes from the opera played simultaneously. The waspish Beckmesser is taken to be a caricature of the Viennese critic Hanslick (1825–1904), a fierce opponent of Wagner's music.

Melisma A melodious succession or flourish of notes sung to a single syllable. The term is used particularly in connection with *plainsong, and the type of *organum known as 'melismatic' organum.

Melodia [Italian] Melody.

Melodic and rhythmic devices See *Devices.

Melodic minor scale See *Scale.

Melodic sequence See under *Sequence.

Mélodie This French word can mean **1** a melody, or **2** a solo song with piano accompaniment.

Melodrama Spoken words with musical accompaniment, either as a complete composition or as part of an opera. Examples are the grave-digging scene from Beethoven's opera *Fidelio* and the Wolf's Glen scene from Weber's opera *Der Freischütz*.

Melody Basically, a succession of musical sounds of varying pitches presented one after another (as opposed to harmony – different pitches sounded simultaneously). The sounds are organized in such a way as to achieve a distinctive shape or 'contour', and also usually involved is rhythm – i.e. the duration (long or short) of the various notes in relation to each other. To most people, melody is the most important element or *ingredient in a piece of music. However, response to melody is a very personal matter; what may be accepted as an intriguing, even movingly beautiful melody by one person may be rejected as a banal or even meaningless succession of sounds by another.

Membranophone A term used to describe any musical instrument whose sound is produced by the vibration of a stretched skin or membrane. The most important group of membranophones includes the various kinds of *drum. [See also: *Idiophone; *Chordophone; *Aerophone; *Electrophone]

Même [French] Same.

Meno [Italian] Less. **Meno mosso**, less moved, less quickly.

Mensural music [Latin: *musica mensurata*] A medieval term for music in which the notes have precise time-values in relation to each other, as distinct from *plainsong, in which the rhythm is freely flexible. [See: *Ars Antiqua]

Menuet; **Menuett** See *Minuet.

Menuetto A title which often appears in instrumental scores by late 18th-century composers (but not those from Italy), intended to be the Italian word for *Minuet. It is, however, a made-up word – a mixture of the German word *Menuett* and the true Italian word *minuetto.*

Mer, La (The sea) Debussy's finest orchestral work in *Impressionist style, composed between 1903 and 1905. It consists of three 'symphonic sketches', portraying different moods of the sea. The titles are: 1 *De l'aube à midi sur la mer* (From dawn to midday on the sea); 2 *Jeux de vagues* (Play of the waves); 3 *Dialogue du vent et de la mer* (Dialogue of the wind and the sea).

Messa di voce [Italian: 'placing of the voice'] In singing, the steady sustaining of a long note, perfectly pitched, usually combined with a *crescendo* and then a *diminuendo* to *pianissimo.*

Messe [French; also German] Mass. **Messe des morts**, a mass for the dead, a *Requiem mass.

Messe de Notre Dame (Mass of Our Lady) A *Mass (*c*1340) in four voice-parts by the French *Ars Nova composer, Guillaume de Machaut (*c*1300–1377). It is the earliest-known complete polyphonic setting of the Ordinary of the Mass by a single composer. There are six sections: Kyrie, Gloria, Credo, Sanctus, Agnus Dei, and Ite missa est. In the first and the last three of these, Machaut uses *isorhythmic technique, each of these sections being based on a plainchant *cantus firmus. The Gloria and the Credo, however, are freely composed (i.e. not based on a plainchant).

Messiah (not '*The* Messiah') Oratorio in three parts by Handel, for soprano, alto, tenor, and bass soloists, chorus and orchestra, composed in twenty-four days in 1741 and first performed in Dublin the following year (text from the Bible, selected by Charles Jennens). There is no actual story: a succession of recitatives, arias, and choruses meditate on the Christian idea of salvation – from the Old Testament prophecies, through Christ's life on earth, to the ultimate triumph of Resurrection and Ascension. Mozart wrote *additional accompaniments for use when no organ was available for the continuo. The latter half of the 19th century saw a fashion for mammoth performances with huge choruses and orchestras. At the London première, in 1743, King George II stood throughout the *Hallelujah Chorus, thereby initiating a tradition still observed by audiences today. Other popular numbers include the arias 'I know that my Redeemer liveth' (soprano) and 'The trumpet shall sound' (bass) and the short orchestral **Pastoral Symphony.*

Mesto [Italian] Sad.

Metà [Italian] Half.

Metallophone A percussion instrument consisting of a set of tuned metal bars, graded in size and therefore in pitch, arranged on a frame in a single or a double row, and struck with hammers, usually by hand.

Metamorphosis See *Thematic transformation.

Metre See *Time.

Metronome A mechanical device, patented by Johann Nepomuk Maelzel in 1815, and designed to indicate the exact tempo of a composition by ticking away the number of beats to a minute at any given rate. The traditional metronome has a clockwork mechanism. A rod, fixed at its lower end, acts as an inverted pendulum; behind it, is a vertical scale marked off in numbers. On the rod there is a sliding weight, and the position to which its top edge is set against the scale determines the rod's rate of swing and the number of ticks sounded per minute. If, for example, the weight is set at 120, there will be 120 ticks per minute (two per second).

A composer wishing to indicate the precise speed of a piece writes a **metronome marking** at the beginning of the music: MM (abbreviation for 'Maelzel's metronome') followed by a note (representing the beat) and a number (the number on the scale at which the sliding weight should be set). For example: MM ♩ = 116 indicates 116 crotchet beats per minute; MM 𝅗𝅥 = 60 indicates sixty minim beats per minute.

More recently, electronic metronomes have become available.

Mettez la sourdine [French] Put on the mute.

Mezza; **Mezzo** [Italian] Half.

Mezza voce (abbrev.: **m.v.**) [Italian] 'Half voice', meaning 'half power' in strength or volume.

Mezzo forte (abbrev.: ***mf***) [Italian] 'Half loud' – therefore 'moderately loud'.

Mezzo piano (abbrev.: ***mp***) [Italian] 'Half soft' – therefore 'moderately soft'.

Mezzo-soprano A female *voice with a range lying halfway between that of soprano and contralto.

Mezzo-staccato See under *Staccato.

Mf; ***mf*** Abbreviation of **mezzo forte.*

M.G.; **m.g.** Abbreviation of *main gauche* [French], left hand.

Mi [French and Italian] The note E.

Microtonality A system of composition based on a scale, or scales, containing intervals smaller than a semitone (half-tone) called *microtones. One of the first Western composers to experiment with microtonality, in the 1920s, was the Czech composer Alois Hába; his String Quartet No. 2 (1920) is written in *quarter-tones, while No. 10 (1952) is in *sixth-tones.

Microtone Any interval distinctly smaller than a semitone (half-tone), e.g. a *quarter-tone (= half a semitone), a sixth-tone (= one third of a semitone). Microtones are found, for example, in the music of countries of Eastern Europe, in the music of India, and in Arab music. [See also: *Microtonality]

Middle Ages, Music of the See *Medieval music.

Middle C The note C nearest to the middle of the piano *keyboard. In the treble clef it is written as [music notation] and in the bass clef as [music notation]

Middle pedal Term sometimes used to mean *internal pedal.

Midi, Le See *Le *Matin.*

Midsummer Marriage, The Opera in three acts by Tippett, first produced in London in 1955 (text by the composer). In a deliberate analogy with Mozart's **Magic Flute*, the action revolves around two pairs of lovers. Mark (tenor) hopes to marry Jenifer (soprano), whose father, King Fisher, disapproves. Jenifer, desiring truth rather than love, vanishes into the realm of the supernatural, and King Fisher (baritone), seeking her with the reluctant aid of the clairvoyante Sosostris (contralto), is warned by the Ancients not to meddle in mysteries he does not understand. Meanwhile, in a wood, King Fisher's secretary, Bella (soprano), and her lover, Jack (tenor), witness some Ritual Dances whose nightmarish symbolism terrifies them. Eventually, King Fisher rashly unveils an embodiment of his daughter and her lover in transfigured form. Hoping to free Jenifer, he shoots Mark, but the pair turn to him with a powerful gesture, and it is he himself who dies, leaving them free to wed.

Midsummer Night's Dream, A **1** Incidental music by Mendelssohn for

Shakespeare's play. He composed the Overture in 1826, at the age of 17. The rest of the music was composed in 1842. Four of the items are often played as concert pieces: the Overture, Scherzo, Nocturne, and the famous Wedding March.

2 An opera in three acts by Benjamin Britten, with libretto by the composer and Peter Pears based on Shakespeare's play. It was first performed at Aldeburgh in 1960.

Mighty Handful, The See: The *Five.

Mikado, The Comic opera in two acts by Gilbert (text) and Sullivan (music), first produced in London in 1885. Nanki-Poo (tenor), son of the Mikado of Japan, is in love with Yum-Yum (soprano), a ward of Ko-Ko, who himself wants to marry her. Ko-Ko (baritone), sentenced to death for flirting but reprieved and made Lord High Executioner, has been ordered by the Mikado (bass) to behead someone within a month or face execution himself. The Mikado has also ordered Nanki-Poo to wed the ugly old Katisha (contralto). Nanki-Poo contemplates suicide, but Ko-Ko, seeking a victim, urges on him the advantages of a ceremonial beheading. Complications multiply: Ko-Ko unearths an ancient law decreeing that wives must be buried alive with their dead husbands; Pooh-Bah (bass) draws up a false affidavit certifying that Nanki-Poo has been beheaded; Ko-Ko proudly presents this document to the Mikado (not having recognized Nanki-Poo as the Mikado's son); and Katisha discloses the 'dead man's' identity to his father. In the nick of time Nanki-Poo, now safely married to Yum-Yum, makes himself known, and all ends happily with Ko-Ko and Katisha wed.

Mikrokosmos A collection of 153 piano pieces by Bartók, composed between 1926 and 1939 and published in six volumes. The pieces, graded in difficulty, were intended as a complete instruction course – both in piano-playing, and in composing techniques of the first part of the 20th century.

Militaire [French]; **Militare** [Italian] Military.

Military band A band consisting of woodwind, brass, and percussion instruments (the inclusion of woodwind distinguishing it from a *brass band). The number and type of instruments vary considerably from one military band to another, but a fairly typical combination might be: flute and piccolo, oboe, clarinet in E♭, 6 to as many as 14 clarinets in B♭, sometimes alto and bass clarinets, 2 bassoons, alto saxophone in E♭, tenor saxophone in B♭, 2 or more cornets in B♭ or trumpets in B♭, 4 horns in F, 2 tenor trombones and 1 bass trombone, 1 euphonium, 2 basses (bombardons, bass tubas) in E♭ and 2 in low B♭, side (snare) drum, bass drum, cymbals, sometimes kettle drums and other varied percussion – for example, bell lyras (glockenspiels); also string bass when not marching, and playing under cover.

'Military' Polonaise Nickname of Chopin's Polonaise in A for piano, Op. 40 No. 1 (1840), so called because of the strong war-like rhythm of its opening section.

'Military' Symphony Nickname of Haydn's Symphony No. 100 in G major, composed 1793–4 (one of his *'London' Symphonies). The nickname refers to Haydn's inclusion of 'military' percussion instruments – cymbals, triangle, and bass drum (see also *Janissary music) – and also a trumpet call heard towards the end of the slow movement. The four movements of the symphony are: 1 *Adagio* (a long slow introduction) leading to *Allegro* (in sonata form); 2 *Allegretto* (in ternary form – *A B A* + coda – with the 'military' instruments entering for the first time and producing the Turkish or Janissary sounds in section *B*); 3 Menuetto: *Moderato*; 4 Finale: *Presto* (basically in sonata form, but based on a single main theme).

Minaccevole; **Minacciando**; **Minaccioso** [Italian] Menacing, threatening.

Mineur [French] Minor (key).

Miniature score See *Score.

Minim The note which is twice the value of a crotchet, and half the value of a semibreve. (The American name for a minim is a half-note.) A minim is written: 𝅗𝅥 and a minim *rest is shown as ▬ [See also Tables 1 and 2 on page 387]

Minnesinger [German, from *Minne*: 'courtly love'] German aristocratic poet-musicians of the 12th, 13th, and 14th centuries. They were the German counterparts of the *troubadours, whose art inspired them. Among the most notable minnesingers were Walther von der Vogelweide (*c*1170–*c*1230), Neidhart von Reuental (*c*1180–*c*1240), and Oswald von Wolkenstein (*c*1377–1445). [See also: *Minstrel; *Meistersinger; *Barform]

Minor A word meaning 'less' or 'smaller'. A **minor interval** is a chromatic semitone less than a major one – for example, C–E is a major 3rd, C–E♭ is a minor 3rd (see *Intervals). A **minor triad** is one which has a minor 3rd and perfect 5th above the root (see *Triad). The main characteristic of a **minor scale** is that the third degree lies a minor 3rd above the tonic (see *Scale). A **minor key** is the key based on the minor scale of the same name, and sharing the same key signature as its relative major (see *Relative keys; and the table of Key signatures on page 389). [See also: *Major; *Mode, 2]

Minore [Italian] Minor (key). Also used as a heading (e.g. in variations, or for the middle section of a piece in ternary form) to indicate a sudden switch from major to minor. [See also: *Maggiore]

Minstrels Name commonly used to describe any kind of professional musician of Medieval times – but especially an instrumentalist. Minstrels were often employed by *troubadours, *trouvères, and *minnesingers to play accompaniments to their songs. Some found steady employment at a court or castle; others wandered freely from one place to another earning their money 'on the road'. A successful minstrel, however, was far more than a mere musician. As a 12th-century manuscript points out, he was expected '... to be good at story-telling and rhyming, and trials of skill. He must know how to play the drum, the cymbals and the hurdy-gurdy; to juggle with apples, and to throw and catch knives; to imitate birdsong; to perform card-tricks, and to jump through four hoops; to play the citole and the lute, the harp and the fiddle, and many other instruments ...' [See also: *Jongleur]

Minuet [French: *menuet*; German: *Menuett*; Italian: *minuetto*] A graceful French dance, moderate in speed and with three beats to a bar, which first became fashionable at the court of Louis XIV (the 'Sun King') around the middle of the 17th century. Lully, court composer to Louis XIV, began to include minuets in his ballets and operas. Like many French fashions, the minuet soon spread to other countries. From about 1700, a rather more stylized version of the minuet was often included as one of the optional extra movements (called *Galanterien*) of the Baroque *suite.

The minuet remained popular during the Classical period (1750–1810). Some minuets were still composed as ballroom dances; but, more importantly, a rather swifter variety of minuet, with a contrasting 'trio', was included in instrumental works such as the symphony, divertimento, serenade, string quartet, and, sometimes, the sonata. [See: *Minuet and Trio form; *Sonata; *Scherzo; also *Menuetto]

Minuet and Trio form Baroque composers often wrote *minuets in pairs – the second minuet forming some kind of contrast to the first. To make a longer piece, the two were performed in alternation, or 'sandwich fashion':

Minuet I	Minuet II	**Minuet I**

Originally, whereas Minuet I was played by the whole orchestra, Minuet II was often scored for three instruments only. For this reason, the second minuet became known as the *trio* (Italian for 'three'). The custom was to omit any repeats in the first minuet when it was played again after the trio. Other dances, such as gavottes and bourrées, and sometimes pieces which were not dances at all, were similarly composed in pairs to be performed in the same way. As all these pieces were written to the same basic plan, the name 'minuet and trio' eventually came to describe the form itself. The overall shape of a piece or movement in minuet and trio form is *ternary:

A¹: Minuet section – ending in the tonic key;
B: Trio (Minuet II) – a contrast, usually in a new key;
A²: Minuet section again – this time without repeats.

However, each of the main sections (both minuet and trio) is in fact a complete binary or ternary design in itself:

A¹: Minuet	**B: Trio** (a contrast)	**A²: Minuet (without repeats)**
‖: a :‖: b(a) :‖	‖: c :‖: d(c) :‖	‖ a ‖ b(a) ‖

In the second half of the 18th century, composers included a Minuet and Trio in works such as symphonies, string quartets and other chamber works, and also in some sonatas. The music below is the third movement of Mozart's *Eine *Kleine Nachtmusik* for strings. The minuet section, in G major, is in binary form; the contrasting trio section, in D major, is in ternary form.

In the symphonies of Haydn and Mozart, the Minuet and Trio is usually placed third in the order of movements, forming a contrast to the slow second movement and the swift, more boisterous, finale. Although the trio section is no longer for three instruments only, there is usually a noticeable change in orchestration (often featuring solos for wind instruments) and a lightness of musical texture to contrast with the fuller sound of the minuet section.

Beethoven used the Minuet and Trio in his earlier works, but later transformed the style and character of the movement into the much swifter, more vigorous, **Scherzo and Trio** (*scherzo* meaning 'a joke') – usually, however, still keeping to the same basic plan:

Scherzo : Trio (a contrast) **: Scherzo** (without repeats)

[See also: *Alternativo; *Menuetto]

Minuetto [Italian] *Minuet. **Tempo di minuetto**, at the speed, and in the style, of a Minuet.

'Minute' Waltz Nickname of Chopin's Waltz in D flat for piano, Op. 64 No. 1 (1846), which is supposed to take one minute in performance – but in fact, if played *musically*, takes around a minute and a half. The piece is also known as the 'Dog' Waltz – the story being that Chopin is supposed to have written it while watching a puppy chase its tail.

'Miracle' Symphony Nickname by which Haydn's Symphony No. 96 in D is usually known. It used to be said that at the end of the first performance of this symphony in London in 1791, many in the audience ran forward to congratulate Haydn and so miraculously escaped being crushed when a huge chandelier fell down onto where they had been sitting. However, it has now been discovered that this incident in fact happened in 1794, during Haydn's second visit to London, after the first performance of his Symphony No. 102 in B flat – so it is really that symphony to which the nickname 'Miracle' should be attached. [See also: *'London' Symphonies]

Miroirs (Mirrors) A group of five piano pieces by Ravel, composed in 1904–5. The titles are: 1 *Noctuelles* (Moths); 2 *Oiseaux tristes* (Melancholy birds); 3 *Une barque sur l'océan* (A boat on the ocean); 4 *Alborada del gracioso* (The jester's morning-song); 5 *La vallée des cloches* (Valley of the bells). Ravel later made orchestral versions of the third and fourth pieces.

Mirror canon See under *Canon.

Mirror fugue A *fugue so planned and written that it can also be played with each part or voice inverted (turned upside down) – as if a mirror were held beneath the printed music. Two famous examples are Contrapunctus 12 and 13 in Bach's *The *Art of Fugue*.

Contrapunctus XII

Missa [Latin] *Mass.

Missa Papae Marcelli (Mass for Pope Marcellus) Mass for six voices by Palestrina (from his second book of masses, published in 1567), written for – or possibly in memory of – Pope Marcellus II who died in 1555 only three weeks after he was elected. At that time, the church authorities were concerned that composers were making choral pieces sound too complicated, weaving the voice-parts together in such elaborate counterpoint that the words were unintelligible. It is believed that Palestrina may have written this mass to demonstrate that it was perfectly possible to compose a dignified and beautiful choral work in a much simpler style which allowed every word of the text to stand out clearly.

Misterioso [Italian] Mysterious.

Mistico [Italian] Mystic, mystical; mystically.

Misura [Italian: 'measure'] **1** A *bar or measure. **2** Beat. **Senza misura**, 'in free time'. **Alla misura** or **misurato**, 'in strictly measured time'.

Mit [German] With.

Mixed cadence See under *Cadences.

Mixed consort See *Consort.

Mixed media See *Multimedia.

Mixed voices If a composition is described as being for mixed voices, or unequal voices, it is to be performed by a mixture of adult male and female voices.

Mixolydian mode See *Church modes.

Mixture stops See under *Organ.

Mládí [Czech: 'Youth'] A suite, in four movements, for wind sextet (flute interchanging with piccolo, oboe, clarinet, horn, bassoon, and bass clarinet), composed by Janáček in 1924.

MM Abbreviation for 'Maelzel's *metronome'.

Modal Term commonly used to describe music which makes use of harmonies and/or melodies based on a mode rather than a major or minor scale (see *Church modes). The word is also used to describe the rhythms, based on strict patterns (rhythmic modes), used by Medieval composers (see under *Ars Antiqua).

Mode **1** Usually referring to one of the scales in the medieval system of *church modes (ecclesiastical modes). **2** The word *mode* may also be used in a wider sense, as in 'major mode' (meaning, in a major key) and 'minor mode' (in a minor key).

Moderato [Italian] Moderate (in speed). For example: *Allegro moderato*, moderately quick – that is, less fast than *Allegro.

Modéré [French] Moderate. **Modérément**, moderately.

Modern jazz A general term used to describe all types and styles of *jazz which developed during the 1940s and after, experimenting with melodies, harmonies, and rhythms which are more adventurous and complex than those used in *mainstream.

Modern music See *Twentieth-century music.

'Modern' rondo form See *Rondo.

Modified sonata form See *Abridged sonata form.

Modo [Italian] Mode, manner. **In modo di**, in the manner of.

Modulating sequence See under *Sequence.

Modulation The change of key during the course of a composition; the passing from one key to another. Although a piece may begin and end in C major (in which case C major is then referred to as the *tonic key*) the music will invariably modulate to other keys at certain points. The smoothest and most natural-sounding modulation will be to any key which is closely related to the tonic key. [See: *Related keys; also, *Remote keys]

Möglich [German] Possible. (For example: *so rasch wie möglich*, as quick as possible.)

Moins [French] Less.

Moll [German] Minor, meaning 'minor key'. (For example: *a-moll*, A minor.) [See also: *Dur]

Molto [Italian] Much, very (e.g. *molto allegro*, very fast). **Moltissimo**, extremely, most.

Moment musical (*Moments musicaux*) [French: 'Musical moments'] Six piano pieces by Schubert (Op. 94; D780), composed in about 1828. Schubert's actual title for the set, in incorrect French, was *Momens musicals*.

Monody (monodic style) The name given to a musical style which evolved in Italy around 1600, in reaction against the complicated contrapuntal style of the 16th century. It consisted of a recitative-like melody for a single voice, supported by a fairly simple *continuo accompaniment. The vocal line reflected the expressive and dramatic meaning of the text, often closely following the natural speech-rhythms of the words. The new monodic style, which at first was called *Le *Nuove Musiche* ('the new music'), was used in solo song, and also in early operas (see *Camerata, and *Opera). As a brief example of monody, here is the ending of Giulio Caccini's song 'Amarilli', included in his collection entitled *Le Nuove Musiche* (1602):

Monophonic [from Greek: 'single sound'] A term describing a musical *texture which consists of a single melodic line, without supporting harmonies. For example: *plainsong, most medieval songs and dances (see, for instance, *Estampie), and much folk-music. [See also: *Homophonic; *Polyphonic; and *Heterophony]

Monothematic A piece or a movement is described as monothematic if the composer bases the music on one theme rather than on several.

'Moonlight' Sonata Nickname of Beethoven's Piano Sonata No. 14 in C sharp minor, Op. 27 No. 2 (1801) subtitled 'quasi una fantasia'. It took on this nickname when the poet Heinrich Rellstab wrote that the slow first movement, *Adagio sostenuto*, reminded him of Lake Lucerne by moonlight. The second movement, *Allegretto*, is in minuet and trio form, and the third movement, *Presto agitato*, is in sonata form. [See also under *Sordino]

Morbido [Italian] Soft, gentle. **Morbidezza**, softness, gentleness.

Morceau [French] Piece, or composition.

Mordent See *Ornaments.

Morendo [Italian: 'dying'] Indication that the music becomes softer and softer, usually implying that it also becomes gradually slower.

Moresca (morisca) [Italian: 'Moorish dance'] A dance popular during the 15th and 16th centuries in which the performers made themselves up to look like Moors, blackening their faces and wearing colourful Moorish-style costumes. They also tied small bells to their legs, as in the English **morris dance** which originally was a variety of the moresca.

Mormorando [Italian] Murmuring.

Morris (morris dance) The name given to a group of traditional English folk-dances, performed by male dancers. The dances vary according to locality. A familiar one is the 'Whitsuntide Morris', usually for six dancers, three facing three. The dancers wear small bells strapped to their legs to emphasize the rhythm of the dance, and wave a handkerchief in each hand or carry a stick in one or both hands.

Mosso [Italian] Moved (in speed). Also used as a warning by a composer against taking too slow a tempo or dragging (e.g. *Andante mosso*, 'moving along, not too slow'). **Meno mosso**, less moved, less quickly. **Più mosso**, more moved, quicker. **Un poco mosso**, a little moved (and so, rather quicker).

Motet The term *motet* has been used by composers since the 13th century. The name comes from the French *mots*, meaning 'words'. And the earliest motets were created merely by adding new Latin words to the upper voice-part in a *clausula section of an organum (this voice-part, originally called *duplum*, was now called *motetus*). The motet created in this way might be sung during a performance of the complete organum, or it might be performed separately as a piece in its own right. The idea of composing and singing motets – either as part of the church services, or for performance outside church – became increasingly popular during the 13th century. A motet might exist in several different versions. For instance, a composer might take a sacred motet, perhaps from a two-voice organum, and add a third voice-part (called *triplum*) in quicker notes, and with quite different words. He would make sure his melody fitted with either the *motetus* or the *tenor* (which was now played rather than sung), but not necessarily both – resulting in frequent discordant clashes between the three parts. Later on, someone else might write new words to the *triplum* part – and these might be secular rather than sacred, and perhaps in French rather than Latin. A motet in which two texts are sung simultaneously is described as 'polytextual'. Many motets of the 14th and early 15th centuries tend to be *isorhythmic in structure (many examples by Machaut, Dunstable, and Dufay).

By the beginning of the Renaissance period (1450–1600) the motet was considerably changed in character. It had now become a sacred choral composition to a Latin text of the composer's own choosing – and this single text was sung in all the voice-parts (which numbered from four to six or more). The texture of the music was mainly polyphonic, with much use of imitation – a melodic idea introduced in one voice-part would then be imitated, or copied, by the other voice-parts in turn. Sometimes composers intended the voices to be accompanied by instruments, but most often a Renaissance motet was performed **a cappella*. Included among the most notable Renaissance composers of motets are Josquin, Tallis, Palestrina, Lassus, Byrd, Victoria, and Giovanni Gabrieli. The finest motets of the Baroque period include those by Schütz, and the six great motets of J. S. Bach – four of them in eight voice-parts for double chorus (*Singet dem Herrn*; *Der Geist hilft*; *Fürchte dich nicht*; *Komm, Jesu, komm*), one in five voice-parts (*Jesu meine Freude*), and one in four voice-parts with continuo (*Lobet den Herrn*). After 1750 the motet became less important, though fine examples were composed by Mozart, Bruckner, and Brahms, and, among 20th-century composers, Vaughan Williams and Poulenc.

Motetus **1** Motet. **2** In the 13th-century motet, the name given to the second voice-part (that added next above the tenor) and originally called *duplum.

'Mother Goose' Suite (*Ma mère l'oye*) A suite for piano duet by Ravel, composed between 1908 and 1910; based on fairy tales by Perrault and other 17th-century French writers. There are five movements: 1 *Pavane de la belle au bois dormant* (Sleeping Beauty's Pavan); 2 *Petit poucet* (Tom Thumb); 3 *Laideronette, l'impératrice des pagodes* (Little Ugly One, Empress of the Pagodas); 4 *Les entretiens de la belle et de la bête* (The conversations between Beauty and the Beast); 5 *Le jardin féerique* (The Fairy Garden – the Prince awakens Sleeping Beauty). Ravel later orchestrated the suite, adding other pieces and linking passages, so that it could be performed as a ballet.

Motif See *Motive.

Motion The movement or progress of the notes in one or more melodic parts or voices. If a melody moves by **conjunct motion**, the notes progress by step (see music example (a), below). In **disjunct motion** the notes progress by leap (b). Both these types of motion are shown in (c) – from the hymn-tune *Darwall's 148th* ('Ye holy angels bright').

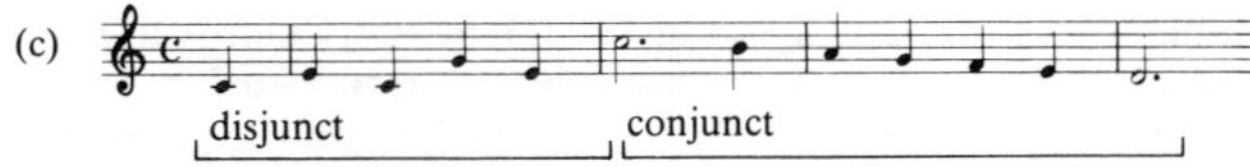

'Motion' also describes the movement of two melodic parts or voices in relation to each other. For example:
parallel motion: the two parts or voices move up or down always keeping exactly the same interval apart (see (d), below, which is in parallel 3rds – though any interval might be used);
similar motion: both parts take the same general direction (both rising, or both falling) but without keeping exactly the same distance apart (e);
contrary motion: the parts move in opposite directions – as one part rises, the other falls (f);
oblique motion: one part keeps the same note as the other part moves (g).

[See also: *Retrograde motion]

Motive [French: *motif*; German: *Motiv*] A brief melodic and/or rhythmic musical idea – often a small but significant fragment of a theme, with recognizable shape and musical character and identity. Motives are used as basic components in building up the texture of a composition (especially, for example, in the development section of a piece or a movement in *sonata form). One of the best-known examples is the four-note motive which is heard at the beginning of Beethoven's Fifth Symphony, and which assumes great importance, both rhythmic and melodic, throughout the work:

The following example shows the three motives which Beethoven presents at the beginning of his **Pastoral Symphony*; each of them plays an important part in the structure of the first movement.

[See also: *Leading motive]

Moto [Italian] Movement, motion, speed. **Con moto**, with movement, 'moving along fairly briskly'. **Moto perpetuo**, perpetual motion (see *Perpetuum mobile).

Motown An all-black record company set up in 1960 by Berry Gordy in Detroit (the 'Motortown'), Michigan. Among his other Detroit-based labels was Tamla, which later merged with Motown. The style of the music, produced by a staff of song-writers, was a mix of gospel, pop, and rhythm and blues. Included among the many black musicians who made hits on these labels were Martha and the Vandellas, Marvin Gaye, Smokey Robinson, Stevie Wonder, and Diana Ross and the Supremes.

Motto (motto theme) A distinctive theme heard at or near the beginning of a composition and then recurring at key points during the course of the music. It may have symbolic or programmatic significance, and may be changed in character at each reappearance (see *thematic transformation). Tchaikovsky makes use of a motto theme in his Fourth Symphony (music example (a), below) and also in his Fifth Symphony (b):

'Mourning' Symphony (*Trauersymphonie*) Nickname of Haydn's Symphony No. 44 in E minor, composed in 1771, the general mood of which is sombre and mournful. The second movement, Minuet, is written as a strict canon between the top and bottom parts of the musical texture. Haydn requested that the slow third movement should be played at his funeral.

Mouth organ (harmonica) A small oblong-shaped wind instrument with square holes down the length of one side leading to free reeds (thin metal tongues) inside the instrument. The player obtains the different notes by moving the instrument sideways across the lips and alternately blowing and sucking, unwanted holes being blocked by the tongue. Concertos for harmonica (mouth organ) and orchestra have been composed by Malcolm Arnold, Arthur Benjamin, and Villa-Lobos. [See also: *Sheng; *Shō]

Mouthpiece The part of a wind instrument which is held between or against the player's lips and into which the player blows.

Mouvement [French] **1** *Movement. **2** Speed, pace, tempo. The French term **au mouvement** has the same meaning as the Italian term ***a tempo**.

Movement The individual pieces which make up compositions such as sonatas, symphonies, suites, concertos, string quartets, and so on. These pieces contrast with each other in mood and character, and also in speed ('rate of movement'). A symphony, for instance, may be in four movements: 1 *Allegro moderato* (moderately quick); 2 *Adagio* (slow); 3 Scherzo: *Allegro* (quick); 4 Finale: *Presto* (very fast). It is because of this distinction of speed that each of these individual pieces is known as a 'movement' within the structure of the complete work. [See also: *Cyclic form]

Movimento [Italian] **1** *Movement. **2** Motion, speed, pace, tempo.

Mp; ***mp*** Abbreviation of **mezzo piano*.

Mṛdaṅgam (mridanga) A south Indian double-headed barrel *drum, played with the hands only. The name means 'made of clay' but the body is now carved from a single block of wood. The mṛdaṅgam provides both treble and bass drums in a single instrument. A hard paste is fixed permanently to the smaller drumhead played by the right hand so that it produces a fairly high, clear sound of definite pitch. Before each performance, the larger drumhead played with the left hand is weighted with dough, so that it produces a much lower, resonant sound of indefinite pitch.

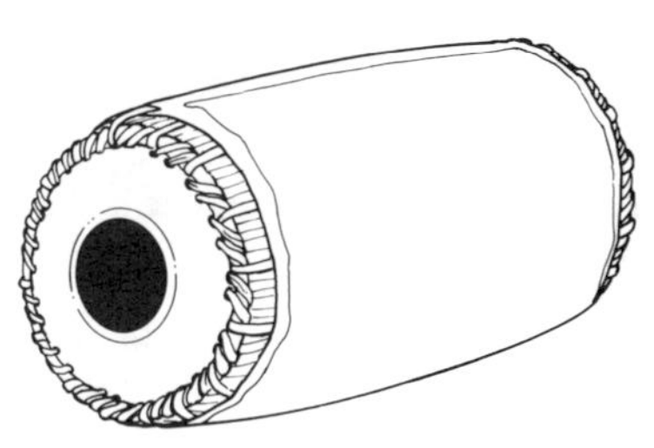

mṛdaṅgam

M.S.; **m.s.** Abbreviation of *mano sinistra* [Italian], left hand.

Multimedia (mixed media) A term used, particularly in the 1960s, to describe a composition (excluding ballet or opera) in which music is merged with other arts or media, such as dance, mime, movement, drama, poetry, film or slides, pre-recorded tape, electronic sounds, lighting effects. The performance of such a work often involves aleatory or 'chance-choice' elements (see *Aleatory music), and perhaps also some degree of audience participation.

An example of a multimedia composition is *HPSCHD* by John Cage and Lejaren Hiller. The title stands for 'harpsichord', and the work's first performance, in May 1969, included seven harpsichords and fifty-one computer-generated sound-tapes (relayed over fifty-eight loudspeakers), together with lighting effects and films and slides projected onto huge sheets in the centre of the performing area and onto a continuous screen running around the rim of the huge circular ceiling. Any part in the musical texture (harpsichord or sound-tape) could commence at any time. Also involved in the lengthy performance was an 'audience' of several thousand spectators who were invited to come and go at will, and freely wander around and even through the performing area.

Munter [German] Lively, brisk, cheerful.

Musette **1** A French type of bagpipe popular during the 17th and 18th centuries. **2** A rustic type of *gavotte whose melody is sounded against a bagpipe-like drone. In the Baroque *suite, a musette was sometimes used as a 'trio' to a gavotte, providing a movement in *minuet and trio form – for example, the fifth movement of Bach's English Suite No. 3:

Another well-known example is the trio of the third movement of Prokofiev's **Classical Symphony*.

Musica [Italian, also Latin] Music.

Musica ficta (*Musica falsa*) [Latin: 'false music'] Terms used in connection with the music of the 10th to the 16th centuries, and referring to the practice of inserting chromatic alterations – sharps and flats lying outside the mode in which the music was written – and thereby modifying the mode. The practice increased during the 16th century, and this was largely responsible for the crumbling away of the modal system. Modes lost their individual characters and 'flavours' and, basically, came to sound like two modes only – the Ionian, and the Aeolian (with the sixth and seventh notes sharpened as required). From these, in the 17th century, grew the major-minor key system upon which harmony was based for the next two and a half centuries or more.

Musical comedy A form of stage entertainment, popular in Britain and the USA during the late 19th and 20th centuries, consisting of a play in which spoken dialogue is interspersed with musical items (songs, choruses, dances). It grew from the light opera and *operetta. After about 1945 it became usual to call such a work a 'musical play' or simply a **musical**. Well-known composers include Jerome Kern, George Gershwin, Richard Rodgers, Frederick Loewe, Leonard Bernstein, Andrew Lloyd Webber.

Musical devices See *Devices.

Musical forms See *Form.

Musical glasses (armonica, harmonica, glass harmonica) An instrument taking various forms – in one of which, the sounds are produced by rubbing a damp finger round the rims of drinking glasses or glass bowls tuned to different notes by being partially filled with liquid.

Musical Joke, A (*Ein musikalischer Spass*) A divertimento in four movements (K522; 1787) by Mozart, for two horns and strings. Mozart pokes fun at every kind of mediocre musician of his day – including composers. For example, in the second movement (Minuet) there are hilariously wrong notes from the horns; in the final movement the music can't make up its mind when to stop – and when the end is finally reached, the orchestra finishes in five different keys at once.

Musical Offering, The (*Das musikalisches Opfer*) A work by J. S. Bach, composed in 1747, and consisting of two ricercars (one in three parts, the other in six), ten canons, and a trio sonata for flute, violin, and continuo. All these are based on a 'royal theme' given to Bach by King Frederick the Great of Prussia (to whom the work was dedicated);

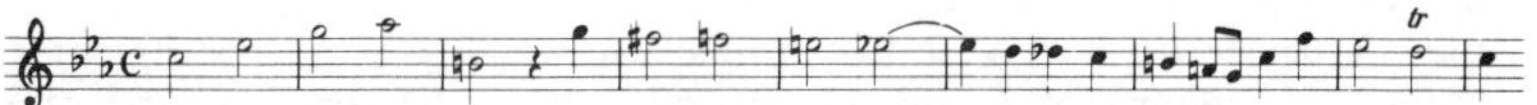

Musica mensurata; **Musica mensurabilis** [Latin] *Mensural music.

Music-drama The term preferred by Wagner to describe his operas. Music and drama are given equal importance, and instead of structuring acts in separate musical 'numbers' (recitatives, arias, choruses) Wagner uses a technique which he described as 'endless melody', in which the music flows almost continuously from the beginning of an act to its conclusion. Wagner explained that his aim was a perfect merging of all the theatrical arts: singing, acting, design (costumes and scenery), lighting and stage effects – all blending together, the total effect powerfully heightened by the varied and vividly expressive sounds of a huge orchestra. [See also: *Leading-motive]

Music for Strings, Percussion, and Celesta A work in four movements by Bartók, composed in 1947 for the tenth anniversary of the Basel Chamber Orchestra. The work is written for a large string section which is divided into two equal groups, placed to left and to right of the conductor. Harp, celesta, and percussion (chromatic kettle drums, snare drums, bass drum, cymbals, tam-tam, xylophone, and piano) are positioned in the centre. The three-dimensional spatial positioning of the instruments on the tiered concert platform is important to the way Bartók combines and contrasts their sounds throughout the music. The four movements are: 1 *Andante tranquillo*; 2 *Allegro*; 3 *Adagio*; 4 *Allegro molto*.

Music for the Royal Fireworks See **Fireworks Music*.

Musik [German] Music.

Musikalischer Spass, Ein See *A *Musical Joke*.

Musikalisches Opfer, Das See *The *Musical Offering*.

Musique [French] Music.

Musique concrète [French: 'concrete music'] The name given in the late 1940s by the French composer, Pierre Schaeffer, to music composed in a 'concrete' way directly onto tape, rather than in an abstract way by writing down notes on paper. In his experiments in the Studio d'Essai of French Radio, Schaeffer recorded natural sounds (such as the sound of a bell, the cork popping out of a bottle, a human voice, and so on). He transferred these recordings from tape to tape, combining them, superimposing one on top of another, changing the pitch by altering the speed of the original tape, playing a recording backwards – so that often the original sounds became unrecognizable. The resulting composition was a montage of sounds stored on tape which could be played back at will without need of any 'performer'. Many of the techniques of *musique concrète* subsequently played a large part in *electronic music. However, a pure *musique concrète* composition is based on natural sounds only. For example, the sole sound-source of *Intermezzo* by Mimaroglu (born in Turkey) is an elastic band; that of *Water Music* by the Japanese composer, Takemitsu, consists entirely of water drops.

Musique de table [French] *Table music.

Muta [Italian: 'change'] Indication in orchestral parts **1** to change the tuning of kettle drums (e.g. *muta in G*, change tuning to the note G), or **2** in earlier scores, to change *crooks on horns and trumpets (e.g. *muta in D*, change to the crook pitched in D). Also **3** to change instruments (e.g. *Flauto II muta in piccolo*, indicating that the second flute player changes from flute to piccolo).

Mutation stops See under *Organ.

Mute A device used to alter the normal tone-quality of an instrument and reduce the volume of sound. On instruments in the string section of the orchestra a small comb-like device is clipped onto the bridge, dampening the vibrations and bringing a hushed, silvery quality to the tone. On brass instruments a mute, varying in size and shape and made of a substance such as wood, metal, or cardboard, is wedged into the bell of the instrument. With the exception of the flute, woodwind instruments may be muted, usually by stuffing a handkerchief into the bell. Drums, also, may be muted – particularly kettle drums (e.g. by placing a cloth on the drumhead, opposite the striking point). On the piano, the left pedal (soft pedal, or *una corda* pedal) serves as a mute. [See also: *Sordino]

M.V.; ***m.v.*** Abbreviation of **mezza voce*.

My Country (My Fatherland) See **Má vlast*.

Nach [German] After, following, to, at.

Nachtanz [German: 'after-dance'] A 16th-century term for a quick dance in triple time performed immediately after a slower dance in duple time (e.g. a galliard following a pavan, or a saltarello following a passamezzo). Dances were commonly paired in such a way, the second dance often based on the same tune as the first but transformed into triple time.

Nachtmusik [German] Night-music; serenade. The most famous example is Mozart's *Eine *Kleine Nachtmusik*.

Nachtstück [German] Night-piece. Same as *Nocturne.

Nāgasvaram A south Indian double-reed instrument – a large, powerfully-toned shawm with a conical tube usually made of wood (occasionally of silver or gold) and a metal bell. There are seven finger-holes. The nāgasvaram is the south Indian counterpart of the north Indian *shahnāī.

Nakers [from Arabic: *naqqara*] Medieval bowl-shaped drums, of Arabic origin. They were about 26 cm in diameter and used in pairs, usually slung around the player's waist, and played with two sticks. Nakers were the ancestors of modern orchestral *kettle drums.

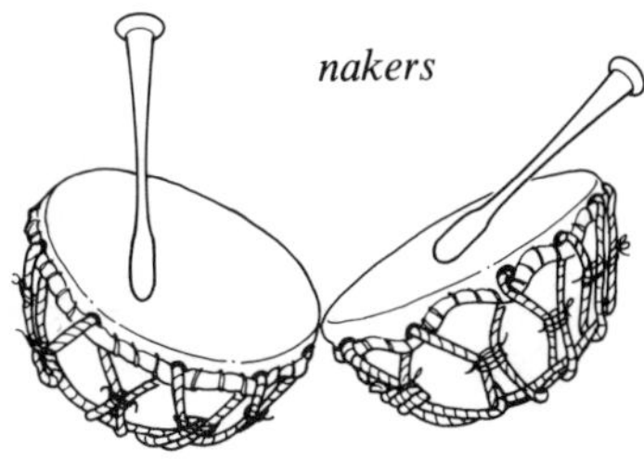

Nat. Abbreviation standing for **naturale* [Italian] or *naturel* [French] or *natürlich* [German].

Nationalism A term commonly used to describe a musical movement of the second half of the 19th century, which was a type of Romanticism. Music had become powerfully dominated by German influences, and composers of certain other countries – particularly Russia, and also Bohemia (now part of Czechoslovakia) and Norway – decided to break free from these influences and discover a distinctive musical style which would be expressive and characteristic of their own particular country. They achieved this by incorporating 'national' ingredients into their music – by using the tunes and rhythms of their nation's folk-music, and by taking scenes from their country's life, history, legends, and folk-tales as a basis for compositions such as operas, songs, and *symphonic poems.

The first composer to write a work deliberately expressing the nationalist spirit was the Russian composer, Glinka, in his opera *A Life for the Tsar* (1836). His lead was enthusiastically taken up in the 1860s by the group of

Russian composers known as 'The *Five'. In Bohemia, Smetana was inspired to write nationalist works such as his opera *The *Bartered Bride* and his cycle of six symphonic poems entitled **Má vlast*. In Norway, Grieg (who had received his musical training in Germany) determined to base his music on ingredients from his country's folk-music – heard especially in his *Norwegian Dances*, his songs, and in many of his *Lyric Pieces* for piano.

Other well-known composers who have incorporated 'national' ingredients into some or many of their compositions include: Dvořák in Bohemia; Albéniz, Granados, and Falla in Spain; Sibelius in Finland; Vaughan Williams in England; Bartók and Kodály in Hungary; Copland in the USA; and Villa-Lobos in Brazil (see **Bachianas brasileiras*).

Natural **1** Describing a note which is neither sharpened nor flattened and so corresponds to a white note on the piano keyboard (the white notes of the keyboard are sometimes referred to as 'naturals'). **2** The sign (♮) which is placed in front of a note, cancelling a previous sharp or flat and so restoring the note to its normal 'white-note' pitch. [See also: *Accidentals]

Naturale [abbrev.: **nat.**) [Italian] In the natural, ordinary way (generally, cancelling some previous instruction to sing or play in some special way, e.g. *falsetto, sul ponticello*).

Natural horn; **Natural trumpet** The older type of horn and trumpet, having no valves (or slide or keys). [See also under *Brass instruments]

Naturel (abbrev.: **nat.**) [French] Same as the Italian **naturale*.

Natürlich (abbrev.: **nat.**) [German] Same as the Italian **naturale*.

Nāy (ney) In Arab music of the Middle East and north Africa, an end-blown flute, made from cane, bamboo, wood, or metal. It has usually six finger-holes (the player using the first three fingers of each hand) and there is sometimes also a thumb-hole at the back. Archaeologists working in Egypt have discovered evidence that the nāy has been used for at least 3,000 years.

Neapolitan sixth chord A chord which is the first inversion of the major triad on the flattened supertonic of the major or minor scale. In the music example, in C major, the flattened supertonic is D♭; the major triad will therefore consist of D♭–F–A♭, which in first inversion becomes F–A♭–D♭.

Nebenstimme [German] A term introduced by Schoenberg for the second most important voice or *part in a complicated musical texture, and indicated at the appropriate points throughout the score by the symbol N (the main voice or part being called **Hauptstimme*).

Neck The projecting part of a string instrument along which the *fingerboard is laid.

Neoclassicism A term, meaning 'the new classicism', which is used to describe a style in 20th-century music (from about 1920 onwards) in which the composer shows a strong reaction to the Romantic style of the 19th century by returning to the musical forms, and principles of style, of earlier periods. For instance, instead of composing for a huge orchestra in a rich but rather weighty style, the composer writes for a smaller orchestra, selecting instrumental timbres (tone-colours) which are sharply contrasted; also avoiding the expression of intense emotion and, instead, aiming for a 'cool' clear texture characteristic of music written before the Romantic period.

As the adjective **neoclassical** suggests, a composer writing in this style may take as a model a composer of the Classical period proper, such as Haydn or Mozart. Or, the composer may look even further back in time – for example, to the style of Baroque composers such as Bach and Handel. But although a composer writing in neoclassical style may turn to the past for inspiration, the resulting composition will still have a definite 20th-century flavour – perhaps by the inclusion of abrupt changes of key, unexpected melodic 'twists', clashing harmonies containing deliberate 'wrong' notes, or a surprising choice of instruments.

Prokofiev's **Classical Symphony* is usually considered to be an early example of neoclassicism. Stravinsky became one of the leading exponents of the style, in works such as his ballet **Pulcinella*, the Octet for wind instruments, **Symphony of Psalms*, Concerto in $E\flat$: *'Dumbarton Oaks', and his 'Neo-Mozartian' opera *The *Rake's Progress.*

Nera [Italian: 'black'] A crotchet ('black' note).

Net; **Nette** [French]; **Nett** [German]; **Netto** [Italian] Distinct, clear.

Neumes Early *notation signs drawn above the words of plainchants in medieval manuscripts. Until the 9th century, choirbooks contained nothing but the words of the various chants. Singers had to know the melodies by heart and perform them from memory. As more chants were composed it became necessary to remind singers of the different melodies, and so *neumes* – consisting of dots, lines, and curves – were drawn above the words (as on the left, below). These served as 'memory aids' by indicating (but only very approximately) the rise and fall of a melody. By the beginning of the 13th century, square-shaped neumes were being widely used. These were now drawn on a four-lined stave, so that the pitch of each sound could be precisely given (right, below). This way of notating plainsong melodies is still in use today.

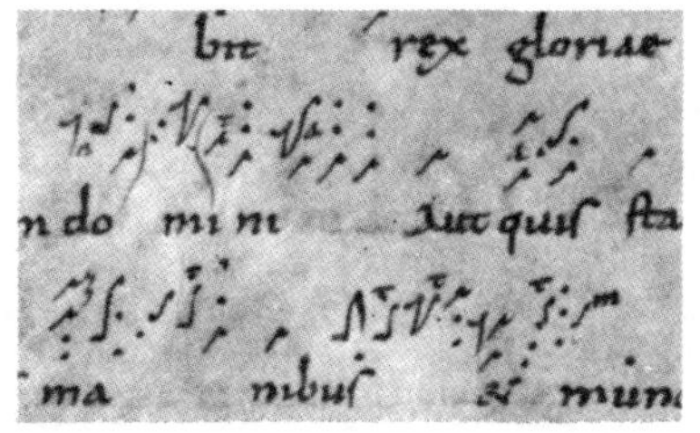

New Music, The [from German, *neue Musik*] A term introduced during the 1920s to describe the various new (often startling) sounds, new trends, and new techniques being used in 20th-century music – especially *atonality and *twelve-note technique.

It is interesting to notice that the word 'new' has been specifically applied at three points during the history of Western music, occurring roughly 300 years apart – on each occasion to describe sudden, important changes taking place in musical style:

*c*1300 **Ars Nova* (The New Music, The New Art)
*c*1600 *Le *Nuove Musiche* (The New Music)
*c*1900 *The New Music*

New Orleans jazz A style of *jazz, originating in the early part of the 20th century, and performed by a small group of players. It was named after the city where many of its originators first worked. The style has undergone a revival since the 1940s (see *Traditional jazz). Famous names of New Orleans jazz include cornet and trumpet player Louis Armstrong ('Satchmo', or 'Satchel-mouth'), cornet player and leader Joe 'King' Oliver, trombonist Kid Ory, pianist 'Jelly Roll' Morton, and clarinettist and saxophonist Sidney Bechet.

'New World' Symphony See **From the New World.*

Nicht [German] Not.

Niente [Italian] Nothing. **A niente** (after a diminuendo indication), fading away to nothing. **Quasi niente**, as if nothing, almost nothing (so softly as to be barely heard).

Night on the Bare Mountain (St John's Night on the Bare Mountain) A symphonic poem composed by Musorgsky in 1867 (altered and revised several times) inspired by a story by Gogol called *St John's Eve* (i.e. Midsummer's Eve), describing a witches' sabbath on Bare Mountain near Kiev in southern Russia. The music became famous in an orchestral arrangement by Rimsky-Korsakov, but is occasionally now performed in Musorgsky's original version in which the orchestration is rather more stark.

Nights in the Gardens of Spain (Noches en los jardines de España) A work for solo piano and orchestra in *Impressionist style, composed by Manuel de Falla between 1911 and 1915. The three movements have the titles: 1 *En el Generalife* (In the Generalife); 2 *Danza lejana* (Dance in the distance); 3 *En los jardines de la Sierra de Córdoba* (In the gardens of the Sierra de Córdoba).

Ninth See under *Intervals.

Ninth chord (chord of the ninth) A chord consisting of root, 3rd, 5th, 7th, and 9th – making four 3rds stacked one above another. It most often occurs as a **dominant ninth** (being then built upon the *dominant of the scale).

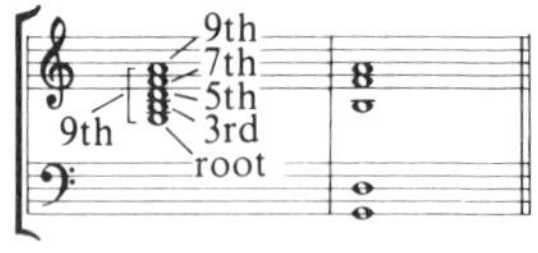

Nobile [Italian] Noble. **Nobilmente**, nobly; in a noble, impressive manner. **Noblezza**, nobility.

Noces, Les (The wedding) A ballet ('Four Russian scenes with singing and music') by Stravinsky, first produced in Paris in 1923 (choreography by Nijinska). The work is scored for soprano, mezzo-soprano, tenor, and bass soloists, four pianos, and seventeen percussion instruments. The four scenes are: 1 The tresses; 2 In the home of the bridegroom; 3 Departure of the bride; 4 The wedding feast.

Noch [German] Still; yet; more. **Noch einmal**, once more, over again. **Noch und noch**, more and more.

Noches en los jardines de España See **Nights in the Gardens of Spain.*

Nocturne [French] A 'night-piece', often expressing the associated ideas of calm, mystery, or moonlight. The first nocturnes were composed for piano solo by the Irish composer John Field. The idea was later taken up by Chopin, who composed twenty-one nocturnes expressing a wide range of moods. In a typical Chopin nocturne, the left hand plays *broken chord patterns relying on careful use of the sustaining pedal, while above, the right hand sings a flowing (often poignant) melody. Other composers who have written nocturnes for piano include Fauré (thirteen nocturnes) and Scriabin (four nocturnes, including one for the left hand only, Op. 9 No. 2; also a *Poème-Nocturne*).

Nocturnes Three orchestral pieces in *Impressionist style by Debussy, composed between 1897 and 1899. Their titles are: 1 *Nuages* (Clouds); 2 *Fêtes* (Festivals); and 3 *Sirènes* (Sirens), which includes a female chorus, singing wordlessly to suggest the voices of the sirens which, according to legend, lured sailors to wreck their ships upon the rocks.

Noël [French] Christmas carol; also a 17th- and 18th-century title for a Christmas organ piece, often variations on well-known Christmas melodies.

Noire [French: 'black'] A crotchet ('black' note).

Non [Italian] Not.

Nonet [German: *Nonett*; French: *nonette*; Italian: *nonetto*] *Chamber music for nine solo performers. Examples are: Spohr's Nonet, Op. 31 (1815), for flute, oboe, clarinet, horn, bassoon, violin, viola, cello, and double bass; and Bax's Nonet (1930) for flute, oboe, clarinet, harp, string quartet, and double bass.

Non-harmonic note (unessential note) A note which does not form part of the chord or harmony against which it is sounded. Examples of non-harmonic notes are passing notes, appoggiaturas, suspensions, and auxiliary notes.

Nota [Italian] Note.

Notation Any method by which sounds may be expressed or noted down on paper to record them for future performance. Our present conventional system of notation uses a five-line *stave, *clef, notes and rests (see page 387), *bar-lines, and so on. But there are many other ways of notating sounds; for example, the *neumes used by medieval composers; or the signs and symbols newly invented by certain 20th-century composers who find previous systems inadequate to express precisely the types of sound they require. [See also: *Graphic score]

Note **1** A single sound which has recognizable pitch and duration. **2** A written sign or symbol representing such a sound (see Tables 1 and 2 on page 387). **3** A key on a keyboard pressed down to produce a sound – for example, the black and white notes (keys) of a piano keyboard.

Americans, however, use the word 'tone' to mean **1**, above – you *see* a note, but *hear* a tone.

The various parts of written or printed notes are given these names:

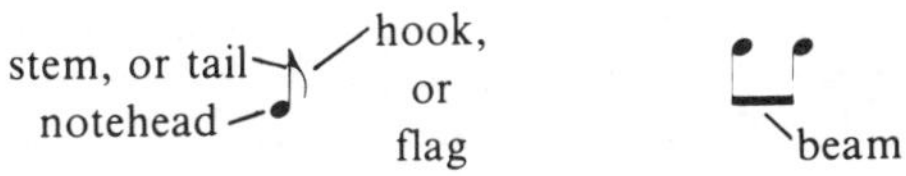

stem, or tail
notehead
hook, or flag
beam

[For names of notes in different languages, see Table 7 on page 390]

Note-against-note style A term used in counterpoint meaning that for every note in a given part there is a note of the same value in each added part. The same term is therefore also used to describe the kind of musical texture in which the various parts mainly keep in step with each other rhythmically (rather than following separate, individual rhythms). Note-against-note style is characteristic of early *organum, the 13th-century *conductus, and many pieces written in *fauxbourdon by 15th-century composers.

Note-cluster (tone-cluster) A term used by 20th-century composers to describe a chord which is made up of several adjacent notes sounded simultaneously.

Note-clusters are particularly effective in piano music. (In America they are known as tone-clusters or cluster chords.)

Notehead See under *Note.

Note row See under *Twelve-note technique.

Notes and rests See Table 1 on page 387; and also: *Rest, *Semibreve, *Breve, *Minim, *Crotchet, *Quaver, *Semiquaver, *Demisemiquaver, *Hemidemisemiquaver, *Semihemidemisemiquaver.

Notre Dame School, The See under *Ars Antiqua.

Notturno [Italian: 'nocturnal', and therefore 'night music'] A term used by 18th-century composers such as Haydn and Mozart mainly for a composition in several movements, similar to a *divertimento or *serenade, intended for outdoor performance – not in the evening, but at night (generally around 11 p.m. to midnight). Examples include Mozart's *Notturno* (K286) for four orchestras, and his **Serenata notturna* (K239).

Novelette [German: 'short novel', 'short story'] A title first used by Schumann for a piano piece in which the music seems to relate a story (e.g. his eight *Noveletten*, Op. 21).

Noye's Fludde One-act setting of Chester Miracle Play, for children and adults, by Britten, first produced in Orford Church, Suffolk, in 1958 as part of the Aldeburgh Festival. The text is based on the story of Noah and his Ark as told in Genesis 6–8. The parts of the Voice of God (spoken role), Noye (bass-baritone) and Mrs Noye (contralto) are intended for adult professionals, who also form the core of the orchestra. The remaining roles, both vocal and instrumental (including the chorus of animals and birds), are taken by children or amateurs. The score includes three hymns in which the congregation participates.

Nozze di Figaro, Le See *The *Marriage of Figaro.*

Nuits d'été, Les (Summer nights) A *song-cycle by Berlioz (Op. 7; 1840–41) setting six poems by Théophile Gautier. The six songs are: 1 *Vilanelle* (Country song); 2 *Le Spectre de la rose*; 3 *Sur les lagunes* (On the lagoons); 4 *Absence*; 5 *Au cimetière* (In the cemetery); 6 *L'île inconnue* (The unknown isle). The original version of *Nuits d'été* was for mezzo-soprano or tenor and piano, but Berlioz later orchestrated each song, making this the first important orchestral song-cycle.

'Number' opera A term describing any kind of opera which is structured in single, self-contained 'numbers' (that is, separate pieces such as arias, duets, choruses) interspersed with recitative or spoken dialogue.

Nuove Musiche, Le [Italian: 'The New Music'] A term which was originally used to describe the new *monody or monodic style of composition, consisting of recitative-like melody with simple accompaniment, which appeared in Italy around the year 1600 – an important landmark in musical history which saw the rise of opera and oratorio. The name for this style, *Le Nuove Musiche*, was taken from the title of a collection of vocal pieces in monodic style, published in 1602, by the Italian composer Giulio Caccini, a member of the Florentine *Camerata. [See also: The *New Music]

Nuovo [Italian] New. **Di nuovo**, anew, again, once more.

Nut **1** On string instruments such as violins, guitars, lutes, etc., the small ridge over which the strings pass as they leave the tuning-pegs, and which keeps them from touching the fingerboard. Grooves cut into the nut keep the strings in place and at fixed distances apart from each other. **2** In connection with the bow of a string instrument, 'nut' means the same as *heel.

Nutcracker, The (*Casse-noisette*) Ballet in two acts and three scenes, composed by Tchaikovsky, first produced in St Petersburg (now Leningrad) in 1892 (story based on Hoffmann's *Der Nussknacker und der Mäusekönig*; choreography by Ivanov). As a Christmas present, Drosselmeyer gives his goddaughter, Clara (sometimes known as Marie, or Masha), a nutcracker. Falling asleep, she dreams that she is defending it against the Mouse King, whom she kills by throwing her slipper at him. The nutcracker turns into a handsome prince, and Clara accompanies him on a journey to the Kingdom of Sweets. There they are greeted by the Sugar-Plum Fairy and entertained to a sumptuous banquet and a divertissement of dances.

The famous *Nutcracker Suite*, based on music from the ballet, consists of: 1 Miniature Overture (*Ouverture miniature*); 2 March (*Marche*); 3 Dance of the Sugar-Plum Fairy (*Danse de la fée-dragée*); 4 Russian Dance (*Danse russe, Trepak*); 5 Arab Dance (*Danse arabe*); 6 Chinese Dance (*Danse chinoise*); 7 Dance of the Flutes (*Danse des mirlitons*); 8 Waltz of the Flowers (*Valse des fleurs*).

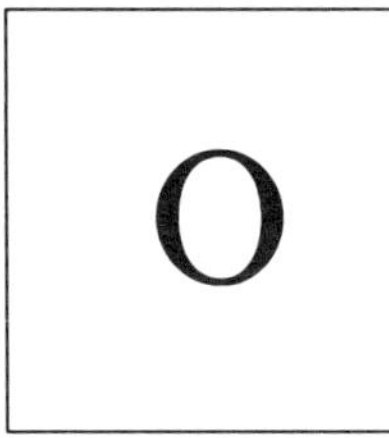

O; od [Italian] Or.

○ Sign used in printed music to indicate: **1** to a player of a bowed string instrument, that either an open string or a harmonic should be played; **2** to a harpist, that a harmonic should be played; **3** to a horn player that an open note should be played (as opposed to a stopped note, often indicated by +).

Obbligato [Italian: 'obligatory' or 'essential'] Originally, this term referred to an instrument or instrumental part which was essential to the effect of the music – for instance, an aria for soprano, strings, and *oboe obbligato*. During the 19th century though, by some misunderstanding of its true meaning, this Italian word came to be used by composers to refer to an *optional* instrument or part which is not absolutely essential to the music and can therefore be omitted.

Oberwerk [German] Swell organ. [See under *Organ]

Oblique motion See *Motion.

Oboe A double reed *woodwind instrument which, together with the flute, clarinet, and bassoon, is one of the four main orchestral woodwinds. The tube of the oboe, about 60 cm long, is conical and ends with a moderately-flared bell. The double reed consists of two thin strips of cane, their ends finely tapered. These are bound round a small metal tube, called a staple, and fitted into a cork which fixes firmly into the top of the instrument. As the player blows, the two reeds vibrate against each other, causing the air column inside the oboe to vibrate, and so produce a note. The different pitches are obtained by opening and closing holes, cut into the side of the oboe, by means of a system of keys and levers operated by the fingers (see *Boehm system).

oboe

The range of the oboe is just over two and a half octaves.

Range: 

The sound of the oboe is reedy, and penetrating – the reason why, before a concert begins, it is the oboe which sounds the note A to which all the other players tune their instruments. When playing slowish melodies, the oboe tends to sound rather plaintive and melancholy. In swifter, rhythmic tunes it can sound crisp and lively, with a marvellous edge and bite to the tone.

The oboe developed from the *shawm during the 17th century. By 1700, almost all orchestras included oboes (usually a pair), and it was in fact around the oboe that, in due course, the woodwind section was built up. The oboe is frequently used in chamber music – almost always in works for wind ensemble – and is a regular member of the military band and the symphonic band.

Famous orchestral solos for oboe can be heard at the beginning of the *Scène* from Tchaikovsky's *Swan Lake* and the slow movement of his Fourth Symphony, the slow movement of Beethoven's **Eroica Symphony*, the slow movement of Schubert's Ninth Symphony, and Handel's *The *Arrival of the Queen of Sheba* (two oboes). Works for solo (unaccompanied) oboe include Britten's *Six Metamorphoses after Ovid* and Berio's *Sequenza VII*. Among the many concertos for oboe and orchestra are those by Albinoni, Vivaldi, Handel, Marcello, Mozart, Richard Strauss, Vaughan Williams, and Martinů; also, Bach's Double Concerto for oboe and violin, and Henze's Double Concerto for oboe, harp, and strings. Chamber works with oboe include Mozart's Oboe Quartet in F, Bax's Oboe Quintet, Bliss's Oboe Quintet, Britten's Phantasy Quartet, and Poulenc's Oboe Sonata. Also, works by Mozart for wind ensemble – especially the Serenades in B♭ (K361), in E♭ (K375), and in C minor (K388); and the Divertimentos in E♭ (K252) and in B♭ (K270) each for two oboes, two horns, and two bassoons.

Among instruments closely related to the oboe are the *cor anglais, *bassoon, *oboe da caccia, *oboe d'amore, and *heckelphone. [See also: *Hichiriki]

Oboe da caccia [Italian: 'oboe of the hunt'] An 18th-century tenor oboe with a large open bell. Its range is similar to that of the cor anglais. Bach asks for oboe da caccia in certain items in his *St Matthew Passion*, e.g. 'Ah, Golgotha!' (No. 69, alto recitative) and 'See the Saviour's outstretched hands!' (No. 70, alto aria) – each of these items including a pair of oboi da caccia in the accompaniment.

Oboe d'amore [Italian: 'oboe of love'] A type of oboe (the alto member of the oboe family) originating in Germany around 1720. It is pitched a minor 3rd lower than the normal orchestral oboe, and has a pear-shaped bell like that of the cor anglais. Bach asks for oboe d'amore in certain sections of his B minor Mass, e.g. *Qui sedes* (No. 9, alto aria) and *Et in Spiritum sanctum Dominum* (No. 18, bass aria, with two oboi d'amore and continuo).

Oboe quartet Chamber music for oboe plus string trio (violin, viola, cello); e.g. Mozart's Oboe Quartet in F major, K370, composed in 1781.

Oboe quintet *Chamber music for oboe plus string quartet (two violins, viola, cello). Examples are Bax's Oboe Quintet (1922) and Bliss's Oboe Quintet, Op. 44 (1927).

Oboi [Italian, plural] Oboes. (The Italian singular, like the English, is *oboe*.)

Octave The *interval of an 8th; the distance between the first and eighth notes (which share the same letter-name) of any *diatonic scale, major or minor. For example: C to the next C, above or below. Contained within any octave are thirteen notes separated by twelve semitones. [See also: *Octave signs, below]

Octave signs Composers use various terms and signs to indicate that a note, or a passage of notes, is to be played one octave higher or lower than the pitch at which it is printed. This saves printing many leger lines, and also makes the music easier to read on the part of the performer. Octave signs include:

Ottava alta (high octave) *Ottava sopra* (octave above) *8va*⁻ – – – – – – – – – – – ┐	Play the note or notes one octave higher than the printed pitch
Ottava bassa (low octave) *Ottava sotto* (octave below) *8va*_ – – – – – – – – – – – ┘	Play the note or notes one octave lower than the printed pitch

All'ottava, all'8va (at the octave): play the notes one octave higher (if the term is printed above the notes) or one octave lower (if printed below the notes).

Coll'ottava, coll'8va, or *con 8*: at the same time as the written note, play the note one octave lower (if the passage is written in the bass clef), or one octave higher (if written in the treble clef).

Coll'ottava bassa: with the written note, play the note one octave lower.

Octet [French: *octette, octuor*; German: *Oktett*; Italian: *ottetto*] **1** Music composed for eight solo instruments or voices. **2** A group which performs such a composition. Examples include: Beethoven's Wind Octet (in E♭, Op. 103; *c*1793) for 2 oboes, 2 clarinets, 2 horns, 2 bassoons; Mendelssohn's String Octet (in E♭, Op. 20; 1825) for 4 violins, 2 violas, 2 cellos; Schubert's Octet (in F, 1824) for clarinet, bassoon, horn, 2 violins, viola, cello, double bass; and Stravinsky's Octet (1923) for flute, clarinet, 2 bassoons, 2 trumpets, tenor and bass trombones. [See also: *Chamber music]

Octuor [French] *Octet.

Octuplet A group of eight notes performed evenly in the time taken by six notes of the same kind.

Od [Italian] Or.

Ode A lyrical poem, often in honour of a particular person or occasion. A musical setting of an ode is usually of a ceremonious character, with contrasting sections of music for soloists, chorus, and orchestra. Four compositions by Purcell and one by Handel have the title *Ode for St Cecilia's Day* (St *Cecilia being the patron saint of music). Another well-known ode by Purcell is **Come, ye Sons of Art, Away*.

Oder [German] Or; or else; otherwise.

Odhecaton [from Greek for 'song' and 'hundred'] A collection of 'A Hundred Songs' (though actually only ninety-six) published in 1501 by Petrucci. *Odhecaton* was the earliest printed collection of polyphonic music. It contains secular compositions, dating from around 1470 to 1500, by composers such as Compère, Isaac, Josquin des Prez, Ockeghem, and Obrecht.

Oeuvre [French] A work. (Same meaning as *Opus.)

Offen [German] Open.

Offertorium [Latin: 'offertory'] The fourth item of the Proper of the *Mass, sung as the bread and wine are placed upon the altar. The term is also applied to a motet which may be sung at this point, or a piece played on organ or other instruments.

Office A service forming part of the Divine Office (Canonical Hours, Daily

Hours) of the Roman Catholic Church. Divine Office occurs eight times daily, approximately every three hours. The eight services (apart from the *Mass) are: 1 *Matins; 2 Lauds; 3 Prime; 4 Terce; 5 Sext; 6 None; 7 *Vespers; 8 Compline.

Ohne [German] Without.

Oiseau de feu, L' See *The *Firebird.*

Oktave [German] *Octave.

Oktett [German] *Octet.

'Older' rondo form See *Rondo.

Old Hall Manuscript An important collection of sacred polyphonic music (Mass movements, motets, antiphons, sequences) by more than twenty composers of the late 14th and early 15th centuries, nearly all of them English. It used to be kept at the College of St Edmund at Old Hall, near Ware. It is now housed in the British Library.

Old Hundredth The hymn-tune usually sung to the words 'All people that on earth do dwell' or 'Praise God from whom all blessings flow'. It is a very old tune which first appeared in the Geneva Psalter of 1551. It was used in the Anglo-Genevan Psalter of 1561 as a setting of the 100th Psalm – hence its name. Several composers have based organ pieces on this tune. Vaughan Williams made a festive arrangement of 'The Old Hundredth Psalm Tune' for choir, congregation, organ, orchestra, and 'all available trumpets', which was first performed at the Coronation of Queen Elizabeth II in 1953.

Ondeggiando; **Ondeggiamente** [Italian] Undulating, swaying, waving.

Ondes Martenot (ondes musicales) [French: 'Martenot's waves', or 'musical waves'] An electronic instrument, invented in the 1920s by French musician Maurice Martenot, which uses a valve oscillator to produce the sound through an amplifier and loudspeaker. The pitch is infinitely variable over a range of almost six octaves. There is a piano-type keyboard, and the performer may play the instrument by sliding a finger-ring attached to a ribbon above the keyboard (in this case using the keyboard merely as a guide to the whereabouts of the desired pitches), or by actually depressing keys on the keyboard. The keys can also be manipulated sideways to a certain extent, to produce effects of vibrato and glissando. The instrument is purely melodic – single pitches and glissandos can be played, but not chords. The volume can be controlled, and variations of timbre or tone-colour achieved, by the performer's left hand. The characteristic, and often haunting, sound of the ondes Martenot can be heard in Honegger's *Joan of Arc at the Stake*, and in certain works by Messiaen, such as the *Turangalîla-symphonie* and *Trois petites liturgies de la Présence Divine* (especially during the second half of the third liturgy).

Ongarese [Italian] Hungarian. **All'ongarese**, in Hungarian (gypsy) style.

On Hearing the First Cuckoo in Spring A tone poem for small orchestra (1912) by Delius, describing the freshness and beauty of the countryside awakening in Spring. One of the melodies included is a Norwegian folk-tune. The repeated call of the cuckoo is heard on the clarinet. [See also: *Summer Night on the River]

On Wenlock Edge A *song-cycle for tenor, string quartet, and piano, composed by Vaughan Williams in 1908–9, setting six poems from A. E. Housman's *A Shropshire Lad.* The titles of the songs are: 1 On Wenlock Edge; 2 From far, from eve and morning; 3 Is my team ploughing?; 4 Oh, when I was in love with you; 5 Bredon Hill; 6 Clun. Vaughan Williams later arranged the work for tenor and orchestra.

Op. Abbreviation standing for *Opus.

Open In brass parts, the instruction 'open' (or the French word *ouvert*) indicates a return to normal playing after playing muted or stopped notes.

Open form Describing a composition as being in 'open form' means that although certain details of the music (such as speed, dynamics, expression) may be fixed by the composer, the actual order or sequence of large musical events – sections of the music, or perhaps pages of the score – is determined either by chance (perhaps by throwing a dice) or according to the choice of the performer(s). In this way the composer, having completed the composing of the piece, leaves the form or structure 'open' to future decisions – either chance, or choice. Stockhausen's *Piano Piece XI* (1956), for example, consists of nineteen fragments of music, any of which the pianist may select and play in any order. At the end of each fragment there are printed markings of speed, loudness, and touch which must be applied to whichever fragment the pianist chooses to play next. Any fragment may be played twice (the second time an octave higher or lower than the first) and the piece ends when any fragment has been chosen and played for a third time.

Open note On string instruments, the note obtained from a string which is not stopped by the finger and therefore vibrates along its entire length (called an 'open string'). On valved brass instruments, open notes are those obtained without using (depressing) any valves; they are therefore 'natural harmonics' – notes of the *harmonic series. In brass parts, however, 'open' indicates a return to normal playing after playing muted or stopped notes.

Open position See *Spacing.

Open score See *Score.

Open string An unstopped string on any instrument. [See: *Open note]

Oper [German] Opera; also opera house or opera company.

Opera [from Italian; French: *opéra*; German: *Oper*] A play, set to music, sung and acted, with scenery, costumes, and lighting. Some operas (*grand opera) employ music throughout; others include spoken dialogue. The story is often told in a series of recitatives, punctuated by arias and choruses (the *'number' opera), but many composers have preferred a less fragmented, more continuous plan. Music has been associated with drama from early times. The ancient Greeks used it: so did the writers of medieval miracle plays. The 16th-century liturgical dramas had music accompanying the acting, as well as *intermedii* between the scenes. These *intermedii* were light diversions, unconnected with the main play. They were often elaborate and employed voices and instruments.

Italy to the mid 19th century Opera proper is thought to have begun in Italy towards 1600. The Florentine *Camerata, tired of complicated polyphony, replaced it with a plain *monody which came to be known as *Le *Nuove Musiche* (The New Music). The first real operas were **Dafne* (1597) by Peri and Corsi, and **Euridice* (1600) by Peri and Caccini. The Venetian composer Monteverdi, in operas notable for their balanced design and wide emotional range, displayed a flair for characterization and a feel for theatrical effect. His *Orfeo* (1607; see **Orpheus*) made use of a vast and varied orchestra, while his *L'incoronazione di Poppea* (1642) injected some humour into the **opera seria* form. The works of his pupil Cavalli (e.g. *Ormindo*, 1644) contain fine arias. Alessandro Scarlatti established the **da capo aria* and the Italian *overture and added wind to the normal string orchestra. The early 18th century saw the birth of **opera buffa*, either with *recitativo secco* (see *recitative) or with spoken dialogue. Examples of the form were composed by Pergolesi (*La *Serva padrona*, 1733), Piccinni, Paisiello, and Cimarosa (*Il matrimonio segreto*, 1792). Rossini was a master of the catchy tune and the invigorating rhythm (*The *Barber of Seville*, 1816), but he also wrote serious operas (*Otello*, 1816; **William Tell*, 1829). He composed for a generation of singers of outstanding voice and virtuosity, who were well served also by the rapturous **bel canto* style of Bellini (*Norma*, 1831; *I puritani*, 1835) and, at his best, by the uneven Donizetti (**Lucia di Lammermoor*, 1835; *Don Pasquale*, 1843).

France to the late 19th century The first major opera composer in France was the Italian-born Lully. His works (e.g. *Armide*, 1686) were rather formal, but his recitative was tailor-made for the French language, he used the orchestra imaginatively, and he raised the chorus and ballet to positions of importance. He also made use of the French *overture. In the early 1700s the rigidity of opera seria was countered by the new **opéra comique*. Rameau (e.g. in *Les Indes galantes*, 1735) breathed new life into French opera. In 1784, Grétry's *Richard Coeur de Lion* (an early example of the *'rescue' opera) went so far as to use a *leading-motive (leitmotif). The style of Boieldieu, composer of *La Dame blanche* (1825), was so Germanic as to constitute a link between Weber and Wagner. In operas like *Fra Diavolo* (1830), Auber combined Italian sparkle with French elegance, while Berlioz produced the astonishingly original *Les Troyens* (1856–8), a 'number' opera on an epic scale. Even the naturally unpretentious Gounod rose to the grand manner in **Faust* (1859), and in **Carmen* (1875) Bizet created the most captivating of all *opéras comiques*. Offenbach composed the satirical *Orpheus in the Underworld* (1858; see **Orpheus*) and the tuneful **Tales of Hoffmann* (1881). Also in Paris were the Italian Cherubini, whose *Les Deux Journées* (1800; known as *The Water Carrier*) influenced Beethoven's **Fidelio*; and Meyerbeer, a German Jew, whose love of spectacle is conspicuous in his *Robert le Diable* (1831).

Germany and Austria to the mid 19th century In the 17th century most operas staged in Germany were by Italians, but in 1725 Telemann scored a hit with *Pimpinone*, an intermezzo (see *Intermezzo 2) as lively as Pergolesi's *La serva padrona* of eight years later. The *Singspiel, virtually created by Hiller, sent opera seria temporarily into decline. Gluck formulated the operatic 'reforms' published in the preface to his *Alceste (1767): the music should be finely balanced to serve the drama; melodies and harmonies should be 'classically' simple and free from excessive ornamentation; continuity should be greater (he abandoned the da capo aria, and gave his recitatives orchestral support in a *stromentato* style sometimes flowering into *arioso); the characters should be plausibly human, not symbolic heroes; and the plot itself should not strain credibility (see *Orfeo ed Euridice*, under **Orpheus*). Haydn was hampered by poor libretti, but some of his fifteen surviving operas (e.g. *Il mondo della luna*, 1777) combine the *seria* with the *buffa* and contain some fine ensembles. Mozart, as always, is incomparable. In his German Singspiele (*The *Abduction from the Seraglio*, 1782; *The *Magic Flute*, 1791) and his Italian works (*Idomeneo*, 1781; *The *Marriage of Figaro*, 1786; **Don Giovanni*, 1787; **Così fan tutte*, 1790) his genius for characterization and his feel for texture, both vocal and instrumental, are heightened by an unrivalled understanding of symphonic principles of design. Beethoven's **Fidelio* (1814) is the supreme 'rescue' opera, while the 'Wolf's Glen' scene in Weber's *Der *Freischütz* (1821) is a chilling manifestation of Romantic horror.

Verdi, Wagner, and Richard Strauss The leading figure in late 19th-century

Italian opera was Verdi, a forthright man who preferred the simple and natural to the complex and mystic. From *Nabucco* (1842) to the sumptuous **Aida* (1871), his operas are melodious and colourful (see **Rigoletto*, 1851; *La *Traviata*, 1853; *Il *Trovatore*, 1853). In his late works, the Shakespearean **Otello* (1887) and **Falstaff* (1893), the continuity is greater, the role of the orchestra more substantial. The German Wagner called his operas 'music-dramas', wrote his own texts (usually based on ancient Scandinavian or German legends), and regarded the music and drama as an inseparable unity. The *leading-motive became a crucial structural feature, and the orchestra was as important as the singers. He aimed to write 'unending melody' and was unsurpassed in the creation of atmosphere (see *The *Flying Dutchman*, 1843; **Tannhäuser*, 1845; **Lohengrin*, 1850; **Tristan and Isolde*, 1865; *Die *Meistersinger*, 1868). His huge four-part cycle *Der *Ring des Nibelungen* took more than twenty years to write. Richard Strauss (*Elektra*, 1909; *Der Rosenkavalier*, 1911) inherited some of Wagner's opulence. The operettas of Johann Strauss II (e.g. *Die *Fledermaus*, 1874) date from this period, while the decades around 1900 saw the **verismo* style of Puccini (*La *Bohème*, 1896; **Tosca*, 1900; **Madama Butterfly*, 1904), Mascagni (**Cavalleria rusticana*, 1890), and Leoncavallo (**Pagliacci*, 1892).

Nationalism The Russian Glinka used folk-like tunes and the sound of the balalaika in his *A Life for the Tsar* (1836; also known as *Ivan Susanin*), while the oriental atmosphere of his *Russlan and Ludmilla* (1842), in which he used the whole-tone scale, foreshadowed the patriotic pageantry of Borodin's **Prince Igor* (1890). *Nationalism is apparent also in Musorgsky's **Boris Godunov* (1874), but not in Tchaikovsky's operas (e.g. *Eugene Onegin*, 1879), which are international. The spirit of Bohemia is strong in Smetana (*The *Bartered Bride*, 1866), Dvořák (*Rusalka*, 1901) and Janáček (*Jenůfa*, 1904; *Katya Kabanova*, 1921).

Britain to c1900 English opera grew from the **masque*. The greatest real opera of the 17th century was Henry Purcell's **Dido and Aeneas* (*c*1689) – a strikingly dramatic work, almost Monteverdian in its depth of emotion. In the early 1700s Handel established serious opera in England with a succession of richly varied works including **Giulio Cesare* (1724) and *Alcina* (1735). Many of his best arias were written for castrati, and he favoured *opera seria*, even though it was considered old-fashioned in his day. *The *Beggar's Opera* (by Gay and Pepusch, 1728) was akin to French *opéra comique* and was welcomed for its spicy satire, as were Arne's comic operas (e.g. *Thomas and Sally*, 1760) for their homely charm. 19th-century composers of opera included Balfe (*The Bohemian Girl*, 1843) and Stanford (*Shamus O'Brien*, 1896). From 1871, Gilbert and Sullivan produced their popular operettas (see *The *Pirates of Penzance*, 1879; *The *Mikado*, 1885).

The 20th century Like other forms of music, opera has been affected by 20th-century trends. Audiences of the day were puzzled by the misty *Impressionism and constant recitative of Debussy's *Pelléas et Mélisande* (1902), by the lack of action in Bartók's *Duke Bluebeard's Castle* (1918), the *Sprechstimme in Berg's **Wozzeck* (1925), the biting satire of Weill's *The *Threepenny Opera* (1928) and the *neoclassicism of Stravinsky's *The *Rake's Progress* (1951). Easier on the ear were the haunting tunes and jazzy rhythms of Gershwin (whose opera **Porgy and Bess* is almost a musical) and Bernstein (whose musical **West Side Story* is almost an opera). England came into its own with works by Britten (e.g. **Peter Grimes*, 1945; *Billy Budd*, 1951) and

Tippett (*The *Midsummer Marriage*, 1955; *King Priam*, 1962). Some of Britten's works (**Let's Make an Opera*, 1949; **Noye's Fludde*, 1958) include roles for children. Among other 20th-century operas are Schoenberg's unfinished *Moses und Aron*, Prokofiev's *The Love of Three Oranges* (1921), Hindemith's **Mathis der Maler* (1938) and Henze's *Elegy for Young Lovers* (1961).

Opéra bouffe [French] A 19th-century type of French comic opera, light and witty in style, deriving from the Italian **opera buffa*. A famous example is *Orpheus in the Underworld* by Offenbach.

Opera buffa [Italian: 'comic opera'] A type of opera which developed in Italy during the early 18th century, in contrast to the type known as **opera seria*. An *opera buffa* is based on a light-hearted plot and the characters are drawn from everyday life. Examples are *The *Marriage of Figaro* by Mozart and *The *Barber of Seville* by Rossini.

Opéra comique [French] Although this term literally means 'comic opera', it is used specifically to describe any opera in which the musical numbers are interspersed with spoken dialogue (e.g. Gounod's **Faust* and, in its original form, Bizet's **Carmen*).

Opera semiseria A type of opera which is neither wholly serious, nor wholly comic. The main story of the opera is essentially serious, but comic elements are introduced along the way (usually by lesser characters such as servants). A famous example is **Don Giovanni* by Mozart. [See also: *Opera seria; *Opera buffa]

Opera seria [Italian: 'serious opera'] The main type of opera of the 17th and 18th centuries, based on a serious or even tragic plot, usually drawn from history or mythology, and set to an Italian libretto. An *opera seria* was structured in three acts, and the story was carried forward mainly in *recitativo secco* (see *Recitative). Each passage of recitative was followed by an elaborate aria – lyric or dramatic – expressing the character's thoughts, emotions, and reactions to the situation at that point in the drama. An aria was almost always in *da capo* form (see *Da capo aria). The operas of Handel are of the opera seria type, e.g. **Giulio Cesare* (Julius Caesar). [See also: *Opera buffa; *Intermezzo 2]

Operetta [Italian: 'little opera'] A term which came to be used during the 19th century for a type of opera which was light in style, with spoken dialogue, and with music of a tuneful, popular character. Famous examples of operetta include *Die *Fledermaus* (The bat) by Johann Strauss the Younger; *Die lustige Witwe* (The Merry Widow) by Franz Lehár; and the many operettas of Gilbert and Sullivan (librettist and composer respectively) such as *The *Mikado*, *The *Pirates of Penzance*, and *The Yeoman of the Guard*. [See also: *Opéra bouffe]

Ophicleide A 19th-century brass instrument which was the bass member of a family of keyed bugles. It had nine to twelve keys, and was usually pitched in C or B♭. The ophicleide was often used in bands and sometimes in the orchestra, until its place was taken by the tuba. (It is included, for example, in Mendelssohn's score of his Overture to *A Midsummer Night's Dream*.)

Opus (usually abbreviated to **Op.**, plural: *Opp.*) [Latin: 'work'] Term used by many composers to identify their works either in order of composition or in order of publication. For instance, Beethoven's Fifth Symphony is identified as Op. 67, his Piano Concerto No. 5 (The 'Emperor') as Op. 73. Sometimes two or more pieces are composed and/or published as a group, in which case the opus is subdivided. For example, Chopin's 'Revolutionary' Study is identified as Op. 10 No. 12, his Prelude in D♭ as Op. 28 No. 15.

A high opus number need not necessarily indicate a late work; it may be attached to an early work which remained unpublished until later in the composer's life. **Op. post.** (or **Op. posth.**) indicates a posthumous work which was published and received its opus number after the composer's death.

Oratorio An extended musical setting of a quite lengthy text – usually tracing a religious story, most often taken from the Bible. Oratorio emerged around 1600 (at about the same time as opera) and took its name from St Philip Neri's Oratory ('hall of prayer') in Rome where, in the early years of the 17th century, the first oratorios were performed.

A typical oratorio is scored for solo voices, chorus, and orchestra; and the music is structured in separate musical items or 'numbers'. For the soloists there are *recitatives (used, as in opera, as a means of swiftly telling the story), and also *arias and duets. The choruses may be reflective, or they may vividly describe the more dramatic and exciting events in the story. The main function of the orchestra is to accompany the voices, though there may be an overture and perhaps one or two orchestral interludes.

The earliest oratorios were often acted out, with costumes and scenery; and their music was often in a similar style to that of the operas of the period. In time, however, oratorios ceased to be acted, and were given musical presentation only, in churches and concert halls rather than theatres.

[See also: *Lauda; *Passion; *Cantata; **Christmas Oratorio*; *Testo]

The following list includes some notable oratorios, from 1600 to the present.

Cavalieri: *Rappresentatione di Anima e di Corpo* ('The Representation of the Soul and the Body'), 1600 [while some authorities count this as the earliest oratorio, others maintain that it is the earliest surviving opera – a 'sacred opera' or 'sacred representation' – since it was intended for stage production with acting, costumes, and scenery, and includes secular dances and items in madrigal style].

Carissimi: *Jephte* (*c*1645). Schütz: *Christmas Story* (1664). Handel: **Israel in Egypt* (1739), **Messiah* (1741), *Samson* (1741), **Judas Maccabaeus* (1747), *Solomon* (1749), *Jephtha* (1752). Haydn: *The *Creation* (1796–8), *The *Seasons* (1799–1801).

Berlioz: *L'*Enfance du Christ* (1850–54). Mendelssohn: **Elijah* (1846). Stainer: *The Crucifixion* (1887). Elgar: *The *Dream of Gerontius* (1899–1900). Honegger: *Le Roi David* (1921). Walton: **Belshazzar's Feast* (1930–31). Tippett: *A *Child of Our Time* (1939–41). Stravinsky: *Oedipus rex* (1927), an 'opera-oratorio' with minimal acting and staging.

Orb and Sceptre A march for orchestra by Walton, composed for the coronation of Elizabeth II in 1953. [See also: **Crown Imperial*]

Orchésographie See under **Capriol Suite*.

Orchestra [French: *orchestre*; German: *Orchester*; Italian: *orchestra*] An organized and balanced group of bowed string instruments (with more than one player per part), to which may be added a number of woodwind, brass, and percussion instruments. Orchestras, in fact, vary greatly in the actual number, and different kinds, of instruments included, according to the period and type of whatever composition is being performed. The modern orchestra, often called *symphony orchestra, is made up of four **sections** of instruments: *strings* (with more than one player per part), *woodwind, brass, percussion.* In each of these four sections, the instruments share a 'family likeness' or similar method of playing or sound production. One or more harps may also be included; and, occasionally, additional instruments such as piano or organ – though these are not strictly orchestral instruments and are counted as 'visitors'.

The word orchestra comes from Greek, *orkhēstra*, meaning 'dancing place', and in the open-air Greek theatre of the 5th century BC this was the space in front of the main acting area which was used by the chorus (who danced, sang, and chanted) and by the instrumentalists. A long while later, towards 1600 in Italy, the first operas were being performed. As their composers believed they were imitating the ancient Greek dramas, the word 'orchestra' was used to describe the space between audience and stage which was occupied by the accompanying instrumentalists. It then came to refer to the instrumentalists themselves, and eventually to the collection of instruments they played.

In the 17th century, orchestras were very variable and haphazard – composers often including whatever instruments might be available. For a while, viols and violins played side by side, but before long the viols dropped out due to the greater power, brilliance, agility, and range of expression of the violin. By the beginning of the 18th century the string section had become established as a self-contained unit, consisting of first violins, second violins, violas, cellos, and double basses (the first violins generally playing higher notes than the seconds, the double basses doubling the cellos – playing exactly the same written notes but sounding an octave deeper).

The string section thus became the firm basis of the orchestra, to which a composer might add other instruments, singly or in pairs, as occasion offered – flutes (or recorders), oboes, bassoons, perhaps horns, and occasionally trumpets and kettle drums. And there was always a keyboard continuo instrument – harpsichord or organ – the player building up chords on the bass-line to fill out the harmonies, and also decorating the texture of the music (see *Continuo; also *Figured bass).

Towards the end of the 18th century composers began to include a pair of clarinets along with pairs of flutes, oboes, and bassoons to form a self-contained woodwind section. The orchestra now commonly consisted of: 2 flutes, 2 oboes, 2 clarinets, 2 bassoons; 2 horns, 2 trumpets; 2 kettle drums; and strings (the keyboard continuo now falling out of use).

During the last years of the 18th century and the early years of the 19th, this formation of the orchestra was accepted as standard. It is often called the 'Classical orchestra' since Haydn's last symphonies, and the early symphonies

late 18th-century orchestra

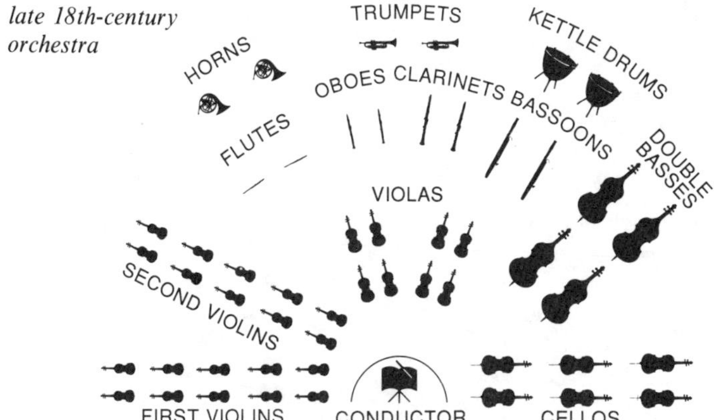

of Beethoven and Schubert, are scored for precisely this combination of instruments.

During the 19th century, the orchestra increased in both size and range. In the earlier part of the century, the standard number of horns became four, often with two crooked in one key and the other two crooked in another key (see *Crook) to obtain a wider range of notes – all the notes chosen, of course, so that they would sound in the key of the piece. The invention of the *valve system, around 1815, finally offered horns and trumpets a full range of notes and much greater flexibility. Trombones, previously used only in church music and operas, now found a regular place in the orchestra, and the tuba, introduced in the 1830s, became the bass of a now complete brass section.

Woodwind instruments were improved by the development of new key mechanisms (e.g. see *Boehm system). And by the 1850s, in addition to the four standard woodwinds (flutes, oboes, clarinets, bassoons) composers often included parts for 'extra' woodwind – piccolo, cor anglais, bass clarinet, and double bassoon – so extending the range of the woodwind section in both pitch and tone-colour.

This enlarging of the woodwind and brass sections meant that, in order to balance the sound, the number of string players also needed to be increased. Sometimes one (or more than one) harp was also included. As far as the percussion section was concerned, scores ranged from those which included kettle drums only, to others which called for an extremely varied and colourful choice of both pitched and unpitched percussion (see *Percussion instruments).

It is the orchestra of this size and range and proportions (made up of ninety or more players) that has become known as the modern orchestra, full orchestra, or symphony orchestra. The diagram below shows such an orchestra, needed to play certain scores by composers of the second half of the 19th century. It also shows a typical layout of the instruments, according to the four sections of the orchestra: strings spread out across the front, woodwind in the centre, with brass and percussion behind.

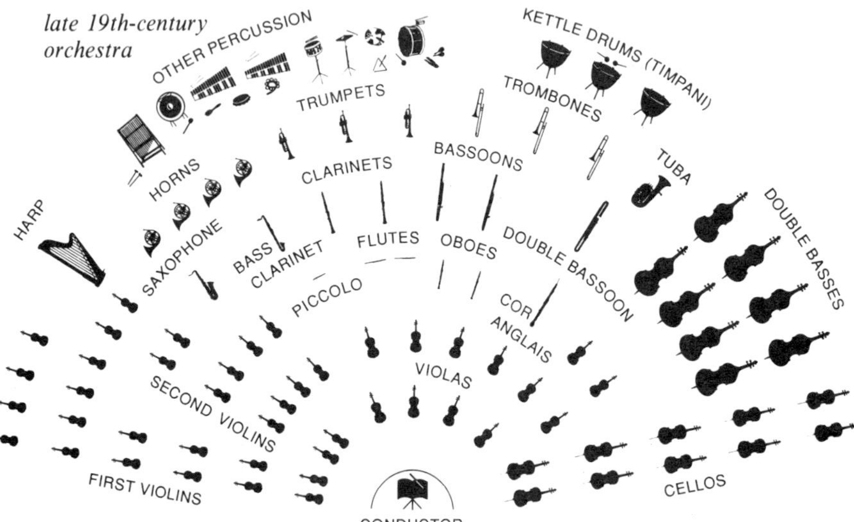

At the end of the 19th century and the beginning of the 20th, some composers occasionally scored works for a vastly expanded orchestra – see, for example, **Also sprach Zarathustra* and *Ein *Heldenleben* by Strauss, *'Symphony of a Thousand' (Symphony No. 8) by Mahler, *The *Rite of Spring* by Stravinsky, *The *Planets* by Gustav Holst, and **Gurrelieder* by Schoenberg. At the same time however (from *c*1910) other composers chose, or were driven by financial pressure, to score works for a much smaller orchestra – consisting, for example, of a smallish string section plus one or two each of various kinds of woodwind and brass instruments, and perhaps a colourful and varied selection of percussion instruments played by one or two performers. (See also: *Neo-classicism.)

Other 20th-century trends have included the use of an even greater variety of colourful and even exotic percussion instruments, the discovery of new colouristic effects from familiar instruments, and also the inclusion of electronic sounds – which may be pre-recorded on tape or manipulated 'live' during performance, and combined with instruments and perhaps voices, sounding naturally or transformed by electronic means, in 'live' performance or on pre-recorded tape.

[See also: *Chamber orchestra; *String orchestra; *Orchestral devices; *Orchestration; *Score; *Scoring; *Transposing instruments; *Conducting; *Leader. For foreign names of instruments, and their abbreviations, most often found in orchestral scores, see Table 15 on page 396–397]

Orchestral chimes Same as *Tubular bells.

Orchestral devices (orchestral effects) Various special effects (which may be colourful, intriguing, even dramatic) used by composers of orchestral or ensemble music, exploiting the various possible timbres (tone-colours or sound-qualities) of the instruments, singly or in combination. For examples, see the following entries: *Pizzicato; *Mute; *Glissando; *Sforzando; Col *legno; Sul *ponticello; Sul *tasto; *Harmonic 2; *Divisés, divisi; *Flutter-tonguing. See also under: *Bowing; *Stopping; *Antiphonal; *Mannheim School.

Many colouristic effects are used by some 20th-century composers, ranging from instruments being played at the extremes of their registers (often forcefully, even harshly) to new effects from string instruments such as tapping or striking the body of the instrument with the bow or fingertips, bowing the strings *behind* the bridge (i.e. between the bridge and the tailpiece), and bowing *on* the tailpiece, and new effects from wind instruments such as noisily clicking the keys on a woodwind instrument or swiftly depressing and releasing the valves on a brass instrument (without blowing) to produce a rattling noise, playing on the double reed alone of a woodwind instrument or on the detached mouthpiece of a brass instrument, and whispering, speaking, singing, or shouting into an instrument.

Orchestral rattle See *Ratchet.

Orchestral score See *Score.

Orchestration The art and technique of writing and arranging music for orchestra. A skilful and imaginative orchestrator will have a thorough knowledge of instruments: their ranges, characteristic *timbres, technical capabilities, and the many ways in which instrumental sounds may be combined together – blended or contrasted – to create various kinds of musical texture. It is also necessary to be able to judge the balance of sounds (ensuring that softer instruments are not 'drowned' by louder ones), to be familiar with the layout of an orchestral *score, and to be able to notate the required notes accurately for all the instruments, especially those known as *transposing instruments.

Orchestre [French] *Orchestra.

Ordinario (abbrev.: **ord.**) [Italian] Ordinary; in the ordinary way; normal. **Tempo ordinario**, at a normal, reasonable speed.

Ordinary See *Mass.

Ordre [French] Term, meaning *suite, used by the French composer François Couperin and his contemporaries. Couperin's twenty-seven *ordres* include dances, such as the *allemande, *courante, *sarabande, *gavotte, and *gigue; also many non-dance pieces with picturesque titles, e.g. *Le Rossignol en amour* (The nightingale in love), *Soeur Monique* (Sister Monica), *Les Papillons* (The butterflies), and *Les Petits Moulins-à-vent* (The little windmills).

Orfeo; Orfeo ed Euridice See under *Orpheus.

Organ [French: *orgue*; German: *Orgel*; Italian: *organo* The oldest keyboard instrument – existing, in primitive form, in the 3rd century BC. The *console*, at which the player sits, usually consists nowadays of several five-octave *manuals* (keyboards for the hands) and a *pedal-board* of about two and a half octaves (a keyboard played with the feet). The pedal-board is made of wood; its layout is similar to that of the black and white keys on the manuals. The sound is produced by pipes – some made of metal, others of wood. These are lined up in rows (known as *ranks* or *registers*) on the tops of *wind chests*, which are kept filled with air by an electrically-operated blower. Formerly the blowing was done by hand. The degree of wind pressure affects the tone, which is regulated by a specialized treatment of the pipes known as 'voicing'.

There are two main types of organ-pipe. The *flue pipes* work like the *recorder; air enters at the base and is set vibrating by a lip in the wall of the pipe. The *reeds* contain resonators, which beat against a 'shallot' inside the pipe (much as a *clarinet reed beats against the mouthpiece). Each rank of

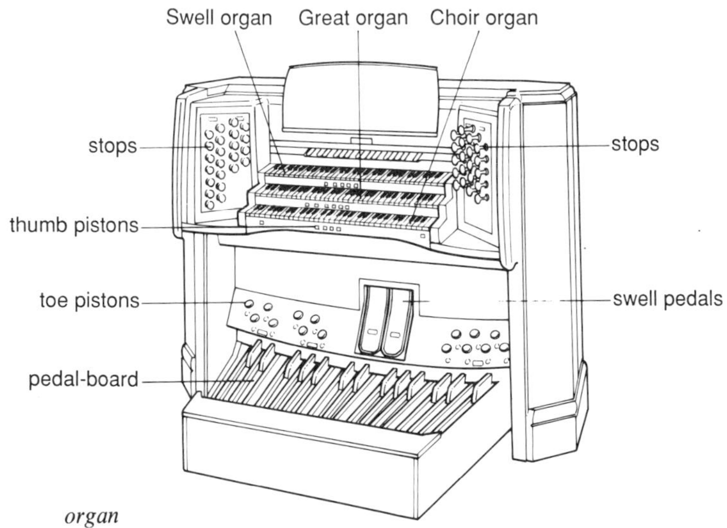

organ

pipes has its own distinctive tone, and is brought into play by a *stop* operated from the console. Each keyboard (manual or pedals) controls a separate division of the organ, with its own pipes and stops; every key has a pipe for every stop in its own division. By selecting and drawing (pulling out) stops (a process known as registration), the player determines which ranks of pipes are used, blending them like colours from an artist's palette. The pipes in any one rank become successively smaller as the pitch of the notes rises.

Ranks in which the lowest pipe (sounding the C two octaves below middle C) is 8 feet long are known as *foundation stops*; they sound the notes at the written pitch. A 4-foot rank (in which the corresponding pipes are half as long as those in an 8-foot rank) gives notes an octave higher than those written, a 2-foot two octaves higher, a 16-foot an octave lower than written, and so on. The figure indicating the pitch of the rank (e.g. 8, 4, 2) is shown on the stop handle. A stopped pipe (one with a cap on the top) sounds an octave lower than its length implies (for example, 'Stopped Diapason 8' is derived from a 4-foot rank).

There are also *mutation stops*, tuned to intervals between the octaves, such as the twelfth ($2\frac{2}{3}$ feet) and the seventeenth ($1\frac{3}{5}$ feet). Their tone is weaker than the main stops; they merely accentuate harmonics of the note played (see *harmonic series), adding sparkle to the tone. Often several mutation stops are grouped together and controlled by a single stop handle. This is known as a *mixture*, and it gives an impressive sound when added to a background of more basic tone. All stops which bring ranks of pipes into play are called *speaking stops*. In addition, there are *couplers*, also activated by stop handles. Some of these add an octave above or below the note played; others bring the effects of one manual through to another, or those of the manual through to the pedals, increasing the variety of tone and the amount of volume available. Some organs have thumb pistons (push-buttons sited between the manuals), and perhaps toe pistons, which bring into play set combinations of stops. Adjustable pistons also exist, which enable the organist to pre-set a personal selection of stops and to vary it at will.

The manuals of an organ are identified by names. The most powerful, basic tone is provided by the *Great Organ*. A two-manual instrument has the Great, and, at a higher level, the *Swell*, whose pipes are enclosed in a wooden box with one side slatted like a Venetian blind. By using a Swell pedal (a treadle-shaped device behind the pedal-board) the organist can open and close the slats to obtain *crescendo* and *diminuendo* effects. A three-manual instrument will have, in addition, the *Choir Organ*, played from a manual below the Great, and consisting of soft stops suitable for accompanying small groups of singers. A really large organ may have a fourth manual, the *Solo*, above the Swell, and even a fifth, *Echo Organ*, above that. The Solo Organ has stops suitable for solo melodies, accompanied on another manual. The Echo Organ is a small division, often placed apart from the main instrument. Designed to give echo effects, it is enclosed in a slatted box (like the Swell, and sometimes the Choir and Solo manuals). Each manual has its own bank of stop handles in jambs to the sides of the console. The specification (i.e. the number and type of stops) varies greatly from one instrument to another. A small village organ may have only six or eight speaking stops; the organ in Liverpool Anglican Cathedral has 168.

Every stop has its own *slider* between the wind chest and its rank of pipes. When a stop is drawn, the slider moves sideways, so that holes bored in it coincide with the bases of the pipes. Also at the base of each pipe is a valve (or *pallet*). In organs with mechanical action, when a key is depressed, a set of rods (*trackers*) opens the pallet, allowing air from the wind chest to enter the pipes of all stops drawn on that manual governed by that key. Many organs have electric action.

The diagram below is of a small two-manual organ with pedals.

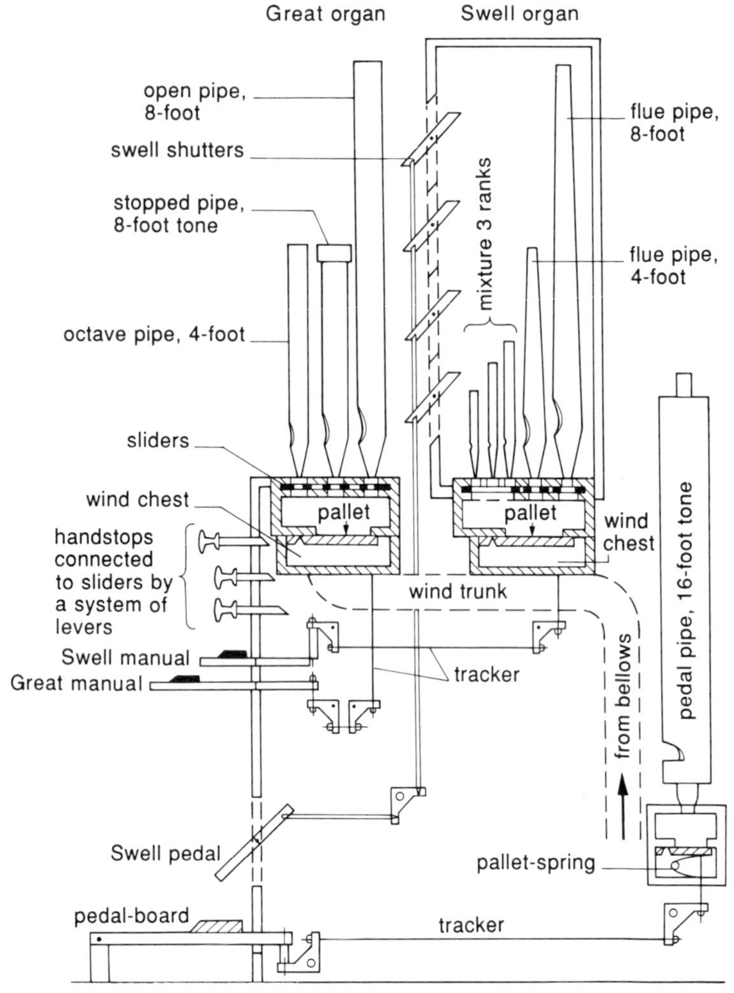

cross-section through an organ

The ancient organ (the *hydraulis*) was worked by water pressure, but pneumatic bellows were introduced in the 4th century AD. In the 10th century, a huge organ was built at Winchester, requiring seventy men to operate its twenty-six bellows. Pedals and stops were added to organs on the continent of Europe in the 15th century, although British organs lacked pedals until the late 1700s.

The 20th century has seen the invention of electronic organs, whose tone is produced, not by pipes, but by rotating discs with electro-magnetic pick-ups. They co-exist with pipe organs. [See also: *Portative organ; *Positive organ; *Regal]

Organetto [Italian] The 14th-century name for a small portable organ. [See: *Portative organ]

Organistrum [Latin] A *hurdy-gurdy.

Organo [Italian] Organ. **Organo pieno, organo pleno**, *full organ.

Organ point Same as *Pedal point.

Organum A general name given to the earliest experiments in composing polyphony, from the 9th century to the early part of the 13th. Their aim was to adorn various plainchants by adding one or more extra voice-parts to the existing melodies. Over this lengthy period of time, organum developed in four stages:

(1) **Parallel organum** (9th and 10th centuries) In this earliest – and simplest – kind of organum, the composer called his borrowed plainsong melody the 'principal voice'. Below it, he added another voice-part which he called the 'organal voice'. This, however, merely copied, or 'shadowed', the principal voice by proceeding at the interval of a 5th or a 4th below it in parallel *motion (except at the beginning and end of a phrase where oblique *motion might briefly occur):

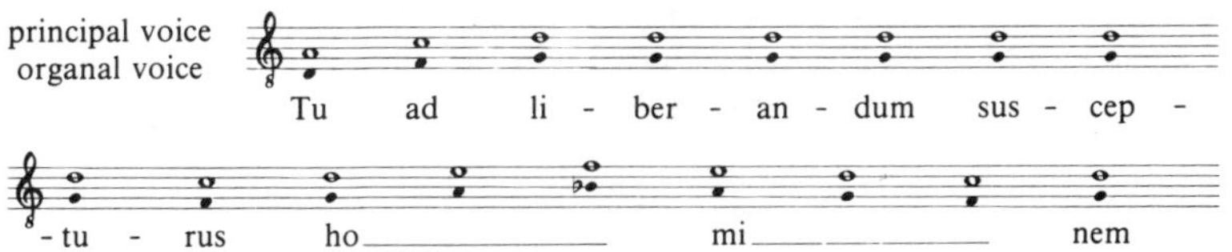

Sometimes, to make a grander and richer effect, either or both of these voice-parts might be duplicated an octave higher or an octave lower.

(2) **Free organum** By the 11th century, besides parallel motion, composers were allowing the two voice-parts to move more freely in oblique, contrary, and similar *motion, The organal voice was still added in *note-against-note style, but was now usually above, rather than below, the principal voice:

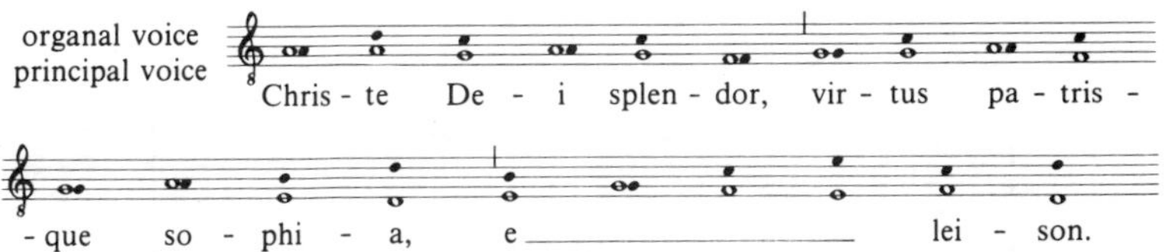

(3) **Melismatic organum** By the middle of the 12th century an important change had taken place in organum. The principal voice, which sang the plainchant *cantus firmus, now held on to each note for a much greater length of time. For this reason, composers began to call the principal voice the *tenor* (from Latin, meaning 'hold'). Above this tenor, the organal voice would now weave flowing phrases of three, four, or many more, notes above each single note of the plainchant. A melodious flow of notes sung to a single syllable is

called a *melisma*, and so this style of organum is known as melismatic organum:

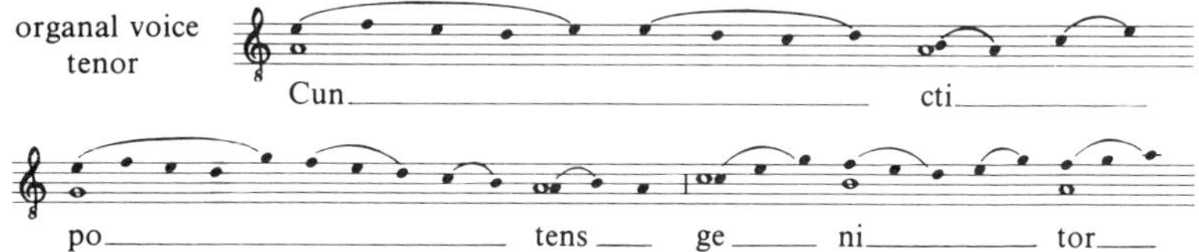

(4) **Measured organum** The composing of organum reached its most elaborate stage towards the end of the 12th century in music by composers of the Parisian 'Notre Dame School' (see under *Ars Antiqua). Having chosen a suitable plainchant as a cantus firmus, the composer would take the opening solo portion of the chant as his *tenor*, drawing out the notes into extremely long values (see music example (a) below). Above this tenor he would add a solo part called the *duplum* ('second voice') in quicker notes – rather as earlier composers had done when writing melismatic organum. But the important difference here is that in Notre Dame music, upper voice-parts are *measured* (arranged in precise units of musical time) the voices weaving dance-like phrases based on rhythm-patterns, all in triple time, which were in fact borrowed from poetry. When the composer came to a solo portion of chant with a melisma to each syllable, he would then set the tenor also moving in rhythm (see (b) below). A section of organum where the tenor *also* moved in rhythm was called a **clausula*. During this, the tenor notes were arranged in a short rhythmic pattern, repeated throughout.

(a)

(b)

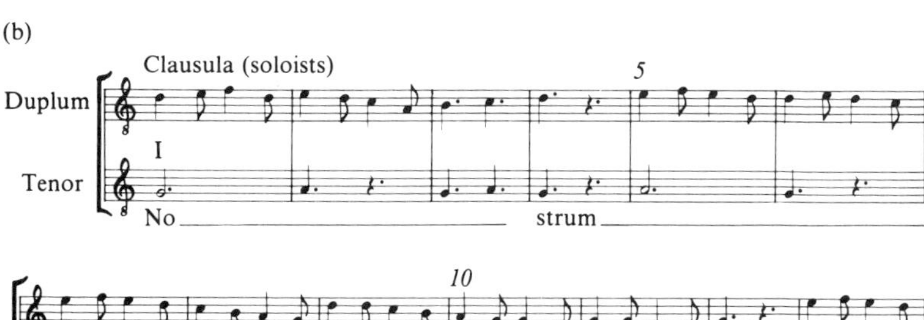

(etc.)

An organum written in two voice-parts was called an *organum duplum*. The Notre Dame composer, Pérotin, was first to use three voice-parts (*organum triplum*) and, on at least two occasions, four voice-parts (*organum quadruplum*). [See also: *Motet]

Orgel [German] Organ.

Orgelbüchlein [German: 'Little organ book'] A collection of forty-six short chorale preludes by J. S. Bach, mostly composed between 1713 and 1717. The settings are comparatively simple, since Bach intended them for teaching purposes and for pedalling practice. Among the best-known chorales included in the collection are: *Von Himmel hoch* (From heaven above); *In dulci jubilo* (In sweet joy), one of the oldest and best-known Christmas carols, dating from the 14th century; *Christ lag in Todesbanden* (Christ Lay in Death's Bonds) – see under the German title for this chorale melody; and *Ich ruf' zu dir, Herr Jesu Christ* (I call on Thee, Lord Jesus Christ).

Orgue [French] Organ.

Ornaments and grace notes These are notes which are extra to the main notes of a melodic line, serving to 'grace' (decorate or embellish) it – also sometimes serving to enhance the harmony, or to make the rhythm more incisive. Ornaments may be indicated by special signs, or they may appear as small-sized notes printed among the main notes. The most important ornaments are shown below, together with an indication as to how they may be performed. But the interpretation of certain ornaments (particularly in music up to the 18th century) requires detailed study, and at least two important factors may need to be taken into account: the speed of the music, and the period when it was composed. For example, a trill in slow music will include more alternations of the two notes than a trill in fast music; and a trill in music by Bach will not be performed in exactly the same way as a trill in music by Chopin. Similarly, a mordent in a piece by Bach will begin *on* the beat; whereas in a piece by Chopin it will begin *before* the beat.

tr or *tr*〰 *Trill* (or *shake*) essentially, this consists of the alternation of the main written note with the note above it:

Allegro

Adagio

Inflected notes (sharp, flat, natural, etc.) may be indicated above and/or below the trill sign. For example:

𝆗 *Upper mordent* [from Italian: 'biting'] the main note, the note above, the main note again:

Lower mordent the main note, the note below, the main note again:

Appoggiatura [a 'leaning' note] usually steals half the value of the main note; often two-thirds if the main note is a dotted note:

Acciaccatura [a 'crushed' note] crushed in quickly, either on the beat, or just before it:

or

∾ *Turn* consisting essentially of four notes 'turning' around the main note – the note above, the main note, the note below, the main note again:

but

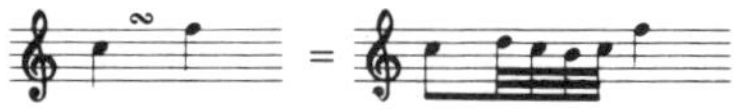

or ∽ or *Inverted turn* the note below, the main note, the note above, the main note again:

Inflected notes (sharp, flat, natural, etc.) may be indicated above and/or below the sign. For example:

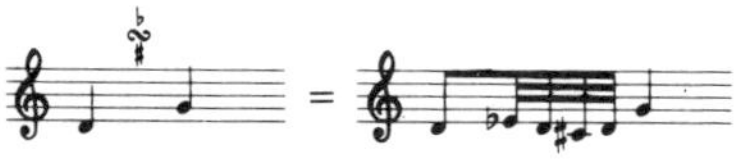

[See also: *Slide, 3]

Orpheus In the Greek legend Eurydice, wife of the poet and musician Orpheus, is bitten by a serpent and dies. Orpheus follows her to the Underworld and charms Pluto into releasing her, but he is warned that he must not look at her as he leads her back to earth. The temptation is too strong. He turns to face her, and she vanishes back to Hades. The story has attracted many composers.

Monteverdi's *Orfeo* (five acts, text by Striggio, first produced at Mantua in 1607) begins with the rejoicing after the wedding of Orfeo and Euridice, which is cut short by the arrival of a messenger bearing the news of Euridice's death. It ends, unlike the original legend, with Orfeo's father, Apollo, reassuring his son that both he and Euridice will become immortal and be reunited among the stars.

Gluck's *Orfeo ed Euridice* (three acts, libretto by Calzabigi, first produced in Vienna in 1762) begins with the mourning at Euridice's tomb and, in a rather contrived happy ending, Amor, the god of love, restores Euridice to her husband a second time. (Gluck revised this setting extensively during a stay in Paris in 1774.)

Offenbach's *Orpheus in the Underworld* (*Orphée aux enfers*) (two acts, text by Crémieux and Halévy, first produced in Paris in 1858) is intentionally an absurd parody of the legend. Orphée is a violinist, married to Eurydice, who detests his fiddle-playing above all things. She prefers the company of Aristée, a shepherd and bee-keeper, who turns out to be Pluto in disguise. When Pluto spirits her away to Hades, Public Opinion (an actual character in the opera) forces the unwilling Orphée, who would much prefer that Eurydice stayed in Hades, to try to get her back. As Orphée leads Eurydice back to earth, Jupiter hurls a thunderbolt. Startled, Orphée looks round – and so Eurydice must remain in Hades forever.

Monteverdi's version is notable for its huge and motley orchestra, Offenbach's for its lively overture, which includes the famous *Cancan* from Act 2.

Liszt composed a symphonic poem, *Orpheus*, to be performed as an introduction to his production of Gluck's opera *Orfeo ed Euridice* at Weimar in 1854.

Stravinsky's ballet *Orpheus* (first produced in New York in 1948) is a modern treatment of the original legend.

Osanna See *Mass.

Ossia [Italian; really *o sia*, meaning 'or else', 'or it may be'] In printed music, this word is used to indicate an alternative version of a passage of music – usually easier to perform.

Ostinato [Italian: 'obstinate', 'persistent'] A musical pattern which is obstinately and continuously repeated during a section of a piece or even throughout a complete piece. The repeating idea may be a rhythmic pattern, a scrap of tune, or even a complete melody. Two well-known examples of ostinato are the three-note idea played ninety-eight times by the horns during the *Carillon* from Bizet's *L'Arlésienne Suite* No. 1, and the snare-drum rhythm repeated persistently throughout Ravel's *Bolero*:

Bizet: *Carillon*

(Horns)

ff

(etc.)

Ravel: *Bolero*

If an ostinato pattern occurs in the bass, it is known as a *basso ostinato* or *ground bass. [See also: *Chaconne and Passacaglia]

Otello Opera in four acts by Verdi, first produced in Milan in 1887 (libretto by Boito based on Shakespeare's tragedy *Othello*). Otello (tenor), a Moor and governor of Cyprus, has as his adviser the evil-minded Iago (baritone), who is secretly scheming to destroy him. With the help of Roderigo (tenor), Iago makes Otello's lieutenant, Cassio, drunk, and Otello dismisses him from his service. He then persuades the dejected Cassio (tenor) that if he speaks to Otello's wife, Desdemona, she will intercede with her husband and have him reinstated. Finally, by planting Desdemona's handkerchief in Cassio's room, he convinces Otello that Desdemona is in love with Cassio. When Desdemona (soprano) pleads on Cassio's behalf, Otello sees it as proof of her infidelity and, unmoved by her protestations of innocence, murders her. No sooner has he done so than Iago's wife, Emilia (mezzo-soprano), arrives hotfoot to tell him of Desdemona's innocence and of Iago's devilish plot. Appalled to find that he has killed his wife for no reason, Otello stabs himself to death. The opera follows Shakespeare's plot closely, though the early Venetian scenes are omitted and the entire action is set in Cyprus. Rossini also wrote an operatic version of *Otello*.

Ôtez [French] Take off; remove. **Ôtez la sourdine**, remove the *mute.

Othello For Dvořák's *Othello*, see **Carnival Overture*. For the opera by Verdi, see **Otello*.

Ottava (often abbreviated to *8va* or simply *8*) [Italian] Octave. [See also: *Octave signs]

Ottavino [Italian] The piccolo.

Ottetto [Italian] *Octet.

Ottoni (*strumenti d'ottone*) [Italian] The brass; brass instruments.

Ou [French] Or.

Ours, L' See *'Bear' Symphony.

Outer parts (outside parts) The highest and lowest notes in a chord, or in a series of chords. For example, in choral music the outer parts are generally the soprano and the bass.

Ouvert [French] Open. [See also under *Estampie]

Ouverture [French]; **Ouvertüre** [German] *Overture.

Overblowing In the playing of wind instruments, adjusting the pressure of the breath and the lips so that only a portion of the air column vibrates, and therefore an upper harmonic is sounded. Woodwind instruments such as the flute, oboe, and bassoon, when overblown, produce the second harmonic – sounding exactly an octave higher than the fingered note. However, the clarinet, when overblown, sounds the third harmonic – a 12th (one octave and a 5th) above the fingered note. (See *Harmonic series.) Usually, to assist in overblowing, there is a special key (an 'octave key' on the oboe, a 'speaker key' or 'register key' on the clarinet) which opens a small hole or vent in the body tube.

Taking, as an example, a scale played on the oboe: having sounded the notes in the lower register, the player duplicates the same fingering, but by using the octave key, and overblowing, sounds the notes in the second register.

Overstringing A method of stringing a piano in such a way that one large group of strings crosses diagonally over another one on a higher level. This improves the resonance, distributes the string tension more evenly, and (particularly in upright pianos) accommodates lengthier strings within a smaller space. An instrument that is built in this way is said to be **overstrung**.

Overtones Same as harmonics (see *Harmonic series) except that the first harmonic (called the fundamental) is not generally considered to be an overtone. And so in the harmonic series the second harmonic is the first overtone, the third harmonic is the second overtone, and so on.

Overture [French: *ouverture*; German: *Ouvertüre*; Italian: *sinfonia*, *overtura*] An 'opening piece'; a piece of instrumental music composed as an introduction to a dramatic work such as an opera or an oratorio, or as an independent piece to be performed in the concert hall. The very earliest operatic overtures were often little more than fanfare-like snatches of music, calling the audience's attention to the fact that the opera was about to begin (e.g. the *Toccata* which serves as overture to Monteverdi's opera *Orfeo*, composed in 1607). Gradually, overtures became more elaborate, and towards the end of the 17th century two different forms became accepted as standard. The first, associated with Lully (court composer to Louis XIV) is known as the **French overture**. The second, introduced by Alessandro Scarlatti, is the **Italian overture** (also called **Sinfonia**). Here is the basic plan for each of these two types:

	French overture
1	a **slow** section, majestic and dignified, featuring dotted rhythms, leading to:
2	a **quick** main section, usually in fugal style, often ending with a short slow passage similar in mood to the opening section.

	Italian overture (Sinfonia)
1	a **quick** movement, often in fugal style (*Allegro*)
2	a **slow** movement (*Adagio*)
3	Finale – a **quick** movement, often in a dance-like rhythm (*Allegro* or *Presto*)

In the slow music of a French overture, although dotted rhythms might be written as ♩. ♪, all dotted notes were usually played as if they were *double*-dotted notes, with each following short note given only half its written value (e.g. ♩.. 𝅘𝅥𝅯). This enhanced the solemn and stately effect characteristic of the music. In some later French overtures the final slow section is quite lengthy; in others, this section is replaced by a stately dance such as a minuet or a gavotte. (Handel's Overture to his oratorio *Samson* ends with a minuet; his Overture to *Messiah*, however, matches the plan shown above, left.) Occasionally, a French overture is followed by an entire suite of dances (e.g. the four 'Overtures' or Orchestral Suites by Bach).

The Italian overture (Sinfonia), with its three contrasting movements, was an important ancestor of the *symphony. Examples of this type of overture are Alessandro Scarlatti's Overture to *La caduta de' Decemviri*, and William Boyce's Overture to the Ode for New Year, 1756: *Hail, hail, auspicious day* (Boyce later published the same music as the first of his Eight Symphonies in eight parts).

From the time of Mozart onwards, the overture became a one-movement work, often structured in *sonata form or *abridged sonata form, perhaps with a slow introduction but with no repeat of the exposition. An important development in the overture was that composers now often aimed to link the music more closely, in both mood and theme, to the following drama, preparing the audience for the mood and emotional character of the plot. This type of overture is described as **allusive** if it hints at, or 'alludes to', important tunes or situations from the drama which follows. Examples are the overtures to Mozart's operas *Don Giovanni* and *The Magic Flute*, Weber's Overture to *Der Freischütz*, and almost all of Wagner's Overtures (some of which he preferred to call *Vorspiel* or 'Prelude').

Some 19th-century overtures to light operas or operettas merely consist of a whole string of tunes taken from the stage-work they introduce. These are often called **potpourri** or **medley overtures**. The overtures to operettas by Offenbach and Sullivan are often of this type – as also are many overtures to 20th-century 'musicals'.

The 19th-century **concert overture** is an independent piece of music, complete in itself, composed with concert performance in mind and having no connection with an opera or any other work. This idea is usually credited to Mendelssohn, though it really originated earlier in the 19th century with the inclusion at concerts of some of Mozart's operatic overtures, and Beethoven's *'Egmont' Overture and his three *'Leonora' Overtures. A concert overture is very often *programmatic, such as Mendelssohn's *The *Hebrides* (*Fingal's Cave*) and Elgar's **Cockaigne*. Or it may have been composed to commemorate a particular event – for example, Tchaikovsky's **Eighteen-Twelve Overture*, Brahms's *Academic Festival Overture*, and Shostakovich's *Festive Overture* (composed in 1954 to celebrate the 37th anniversary of the October Revolution).

Ovvero [Italian] Or; or else; or indeed; otherwise.

'Oxford' Symphony Nickname of Haydn's Symphony No. 92 in G, composed in 1789. It was not specially composed for Oxford, but was performed there at the University when Haydn received his honorary doctorate in 1791.

P; ***p*** Abbreviation standing for *piano* [Italian] meaning 'soft', 'quiet'. **P** is also sometimes used as an abbreviation standing for: **1** pedal (in keyboard music); **2** *positif* (in French organ music); **3** Pincherle (Marc Pincherle), a French musicologist who in 1948 published a book about the Italian composer, Antonio Vivaldi. Linked to the title of any concerto, sonata, or symphony by Vivaldi, the letter **P** followed by a number identifies that particular piece in the *thematic catalogue included in Pincherle's book. [See also: *RV]

Pacific 231 A 'symphonic movement' by Honegger, composed in 1923. The title refers to a huge and powerful type of American railway engine. Honegger explained that the music is intended to suggest 'the calm breathing of the engine awaiting departure, the effort and strain as it slowly begins to heave itself forward, then a gradual gathering of speed until the 300 ton monster is hurling itself at 120 kilometres an hour through the night ...'

Padoana (other spellings include: *padouana*, *padovana*, *paduana*) [Italian: 'Paduan', 'from Padua'] Names used in the 16th and 17th centuries for dances of various types – some in dignified duple metre, similar to the *pavan; others in triple metre or swift $\frac{6}{8}$ time.

Padovana [Italian] **1** See *Pavan. **2** Another spelling of *Padoana.

Paduana **1** German for *Pavan. **2** Another spelling of *Padoana.

Paean [Greek] A song of praise.

Paganini Rhapsody See *Rhapsody on a Theme of Paganini.*

Pagliacci (Clowns) (often, wrongly, called '*I* Pagliacci') Opera in a prologue and two acts by Leoncavallo, first produced in Milan in 1892 (libretto by the composer inspired by an actual court case). A troupe of players has arrived to stage a Harlequinade. In the prologue to the opera a clown, Tonio (baritone), explains that their play is not just make-believe: the characters are real people, the story true. On comes the troupe with its leader, Canio (tenor). Tonio, falling for Canio's wife Nedda (soprano), makes passes at her, but is rebuffed. She means to run away with her lover, Silvio (baritone). Tonio hears them making their plans and summons Canio, who is devastated. But the show must go on. They act their Harlequinade, with Canio in the role of a husband who suspects his wife of unfaithfulness. Gradually his tortured mind confuses the play with reality. He demands from Nedda the name of her lover, and when, terrified, she tries to escape, he stabs first her and then Silvio, who has rushed to her aid. The opera is often paired with Mascagni's **Cavalleria rusticana* to provide an evening's entertainment. [See also: *Verismo]

Pallet See under *Organ.

Pandora Same as *Bandora.

Panpipes One of the oldest wind instruments, consisting of a number of pipes bound or fixed together side by side. The pipes are graded in size and therefore in pitch. The sounds, rather hollow in tone-quality, are made by blowing across the top of the pipes. In Greek mythology this instrument was attributed to the god Pan, hence its name.

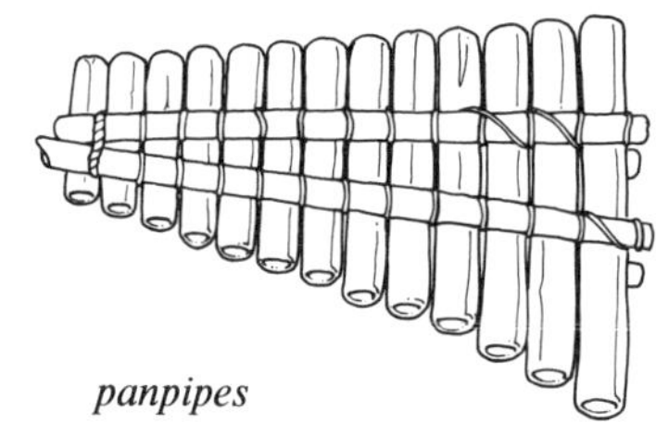
panpipes

Papillons (Butterflies) Twelve short, dance-like piano pieces, Opus 2, by Schumann, composed between 1829 and 1831. [See also: **Carnaval*]

Parallel chords A sequence of chords, identical in structure, built on different degrees of the scale so that they proceed in parallel motion. Also called a 'chord stream'. The device is frequently used by 20th-century composers (e.g. Debussy, Vaughan Williams).

Parallel fifths and octaves (consecutive fifths and octaves) These result when one part or voice in the musical texture moves in parallel *motion with another at the interval of a perfect fifth or octave. From the 16th century to the late 19th century such effects were considered to be incorrect. However, parallel fifths and octaves formed the basis of medieval parallel *organum; and they have been frequently and effectively used by 20th-century composers. [See also: *Exposed fifths and octaves]

parallel fifths   parallel octaves

Parallel key See under *Related keys.

Parallel motion See *Motion.

'Paris' Symphonies A set of six symphonies, Nos. 82 to 87, composed by Haydn in 1785–6. They were commissioned by le Comte d'Ogny for the masonic concert society called Le Concert de la Loge Olympique in Paris, and were first performed there in 1787. Three of the 'Paris' Symphonies have earned individual nicknames: No. 82 in C, 'The *Bear'; No. 83 in G minor, 'The *Hen', No. 85 in B flat, 'La Reine' – 'The Queen', or 'The Queen of France', (this was a favourite symphony of Marie Antoinette).

'Paris' Symphony Nickname of Mozart's Symphony No. 31 in D major (K297), composed in 1778 when Mozart was staying in Paris and first performed there at a *concert spirituel.* This symphony has no Minuet, and so is in three movements instead of the usual four: 1 *Allegro assai*; 2 *Andantino*; 3 *Allegro.*

Parlando; **Parlante** [Italian: 'speaking'] In a speaking manner; imitating the character of speech.

Parody mass It was quite common during the 16th century for a composer to base the music of a *mass on a pre-existing composition such as a motet or a chanson (either his own, or perhaps someone else's). A mass of this type is known as a 'parody mass' – the word 'parody' here being used in the sense of 'borrowing', not 'making fun of'.

Paroles [French] Words. **Chanson sans paroles**, song without words.

Part **1** Any instrument or voice in a composition, or the music written for it (e.g. violin part, trumpet part, tenor part). In an orchestral piece, *score and parts includes a full score for the conductor and separate parts for the orchestral players. **2** Each of the melodic lines, or individual strands of music, which weave along together in a composition written in *contrapuntal or polyphonic style (e.g. a three-part fugue, a four-part madrigal, an eight-part motet). [See also: *Voice 2; *Voice-parts; *Partsong]

Parte (plural: *parti*) [Italian] *Part. **Colla parte** ('with the part') is a warning to accompanists to follow the soloist closely.

Parthenia, or **The Maydenhead** A collection consisting of 'the first musicke that ever was printed for the Virginalls', published in late 1612 or early 1613. It contains twenty-one pieces by the three leading Tudor composers of music for *virginals: William Byrd (1543–1623), John Bull (1563–1628), and Orlando Gibbons (1583–1625). [See also: *Fitzwilliam Virginal Book]

Parthenia In-violata A collection of keyboard pieces, published twelve years or so after *Parthenia and intended as a companion volume. All the pieces are by anonymous composers, and each includes a separate part to be played on a bass viol.

Partials See *Harmonic series.

Partita [Italian] Name used during the 17th and 18th centuries to mean either a *suite or a set of *variations. Bach's six keyboard Partitas are suites, and so are his three Partitas for unaccompanied violin; he also composed partitas for organ which are sets of variations on *chorales (e.g. the chorale partita on *Sei gegrüsset, Jesu gütig*, BWV768).

Partition [French]; **Partitur** [German]; **Partitura** [Italian] *Score.

Partsong A song written in several *voice-parts – these parts taken either by solo singers or by groups of voices. A partsong is usually written in *chordal style (rather than contrapuntal style), with the melodic interest restricted mostly (if not entirely) to the highest voice-part.

Part-writing A term, used especially in connection with contrapuntal music, referring to the way in which the various parts in the musical texture are put together, and also the way in which they proceed, as melodic lines, in relation to each other. (The American term 'voice-leading' has the same meaning.)

Pas [French] Pace or paces, step or steps. And so in ballet a **pas de deux** is a dance for two performers; a **pas de trois**, a dance for three; and so on. A **pas seul** is a dance for a single performer. **Pas d'action** describes a dance or a scene which is especially dramatic in character.

Paspy Old English way of spelling *Passepied.

Passacaglia [Italian; French: *passacaille*] See *Chaconne and Passacaglia.

Passage work Any part of a composition which may not be of particular musical importance but serves as a link (or 'passage') between important musical ideas. It may, however, be based upon material heard earlier, and may include modulation (or change of key). Passage work usually has an air of 'busyness' – particularly when it occurs in a *concerto, in which case it may feature a display of technical brilliance (perhaps incorporating swift scales and arpeggios) from the soloist.

Passamezzo [Italian: 'step and a half'] A mid 16th-century Italian dance, similar to a *pavan, which became popular throughout Europe. The speed was moderate, with two or four beats to a bar. Most often, the music consisted of variations composed upon one or the other of two standard bass-lines, each with its own scheme of harmonies, repeated several times over as an ostinato or *ground bass. The two patterns were known as the *passamezzo antico* (see music example (a) below) and the *passamezzo moderno* (see (b)).

Very often, either bass-line would be filled in with notes of shorter value.

A passamezzo was usually followed by a dance in triple time, such as a saltarello, sometimes based on the melody of the passamezzo but transformed into three-time (compare music (a), above, with the music given under *Saltarello).

[See also: *Folía; *Romanesca; *Ruggiero]

Passepied [French: 'pass-foot'] A French dance of the 17th and 18th centuries of lively character and in swift $\frac{3}{8}$, $\frac{3}{4}$, or $\frac{6}{8}$ time. It was sometimes included as one of the movements of the Baroque *suite. For example, Bach includes a pair of passepieds (to be performed alternately, with the first repeated after the second) in his English Suite No. 5; and another pair in his Orchestral Suite No. 1:

(English composers used the spelling 'paspy'.)

Passing note A *non-harmonic note which passes from one harmony note to another in a single direction, and usually by step. (In the examples below, passing notes are marked *.)

Passion (Passion music) A musical setting of the story of the Crucifixion of Jesus Christ as related in the four gospels (the word 'passion', which comes from Latin by way of Old French, originally meant 'suffering'). The earliest examples of Passion music, dating from the 12th century, are in plainsong. In the 15th century, composers began to make polyphonic settings. Many Passions composed from the 17th century onwards may be considered to be oratorios of a rather special kind. The two finest and most elaborate examples are by J. S. Bach: the *St John Passion* (1724) for solo voices, chorus, and orchestra, and the *St Matthew Passion* (1727 or 1729) for solo voices, two choruses, and two orchestras. Each of these is in the form of an oratorio, and besides recitatives, arias, and choruses, Bach includes settings of chorales which he places at key points to intensify the most solemn and deeply-moving moments in the story (see *'Passion Chorale'). Besides the Biblical narrative, Bach uses additional poetic texts for arias and large choruses.

Outstanding among many other settings of the Passion are those by Lassus and Schütz. A more recent setting is Penderecki's *St Luke Passion*, first performed in 1966.

[See also: *Testo; *Turba]

'Passion Chorale' A chorale particularly associated with the Passion. The best-known example is *O Haupt voll Blut und Wunden* ('O Sacred Head sore wounded'; also translated as 'Be near me, Lord, when dying') the melody of which is adapted from a song by Hans Leo Hassler (1562–1612). This is the principal chorale which Bach uses in the *St Matthew Passion*. It occurs five times in all, each time in a different key, and Bach harmonizes it in four different ways.

Passione [Italian] Passion; emotion. **Con passione**, with passion, with deep feeling.

Pastoral; Pastorale [Italian]; **Pastourelle** [French] **1** Describing music which represents country life. **2** From the 15th century to the 18th, a type of stage-work based on a rural theme. **3** A piece in $\frac{6}{8}$ or $\frac{12}{8}$ time, with a lilting rhythm, and frequently imitating the drone of a shepherd's bagpipe. Such pieces have often been used in Christmas music, associated with the shepherds in the field on Christmas Night. Examples are the final movement of Corelli's *'Christmas Concerto' (in G minor, Op. 6 No. 8), the *Pastoral Symphony* in Handel's **Messiah*, and the *Sinfonia* which opens part two of Bach's **Christmas Oratorio*.

Pastorale from Corelli: 'Christmas Concerto'

'Pastoral' Sonata Nickname of Beethoven's Piano Sonata No. 15 in D, Op. 28, composed in 1801. The movements are: 1 *Allegro*; 2 *Andante*; 3 Scherzo and Trio (*Allegro vivace*); 4 Rondo: *Allegro ma non troppo*.

Pastoral Symphony **1** Beethoven's title for his Symphony No. 6 in F major, Op. 68, composed in 1808. It is an example of *programme music. The symphony has five movements, entitled: 1 Awakening of happy feelings upon arriving in the countryside (*Allegro ma non troppo*); 2 Scene by the brook (*Andante molto mosso*); 3 Peasants' merry-making (*Allegro*, a scherzo and trio); 4 Thunderstorm (*Allegro*); 5 Shepherds' song – happy and thankful feelings after the storm (*Allegretto*). Beethoven commented that the music was 'an expression of feelings rather than tone-painting', though the birdcalls (nightingale, quail, and cuckoo) which close the slow movement, the peasants' merry-making in the scherzo, and the storm which erupts in the fourth movement, are all clearly pictorial.

2 Title given by Vaughan Williams to his third symphony, completed in 1921. There are four movements, the last including a wordless part for solo soprano.

3 A short orchestral piece, occurring in Part One of Handel's oratorio **Messiah*. It sets the mood for the following three recitatives and chorus describing the shepherds receiving the news of Christ's birth. Handel also added the title **Pifa* to this piece. [See also: *Pastoral 3]

Patetica; **Patetico** [Italian]; **Pathétique** [French] Pathetic, moving, emotional, arousing sympathetic sorrow.

'Pathétique' Sonata Beethoven's Piano Sonata No. 8 in C minor, Op. 13, (composed around 1797–8) which he entitled *Grande Sonate Pathétique* (*pathétique* in the sense of 'stirring the emotions', rather than 'pathetic'). The sonata has three movements: 1 *Grave – Allegro molto e con brio*; 2 *Adagio cantabile*; 3 Rondo: *Allegro*. The first movement, in sonata form, begins with a slow introduction whose theme reappears twice during the course of the movement. The second, in A♭ major, is in simple rondo form; and the third is in sonata-rondo form.

Pathétique Symphony Tchaikovsky's last symphony, No. 6 in B minor, Op. 74, composed in 1893. The title (best translated as 'emotional' rather than 'pathetic') was authorized by the composer. The symphony is in four movements. The first (*Adagio – Allegro non troppo*) is in sonata form, the second (*Allegro con grazia*) is in $\frac{5}{4}$ time, and the third (*Allegro molto vivace*) is a march-like scherzo. The slow movement (*Adagio lamentoso*) is placed last.

Patron saint of music St *Cecilia.

Pauken [German] Kettle drums.

'Paukenschlag' See *'Surprise' Symphony.

'Paukenwirbel' Symphonie See *'Drum Roll' Symphony.

Pause The sign 𝄐 printed above or below a note or a rest, indicating that it should be held for longer than its normal value. In music for a soloist, a pause sign may indicate that a *cadenza should be improvised at that point. A pause is also sometimes called a 'hold' or a *fermata*. However, the French word *pause*, the German word *Pause*, and the Italian word *pausa* each mean *rest – the term for 'pause' in each case being *point d'orgue*, *Fermate*, and *fermata*.

Pavan (pavane, paven, pavin; Italian: *pavana*, *padovana*; French: *pavane*; German: *Paduana*) A dignified 16th-century court dance in which couples advanced in slow, majestic procession. The music was in two or four beats to a bar, slow to moderate in speed. It was once thought that the name came from the Latin word *pavo* meaning 'peacock', matching the idea of women in colourful, long-flowing dresses strutting beside their partners; but it is more likely that it derived from the Italian word *padovana* – 'from the town of Padua'. A pavan was often followed by a nimble *galliard, sometimes based on the same theme transformed into three-time.

In a stylized form (not intended for dancing) the pairing of pavan and galliard became very popular with Tudor keyboard composers (e.g. Byrd, Bull, and Gibbons). And from this pairing of contrasted dances stemmed the idea of the *suite.

Pavane: *La Bataille* (The battle) from Susato: *Danserye*

(etc.)

Pavane pour une infante défunte (Pavan upon the death of a Spanish princess) A piano piece by Ravel, composed in 1899; then arranged by him for orchestra in 1910. The title refers to the old custom at the Spanish court of solemnly dancing a ceremonial pavan upon the death of a member of the royal family.

Pavillon [French] The *bell of a wind instrument (especially a brass instrument). **Pavillon en l'air** ('bell upwards') is a direction to a wind player to raise the instrument so that the sound from the bell travels more directly and vividly towards the listener.

Peasant Cantata The nickname of Bach's secular cantata: *Mer hahn en neue Oberkeet* ('We have a new magistrate'), for solo voices, choir, horn, flute, strings, and continuo. It was composed in 1742 to mark the installation of a new magistrate in a country district in Saxony. Bach includes several popular tunes of the day, and the libretto (by Picander) is written in local dialect.

Ped. Abbreviation of *Pedal. In organ music it indicates a note or notes to be played by the feet on the pedals or pedal-board of the organ. In piano music it indicates points where the sustaining pedal should be depressed, and is often printed as 𝆮 ✽ (the asterisk indicating the point at which the pedal should be released).

Pedal [from Latin, meaning 'foot'] **1** Any kind of lever or mechanism operated by the foot or feet, as on the piano, organ, harp, harpsichord, chromatic (pedal-tuned) kettle drums. [See: *Ped.] **2** Short for *pedal point. **3** On brass instruments a pedal, or pedal note, is the lowest note (fundamental) of a harmonic series which the instrument is capable of sounding and which is of practical use.

Pedal-board The name given to the pedals of the *organ – which, in design and purpose, are a 'keyboard for the feet'. (Very occasionally, pianos, harpsichords, and clavichords have been fitted with a pedal-board.)

Pedal clarinet See *Contrabass clarinet.

Pedale [Italian] Pedal. **Con pedale** (often abbreviated to **con ped.**), direction to a pianist to make use of the sustaining pedal.

Pedalier [French] The pedals or pedal-board of the *organ.

Pedalklavier [German] The pedals or pedal-board of the *organ.

Pedal notes (on brass instruments) See *Pedal 3.

Pedal point (pedal, organ point) A note which is sustained or continuously repeated in the bass, beneath changing harmonies. Most often, the note sounding as the pedal point will be the dominant ('dominant pedal') or the tonic ('tonic pedal'). [See also: *Inverted pedal; *Internal pedal; *Double pedal]

Pedal steel guitar See under *Hawaiian guitar.

Peer Gynt Incidental music by Grieg composed in 1874–5 for Ibsen's play of the same title. Grieg later arranged eight of the pieces to make two orchestral suites. Suite 1 (Op. 46) contains: Morning, Death of Åse, Anitra's Dance, and In the Hall of the Mountain King. Suite 2 (Op. 55) contains: Ingrid's Lament, Arabian Dance, Return of Peer Gynt, and Solveig's Song. Grieg made versions of both suites for piano solo, and also for piano duet.

Pegbox The part of a string instrument, at the end of the neck, in which the **pegs** holding the strings are fitted. The player tunes the instrument by turning the pegs, and so tightening or slackening the strings.

Pelléas et Mélisande **1** An opera in five acts by Debussy, composed between 1893 and 1902, and based on the play of the same title by the Belgian dramatist, Maeterlinck. **2** Incidental music, Opus 80, by Fauré, composed in 1898 for a London production of Maeterlinck's play. Later, four of the pieces were published as a concert suite. **3** A lengthy symphonic poem, Opus 5, composed by Schoenberg in 1902–3, based on the story of Maeterlinck's play. **4** Incidental music, Opus 46, composed by Sibelius in 1905 for a production of the play in Helsinki. The same year, Sibelius arranged nine of the pieces as a suite for small orchestra.

Pensieroso [Italian]; **Pensif** [French] Pensive; in a thoughtful manner.

Pentatonic scale Any scale consisting of five notes, completed by the octave of the first. The most familiar type is constructed from a series of major 2nds (tones) and minor 3rds. (Of the two examples given opposite, the second makes use of just the black notes on the piano.) However, there are many other ways of dividing the octave to form pentatonic scales – involving, for example, the intervals of a semitone and a major 3rd. Pentatonic scales form the basis of much European folk-music, particularly Celtic and Scottish (the well-known tune, *Auld Lang Syne*, is built from a pentatonic scale). They are also the basic scales of the music of many other cultures, e.g. China, Japan, Indonesia, and parts of Africa.

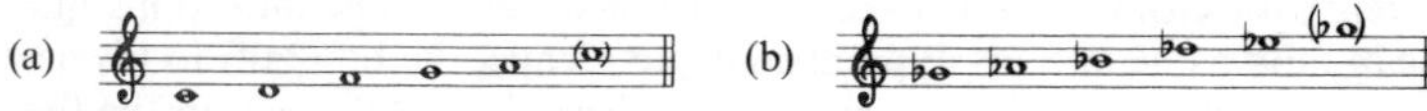

Per [Italian] By; for.

Percussione [Italian] The percussion section of the orchestra.

Percussion instruments Instruments that are sounded by being struck, clashed, shaken, or scraped. Some of them are among the oldest of all instruments. Percussion instruments may be divided into two groups.

The first group contains **pitched**, or **tuned**, percussion instruments – those which can play one or more notes of **definite pitch**, and so could possibly play a tune. Included in this group are: kettle drums (timpani), glockenspiel, xylophone, tubular bells, celesta, vibraphone, marimba, temple blocks, bongos, antique cymbals, and certain gongs.

The second, much larger, group of percussion instruments contains those which are **unpitched**, or **non-tuned**. These instruments produce sounds of **indefinite pitch** – although the sound produced may be highish (e.g. triangle) or lowish (e.g. bass drum) it has no precise pitch, and could not match exactly any note played, for example, on the piano. These percussion instruments of indefinite pitch are used purely for rhythm, for impact, and the distinctive timbre ('colour') of their sounds. Included in this group are: bass drum, snare (side) drum, tenor drum, cymbals, triangle, tambourine, castanets, Chinese block, tam-tam and certain gongs, whip, sleigh bells, maracas, güiro, and ratchet (rattle).

[See also: *Membranophone; *Idiophone]

Perdendosi [Italian: 'being lost'] Dying away.

Perfect cadence See *Cadences.

Perfect intervals See under *Intervals.

Perfect pitch The same as *Absolute pitch.

Perpetual canon See *Infinite canon.

Perpetuo [Italian] Perpetual, continuous.

Perpetuum mobile [Latin: 'perpetual motion' or 'continuously moving'; Italian: *moto perpetuo*] Title sometimes used for rapid, bustling pieces which flow without pause in quick notes, usually all of the same value.

Pesante [Italian] Heavy, weighty.

Pesca [Italian] A fishing song. [See also under *Caccia]

Peter and the Wolf A 'musical tale for children' by Prokofiev (Op. 67; 1936) for narrator and orchestra, describing how a Russian boy named Peter, with the help of his friends (a cat and a bird), tricks and captures a fierce wolf. Prokofiev composed the piece as a means of introducing children to the sounds of the main instruments of the orchestra. Each character taking part in the story is represented by one or more instruments: the Bird – flute; the Duck – oboe; the Cat – clarinet; Grandfather – bassoon; the Wolf – three horns; Peter – the string section of the orchestra; the gunshots of the Hunters – kettle drums and bass drum.

Peter Grimes Opera in a prologue and three acts by Britten, completed in 1945 (libretto by Montagu Slater after Crabbe's poem *The Borough*). An inquest in a fishing village in Suffolk acquits the fisherman Grimes (tenor) of suspected cruelty after a young apprentice vanishes mysteriously at sea. The coroner, however, urges him not to take on another boy. The widowed schoolmistress

Ellen Orford (soprano) supports Grimes against the hostility of the villagers and helps him to find a new apprentice, but the new boy is ill-treated and Ellen quarrels with Grimes, who strikes her. The villagers follow him to his hut on the cliff, and as he and his apprentice try to escape, the boy falls to his death. Grimes, his mind disordered, vanishes for three days. At dawn on the fourth day his boat is seen on the beach, and he appears, exhausted. Balstrode, a retired sea captain (baritone), persuades him that there is only one way to escape the fury of the Borough. He must put out to sea in his boat and sink it. With a heavy heart Grimes sails away. As the fisherfolk awake, the boat goes down, and Grimes is drowned.

Five orchestral pieces from the opera are sometimes played, consisting of *Four Sea Interludes* (1 *Dawn*; 2 *Sunday Morning*; 3 *Moonlight*; 4 *Storm*) and a *Passacaglia*.

Petit; **Petite** [French] Small. **Petite flûte**, piccolo.

Petrushka Ballet in four scenes composed by Stravinsky, first produced in Paris in 1911 (libretto by Benois; choreography by Fokine). At St Petersburg a happy crowd is celebrating the Shrovetide fair. A puppet owner, the Charlatan, brings three of his dolls to life – Petrushka, a Ballerina, and a Moor. Petrushka is in love with the Ballerina; she, however, prefers the Moor, so Petrushka attacks him. Later Petrushka, shut in his poky room, is visited by the Ballerina, but she flees when he makes timid advances to her. The scene changes to the Moor's room, where he and the Ballerina are dancing together. Petrushka enters but is chased away. Finally, back at the fair, the Moor stabs Petrushka, who dies. The Charlatan is untroubled (after all, it is only a puppet), but Petrushka's ghost hovers above, mocking the crowd. A *suite from the ballet was first performed in 1914, and in 1946 Stravinsky re-scored the entire work for a smaller orchestra (the arrangement was published in 1947). In 1921 he made a virtuoso piano transcription of three of the movements for Artur Rubinstein.

Peu [French] A little. **Peu à peu**, little by little.

Pezzo [Italian] A piece of music, a composition.

Pf.; **Pft.**; **Pfte.** Abbreviations all standing for *pianoforte* – the instrument more commonly called the *piano.

Phantasie [German] Fantasy, or *fantasia. **Phantasiestück** (plural: *Phantasiestücke*), a fantasy piece, fanciful in mood, and free in form and style.

Phrase A portion or division of a melody, consisting of a group of notes giving a strong impression of 'belonging together'. A *phrase mark* (a curved line, or *slur) may be drawn above or below the music to indicate the number of notes or bars making up the phrase. The most usual length for a phrase is four bars, but phrases of eight bars, two bars, or just a single bar are also quite common. Phrases consisting of three, five, or seven bars are rather rarer. When two or more consecutive phrases arrive at a main musical 'stopping place' (usually marked by a perfect or plagal cadence) they are said to have formed a *sentence*. [See also: *Phrasing]

Phrase mark See *Phrase.

Phrasing **1** The subdivision of a piece of music into the basic musical 'components' which the composer has used to structure or build up the music: sentences, *phrases, motives, figures. Also **2** the art of performing a piece of music – and *shaping* the music, with skill and musicianship – in such a way that this structure is clearly yet sensitively brought out. This not only involves shaping phrases, and parts of phrases, so that the notes sound as if they 'belong together', but involves other essential factors such as contrasts of *staccato* and *legato*, dynamics, *crescendo* and *diminuendo*, variation of tone, etc. Also (according to type of performer) factors such as: control of breath in singing and the playing of wind instruments; observance and execution of the various types of *bowing on string instruments; control of touch, tone, and pedalling in piano-playing; and so on.

Phrygian cadence A type of imperfect cadence, occurring in minor keys only, and consisting of the subdominant chord in first inversion followed by the dominant chord in root position. It takes its name from the Phrygian mode, in which the interval between the *final* and the note above is a semitone (in the example, the bass notes F–E). A Phrygian cadence often occurs, functioning as an imperfect cadence, as a link between one movement and the next in Baroque sonatas and concertos (e.g. Corelli, Handel).

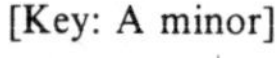

Phrygian mode See *Church modes.

Piacere See **A piacere*.

Piacevole [Italian] Pleasant, pleasantly; pleasingly.

Piangendo [Italian] Lamenting, weeping.

Piangevole [Italian] Sad, plaintive.

Pianissimo (abbrev.: **pianiss.**, **PP**, or ***pp***) [Italian] Very soft. **PPP** or ***ppp*** means 'extremely soft'. [See the table of Dynamic markings on page 390]

Piano [Italian] **1** Soft, quiet (abbrev.: **P** or ***p***). **2** The customary abbreviation for **pianoforte** [Italian; German: *Klavier*]. By 1700, Cristofori, in Florence, had made the first real piano – a so-called *gravicembalo col piano e forte* (a 'harpsichord with soft and loud'). The sounds were produced by leather-headed hammers hitting strings (not, as in the *harpsichord, by quills plucking them), and the dynamics could be controlled by the amount of force with which the player struck the keys. There were two strings to each note (to give added resonance), an *escapement* (which caused the hammer, having struck the string, to fall away from it immediately, leaving it free to vibrate), and **dampers* (see also under *sordino) to silence the notes when the keys were released. The range of Cristofori's instruments varied between four and 4½ octaves. His ideas were developed in Germany by Silbermann, whose later instruments impressed J. S. Bach, and in England by Zumpe. The earliest pianos were of harpsichord shape, but, in about 1760, Zumpe made a **square piano** (really rectangular, with the *keyboard set into one of the long sides and the strings parallel to the keyboard). There was no *backcheck* to catch the hammers on the rebound, and no escapement, but there were two handstops (one for each half of the keyboard), and these raised all the dampers throughout the instrument, so that the sounds did not stop when the player's fingers left the keys. In 1783, the Englishman John Broadwood introduced a *damper pedal*, which had the same effect as Zumpe's handstops but was operated, more conveniently, with the foot (usually the left one). Probably the first French piano was one made by Érard, in Paris, in 1777.

The action of a piano consists of the keyboard, the strings, and the mechanism which produces the sound. The 18th-century *Viennese action*, used by Stein and others, was light, with treble and bass well balanced and the dampers controlled by a knee lever. The *English action* was heavier, the keys had to be pressed down farther, and the bass notes were often more powerful than the treble. French pianos were especially thin in tone. The word ***fortepiano*** is used to describe these early instruments with wooden frames and leather-covered hammers.

Mozart had to make do with a five-octave range, but, in the 1790s, Broadwood extended the range to six octaves. The additional strings increased the overall tension on the wooden frame, and, in 1800, Hawkins of Philadelphia reinforced the frames of his pianos with iron. The first fully iron frame, cast in one piece, was used in 1825 by Babcock, whose lead was followed by Steinway. Hawkins invented the **upright piano**, in which the strings were perpendicular to the keys, and used the process known as **overstringing*. In 1821, Érard patented a *double escapement*, making possible the very rapid repetition of single notes. Around 1850, the range reached the seven and a quarter octaves common today.

The **grand piano** is usually best for tone. Its *soundboard* (which acts as a resonator, rather like the body of a violin) is parallel to the floor, at an acoustically effective distance, and the dampers drop onto the strings (which are horizontal) by the natural force of gravity. The full-length concert grand can measure nine feet (about 2.75 metres) or more, the baby grand less than five feet (about 1.52 metres).

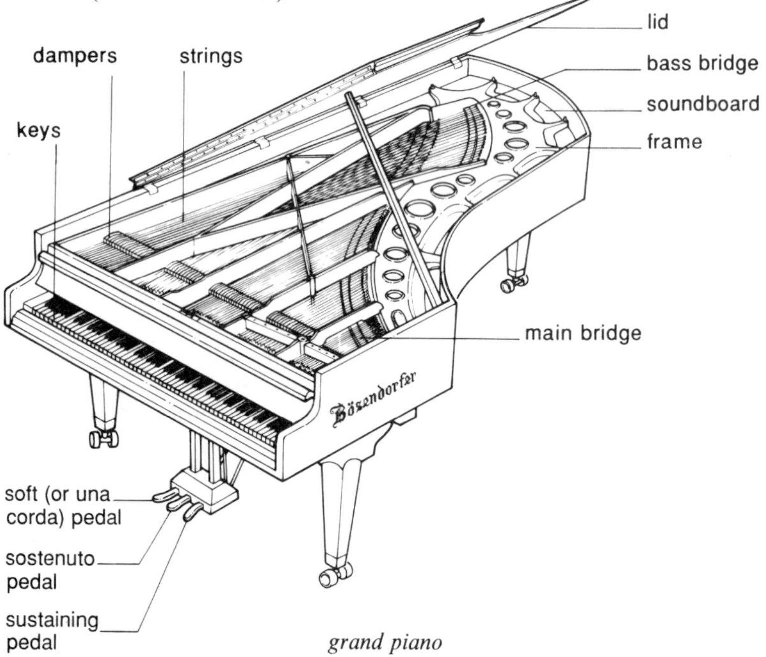

grand piano

In the modern piano, when a key is struck, a hammer, with a striking surface of wool felt, is thrown at a string. An escapement causes it to rebound, and a backcheck prevents it from hitting the string a second time. When the key is released, the sound is terminated by a damper. The bass strings are wrapped in copper, with one string each for the very lowest notes, and two each for the next few. All the other notes have three unwrapped steel strings each. The strings are stretched over *bridges*, which transmit the vibrations to the soundboard.

The diagrams below show the action of the grand piano and the upright piano.

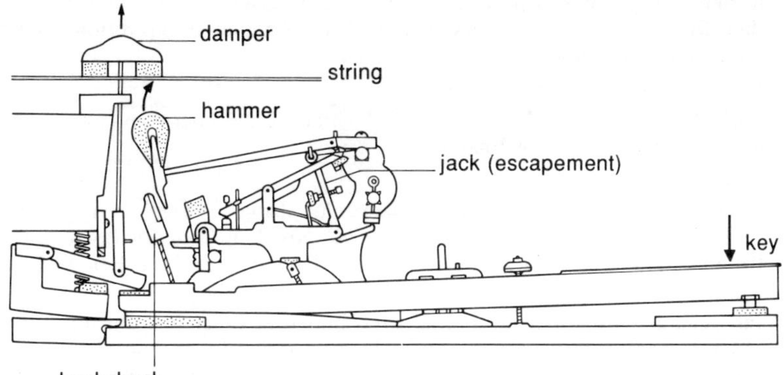

action of a modern grand piano

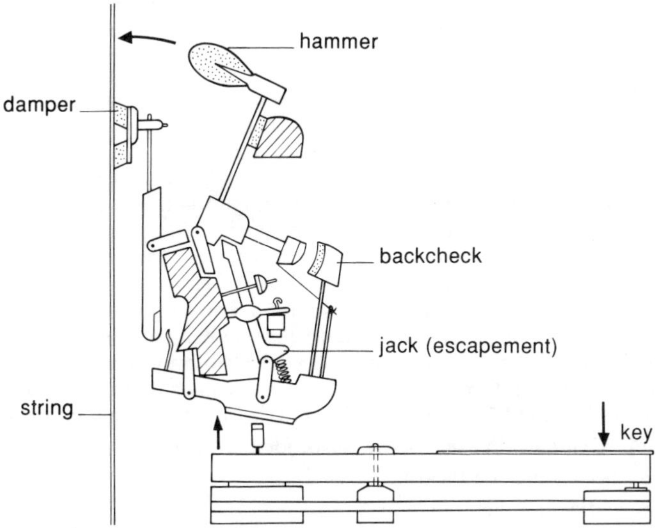

action of a modern upright piano

A piano may have two, or three, pedals. The *sustaining* (or *damper*) *pedal*, worked by the right foot, lifts the dampers off *all* the strings, adding to the resonance, and enabling the pianist to achieve an unbroken *legato* even when moving the hands freely over the keyboard. In 1874, Steinway perfected a *sostenuto pedal* (the middle one, in instruments which possess three). Its mechanism catches only the dampers already raised, so that one chord can be sustained against subsequent harmonies which are not affected. The *soft* (left) *pedal* (used only when a composer asks for it) is designed to produce veiled effects. In a grand piano it moves the keyboard and the entire action slightly to the right, so that the hammers hit only two of the strings for notes which have three, or one string for any other note. The indication for using the soft pedal is **una corda* (sometimes *u.c.*). *Tre corde* (or **t.c.*) signifies its release. In most upright pianos the soft pedal lifts the hammers closer to the strings, reducing their force of impact; in others, a strip of felt is moved into position between the hammers and the strings.

Piano accordion See *Accordion.

Pianoforte [Italian: 'soft-loud'] The full name of the instrument more commonly called simply 'the *piano'.

Pianola See *Player piano.

Piano quartet *Chamber music for piano plus string trio (violin, viola, cello). Fine examples are Mozart's Piano Quartet No. 1 in G minor (K478; 1785), Brahms's Piano Quartet No. 3 in C minor (Op. 60; 1875), and Fauré's Piano Quartet No. 1 in C minor (Op. 15; 1879).

Piano quintet *Chamber music for piano plus four other instruments – most often a string quartet (2 violins, viola, cello). There are fine examples by Schumann (in E♭, Op. 44; 1842), Brahms (in F minor, Op. 34; 1864), Dvořák (in A, Op. 81; 1887), Franck (in F minor; 1879), and Shostakovich (in G minor; 1940). However, the most familiar piano quintet, Schubert's *'Trout' Quintet (in A; 1819), is for piano, violin, viola, cello, and double bass; and Mozart wrote a Quintet (in E♭, K452; 1784) for piano and wind (oboe, clarinet, horn, bassoon) – an example followed by Beethoven in his Quintet in E♭ (Op. 16; 1796) for the same combination of instruments.

Piano roll See under *Player piano.

Piano score See *Score.

Piano trio *Chamber music composed for piano, violin, and cello; also, the name given to a group which performs such a composition. Haydn composed forty-five piano trios; Mozart composed six (and also a Trio for piano, clarinet, and viola, K498). Beethoven composed six piano trios, including the *'Ghost' Trio and the *'Archduke' Trio (and also a Trio for piano, clarinet, and cello). Brahms composed three piano trios (also a Trio for piano, violin, and horn, and a Trio for piano, clarinet, and cello). Other notable piano trios include the two by Schubert (in B♭, and in E♭), the two by Mendelssohn (in D minor, and in C minor), Dvořák's 'Dumky' Trio (see under **Dumka*), Ravel's Piano Trio (1914), and Shostakovich's Piano Trio No. 2 in E minor (1944).

Piatti [Italian] Cymbals. **Piatto sospeso**, suspended cymbal.

Picardy third See *Tierce de Picardie.

Piccolo [abbreviation of the Italian, *flauto piccolo*, meaning 'small flute'] A woodwind instrument which is really a half-sized *flute. As the method of fingering is the same on both instruments, all flautists are equally able to play the

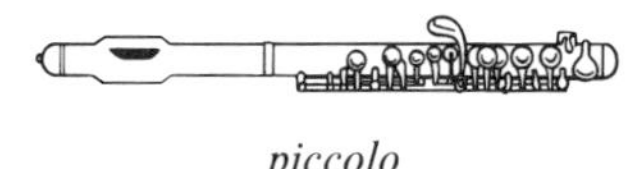

piccolo

piccolo. Its range lies an octave higher than the flute, and the upper notes are piercingly brilliant and penetrating. Music for piccolo is written one octave lower than it actually sounds.

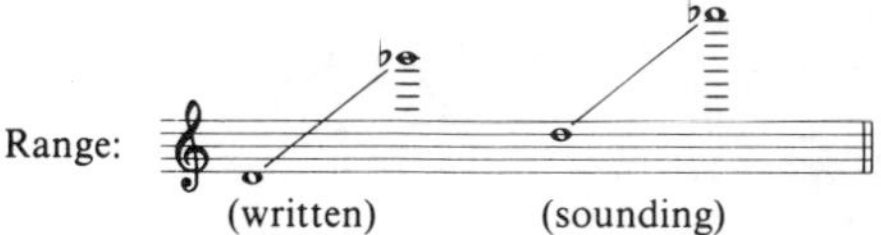

Compositions in which the piccolo can be heard include the first movement of **Lieutenant Kijé* by Prokofiev, Malcolm Arnold's English Dance No. 5, *Dance of the Firebird* from Stravinsky's ballet *The *Firebird*, and Sousa's March *The Stars and Stripes Forever* (solo, during the repeat of the main tune).

Pictures at an Exhibition A suite of descriptive pieces for piano solo by Musorgsky, composed in 1874. Each of the ten pieces describes a picture from a memorial exhibition displaying paintings, drawings, and sketches by the Russian artist, Victor Hartmann, who died in 1873. The work is introduced by a short 'Promenade', which comes again before some of the pieces – as if to suggest the composer strolling from picture to picture. The titles of the ten 'Pictures' are: 1 The Gnome; 2 The Old Castle; 3 In the Tuileries Gardens; 4 Bydlo (a Polish ox-drawn cart); 5 Ballet of the Unhatched Chicks; 6 Samuel Goldenberg and Schmuyle (two Polish Jews); 7 The Market-place at Limoges; 8 Catacombs; 9 The Hut on Fowl's Legs; 10 The Great Gate of Kiev.

Pictures at an Exhibition is often heard in Ravel's brilliant arrangement for full orchestra. Other orchestral versions include those by Sir Henry Wood, and Stokowski; and there is a version for brass and percussion by Elgar Howarth.

Pieno; **Piena** [Italian] Full, whole, complete. **A voce piena**, with full voice. **Organo pieno** or **organo pleno**, *full organ.

Pierrot lunaire ('Pierrot by Moonlight', or 'Moonstruck Pierrot') A song-cycle in *Expressionist style, Opus 21, by Schoenberg, composed in 1912. It is a setting of twenty-one poems by the Belgian poet, Albert Giraud, for female 'singing narrator' (using the technique of *Sprechgesang, or 'speech-song') and five players using eight instruments: piano, flute and piccolo, clarinet and bass clarinet, violin and viola, cello. No two songs use exactly the same combination of instruments. The poems were translated from the original French into German by O. E. Hartleben.

Pietoso [Italian] Compassionate, sympathetic.

Pifa [Italian] Title for a piece imitating the sounds of shepherds' pipes or **pifferi*. Handel added the subtitle 'Pifa' to his **Pastoral Symphony* in *Messiah*.

Pifferi Old Italian name for various types of popular wind instruments, such as shepherds' pipes, shawms, bagpipes. [See also: *Pifa]

Pines of Rome, The (*Pini di Roma*) A symphonic poem for large orchestra by Respighi, composed in 1923–4. It is in four sections, each describing a landscape near Rome which features pine-trees: 1 The Pines of the Villa Borghese; 2 The Pines near a Catacomb; 3 The Pines of the Janiculum; 4 The Pines of the Appian Way. At the end of the third section, a recording of a nightingale's song is played against a hushed orchestral background. [See also: *The *Fountains of Rome*; **Roman Festivals*]

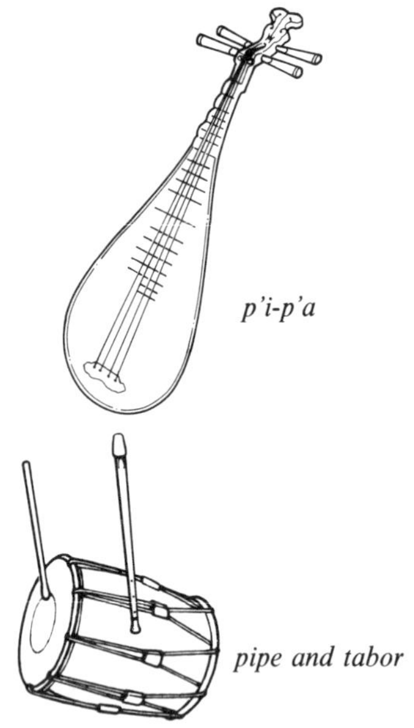

P'i-p'a A Chinese plucked lute, originating in Central Asia (probably Persia) and introduced into China around AD 400. It is pear-shaped and short-necked. There are four strings of silk or nylon, and sixteen or more frets on the belly and the neck. The p'i-p'a has a range of three and a half octaves. (The Japanese *biwa developed from the p'i-p'a.)

Pipe and tabor A combination of two instruments, dating from the 13th century, and consisting of a simple pipe (often with only three holes) and a two-headed drum, both played by the same person – a simple sort of 'one-man band', often used to accompany dancing. The player held the pipe in one hand and beat time on the tabor, which was suspended from the shoulder or slung around the waist.

Pirates of Penzance, The Comic opera in two acts by Gilbert (text) and Sullivan (music), first produced at Paignton, Devon, in 1879. Frederick (tenor), apprenticed by mistake to a band of pirates, is 21 and has been freed from his indentures. He falls in love with one of Major-General Stanley's daughters, Mabel (soprano), whom he sees among a bevy of beautiful maidens, but the pirates are determined to marry the maidens themselves. General Stanley (baritone) saves his daughters by pretending to be an orphan and gaining the pirates' sympathy. Frederick engages a band of policemen to capture his former colleagues, but before they can do so the pirates return to inform him that he was born on February 29 and thus, being only 5¼, is still apprenticed to them. His sense of duty prompts him to rejoin them and to expose the General's lie. The pirates attack the General's home and tussle with the police, who call on them to surrender in the name of the Queen. Such is their loyalty that they quickly comply; for really the pirates are all noblemen who have gone wrong. They resume their ranks and duties and marry the maidens, including (with his blessing) the General's daughters.

Piston **1** On brass instruments, the same as *valve. **2** Many organs now have pistons – buttons which, with one swift touch of the foot or a thumb, change whole groups of stops at once, so that the flow of the music remains uninterrupted. **3** In French scores, *piston* is short for *cornet à pistons* – the modern cornet.

Pitch The relative height (highness) or depth (lowness) of a musical sound, determined by its frequency (number of vibrations per second). [For the terms 'definite pitch' and 'indefinite pitch', see under *Percussion]

Pitch class The set of pitches which share the same letter-name, at whatever octave they occur. And so, on the piano keyboard for example, all the Cs are members of the pitch class C, all the Ds are members of the pitch class D, and so on.

Pitch-names See Tables 9 and 10 on page 391.

Più [Italian] More. As in **più forte**, more loud, louder; **più lento**, more slowly, slower. **Più più**, more and more. **Il più** means 'the most' – **il più forte possible**, as loud as possible. [See also: *Piuttosto]

Piuttosto [Italian] Somewhat, rather, rather than; sooner. [See also: *Tosto]

Piva [Italian] **1** Bagpipe. **2** A swift Italian dance of the 15th and 16th centuries, with leaps and turns. In the 16th century it often appeared as the third of a suite of three dances, e.g. pavan, saltarello, and piva.

Pizzicato (abbrev.: **pizz.**) [Italian for 'nipped'] Plucked. An indication to string players to pluck the string(s) with the fingertips instead of using the bow (see also *arco). Some 20th-century composers (Bartók in particular) occasionally ask for a strong *pizzicato* which causes the string to slap against and rebound off the fingerboard.

Placito [Italian] Pleasure. **A bene placito**, at the performer's pleasure, as the performer pleases.

Plagal cadence See *Cadences.

Plainsong (plainchant) [Latin: *cantus planus*] The traditional monophonic melodies to which the texts of the Roman Catholic liturgy are sung. Those adopted for general use are referred to as Gregorian Chant (after St Gregory the Great, who was Pope from 590 to 604). Many of the chants reached their final form in the 8th and 9th centuries.

The various chants divide into two main categories: those for the *Mass, and those for the *Office. Each chant is written in one of the *church modes, and the music is monophonic – the voices sing in unison, with no supporting chords or harmonies, and there is no instrumental accompaniment. The chant melodies move smoothly, rising and falling in small steps rather than wide leaps; and the rhythm flows gently and irregularly, mainly matching the rhythm and stress of the Latin words to which this music is sung. Some chants are sung antiphonally – one choir singing in alternation with another; others are sung in response style, with one or more soloists answered by the full choir. [For musical examples of plainsong, see under: *In nomine; *Dies irae; *Organum]

Planets, The A suite for large orchestra, Opus 32, by Gustav Holst, composed between 1914 and 1916. Each of the seven pieces describes the astrological character and associations of a certain planet. The titles are: 1 Mars, the Bringer of War; 2 Venus, the Bringer of Peace; 3 Mercury, the Winged Messenger; 4 Jupiter, the Bringer of Jollity; 5 Saturn, the Bringer of Old Age; 6 Uranus, the Magician; 7 Neptune, the Mystic. Holst scores *The Planets* for a very large orchestra which includes: 4 flutes, alto flute and 2 piccolos, 4 oboes, bass oboe and cor anglais, 3 clarinets and bass clarinet, 3 bassoons and double bassoon; 6 horns, 4 trumpets, 3 trombones (2 tenors, 1 bass), tenor tuba and bass tuba; 6 kettle drums, bass drum, snare drum, cymbals, triangle, tambourine, glockenspiel, xylophone, celesta, tubular bells, tam-tam; organ; 2 harps; a very large string section; and also, in the final piece, wordless female chorus.

Player piano A type of piano which is able to 'play itself'. A perforated roll of paper (**piano roll**) gradually unwinds, and works the hammers of the piano by means of air pressure forced through the holes in the paper. The air pressure is built up either by foot pedals worked by the 'pianist' or by an electric motor. Player pianos were popular from the 1870s to the 1920s. One of the best examples was patented in 1897 under the name of **Pianola**; a more elaborate type, called the **reproducing player piano**, was able to recreate all the subtly-graded dynamics and nuances of an original performance. Piano rolls were made of performances by many famous pianists and composers, including Paderewski, Rachmaninov, Debussy, Mahler, Gershwin, and Richard Strauss.

Plectrum A small flat piece of horn, metal, hard plastic, etc., held between fingers and thumb and used to pluck the strings of an instrument such as the guitar or mandolin. Also the piece of quill or pointed leather set into the top of a jack in plucked-string keyboard instruments such as the *harpsichord.

Plein [French] Full, whole, complete. **Plein jeu**, *full organ.

Pleno [Italian] Same as *Pieno.

Plötzlich [German] Sudden, immediate; abrupt.

Plus [French] More. **De plus en plus**, more and more.

Pochette [French: 'little pocket'] The same as *Kit.

Pochettino; **Pochetto**; **Pochino**; **Pochissimo** See under *Poco.

Poco [Italian] Little; rather, slightly. For example: *poco lento*, rather slow; *poco rallentando*, slowing down slightly. **Poco a poco**, little by little, gradually. **Pochetto, pochino**, very little. **Pochettino**, very little indeed. **Pochissimo**, as little as possible.

Poème électronique Edgard Varèse's last completed work, composed for the Brussels Exposition of 1958. It is for three-track tape, and includes electronic sounds, bells, drums, organ, and voices, electronically transformed.

Poi [Italian] Then. As in *Scherzo D.C. e poi la Coda* – repeat the Scherzo and then (play) the Coda. **Poi a poi**, by degrees.

Point (point of imitation; other spellings include 'pointe', 'poynte', 'poynct') **1** A term used in England, from the 16th century to the beginning of the 18th, to describe a melodic idea or a complete theme suitable for treatment in imitative style (see *Imitation). **2** The same term was used, by extension, to describe a passage or a section of a piece written in imitative style (particularly a *motet or a *madrigal). A point may be of any length, and usually concludes with a cadence. Typically, while a chord is held at the end of a point, one of the voice-parts will set off with the theme of the next point, soon imitated by the other voice-parts. By overlapping points in this way, the composer creates a continuous, 'seamless' musical texture.

Point d'orgue [French] **1** An organ point or *pedal point. **2** A fermata or *pause sign (𝄐). **3** A *cadenza in a composition such as a concerto (often indicated by a pause sign).

Pointillism Term describing a 20th-century technique in composing in which each player, usually treated as a soloist, is given brief wisps of music to play – often a single note only now and then. So the music consists largely of individual 'points' of sound – scintillating dabs of instrumental colour. The style is named after the technique of Pointillist artists, such as Seurat, who painted pictures by precisely applying countless separate dots, or 'points', of pure colour (red, blue, and yellow). The first composer to explore Pointillism was Webern (for example, in his *Five Pieces for Orchestra*, Op. 10).

Polacca [Italian] *Polonaise.

Polka A lively Czech couple-dance in swift duple time, originating in Bohemia during the 1830s and soon spreading to other countries. In the ballrooms of Vienna it became almost as popular as the waltz. The polka takes its name from the Czech word *půlka* meaning 'half', and one story connected with the polka is that it was invented by a servant girl who was forced to take very small steps as she made up the dance owing to the restricted space in her tiny attic room. The following rhythm is characteristic of the dance:

2/4 ‖: 1 2 3 (hop) | 1 2 3 (hop) :‖

Well-known polkas include the Polka from Smetana's *The *Bartered Bride*, Dvořák's Slavonic Dance No. 3 in A♭, *Thunder and Lightning Polka* by Johann Strauss the Younger, the Polka from Weinberger's opera *Shvanda the Bagpiper*, and the Polka from **Façade* by William Walton.

Polka from Smetana: *The Bartered Bride*

Polonaise [French for 'Polish' or 'Polish dance'] A stately Polish processional dance, with three beats to a bar, moderately fast in speed. Bach included examples in his French Suite No. 6, Orchestral Suite No. 2, and Brandenburg Concerto No. 1. During the 19th century, characteristics of the polonaise became the repetition of rhythmic patterns (e.g.), and the use of feminine cadences ending on the third beat of a bar (as in the music below). The most famous examples are Chopin's sixteen Polonaises for solo piano (including the *'Military' Polonaise, and the *'Heroic' Polonaise).

Chopin: 'Military' Polonaise, final bars

Polovtsian Dances See under **Prince Igor*.

Polychoral A term describing a composition in which the voices and/or instruments are divided into two or more groups, performing mainly in alternation, but also combining together at times with rich and powerful effect. The sounds within each group might be blended, but the groups contrasted one against another (e.g. in pitch and timbre). The style is especially associated with Giovanni Gabrieli, and other Venetian composers of the late 16th and 17th centuries. Composers often referred to the technique of composing music in this style, and also to the groups performing it, as *cori spezzati*, meaning 'broken choirs' or 'divided choirs' (see *Coro).

Polymetre (adjective: **polymetric**) **1** The simultaneous use of two or more different metres. For example, one part in the musical texture may be in $\frac{3}{4}$ while, simultaneously, another part is proceeding in $\frac{4}{4}$. **2** The same word may also be applied to the *successive* use of different metres, perhaps changing from one bar to the next – for example: a bar in $\frac{3}{4}$, followed by one in $\frac{2}{4}$, followed by $\frac{5}{8}$, and so on. [See also: *Polyrhythm]

Polyphonic [from Greek: 'many sounds', 'music in more than one part'] A term describing a musical *texture which consists of two or more melodic lines, mainly of equal importance and independence, weaving along together. (Another word used with much the same meaning is 'contrapuntal'.) The following example is from the Benedictus of the Mass 'Gloria tibi Trinitas' by the 16th-century composer, John Taverner.

Music composed in this type of style and texture is called **polyphony**; and the earliest examples, by Medieval composers, are known as *organum. [See also: *Homophonic; *Monophonic]

Polyrhythm Two or more different (and often complex) rhythms going along at the same time, strongly conflicting against each other and creating a kind of 'rhythmic counterpoint'. **Polyrhythmic** effects may be heard in certain medieval polyphonic pieces (e.g. late 14th-century motets), in a great many 20th-century compositions (particularly by composers such as Ives, Bartók, and Stravinsky), and also in pieces of modern jazz.

Polytextual Term describing a vocal composition in which two or more different texts (separate sets of words) are sung simultaneously. Many medieval motets, for example, are polytextual.

Polytonality The use of two or more keys simultaneously. (If two keys only are involved, it is sometimes called **bitonality**.) **Polytonal** music may have the melody in one key, while the harmony is in another (as in the example, opposite); or two or more tunes may weave along together in counterpoint, each tune in its own separate key. Many 20th-century composers have made use of polytonality, notably Ives, Bartók, Stravinsky, Milhaud, and Holst.

Pommer German name for *shawm.

Pomp and Circumstance Elgar's title (quoting from Shakespeare's play *Othello*) for his five orchestral marches, Opus 39: No. 1 in D and No. 2 in A minor (both composed in 1901), No. 3 in C minor (1904), No. 4 in G (1907), and No. 5 in C (1930). Elgar used part of the famous first march – to words by A. C. Benson, beginning 'Land of Hope and Glory' – as the final section of his *Coronation Ode* (1902). When this march is played at the last night of the Henry Wood Promenade Concerts in London each summer, the entire audience joins in by singing Benson's words.

Pomposo [Italian] Pompous, grand.

Ponticello [Italian] The bridge of a string instrument. **Sul ponticello**, indication to a string player to bow the string(s) very close to the bridge, producing a rather eerie tone-quality, especially when combined with bowed *tremolo.

Pope Marcellus Mass See **Missa Papae Marcelli.*

Pop music A general term used since the 1950s to describe any style of music which is not classed as so-called 'serious' or 'classical' music (e.g. ballad, country, folk, reggae, rhythm and blues, rock), and which has been composed with the main aim of achieving immediate popularity, and vast sales. The ultimate goal of the composer and lyrics-writer of a pop song or pop number is that, recorded by a noted pop singer or pop group, it will rise to 'number one in the charts' to become currently 'top of the pops'.

Popolare [Italian] Popular.

Porgy and Bess Opera in three acts by George Gershwin, first staged in Boston, Massachusetts, in 1935 (liberetto by Du Bose Heyward and Ira Gershwin). The action takes place in Catfish Row, a Negro tenement in Charleston, South Carolina. Porgy (baritone), a crippled beggar, falls in love with Bess, the wife of the brutal docker Crown (baritone). When drunk, Crown kills Robbins (tenor) and goes into hiding. A gambler, Sporting Life (tenor), tries to persuade Bess to elope with him to New York, but Bess (soprano) plans to marry Porgy. Crown returns, and, as a storm rages, he taunts the two lovers, but rushes out to help Clara (soprano), whose husband's boat has capsized. When Crown returns to claim Bess, Porgy kills him. Summoned to identify the body, Porgy refuses, and is locked up for contempt of court. Bess goes off with Sporting Life to New York, and the opera ends with Porgy leaving Catfish Row in pursuit.

Portamento [Italian: 'carriage', 'bearing'] The effect of smoothly carrying one note into the next, or of sliding continuously from one pitch to another, in legato style. The effect is possible with the voice, on a bowed string instrument, and on the trombone.

Portando; **Portato** [Italian: 'carrying', 'carried'] Terms meaning the same as mezzo-staccato (see under *Staccato).

Portative organ A small organ very popular in Medieval times – small enough to be carried as it was played (*portative*, like *portable*, from a Latin word meaning 'carry'). There were often two rows of pipes, offering a range of up to two octaves from middle C. One hand played on the keys, while the other hand or arm worked the bellows. The instrument was useful for domestic music-making, and also for music out-of-doors, e.g. processions, or dancing in the open air.

portative organ

Portato See *Portando.

Port de voix; **Porter la voix** [French: 'carrying of the voice', 'to carry the voice'] Terms meaning the same as the Italian **portamento*.

Portsmouth Point A concert overture composed by Walton in 1925. It was inspired by an etching by Thomas Rowlandson (1756–1827), depicting a lively scene on the quay at Portsmouth.

Posaune (plural: *Posaunen*) [German] Trombone.

Positif [French]; **Positiv** [German] The choir organ. [See under *Organ]

Position **1** In connection with a chord, referring to which note is in the bass. If the root is in the bass, the chord is said to be in 'root position'; if any other note of the chord is in the bass, the chord is said to be 'in inversion' (see under *Chord). **2** In connection with the playing of bowed string instruments (the violin, cello, etc.), the different points along the fingerboard to which the left hand is shifted to obtain the various pitches. Taking the G string as an example, in first position the fingers, in turn, stop the string to sound the notes A, B, C, D; shifting to second position, the notes sounded are B, C, D, E; and so on. (In higher positions on the cello, the thumb is also used.) **3** On the *trombone, the placement of the slide according to the seven playing positions – the home position (with the slide fully drawn in) being called the first position.

Positive organ The name for a small Medieval or Renaissance organ, rather larger than a *portative organ, but small enough to be moved from one place to another (*positive* from a Latin word meaning 'placed in position' – on a table or on the floor). A later form of positive organ was called a **chamber organ** or **cabinet organ**.

Possibile [Italian] Possible. As in **il più piano possibile**, as soft as possible.

Post horn A simple brass instrument consisting of a lengthy tube (either straight or coiled) which was once used on mail coaches to sound signals to announce arrival or departure. Originally, it had no valves or keys, and so (like a bugle) could only sound notes of the harmonic series. Mozart included the post horn in the sixth of the seven movements of his Serenade No. 9 in D, K320 (nicknamed the 'Posthorn' Serenade), and two post horns in the third of his German Dances, K605 ('Sleigh-ride').

Posthumous (abbrev.: **Post.** or **Posth.**) [From Latin, meaning 'after death'] Term used to describe a composition which was not published during the composer's lifetime.

Postlude **1** A movement or the final section of a movement concluding a composition. [See also: *Epilogue] **2** The name often given to the organ piece played at the end of a service (i.e. the final *voluntary).

Potpourri [French: 'rotten pot'] A medley of popular tunes, songs, or operatic airs, loosely strung together. Some overtures to light operas or operettas consist of a whole string of tunes taken from the stage work they introduce, and these are often called potpourri (or medley) overtures. (The overtures to operettas by Sullivan and Offenbach are often of this type.)

Poule, La **1** Harpsichord piece by Rameau (included in Suite No. 2 of his *Pièces de clavecin*, Book of 1731) which imitates the clucking of a hen. [See also: *The *Birds*] **2** Haydn's Symphony No. 83 in G minor. [See: *'Hen' Symphony]

Pour [French] For.

Poussez [French] Push forward – hurry, increase the speed.

Poynct; **Poynte** Alternative spellings of *Point.

PP; ***pp*** Abbreviation standing for **pianissimo*.

Pr. Abbreviation for *Principale.

Praeludium [Latin] *Prelude.

'Prague' Symphony Nickname of Mozart's Symphony No. 38 in D major (K504) composed in 1786; so called because it was first performed when Mozart visited Prague in 1787. This symphony has no Minuet, and so is in three movements instead of the more usual four: 1 *Adagio* (a quite lengthy slow introduction) leading to *Allegro*; 2 *Andante*; 3 Finale: *Presto*. All three movements are in sonata form.

Präludien [German] Preludes.

Préambule [French]; **Praeambulum** [Latin] A preamble or *prelude.

Precipitando [Italian] Dashing, hurrying, rushing. **Precipitato**, rushed. **Precipitoso**, hasty, headlong, impetuous.

Preciso [Italian] Precise, exact.

Pre-Classical A term applied in a general sense to any music before the late 18th century, but more specifically to the music of those composers (working around 1740–60) who led the way to the Classical style of Haydn and Mozart – particularly C. P. E. Bach and members of the *Mannheim School.

Prelude **1** An instrumental piece which introduces (is 'played before') another piece, or group of pieces, or a large-scale work – as in the case of a prelude to a fugue, or a suite, or an act of an opera. **2** An independent piece, particularly for piano – for example, the Twenty-four Preludes of Chopin, the Twenty-four Preludes of Rachmaninov.

Prélude à 'L'Après-midi d'un faune' (Prelude to 'The Afternoon of a Faun') Debussy's first important composition, completed in 1894, in *Impressionist style. He composed it after reading Mallarmé's poem, *L'Après-midi d'un faune*, which describes a young faun lying under shady trees in the intense heat of a summer's afternoon. His drowsing is interrupted by a vision of nymphs running through a cool glade. Debussy originally intended to compose three pieces (*Prélude*, *Interlude*, and *Paraphrase finale*) but only the first was completed.

Préludes, Les A *symphonic poem by Liszt, first performed in 1854. Liszt explained the title, taken from a poem by Lamartine, as meaning that life is merely a series of preludes to the unknown life hereafter. The music is not structured according to any set musical form. Instead, Liszt brings unity to the piece by using the device called *thematic transformation – the main theme reappearing several times throughout the symphonic poem, but continually transformed, or changed, in mood and character.

Premier; **Première** [French] First.

Preparation A term used in connection with discords. The composer 'prepares' the listener's ear for a discord by sounding the dissonant note as a consonant note in the same part in the preceding chord:

[See also: *Resolution]

Prepared piano An idea invented in 1938 by the American composer John Cage, in which, to perform some of his compositions, a piano must be very elaborately 'prepared'. Nuts, bolts, and screws, pieces of rubber and plastic are fixed between, under, and over certain strings in the piano – a process which may take two or three hours before performance can begin. The result of this preparation is twofold. The tone-qualities of prepared strings are affected according to the various kinds of material used – producing richly varied sonorities which may suggest the sounds of Eastern bells, gongs, and drums. Also, wedging the materials between the strings produces a tightening effect, so raising the pitch. A key normally sounding C may instead produce a sound several notes higher. A further important effect is that, after preparation, the separate strings of a note may not reach equal tension – thus resulting in two, or even three, sounds of quite different pitch played by a single key. Included among Cage's many compositions involving prepared piano are his *Sonatas and Interludes* for prepared piano (1946–8) and his *Concerto* for prepared piano and chamber orchestra (1951).

Près de la table [French] In harp music, instructing the player to pluck the strings 'near to the soundboard', resulting in a rather metallic tone-quality.

Pressez [French] Hurry; increase the speed.

Presto [Italian] Quick, nimble – usually taken to mean 'very fast'. **Prestissimo**, extremely fast. **Presto possibile**, as fast as possible.

Prima; **Primo** [Italian] First. For example: *prima donna* ('first lady'), the leading female singer in an opera; *violino primo*, first violin(s). **Primo** and **Secondo** are terms referring to the upper and lower parts in a piano *duet. **Prima volta**, first time (see *Volta). **Tempo primo** (often abbreviated to *Tempo Imo* or *Tempo I*), first speed – the same speed as at the beginning. **Come prima**, as at first.

Primary triads (primary chords) Of the seven triads which can be built on the notes of any major or minor scale, three are more important than the rest. And so, in the same way that we speak of the three 'primary colours', these are called primary triads. They are the three triads built on these notes of the scale: the tonic (I), the subdominant (IV), and the dominant (V). For example:

Primary triads of C major

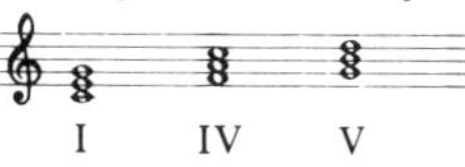

Primary triads of C minor

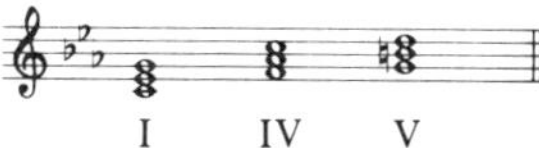

Primo See *Prima.

Prince Igor Opera in a prologue and four acts by Borodin, left incomplete but finished by Rimsky-Korsakov and Glazunov (libretto by Borodin), first produced at St Petersburg in 1890. Prince Igor (baritone) and his son Vladimir go to war against the Polovtsians and are captured by Khan Konchak (bass). Vladimir (tenor) falls in love with Konchak's daughter Konchakovna (mezzo-soprano), and when Igor escapes and returns to his people, Vladimir remains behind and marries her. The Polovtsian Dances, from Act II, are sometimes sung at choral and orchestral concerts or (less effectively) played by the orchestra alone. In 1953 a selection from the opera was adapted for the Broadway musical *Kismet*.

Principale [Italian] Principal; chief. Also, in a concerto, referring to the solo instrument(s) – for example, in a Mozart Horn Concerto: *Corno principale* (abbrev.: *Cor. pr.*), solo horn.

Principal subject The main theme (the recurring rondo theme) in a piece or movement in sonata-rondo form. [See: *Rondo 2]

Programmatic; **Programme** See *Programme music.

Programme music Any music which is intended to 'tell a story', or is in some way descriptive or illustrative so that it conjures up pictures in the mind of the listener, is called programme music, or is said to be **programmatic**. The 'story-line' or the descriptive idea which initially fired the composer's imagination, and on which the music was then based, is itself called the **programme**. (Music without any such background, but which is intended to be enjoyed simply for its own sake, purely as sound, is called *absolute music or abstract music.)

Examples of descriptive or illustrative music date back as far as the 14th century. However, it was not until the 19th century, when closer links were formed between music and literature and painting, that composers keenly took up the idea of programme music and extensively explored its possibilities – especially in orchestral form in types of composition such as the *symphonic poem, the *programme symphony, and also, in many cases, in the concert overture (see under *Overture).

Programme symphony A composition structured in the form of a *symphony, in several movements, and based upon a programme (see *Programme music) – i.e. it is in some way descriptive or even attempts to 'tell a story'. Examples are Beethoven's **Pastoral Symphony*, Berlioz's **Symphonie fantastique*, and Liszt's **Faust Symphony*.

Progression Movement of one note to another note or one chord to another chord.

Progressive jazz A *jazz term used to describe the attempts in the 1940s and 1950s to revive the big band tradition (see *Swing). The music, for large jazz ensemble, featured complex melodies and rhythms, and often extremely dissonant harmonies and dense textures. Usually, there was little improvisation. The most notable exponent of progressive jazz was Stan Kenton.

Promenade concerts Originally, concerts at which the audience could stroll or walk about ('promenade') while listening. Nowadays, a concert offering a certain number of cheaper tickets to people willing to stand rather than take seats. The present London Promenade Concerts (familiarly known as the 'Proms'), centred at the Royal Albert Hall, take place annually from mid-July to mid-September. These were founded by Robert Newman in 1895 and were conducted, until 1944, by Sir Henry Wood. The BBC took over the organization of the Proms in 1927.

Prometheus See *The *Creatures of Prometheus.*

Proper See *Mass.

'Prussian' Quartets **1** Set of six string quartets, Opus 50, composed by Haydn in 1787. The first edition printed a dedication to Friedrich Wilhelm II, King of Prussia. [See: *'Frog' Quartet] **2** Nickname for the last three of Mozart's 23 string quartets, composed in 1789–90 for the King mentioned above. They are Nos. 21 in D (K575), 22 in B flat (K589), and 23 in F (K590). In each quartet Mozart made the cello part more important than usual since the King was an enthusiastic cello player.

Psalmus hungaricus (Hungarian Psalm) A work by Kodály for solo tenor, chorus (and optional children's chorus), orchestra, and organ. It is a setting of Psalm 55, translated into Hungarian by the 16th-century poet, Mihály Vég. Kodály composed the work in 1923 to mark the 50th anniversary of the union of the cities Buda and Pest.

Psaltery A plucked string instrument (of the zither type) very popular in Medieval times. The metal strings, stretched over a flat, hollow soundbox, were plucked either with the fingers or with goose quills, held one in each hand. The psaltery was used to accompany the voice, in ensemble music, and also as a solo instrument. [See also: *Qānūn]

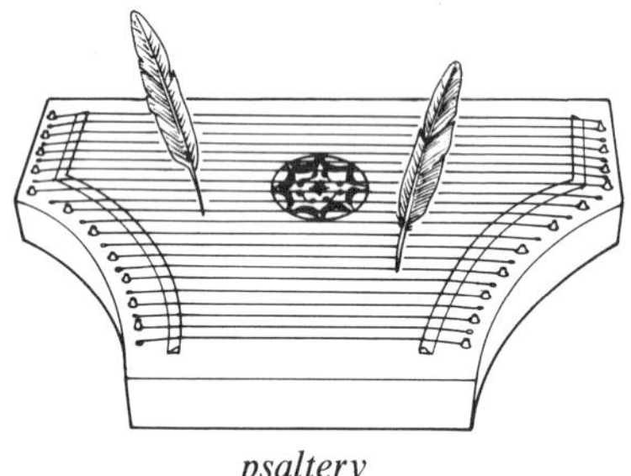

psaltery

Psychedelic rock See under *Rock.

Puis [French] Then.

Pulcinella Ballet with song in one act, for soprano, tenor, bass, and chamber orchestra, composed by Stravinsky; first produced in Paris in 1920 with choreography by Massine and décor by Picasso. The story is based on the character of Pulcinella, the traditional hero of many Italian comedies of the 16th and 17th centuries. Stravinsky based his music on several tunes which, at the time, were thought to be by the Italian composer Pergolesi (1710–36). However, it is now known that many of the tunes were by other, less famous, composers. Stravinsky keeps many of these tunes intact, but gives the music a definite 20th-century flavour by spicing the accompaniment with dissonances, and choosing unusual combinations of instrumental timbres (see *Neoclassicism). Stravinsky arranged a suite of pieces from the ballet for chamber orchestra (1922, revised 1947). His *Suite italienne* (1932) is also arranged from *Pulcinella*, and this exists in two versions: for cello and piano (five movements), and for violin and piano (six movements).

Pulse In simple *time, the word 'pulse' is used in the same sense as *beat – so in music in $\frac{3}{4}$ time, for example, there are three beats, or three pulses, in each bar. However, in compound *time, each dotted note consists of three pulses; $\frac{6}{8}$ time, for example, has six pulses per bar, but only *two* beats.

Pult (plural: *Pulte*) [German] *Desk.

Puncta; **Punctus** See under *Estampie.

Punk rock See under *Rock.

Punta [Italian] Point.

Punta d'arco; **Punto del arco** [Italian] Directions to string players to use the 'point of the bow' – to use only the last few centimetres of the bow on the string.

Pupitre [French] *Desk.

Puzzle canon (riddle canon) A *canon which cannot be performed until some verbal puzzle or riddle, provided by the composer, has been solved. 15th-century composers in particular were very fond of such musical 'tricks'. An example occurs in the Agnus Dei III of Dufay's Mass 'L'Homme armé' where the riddle reads: 'let the crab proceed full and then return half'. This indicates that the tenor voice should first sing the melody backwards (in retrograde, or **cancrizans*) in full note-values; and then forwards, from beginning to end, in halved note-values.

Pyiba; **Pyipar** Other spellings of *P'i-p'a.

Qānūn (kanun) The Arabic psaltery (an instrument of the zither type) consisting of a shallow box designed in the shape of a trapezium, over which are stretched up to 100 strings of metal, gut, or nylon. These are arranged in triple courses (sets of three strings, each set tuned in unison). The qānūn rests on the lap of the player, who plucks the strings by means of plectrums fastened to the forefinger by rings.

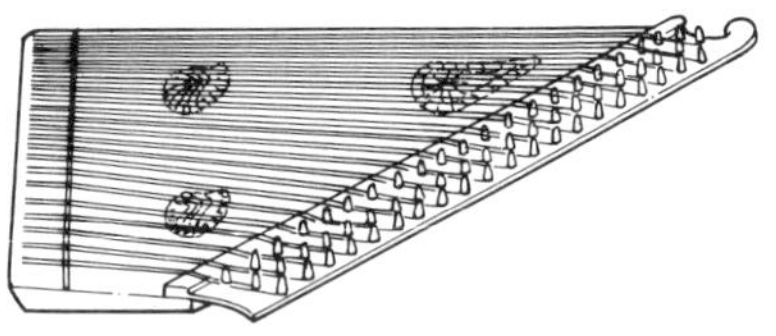

qānūn

Qin See *Ch'in.

Quadrat [German] The natural sign (♮).

Quadrille A dance, for four or more couples, very popular at the beginning of the 19th century, first in France, and then in England and Germany. The dancers formed a square (as in an American 'square dance'). A quadrille was made up of five different sections of music, alternating between $\frac{6}{8}$ and $\frac{2}{4}$, and the tunes were often adaptations of well-known melodies from operas, country dances, or popular songs. The famous dance known as *The Lancers*, invented in 1856, is a type of quadrille.

Quadro [Italian] The natural sign (♮).

Quadruple counterpoint See under *Invertible counterpoint.

Quadruple fugue A *fugue based on four subjects, treated first separately and then in combination. [See also: *Double fugue; *Triple fugue]

Quadruple stop; **Quadruple stopping** See *Stopping 1.

Quadruplet A group of four notes played or sung evenly in the time of three notes of the same kind.

Quadruple time; **Quadruple metre** Any kind of *time (or metre) which has four beats to each bar. The beat may be a plain note (such as ♩ or 𝅗𝅥) or it may be a dotted note (such as ♩. or 𝅗𝅥.). [See the articles on *Time and *Time signature, and also the table of Time signatures on page 389]

Quadruple woodwind See under *Woodwind instruments.

Quadruplum In a medieval polyphonic piece in four parts, quadruplum was the name given to the fourth part lying above the tenor *cantus firmus* (the tenor itself being counted as the first part). [See: *Tenor, 3; also *Duplum and *Triplum]

Quarter-note *Crotchet.

Quarter-tone A *microtone which is half a semitone. (There are therefore two quarter-tones to each semitone, and four quarter-tones to each whole tone.) The music of certain Eastern nations makes much use of quarter-tones (e.g. Arab music, and Hindu music). In Western music, the smallest interval normally used is that of a semitone, though some 20th-century Western composers (e.g. Ives, Bloch, Bartók, Stockhausen, and particularly the Czech composer Alois Hába) have occasionally experimented with quarter-tones in their music.

Quartet [German: *Quartett*; French: *quartette*, *quatuor*; Italian: *quartetto*] **1** Music composed for four solo instruments or voices. **2** A group which performs such a composition. [See also: *String quartet; *Piano quartet; and under *Chamber music]

Quasi [Italian] Almost, as though, like, in the style (manner) of.

Quatre [French] Four. **À quatre voix**, for four voices; or, in four voice-parts. **À quatre mains**, for four hands.

Quattro [Italian] Four. **A quattro** (*a 4*), for four voices or instruments; or, in four instrumental parts or voice-parts. **A quattro mani**, for four hands.

Quatuor [French] **1** *Quartet. **2** Also sometimes used to mean the string section of an orchestra.

Quatuor à cordes [French] *String quartet.

Quaver The note which is half the value of a crotchet, and twice the value of a semiquaver. Eight quavers are equal to one semibreve. (The American name for a quaver is an eighth-note.) A single quaver is written: ♪; a group of two: ♫; and a quaver *rest is shown as 𝄾 [See also Tables 1 and 2 on page 387]

'Queen, The'; **'The Queen of France'** See *'Paris' Symphonies.

Queen of Sheba See *The *Arrival of the Queen of Sheba.*

Querflöte Older German name for the transverse flute (i.e. the ordinary flute), used to distinguish it from the recorder which was referred to as the *Blockflöte*.

Questa; **Questo** [Italian] This. **Queste**, **questi**, these.

Quickstep **1** A lively march requiring quick steps. **2** A ballroom dance which is basically a swift version of the *foxtrot.

Quieto [Italian] Quiet, calm, peaceful.

'Quinten' Quartet See *'Fifths' Quartet.

Quintet [German: *Quintett*; French: *quintette*, *quintuor*; Italian: *quintetto*] **1** Music composed for five solo instruments or voices. **2** A group which performs such a composition. [See also: *String quintet; *Piano quintet; *Oboe quintet; *Clarinet quintet; and also under *Chamber music]

Quintuor [French] *Quintet. **Quintuor à cordes**, string quintet.

Quintuplet (quintole, quintolet) A group of five notes performed evenly in the time normally taken by (a) four notes, or (b) three notes, of the same kind:

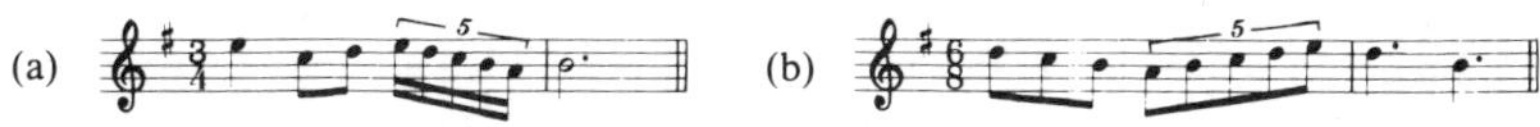

Quintuple time; **Quintuple metre** See under *Time.

Quodlibet [Latin: 'if you please'] A piece of music cleverly woven together from two or more popular tunes. The tunes may be played or sung successively, or woven together in *counterpoint. The finest example of a quodlibet is the final variation of Bach's *'Goldberg' Variations, which uses two popular tunes of his day: 'Long have I been away from you' and 'Cabbage and turnips have driven me away from home'.

R Abbreviation standing for: **1** 'right hand' (in piano music); **2** *ripieno; **3** ritardando; **4** rinforzando. **5** Also an abbreviation standing for Mario Rinaldi, who published a catalogue of the music of Vivaldi; when linked to a work by Vivaldi it indicates that piece's numbered entry in Rinaldi's catalogue. Confusingly, however, a letter R is also sometimes used to identify a piece in the more recent catalogue of Vivaldi's music by Peter Ryom, though this is usually indicated by the more precise abbreviation ***RV**. [See also: *P 3]

Rabāb An Arabic word, used (in various spellings) to describe a variety of bowed string instruments (bowed lutes or fiddles) found in Islamic countries. These instruments usually have three strings, and occur in various shapes (e.g. rectangular, pear-shaped, narrow boat-shaped, trapezoidal). One form of rabāb, which became popular in Europe in the 10th century, was commonly called the *rebec (one of the important ancestors of the violin).

Racket (Rackett) A low-pitched double-reed woodwind instrument of the Renaissance and Baroque periods, shaped rather like a pep-perpot. Its great length of tube was folded inside a cylinder less than a foot (30 cm) high, which had finger-holes pierced in the side. The characteristic tone is buzzy yet penetrating.

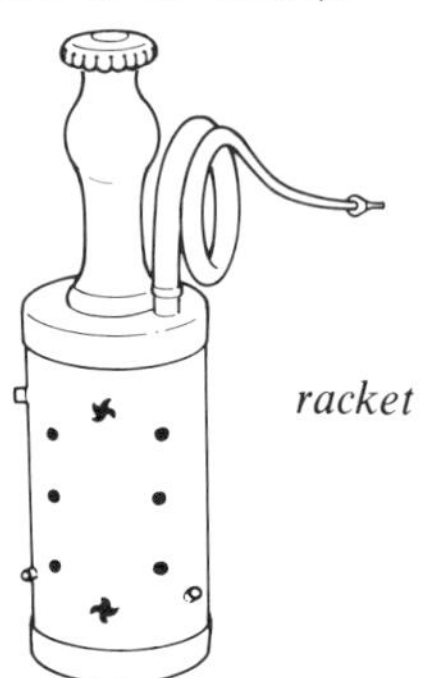

racket

Radetzky March Orchestral piece, Opus 228, by Johann Strauss the Elder; composed to celebrate the victory in August 1848 of the Austrian army, commanded by General Radetzky, in the war against Italy. The *Radetzky March* is often played at the last night of the Sir Henry Wood Promenade Concerts in London; the audience joins in by clapping the beat of the main march-tune.

Raganella [Italian] Ratchet.

Ragtime A style of dance music, originating in the USA towards the end of the 19th century. It became mainly a style of piano-playing, featuring a strongly syncopated tune in the right hand above a steady march-like beat ($\frac{2}{4}$ or $\frac{4}{4}$) in the left hand (see the example below). The most famous composer of piano rags was Scott Joplin (1868–1917). Well-known examples of his rags are *Maple Leaf Rag* (1899), *Elite Syncopations* (1902), and *The Entertainer* (1902).

Characteristic features of ragtime were important ingredients in the emergence of *jazz.

Stravinsky composed two pieces inspired by ragtime: *Ragtime* for eleven instruments (1918), and *Piano-Rag-Music* (1919).

'Raindrop' Prelude Nickname of Chopin's fifteenth piano prelude in D flat, from his set of Twenty-four Preludes in all the keys, Op. 28 (published in 1839). The story goes that Chopin composed this music during a storm when he was staying in a disused monastery on the island of Majorca, and that the repeated note A flat (in the central section of the piece, G sharp) represents raindrops steadily dripping from the roof.

Rake's Progress, The Opera in three acts and an epilogue by Igor Stravinsky, first produced in Venice in 1951 (libretto by Auden and Kallman inspired by Hogarth's engravings). Tom Rakewell (tenor), betrothed to Anne Trulove (soprano), is visited by a stranger, Nick Shadow, who claims to bring him news of a fortune left to him by an uncle. Shadow (baritone) persuades Tom to take him as his servant and go with him to London to collect the money. He will claim his own wages in a year and a day. In London, Shadow persuades Tom first to marry a bearded lady from a circus, Baba the Turk (mezzo-soprano), and then to invest in a bogus machine which supposedly turns stones into bread. Tom becomes bankrupt and his belongings are auctioned. After the agreed year and a day Shadow (who is really the Devil personified) takes Tom to a graveyard at night and claims his soul, but he is content to gamble for it. Tom wins, and Shadow sinks into a grave. Tom, however, now driven mad, is taken to Bedlam and dies there thinking that he is Adonis and that Anne, who comes to visit him, is Venus. The Epilogue points the moral 'For idle hands and hearts and minds the Devil finds a work to do'. Its accompanied recitatives and arias, and its reminiscences of Mozart in up-dated harmony, make this opera a prime example of *Neoclassicism.

Rákóczi March A Hungarian national tune, named after Prince Ferencz Rákóczi who led the Hungarians in revolt against Austria in 1703–11. Berlioz used the tune in the *Marche hongroise* (Hungarian March) in scene 3 of his cantata *The *Damnation of Faust*, and Liszt used it in one of his **Hungarian Rhapsodies* (No. 15 for piano).

Ralentir [French] Slow down; slacken in speed.

Rallentando (abbrev.: **rall.**) [Italian: 'slackening'] Slowing down gradually, and therefore the same as **ritardando*. [But see: *Ritenuto]

Range The total number of notes or pitches, extending from low to high, which a particular voice or instrument is capable of producing. [See the table of Ranges of voices and instruments on page 394]

Rank A set of organ pipes, graded in size and therefore in pitch, and all producing sounds of a similar tone-colour. A rank is controlled by a *stop. However, a rank is itself sometimes referred to as a stop, sometimes as a register.

Rap (rapping) A style of popular music which originated during the 1970s among black American musicians in New York. It consists of improvised rhyming verses, often delivered in a dead-pan tone of voice, and performed to a rhythmic accompaniment.

Râpe-guero [French] The same as *güiro.

Rappresentatione di Anima e di Corpo See under *Oratorio.

Rapsodia [Italian]; **Rapsodie** [French] *Rhapsody.

Rapsodie espagnole (Spanish Rhapsody) A descriptive orchestral suite by Ravel, composed in 1907–8. It is in four movements: 1 *Prélude à la nuit* (Prelude to the night); 2 *Malagueña*; 3 *Habanera*; 4 *Feria* (Fair).

Rasch [German] Quick, brisk, impetuous. **Rascher**, quicker.

Ratchet (orchestral rattle) A percussion instrument consisting of a ratchet wheel, or cog-wheel, whose teeth cause one or more flexible blades of wood or metal, fixed at one end, to vibrate stridently. In one version, the wheel is made to revolve by turning a handle. In another, it remains stationary while the blades in their frame are twirled around (as in the football variety of rattle). The instrument may be heard in Strauss's **Till Eulenspiegel* (bars 137–9 and 145–7, the 'market scene'), towards the end of *The Gnome* from Ravel's orchestration of Musorgsky's **Pictures at an Exhibition*, and during the first section of Respighi's *The *Pines of Rome* (e.g. at bars 36–53).

Ratsche [German] Ratchet.

Rattle For the rattle occasionally used in the orchestra, see *Ratchet.

Rauschpfeife [German] A type of shawm of the 16th and early 17th centuries in which the double reed was enclosed in a cap. The sound was loud and penetrating.

Ravvivando [Italian: 'reviving'] Quickening; becoming animated.

'Razor' Quartet Nickname of Haydn's String Quartet in F minor, Op. 55 No. 2, composed around 1789. This is the fifth of the *'Tost' Quartets. It owes its nickname to a story that when Haydn was visited by the London publisher John Bland, he offered his best string quartet in exchange for a good English razor.

'Razumovsky' Quartets Three string quartets by Beethoven, Opus 59 (No. 1 in F, No. 2 in E minor, No. 3 in C) composed in 1805–6 for the Russian ambassador to the Austrian court in Vienna, Count Andrey Razumovsky. Beethoven includes a Russian folk-tune (marked 'Thème Russe') in the finale of the first quartet, and another in the third movement of the second quartet.

Re [Italian]; **Ré** [French] The note D.

Reading Rota See *_Sumer is icumen in._

Real answer See under *Fugue.

Real sequence See under *Sequence.

Rebab Another version of the name *rabāb.

Rebec (rebeck) A medieval bowed string instrument, slender and pear-shaped, made in various sizes to form a family. The number of strings varied between one and five, though the most common number was three. The tone was rather nasal and 'reedy'. A popular choice of instrument to accompany songs or dancing. The rebec, which derived from the Arab *rabāb, was one of the important ancestors of the violin.

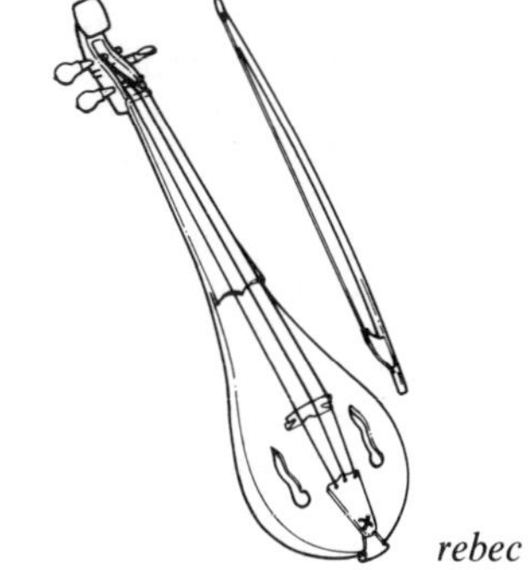

rebec

Recapitulation See *Sonata form.

Recercar See *Ricercare.

Rechte [German] Right. **Rechte Hand** (in piano music), right hand.

Recit. Short for *Recitando or *Recitative.

Récit [French] **1** The swell organ (see under *Organ). **2** An accompanied solo (for instance, an organ piece which has a distinctive melody played on a solo stop). **3** A 17th-century French term (from *récitatif*) for a solo vocal piece, usually in the style of an aria.

Recital A concert given by a single performer (e.g. a piano recital) or by two performers of which one is usually a pianist – such as a violin recital (violin and piano) or a song recital (voice and piano).

Recitando [Italian] Reciting; in the manner and style of a *recitative.

Recitative [Italian: *recitativo*; French: *récitatif*; German: *Rezitativ*] A declamatory style of vocal writing in which the voice – half singing, half reciting – rises and falls according to the meaning of the text and closely follows the natural speech-rhythms of the words. Recitative is used especially in opera and oratorio, as a means of swiftly carrying forward the plot (whereas an *aria is often reflective, tending to hold up the story). By the end of the 17th century, two main types of recitative had developed. In the first type, called **recitativo secco** ('dry' recitative), the voice is accompanied only by continuo instruments – for example, the rhythmically flexible vocal line may be punctuated by chords on a harpsichord, with a cello strengthening the bass-line. The second type, called **recitativo accompagnato** ('accompanied' recitative) or **recitativo stromentato** ('instrumented' recitative), may be used when the composer feels that the emotional or dramatic nature of the words needs heightening by a simple accompaniment for orchestra or at least for instruments besides those of the continuo group. Good examples of both these types of recitative can be found in numbers 14–16 of Handel's *Messiah*. No. 14 ('And there were shepherds') begins *secco*; then (at 'And lo!') becomes *stromentato*. No. 15 ('And the Angel said') is *secco*. No. 16 ('And suddenly there was with the Angel') is *stromentato*.

[See also: *Arioso 2]

Recorder [French: *flûte à bec, flûte douce*; German: *Blockflöte*; Italian: *flauto dolce*] A woodwind instrument, in use from the 14th century to the 18th, and revived in the 20th century. The recorder is an end-blown flute, held vertically (as distinct from a transverse or side-blown flute, held horizontally). It has a beak-shaped whistle mouthpiece, and seven finger-holes plus a thumb-hole at the back. In the 16th century, recorders were made in several sizes to form a complete family. Those usually making up a *consort of recorders were the descant, treble, tenor, and bass; to these might be added the sopranino and the great bass. (In the USA and Germany the descant is called 'soprano' and the treble is called 'alto'.) In England, the recorder was often called the 'English flute' to distinguish it from the 'German flute' or transverse flute. Bach and Handel, in their scores, often called the recorder simply *flauto*, and the transverse flute *flauto traverso* or simply *traversa*.

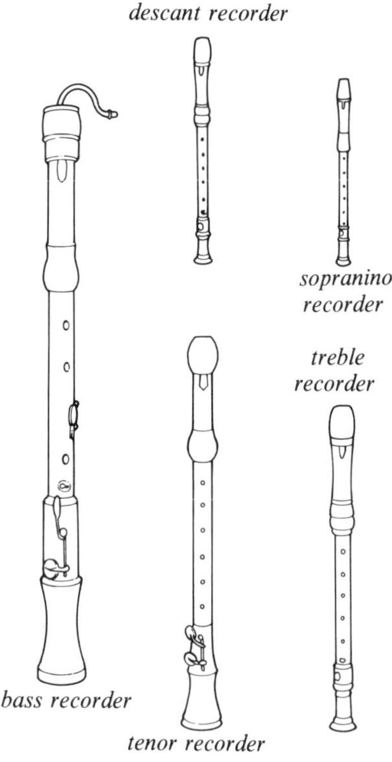

Recte et retro [Latin: 'forwards and backwards'] The presentation of a theme together with its *retrograde version. [See also under *Canon]

Redundant entry See under *Fugue.

Reed A thin, flexible strip of cane or metal, used to produce the sound in various types of musical instrument. A reed is made to vibrate by the passage of a stream of air. A **single reed** (or **single beating reed**) of cane is used in the clarinet and saxophone; also in the reed-stops (metal reed) of the organ. A **double reed** (or **double beating reed**) is used in the oboe, cor anglais, and bassoon – the double reed consisting of two strips of cane which vibrate against each other as the stream of air passes between them. A **free reed** is a thin tongue, usually of metal, which is fixed at one end and free to vibrate in a slot at the other end; instruments which use free reeds include the accordion, mouth organ, and harmonium.

Reel A swift dance with whirling music in duple time in which two or more couples, standing face to face, perform dance steps of two basic kinds: a 'setting' step (on the spot) and a 'travelling' step (tracing a particular pattern). The reel is popular in Scotland and Ireland (the Irish reel being much swifter), and also in Scandinavia. Early settlers took the reel to America, where one variety is known as the Virginia Reel.

Refrain A recurring section of music. If a song has a refrain it will consist of a section usually repeated at the end of each verse, and to the same words and music. The word refrain is also used to describe recurring sections of music in certain instrumental pieces. [See under *Rondo]

Bible regal

Regal A small type of portable organ whose 'snarling' sounds – buzzy yet penetrating – were caused by reeds beating in very short pipes called resonators. One special form was called a 'Bible regal' since, when closed up, it resembled a large Bible. When opened out and placed on a table, the two halves of the 'Bible' became the bellows. Regals were popular from the mid 15th century to the 17th century.

Reggae A type and style of popular music originating in Jamaica in the 1960s. The music is in four beats to a bar, and features strong accents on beats two and four – emphasized by occasional rests (silences) on the first or third beats. The instruments are likely to be electric guitars (lead, rhythm, and bass), organ, piano, and drums. The melodies of reggae are often subtly rhythmic. Harmonies tend to be restricted to a few common chords; the music seldom, if ever, modulates. The bass-patterns, frequently syncopated, are shapely and melodic – claiming almost as much interest as the melodies themselves.

The words of reggae songs often make strong comment on political issues and social injustice. Reggae's most outstanding song-writer and performer was the Jamaican, Bob Marley (1945–81), who formed the band called the Wailers.

Register **1** The rank or set of pipes controlled by an organ stop (see under *organ); also, each complete set of strings in a *harpsichord. **2** The different parts of the range of a human voice, described according to their tone-quality and method of production: *chest voice, middle (or medium) voice, and *head voice.

Registration In organ-playing and harpsichord-playing – the selection, combination, and use of the various registers (i.e. stops) to obtain variety and contrasts in volume and tone-colour.

Rehearsing and directing (an ensemble, choir, orchestra) See *Conducting.

'Reine, La' See *'Paris' Symphonies.

Rejoice in the Lord alway See *'Bell' Anthem.

Related keys The main key, or 'home' key, of a composition (the key in which it begins and ends) is called the *tonic key*. For whichever key this may be, there are certain other keys which are closely related. *Modulation between these keys will sound particularly smooth and natural. The tonic key of any piece may be thought of as the *key-centre* around which these related keys revolve. The closely related keys to any tonic key are:

the **relative key* (major or minor as the case may be) which shares the same key signature as the tonic key;

the *dominant key*, and its relative key (both having a key signature containing either one sharp more, or one flat less, than the tonic key);

the *subdominant key*, and its relative key (both with a key signature of one flat more, or one sharp less, than the tonic key);

and also the *parallel key* (major or minor as the case may be) which shares the same tonic note or key-note (e.g. the parallel key to C major is C minor, and vice versa).

[See also: *Remote key; and the table of Key signatures on page 389]

Relative keys Any pair of keys (one major, one minor) sharing the same key signature. For example: F major and D minor both have a key signature of one flat – B♭. F major may therefore be referred to as the **relative major** of D minor, and D minor as the **relative minor** of F major (see the table of Key signatures on page 389). [See also: *Related keys]

Relative pitch See under *Absolute pitch.

Remote key A key which is not closely related to the tonic key of the piece (see *Related keys). A remote key will have two or more sharps or flats more, or less, than the tonic key.

Renaissance music The word 'Renaissance' (French for 'rebirth' or 'revival') is used to describe music composed from about 1450 to around 1600 – that is, the period in the *history of Western music between the Medieval period and the Baroque. In general, the Renaissance was a time of exploration and discovery – by travel, and through scientific enquiry. There was keen enthusiasm for the rebirth of learning and for the revival of the artistic and cultural values of the ancient Greeks and Romans. Much of this was reflected in the works of Renaissance architects and painters, writers, and composers.

One of the main differences between Medieval and Renaissance music is that of musical texture. A Medieval composer tends to sharply contrast the separate strands in his music one against another. A Renaissance composer aims more to blend them together. He may use a simple *chordal style, planning his music in clear-cut sections. Or he may write in a *polyphonic (or contrapuntal) style, weaving together the strands of his music to make a continuous, 'seamless' texture. To do this, he uses the important musical device known as *imitation. One voice-part brings in a snatch of tune, then is immediately imitated by another voice-part copying (imitating) the same musical idea.

Composers now usually wrote in four voice-parts, now adding a lower part (bass part) and so extending the range and fullness of sound. Music was still based on modes (see *church modes), but these were gradually used more freely as composers introduced more chromatic alterations or 'accidentals' (see under *musica ficta). Whereas the most commonly heard intervals in Medieval music had been the 4th, 5th, and octave, Renaissance composers based their harmonies on triads. There was a greater concern with the smooth progression of chords, any discords being carefully planned rather than happening by chance (see *concords and discords; also *preparation and *resolution).

Some of the finest pieces by Renaissance composers were settings of the *Mass and motets composed for the church – most of them intended to be performed **a cappella*. English composers also wrote *anthems. It was during the second half of the 16th century that polyphonic church music reached its peak in beauty and expressiveness, especially in the works of Palestrina (Italy), Lassus (Netherlands), Byrd (England), and Victoria (Spain).

However, composers now also took a keener interest in writing secular (non-sacred) music. Types of vocal piece included the Italian *frottola, the German polyphonic *lied, the Spanish *villancico, the French polyphonic *chanson, and Italian and English madrigals (see *madrigal, 2; also *ballett, *ayre, and *word-painting). The Lutheran *chorale originated in the 16th century, and this was to play an important role during the Baroque period.

Renaissance instrumental pieces included arrangements of vocal pieces, and also pieces specially written for instruments – see *canzona, *ricercare, *fantasia, and *In nomine. Pieces were also composed in the form of *variations, and on a *ground bass (see also *romanesca and *ruggiero). English composers of Tudor times, in their music for *virginals, discovered an effective style truly suited to the keyboard (see also *Parthenia and *Fitzwilliam Virginal Book). Popular Renaissance dances included the *basse danse, *pavan, *galliard, *passamezzo, *saltarello, *branle, and volta (see *volta 2). An exciting development towards the end of the Renaissance period was the Venetian *polychoral style.

The following lists many of the instruments popular during the Renaissance (some remaining popular from Medieval times). Several Renaissance instruments were made in various sizes and pitches, to form a family – for example, viol, recorder, crumhorn, shawm.

Strings (bowed)
viols
lira da braccio
lira da gamba
violin
tenor violin

Strings (plucked)
16th-century lute
archlute
guitar
vihuela
bandora
cittern
harp

Wind
recorders
flute
shawm
crumhorn
racket
Rauschpfeife
trumpet
cornett
sackbut (trombone)
serpent

Percussion
tabor
tambourine
kettle drums
snare (side) drum
triangle
cymbals

Keyboard
clavichord
harpsichord
virginals
church organ
chamber (positive) organ
regal

The most important composers of the Renaissance include: Josquin des Prez, Isaac, and Lassus (Netherlands); Tallis, Byrd, Morley, Bull, Dowland, Weelkes, and Gibbons (England); Victoria (Spain); Palestrina, Giovanni Gabrieli, and Monteverdi (Italy).

[See also: *Early music; and the time-chart of composers on pages 398–413]

Renforcer [French: 'to reinforce'] Strengthen, increase.

Repeat signs (repeats) The signs ‖: and :‖ marking the beginning and end of a section of music, indicating that the music between the signs should be repeated. If the first of these signs does not occur, then a repeat is made from the beginning of the piece or movement. Performers sometimes choose to ignore certain repeat marks – in particular those indicating the repeat of the exposition section of a piece in *sonata form. [For other information about repeats, see *Volta 1; *Da capo; *Dal segno; *Al segno; *Replica; *Ripetizione; *Bis; *Minuet and Trio form. For signs and markings indicating repetition of notes, figures and bars of music, see the table of Abbreviations on pages 392–393]

Repetition See under *Form. (For abbreviations used for repetition of notes and bars of music, see Table 11 on pages 392–393.)

Repetizione A misspelling of *Ripetizione.

Replica [Italian] Repeat. **Si replica**, to be repeated. **Senza replica**, without repetition.

Reprise **1** Repetition. **2** A name sometimes used for the recapitulation section in *sonata form.

Reproducing piano See *Player piano.

Requiem (Requiem Mass) A setting of the Latin text of the Mass for the Dead, which begins with the word *requiem*, meaning 'rest'. The items, or sections, of the Requiem are normally as follows: 1 Introit: *Requiem aeternam dona eis Domine* (Eternal rest grant them, O Lord); 2 *Kyrie* (Lord have mercy); 3 Sequence: **Dies irae* (Day of wrath); 4 Offertory: *Domine Jesu Christe* (O Lord Jesus Christ, King of Glory); 5 *Sanctus* (Holy, holy, holy); 6 *Agnus Dei* (O Lamb of God); 7 Communion: *Lux aeterna* (May eternal light shine upon them). Also sometimes included are: *Libera me* (Deliver me, O Lord, from death eternal) and *In Paradisum* (Into Paradise may the Angels lead you) from the Order of Burial.

There is a traditional plainsong setting of the Requiem Mass; also settings by many composers, including Palestrina, Lassus, Victoria, Mozart, Berlioz, Verdi (*'Manzoni' Requiem), Fauré, and Benjamin Britten (**War Requiem*). In such settings, the text of the lengthy sequence *Dies irae* may be split up into separate self-contained sections. For example: *Dies irae; Tuba mirum* (A trumpet, spreading wondrous sound); *Rex tremendae majestatis* (O King of tremendous majesty); *Confutatis maledictis* (When the wicked are confounded); *Lacrymosa* (Sorrowful that day).

[See also: *A *German Requiem*]

'Rescue' opera A term which is sometimes used to describe the type of opera in which the hero or heroine, having suffered various trials and dangers and been captured, perhaps imprisoned and faced with death, is finally rescued. The supreme example is Beethoven's opera **Fidelio*.

Resolution Passing in a satisfactory way from discord to *concord. In bar 2 of the music example the dissonant note D (a *suspension) is **resolved** by passing (falling) to middle C to form a concord. [See also: *Preparation]

Responsorial A manner of performance which features the alternation of a soloist and a group (as distinct from *antiphonal performance in which two groups are heard in alternation). Also sometimes described as *call-and-response.

Rest A silence, or (in musical notation) a sign used to indicate it. Rests have definite time-values in the same way as notes, and there is a particular sign for each time-value (see the table of Notes and rests on page 387).

Restatement A name sometimes used for the recapitulation section in *sonata form.

'Resurrection' Symphony Mahler's Symphony No. 2 in C minor, in five movements, composed between 1888 and 1894. The third movement (Scherzo) is based on themes from his song 'St Anthony of Padua's Sermon to the Fishes' from *Des *Knaben Wunderhorn*. The fourth movement is a setting for alto voice and orchestra of *Urlicht* ('Primordial Light') from the same collection. And the fifth movement includes a setting for soprano and alto soloists, chorus, and orchestra of the *Auferste h'n* ('Resurrection') chorale by the 18th-century German poet, Klopstock.

Retardation A type of *suspension in which the dissonant note resolves upwards, instead of downwards.

Retenu [French] Held back. **En retenant**, holding back. Both these terms are used in the same sense as the Italian word **ritenuto*.

Retrograde (retrograde motion) A term meaning reverse or backward motion; for example, taking a melody (or a phrase, or a section of music) and performing it backwards – beginning with the final note and ending with the first. The entire texture of the music (i.e. including the harmonies) may be presented in retrograde. The term **cancrizans** ('crab-like') has the same meaning (even though crabs move sideways rather than backwards!).

Retrograde inversion means the music is presented in retrograde (backwards) and in *inversion (upside down) at the same time.

Below, a scrap of melody, (a), is shown in retrograde, (b); then in inversion, (c) (preserving the *number* of each *interval, but not necessarily the *quality*); and then in retrograde inversion, (d).

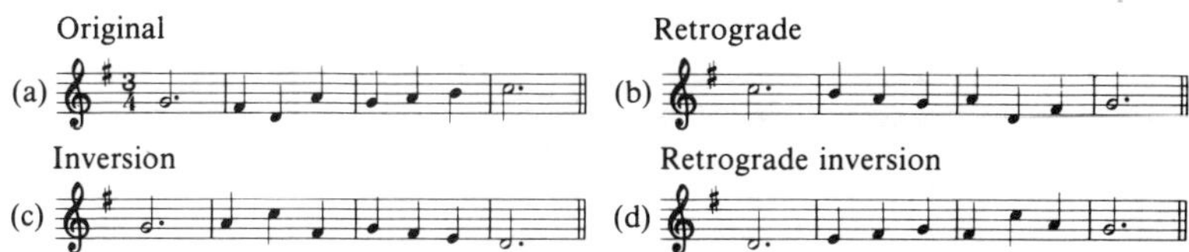

[See also: *Al rovescio; under *Canon; and under *Twelve-note technique]

Rêverie [French: 'dreaming'] A quiet, usually fairly slow piece, with a dream-like, meditative atmosphere.

Revidiert [German] Revised.

'Revolutionary' Study Nickname of Chopin's Study (Étude) No. 12 in C minor from his first set of Twelve Studies for piano, Op. 10. This piece was composed in a mood of anger when, during his journey to Paris in 1830, he heard the news that Warsaw had been captured by the Russians. After a nine-bar introduction, the angry theme crashes out *con fuoco* above roaring semiquavers.

Rezitativ [German] *Recitative.

Rf; rfz Abbreviations of either **rinforzando* or *rinforzato*.

R.H.; r.h. Abbreviation standing for 'right hand', and also for *rechte Hand* [German] which has the same meaning.

Rhapsodie [German] Rhapsody.

Rhapsodie espagnole (Spanish Rhapsody) A work for solo piano composed by Liszt in 1863. It is based on two well-known Spanish themes: the **folía* (or 'Folies d'Espagne') and the *jota aragonesa* (see *jota). The piece was arranged for piano and orchestra by Busoni.

Rhapsody A word which comes from Greek (with a meaning something like 'songs strung together') and used by 19th- and 20th-century composers as a title for pieces which are generally free in form and design, and often feature abrupt contrasts and changes of mood. Many rhapsodies are based on folk or national melodies. Examples include Liszt's **Hungarian Rhapsodies*; certain pieces for piano solo by Brahms, and also his **Alto Rhapsody*; the orchestral rhapsody **España* by the French composer Chabrier; the two *Romanian Rhapsodies* for orchestra by Enescu; Gershwin's **Rhapsody in Blue*; and Rachmaninov's **Rhapsody on a Theme of Paganini*.

Rhapsody in Blue A work for piano and jazz band, or piano and symphony orchestra, composed by George Gershwin in 1924. Paul Whiteman, the American band-leader, had suggested that Gershwin should write 'a jazz-influenced concert piece' for a concert he was arranging called 'An Experiment in American Music'. Gershwin's title refers to the fact that throughout, the music is 'coloured' by what jazz musicians call *'blue' notes. The piece was orchestrated, not by Gershwin, but by another American composer called Ferdé Grofé – first for jazz band, and later in a version for full symphony orchestra.

Rhapsody on a Theme of Paganini A work for solo piano and orchestra, Opus 43, composed by Rachmaninov in 1934. It consists of twenty-four variations on the theme of Paganini's Caprice No. 24 in A minor for solo violin:

Rheingold, Das (The Rhinegold) See *Der *Ring des Nibelungen.*

'Rhenish' Symphony Schumann's Symphony No. 3 in E flat, Op. 97, composed in 1850 after a trip along the River Rhine. There are five movements; the fourth, featuring solemn and majestic music for trombones, was inspired by the installation of a cardinal at Cologne Cathedral.

Rhinegold, The See *Der *Ring des Nibelungen.*

Rhumba See *Rumba.

Rhythm The aspect of music which is concerned with the way in which a composer groups together musical sounds in relation to time, mainly with regard to duration (the lengths, long or short, of different sounds in relation to each other) and stress or *accent. Also involved are *phrasing and the tempo (or speed) of the music. Usually, going along in the background (either heard, or merely felt) is a regular beat or pulse; this is the steady 'heart-beat' of the music against which the ear measures rhythm. Together with melody and harmony, rhythm is one of the three most important elements or *ingredients of music. [See also: *Time; *Syncopation]

Rhythm and blues (often abbreviated to **R'n'B**) A style of popular music, developing in the USA in the late 1940s, and combining ingredients of blues and jazz – the melodic style of the blues and the powerful, driving rhythm of certain types of jazz. It began mainly as dance music. Rhythm and blues is in quadruple time, with the second and fourth beats emphasized. It is performed by an ensemble of vocalists and instrumentalists, usually including electronically amplified instruments. The music is generally in a major key, often incorporating *'blue' notes. During the 1950s, rhythm and blues played an important part in the birth of rock and roll.

Rhythmic modes See under *Ars Antiqua.

Rhythm section In any jazz ensemble, the group of instruments primarily supplying the basic beat – drums (percussion), piano, banjo, guitar, double bass.

Ricercare (*ricercar, recercar, ricercata,* also many variations in spelling of these) [Italian: 'seeking out', 'searching out'] A term used from the 16th century to the 18th to describe instrumental compositions of two basic types. **1** A contrapuntal piece in fugal style (particularly for organ). In its simplest form this type of ricercare was the instrumental counterpart of the vocal motet. In more elaborate form, it was designed in several sections of music, each introducing a separate theme and 'seeking out' its contrapuntal possibilities, making use of such devices as *inversion, *augmentation, *diminution; perhaps presenting two or more of the themes in combination. This type of ricercare had important influence on the development of the *fugue. [See also: *Fantasia] **2** Any kind of prelude or 'study', not necessarily in contrapuntal style, serving as an introduction to the performance of a larger piece. This type of ricercare was often written for lute or viol.

Ricochet; Jeté [French: 'rebound' and 'thrown'] Two names for a type of *bowing stroke on string instruments in which the upper part of the bow is 'thrown' onto the string so that it bounces several times, *staccato*, during the down-stroke.

Riddle canon See *Puzzle canon.

'Rider' Quartet ('Horseman' Quartet) Nickname for Haydn's String Quartet in G minor, Op. 74 No. 3 (1793), so called because of the vigorous 'riding' rhythms of the final movement.

Riduzione [Italian] Arrangement (e.g. an arrangement for piano of an orchestral score).

Riff In jazz, a melodic phrase (frequently two or four bars long) repeated persistently, over changing harmonies, throughout part or all of a piece.

Rigaudon (rigadoon) A lively dance, in duple time and with a leaping step, which originated during the 17th century in southern France. It was popular in French operatic ballets (by composers such as Rameau and Campra) and was sometimes included as one of the movements of the Baroque *suite. In England, it was called a rigadoon. The following example is from *Musick's Handmaid*, part 2, by Purcell.

Rigoletto Opera in three acts by Verdi, first produced in Venice in 1851 (libretto by Piave based on Hugo's *Le Roi s'amuse*). Rigoletto (baritone), jester to the Duke of Mantua, helps his rakish master as he pursues his courtiers' womenfolk. Count Monterone, whose daughter has suffered the Duke's attentions, puts a curse on him. The Duke (tenor) falls for Gilda (soprano), whom the courtiers believe to be Rigoletto's mistress but who is really his daughter. Unaware of this, the Duke arrives to seduce her, disguised as a student and using a false name. Rigoletto pays the seedy innkeeper Sparafucile (bass) to murder the Duke, taking care not to disclose the intended victim's identity. Soon the Duke, again in disguise, visits the inn and makes advances to Sparafucile's sister Maddalena (contralto), but Rigoletto and Gilda overhear him from the street outside. At Rigoletto's bidding Gilda dresses as a man and prepares to go home to Verona. But returning in the hope of seeing the Duke once more, she overhears Maddalena begging her brother to spare their handsome guest, and Sparafucile (who must have a body to produce) promising to kill instead the first person who visits the inn. She makes a bold decision. To save her lover she will sacrifice herself. She enters, and is stabbed. When Rigoletto arrives to claim the Duke's body Sparafucile drags out a sack. In it the horrified jester finds not the Duke but his own daughter, who with her dying breath begs his forgiveness. Monterone's curse is fulfilled.

Rigore [Italian] Rigour, strictness. **Senza rigore**, without strictness (therefore, 'freely').

Rigoroso [Italian: 'rigorous'] Firm and exact in time and rhythm.

Rim-shot See under *Snare drum.

Rinforzando [Italian: 'reinforcing'] Emphasizing. **Rinforzato**, emphasized. Indication of a sudden crescendo to bring out a short phrase; or of a sudden accent on a single note or chord. Each of these words may be abbreviated to either ***rf.***, ***rfz.***, or ***rinf.*** [See also: *Sforzando]

Ring des Nibelungen, Der (The Ring of the Nibelung) Cycle of four operas by Wagner, first produced on four successive evenings at Bayreuth in 1876 (text by the composer after Norse and German legends). The action functions on three levels. In Valhalla dwell the gods (the chief god, Wotan; Loge, the god of fire; the goddesses Freia and Fricka – wife of Wotan). On earth are the mortals, among them Siegmund, Sieglinde, and, later in the cycle, their son, Siegfried. Below, in a shadowy realm, live the Nibelungs, a race of dwarfs, including the power-hungry Alberich and his brother, Mime.

In *Das Rheingold* (The Rhinegold) the dwarf Alberich steals from the Rhinemaidens the Rhinegold, from which whoever forges a Ring (and renounces love!) shall be master of the world. The giants Fasolt and Fafner (basses) have built the castle of Valhalla, at the behest of Wotan (bass-baritone), who has promised them in payment Freia, the goddess of youth. The wiles of Loge (tenor) release Wotan from the bargain and the giants agree to accept the Rhinegold instead. Meanwhile Mime (tenor) has fashioned the Ring and made Alberich a magic helmet, the Tarnhelm, which will make him invisible or enable him to assume other shapes. Loge tricks Alberich (bass-baritone) into giving him the gold, the helmet, and the Ring. In revenge, Alberich curses the Ring and all who will hold it. Erda, the earth goddess, warns Wotan that to escape the curse he must rid himself of the Ring. He gives it to the giants. They fight over it, and Fasolt dies.

The second opera, *Die Walküre* (The Valkyrie), introduces the Valkyries (warrior-women and daughters of Wotan, who ride through the heavens on horseback bearing the bodies of dead heroes to Valhalla). Wotan has begotten on earth a son, Siegmund, and a daughter, Sieglinde. He intends that Siegmund shall recover the Ring from Fafner and restore it to the Rhinemaidens, thus freeing the gods from the curse. Siegmund will find a sword, which will deliver him from death. Stumbling through a forest in a storm, Siegmund (tenor) is sheltered by Sieglinde (soprano) in the hut of her husband, Hunding. Unaware of their relationship the two fall in love, and Hunding (bass) challenges Siegmund to a duel. Sieglinde shows Siegmund a sword buried in a tree-trunk. Only a hero can draw it out. It is the weapon Wotan promised. Fricka (mezzo-soprano), siding with Hunding, compels Wotan to withdraw his protection from Siegmund, who is killed when Wotan intervenes in the fight and shatters the sword. A Valkyrie, Brünnhilde (soprano), gathers up the pieces and gives them to Sieglinde to pass on to Siegfried, the son she will soon produce. This offends the gods. Brünnhilde is banished to a rock, where she must sleep surrounded by leaping flames through which only the most courageous hero may pass to set her free. (The famous orchestral *Ride of the Valkyries* introduces Act 3 of this opera.)

The third opera, *Siegfried,* opens in a forest cave. Mime ponders how to regain the Ring, which is guarded by Fafner, who, by means of the Tarnhelm, has turned himself into a dragon. Sieglinde has died giving birth to Siegfried, and Mime has tended him from babyhood, hoping to use him to kill Fafner and recover the gold. Wotan appears, disguised as a Wanderer, and reveals that the sword can be reforged only by a hero who knows not fear. That hero will behead Mime. Siegfried (tenor) reforges the sword, slays Fafner, and regains the helmet, gold, and Ring. Mime offers Siegfried a poisoned broth, but, warned by a Woodbird not to trust the dwarf, Siegfried declines it. He kills Mime with the sword (another victim of the curse!) and takes the ill-fated Ring. Told by the Woodbird of Brünnhilde's plight, he makes for the Valkyrie's rock. Wotan (as the Wanderer) tries to obstruct him, but Siegfried passes through the flames, wakes Brünnhilde, and claims her for his own.

The final opera, *Götterdämmerung* (Twilight of the Gods), finds Siegfried in the Hall of the Gibichungs with their king, Günther (baritone), and his sister, Gutrune (soprano). Tempted by his scheming half-brother Hagen (bass), Günther covets Brünnhilde for his bride. Hagen promises that Siegfried, who alone can fetch Brünnhilde, will do so if he can marry Gutrune. A magic potion, administered by Hagen, deprives Siegfried of all memory of Brünnhilde. He falls in love with Gutrune. Using the Tarnhelm, he takes the form of Günther, passes again through the flames, wrests the Ring from Brünnhilde's finger, and brings her to the waiting king. Resuming his own shape, he still fails to remember the bewildered Brünnhilde, who, seeing the Ring on his finger, assumes he has stolen it from Günther. Encouraged by Hagen she plots Siegfried's death. By means of a second potion, Hagen then restores Siegfried's memory and persuades him to tell the story of his life. When Günther hears of Siegfried's vow of love to Brünnhilde, he starts up in dismay. Hagen kills Siegfried with his spear and defiantly claims the Ring, but as he tries to snatch it from Siegfried's finger the corpse's arm rises in chilling menace. Brünnhilde now understands all. She has a funeral pyre built, and when Siegfried's body has been placed on it she takes the Ring and sends two ravens to tell Wotan of Siegfried's death and to bid Loge set fire to Valhalla. Then she hurls the firebrand into the pyre and, mounting her horse, rides into the flames. The Rhine overflows, drowning the evil Hagen, while, in the heavens, Loge's fire destroys Valhalla and the gods, initiating a new age of love.

Ripetizione [Italian] Repetition. (The word is sometimes incorrectly spelt 'repetizione'.) **Senza ripetizione**, without repeat(s). **Alla ripetizione dal 𝄋 al ⊕** – 'during the repeat, skip from the sign 𝄋 to the sign ⊕'.

Ripieno [Italian: 'filling'] In Baroque compositions (particularly the *concerto grosso*), *ripieno* refers to the full orchestra – as distinct from *concertino* which refers to the group of soloists. **Senza ripieni** does not mean 'without orchestra', but indicates a passage to be played by only a few of the string players – those sitting at the leading desks.

Ripresa [Italian] Repeat or repetition.

Risoluto [Italian] Resolute; in a determined manner.

Rit. An abbreviation normally standing for **ritardando* – though some composers, confusingly, also use it as an abbreviation of **ritenuto.*

Ritardando [Italian: 'delaying'] Slowing down gradually (and therefore the same as **rallentando*). Often abbreviated to **ritard.**, or simply **rit.** [But see: *Ritenuto]

Ritenuto [Italian] Held back. Immediately slowing down (not gradually, as is the case with *ritardando* and *rallentando*). Often abbreviated to **riten.**, sometimes (confusingly) to ***rit.**

Rite of Spring, The (*Le Sacre du printemps*) Ballet by Stravinsky, with choreography by Nijinsky, and subtitled 'Pictures from Pagan Russia'; first produced in Paris in 1913. In his autobiography, Stravinsky tells how he received the idea for the ballet: 'One day, I had a fleeting vision which came as a complete surprise. I saw in my imagination a solemn pagan rite: elders, seated in a circle, watched a young girl dance herself to death. They were sacrificing her to propitiate the god of spring.'

The first performance of the ballet caused a riot – fights broke out between admirers of Stravinsky and others convinced that he was 'destroying music'. The noise made by the audience drowned the sound of the huge orchestra so that dancers were forced to count the beats aloud in order to continue dancing. The music was described as 'savage primitivism' – but this was Stravinsky's deliberate intention, in order to match the pagan scenario. The music is characterized by harmonies that are extremely dissonant – often polytonal – and savage, pounding rhythms, the number of beats often changing bar by bar. There are frequent ostinato patterns, and polyrhythmic effects. Stravinsky's melodies, however, are basically simple (sometimes folk-like) and constructed from short motives, repeated and varied with shifts of stress and accent.

In spite of the notoriety of its first performance, *The Rite of Spring* was soon acclaimed a masterpiece. The music is now often performed as a concert piece. The ballet divides into two parts, each made up of several scenes: First part: *The Adoration of the Earth* Introduction, Dance of the Youths and Maidens, Ritual of Abduction, Spring Round Dances, Rituals of the Rival Tribes – Procession of the Sage – The Dance of the Earth; Second part: *The Sacrifice* Introduction, Mystic Circles of the Maidens, Glorification of the Chosen Maiden, Evocation of the Elders – Ritual of the Elders, Sacrificial Dance of the Chosen Maiden.

The large orchestra needed for *The Rite of Spring* includes: 3 flutes, 1 alto flute and 2 piccolos, 4 oboes and 2 cors anglais, 3 clarinets, 1 small clarinet and 2 bass clarinets, 4 bassoons and 2 double bassoons; 8 horns, 4 trumpets, 1 small trumpet in D and 1 bass trumpet, 3 trombones, 2 tenor Wagner tubas in B♭, 2 bass tubas; 5 (at least) kettle drums, bass drum, cymbals, tam-tam, triangle, tambourine, güiro, antique cymbals in A♭ and B♭; and a large section of strings.

Ritmico [Italian] Rhythmical.

Ritmo [Italian] Rhythm. [See also under: *Battuta]

Ritornello [Italian: 'little return'] **1** A 17th-century term for brief instrumental passages serving as introduction, interludes, or postlude in a vocal composition (e.g. a song or an anthem). **2** A brief instrumental passage played between scenes, or between sections of a single scene, in a 17th-century opera. **3** A term now used to describe the recurring main theme, played by the *ripieno* group, in a Baroque *concerto grosso* or solo concerto (see *Ritornello form).

Ritornello form [from Italian: *ritornello*, 'little return'] The name given to the musical *form or structure often used to build up the quicker movements (occasionally the slower movements also) in a Baroque *concerto grosso* or solo concerto. The ritornello itself – the main theme which will return throughout the movement – is introduced by the orchestra (the *ripieno* group), usually also with the soloist(s) joining in. It then returns at other points during the movement. It may reappear in full, or it may be shortened, or varied. Its first and last appearances are in the tonic key of the movement; at other times it is generally in a key other than the tonic.

Appearances of the ritornello are separated by *episodes* which feature the soloist (or solo group). An episode may introduce new musical ideas, or it may be based on one or more ideas taken from the ritornello.

Ritornello form was not confined to concertos; Baroque composers often used the same structure in other types of music – for example, to build up arias and choruses in works such as operas, oratorios, and cantatas.

Ritual Fire Dance, The The best known of the dances from Falla's ballet *El *Amor brujo*.

Rock (rock music) A general name for a type of popular music originating in the USA (where it was first called rock and roll, or rock 'n' roll) in the early 1950s, eventually spreading throughout the world, and developing through several styles and with various off-shoots. Its main roots lay in white *country music and black *rhythm and blues. Famous early exponents included Bill Haley and the Comets, Elvis Presley, and Chuck Berry; during the 1960s, its status and popularity were greatly increased by such British groups as the Beatles and the Rolling Stones.

The sounds of rock are generally characterized by an energetic driving rhythm and a heavy insistent beat (the essential backbone of the music), and the use of powerfully electronically amplified instruments. The singer(s) may use extremes of vocal range, and often an earthy, gutsy, even raucous tone-quality; other vocal sounds and techniques may be used such as speaking, shouting, falsetto, portamento. The music is often in $\frac{4}{4}$ time, which may be sounded as eight even quavers, often with strong accents on the second and fourth main beats. Riffs may be featured. Melodies may make use of *'blue' notes, or at times, rather than being clearly in a major or minor key, may show the influence of modes (for example, Aeolian, Dorian, Mixolydian – see under *church modes). Harmonies may be based on a few common chords, or may be dissonant and quite complex; an entire piece may be structured on just two or three chords.

Included among the names given to later developments and off-shoots of rock are the following. **Folk rock** (most famous exponent, Bob Dylan) – rock with a strong folk-song flavour and lyrics dealing with social themes and personal problems and misfortunes. **Heavy rock** or **hard rock** – rock with a particularly powerful beat, making strong use of riffs and crashing guitar chords often played off the beat. **Psychedelic rock** or **acid rock** – which includes electronic sounds and attempts to create a weird, colourful, hallucinatory, and atmospheric mood similar to that experienced by someone having taken a mind-altering drug such as LSD ('acid'). **Punk rock** – originating in the USA in 1964, and arriving (exploding) in Britain in 1976; the style featured simplicity of melody and harmonies, with strong protest lyrics (venomous, provocative, crude, deliberately offensive) expressing youth rebellion against social conditions, unemployment, and absolutely any form of authority. Essential to the total effect was the aggressive punk image – bizarre and outlandish attire, spiky hair, and scowling or leering expression. The first top-selling punk record was *God Save the Queen* by the Sex Pistols. **Heavy metal** – less melody-based than heavy rock, and projecting an image of 'the wild side of life' (satanic make-up, leotards, leather, studs, and metal); bands with names such as W.A.S.P., Anthrax, Metallica, Iron Maiden. Influenced mainly by Van Halen, Alice Cooper, and Kiss for the image, and Black Sabbath, Deep Purple, and Led Zeppelin for the music – the louder the better.

The term rock (rock music) has now largely lost any specific meaning and often tends to be applied indiscriminately to almost any type of pop music which does not fit into a special self-evident category (as, for example, does *reggae).

Rococo [from French, *rocaille*: 'fancy rock-work' in architecture, involving S-shaped curves, shells, etc.] A term borrowed from architecture and the visual arts and applied to certain music of the second and third quarters of the 18th century (e.g. by Couperin, Telemann, Domenico Scarlatti) which is light in style, delicate, graceful, and highly ornamented. Rococo style is very similar to (if not exactly the same as) *Gallant style.

Rodeo A 'cowboy ballet' composed by Aaron Copland in 1942 for the choreographer, Agnes de Mille. The music includes several traditional cowboy tunes. Copland later selected 'Four Dance Episodes' from the ballet score to be played as a suite at concerts. Their titles are: 1 Buckaroo Holiday; 2 Corral Nocturne; 3 Saturday Night Waltz; and 4 Hoe-Down. [See also: **Billy the Kid*; **Appalachian Spring*]

Roll The rapid reiteration of a note or sound on percussion instruments such as kettle drum, snare drum, cymbal. For example, to play a roll on a kettle drum the player uses both sticks alternately and very swiftly. A roll may increase and/or decrease in loudness, and (particularly when *crescendo*) is one of the valuable means by which a composer may build up tension or a feeling of expectancy.

Roman Carnival Overture See *Le *Carnaval romain*.

Romance [French; Italian: *romanza;* German: *Romanze*] A title used, often loosely by composers, for instrumental or vocal compositions which are lyrical in character and tender or even sentimental in mood. Examples include the *Romanze* from Mozart's *Eine *Kleine Nachtmusik*, and also his Piano Concerto No. 20 in D minor (K466); Beethoven's two *Romances* for violin and orchestra; Schumann's three *Romanzen* for piano, Op. 28; the *Romance* for harmonica, strings, and piano, and also *The *Lark Ascending* for violin and orchestra, both by Vaughan Williams.

Romanesca The bass-line (see below) of a 16th-century song popular in Italy and Spain. (In Spain it was known as *Guárdame las vacas*, 'Watch over the cows for me'.) This bass-line, together with its scheme of harmonies, came to be used in a great many other songs, dances, and instrumental pieces by composers during the 16th and 17th centuries. In such pieces it was used as an ostinato or *ground bass, with new melodies composed (sometimes improvised) above it to make a set of continuous *variations. Among the many composers who used it were the Spanish composer Diego Ortiz and the Italian composers Monteverdi and Frescobaldi. Here is the romanesca bass in its simplest form:

Romanesca bass

[See also: *Ruggiero; *Passamezzo; *Folía]

Roman Festivals (*Feste romane*) The third of Respighi's three symphonic poems describing Rome, past and present; composed in 1928. The work is scored for a large orchestra, and is in four sections: 1 Games in the Circus Maximus; 2 The Jubilee (pilgrims approach the Holy City of Rome); 3 The October Harvest Festival; 4 The Epiphany. [See also: *The *Fountains of Rome; The *Pines of Rome*]

Romanticism (Romantic music) These terms are used in connection with music composed from about 1810 to around 1910 – that is, the period in the *history of Western music which followed the Classical period.

Classical composers had aimed to strike a perfect balance between expressiveness and formal structure; 19th-century Romantic composers altered this balance. Mainly, they sought a greater freedom in the form and structure of their music and aimed for a deeper, much more intense expression of moods, feelings, and emotions. This was especially achieved by widening the range of musical materials, e.g. of pitch, dynamics (volume), and instrumental timbres. Harmonies became much richer, and a more powerful use of chromatic discords, together with swifter and more adventurous modulations, eventually led to the weakening, and then the disintegration, of the major-minor key system. The most important musical form was still *sonata form, but now on a larger time-scale, often with some modification and a more searching *development of musical material.

Fantasy and vivid imagination are very important ingredients in Romantic style. Many composers read widely and took an interest in the other arts – their compositions often being inspired by poems, novels, plays, or paintings. Other sources of inspiration which particularly fascinated Romantic composers include: distant countries and the remote past; nature and the seasons; rivers, lakes, and forests; night, moonlight, and dreams; legends and fairy tales; magic, mystery, and the supernatural; and, of course, love – especially the joy and pain of young love.

During the Romantic period, the orchestra increased enormously, both in the number of instruments employed and in the range of pitches and timbres they could provide (see under *orchestra). The *symphony and the *concerto were written on a larger, grander scale, and a keener interest in *programme music led to a new musical form – that of the * symphonic poem, invented by Liszt. Outstanding among the many Romantic composers of *opera were Verdi in Italy, and Wagner in Germany – Wagner preferring to call his lengthy operas *music-dramas, and using the device of the *leading-motive as a crucial structural and dramatic feature.

However, alongside these large and sometimes spectacular musical canvases, occasionally involving a huge number of performers, Romantic composers also wrote works for just one or a few musicians. These included a rich variety of poetic *'character' pieces for piano (the most favoured instrument), *chamber music, and a vast number of songs expressing every possible mood and emotion (see *lied, and also *song-cycle).

Although several of the leading Romantic composers were German or Austrian, composers of many other nations made important and varied contributions. In some cases, they deliberately reacted against the powerful German influences by creating a distinct musical style (often relying on folk-tunes and national ingredients) which was expressive and characteristic of their own particular country (see *Nationalism).

The earliest indications of 19th-century Romantic style may be heard in Beethoven's later works, and in most of the works of Schubert. Among other outstanding Romantic composers are Weber, Berlioz, Mendelssohn, Schumann, Chopin, Liszt, Wagner, Verdi, Brahms, Tchaikovsky, Rimsky-Korsakov, Smetana, Dvořák, Grieg, Elgar, Mahler, and Richard Strauss. [See the time-chart of composers on pages 398–413; see also: *Twentieth-century music]

'Romantic' Symphony Bruckner's Symphony No. 4 in E flat, composed in 1874, and revised in 1878–80 and 1886 (a slight rescoring of the previous revision).

Romanza [Italian]; **Romanze** [German] *Romance.

Romeo and Juliet Several composers have written works inspired by Shakespeare's tragedy *Romeo and Juliet*. They include: **1** a 'dramatic symphony' (Op. 17; 1839) by Berlioz, for alto, tenor, and bass soloists, chorus, and orchestra; **2** an opera in five acts (1864) by Gounod; **3** a Fantasy-Overture (symphonic poem) by Tchaikovsky, composed in 1869, then revised in 1870 and 1880; **4** a full-length ballet (Op. 64; 1935–6) by Prokofiev; he later arranged several of the pieces from the ballet score to make a piano suite (Op. 75) and three suites for orchestra (Op. 64b, Op. 64c, and Op. 101).

The same story – but set in 20th-century New York instead of 16th-century Verona – formed the basis for Leonard Bernstein's musical, **West Side Story* (1957).

Ronde [French] **1** *Semibreve. **2** A *round dance, often with a vocal accompaniment provided by the dancers themselves.

Rondeau [French] **1** *Rondo. **2** One of the three main forms of poetry and music (along with the *ballade and the *virelai) used by French composers from the 13th century to the 15th (e.g. Guillaume de Machaut, and Guillaume Dufay). Early rondeaux were *monophonic; later examples were composed in *polyphonic style in three parts (voice and two instruments). The following shows the plan of a medieval rondeau setting an eight-line poem and constructed from just two strains of music. Capital letters indicate the refrain – repeating the same words to the same music.

1	2	3	4	5	6	7	8
A	**B**	**a**	**A**	**a**	**b**	**A**	**B**

An example is the rondeau *Prendés i garde* by Guillaume d'Amiens, a trouvère of the late 13th century.

Rondo (rondo form) A musical *form or structure in which the main theme keeps recurring ('coming round') with contrasting sections of music heard in between. There are two main types of rondo form: **1 simple rondo form** (also sometimes called 'older' rondo form, rondeau – see below) and **2 sonata-rondo form** (also called rondo-sonata form, 'modern' rondo). However, a piece or movement in *either* of these two forms may be described simply as 'a rondo', or as being 'in rondo form'.

1 Simple rondo form In a simple rondo the recurrences of the main theme (**A**) are separated by contrasting sections of music called *episodes. The diagram below shows the plan for a simple rondo with two episodes, **B** and **C** (though in some cases there may be three or more episodes, and so the main theme then comes round four or more times).

A¹ the main rondo theme	**B** episode 1: a contrast	**A²** rondo theme again	**C** episode 2: another contrast	**A³** rondo theme, last time

The main rondo theme is always in the tonic key, while each contrasting episode visits a *related key. A *link may be used to join sections smoothly together. Each time the rondo theme returns it may be shortened or varied in some way, and its final appearance may be followed by a *coda.

An example of a movement in simple rondo form is the final (third) movement of Mozart's Horn Concerto No. 3 in E♭ major (K447):

A^1 main rondo theme, in the tonic key:

B first contrasting episode, beginning in the tonic key, modulating to the dominant key (B♭ major):

A^2 rondo theme again, in the tonic key.

C second contrasting episode, in the subdominant key (A♭ major):

A^3 rondo theme, last time – rounded off by a coda.

17th-century French composers used the word **rondeau** as a title for a piece in simple rondo form, referring to the main theme as the *refrain* or the *rondeau*, and calling each episode a *couplet*. Such pieces often occur in the ballets and operas of Lully and Rameau. The rondeau was also the favourite form for the harpsichord pieces of *Les *Clavecinistes*.

2 Sonata-rondo, Sonata-rondo form As the name suggests, sonata-rondo form is a mixture of *sonata form and simple rondo form, combining certain ingredients of each. The basic plan for a sonata-rondo, which is symmetrical in structure, may be shown simply as **A B A C A B A**.

Like simple rondo form, sonata-rondo depends upon a recurring main theme (**A**) which appears at least three times. But both this theme and the second theme (**B**), which occurs twice, are referred to as *subjects* since they may be used for *development during the central section (**C**).

Like sonata form, sonata-rondo has two subjects (the second subject returning, during the recapitulation, in the tonic key), and the total structure divides into three main sections. However, exposition and recapitulation both end with a return of the principal subject (the rondo theme), or at least some reference to it. And the central section of a sonata-rondo may consist of *development of previous material, or an *episode introducing new material, or a combination of both. There is usually a bridge passage, as in sonata form, connecting the principal subject to the second subject. At other points, a link may be used to join sections smoothly together.

The following diagram gives the basic plan for a piece or a movement in sonata-rondo form.

Exposition:

A¹ Principal subject (the recurring rondo theme) in the tonic key.
Bridge passage, changing key and leading to:

B Second subject (usually in the dominant or the relative major).

A² Principal subject (rondo theme) in the tonic key.

Central section:

Very often an *episode* (introducing new material) in another *related key; or a *development* of any previous material; or, occasionally, a combination of both.

Recapitulation:

A³ Principal subject (rondo theme) in the tonic key.
Bridge passage, now altered to lead to:

B Second subject – now *also* in the tonic key.

A⁴ Principal subject (rondo theme), perhaps shortened, *and/or* a
Coda making some reference to the principal subject.

Sonata-rondo form is frequently used to structure the final movement of instrumental works such as sonatas, symphonies, concertos, string quartets, and other chamber works. Two fine examples are the third movement of Beethoven's *'Pathétique' Sonata, and the finale of his Violin Concerto. In each of these sonata-rondos, the central section (**C**) is an episode introducing new, contrasting material. An example of a sonata-rondo with development in the central section is the last movement of Beethoven's Piano Sonata in E minor, Op. 90.

Rondo-sonata form See *Rondo.

Root; Root position See under *Chord.

Rosalia See under *Sequence.

Rosamunde Incidental music composed by Schubert in 1823 for a performance of a play with that title. Included is an overture, a song and three choruses, two ballets, and three entr'actes. Some people now believe that Schubert may originally have intended the first entr'acte, in B minor, as the fourth movement of his Symphony No. 8 in B minor, nicknamed the *'Unfinished' Symphony. The third entr'acte, *Andantino* in B flat, is based on a melody Schubert had used twice before – in the slow movement of his String Quartet No. 13 in A minor (D804), and as a theme for variations in his sparkling Impromptu in B flat for piano (D935; Op. 142 No. 3).

Rota Medieval term for a round. [See **Sumer is icumen in*]

Round **1** A simple type of *infinite canon at the unison in which the melody comes 'round' again and again. Examples include *Three blind mice, London's burning, Frère Jacques.* **2** Short for *round dance.

Round dance A dance in which the performers, usually alternately male and female and holding hands, dance round in a circle.

Row Short for note row. [See under *Twelve-note technique]

Royal Fireworks Music See **Fireworks Music.*

Rubato (*tempo rubato*) [Italian: 'robbed'; 'robbed time') An indication that to achieve sufficient expression the music should be performed flexibly (rather than rigidly, in strict time) with an easing or lingering on certain notes of a phrase, perhaps a gentle pressing forwards on others.

Ruff See under *Snare drum.

Ruggiero The bass-line (see below) of a 16th-century song, together with its scheme of harmonies, which (like the *romanesca and *passamezzo basses) came to be used in many other songs, dances, and instrumental pieces by composers during the 16th and 17th centuries. The romanesca bass was used as an ostinato or *ground bass, with new melodies composed (sometimes improvised) above it to make a set of continuous *variations. Among the many composers who used it were the Spanish composer Diego Ortiz and the Italian composer Frescobaldi.

Ruggiero bass

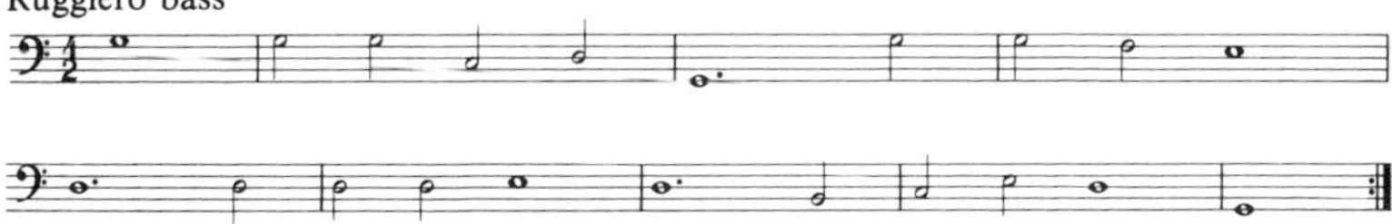

[See also: *Romanesca; *Passamezzo; *Folía]

Ruhig [German] Calm, peaceful.

Rührtrommel [German] Tenor drum.

Rumba (rhumba) A swift Afro-Cuban dance which first became popular in the USA and Europe in the 1930s. The music is strongly rhythmic, and often features the syncopated pattern (played on maracas, claves and other Cuban percussion instruments) of 3 + 3 + 2:

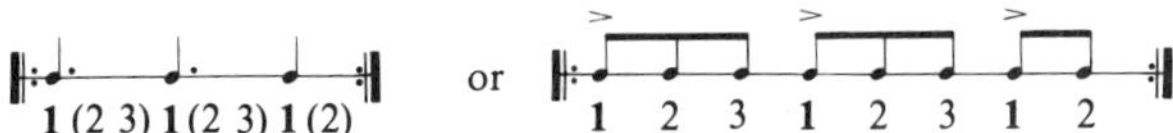

The dance emphasizes movements of the hips and shoulders rather than the feet.

Russe The French word for 'Russian'.

Russian Five, The See The *Five.

'Russian' Quartets Nickname for Haydn's set of six string quartets, Opus 33, composed in 1781 and dedicated to Tsar Paul I of Russia. They are also known as 'Gli Scherzi' ('The Scherzos', or 'The Jokes') since each minuet movement is marked either *scherzo* or *scherzando*, and also as the 'Jungfern' ('Maiden') Quartets because a girl was pictured on the cover of the edition printed in 1782. Two of the six quartets have individual nicknames: No. 2 in E flat, 'The *Joke'; and No. 3 in C, 'The *Bird'.

Rute (*Ruthe*) [German] A switch (consisting, for example, of a bundle of birch rods resembling a small witch's-broom) or a thin, split cane, sometimes required to strike the bass drum with – either on the shell, or on the drum-skin. The effect is heard, for example, in the third movement of Mahler's *'Resurrection' Symphony.

RV Abbreviation of *Ryom Verzeichnis* (Peter Ryom's catalogue, 1974/79) of the works of the Italian composer Antonio Vivaldi. Linked to the title of any composition by Vivaldi, **RV** followed by a number identifies that piece according to its numbered entry in Ryom's catalogue. [See also: *P 3 and *R 5]

Rythmé [French] Rhythmical; with well-marked beats.

S Abbreviation standing for: **1** Schmieder (see under *BWV); **2** *segno; **3** sinistra (see under *mano); **4** soprano (SATB: soprano, alto, tenor, bass); **5** subito; **6** solo.

Sabre Dance See **Gayaneh.*

Sackbut (sagbut) [from Old French: *saqueboute*, 'pull-push'] English name (used until the 18th century) for the early form of trombone, which evolved around 1460. The bell was less flared, giving a softer, rounder, more mellow tone than the modern trombone. Sackbuts were made in different sizes, and in ensemble music were often combined with *cornetts. An example is Matthew Locke's *Music for His Majesty's Sackbuts and Cornetts*, composed in 1661.

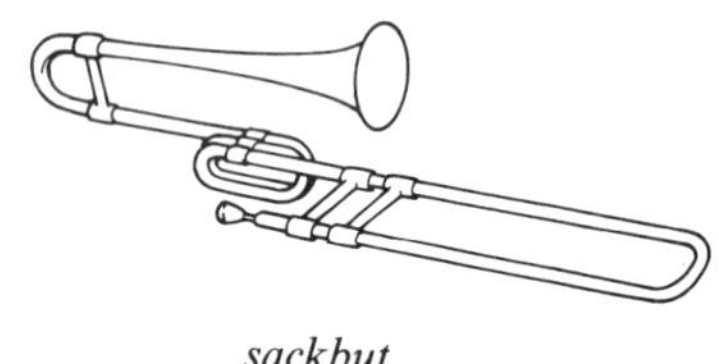

sackbut

Sacre du printemps, Le See *The *Rite of Spring.*

St Anthony Variations See **Variations on a Theme by Haydn.*

St Cecilia See *Cecilia, Saint.

St John Passion; St Matthew Passion See *Passion.

St Paul's Suite A suite for string orchestra by Gustav Holst, composed in 1912–13 for the string orchestra of St Paul's Girls' School in Hammersmith, London, where Holst was music-teacher at the time. The suite is in four movements: 1 Jig; 2 Ostinato; 3 Intermezzo; 4 Finale: 'The Dargason' (an old English dance-tune against which, on two occasions, the well-known folk-melody 'Greensleeves' is woven in counterpoint).

Saite [German] String. **Saiten**, strings. **Saiteninstrumente**, string instruments (including all types – whether bowed, plucked, or hammered).

Salmo [Italian] Psalm.

'Salomon' Symphonies Haydn's last twelve symphonies, Nos. 93 to 104, composed for the London impresario, Salomon. They are also known as Haydn's *'London' Symphonies.

Salón México, El A descriptive orchestral piece by Aaron Copland, composed in 1933–6 (originally inspired by a visit to Mexico in 1932). Copland includes several popular Mexican tunes to evoke the smoky atmosphere of the dance hall called *El Salón México*. The music is brilliantly orchestrated.

Saltando [Italian: 'leaping'; French: *sautillé*] A type of *bowing stroke on string instruments in which crisp, short strokes are made with the middle of the bow, causing it to bounce slightly on the string. Other terms, with the same meaning, are **saltato** and **spiccato**.

Saltarello [Italian: 'little hop'] A fast Italian dance in either triple time or $^{6}_{8}$ or $^{12}_{8}$ time, with a sprightly hopping or jumping rhythm. The earliest examples are found in a manuscript dating from the late 14th century. The saltarello became particularly popular during the 16th century and was often performed immediately after a *passamezzo, so that the two dances formed a linked, contrasting pair. Sometimes, the music of the saltarello was a transformation of that of the preceding dance (compare the music below with that given under *Passamezzo).

Nikolaus Ammerbach (*c*1530–1597): Saltarello

[See also: *Italian Symphony]

Saltato See *Saltando.

Samba A dance, which originated in Brazil, in lively duple metre and with highly syncopated rhythm patterns. It became popular as a Latin-American ballroom dance in the early 1940s.

Samisen See *Shamisen.

Sanctus See *Mass.

Sanft [German] Soft, gentle.

San-hsien A Chinese three-string plucked lute, with small snake-skin covered soundbox and long, fretless neck. The name means 'three strings'.

Sans [French] Without.

Sarabande [French] A dance which originated in Spain and Latin America in the 16th century. At that time it was fast and wild. It was introduced into Italy in the early 17th century, and a slower, more stately version in triple time became the third of the four standard dance movements of the Baroque keyboard *suite. One of the characteristics of the sarabande is that there is often an accent or a 'halting' on the second beat of the bar. The following example is the Sarabande from Handel's Keyboard Suite XI (No. 4 of the 1733 collection).

(Handel bases this Sarabande on the well-known **Folía* dance-tune; he extends the piece by writing two variations on these sixteen bars.)

Sāraṅgī A fiddle used in north Indian folk and classical music. The body, which is usually carved from a single block of wood, is waisted; the neck is short and wide, and without frets. There are three or four gut melody strings played with a bow, and two dozen or more sympathetic strings (see *Sympathetic vibrations). The player holds the instrument upright, and stops the side of the strings with the fingernails of the left hand.

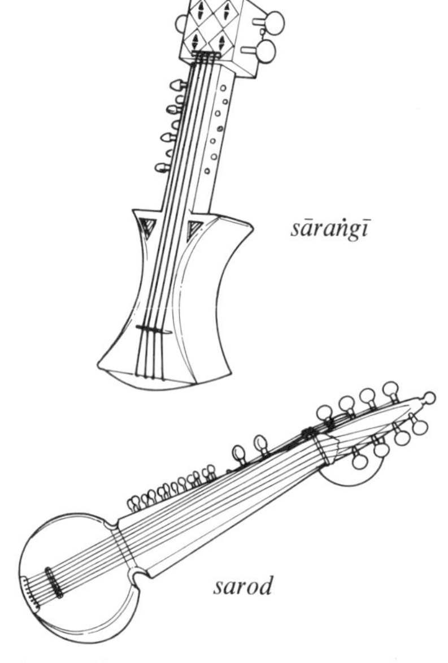
sāraṅgī

sarod

Šárka See **Má vlast*.

Sarod An Indian type of long-necked plucked lute. The hollow body is pear-shaped and carved from a single piece of wood; and the fingerboard, which has no frets, is of metal. There are usually eight metal playing strings (four melody strings and four drone strings) plucked with a plectrum made from coconut shell, and also a set of about fifteen sympathetic strings (see *Sympathetic vibrations). The sarod has two 'resonating chambers'. The larger one (the body) is covered with skin or parchment; the smaller one (below the top of the instrument) is usually covered with metal.

Sarrusophone A wind instrument, made of brass, with a conical bore, and a double-reed mouthpiece. It was invented in 1856 by a French bandmaster named Sarrus. Even though made of brass, the sarrusophone is more properly classed as a 'woodwind' instrument, due to its reed mouthpiece. Sarrusophones are built in various sizes, the lowest-sounding occasionally included in orchestral scores – especially by French composers – in place of a double bassoon (e.g. Ravel's **Rapsodie espagnole*).

Sassofono [Italian] Saxophone.

S. A. T. B. Abbreviations in music for voices for soprano, alto (contralto), tenor, bass.

Satz (plural: *Sätze*) [German: 'sentence'] A piece; or a movement (of a sonata, symphony, etc.). Can also be used in the sense of theme or *subject: for example, **Hauptsatz**, main theme or first subject.

Sautillé [French] Same as *Saltando.

Saxhorns A family of brass instruments of various sizes and pitches, patented in 1845 by Adolphe Sax. Each has three valves, a mainly conical bore, and usually the bell points upwards.

Saxophone A wind instrument, invented during the 1840s by the Belgian clarinettist and instrument-maker, Adolphe Sax. The saxophone's conical tube is made of metal – but it has a single-reed mouthpiece like the clarinet, and a system of key-work opening and closing holes cut along the length of its tube. Both are characteristics of woodwind instruments rather than brass.

tenor saxophone

Saxophones are made in as many as eight different sizes and pitches. Of these, the three most commonly used are the alto saxophone in E♭, the tenor in B♭, and the baritone in E♭. All saxophones are treated as *transposing instruments; their music is always written in the treble clef, and within the same written range:

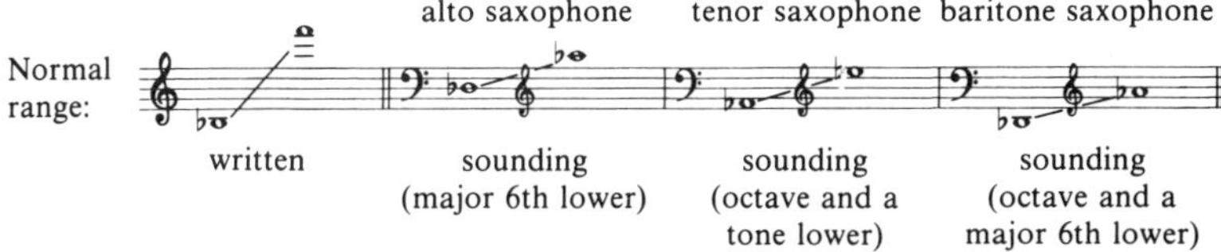

Saxophones are regularly used in military bands, dance bands, and jazz ensembles (a jazz big band will include a whole section of saxophones). They are also sometimes used in orchestral music. Examples include: the second part of Bizet's *Prélude* to *L'Arlésienne* (alto saxophone), *The Old Castle* in Ravel's orchestration of Musorgsky's *Pictures at an Exhibition* (alto saxophone), the middle section of *The Wedding of Kijé* from Prokofiev's **Lieutenant Kijé* (tenor saxophone), and *The Dance of Job's Comforters* (three saxophones) from *Job* by Vaughan Williams. Glazunov wrote a Quartet for Saxophones (soprano, alto, tenor, baritone), and a Concerto in E♭ for alto saxophone and strings. Debussy wrote a *Rapsodie* for alto saxophone and piano (later orchestrated), Ibert composed a *Concertino da camera* for alto saxophone and eleven instruments, and Frank Martin wrote a *Ballade* for alto saxophone and orchestra. Included among the names of many fine jazz saxophonists are Charlie Parker (alto saxophone), Coleman Hawkins and Ornette Coleman (tenor saxophone), and two members of Duke Ellington's orchestra: Johnny Hodges (alto) and Harry Carney (baritone).

Scale [from Latin, *scala*: a ladder, staircase, or a flight of steps] A succession of single notes, lying within an octave, the notes arranged in order of pitch, moving upwards, or downwards. There are many different kinds of scale on which music can be based. Before *c*1600, Western music was based on the medieval system of modes (see *Church modes). From about 1600 to about

1900 (and after, in the case of some composers) Western music has largely been based on two main kinds of scale: *major*, and *minor*.

The **major scale** is a mixture of tones and semitones (shown as S and T, below) which are arranged according to a strict pattern – the two semitones occurring between the third and fourth, and seventh and eighth notes. Here as examples are the scales of C major and G major:

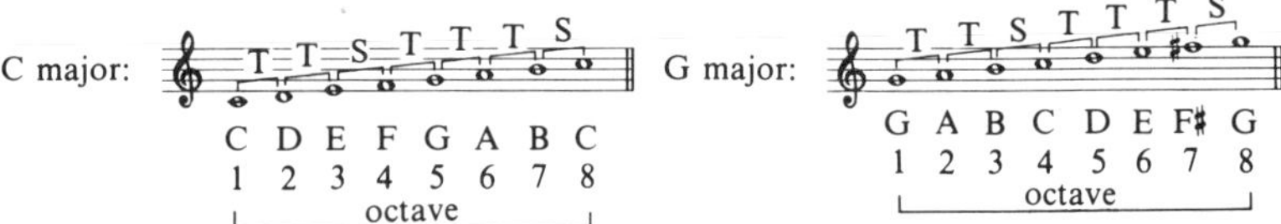

It is possible to have a major scale beginning on *any* note – but this same pattern of tones and semitones must be strictly kept.

The **minor scale**. The most important difference between the major scale and the minor scale is that in the minor scale, the third note is lowered by a semitone, making it a *minor* 3rd above the first note:

C major scale begins: T T S T

major 3rd
(tone + tone)

C minor scale begins: T S T T

minor 3rd
(tone + semitone)

There are two different patterns for the minor scale. One is called the harmonic minor scale; the other is called the melodic minor scale.

The *harmonic minor scale* – so called because its notes are likely to be used in building chords and harmonies – lowers the sixth note as well as the third. This produces a rather awkward step of a tone and a half (= three semitones) between the sixth and seventh notes:

C minor, harmonic: T S T T S T½ S

The *melodic minor scale* – so called because its notes are likely to be used in building melodies – smooths away this awkward step by changing the sixth note when moving upwards, but lowering both sixth and seventh notes when moving downwards:

C minor, melodic: T S T T T T S T T S T T S T

Another kind of scale is the **chromatic scale**, which proceeds entirely by semitones, so dividing the octave into twelve equal steps of one semitone each (a 'ladder' whose steps are all the same distance apart):

Chromatic scale:

(For the use of the chromatic scale in 20th-century serial music, see under *Twelve-note technique.)

There are a great many other kinds of scale on which music can be based. Among the most important are the *pentatonic scale, and the *whole-tone scale; scales may also be constructed using *microtones.

[See also: *Degree]

Scale degrees See *Degree.

Scat singing (scatting) A type of singing, sometimes used by jazz singers, in which nonsense words and syllables and improvised sounds are used instead of normal words.

Scena [Italian] In opera, a lengthy and usually dramatic vocal solo consisting of a sequence of several linked sections – e.g. orchestral introduction, recitative (or arioso) passages, one or more arias.

Scenes from Childhood See **Kinderscenen.*

Scharf [German] Strong, sharp. **Scharf betont**, sharply accented.

Scheherazade German spelling of **Sheherazade.*

Schellen [German] *Sleigh bells or jingles.

Schellentrommel [German] Tambourine.

Scherzando [Italian] Joking, playful.

Scherzetto; Scherzino [Italian] A short or small-scale *scherzo.

Scherzi, Gli See *'Russian' Quartets.

Scherzo [Italian: 'joke', 'jest'] A movement (most often the third one) of symphonies, chamber works, and also many sonatas. Originally, in such works, composers had written a minuet. Haydn, however, in his later symphonies, increased the pace of the minuet and brought an earthy, outdoor flavour to what had once been an elegant, courtly dance. Beethoven increased the pace still further, and eventually transformed the minuet into the brisk and vigorously rhythmic scherzo, while still keeping to the same basic plan (see *Minuet and Trio form). At first, like the minuet, the scherzo was written in triple time – but the speed is often so swift that the music may be counted as one-in-a-bar. Not all scherzos are humorous, but they are often dramatic in character and include a strong element of surprise. Sometimes a composer writes a scherzo as an independent, self-contained composition (examples are Brahms's Scherzo, Op. 4, and Chopin's four scherzos for solo piano). In the 17th century, the word was used as a title for vocal pieces in a light style (e.g. Monteverdi's *Scherzi musicali* of 1607).

Scherzoso [Italian] Playful.

Schlag [German] Beat.

Schlaginstrumente; Schlagzeug [German] Percussion instruments.

Schleppend [German] Dragging.

Schlummerlied [German] Slumber-song.

Schluss [German] **1** Conclusion; end. **2** Cadence.

Schmetternd [German: 'blaring'] An indication to a horn player to blow the note(s) with considerable force to produce a particularly 'brassy', blaring tone-quality.

Schnell [German] Quick. **Schneller**, quicker.

Schöne Müllerin, Die (The fair maid of the mill) A *song-cycle for male voice and piano (D795) composed by Schubert in 1823 and consisting of settings of twenty poems by Wilhelm Müller. The sequence of songs tells how a young man happily courts the beautiful daughter of a miller, but becomes embittered when she eventually rejects his love. The titles of the songs are: 1 *Das Wandern* (Rambling); 2 *Wohin?* (Whither?); 3 *Halt!* (Halt!); 4 *Danksagung an den Bach* (Giving thanks to the brook); 5 *Am Feierabend* (Evening leisure after work); 6 *Der Neugierige* (The inquisitive one); 7 *Ungeduld* (Impatience); 8 *Morgengruss* (Morning greeting); 9 *Des Müllers Blumen* (The miller's flowers); 10 *Tränenregen* (Shower of tears); 11 *Mein!* (Mine!); 12 *Pause* (Pause); 13 *Mit dem grünen Lautenband* (With the green lute-ribbon); 14 *Der Jäger* (The hunter);

15 *Eifersucht und Stolz* (Jealousy and pride); 16 *Die liebe Farbe* (The favourite colour); 17 *Die böse Farbe* (The hateful colour); 18 *Trockne Blumen* (Withered flowers); 19 *Der Müller und der Bach* (The miller and the brook); 20 *Des Baches Wiegenlied* (The brook's cradle-song).

Schöpfung, Die See *The *Creation.*

Schottische [German for 'Scottish'] A ballroom dance, a *round dance, usually in $\frac{2}{4}$ time and similar to a polka but slower. There is, though, no known connection with Scotland, nor with the *écossaise.

Schübler Chorales Six *chorale preludes by Bach, so called because they were published, around 1748, by Schübler. They are Bach's own arrangements for organ of movements from his cantatas (see **Wachet auf*).

Schwanengesang (Swan song) Schubert's last songs, composed in 1828, setting seven poems by Rellstab, six by Heine, and one by Seidl. They were published after Schubert's death, and given the overall title *Schwanengesang* by the publisher – though the fourteen songs do not make up a genuine song-cycle. Included are the famous *Ständchen* (Serenade) and the dramatic *Der Doppelgänger* (The ghostly double).

Schwellwerk [German] Swell organ. [See under *Organ]

Schwung [German] Swing. **Mit Schwung**, with strong rhythmic swing.

Scordatura Abnormal tuning of a string instrument, in order to obtain extra notes (such as tuning the lowest string of a cello to B instead of the normal C), to make it easier to play certain passages or chords (e.g. on a guitar or lute), or to achieve an unusual tone-quality (e.g. in **Danse macabre* by Saint-Saëns, where the top string of the solo violin is tuned to E♭ instead of E♮).

Score [French: *partition*; German: *Partitur*; Italian: *partitura*] The word 'score' comes from the Old English *scoru* meaning 'marked with scratches or lines', and it was originally used by musicians to refer to the way lines were marked or scratched with a pen down through the staves of music to form bar-lines. Later, 'score' came to mean a complete copy of a composition, either in manuscript or in print, with all the parts arranged one above another so that they can all be taken in at a glance. There are several different types and sizes of score.

A **full score** (or **orchestral score**) shows all the staves of music for all the instruments taking part in a composition (the players themselves having only the *part to be played by their instruments) and it is printed on large-sized pages for easy reading, e.g. by the conductor during performance. The instruments are arranged down the page according to the four sections of the orchestra – the order always being: *woodwind, brass, percussion, strings*. In a typical score for full orchestra or symphony orchestra the order is as shown on the right.

Woodwind:	Piccolo
	Flutes
	Oboes
	Cor anglais
	Clarinets
	Bass clarinet
	Bassoons
	Double bassoon
Brass:	Horns
	Trumpets
	Trombones
	Tuba
Percussion:	Kettle drums (timpani)
	Other percussion
Strings:	First violins
	Second violins
	Violas
	Cellos
	Double basses

When a harp is included, its music comes between the percussion and the strings. If voices are included, or a featured solo instrument (e.g. in a concerto), then these staves of music are placed immediately above the strings (though in older editions, the voice parts may be printed between violas and cellos, so splitting the string section in two).

A **miniature score** (or **pocket score** or **study score**) reproduces all the information shown in a full score but at a reduced size (often about 13.5 cm by 19 cm) making it convenient for study purposes or for taking to a concert. In a **piano score** all the orchestral and/or vocal parts are reduced (and often simplified) to a version of the music which may be played on a piano. A **vocal score** gives separate staves for all the vocal parts in an opera or other work for voices and orchestra, but with the orchestral parts reduced to a two-stave arrangement which can be played on a piano or organ (singers use vocal scores when learning their parts, and also to rehearse from). In an **open score** each part or 'voice' of a polyphonic composition is presented on a separate stave (even though the music might be intended for solo keyboard). The term **short score** is used to mean either (1) a reduction or condensation to very few staves (often two) of a work normally taking many more staves, or (2) a composer's 'sketch' score of a complete composition, showing on a few staves his main intentions which he will later elaborate and orchestrate in the form of a full score. [See also: *Transposing instruments; and the table of Foreign names for instruments, most often found in scores, on pages 396–397]

Scored for See under *Scoring.

Score-reading Strictly, the term means taking a musical *score to the piano and playing it over, reproducing all the notes in every possible detail. Or even silently reading the score, page by page, and mentally hearing the total effect of the music without a single note being actually sounded. But musicians often use the term 'score-reading' to mean *following* a score – noticing certain musical information given in the score and following (or 'keeping up with') the music as it is being performed.

Scoring The process of devising and determining the orchestral colouring (or *orchestration) of a composition – deciding which instruments shall play at which times and how their sounds will combine and balance – and then correctly setting their notes down on paper in the form of a full *score. Many composers first sketch out a composition in the form of a short score (see under *score), later attending to the more detailed process of scoring. The word 'scoring' may also be used in a critical sense – for example: 'good scoring for clarinets', 'muddy scoring for lower brass and strings'. And the term 'scored for' is often used when mentioning the combination of instruments a composer has chosen for a piece or a section of a piece – for example, 'scored for oboes, horns, and strings'.

Scorrevole [Italian] Gliding; freely flowing.

Scotch snap See *Lombard rhythm.

Scottish Symphony (Scotch Symphony) Mendelssohn's title for his Symphony No. 3 in A minor, Op. 56, completed in 1842. The music was inspired by a visit to Scotland in 1829. The symphony is in four movements which are played without a break: 1 *Andante con moto* leading to *Allegro un poco agitato* – 2 *Vivace non troppo* – 3 *Adagio* – 4 *Allegro vivacissimo*. [See also: *The *Hebrides; *Italian Symphony*]

Sea Pictures A song-cycle, Opus 37, for alto voice and orchestra, composed by Elgar in 1897–9. The titles of the songs (with poets mentioned in brackets) are: 1 Sea slumber-song (Roden Noel); 2 In haven (C. Alice Elgar – the composer's wife); 3 Sabbath morning at sea (Elizabeth Barrett Browning); 4 Where corals lie (Richard Garnett); 5 The swimmer (A. Lindsay Gordon).

Seasons, The **1** An oratorio [German title: *Die Jahreszeiten*] composed by Haydn between 1799 and 1801, to words translated and adapted by Baron van Swieten from the English poem *The Seasons* by James Thomson. The oratorio is in four parts (Spring, Summer, Autumn, Winter) and is scored for soprano, tenor, and bass soloists, choir, and orchestra. **2** A ballet, Opus 67, by Glazunov, composed in 1899.

[See also: *The *Four Seasons*]

Sea Symphony, A Title given by Vaughan Williams to his first symphony (1903–9) for soprano and baritone soloists, chorus, and orchestra. The four movements, each of which sets words by the American poet Walt Whitman, are entitled; 1 A song for all seas, all ships; 2 On the beach at night alone; 3 (Scherzo) The waves; 4 The explorers.

Sec [French] 'Dry'; short and detached (and so similar to **staccato*). Also an indication to damp or silence the sound immediately (e.g. in playing a cymbal clash).

Secco [Italian: 'dry'] **1** The same as **staccato*. **2** Short for **recitativo secco*.

Second **1** As a noun, see *Intervals. **2** As an adjective, 'second' describes another instrument or voice of the same type, whose music is generally pitched lower than the 'first'. For example: second violin, second oboe, second soprano.

Seconda; Secondo [Italian] Second. For example: *seconda *volta*, second time; *violino secondo*, second violin(s). *Secondo* may also refer to the lower part of a piano *duet, the upper part being called *primo*.

Secular Term used generally to describe music which is non-sacred (e.g. a secular *cantata consists of a setting of a non-religious text).

Segno [Italian: 'sign'] A sign usually printed as 𝄋 (a decorated letter 'S') and used to indicate the beginning or end of a repeated section of music. [See also: *Dal segno; *Al segno; *Da capo; *Fino. And also under *Ripetizione]

Segue [Italian] 'Follows'. It may be used as a direction to go on to the next section, piece, or movement immediately, without a pause. Or as a direction to continue in the same style or manner – e.g. a pattern of broken chords. [See example 15 of Table 11 on pages 392–393]

Seguente [Italian] 'Following'. For example, *attacca il seguente* means go straight on with what follows, without a pause.

Seguidilla (*seguidillas*) A Spanish dance and song, in moderately quick triple time. It is accompanied by guitar and castanets, and is similar to the *bolero, but faster. Sung sections, called *coplas*, alternate with lively dance sections in a more definite rhythm. Albéniz composed a *Seguidillas* for solo piano; the famous example in Act I of Bizet's **Carmen*, however, is not a typical seguidilla.

Albéniz: *Seguidillas*

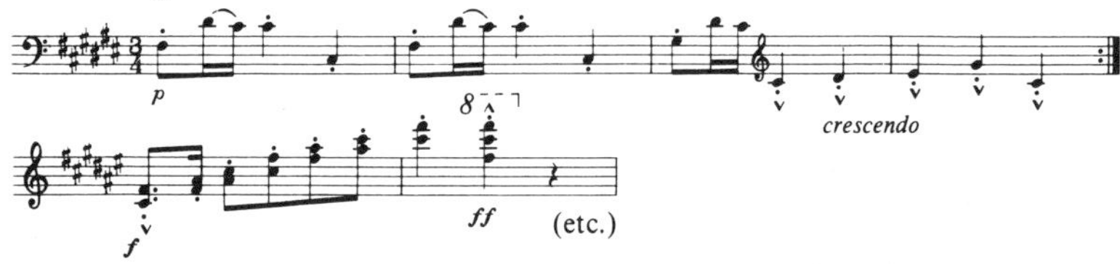

Sehnsucht [German] Longing, yearning. **Sehnsuchtsvoll**, full of longing.

Sehr [German] Very.

Semibreve [from Latin: 'half a breve'] The longest note commonly used in modern notation, which has the value of two minims or of four crotchets. (The American name for a semibreve is a whole note.) A semibreve is written: 𝅝 and a semibreve *rest is shown as 𝄻 [See also Tables 1 and 2 on page 387]

Semichorus A part of a chorus or choir (though usually less than half of it) used for purposes of contrast in tone-quality and volume – perhaps to create *echo effects or *antiphonal effects between semichorus and the main chorus.

Semidemisemiquaver Name sometimes used for *hemidemisemiquaver.

Semihemidemisemiquaver The note, only occasionally used, which is half the value of a hemidemisemiquaver. Thirty-two semihemidemisemiquavers are equal to one crotchet; and 128 semihemidemisemiquavers equal one semibreve. (The American name for a semihemidemisemiquaver is 128th-note.) The examples below show (a) a single semihemidemisemiquaver (five hooks to the stem); (b) a group of eight semihemidemisemiquavers (equal to one semiquaver); and (c) a semihemidemisemiquaver rest. Passages including semihemidemisemiquavers can be found in the slow movement (in $\frac{3}{8}$ time) of Beethoven's Third Piano Concerto.

Semi-opera Name given to an English theatrical work of the 17th and 18th centuries, spectacularly staged, but in which music plays a less dominant role than in a full opera. Examples are Purcell's *King Arthur* (1691) and *The *Fairy Queen* (1692, revised 1693).

Semiquaver The note which is half the value of a quaver, and twice the value of a demisemiquaver. There are four semiquavers in a crotchet, sixteen semiquavers in a semibreve. (The American name for a semiquaver is a sixteenth-note.) A single semiquaver is written: 𝅘𝅥𝅯 (with two hooks on the stem); a group of four: ♬♬ ; and a semiquaver *rest is shown as 𝄿 [See also Tables 1 and 2 on page 387]

Semitone A half-tone or half-step – the smallest *interval normally used in Western music. The octave divides into twelve semitones, as shown on the piano *keyboard – where the step from any note to its nearest neighbour (black or white as the case may be) is one semitone. [See also: *Chromatic semitone]

Semplice [Italian] Simple, unaffected. **Simplicità**, simplicity.

Sempre [Italian] Always; still; continually.

Sentence See under *Phrase.

Sentimento [Italian] Sentiment, feeling.

Senza [Italian] Without.

Septet [German: *Septett*; French: *septette, septuor*; Italian: *septetto*] **1** Music composed for seven solo instruments or voices **2** A group which performs such a composition. Examples are: Beethoven's Septet in E♭ (Op. 20; 1800) for clarinet, bassoon, horn, violin, viola, cello, double bass; Ravel's Septet (1905), entitled *Introduction and Allegro*, which is for harp, flute, clarinet, and string quartet; and Stravinsky's Septet (1953) for clarinet, bassoon, horn, piano, violin, viola, and cello. [See also: *Chamber music]

Septuor [French] *Septet.

Septuplet (septolet, septimole) A group of seven notes to be performed evenly in the time normally taken by either four, or six, notes of the same kind.

Sequence **1** The immediate repetition of a melodic pattern at a slightly higher or lower pitch. In a **melodic sequence** repetition takes place in the melody alone; if repetition occurs in all the parts in the musical texture, it is called a **harmonic sequence**. If, during repetition, all *intervals are exactly preserved in quality, resulting in change of key, it is called a **real sequence**. But if the quality of intervals is variable, and the music remains in the same key, it is called a **tonal sequence**. The term **modulating sequence** is used when change of key occurs, but without necessarily preserving the quality of all the intervals. A sequence in which the repetitions successively rise in pitch is often called a **rosalia**.

2 In Gregorian chant, the Sequence is a type of hymn. The text, except for the first and last lines, usually consists of a series of couplets or pairs of lines, each pair sung to the same music. Examples include the 'Golden Sequence' *Veni sancte spiritus* for Whitsunday, the **Stabat Mater*, and the **Dies irae* of the *Requiem Mass.

Seraglio, Il See *The *Abduction from the Seraglio.*

Serena [Italian] Serene; peaceful.

Serenade [from Italian, *serenata*: 'evening music', and also *sereno*: 'the open air'] **1** A love-song to be sung in the evening below the window of the beloved, often to the accompaniment of guitar or mandolin. **2** An instrumental composition in several movements intended, by 18th-century composers, for evening entertainment – often for performance in the open air. The serenade descended from the suite, the symphony, and the concerto. Like the *divertimento, the serenade was usually composed in a light, entertaining style. Famous examples are Mozart's *Eine *Kleine Nachtmusik*, *'Haffner' Serenade, **Serenata notturna*, and Serenade in B♭ (K361) for thirteen wind instruments. Among 19th-century composers, Brahms composed two orchestral serenades (Op. 11 and Op. 16), and Dvořák, Suk, Tchaikovsky, and Elgar each composed a *Serenade for Strings*. 20th-century examples include Stravinsky's *Serenade* for piano, Schoenberg's *Serenade*, Op. 24, for clarinet, bass clarinet, mandolin, guitar, violin, viola, and cello (with a part for baritone voice in the fourth of the seven movements), and Britten's **Serenade* for tenor, horn, and strings.

Serenade for tenor, horn, and strings A song-cycle, Opus 31, composed by Benjamin Britten in 1943 for Peter Pears (tenor) and Dennis Brain (horn). A *Prologue* and *Epilogue*, played by the horn alone, frame six songs: 1 *Pastoral* ('The day's grown old' by Cotton); 2 *Nocturne* ('The splendour falls on castle walls' by Tennyson); 3 *Elegy* ('O rose, thou art sick' by Blake); 4 *Dirge* (a setting of 'The Lyke-Wake Dirge' by an anonymous 15th-century poet); 5 *Hymn* ('Queen and huntress, chaste and fair' by Jonson); 6 *Sonnet* ('O soft embalmer of the still midnight' by Keats). Each poem is in some way connected with thoughts of evening or nightfall – the glowing haze of sunset, mysterious lengthenings of shadows, the coming of darkness, and sleep.

Serenade to Music A work by Vaughan Williams, composed in 1938 for Sir Henry Wood's golden jubilee as a conductor. Lines from Act V Scene 1 of Shakespeare's *The Merchant of Venice* (beginning 'How sweet the moonlight sleeps upon this bank') are set for sixteen solo voices (four each of sopranos, altos, tenors, and basses) and orchestra. Vaughan Williams later arranged the music for four solo voices and orchestra, and also for orchestra alone.

Serenata **1** A *serenade. **2** In the early 18th century, a title given to a secular cantata or a short opera composed in homage to a patron or to honour the birthday of a royal personage.

Serenata notturna Mozart's title for his sixth *serenade, in D major, K239, composed in 1776. It is composed for two small orchestras – the first consisting of two violins, viola, and double bass, and the second made up of first and second violins, viola(s), cello(s), and kettle drums. The work is in three movements: 1 *Marcia: Maestoso*; 2 *Menuetto*; 3 *Rondo: Allegretto*.

Seria [Italian] Serious; tragic. **Serioso, seriosamente**, seriously. [See also: *Opera seria]

Serialism; Serial music See *Twelve-note technique.

Series A succession of pitches (i.e. notes) presented in a particular order and used as the basic material for a composition – for example, the note row in a piece composed in *twelve-note technique.

Sérieux; Sérieuse [French] Serious; of serious intent.

Serious Songs See **Vier ernste Gesänge*.

Serpent A low-sounding wind instrument (the bass of the *cornett family); invented in the 16th century and remaining in use until around 1850. The serpent consisted of a long wooden tube (shaped like a serpent) bound round with leather; it had finger-holes, and a cup-shaped mouthpiece similar to that of the modern trombone. (Even though made of wood, the serpent is classed as a 'brass' instrument, due to its cup-shaped mouthpiece.)

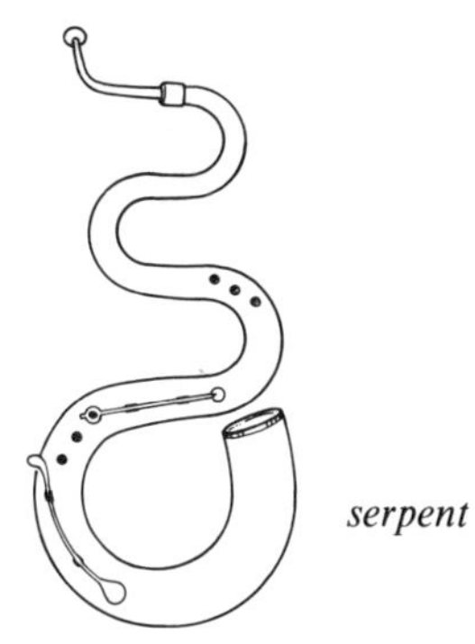
serpent

Serré [French] Hurried. **Serrez**, hurry, press onward; **en serrant**, hurrying.

Serva padrona, La (The maid as mistress) Comic opera in two acts by Pergolesi (libretto by Federico), first produced in Naples in 1733 as an *intermezzo between the acts of the opera *Il prigionier superbo*. Only three characters take part. Serpina (soprano), maid to the rich old bachelor Uberto (bass), plans to become mistress of the house. With the help of another servant, Vespone (silent role), who pretends to elope with her, she cunningly inveigles Uberto into marriage.

Sestetto [Italian] *Sextet.

Seventh See *Intervals.

Seventh chord (chord of the seventh) Any *chord consisting of root, 3rd, 5th, and 7th – making three 3rds stacked one above another. A seventh chord built upon the dominant (fifth degree) of any major or minor scale is called a **dominant seventh**; all others are called **secondary sevenths**. [See also: *Diminished seventh chord]

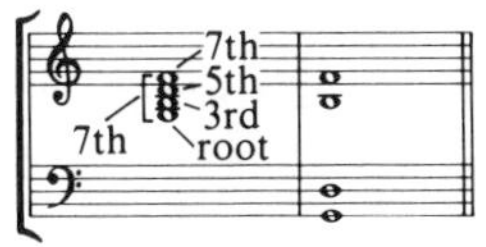

Sevillana A folk-dance from the Spanish town of Seville.

Sextet [German: *Sextett*; French: *sextette, sextuor*; Italian: *sestetto*] **1** Music composed for six solo instruments or voices: **2** A group which performs such a composition. [See: *String sextet; and also under *Chamber music]

Sextuor [French] *Sextet.

Sextuplet (sextolet) A group of six notes to be performed evenly in the time normally taken by four notes of the same kind. A sextuplet may be notated as two groups of three notes, as at (a), below; or as three groups of two, as at (b).

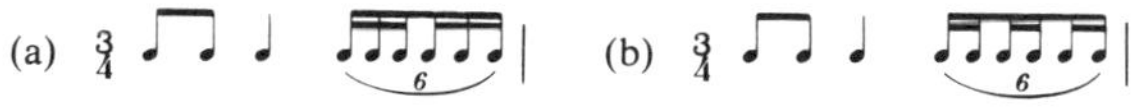

(a) (b)

sf; sfz Abbreviations of either **sforzando* or *sforzato*.
Sforza [Italian] Force.
Sforzando; Sforzato (both usually abbreviated to either ***sf*** or ***sfz***) [Italian] Forcing, forced – indicating that a note or chord is to be strongly accented, attacked with emphasis. *Forzando* and *forzato* (both abbreviated to ***fz***) mean exactly the same. [See also: **sfp*]
sfp A dynamic marking (standing for *sforzando-piano*) indicating that the note or chord is to be accented, attacked with emphasis – and then the volume immediately reduced to *piano* (soft).
sfz Abbreviation standing for either **sforzando* or *sforzato*.
Shahnāī (shanai) A powerfully-toned north Indian shawm, with a double reed, and usually seven to nine holes (the lowest two used for tuning). The main part of the tube is cylindrical and made of wood; to this is attached a flaring metal bell. [See also: *Nāgasvaram]

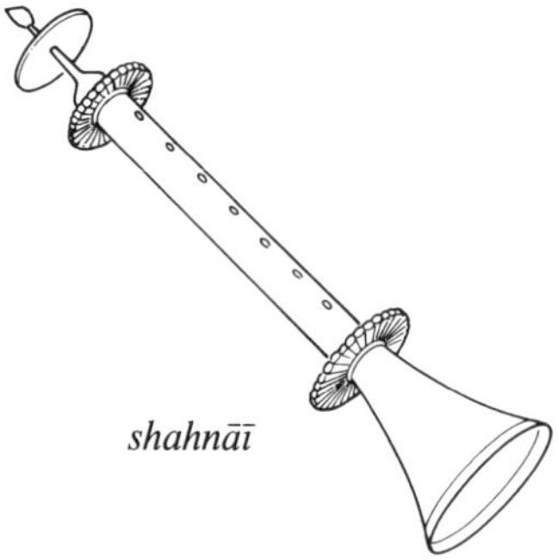

shahnāī

Shake Older name for trill. [See: *Ornaments]
Shakuhachi A heavy, Japanese bamboo flute. It is held vertically and end-blown (like the recorder). The shakuhachi has only five holes (four finger-holes and one thumb-hole) yet it has a range of three octaves or more, with all the chromatic notes in the range obtainable by partly covering the holes, special fingering techniques, and *overblowing.

shakuhachi

Shamisen (samisen) A Japanese long-necked plucked lute, with a flat back and a skin-covered belly. There are no frets, and its three strings, of silk or nylon, are plucked with an ivory plectrum.

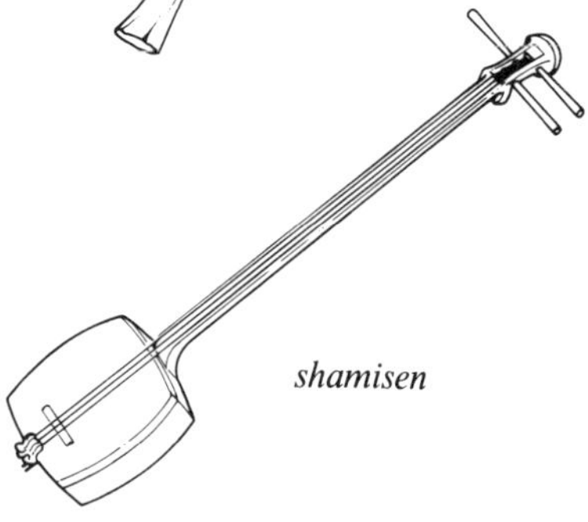

shamisen

Shanai See *Shahnāī.

Shanty [from French, *chantez*: 'sing'] A *work-song, usually with a strong rhythm, sung by sailors in the days of sailing ships, while performing tasks such as hauling ropes or hoisting sails. The verses were usually sung by a solo voice, with everyone joining in the chorus. Well-known examples are: *The Drunken Sailor* (windlass and capstan shanty), *Haul away Joe* (fore-sheet shanty) and *Fire down below* (pumping ship shanty).

Sharp **1** The sign ♯ which raises the pitch of a note by a semitone. [See also: *Accidentals; *Key signature] **2** Describing any musical sound which is higher in pitch than it should be.

Sharpen To raise the pitch of a note by a semitone – but not *necessarily* by means of a sharp sign (♯). For example, if the note F is sharpened it becomes F sharp; but if B flat is sharpened, it becomes B natural. [See: *Keyboard, diagram 2]

Shawm A double-reed woodwind instrument (the ancestor of the oboe) with a flaring bell and powerful sound – slightly buzzy, yet brilliant and penetrating. The shawm originated in the Middle East, and was brought to Europe at the time of the Crusades. During the Renaissance period, shawms were built in several sizes – the most common being alto, tenor, bass, and great bass, though smaller sizes (treble and sopranino) were also made. [See also: *Bombard; *Pommer; *Rauschpfeife; *Shahnāī; *Nāgasvaram]

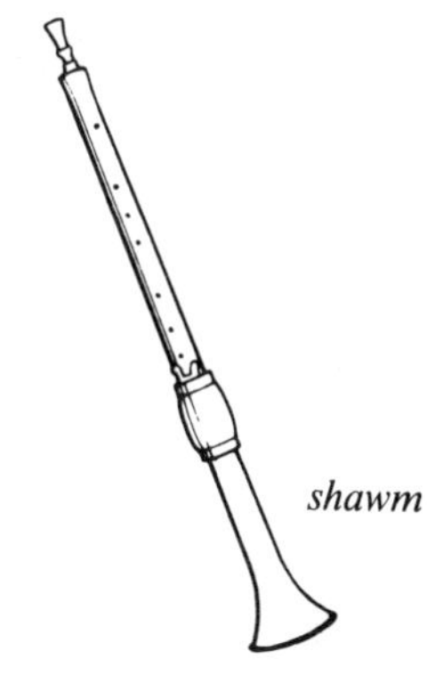

shawm

Sheep may safely graze [German: *Schafe können sicher weiden*] A soprano aria, with two recorders and figured bass, from Bach's secular cantata *Was mir behagt* (composed probably in 1713). The piece is often heard in other arrangements, e.g. for orchestra, for solo piano, for piano duet.

Sheherazade A symphonic suite, Opus 35, composed by Rimsky-Korsakov in 1888. The music, richly and brilliantly orchestrated, is programmatic, being based on the *Arabian Nights* (or *Thousand and One Nights*) in which Sheherazade must each night tell a different story to her husband, the sultan, in order to delay her threatened execution. Although Rimsky-Korsakov denied that his music described specific stories from the collection, the following titles have become attached to the four movements of the suite: 1 The sea and Sinbad's ship; 2 The story of the Kalandar Prince; 3 The young Prince and the young Princess; 4 Festival at Baghdad – The sea – The ship is dashed to pieces on a rock surmounted by a bronze warrior. At various times during the suite, the voice of Sheherazade is suggested by a solo violin.

Sheng A Chinese mouth organ which has been in use for over 2,500 years. It usually has seventeen bamboo pipes mounted in an incomplete circle on a wind-chest which is most often made of copper. Each pipe contains a free reed of metal, carefully tuned with a drop of wax. For each pipe there is a finger-hole, and as the player blows, a pipe sounds only when its finger-hole is stopped. (A similar, though rather smaller, instrument is the Japanese *shō.)

Shō A Japanese mouth organ which usually has seventeen bamboo pipes mounted in an incomplete circle on a wooden wind-chest. Each pipe contains a free reed of metal which is precisely tuned with a carefully gauged drop of wax. The shō can play eleven chords. A continuous sound is produced by the performer alternately exhaling and inhaling. Moisture (which, if allowed to collect inside, would prevent the reeds from speaking) is kept in check by warming the instrument over a charcoal fire at times when it is not being played. (A similar, but larger instrument, is the Chinese *sheng.)

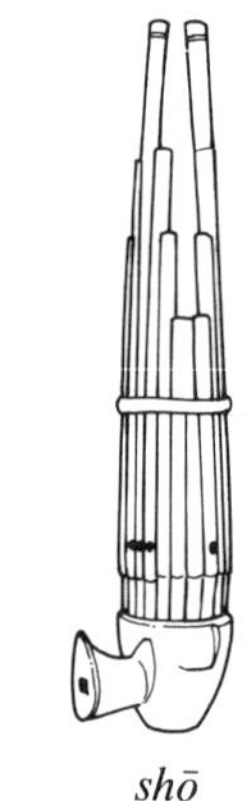

shō

Short octave (short-octave tuning) Until the late 17th century, keyboards on many organs and stringed keyboard instruments (e.g. harpsichord, virginals, clavichord) were designed with a 'short' (or 'broken') octave in the bass. In the example on the right, the lowest key (which looks as if it should sound the note E) would in fact sound low C. The 'F sharp' key would sound D, and the 'G sharp' key would sound E. The remaining keys would sound the notes normally expected. The purpose of the short octave was to save space and expense by omitting low notes which were unlikely, at that time, to be needed.

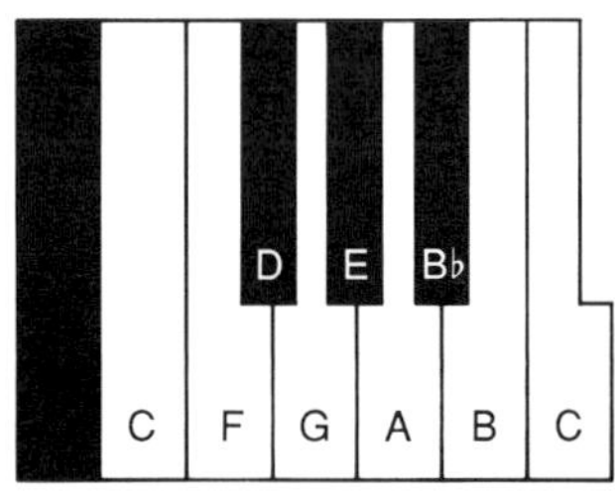

short octave

Short score See under *Score.

Si [French and Italian] The note B natural.

Siciliana; Siciliano [Italian]; **Sicilienne** [French] A type of Sicilian pastoral dance in moderate $\frac{6}{8}$ or $\frac{12}{8}$ time, with a lilting, swaying rhythm (the figure ♩. ♪ ♩ is characteristic). The rhythm of the siciliana was often used by Baroque composers in instrumental and vocal pieces or movements (e.g. *La Paix* in Handel's *'Fireworks Music'; the alto aria *Erbarme dich mir* in Bach's **St Matthew Passion*).

Handel: *La Paix* from 'Fireworks Music'

(etc.)

Side drum See *Snare drum.

Siegfried See *Der *Ring des Nibelungen.*

Siegfried Idyll A work for small orchestra composed by Wagner in 1870 as a birthday present for his wife Cosima, and first performed by a group of fifteen players (with Wagner conducting) outside her bedroom door at their villa at Triebschen on Christmas morning, 1870. The title refers to their son, Siegfried, then just over one year old, and the music is based on certain themes from Wagner's opera, *Siegfried,* together with a cradle-song. Wagner intended the piece for private performance only; but in 1878, having run into financial difficulties, he arranged the work for a larger orchestra and published it to help pay off his debts.
Sight reading The skill and art of performing a piece of music seen for the first time (i.e. at 'first sight' – without having studied or practised it beforehand).
Signature See *Key signature and *Time signature.
Silence [French] A rest.
Silofono [Italian] Xylophone.
Sim. Abbreviation of **simile.*
Similar motion See *Motion.
Simile (abbrev.: **sim.**) [Italian] Same, similarly, in the same way. An indication, after some kind of instruction has been given, that the performer is to continue in exactly the same way (for example, following the same kind of phrasing, bowing, pedalling, etc.).
Simple Symphony A work for string orchestra, Opus 4, composed by Benjamin Britten in 1933–4. The music is based on a handful of tunes which he had written as a boy. The four movements are: 1 Boisterous Bourrée; 2 Playful Pizzicato; 3 Sentimental Sarabande; and 4 Frolicsome Finale.
Simple time See under *Time, and also the table of Time signatures on page 389.
Sin' See **Sino.*
Sinfonia [Italian] **1** *Symphony. **2** During the 17th and early 18th centuries, the name given to an overture 'in the Italian style' to an opera (see under *Overture) or to the instrumental introduction to a scene in an opera. **3** During the same period, the term might also be used for any instrumental piece serving as a prelude or introduction (e.g. the *Sinfonia* which opens Bach's keyboard Partita No. 2). **4** Nowadays the term is sometimes used as the performing name of an orchestra (e.g. the Sinfonia of London). [See also: *Symphonia]
Sinfonia antartica ('Antarctic Symphony') Title given by Vaughan Williams to his Symphony No. 7 (1949–52), which he based on music he had written in 1948–9 for the film 'Scott of the Antarctic'. The symphony is scored for a large orchestra (including organ, and a *wind machine) and there are wordless parts for solo soprano and women's chorus. There are five movements: Prelude, Scherzo, Landscape, Intermezzo, and Epilogue. In the score, each movement is headed with an appropriate quotation of poetry or prose.
Sinfonia concertante See *Concertante.
Sinfonia da requiem A symphony, Opus 20, composed by Benjamin Britten in 1940 in memory of his parents. The work is in three movements, each with a descriptive title taken from the *Requiem Mass: 1 *Lacrymosa*; 2 *Dies irae*; 3 *Requiem aeternam.*
Sinfonie [German] *Symphony.
Sinfonietta [Italian] **1** A short or small-scale *symphony. **2** The name sometimes given to a small orchestra (e.g. Bournemouth Sinfonietta).
Sinfonische Dichtung [German] *Symphonic poem.

Singbar; Singend [German] Both these terms are used to mean 'in a singing style'. (Same as Italian: *cantabile.*)

Single reed See *Reed.

Singspiel [German: 'song-play', 'play with singing'] A German opera (often comic) in which musical numbers are interspersed with spoken dialogue – originally imitating the English *ballad opera, but later developing independently. The finest examples are Mozart's *The *Abduction from the Seraglio* (1782) and *The *Magic Flute* (1791).

Sinistra; Sinistro [Italian] Left. **Mano sinistra**, left hand. **Colla sinistra**, with the left (hand).

Sino [Italian] Until, up to, as far as. **Sin' al fine**, up to the end; **sin' al segno**, as far as the sign, up to the sign (each of these phrases indicating the point up to which a section of a composition is to be repeated).

Si replica [Italian] To be repeated.

Sistrum A type of rattle, probably originating in ancient Egypt; often consisting of wooden or metal discs strung loosely on a frame.

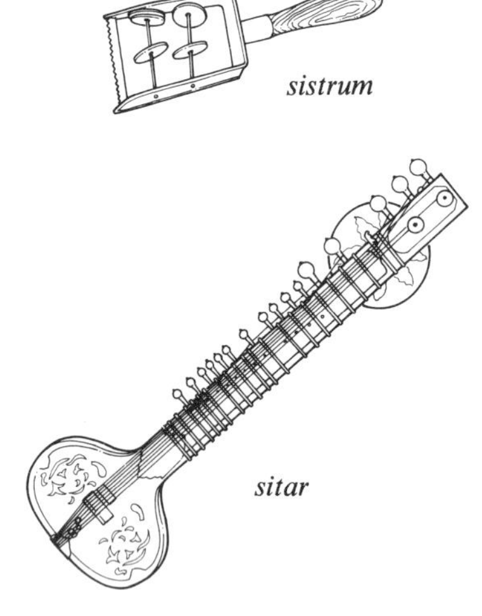

sistrum

sitar

Sitar A type of large long-necked lute – one of the most important instruments of the Indian subcontinent (especially in the north). The hollow neck is made of wood, and the body, made of half a hollow gourd, has a thin wooden belly or table. There may also be an upper gourd. The sitar has sixteen to twenty-four curved, movable frets made of metal. There are seven metal strings, plucked with a wire plectrum worn on the forefinger. Five of these strings are melody strings, and the remaining two are drone strings. Running under the main strings there is also a set of a dozen or more sympathetic strings (see *Sympathetic vibrations). Among notable players of the sitar are Ravi Shankar, Ustād Vilayat Khan and, his son, Shujaat Khan.

Six, Les [French: 'The Six'] Name given in 1920 by the music critic, Henri Collet, to a group of six composers (five male, one female) working in Paris. They were: Darius Milhaud, Francis Poulenc, Arthur Honegger, Georges Auric, Louis Durey, and Germaine Tailleferre. *Les Six* became closely associated with the writer, Jean Cocteau, who urged that 'French music should be freed from foreign, and in particular German, taints'.

Six-four chord ($^6_4$ chord) A chord which is the second inversion of a major or minor triad. It therefore consists of a bass note with a 6th and a 4th above it. [See also under *Chord; also *Six-three chord]

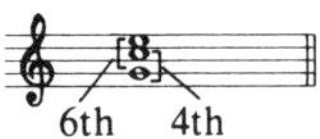

Sixteen-foot See *Foot.

Sixteenth-note *Semiquaver.
Sixth See *Intervals.
Sixth chord Same as *six-three chord.
Six-three chord ($^6_3$ chord, or sixth chord) A chord which is the first inversion of a major or minor triad. It therefore consists of a bass note with a 6th and a 3rd above it. [See also under *Chord; also *Fauxbourdon; *Six-four chord]

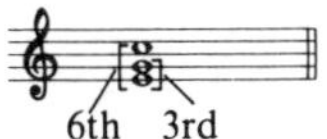

Sixth-tone A *microtone which is one third of a semitone, and one sixth of a whole tone.
Sixty-fourth-note *Hemidemisemiquaver.
Slancio [Italian] Impetus, impetuosity, dash.
Slapstick Another name for *whip.
Slavonic Dances Sixteen dances in two sets of eight (Op. 46, 1878; and Op. 72, 1886) by Dvořák. They were originally written for piano duet, but later scored for full orchestra. Dvořák used the rhythms of various Czech folk-dances; however, the melodies, though very much in the style of Czech folk-music, were all of his own invention.
Sleepers, Wake! See **Wachet auf.*
Sleeping Beauty, The (*La Belle au bois dormant*) Ballet with prologue, in three acts and four scenes, composed by Tchaikovsky, first produced in St Petersburg (now Leningrad) in 1890 (story by Petipa and Vsevolojsky, based on a fairy tale by Perrault; choreography by Petipa). The ballet was once known in Britain as 'The Sleeping Princess'. Angry at not being invited to Princess Aurora's christening, the wicked fairy Carabosse puts a curse on her. One day she will prick her finger on a spindle and die. The Lilac Fairy modifies the curse, so that Aurora will not die, but will sleep for a hundred years and be woken by the kiss of a young Prince. On Aurora's twentieth birthday an old woman gives her a spindle and some thread. She promptly pricks her finger, and as she falls asleep the old woman throws off her hood and reveals herself as the wicked Carabosse. A hundred years pass. Then, one day, Prince Désiré arrives with a hunt. When he is alone the Lilac Fairy shows him a vision of the Sleeping Beauty and leads him to her. Overcome, he kisses her, and she awakes. Amid general rejoicing, they wed. An orchestral *suite of pieces from the ballet is sometimes played at concerts, usually consisting of Introduction – Lilac Fairy; Andante – Adagio; Puss in Boots; Panorama; Valse.
Sleeping Princess, The See *The *Sleeping Beauty.*
Sleigh bells (jingles, jingle bells) A percussion instrument consisting of several small metal bells, each with a slit and each containing a metal or clay pellet. They are usually fastened to a strap or a metal frame, and may be shaken or the frame tapped with the hand or against the hand. Sleigh bells are used by Mahler at the beginning of his Fourth Symphony, by Prokofiev in the *Troika* (sleigh ride) from his suite **Lieutenant Kijé*, and by Carl Orff in the song 'Chramer, gip die varwe mir' from **Carmina burana.*

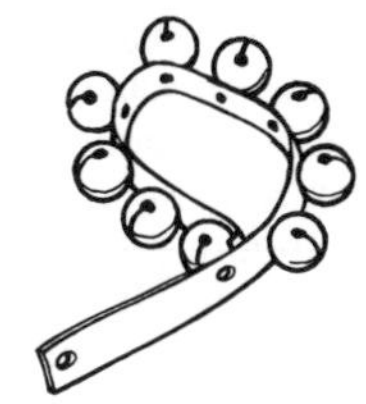
sleigh bells

Slentando [Italian] Slowing down. (Same as **rallentando*.)

Slide **1** The movable part of the tube of the trombone. **2** In violin-playing, a gliding movement of a finger along the string, passing swiftly and smoothly from one note to another. **3** A certain type of ornament (indicated in many ways) in which the main note is preceded by two grace notes, moving by step, ascending or descending. The grace notes take their value from the main note (i.e. the first is played on the beat). For example:

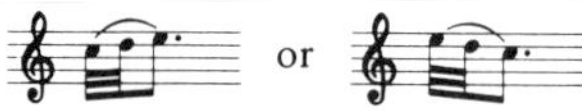

Slur A curved line drawn over or under two or more notes. It is used for several purposes. A slur may indicate: **1** a whole group of notes which make up one *phrase; **2** that all the notes it includes are to be performed *legato; **3** (in string music) that the notes are to be played with one stroke of the bow; **4** (in vocal music) that they are to be sung in one breath, or to the same syllable; **5** (in wind music) that they are to be played legato without any further attack by *tonguing.

A slur joining two notes of the same pitch is called a *tie. A slur joining notes which have staccato dots indicates that they should be performed mezzo-staccato (see under *Staccato).

Smorzando (abbrev.: **smorz.**) [Italian] Dying away (usually implying that the music becomes slower as well as softer).

Snare drum (side drum) A small, shallow, cylindrical *drum which came to the orchestra from the military parade ground (it is also called side drum, being slung to the player's side while marching). The snare drum has two drumheads, of calfskin or plastic: the upper *batter-head*, and the lower *snare-head*. The snare-head has **snares** of gut or metal stretched across it. As the batter-head is played, usually with two hard-headed sticks, the snares vibrate against the snare-head. The sound is bright and crisp, and of indefinite pitch. Occasionally, composers ask for the drum to be played with the snares lifted away from the snare-head so that only the two skins vibrate, producing a less bright, more hollow sound.

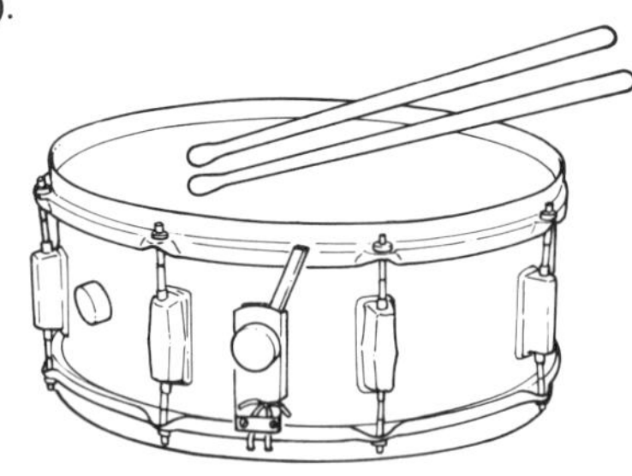

snare drum

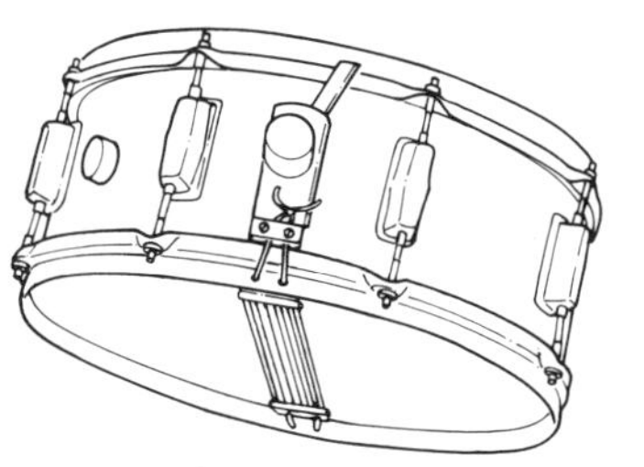

Basic snare drum strokes include the roll, flam, drag, ruff, and rim-shot. The **roll** is played by smoothly and swiftly alternating double strokes with each stick – two with the left stick, then two with the right, and so on. A **flam** consists of an accented stroke preceded by a single swift unaccented stroke. If an accented stroke is preceded by two swift unaccented strokes, it is called a **drag**; if by three, it is called a **ruff**.

flam: drag: ruff:

The **rim-shot**, which produces an explosive sound like a gun-shot, is played by sharply striking both rim and skin simultaneously with one stick; or by placing the left stick with the tip on the skin, the middle of the stick on the rim, then sharply striking the left stick with the right.

Other effects include playing 'on the rim' – using the wooden sticks on the wooden or metal rim of the drum instead of (or alternating with) playing on the skin, and also the use of wire brushes and other sticks of various types.

The snare drum is given an important part in Ravel's *Bolero* where it plays a persistent *ostinato rhythm throughout (the first snare drum is joined, at figure 16 in the score, by a second snare drum), and the instrument is particularly featured in the first movement of Nielsen's Fifth Symphony, at the climax of which the player is instructed to improvise freely 'as if at all costs to stop the progress of the music'. The tone-quality of a snare drum being played when the snares have been released (so only the skins vibrate) can be heard in the second movement, *'Giuoco delle coppie'*, from Bartók's Concerto for Orchestra.

[See also: *Coperto; *Drum kit]

Soave [Italian] Gentle, soft, suave. **Soavamente**, gently.

Sofort [German] Immediately, at once.

Soft pedal The left pedal on the *piano.

Soggetto [Italian] **1** Theme or subject. **2** A fugue subject of moderate length.

Soir, Le See *Le *Matin.*

Sol [French and Italian] The note G.

Soldier's Tale, The See *L'*Histoire du soldat.*

Solenne [Italian]; **Solennel**; **Solennelle** [French]; **Solennis**; **Solemnis**; **Sollemnis** [Latin] Solemn, grave.

Sol-fa See *Tonic sol-fa.

Soli The plural of the Italian word *solo.

Solo [Italian: 'alone'] **1** Describing a composition for a single performer (e.g. piano solo). **2** In early concertos, the term is applied to passages for the soloist, or group of soloists (**soli**), as opposed to passages marked *tutti* ('everyone'). **3** In orchestral music, marking a passage to be played by one instrument only of a type (e.g. first flute, first horn) and usually also indicating to the conductor that the part so marked should be 'brought out'.

Soloklavier [German] The solo organ. [See under *Organ]

Solo organ See under *Organ.

Sombrero de tres picos, El See *The *Three-Cornered Hat.*

Somma; Sommo [Italian] Greatest, highest, utmost.

Son [French] Sound.

Sonagli [Italian] *Sleigh bells or jingles.

Sonata [Italian: 'sounded', 'played' (plural: *sonate*); French: *sonate*; German: *Sonate*] The most important type of instrumental music from the Baroque period to the present day. The title 'sonata' has been used by composers since the end of the 16th century, and although it has changed in meaning over the years it has almost invariably been used to describe an instrumental work – either for a soloist, or a small group of players. It is most commonly used to mean a work, usually in three or four contrasting *movements, either for piano alone (piano sonata) or for piano with one other instrument (e.g. violin sonata – violin and piano; clarinet sonata – clarinet and piano; etc.), and with one or more movements structured in *sonata form.

The earliest sonatas Until the 16th century, instruments were used mainly to accompany voices. But just before 1600 – in Italy in particular – composers took a greater interest in writing pieces for instruments alone. At first they took vocal pieces as their models. An instrumental arrangement of a French *chanson* (song) was given the title *'canzona', and was built up in several sections of music, contrasted in speed, rhythm, metre, and texture. A piece for instruments in the rather more solemn style of church music was called a sonata – but at this time the title simply implied a piece to be 'played' or 'sounded' (*sonata*) rather than sung (*cantata*).

Baroque sonatas Around 1600, the word 'sonata' took on a more definite meaning. Many Baroque sonatas were for two melody instruments (often violins) with *continuo accompaniment. The continuo part consisted of a bass-line (the *basso continuo*) to be played on a low instrument such as a cello or viola da gamba. But the composer expected another continuo player, on harpsichord or organ, to fill in the harmonies by building up chords on the bass-line. Often, composers wrote figures beneath the bass-line to indicate the notes of the chords which were expected, and so such a bass-line is called a *figured bass.

Composers called these works **trio sonatas**, referring to the three parts of the musical texture which were actually printed (the two melody-parts, and the figured bass) – but in fact *four* players were needed. Sometimes one or both violins might be replaced by a woodwind instrument such as recorder, flute, or oboe.

Sonatas were also written for a single melody instrument with continuo. Although *three* players are then needed, such sonatas are often called **solo sonatas** since they feature a solo melody instrument.

Baroque composers tended to divide all these sonatas (both 'trio' and 'solo') into two main types. These were the **sonata da camera** or 'chamber sonata', intended for performance in the room of a home; and the **sonata da chiesa** or 'church sonata' (in which continuo instruments were likely to be organ, and perhaps bassoon rather than cello). Both types of sonata often had four movements, usually all in the same key, but contrasted in speed (for example, slow : fast : slow : fast). Many of the movements were in *binary form. Chamber sonatas were really *suites, and so included dances; church sonatas were more serious in mood, with the quicker movements often written in fugal style. Towards the end of the Baroque period, however, the two types of sonata – sonata da camera and sonata da chiesa – tended to merge.

Important Baroque composers of sonatas include Purcell, Corelli, François Couperin, Bach, and Handel. A rather different kind of sonata, a single-movement piece in binary form and written for solo harpsichord, is associated with Domenico Scarlatti.

The Classical Sonata From about 1760 onwards, sonata became the title a composer gave to a work in three or four movements for one or two instruments only – for example, piano; or violin and piano. (If three instruments took part he called the work a trio; if there were four he called it a quartet. But these works, too, are basically sonatas. Similarly, a *symphony is really a sonata for orchestra, and a *concerto is a sonata for one or more solo instruments with orchestra.)

Here is a plan for a sonata in four movements:

1 at a fairly fast speed; almost always structured in what is called *sonata form.
2 at a slower speed, more lyrical and song-like; designed in *binary or

*ternary form, theme and *variations, or sonata form again – perhaps *abridged sonata form.

3 a Minuet, or a brisk *Scherzo (either of these being structured in *minuet and trio form).

4 at a fast speed, often light-hearted in mood; in simple *rondo form, sonata form, a mixture of both (sonata-rondo form), or variations.

Usually, the first and last movements are in the same key (the tonic key), with the second movement in a different, though *related, key. The third movement may be in the tonic key, or in another related key. There is, however, no 'rule' for the number, or order, of the movements. Most sonatas by Haydn and Mozart have three movements only – lacking one of the inner movements on the above plan (or, in the case of Haydn, sometimes the fourth). Of Beethoven's thirty-two piano sonatas, fourteen are in three movements, eleven are in four movements, and seven have two movements only.

The Sonata since Beethoven Many 19th- and 20th-century composers have written sonatas which basically conform to the plan shown above. Others have experimented, developing or altering the basic plan to achieve a more flexible structure – perhaps having the movements merge one into another without a break, or building up the sonata in a single movement only, or making use of the *'cyclic' principle in which initial themes or ideas recur in later movements, usually modified or changed in character. A few 20th-century composers have written sonatas which return to the original meaning of the word: simply a 'sounding-piece' – a 'piece to be played' by one or more instruments.

The following list includes the more important composers of sonatas. (For dates of composers, see the time-chart on pages 398–413.)

Baroque sonatas Sonatas for instrumental ensemble by GIOVANNI GABRIELI (e.g. his **Sonata pian' e forte* for two opposing groups of instruments). Trio sonatas: PURCELL (see *'Golden' Sonata), CORELLI (24 sonate da camera, 24 sonate da chiesa), FRANÇOIS COUPERIN, BACH, and HANDEL. 'Solo' sonatas: CORELLI (12 violin sonatas, Op. 5, the last based on **Folía*), TARTINI (see 'The *Devil's Trill' Sonata), BACH, and HANDEL (15 Sonatas, Op. 1). Sonatas for unaccompanied violin by BACH. Sonatas for solo harpsichord by DOMENICO SCARLATTI.

Classical sonatas Sonatas for clavichord, harpsichord, or fortepiano by C. P. E. BACH and J. C. BACH. HAYDN: about 50 piano sonatas. MOZART: 17 piano sonatas, 5 sonatas for piano duet, Sonata in D for two pianos, 32 violin sonatas. BEETHOVEN: 32 piano sonatas (several with nicknames or titles – e.g. *'Pathétique', *'Moonlight', *'Pastoral', *'Waldstein', *'Appassionata', Les *Adieux, *'Hammerklavier'), 10 violin sonatas (including *'Spring' and *'Kreutzer'), 5 cello sonatas, Horn Sonata.

Romantic (19th century) sonatas SCHUBERT: 21 piano sonatas (several unfinished). SCHUMANN: 3 piano sonatas, 2 violin sonatas. CHOPIN: 3 piano sonatas (No. 2 in B♭ minor including, as its slow movement, the famous Funeral March). LISZT: Piano Sonata in B minor (in one lengthy movement). FRANCK: Violin Sonata in A (composed in *cyclic form). BRAHMS: 3 piano sonatas, 2 violin sonatas, 2 cello sonatas, 2 clarinet sonatas. DVOŘÁK: Violin Sonata in F, Sonatina (meaning 'short sonata') for violin and piano.

20th-century sonatas DEBUSSY: Cello Sonata, Sonata for flute, viola, and harp, Violin Sonata. RAVEL: Violin Sonata, Sonatine in F♯ minor for piano, Sonata for violin and cello. BARTÓK: Sonatina for piano, 2 violin sonatas, Sonata for two pianos and percussion, Sonata for unaccompanied violin.

STRAVINSKY: Piano Sonata, Sonata for two pianos. HINDEMITH: many sonatas – including at least one for each main orchestral instrument, each with piano. POULENC: sonatas (each with piano) for violin, cello, flute, oboe, clarinet; Sonata for piano duet, Sonata for horn, trumpet, and trombone. TIPPETT: 3 piano sonatas, Sonata for four horns. CAGE: Sonatas and Interludes for *prepared piano.

Sonata allegro Term sometimes used to mean *sonata form.

Sonata da camera [Italian] Chamber sonata. [See under *Sonata]

Sonata da chiesa [Italian] Church sonata. [See under *Sonata]

Sonata form One of the most important musical *forms or structures. The name is rather misleading. 'Sonata form' does not refer to the structure of a complete work, but to a special form or structure used to build up a single *movement of a work. Also, sonata form is used in other works besides sonatas, such as symphonies, string quartets and other chamber works. In works like these, especially those by Classical and Romantic composers, the first movement is almost always in sonata form, and sometimes one or more of the other movements as well. Overtures, too, are often structured in this form.

Sonata form grew, in several stages, from *binary form. But in outline it is *ternary, since the overall structure divides into three main sections, called **exposition, development**, and **recapitulation**. (See the diagram below.) There

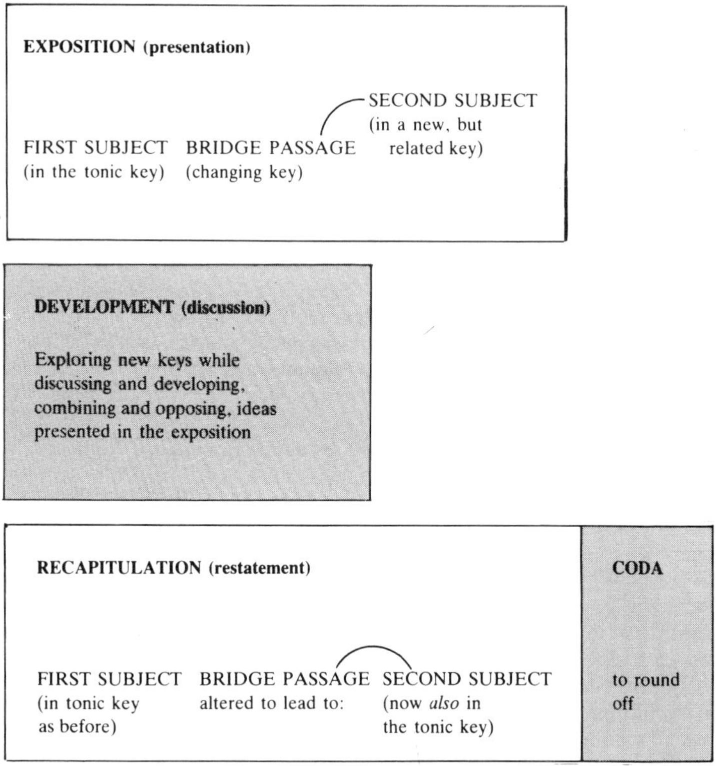

EXPOSITION (presentation)

FIRST SUBJECT (in the tonic key)
BRIDGE PASSAGE (changing key)
SECOND SUBJECT (in a new, but related key)

DEVELOPMENT (discussion)

Exploring new keys while discussing and developing, combining and opposing, ideas presented in the exposition

RECAPITULATION (restatement)

FIRST SUBJECT (in tonic key as before)
BRIDGE PASSAGE altered to lead to:
SECOND SUBJECT (now *also* in the tonic key)

CODA

to round off

may be an introduction – usually in a slow tempo – before the actual sonata form begins.

1 Exposition In this section the composer 'exposes', or presents, his musical material. The main ideas are called **subjects** (in the sense of 'subjects for later discussion'). There are two subjects – though each of these may consist of a **group** of ideas, rather than a single melody. The two subjects are contrasted in key, and usually also in mood and character.

The **first subject** (or **first subject-group**) is presented in the tonic key, and is most often vigorous and rhythmic. This is followed by the **bridge passage**, which modulates (changes key) and leads to:
The **second subject** (or **second subject-group**) in a new, but usually *related key – often the dominant if the tonic is major, or the dominant or relative major if the tonic is minor. The second subject is usually more melodious, less vigorous than the first. The final part of the second subject is called the **codetta** – a 'small coda' or closing section, rounding off the exposition. (Composers sometimes mark the end of the exposition with repeat signs, so the whole of this section may be played again.)

2 Development In this section the composer explores new keys (usually avoiding the tonic key) while discussing and developing any of the musical ideas so far presented. (Entirely new ideas, called 'episodic' material, may also be introduced.)

Any aspect of the musical material – melodic, rhythmic, or harmonic – may be brought under musical discussion or *development. Themes may be broken down into fragments, and the fragments built up in new ways, perhaps subjected to a process of organic growth so that something new unfolds from, or grows out of, something old. Fragments of different ideas may be combined, or set in opposition against each other. A strong feeling of tension and dramatic conflict may be built up, emphasized by modulations through contrasting keys, and reaching a climax when the music purposefully makes for 'home' – the tonic key – and the beginning of the recapitulation section.

3 Recapitulation The composer now 'recapitulates', or restates in a slightly different form, the music of the exposition section. The first subject returns in the tonic key, as before. However, the bridge passage is altered so that the second subject now *also* returns in the tonic key.

The sonata form is then rounded off by a **coda**. This varies in size and importance. In Haydn and Mozart it may be just a repeat of, or a modest extension of, the codetta which closed the exposition. But for Beethoven and later composers, the coda often becomes a 'summing-up' as well as a conclusion. In fact, Beethoven often continues to work out his material so that the coda becomes, in effect, a second development section of considerable weight and importance.

It is important to realize that the above description, and the diagram, give only the 'basic plan' of sonata form. It is a flexible structure, and a composer may make some kind of alteration, or add further interesting details, to achieve a desired musical effect. However, printed overleaf is a particularly clear example of a piece built up in sonata form – the first movement of Mozart's *Eine *Kleine Nachtmusik*. [See also: *Bridge passage; *Development; *Abridged sonata form]

EXPOSITION
First Subject: Part A (whole orchestra in unison)
f
(G major – the tonic key)
First Subject: Part B (1st violins above repeated-chord accompaniment)
5
tr
tr
10
First Subject: Part C
15
Bridge Passage – busily working its way towards D major
tr
tr
20
sf
p
sf
p
crescendo
f
25
Second Subject:
Part A (in D major)
3
p
30
3
(1st vlns)
(2nd vlns)
3
Second Subject: Part B
35
#tr
#tr
p
#tr
#tr
3
40
3
(Part B, repeated)
#tr
p

45
50
Second Subject: Part C
– Codetta (a miniature Coda, ending the Exposition)
55
p
DEVELOPMENT
First Subject: Part A
f (D major)
(expecting E minor . . .
60
Second Subject: Part B
. . . p but C major instead)
65
(A minor)
(expecting G minor . . .
but 'surprise' chord
of E♭ major instead)
70
Linking Passage – working
back to the tonic key of G major
75
(2nd vlns)
RECAPITULATION – in the tonic key
First Subject: Part A
f
First Subject: Part B
80
85
First Subject: Part C

90
Bridge Passage now altered
95
sf
p
cresc.
100
Second Subject: Part A – now also in the tonic key of G major
(1st vlns)
105
Second
Subject: Part B
110
f
115
(Part B, repeated)
120
Second Subject:
Part C – the original Codetta, now expanded into a full Coda
125
130
135

Sonata pian' e forte A *sonata for instrumental ensemble, composed by Giovanni Gabrieli in 1597. The music is for two *antiphonal groups of instruments (cornett + three trombones, and violin + three trombones) and is the first known piece to use contrasts of *piano* and *forte*, which Gabrieli clearly indicates in the score. Each group when sounding alone plays *piano*; but when, at various times, they join together they play *forte*.

Sonata-rondo; Sonata-rondo form See *Rondo.

Sonatina [Italian]; **Sonatine** [French] A short or small-scale *sonata.

Song A vocal composition, usually setting a poem, and most often for solo voice, with or without instrumental accompaniment; one of the very oldest types of musical composition (along with music to accompany dance), found throughout history and in all countries. There is a huge number of types and styles of song – varying, for example, from popular songs to art songs, from the simplest folk-song to the most elaborate and sophisticated *Lied.*

For details of different types of song, of various styles and periods, see: *Aria; *Ayre; *Ballad; *Ballade; *Ballata; *Ballett; *Blues; *Brindisi; *Caccia, 2; *Cantiga; *Canzonet; *Carol; *Catch; *Chanson; *Conductus; *Frottola; *Glee; *Goliard songs; *Gospel; *Lai; *Lauda; *Lied; *Madrigal; *Meistersinger; *Mélodie; *Minnesinger; *Monody; *Noël; *Partsong; *Pop music; *Reggae; *Rock; *Rondeau, 2; *Round; *Song-cycle; *Soul; *Tin Pan Alley; *Troubadours; *Trouvères; *Villancico; *Villanella; *Virelai; *Work-song.

Song-cycle A set or sequence of songs, usually setting poems by a single poet, linked together by being based on the same poetic theme, perhaps even sketching a story. Examples include: Beethoven's **An die ferne Geliebte*; Schubert's *Die *Schöne Müllerin* and **Winterreise*; Schumann's *Frauenliebe und -leben* and **Dichterliebe*; Berlioz's **Nuits d'été*; Mahler's *Das *Lied von der Erde*, **Kindertotenlieder*, and **Lieder eines fahrenden Gesellen*; Vaughan Williams's **On Wenlock Edge*; Schoenberg's **Pierrot lunaire*; and Britten's *Les *Illuminations*, **Serenade* for tenor, horn, and strings, and **Winter Words.*

Song form A term sometimes used, rather loosely, to mean *ternary form. It is unsuitable since few songs are actually in ternary form, most ternary pieces being instrumental not vocal.

Song of the Earth, The See *Das *Lied von der Erde.*

Songs without Words (*Lieder ohne Worte*) The collective name given by Mendelssohn to forty-eight of his piano pieces, composed between 1830 and 1845. They were published in eight groups of six, with the opus numbers: 19, 30, 38, 53, 62, 67, 85, and 102. Mendelssohn's title indicates that each of the pieces is written in the style of a song, with a singable melody supported by a fairly straightforward accompaniment. He gave individual titles to only five of the pieces: No. 18, *Duetto*; No. 23, *Volkslied* (Folk-song); and Nos. 6, 12, and 19 – each called *Venetian Gondola Song*. Others, however, have acquired nicknames. For example: No. 17, 'Funeral March'; No. 30, 'Spring Song'; and No. 34, 'Spinning Song' (also known as 'The Bee's Wedding').

Sonnenquartette See *'Sun' Quartets.

Sonore [French]; **Sonoro**; **Sonora** [Italian] Sonorous (i.e. with a full, richly resonant sound).

Sons bouchés [French] Stopped notes on the horn. The instruction is cancelled by the French word *ouverts*. [See *Stopping, 2]

Sons étouffés See under *Harp.

Sopra [Italian] Above, over, on. **Come sopra**, as above. **Ottava sopra**, play the note or notes one octave higher than the printed pitch. In keyboard music,

m. s. sopra (*mano sinistra sopra*) means cross the left hand over the right; **m. d. sopra** (*mano destra sopra*) means cross the right hand over the left.

Sopranino [Italian] Describing certain instruments of very high range, higher than 'soprano' (e.g. sopranino recorder, sopranino saxophone).

Soprano The highest type of female *voice. Also describing an instrument of high range (e.g. soprano saxophone).

Soprano clef See under *Clef.

Sorcerer's Apprentice, The (*L'Apprenti sorcier*) A symphonic poem by Paul Dukas, composed in 1897. Dukas based the piece, which he described as a 'Scherzo for orchestra', on a ballad called 'Der Zauberlehrling' by the German poet, Goethe. While his master is absent, the apprentice casts a spell on a broom to make it fetch water to fill a huge cauldron. Unfortunately, he is unable to stop the spell so that by the time the Sorcerer returns, the castle is flooded.

The Sorcerer's Apprentice. with Mickey Mouse in the title-role, was one of the pieces featured in Walt Disney's film *Fantasia*.

Sordino (abbrev.: **sord.**) [Italian] *Mute. **Con sordino (sordini)**, with mute (mutes). **Senza sordini**, without mutes (instruction to string or brass players to remove mutes). In piano-playing, **con sordini** ('with the mutes') means use the left pedal (the soft pedal, or *una corda* pedal). However, before the soft pedal was invented, *sordini* referred to the dampers of the piano, and so the direction **senza sordini** (as Beethoven originally marked the first movement of the *'Moonlight' Sonata) means use the right pedal (sustaining pedal) which lifts the dampers away from the strings.

Sospirando; Sospirante [Italian] Sighing; with longing.

Sostenuto [Italian] Sustained. Either in the sense of holding each note or chord for its full value and making sure they flow smoothly, or of holding back the speed slightly (as, for example, in the tempo marking *andante sostenuto*).

Sostenuto pedal See under *Piano.

Sotto [Italian] Under, below, beneath. **Sotto voce**, 'under the voice' – in an undertone, with subdued tone, or even whispered. **Ottava sotto**, play the note or notes one octave lower than the printed pitch. In keyboard music, **m. s. sotto** (*mano sinistra sotto*) means cross the left hand under the right; **m. d. sotto** (*mano destra sotto*) means cross the right hand under the left.

Soul (soul music) A style of vocal popular music which developed during the 1960s among black American musicians. Its roots lie in *gospel and *blues, and it also includes characteristics of *rhythm and blues and *rock. Soul is sung in a fervent, wailing style, the performers vividly conveying strongly-felt emotions. The music, often making use of powerfully-amplified electric guitars and keyboards, is very rhythmic and the beats are heavily accented. Leading performers of soul music include James Brown, Ray Charles, Aretha Franklin, Otis Redding.

Soundboard In instruments such as zithers, the piano and harpsichord, etc., the flat wooden board over which the strings are stretched, and which serves as a resonator, amplifying and enriching the sounds.

Soundholes The holes cut in the table of string instruments to enhance the resonance. In viols they are C-shaped; in violins, violas, cellos, and double basses they are *f*-shaped; lutes and guitars usually have a single, circular soundhole.

Soundpost In instruments such as those of the violin and viol families, a small pillar of pine-wood or spruce, fixed between the table (or belly) and the back of the instrument. Its purpose is partly to counteract the pressure of the bridge (supporting the stretched strings), also to convey the vibrations of the table to the back, thereby enriching the tone-quality. [See under *Anima]

Sound the Trumpet See **Come, ye Sons of Art, Away.*

Soupirant [French Sighing; with longing.

Sourd; Sourde [French] Muffled, or muted. **La pédale sourde**, the soft pedal on the piano.

Sourdine [French] *Mute. (Same as Italian: *sordino.*)

Sous [French] Below, under.

Sousaphone A large bass tuba invented in the 1890s for American bandmaster and composer, John Philip Sousa. The tubing twines round the player's body, and ends, above the head, in a huge bell.

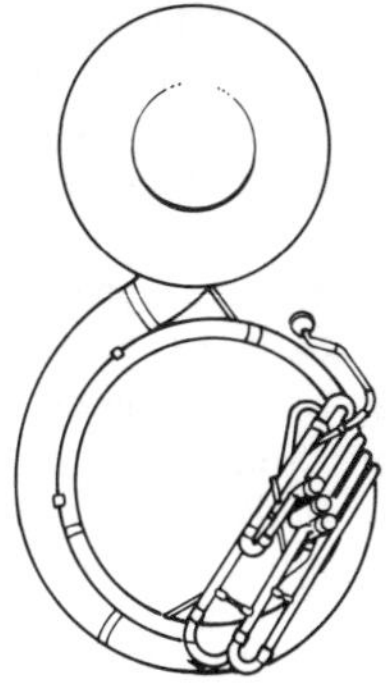

sousaphone

Soutenu [French] Sustained. (Same as Italian: **sostenuto.*)

Spacing The way the notes of a chord are arranged with respect to the intervals (spaces, distances) between them. If the upper notes are as close together as possible, as in (a) and (b) below, or the distance between the lowest and the highest notes is not greater than a 12th, it is called 'close spacing' ('close harmony', 'close position'). When the notes are more widely spread apart, as in (c) and (d), it is called 'open spacing' ('open harmony', 'open position').

(a) (b) (c) (d)

Spanish Caprice (*Capriccio espagnol*) Suite for orchestra, Opus 34, composed in 1887 by the Russian composer, Rimsky-Korsakov. The music, based on tunes and rhythms from a collection of Spanish folk-music which Rimsky-Korsakov discovered, is vividly and brilliantly orchestrated. The suite is in five movements: 1 Alborada; 2 Variations; 3 Alborada; 4 Scene and Gypsy Song (in which several of the instruments are featured in difficult *cadenzas); 5 Fandango Asturiano.

Spanish Rhapsody See **Rapsodie espagnole* (Ravel) and **Rhapsodie espagnole* (Liszt).

Speaker key See *Overblowing.

Spectre de la rose, Le See **Invitation to the Dance.*

Speech-song See *Sprechgesang.

Spianato [Italian: 'smoothed'] Smooth, flowing, even-toned.

Spiccato See *Saltando.

Spike fiddle A type of bowed string instrument with a long neck which pierces the hollow soundbox (body) of the instrument and then emerges from the lower end.

spinet

Spinet The name given in England towards the end of the 17th century to a plucked string keyboard instrument which was a simple type of harpsichord, with a single keyboard and one set of strings, one string per note. Typically, a spinet is wing-shaped, and the strings run diagonally at an angle of 45° to the keyboard. The bass strings are longer than the keyboard, giving the instrument its characteristic shape.

'Spinning Song' Nickname given to Mendelssohn's *Song without Words No. 34 in C, Op. 67 No. 4. It is also known as 'The Bee's Wedding'.

Spirito [Italian] Spirit, life, vigour. **Spiritoso**, spirited, lively.

Spirituals Religious folk-songs of the American Negro, usually to words adapted from the Bible. Some melodies are modal, others use the pentatonic scale. Harmonies are similar to those of the 19th-century hymns, and the rhythm is likely to be syncopated. Many spirituals make use of call-and-response patterns in which a solo singer is answered by a group.

Sprechgesang [German: 'speech-song'] A style of vocal performance midway between speech and song, in which the performer approximates the pitch of each note rather than pitching it precisely. It was first used in 1897 by Humperdinck in his opera *Die Königskinder*; then taken up by Schoenberg in **Gurrelieder* (completed in 1911) and **Pierrot lunaire*, and used by Berg in his two operas, **Wozzeck* and *Lulu*. The example below (the opening of Act III of *Wozzeck*) shows two bars where the singer is to use *Sprechgesang* (each note printed with pitch and time-value but with a cross on its stem) followed by two bars of normal singing.

Marie
3
Und ist kein Be-trug in sei-nem Mun-de er - fun-den wor-den . .

(gesungen)
Herr - Gott! Herr - Gott! Sieh mich nicht an!

Sprechstimme [German: 'speaking part'] The voice part in a composition employing **Sprechgesang*.

Springdans [Norwegian; German: *Springtanz*] A lively Norwegian dance with three beats to a bar – a 'leaping dance', as opposed to a *gangar* or 'walking dance'. Grieg wrote several pieces in this style, e.g. the fifth of his *Lyric Pieces* Op. 38, and the sixth of his Op. 47 set. In the final movement of his Piano Concerto in A minor, the main theme – first presented in the style of a **halling*, with two beats to a bar – is eventually transformed and presented in three beats to a bar as a *springdans*.

'Spring' Sonata (*Frühlingssonate*) Nickname of Beethoven's Sonata in F, Op. 24, for violin and piano, composed in 1801. It is in four movements: 1 *Allegro*;

2 *Adagio molto espressivo*; 3 Scherzo: *Allegro molto*; 4 Rondo: *Allegro ma non troppo*.

'Spring Song' Nickname given to Mendelssohn's *Song without Words No. 30 in A major, Op. 62 No. 6.

Spring Symphony Schumann's title for his Symphony No. 1 in B flat, Op. 38, composed in 1841.

Spring Symphony, A Choral symphony, Opus 44, composed in 1949 by Benjamin Britten, for soprano, alto, and tenor soloists, boys' choir, mixed choir, and orchestra. The music consists of settings of poems connected with Spring by English poets, including Spenser, Nashe, Milton, Herrick, Auden, Peele, Blake, and Beaumont and Fletcher. Towards the end of the finale Britten weaves in a rousing arrangement of the anonymous medieval canon **Sumer is icumen in*.

Square dance An American country dance in which all the dancers form squares, four couples to each square. A 'caller' tells the dancers what to do by calling out the steps and movements, in rhyme and in time with the music. A square dance band is likely to include fiddle (violin), piano, guitar, banjo, accordion or one or two wind instruments, and string bass (double bass).

Square piano See under *Piano.

Stabat Mater [Latin: 'The Mother was standing'] The opening words of a 13th-century sequence (see *Sequence 2), probably written by Jacopo da Todi, and telling of the grief of the Virgin Mary as she stands below the Cross during the Crucifixion. Many composers have used the text for elaborate compositions, including Palestrina, Pergolesi, Haydn, Rossini, Verdi, Dvořák, Szymanowski, and Penderecki.

Staccato [Italian] Short, detached. The performance of a note so that it lasts for only a fraction of its written value; usually indicated by a dot printed above or below the note (see Example 1). **Staccatissimo** ('very short', 'as short as possible') may be indicated by a wedge (Example 2). **Mezzo-staccato** ('half short'), indicating that notes are to be only slightly detached, is shown by a dot plus a horizontal line (Example 3a), or by dots combined with a slur (Example 3b).

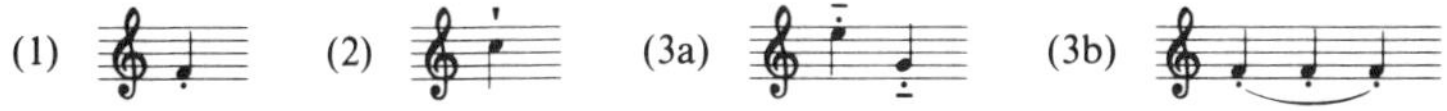

[See also: *Legato]

Staff Same as *Stave.

Ständchen [German] *Serenade.

Stantipes [Latin] *Estampie.

Stark [German] Loud, strong, robust. In brass parts in German scores, *stark anblasen* means 'blow loudly'.

Stave (staff) The five parallel horizontal lines, with the spaces between them, on which musical notes and rests are written. [See also: *Leger lines; *Clef; the *Great stave]

Steel band An ensemble of tuned percussion instruments fashioned from oil-drums, plus other percussion instruments (such as tambourines, maracas, bongos, congas). The steel band originated in Trinidad, West Indies, in the 1930s. The drums are called 'pans', and the barrel of each is cut off at a depth corresponding to the required overall pitch of the instrument. The head (top surface) of each pan has been beaten into a concave shape (a process called 'sinking'), and then marked off into sections, each of which has been hammered with a steel punch ('grooving') so that it will produce a note of specific pitch when struck, in performance, with rubber-headed sticks. Long notes are played by swift alternation of the two sticks, producing the *tremolo* effect characteristic of the sound of the steel band.

The pans (whose names vary) may be divided into three basic groups. Melodies are played on soprano pans (also called first tenors, or ping pongs). Countermelodies are played on double altos (also called double seconds, or second tenors). Harmonies and rhythms are played on single altos, cello pans, and guitar pans. Bass pans provide the bass-notes.

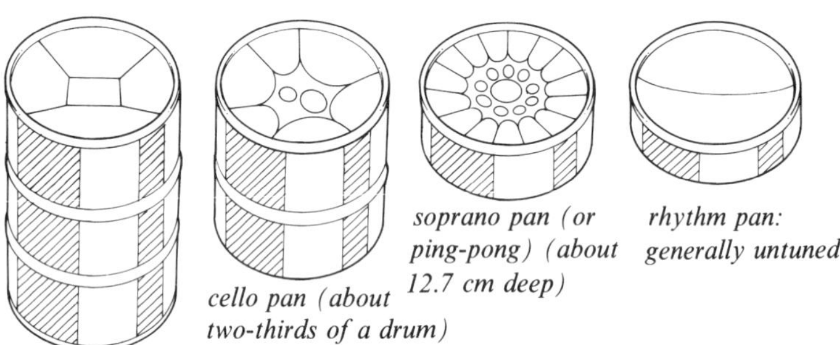

bass pan: five pitches (complete 55 gallon drum)

cello pan (about two-thirds of a drum)

soprano pan (or ping-pong) (about 12.7 cm deep)

rhythm pan: generally untuned

The pans of the steel band are classed as *idiophones, not *membranophones.

Steel guitar See *Hawaiian guitar.

Steg [German] Bridge (of string instruments such as the violin). **Am Steg**, indication to bow very close to the bridge, producing a rather eerie tone-quality, especially when combined with bowed *tremolo.

Stem See under *Note.

Stentando; Stentato, (abbrev.: **stent.**) [Italian] Delaying; holding back.

Step A melodic line moves 'by step' when each note moves to the next alphabetical note, upwards or downwards. [See: *Motion. For steps of the scale, see *Degree]

Sterbend [German] Dying away.

Stesso [Italian] Same. **Stesso tempo**, same meaning as **istesso tempo*.

Stil [German]; **Stile** [Italian] Style.

Stimme [German] Voice, or part. Also, organ stop.

Stimmung [German] **1** Mood. **2** Tuning.

Stinguendo [Italian] Dying away.

Stop On the *organ, a handstop (drawstop or knob) which, when drawn out, allows wind to be admitted to a particular register (rank or set) of pipes. The word 'stop' is also used to describe the register itself.

A *harpsichord may have similar handstops (four to six in number) which provide changes in pitch or tone-quality; later harpsichords are more likely to have pedals, which perform the same function.

[See also: *Stopping]

Stopped notes (on the horn) See *Stopping, 2.

Stopped pipe On the *organ, any pipe which has a stopper or cover at the top. A 'stopped' pipe sounds an octave lower than an open pipe of the same dimensions.

Stopping **1** On string instruments (such as the violin, guitar, lute, etc.) the pressing down of a string onto the fingerboard by a finger of the left hand, to shorten the vibrating length of the string, and so raise the pitch – the shorter the string, the higher the note. On bowed string instruments (the violin, etc.) bowing two, three, and four notes simultaneously is called **double stopping**, **triple stopping**, and **quadruple stopping** respectively, even when open strings may be involved. (In quadruple stopping, however, although the four notes may be written to be played simultaneously, the player bows the lower two strings first then quickly rocks onto the higher two, since the curve of the bridge prevents the bow from being able to touch all four strings at once.)

2 On the natural horn (valveless horn), inserting the right hand into the bell and thereby 'stopping' or closing it to a greater or lesser extent. By this means, notes could be produced extra to the open notes available from the *harmonic series, though these 'stopped' notes were noticeably different in tone-quality. Stopping is also used on the modern horn (valve horn) to produce 'muted' tone; by wedging the hand tightly inside the bell, the note is fully stopped and sounds with a metallic, rather sinister tone-quality if blown loudly, or as if coming from a distance if played softly.

Streich [German: 'stroke'] A bow-stroke. **Streicher** ('bowers'), string players. **Streichinstrumente**, bowed instruments. **Streichquartett**, *string quartet. **Streich-orchester**, string orchestra.

Strepitoso [Italian] Noisy, boisterous.

Stretto [Italian: 'squeezed together', 'drawn together'] Sometimes used in the sense of *accelerando*, and therefore to mean 'increase the speed'. However, *stretto* has a special meaning in *fugue.

Strich [German] Bow-stroke. **Mit breitem Strich**, with a broad stroke.

String bass Same as the *Double bass.

Stringendo [Italian] Pressing on; hurrying.

String instruments Broadly speaking, all types of instruments whose sounds are produced by causing stretched strings (of gut, silk, wire, or plastic) to vibrate. This may be done in one of three ways:

(1) by drawing a bow across the strings (e.g violin, viol, medieval fiddle, rebec, rabāb, sāraṅgī);

(2) by plucking the strings (e.g. harp, guitar, lute, zither, sitar, 'ūd; psaltery, cittern, harpsichord);

(3) by striking the strings (e.g. piano, dulcimer, cimbalom, clavichord).

However, the piano, harpsichord, and clavichord are classed more precisely as *keyboard instruments rather than as string instruments.

In the *orchestra, the **string section** (often called simply 'the **strings**') consists of first violins, second violins, violas, cellos, and double basses.

[See also: *String orchestra; *Violin family; *Stopping, 1]

String orchestra An orchestra consisting entirely of instruments of the string section: first violins, second violins, violas, cellos, and double bass(es).

String quartet A chamber work written for a group of four string instruments, consisting of two violins, one viola, and one cello. Also, the name given to an ensemble which performs such a composition (e.g. the Aeolian String Quartet, the Juilliard String Quartet).

Of all the various types of chamber work, the string quartet has always been the most popular, from Haydn to the present day. (Although Haydn was not the inventor of the string quartet, he is considered to be the composer most responsible for shaping, then bringing to perfection, this most important type of chamber work.) Essentially, a string quartet is a *sonata* for two violins, viola, and cello, and is usually similarly planned in four movements (see under *Chamber music). The following list includes the most notable composers of string quartets.

Classical Haydn: 68 string quartets – many of which have nicknames as well as opus numbers (see *'Sun' Quartets; *'Bird'; *'Joke'; *'Russian' Quartets; *'Frog'; *'Prussian' Quartets, 1; *'Razor'; *'Lark'; *'Tost' Quartets; *'Rider'; *'Fifths'; *'Emperor'; *'Sunrise'). Mozart: 23 string quartets (see *'Haydn' Quartets; *'Hunt'; *'Dissonance'; *'Prussian' Quartets, 2). Beethoven: 16 string quartets (see *'Razumovsky' Quartets; *'Late quartets'; also: *Grosse Fuge).

Romantic Schubert: 15 string quartets (of which the most familiar is nicknamed *'Death and the Maiden'). Mendelssohn, 7 string quartets; Schumann, 3; Brahms, 3; Smetana, 2 (See *'From my Life'); Dvořák, 14 (the most familiar being called the *'American' Quartet).

20th Century Debussy and Ravel each composed one string quartet. Bartók's 6 string quartets are rated among the finest in the repertory. Schoenberg composed a total of 5 string quartets; Hindemith, 7; and Shostakovich, 15. Included among the many other 20th-century composers who have contributed to the string quartet repertory are: Janáček, Webern, Berg (see also *Lyric Suite, 2), Britten, Tippett, Elizabeth Lutyens, Elizabeth Maconchy, Ligeti, Boulez, Penderecki.

String quintet **1** *Chamber music for five string instruments – an extra viola, or cello, or a double bass, added to the normal string quartet of two violins, viola, and cello. Examples are Mozart's String Quintet in G minor, K516, 1787 (two violins, two violas, cello), Schubert's String Quintet in C, 1828 (two violins, viola, two cellos), and Dvořák's String Quintet in G, Op. 77, 1875 (two violins, viola, cello, double bass). **2** The combination of instruments, or ensemble, which plays such a work.

Strings **1** The lengths of stretched gut, silk, wire, or plastic, which, when made to vibrate, produce the sound in all types of *string instrument. **2** The string section of the orchestra (first violins, second violins, violas, cellos, double basses) is often referred to simply as 'the strings'.

String sextet **1** *Chamber music for six string instruments – two violins, two violas, and two cellos. Examples are the two string sextets by Brahms: No. 1 in B♭ (Op. 18; 1860) and No. 2 in G (Op. 36; 1865); and the String Sextet in A (Op. 48; 1878) by Dvořák. **2** The combination of instruments, or ensemble, which plays such a work. [See also: **Verklärte Nacht*]

String trio **1** *Chamber music composed for three string instruments – usually, violin, viola, and cello. Examples include: Beethoven's three String Trios, Op. 9 (1797–8); Hindemith's String Trio No. 1 (1924) and No. 2 (1933); Schoenberg's String Trio, Op. 45 (1946). **2** The combination of instruments, or ensemble, which plays such a work.

Stromentato [Italian: 'instrumented'] Accompanied by instruments (see under *Recitative).

Stromento Older spelling of the Italian word **strumento*.

Strophic A term applied to a vocal composition in which each verse of text is set to the same music (e.g. most hymns and folk-songs). The opposite treatment – with each verse set to new music throughout – is called 'through-composed' (translation of the German term, *durchkomponiert*). In this case, there will be little or no musical repetition. The composer allows the words to determine the structure of the music, and throughout, each line of words is set to fresh music, matching the changing moods or dramatic events in the text. [See also under *Lieder]

Structure (musical structure) Referring to the way in which a composer designs, shapes, and builds up a composition, and therefore much the same in meaning as musical *form.

Strumento [Italian] Instrument. **Strumenti**, instruments. *Strumenti a corde*, string instruments; *strumenti d'arco*, bowed instruments; *strumenti a fiato* or *di vento*, wind instruments; *strumenti di legno*, woodwind instruments; *strumenti d'ottone* or *di metallo*, brass instruments; *strumenti a percossa*, percussion instruments; *strumenti da tasto*, keyboard instruments.

Stück (plural: *Stücke*) [German] Piece, or composition.

Study [French: *étude*; German: *Etüde, Studie*; Italian: *studio*] An instrumental piece intended to develop one or more aspects of a player's technical ability (e.g. octaves, scales, arpeggios, trills, wide leaps). While some studies are simply 'practice-pieces', others rate as fine pieces of music in their own right – such as those of Liszt, e.g. *La *Campanella*, *Waldesrauschen* (Woodland murmurs) and *Gnomenreigen* (Round dance of the gnomes), and, especially, those of Chopin: Twelve Studies Op. 10 (1829–32), Twelve Studies Op. 25 (1832–6), and three 'Nouvelles Études' (1839). Chopin's studies were enthusiasticially described by Schumann as: 'Every one a poem!' (Several of Chopin's studies have acquired nicknames; see: *'Black Key' Study; *'Butterfly': *'Harp'; *'Revolutionary'; *'Winter Wind'.)

Sturm und Drang [German: 'storm and stress'] A name given to a literary and artistic movement in Germany and Austria in the 1760s and 1770s which placed great emphasis on the expression of feeling. The aim was 'to stun, to overcome with emotion'. Several of Haydn's compositions composed around 1770, especially those in minor keys, reflect these ideals – for example, his Symphony No. 26 in D minor ('Lamentation'); No. 39 in G minor; 44 in E minor (*Trauersymphonie*, or *'Mourning' Symphony); 45 in F sharp minor (*'Farewell' Symphony); and 49 in F minor (*La Passione*).

Style galant See *Gallant style.

Subdominant The fourth step or degree of a major or minor scale. It is so called because it lies the same distance *below* the tonic as the dominant lies *above* the tonic (i.e. a perfect 5th in each case). [See: *Degree]

Subito [Italian] Suddenly. For example: *subito piano*, suddenly soft; and *volti subito* (abbrev.: V.S.) – a warning at the bottom of a page of music to turn over quickly.

Subject A main theme on which part or all of a composition is based, so that it serves as an important element in the structure of the music, and may be used for *development (as a 'subject for musical discussion'). [See: *Sonata form; *Fugue]

Submediant The sixth step or degree of a major or minor scale. Whereas the mediant lies a 3rd above the tonic, the submediant lies a 3rd below it. [See: *Degree]

Suite [from French, meaning 'succession', 'followed'] A collection or set of pieces, often dances, grouped together to form a complete work. Renaissance composers had sometimes linked dances in contrasting pairs – a slowish dance in duple or quadruple time followed by a livelier dance in triple time (e.g. a *basse danse followed by a *saltarello, or a dignified *pavan followed by a nimble *galliard). Baroque composers extended this idea into the suite. Many Baroque suites were for harpsichord, and by Bach's time the most common plan for a **keyboard suite** brought together four main dances from different countries:

(1) a German ***allemande**, in $\frac{4}{4}$ time, rather moderate in speed;
(2) either a French ***courante** in $\frac{3}{2}$ or $\frac{6}{4}$ time, moderately fast,
or an Italian *corrente* in $\frac{3}{4}$ or $\frac{3}{8}$ time, rather quicker;
(3) a Spanish ***sarabande**, in slow triple time;
(4) a lively ***gigue** (English 'jig'), usually in compound time.

A suite might begin with a prelude ('opening piece'); and before or after the gigue, the composer might introduce one or more optional extra dances (known as *galanterien* – 'galanteries') such as the *minuet, *bourrée, *gavotte, *passepied, *rigaudon.

All the dances in a Baroque suite were usually in the same key, and almost always in *binary form. Any of the optional dances (galanterien) might be written in pairs (e.g. Gavotte I, Gavotte II). In performance, the second dance was followed by another playing of the first (but with repeats omitted), making a composite movement in *Minuet and Trio form.

Sometimes a suite went by another name. Purcell called his keyboard suites *lessons*; Couperin used the name **ordre*. In Italy, the equivalent of the suite was the *sonata da camera* (see under *Sonata). And Bach, though he composed six 'French' Suites and six 'English' Suites, sometimes used the name **partita*.

Around 1750, as the Baroque period merged into the Classical period, the form of the suite as described above, and also the title itself, became obsolete. But the basic idea of the suite survived in multi-movement types of composition such as the *divertimento, *cassation, and *serenade. During the second half of the 19th century, the name 'suite' was used again when it became popular for a composer to collect together several of the pieces he had written as *incidental music for a play, arranging them as an orchestral suite for concert performance (e.g. Grieg's two **Peer Gynt* suites, the two suites from Bizet's music for *L'*Arlésienne*). Similarly, dances might be selected from a ballet score to form a suite for concert performance (e.g. the ballet suites from Tchaikovsky's **Swan Lake*, *The *Sleeping Beauty*, and *The *Nutcracker*). Other types of 19th- and 20th-century suite may be described as the 'programmatic' suite, consisting of a group of descriptive pieces (e.g. Holst's *The *Planets*), and the suite 'in olden style' – often based on dances of previous centuries (e.g. Grieg's **Holberg Suite*, Ravel's *Le *Tombeau de Couperin*, Warlock's **Capriol Suite*).

Suite bergamasque A suite for solo piano composed by Debussy in 1890, and revised in 1905. The four movements are: 1 *Prélude*; 2 *Menuet*; 3 *Clair de lune* (Moonlight); 4 *Passepied*. The third movement, one of Debussy's most popular compositions, is often played as a separate piece.

Suivez [French: 'follow'] A term that is used in two senses: **1** to mean 'keep with the soloist' (the same as the Italian term *colla *parte*) or **2** to mean 'go straight on without break or pause' (Italian, **attacca*).

Sul; Sull'; Sulla; Sulle All these are Italian for 'on the' or 'over the'. For example: *sul G*, on the G string of the violin; *sul ponticello*, over the bridge (bow the string(s) close to the bridge): *sul tasto* or *sulla tastiera*, over the fingerboard (bow the string(s) near, or over, the end of the fingerboard).

Sumer is icumen in ('Summer is coming in') An *infinite canon, or round, from a manuscript found at Reading Abbey, dating from around 1240. It is also known as the 'Summer canon' and as the 'Reading Rota' – *rota* being the medieval word for a 'round'. It is the earliest known music in six distinct voice-parts, the oldest surviving canon or round, and the earliest example of a *ground bass. Besides the English text (*Sumer is icumen in*) there is also a sacred Latin text, and Latin directions for performing the music. Four of the six voices sing the canon, supported by two bass voices singing the ground bass – or, as it is called in the manuscript, the *pes* (meaning 'foot').

Summer Night on the River A tone poem by Delius, composed in 1911. It is the second of his 'Two pieces for small orchestra' (its companion being **On Hearing the First Cuckoo in Spring*). The river mentioned in the title is the River Loing, which flowed past the bottom of Delius's garden at Grez-sur-Loing, just south of Paris.

'Sun' Quartets Nickname for Haydn's set of six string quartets, Opus 20, composed in 1772; so called because on the cover of the first edition the publisher imprinted his trademark consisting of a sun. These quartets, Haydn's first masterpieces in string quartet writing, are also known by the nickname the 'Great' Quartets (*Die grossen Quartette*).

'Sunrise' Quartet Nickname of Haydn's String Quartet in B flat, Op. 76 No. 4, composed in 1797; so called because of the opening rising phrases played by the first violin.

Suo [Italian] Its own; his or her own. For example, after a passage marked to be performed an octave higher or lower, *suo loco* indicates a return to 'its own place' (to the normal pitch). *A suo arbitrio* means according to his or her (the performer's) own judgement or choice.

Suono [Italian] Sound; tone.

Supertonic The second step or degree of a major or minor scale, so called because it lies one step above the tonic. [See: *Degree]

Sur [French] On.

'Surprise' cadence Another name for Interrupted cadence. [See: *Cadences]

'Surprise' Symphony Nickname of Haydn's Symphony No. 94 in G (one of his *'London' Symphonies) composed in 1791. It is called the 'Surprise' due to a joke which Haydn plays soon after the beginning of the slow second movement. The first half of the theme is played *piano*, then repeated *pianissimo* with *pizzicato* accompaniment – to be abruptly followed by a *fortissimo* chord with a stroke on a kettle drum which, Haydn said, 'would make all the ladies jump!' In Germany, this symphony is called *Symphonie mit dem Paukenschlag* (Symphony with the drum stroke). The four movements of the 'Surprise' Symphony are: 1 *Adagio cantabile* (a short slow introduction) leading to *Vivace assai* (in sonata form); 2 *Andante* (theme and variations); 3 Menuetto: *Allegro molto*; 4 Finale: *Allegro molto* (in sonata form, but with an ingredient from rondo form mixed into the development section).

Suspension The effect which occurs when a note, having formed part of the harmony above one bass-note, is repeated or held over ('suspended') above the next, creating a discord. The discordant effect is resolved as the suspension (the dissonant note) falls into place, one step lower, to make a concord. In a double suspension, two notes are held over. [See also: *Retardation]

Sussurando [Italian] Whispering.

Sustaining pedal Of the pedals on the *piano, the one on the right. [See also: *Una corda and *t.c.]

Svegliando; Svegliato [Italian: 'awakening', 'awakened'] Lively, brisk, alert.

Swan Lake (*Le Lac des cygnes*) Ballet in four acts, composed by Tchaikovsky in 1875–6 (original choreography by Reisinger, later version by Petipa and Ivanov). Von Rothbart, an evil magician, transforms Princess Odette and her companions into swans. The spell, however, allows them to regain human form for a few hours at midnight, and during one of these periods Odette meets Prince Siegfried, who falls in love with her. He vows to marry her, knowing that this will release her from the spell. But when Siegfried attends the ball at which he is to choose his future wife, Von Rothbart arrives with his daughter, Odile. By his magic, Von Rothbart has made her look exactly like Odette. (The same ballerina dances both roles.) Siegfried is deceived and becomes betrothed to Odile, but Odette appears and Siegfried realizes that he has been tricked into breaking his oath. Von Rothbart evokes a storm and the pair are drowned. (A happier version has the swans freed from the spell and restored to human form.)

A short *suite of pieces from the ballet is often played at concerts and usually consists of: 1 *Scène*; 2 *Waltz*; 3 *Dance of the little swans*; 4 *Scène: Pas de deux*; 5 **Csárdás* (Hungarian Dance); 6 *Scène*.

Swan of Tuonela, The A tone poem ('symphonic legend') composed by Sibelius in 1893, and revised in 1897 and 1900. It is the third movement of his *Lemminkäinen Suite*, but is often performed as a separate piece. It is based on a legend from the *Kalevala. Tuonela is the realm of the dead in Finnish mythology. It is surrounded by a dark river with rapid currents leading to a whirlpool. A majestic black swan glides along the river singing a melancholy song – represented in the music by a solo cor anglais.

Swell organ See under *Organ.

Swing A *jazz style, originating in the 1930s (the years 1935–45 are known as the 'swing era'), and characterized by an increase in the number and variety of instruments to form 'big bands' – for example, those of Benny Goodman, Woody Herman, Count Basie, Duke Ellington. A typical big band might include three or four trumpets, two or three trombones, clarinets and saxophones (two altos, two tenors, one baritone), and a rhythm section consisting of piano, bass, guitar, and drums. Swing was 'composed' music (though often still leaving room for some improvisation) and was carefully orchestrated, frequently making strong contrasts between brass (trumpets, trombones) and reeds (clarinets, saxophones). It was played smoothly with a subtle *rubato (or rhythmic 'swing'), yet with polished precision of ensemble. Another characteristic of the style of swing was the riff – a repeated melodic and/or harmonic phrase passed from section to section.

Syllabic A setting of words, for one or more voices, is described as *syllabic* if each syllable is given one note only.

Sylphides, Les (The sylphs) (Originally entitled *Chopiniana*) Ballet in one act, to orchestral arrangements of piano pieces by Chopin, first produced in St Petersburg (now Leningrad) in 1907 (choreography by Fokine). There is no direct story-line; a series of dances portray images in Chopin's fevered mind. The original score consisted of five pieces, orchestrated by Glazunov. A revised version, with additional pieces scored by Maurice Keller, was staged in 1908, and Diaghilev presented the ballet, in its final form, in Paris in 1909. Extra dances have been orchestrated by, among others, Tcherepnin, Liadov, Stravinsky, Roy Douglas, Gordon Jacob, and the conductor Malcolm Sargent. The music usually heard in the West consists of: Nocturne in A flat, Op. 32 No. 2; Valse in G flat, Op. 70 No.1; Mazurka in D, Op. 33 No. 2; Mazurka in C, Op. 67 No. 3; Prélude in A, Op. 28 No. 7; Valse in C sharp minor, Op. 64 No. 2; Grande Valse Brillante in E flat, Op. 18.

Sylvia, or **La Nymphe de Diane** Ballet in three acts and five scenes by Delibes, first produced in Paris in 1876 (libretto by Barbier and de Reinach after Ariosto's pastoral *Aminta*; original choreography by Mérante). Sylvia, a nymph of the goddess Diana, rejects the love of both the shepherd Amyntas, and Orion, the Hunter. Eros intervenes in support of Amyntas, and Sylvia, having first put Amyntas's love to the test, weds him with Diana's blessing. A *suite of pieces from the ballet is sometimes played at concerts, and often includes: *Prélude*; *Les Chasseresses* (The huntresses); *Intermezzo*; *Valse lente* (slow waltz); *Pizzicato*; *Marche et Cortège de Bacchus* (March and Procession of Bacchus).

Sympathetic vibrations These are vibrations set up in one resonating object caused by the vibrations of another. An example of the effect is the note sounded by a wine-glass when the same note is played or sung close by. Certain string instruments (e.g. the *viola d'amore, *sitar, *sāraṅgī) have a separate set of **sympathetic strings**. These are not played upon, but vibrate 'in sympathy' with the main strings when the notes to which they are tuned are sounded. Their purpose is to strengthen the sound of the main strings and to enhance the tone.

Symphonia [Latin, from Greek meaning 'sounding together'] **1** A title used in the late 16th and early 17th centuries for large-scale motets, usually for voices and instruments (e.g. the *Symphoniae sacrae* of Gabrieli and Schütz). **2** During the 17th century, *symphonia* was sometimes used as the title (instead of the more usual *sinfonia*) for an orchestral piece, usually serving as the introduction to an opera, a suite, or a cantata. **3** The same meaning as *symphony. **4** In Medieval times and later, the term *symphonia* was used to describe several instruments, particularly those able to play more than one note at once (e.g. the hurdy-gurdy, and all string keyboard instruments, including the virginals, harpsichord, and spinet). **5** In late Greek and medieval musical theory, *symphonia* meant consonance, or unison.

Symphonic In the style of a symphony. The word is also used to describe music written to be played by an orchestra of some size and power (see *symphony orchestra), or music in which the themes undergo fairly extensive *development.

Symphonic band (concert band) A large type of wind band which first became extremely popular in the USA. It is made up of woodwind, brass, and percussion instruments, and may be regarded as a development and extension of the military band. The actual combination of instruments in a symphonic band is variable but might, for example, include: piccolo and flutes, oboes and perhaps cor anglais, E♭ clarinet, B♭ clarinets, alto and bass clarinets, bassoons, alto, tenor, and baritone saxophones, cornets, trumpets, horns in F, tenor horns (E♭ horns), baritones, trombones, euphoniums, basses (tubas), kettle drums, and other pitched and unpitched percussion. Occasionally, some cellos and double basses are also included.

Symphonic poem [French: *poème symphonique*; German: *symphonische Dichtung, Tondichtung*; Italian: *poema sinfonico*] A symphonic poem, also called a **tone poem**, is a one-movement *programmatic piece for orchestra. The *programme* on which the music is based may be narrative – for example, a legend, an episode from history, or a story, play, or poem which has fired the composer's imagination. Or it may be pictorial, such as a painting, or a scene from nature – perhaps describing life and scenes from the composer's own country, or another country which the composer has visited.

The symphonic poem was invented during the late 1840s by Liszt. It seems likely that his idea stemmed from Beethoven's **Pastoral Symphony* and Berlioz's **Symphonie fantastique* (both programme symphonies), and from programmatic concert overtures such as Mendelssohn's *A Calm Sea and a Prosperous Voyage* and *The *Hebrides (Fingal's Cave)*.

A symphonic poem is sometimes structured in a loose kind of *sonata form; but Liszt's intention, when he introduced the idea, was that the music, rather than following any set musical form or design, should take its shape according to the pattern of ideas and events suggested by the programme – the pictorial or literary idea on which the music is based. However, Liszt often brings unity to a symphonic poem by using the device called *thematic transformation – a main theme reappears several times throughout the piece but is continually transformed, or changed, in mood and character. Liszt composed thirteen symphonic poems, including *Les *Préludes* (first performed in 1854), *Tasso* (1849) and *Mazeppa* (1851), these three being based on poems; **Orpheus* (1853–4), based on the Greek legend; *Hunnenschlacht* (1857), 'The Slaughter of the Huns', based on a painting; *Hamlet* (1858), based on Shakespeare's play; and *Hungaria* (1854) – 'Hungary'.

First to follow Liszt's example was the Czech composer, Smetana, who composed a cycle of six symphonic poems entitled **Má vlast*. Before long the idea had been enthusiastically taken up by many other composers. The idea of the symphonic poem, offering freedom of musical form and the exciting possibility of using a large orchestra as a palette from which to paint a vivid 'sound-picture', appealed particularly to Romantic composers (especially, during the 1890s, to Richard Strauss). Since about 1920, however, it has been less popular with composers.

The two terms 'symphonic poem' and 'tone poem' are generally considered to be interchangeable, though some musicians use the first to describe works which are fairly lengthy and contain *development of themes on a symphonic scale, and reserve the second for less weighty examples which aim merely to express a mood by means of orchestral 'tone-painting' – perhaps using a fairly small orchestra.

Other well-known symphonic poems or tone poems include: FRANCK: *Le *Chasseur maudit* (1882); BORODIN: **In the Steppes of Central Asia* (1880); SAINT-SAËNS: **Danse macabre* (1874); BALAKIREV: **Tamara* (1867–82), *Russia* (1884); MUSORGSKY: **Night on the Bare Mountain* (1867); TCHAIKOVSKY: **Romeo and Juliet* (1869), **Francesca da Rimini* (1876), *Hamlet* (1888); ELGAR: **Falstaff* (1913); RICHARD STRAUSS: **Don Juan* (1888–9), **Till Eulenspiegel* (1894–5), **Also sprach Zarathustra* (1895–6), **Don Quixote* (1896–7), *Ein *Heldenleben* (1897–8); DELIUS: *Paris – A Song of a Great City* (1899), *In a Summer Garden* (1908), **Summer Night on the River* (1911), **On Hearing the First Cuckoo in Spring* (1912), *A Song of Summer* (1930); DEBUSSY: **Prélude à 'L'Après-midi d'un faune'* (1894); DUKAS: *The *Sorcerer's Apprentice* (1897); SIBELIUS: **En saga* (1892), **Finlandia* (1899), *The *Swan of Tuonela* (1895), **Tapiola* (1925); RAVEL: *La *Valse* (1919–20); RESPIGHI: *The *Fountains of Rome* (1917), *The *Pines of Rome* (1924), **Roman Festivals* (1928); BAX: **Tintagel* (1917); HONEGGER: **Pacific 231* (1923); GERSHWIN: *An *American in Paris* (1928).

Symphonie [French] *Symphony. The same spelling is sometimes used in German, though the spelling *Sinfonie* is more common.

Symphonie concertante [French] The same in meaning as the Italian term *sinfonia *concertante.*

Symphonie espagnole (Spanish Symphony) A work for solo violin and orchestra (Op. 21; 1874) by the French composer, Lalo. There are five movements (though in performance, the third is often omitted): 1 *Allegro non troppo*; 2 *Scherzando*: *Allegro molto*; 3 Intermezzo: *Allegro non troppo*; 4 *Andante*; 5 Rondo: *Allegro.*

Symphonie fantastique (Fantastic Symphony) A symphony, Opus 14, subtitled 'Episode from the life of an artist', composed by Berlioz in 1830. It is an outstanding example of *programme music. At the time, Berlioz was passionately in love with an Irish actress named Harriet Smithson. Later they were to be married, but when, at first, she rejected his love, Berlioz expressed his despair in the *Symphonie fantastique*. There are five movements. Here is an outline of the programme which Berlioz attached to the music:

1 *Rêveries, passions* (Dreams, passions) A young musician with vivid imagination dreams of his beloved. In his mind she becomes a melody, an *idée fixe* (a 'fixed idea' or recurring theme) which haunts him continuously:

2 *Un bal* (At a ball) He glimpses her among the whirling dancers at a ball as a brilliant waltz is in progress.

3 *Scène aux champs* (Scene in the fields) He walks in the country. Shepherds' pipes are heard (cor anglais, oboe). He catches sight of his beloved – but she

disappears from view. When the cor anglais resumes its piping, there is no answering call from the oboe. Sunset, distant thunder ...
4 *Marche au supplice* (March to the scaffold) Insane with jealousy, he dreams he has murdered his beloved and is dragged to the scaffold. (The *idée fixe* is heard just before the end – followed by the swift descent of the guillotine.)
5 *Songe d'une nuit du Sabbat* (Dream of a witches' Sabbath) He sees himself, after death, among witches and monsters. His beloved, now transformed into an ugly old hag, dances with them and mocks at him. Funeral bells ... chants for the dead ...

Berlioz gives the five movements of his *Symphonie fantastique* a sense of unity – a feeling of 'belonging together' – by bringing in the theme which he calls the *idée fixe* at certain points during the music, each time transforming it in mood and character to match the situation. Here are two of the transformations of the theme: (a) as it appears in the second movement, and (b) as it appears in the guise of a grotesque dance during the last movement:

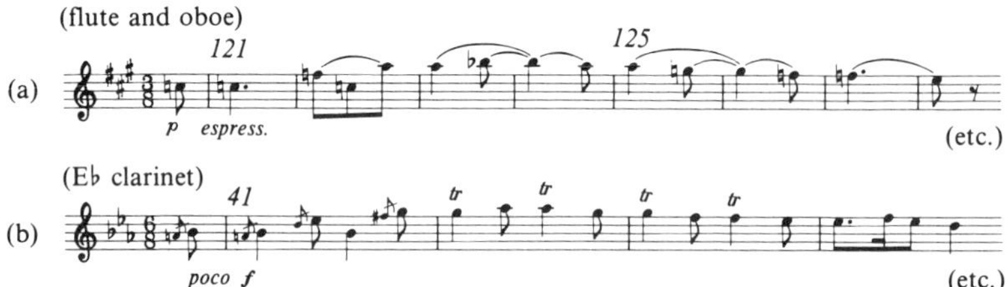

In the last movement Berlioz also brings in the plainchant **Dies irae* (Day of wrath) from the Requiem Mass. [See also: *Thematic transformation]

Symphonie mit dem Paukenschlag See *'Surprise' Symphony.

Symphonie mit dem Paukenwirbel See *'Drumroll' Symphony.

Symphonische Dichtung [German] *Symphonic poem.

Symphony [French: *simphonie, symphonie;* German: *Sinfonie, Symphonie*; Italian: *sinfonia*] The most important form of orchestral music. The word 'symphony', which comes from Greek, really means 'sounding together'. Around 1600, composers were using this word as a title for several different types of piece intended for an ensemble of instruments, with or without voices. In the 17th and early 18th centuries it was often used as a title for an instrumental piece in an opera or oratorio – especially the overture.

Around 1730, the term **symphony** began to take on a more definite meaning – describing a work that is really a 'sonata for orchestra'. Its form and style stemmed mainly from the type of operatic overture known as the 'Italian overture' or *sinfonia* (see under *overture), and the early Classical symphony was similarly structured in three movements which were contrasted in speed: quick – slow – quick. Later, the usual number became four, with a minuet and trio (a dance movement borrowed from the Baroque suite) inserted between the slow second movement and the quick finale.

Many composers helped to shape the Classical symphony, especially Sammartini, Johann Stamitz, and C. P. E. Bach and J. C. Bach (sons of J. S. Bach). But it was Haydn and Mozart who, during the last quarter of the 18th century, polished and enriched this most important musical form.

The four movements of a Classical symphony, well contrasted in speed and mood, are usually set out in the following way:

1 at a fairly brisk speed; built up in *sonata form, perhaps with a slow introduction.
2 at a slower speed, more lyrical and song-like; designed in *binary or *ternary form, theme and *variations, or sonata form again – perhaps *abridged sonata form.
3 at this point, Haydn and Mozart wrote a minuet and trio; Beethoven later transformed this into the vigorous, much brisker scherzo and trio while keeping to the same basic plan (see *minuet and trio form).
4 at a fast speed, often light-hearted in mood; in simple *rondo form, sonata form, or a mixture of both (sonata-rondo form) or theme and variations.

The first and last movements are in the same key (the tonic key). The second movement is in a different, though *related key. The third movement may be in the tonic key, or in another related key.

Besides replacing the minuet with the scherzo, Beethoven made other changes. He increased the time-scale of the symphony, and also its range of expression and dramatic impact. In movements in sonata form, he lengthened both the development section and the coda (sometimes continuing to develop ideas so that the coda amounted to a second development section). He also expanded the size of the orchestra, especially in his last symphony (No. 9, the *'Choral') which introduces solo voices and mixed chorus in the final movement.

During the 19th century, both the symphony and the orchestra which played it continued to expand. Composers followed several interesting trends. One of these was the **programme symphony**, which 'tells a story' or is in some way descriptive. The most famous example is Berlioz's **Symphonie fantastique*, in five movements with descriptive titles (like Beethoven's **Pastoral Symphony*). Berlioz brought unity to his symphony by means of the *idée fixe* – his name for the main theme which recurs at important points throughout the symphony, but each time transformed in character to match the changing situation in the story (see *Thematic transformation).

Other composers realized the need to bring unity to a lengthy symphony. Sometimes they used Berlioz's device of a recurring theme – though instead of *idée fixe* it may be called the *motto theme. (A good example is Tchaikovsky's Fifth Symphony.) A work which uses the same theme (or more than one theme) in several of its movements is described as **cyclic**, or as being in **cyclic form**. Two other well-known symphonies in cyclic form are César Franck's Symphony in D minor and Dvořák's Ninth Symphony (**From the New World*).

Not all Romantic symphonies were programmatic, however. The four symphonies of Brahms, for example, are 'absolute' music – without any programmatic or descriptive background whatsoever. But in many 19th-century symphonies, even though the composer discloses no underlying programme, the mood is often so intense that it seems the music must be based upon emotional or dramatic events which the composer has experienced.

Important symphony composers from the late 19th century onwards include Elgar, Mahler, Sibelius, Nielsen, Vaughan Williams, Stravinsky, Prokofiev, Tippett, and Shostakovich.

The following list includes some notable symphonies, from the mid 18th century to the present day. The total number of symphonies by a composer is indicated in brackets after his name. (For dates of composers, see the time-chart on pages 398–413.)

Pre-Classical G. B. SAMMARTINI [76]: Symphony No. 1 in C (1734) for strings and continuo, Symphony in A for two horns and strings (each in three movements). BOYCE: Eight Symphonies (originally composed as overtures). J. STAMITZ [about 68]: Symphony in D, Op. 3 No. 2, Symphony in E♭, *La Melodia Germanica*, Op. 11 No. 3 (each in four movements). C. P. E. BACH [20]: Symphony in C (Wq 182 No. 3). J. C. BACH [more than 50]: Symphony in D, Op. 18 No. 3, for double orchestra.

Classical HAYDN [104 with numbers, plus Symphonies 'A' and 'B']: Symphony No. 31 in D (*'Hornsignal'), No. 45 in F♯ minor (*'Farewell'), No. 82 in C (*'Bear'), No. 88 in G, No. 92 in G (*'Oxford'), No. 94 in G (*'Surprise'), No. 100 in G (*'Military'), No. 101 in D (*'Clock'), No. 103 in E♭ (*'Drum Roll'), No. 104 in D (*'London'). MOZART [more than 45, in total]: Symphony No. 29 in A, No. 34 in C, No. 35 in D (*'Haffner'), No. 36 in C (*'Linz'), No. 38 in D (*'Prague'), No. 39 in E♭, No. 40 in G minor, No. 41 in C (*'Jupiter'). BEETHOVEN [9]: Symphony No. 1 in C, No. 2 in D, No. 3 in E♭ (**Eroica*), No. 4 in B♭, No. 5 in C minor, No. 6 in F (**Pastoral*), No. 7 in A, No. 8 in F, No. 9 in D minor (*'Choral').

Romantic SCHUBERT [9, but No. 7 only sketched in score]: Symphony No. 4 in C minor (*Tragic), No. 5 in B♭, No. 8 in B minor (*'Unfinished'), No. 9 in C (*'Great'). BERLIOZ [4]: **Symphonie fantastique, *Harold in Italy, *Romeo and Juliet*. MENDELSSOHN [5]: Symphony No. 3 in A minor (**Scottish*), No. 4 in A (**Italian*). SCHUMANN [4]: Symphony No. 1 in B♭ (*'Spring'), No. 4 in D minor (a cyclic symphony). LISZT [2]: **Faust Symphony*. FRANCK [1]: Symphony in D minor (in cyclic form). BRUCKNER [9 with numbers, plus two early works]: No. 4 in E♭ ('Romantic'), No. 7 in E, No. 9 in D minor (unfinished). BRAHMS [4]: Symphony No. 1 in C minor, No. 2 in D, No. 3 in F, No. 4 in E minor. BORODIN [3, the third unfinished]: Symphony No. 2 in B minor. SAINT-SAËNS [3]: Symphony No. 3 in C minor (which includes parts for organ and piano duet). TCHAIKOVSKY [6, plus 'Manfred' Symphony]: Symphony No. 4 in F minor, No. 5 in E minor, No. 6 in B minor (**Pathétique*). DVOŘÁK [9]: Symphony No. 7 in D minor, No. 8 in G, No. 9 in E minor (**From the New World*). ELGAR [2]: Symphony No. 1 in A♭, No. 2 in E♭. MAHLER [10, the last unfinished; Nos. 2, 3, 4, and 8 include voices]: Symphony No. 1 in D, No. 2 in C minor (*'Resurrection'), No. 3 in D minor, No. 5 in C♯ minor, No. 8 in E♭ (*'Symphony of a Thousand'), No. 10 in F♯ ('performing version' created from Mahler's sketches by Deryck Cooke).

20th Century SIBELIUS [7, plus 'Kullervo' Symphony]: Symphony No. 2 in D, No. 4 in A minor, No. 5 in E♭, No. 7 in C (in one movement). NIELSEN [6]: Symphony No. 4 ('Inextinguishable'), Symphony No. 5. VAUGHAN WILLIAMS [9]: Symphony No. 1 (*A *Sea Symphony*), No. 2 (*A *London Symphony*), No. 3 (**Pastoral Symphony*), No. 5 in D, No. 7 (**Sinfonia antartica*). RACHMANINOV [3]: Symphony No. 2 in E minor. STRAVINSKY [5]: *Symphonies of Wind Instruments* (a return to the original meaning of *symphony* – merely 'sounding together'), **Symphony of Psalms*, Symphony in C, Symphony in Three Movements. WEBERN [1]: Symphony, Op. 21 (using twelve-note technique). PROKOFIEV [7]: Symphony No. 1 in D (**Classical Symphony*), No. 5 in B♭, No. 6 in E♭ minor, No. 7 in C. MESSIAEN: *Turangalîla-symphonie* (in ten movements). HINDEMITH [6]: Symphony: **Mathis der Maler*. ROY HARRIS [5]: Symphony No. 3. WALTON [2]: Symphony No. 1 in B♭ minor. TIPPETT [4]: Symphony No. 3. SHOSTAKOVICH [15]: Symphony No. 1 in F minor, No. 5 in D minor, No. 7 in C (*'Leningrad'), No. 10 in E minor, No. 15 in A. BRITTEN [5]: **Simple Symphony*, **Sinfonia da requiem*, *A *Spring Symphony*. PANUFNIK: *Sinfonia rustica*, *Sinfonia sacra*. PENDERECKI: Symphony (1973), *Christmas Symphony* (1982).

'Symphony of a Thousand' The nickname of Mahler's Symphony No. 8 in E♭, composed in 1906. Although it is usual to perform the work with fewer than 1,000 musicians, there have been occasions (including the first performance) when such a huge number has, in fact, been used. Mahler scores the work for 8 solo voices (3 sopranos, 2 altos, tenor, baritone, and bass), boys' voices, 2 choirs of mixed voices, and a very large orchestra consisting of: 4 flutes and 2 piccolos, 4 oboes and cor anglais, 3 clarinets, 2 small clarinets in E♭ and bass clarinet, 4 bassoons and double bassoon; 8 horns, 4 trumpets, 3 trombones and bass tuba, plus 4 extra trumpets and 3 extra trombones (placed apart from the orchestra); kettle drums, bass drum, cymbals, tam-tam, triangle, glockenspiel, deep bells; also celesta, piano, harmonium, organ, 2 harps, and mandolin; and a large string section.

Symphony of Psalms A work in three movements for chorus and orchestra (without violins or violas) by Stravinsky; composed in 1930, and revised in 1948. The text, which is sung in Latin, corresponds to the following Psalms in the Authorized Version: first movement, Psalm 39, verses 12–13; second movement, Psalm 40, verses 1–3; third movement, the whole of Psalm 150.

Symphony orchestra A term implying a large, full orchestra – of such size and proportions that it is capable of performing large scores, such as symphonies by 19th-century composers. [See also: *Chamber orchestra]

Syncopation A rhythmic effect in which the composer alters or displaces the expected stress of the beats, or parts of the beats in a bar. The examples below show the most common ways of creating syncopation.

(1) By placing an accent on a weak beat:

Beethoven: *Eroica Symphony*, first movement

(2) By placing a rest on a strong beat:

Brahms: Hungarian Dance No. 5

(3) By placing an accent between beats ('off the beat', or on a subdivision of the beat):

Tchaikovsky: *Dance of the Cygnets* from *Swan Lake*

(4) By tying (holding on) over a strong beat:

César Franck: Symphony in D minor, third movement

Two or more of the above may be combined.

Some 20th-century composers write music in which the metre is continually changing, perhaps from one bar to the next (see *polymetre). This may give the effect of syncopation – but it is not true syncopation since there is no continuous basic metre underlying the music. True syncopation relies upon the listener sensing a continuous basic metre (either heard, or merely felt) against which the syncopation 'argues'.

Synthesizer An assemblage of various components and electronic devices which creates sounds electronically and produces them through one or more loud-speakers. Most synthesizers are controlled from one or more piano-type keyboards. Every aspect of the sounds which are generated may be modified or changed – including attack (beginning), decay (fading/ending), duration, variations in pitch, intensity (volume), dynamics (loud/soft), and timbre (tone-colour, tone-quality). Thus synthesizers can simulate the characteristic sounds of conventional instruments, and also create entirely new sounds. The sounds may be recorded onto tape and stored, or played live during a performance. Synthesized sounds are now used in live and pre-recorded music of all kinds.

System Two or more staves linked together on the left side by a vertical line, and usually also by one or more brackets.

T Abbreviation standing for: **1** tenor; **2** trill; **3** tutti; **4** tonic; **5** toe (in pedal parts of organ music).

Tablā In the music of North India, a pair of single-headed drums, played by one person, using hands and fingers only. The smaller drum, played with the right hand, is itself called *tablā*, and is barrel-shaped and made of wood. The larger, lower-sounding drum, played with the left hand, is called *bāyā*. This is bowl-shaped and made of clay or metal (often copper). The drum-head of each drum is weighted with a circular spot of black tuning paste.

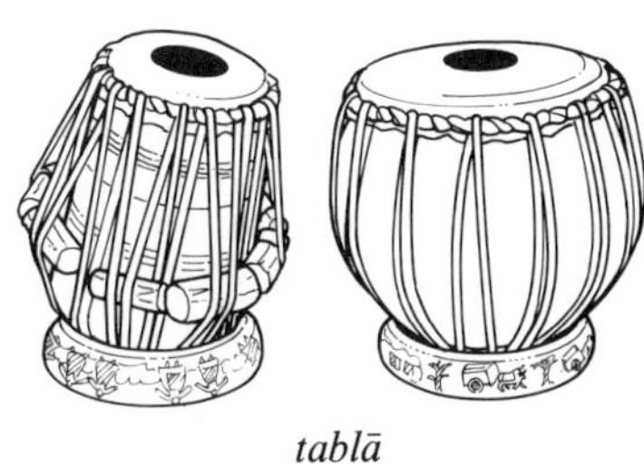

tablā

Tablature A system of notation, used especially in the 15th–17th centuries, in which music for a keyboard instrument or lute was indicated by letters, numbers or other symbols, instead of, or in addition to, conventional note symbols. In a piece for organ, for instance, the music for the right hand might be written as notes on a stave, but that for the left hand written in letters (*a–g*) below the stave. Music for lute might be indicated on a six-line 'stave', but with the lines actually representing the lute strings. Numbers written on the lines indicated the frets on which the fingers should be placed to obtain the required notes. Time-values were indicated by normal note-stems printed above:

Table The front (or top surface) of the main body or soundbox of a string instrument. Also called the **belly.**

Table music [French: *musique de table*; German: *Tafelmusik*] Music intended for performance as background entertainment during a meal or banquet. The German composer Telemann composed three collections of table music, which include both orchestral and chamber works.

Tabor A double-headed drum, dating from Medieval times, and probably originating from Provence. It was cylindrical in shape, often twice as deep as it was wide. [See: *Pipe and tabor]

Tábor See **Má vlast*.

Tace [Italian]; **Tacet** [Latin] 'Silent'. Indication in an orchestral part that the performer does not play during that particular movement or section of the music.

Tafelmusik [German] *Table music.

Tail See under *Note.

Taille [French] **1** Old French name for a middle part in the musical texture, especially tenor; for example: *taille de violons* – 'tenor violin' and therefore meaning 'viola'. **2** Term found in Baroque scores by German composers (e.g. Bach, in certain of his cantatas) referring to the tenor oboe (the part is nowadays usually played on a cor anglais).

Takt [German] **1** Beat. **2** Time (or metre), e.g. $\frac{3}{4}$ *Takt* = $\frac{3}{4}$ time. **3** A bar (or measure) of music.

Talea See under *Isorhythm.

Tales from the Vienna Woods (*Geschichte aus dem Wienerwald*) Famous concert waltz, Opus 325, by Johann Strauss the Younger; composed in 1868.

Tales of Hoffmann, The (*Les Contes d'Hoffmann*) Opera in three acts with prologue and epilogue by Offenbach, first produced in Paris in 1881 (text by Barbier and Carré after stories by E. T. A. Hoffmann). In the Prologue, Lindorf (baritone), in love with Stella, intercepts a letter from her to Hoffmann (tenor). Hoffmann, drinking in a tavern with friends, is urged to tell them of his love affairs, one of which features in each act of the opera. His first love (Act 1) is Olympia (soprano), whom he believes to be the daughter of the scientist Spalanzani (tenor). He dances with her, but Spalanzani's assistant, Coppelius (baritone), smashes her to pieces. She is only a doll. He then falls for Antonia (soprano), whose ill health makes it dangerous for her to sing. The evil Dr Miracle (baritone) causes her dead mother to speak to her from a portrait, urging her to do so. Thus Antonia dies. Finally (Act 3) Hoffmann falls in love with Giulietta (soprano), who is giving a ball in Venice. By means of a magic mirror, Dapertutto (baritone) forces her to steal Hoffmann's reflection, and in trying to recover it Hoffmann kills her lover, Schlemil (bass); but Giulietta mocks him as she passes with another man. The Epilogue reveals Lindorf as Hoffmann's evil genius and Stella (soprano) as his ideal love, but Hoffmann is drunk, and it is Lindorf who leads Stella away. The order of Acts 2 and 3 is sometimes, unjustifiably, reversed.

Tallone [Italian]; **Talon** [French] The heel (or frog or nut) of the *bow used by string players; *au talon*, 'at the heel', is a direction to use that part of the hair of the bow nearest the heel.

Tamara A symphonic poem by Balakirev, begun in 1867 and completed in 1882, based on a poem by Lermontov which tells of Tamara, a beautiful vampire queen, who lures solitary travellers to her castle beside the turbulent river Terek. Sounds of revelry are heard throughout the night, but as the silent dawn breaks, the river bears along on its foaming waters a lifeless body. At a window in the dark tower appears Tamara's shadowy figure, bidding a sighing farewell to her murdered lover.

Tambour [French] Drum. **Tambour militaire**, snare drum (side drum). **Tambour de Basque**, tambourine.

Tambourin [French] **1** The modern orchestral tambourine. **2** In earlier music, the *tabor. **3** Name of an old Provençal dance in duple time, accompanied by a repetitive rhythm on a drum. Rameau composed a *Tambourin* for harpsichord, and there are several orchestral examples in his operas and ballets.

tambourine

Tambourine (timbrel) A percussion instrument of ancient Near-Eastern origin. Essentially, it is a small single-headed frame drum, with pairs of small metal discs, called jingles, set loosely into slots around the frame. The tambourine may be played in a variety of ways. For instance, it may be shaken, so that only the jingles sound; or the drumhead tapped or struck with the fingertips, knuckles, flat of the hand, fist, or against the knee. The tambourine may be set down, drumhead uppermost, and played with drumsticks. One effect called the thumb roll (difficult to achieve) involves rubbing the moistened ball of the thumb upwards across the skin near the frame; friction makes the thumb rebound, causing both drumhead and jingles to sound. The tambourine is heard in *La *Calinda* by Delius, in the *Arab Dance* from Tchaikovsky's ballet *The Nutcracker*, and in Malcolm Arnold's English Dance No. 8.

Tambour militaire [French] Snare drum (side drum).

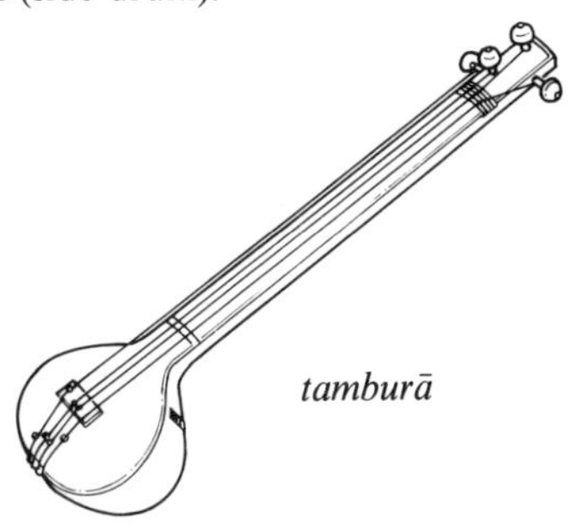
tamburā

Tamburā (tanburā, tānpura) In India, a type of long-necked lute. In Indian classical music, it supplies the accompanying drone. The tamburā has four metal strings, of which two are usually tuned to the upper tonic, one to the lower tonic, and one to the 4th, 5th, or 7th. The strings are strummed separately with the forefinger, and are always played as open strings, never stopped.

Tamburin [German]; **Tamburino** [Italian] Tambourine.

Tamburo [Italian] Drum. **Tamburo piccolo** or **tamburo militare**, snare drum (side drum); **tamburo basco** (or **tamburino**), tambourine.

Tamla See *Motown.

Tam-tam See under *Gong.

Tanburā See *Tamburā.

Tangent See under *Clavichord.

Tango A Latin-American dance, originating in Argentina in the early 19th century. It is very similar to the *habanera. A tango has two beats to a bar, and is based upon a repeated rhythmic figure such as:

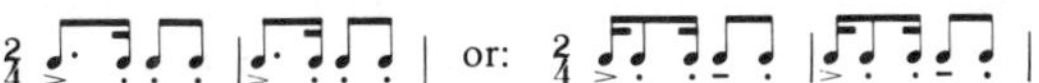

Famous tangos include *Jealousy* by Jacob Gade, *Tango in D* for piano by Albéniz, and *Blue Tango* by Leroy Anderson. Stravinsky includes a Tango in *L'*Histoire du soldat*.

Tannhäuser Opera in three acts by Wagner, first produced in Dresden in 1845, revised version in Paris in 1861 (text by the composer based on a medieval legend). Venus (soprano), the goddess of love, has lured Tannhäuser (tenor) into the Venusberg, where after a year of sensual pleasures he longs to return to his earthly life. He invokes the Blessed Virgin and is transported to a beautiful valley. Pilgrims pass him on their way to Rome, among them the Landgrave of Thuringia (bass) and Wolfram von Eschenbach (baritone). Wolfram tells him that the Landgrave's niece, Elisabeth (soprano), is pining for him on the Wartburg, and he returns there to find that a song contest has been arranged, the winner's prize being Elisabeth's hand in marriage. When his turn comes he cannot resist singing a passionate hymn to Venus. The knights rush on him with swords drawn, and it is only by Elisabeth's intervention that he is saved. The Landgrave sends him to Rome to seek the Pope's absolution, but he is told that he can never be forgiven, not until the Pope's own wooden staff sprouts leaves. Frenziedly he appeals to Venus to take him back, but Wolfram utters Elisabeth's name and the vision of Venus fades. Elisabeth, however, has died of a broken heart. Her funeral procession comes into view, and Tannhäuser, realizing whose it is, falls on her coffin and himself dies. Some pilgrims arrive, bearing the papal staff, which has miraculously broken into leaf. Tannhäuser has been absolved.

Tānpura See *Tamburā.

Tanto [Italian] As much; so much. **Non tanto**, not too much.

Tanz (plural: *Tänze*) [German] Dance.

Tap box See *Woodblocks.

Tapiola A symphonic poem, Opus 112, composed by Sibelius in 1925. In Finnish mythology, Tapio is the god of the forests.

Ṭār An Arabic frame *drum with metal jingles set into the frame, similar to the tambourine.

Tarantella A swift, light dance in very rapid $\frac{6}{8}$ time, which originally came from the town of Taranto in southern Italy – though it was once believed to be a dance performed at frantic speed by someone who had just been bitten by a tarantula spider! Famous tarantellas include that for piano solo by Chopin, and the *Tarantella* from *La *Boutique fantasque*:

Tardo [Italian] Slow. (One of the earliest tempo markings to be used in music.) **Tardamente,** slowly. **Tardando,** slowing down gradually.

Taste [German] A key on a keyboard instrument (e.g. the piano).

Tastiera [Italian] **1** A keyboard. **2** The fingerboard of a string instrument (also called *tasto*). **Sulla tastiera,** the same in meaning as *sul tasto* (see *Tasto 2).

Tasto [Italian] **1** A key on a keyboard instrument (e.g. the piano or the harpsichord). **2** The fingerboard of a bowed string instrument (also called *tastiera*). The term *sul tasto* (or *sulla tastiera*) indicates that the player should bow the string(s) near, or over, the end of the fingerboard, producing a rather flute-like tone-quality.

Tasto solo [Italian] Indication, in a basso *continuo part, that the bass-note(s) should be played alone with no harmony added.

t.c. Abbreviation, either of *tre corde* [Italian: 'three strings'], or of *tutte le corde* [Italian: 'all the strings']. Both are indications, in piano music, to release the left (soft) pedal. [See under *Piano; also *Una corda]

Tecla [Spanish] A key, or a keyboard. **Música para tecla**, music for keyboard (instruments).

TEN

Tedesca The Italian word for 'German'. Also short for *danza tedesca*, German dance. **Alla tedesca,** in the style of a German dance – in a 17th- or early 18th-century piece, referring to the earlier type of allemande (see *Allemande, 1); in a 19th-century piece, usually referring to the *Ländler or the later, waltz-like allemande (see *Allemande, 2).

Te Deum [Latin] Hymn of rejoicing sung in the Roman Catholic Church at *Matins on important feasts of a joyful character and on occasions of thanksgiving. The words begin *Te Deum laudamus, Te Deum confitemur* (We praise Thee, O God. We acknowledge Thee to be the Lord). In the Anglican service, the Te Deum is sung in English translation at Morning Prayer. Settings of the Te Deum, for voices and orchestra, have been composed by Purcell, Handel, Berlioz, Bruckner, Dvořák, Vaughan Williams, and Kodály.

Teil [German] Part, or section, of a composition.

Tema [Italian] Theme, or *subject. **Tema con variazioni**, theme with *variations.

Temperament Any system of tuning in which intervals of the scale are made slightly larger or smaller – are tempered away from – the 'pure' intervals of acoustical theory (see *just intonation). In **mean-tone temperament**, a system generally used from about 1500 to 1700 for tuning keyboard instruments, certain intervals were slightly modified. Music played in keys with not more than two sharps or flats sounded adequately in tune; beyond this range of keys, 'out-of-tuneness' became increasingly apparent. In **equal temperament**, adopted in the 18th century and still in use today, the octave is divided into twelve precisely equal semitones. According to acoustical theory, all of these are out of tune – but so slightly that the effect does not offend the ear. The great advantage of equal temperament is that it makes all keys, and also modulations between them, equally available. [See also: *The *Well-Tempered Clavier*]

Temple block See *Woodblocks.

Tempo [Italian] **1** Speed. **2** Time. **A tempo,** in time (indicating, after a change of speed such as **ritenuto*, a return to the original speed).

Tempo di [Italian] 'At the speed of'. (For example: *tempo di ballo,* at a dancing speed; *tempo di marcia*, at marching pace; *tempo di minuetto,* at the speed of a minuet.)

Tempo markings Indications given to the performer (most often in the form of Italian words or phrases) of the speed of a composition or a section of a piece, or of a change of speed during a composition. The most common terms include:

grave, very slow and solemn	**allegretto**, fairly fast
lento, slow	**allegro**, fast
largo, broad, slow	**vivace**, lively, brisk
adagio, slow, leisurely	**presto**, very fast
andante, at a walking pace	**prestissimo**, extremely fast
moderato, moderate	

For further explanation of these and of many other tempo markings (also French and German) see individual entries. See also entries for terms marking a change of tempo, such as *Accelerando; *Rallentando; *Ritardando; *Ritenuto; *A tempo. See also under *Metronome]

Temps [French] Beat.

Ten. Abbreviation of **tenuto.*

Tenebroso [Italian] Dark; sombre, gloomy.

Tenero [Italian] Tender, fond, delicate. **Teneramente**, tenderly. **Tenerezza**, tenderness, affection.

Tenor [from Latin, *tenere*, meaning 'hold'] **1** A high adult male voice, lower than countertenor, higher than baritone and bass (see *Voice; also under *Clef). **2** In four-part harmony, four-part writing – the *part immediately above the lowest part (soprano, alto, tenor, bass). **3** In early polyphonic music (12th–13th centuries) the part which held, or sustained, the notes of the plainchant *cantus firmus which provided the foundation on which the music was structured. At that time, the tenor was the lowest part (see under *Organum). **4** Old English name for viola (tenor violin).

Tenor C The note C, lying one octave below middle C, which is the lowest note on the viola – the tenor instrument of the string family.

Tenor clef See *Clef.

Tenor drum A double-headed military drum used in bands and sometimes in the orchestra, similar in shape to the snare drum but larger and deeper, and without snares. It is usually played with hard sticks, but occasionally soft-headed sticks are used. The sound is rather hollow and dull, and of indefinite pitch. Berlioz includes six tenor drums in his *Te Deum*. The tenor drum is often used (instead of snare drum) in 'Drake's Drum' from Stanford's *Songs of the Sea*. It can be heard in *The Devil's Dance* from Stravinsky's *L'*Histoire du soldat*, and rolls played on tenor drum can be heard shortly after the beginning of *Intégrales* by Varèse.

Tenore [Italian] Tenor, tenor voice.

Tenor horn A brass instrument, often referred to as the E♭ horn, which is of alto (rather than tenor) pitch. It is the modern version of the alto saxhorn, and is pitched in E♭, a 5th below the cornet. The tenor horn has three valves, and the bell points upwards. It is used in the brass band, but not in the British military band.

Tenor violin **1** The name given to various bowed string instruments whose size lay between that of the viola and the cello; they were used from around 1550, but became obsolete during the 18th century. **2** The old English name for the viola.

Tenth See under *Intervals.

Tenuto (abbrev.: **ten.**) [Italian: 'held'] A warning to a performer that the note should be held for its full time-value (and possibly for a little longer still).

Ternary form A basic musical *form or structure in which the music is built up in *three* sections, presenting 'contrast and return': **A B A**. Sections **A¹** and **A²** use the same music. Section **B** presents some kind of contrast to music **A**, and is called an *episode:

A^1	B	A^2
statement	(an episode) contrast	restatement

In many ternary pieces, A^1 ends with a perfect cadence in the tonic key, so that it sounds rather like a complete short piece in itself. **B** is usually in a new, but *related key; and A^2 is in the tonic key once more. When music **A** returns after music **B**, it may be exactly the same as when it was first heard, or the composer may provide more interest by making changes of some kind – but it will always be recognizable as a return of music **A** after the contrast of music **B**. If A^2 is an *exact* repetition of **A¹**, the composer may decide not to write out the music of **A** all over again. In this case, at the end of **B** will be printed the phrase *Da capo* (or simply *D.C.*), and the word *Fine* will be printed at the end of music **A**.

A ternary piece may begin with a short introduction, and the music may be rounded off with a *coda. A *link may be used to join one section smoothly to the next. Here is a well-known piece by Tchaikovsky designed in ternary form:

Tchaikovsky: *Dance of the Cygnets* from *Swan Lake*

Terpsichore The title of a large and important anthology of 16th-century French dances, about 500 in all, arranged for instrumental ensemble (of four to six parts) by the German composer, Michael Praetorius; published in 1612. Praetorius named the anthology after the Greek muse of dance.

'Terraced' dynamics A term describing the effect, often heard in Baroque music, of sudden changes in dynamic level (volume level) – such as *forte,* a sudden drop to *piano*, followed by an abrupt return to *forte* (i.e. without any effect of *diminuendo* or *crescendo*). The sudden changes (contrasts) of dynamic level form 'terraces' of loud and soft sound.

Terz [German]; **Terza** [Italian] Third.

Terzet [German: *Terzett*; Italian: *terzetto*] A composition (usually in an opera) in which three voices take part, with or without accompaniment. Occasionally also used as a title for a short or lightweight composition for instrumental trio (e.g. Dvořák's *Terzetto* in C major, Op. 74, for two violins and viola).

Tessitura [Italian: 'texture'] A term which may refer to (1) the natural range of any particular singer's voice, or (2) the general range of a vocal or instrumental part in a particular composition, not necessarily including any exceptionally high or low notes.

Testo [Latin: 'text'] In oratorios and settings of the *Passion, the narrative portions of the text – and so, by extension, the role of the Narrator or

Evangelist (e.g. St John, St Matthew) who relates the story, usually in *recitativo secco*. [See also: *Turba]

Tetrachord A series of four notes, adjacent to one another in the musical alphabet. The term is usually applied to the lower four, or upper four, notes of a diatonic scale.

Texture A word used by musicians, likening the way the sounds are woven together in a piece of music with the way the threads are woven in a piece of fabric. A composer may weave the 'fabric' of his music in one of three basic styles: *monophonic texture, consisting of a single melodic line with no supporting harmonies; *polyphonic (or contrapuntal) texture, in which two or more equally important melodic lines weave along at the same time; or *homophonic texture, often consisting of a melody with chordal accompaniment. The texture need not necessarily remain the same throughout a composition – for example, polyphonic and homophonic textures may alternate. And a composer may also vary texture in other ways – for example, contrasting textures which are thin and light with textures which are denser, more weighty, and perhaps richly and intricately decorated. [See also: *Heterophony; *Ingredients of music]

Thematic catalogue A catalogue, or index, listing a group of musical compositions (e.g. the complete works of a particular composer) and which, for the purpose of identification, gives the opening notes (called 'incipits'), or even every main theme, of each composition.

Thematic transformation (metamorphosis) A musical device or technique, bringing unity to a composition, whereby a main theme reappears several times but is continually transformed, or changed, in mood and character. The various transformations may include changes in rhythm, metre, speed, dynamics, melodic shape, pitch or register, harmony, tone-colour (marked changes in orchestration), and style of accompaniment. An example occurs in Berlioz's **Symphonie fantastique*, where the *idée fixe* is transformed each time it appears. Thematic transformation was more fully exploited by Liszt, for example in his Piano Concerto No. 2 in A, his **Faust Symphony* and, especially, in his symphonic poems (see *Les *Préludes*); and also by Wagner in his operas where he intensively applied the device to *leading-motives. It often plays an important part in compositions structured in *cyclic form.

Theme A main musical idea on which part or all of a composition is based – usually in the form of a well-defined melody. In discussing pieces or movements in *sonata form, the word 'theme' is often used with the same meaning as *'subject'. A theme may be a melody which is complete in itself, as in theme and *variations.

Theorbo A type of bass lute or archlute with two sets of strings – one set, rather longer than those of the ordinary lute, to be stopped with the fingers; and another, very much longer set of bass strings which were unstopped (i.e. played as open strings). The theorbo was used during the 17th century and the early part of the 18th as a solo instrument, to accompany the voice, and also as a *continuo instrument in ensemble music.

Thievish Magpie, The (*La gazza ladra*) Opera in three acts by Rossini, first produced in 1817 at La Scala, Milan (libretto by Gherardini). A servant girl, suspected of stealing a silver spoon, is sentenced to death, but her innocence is proved when the spoon is discovered in the nest of a thievish magpie. Rossini's brilliantly orchestrated overture to the opera is often performed at concerts.

Third See *Intervals.

'Third stream' music A term describing music which combines ingredients and characteristics of both jazz and 'classical' music. The term was introduced in the 1950s by the American composer, Gunther Schuller.

Thirteenth See under *Intervals.

Thirteenth chord (chord of the thirteenth) A chord consisting of root, 3rd, 5th, 7th, 9th, 11th, and 13th – making six 3rds stacked one above another. It most often occurs as a **dominant thirteenth** (being then built upon the *dominant of the scale).

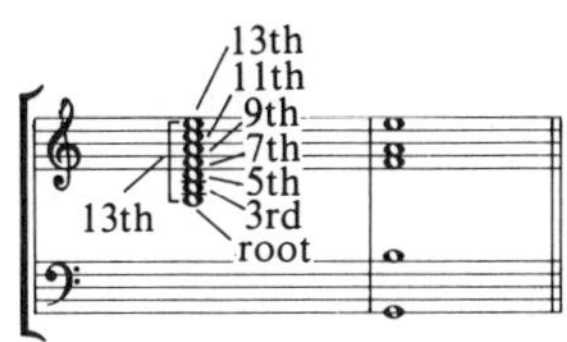

Thirty-second-note *Demisemiquaver.

Thirty-two foot See *Foot.

Thorough bass (through bass) An English term, now virtually obsolete, meaning the same as *basso *continuo*.

Three-Cornered Hat, The (*El sombrero de tres picos*) Ballet in one act composed by Manuel de Falla, first produced in London in 1919 (scenario by Martinez Sierra based on a story by Pedro de Alarcon; choreography by Massine). In a village in Spain a miller and his wife live happily together. Suddenly the provincial governor arrives – the Corregidor, whose symbol of office is his three-cornered hat. He woos the miller's wife, and when he is repulsed he has the miller gaoled and continues to pursue her, but she pushes him into a river. Unable to dry his clothes he borrows a nightshirt from the miller's house, and is promptly arrested by his own soldiers, who take him to be the miller escaped from gaol. The miller himself (who *has* in fact escaped) comes upon the Corregidor dressed in his nightshirt and, suspecting the worst, threatens him. But all ends happily, with the villagers driving the Corregidor away. An orchestral *suite from the ballet exists, and individual items, such as *The Miller's Dance*, are sometimes played.

Threepenny Opera, The (*Die Dreigroschenoper*) Opera in a prologue and eight scenes by Weill, first produced in Berlin in 1928 (text by Brecht, based on a German translation of *The *Beggar's Opera*). The story is similar to the 18th-century original, but is set in Soho in the early 20th century. Macheath becomes Mack the Knife, and there is a Chief of Police called 'Tiger' Brown. The satire is such that Macheath is eventually pardoned because his execution would spoil the Coronation festivities. The music is heavily influenced by jazz.

Three Places in New England An orchestral work in three movements composed between 1908 and 1914 by Charles Ives; also known as 'First Orchestral Set' (*A New England Symphony*). The three movements, corresponding to the title, are: 1 The 'Saint-Gaudens' in Boston Common: Colonel Shaw and his Colored Regiment; 2 Putnam's Camp, Redding, Connecticut; 3 The Housatonic at Stockbridge. (The 'Saint-Gaudens' is a monument; the Housatonic is a river running through Massachusetts and Connecticut.) The music is often discordant and at times Ives makes use of *polytonal and *polyrhythmic effects, resulting in a dense and complex musical texture. Ives also brings in several American patriotic tunes, including Civil War songs and march tunes.

Through-composed See under *Strophic.

Thunder Devices occasionally used in certain compositions to imitate the sound of thunder include: the **thunder sheet**, a large sheet of flexible metal, suspended, and struck with one or two padded drumsticks; and the **thunder machine**, a large rotating drum containing hard balls which strike against the drum-skin (used by Richard Strauss in his *Alpine Symphony*).

Thus spake Zarathustra See **Also sprach Zarathustra*.

Tie (bind) A curved line joining together two notes of the same pitch. The result is a single sustained sound, lasting for the value of both notes added together. Some examples (assuming the crotchet is the beat):

𝅝‿𝅗𝅥 $(= 4 + 2 = 6)$ 𝅗𝅥‿𝅘𝅥 $(= 2 + 1 = 3)$ 𝅘𝅥‿𝅘𝅥𝅮 $(= 1 + \frac{1}{2} = 1\frac{1}{2})$

Tief; **Tiefe** [German] Low, deep.

Tierce de Picardie [French] In some pieces in a minor key, the final tonic chord is a major chord, rather than the expected minor. The effect is known as a *tierce de Picardie*, or 'Picardy third' – referring to the unexpected major 3rd in the final chord. The origin of the term is unknown.

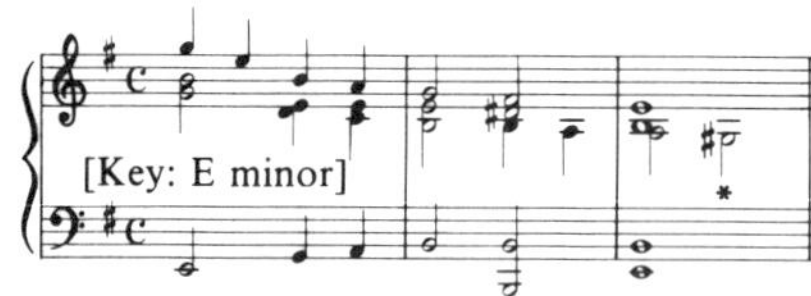

Till Eulenspiegel *Symphonic poem, Opus 28, by Richard Strauss, composed in 1895. The full title is *Till Eulenspiegels lustige Streiche* ('Till Eulenspiegel's merry pranks'), and the music is based on a German folk-tale telling of the adventures of a medieval rogue who gained a wide reputation for playing practical jokes. In German, *Eulenspiegel* means 'owl-glass', and the verb *eulenspiegeln* was coined from Till's name to mean 'to make a fool of someone'. Strauss's symphonic poem depicts several of Till's pranks and escapades, which eventually lead to his arrest and sentence to death by hanging.

Timbales [French] Kettle drums.

Timbre (tone-colour) The characteristic tone or sound-quality of an instrument or a voice. Timbre enables the ear to distinguish the difference between, say, a clarinet, a horn, and a violin – even if all three play exactly the same note. The characteristic timbre of an instrument is the result of several factors, including the materials from which it is made, the method by which it produces its sounds (strings, a reed, etc.), and the way in which these sounds are made to resonate (e.g. the hollow wooden body of the violin). The most important factor, however, is to do with *harmonics*, or *overtones* (see *harmonic series). Some instruments produce more harmonics than others; different instruments emphasize different harmonics. And it is the relative strengths of the harmonics, and the way they mix together, which mainly determine the distinctive timbre of an instrument and also the brilliance (or lack of brilliance) of its sound. [See also: *Ingredients of music; *Orchestral devices]

Timbrel Old English name for *Tambourine.

Time (metre) The number of beats to a bar in a piece of music (or a section of a piece) and their value. This is indicated by bar-lines drawn down through the stave and also, at the beginning, by a *time signature. The time or metre of the music may be **duple**, two beats to each bar; **triple**, three beats to each bar; or **quadruple**, four beats to each bar. The first beat of each bar carries the strongest accent. In quadruple time there are two accented beats – a strong accent on the first beat, and a lesser (secondary) accent on the third beat. Music may be written in more than four beats to a bar, in which case each bar is really made up of some combination of two and three. For example, **quintuple time** (five beats to each bar) may be counted as two plus three, or as three plus two – according to where the secondary accent falls in each bar.

Time may be 'simple' or 'compound'. In **simple time**, each beat is a simple, plain note (that is, not a dotted note) which is divisible into halves. For example, in three-four time (simple triple time) there are three crotchet beats to each bar, and each beat may be divided into two quavers:

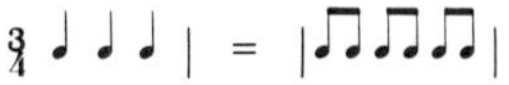

$\frac{3}{4}$ ♩ ♩ ♩ | = | ♫ ♫ ♫ |

In **compound time**, each beat is a dotted note which can be divided into thirds. For example, in six-eight time (compound duple time) there are two dotted crotchet beats to each bar, and each beat may be divided into three quavers:

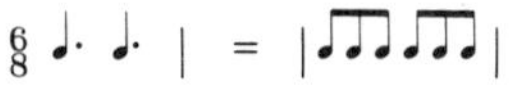

$\frac{6}{8}$ ♩. ♩. | = | ♪♪♪ ♪♪♪ |

[See also the entry for *Time signature, below; and the table of Time signatures on page 389]

Time signature A sign, often consisting of two figures written one above the other, placed after the clef and the key signature at the beginning of a composition, and perhaps also during the course of it. This 'signifies' the *time or metre of the music. The bottom figure indicates what kind of note-value the composer has chosen as a basic unit of measurement by showing it as a fraction of a semibreve: 2 = minim or half-note (half a semibreve), 4 = crotchet or quarter-note (quarter of a semibreve), 8 = quaver or eighth-note (eighth of a semibreve). The top figure indicates the number of units to a bar. So a time signature of $\frac{4}{4}$ indicates four crotchets (quarter-notes) to a bar; $\frac{3}{2}$, three minims (half-notes) to a bar; $\frac{6}{8}$, six quavers to a bar.

Composers sometimes write 𝄴 instead of $\frac{4}{4}$ (often called 'common time') and 𝄵 instead of $\frac{2}{2}$ (also called *alla breve*). 𝄴 is not in fact a capital standing for 'common'. In Medieval times, triple time was shown by O, a circle symbolizing perfection, and duple or quadruple time by C, a broken, or imperfect, circle.

[See also the table of Time signatures on page 389]

Timoroso [Italian] Timid, fearful.

Timpani [Italian] Kettle drums.

Tin Pan Alley The once-popular term used to describe the American pop music industry. The term originated at the beginning of the 20th century, when most of the important publishers of popular songs had offices on 28th Street, between 5th Avenue and Broadway, in New York. This street became known as Tin Pan Alley, and the term eventually became applied to the industry itself and the vast amount of popular music it churned out.

Tintagel A symphonic poem composed by Arnold Bax in 1917. The music gives an impression of the sea, the cliffs, and the ruined medieval castle at Tintagel in Cornwall 'on a sunny but not windless summer day'. Bax also said that he intended his music to evoke legends associated with Tintagel, including those of King Arthur and Tristram and Iseult.

Tirasse [French] A coupler on the *organ, especially a pedal coupler.

Toccata This word comes from the Italian *toccare*, 'to touch' (that is, to touch the keys of an instrument such as an organ, harpsichord, or piano). A piece given this title often challenges the performer's technique by including showy passages which feature arpeggios, rapid runs, swiftly repeated chords, and so on. A toccata may be in several linked sections, contrasting chordal passages with running ones and others in fugal style; or it may be in the same style throughout. The toccata originated in the 16th century, during the Renaissance period. It was retained and developed by Baroque composers. Sometimes a toccata serves as an introduction to a fugue proper – as in Bach's well-known Toccata and Fugue in D minor (BWV565) for organ.

Toccatina [Italian] A short, or small-scale *toccata.

Tod und das Mädchen, Der See **Death and the Maiden.*

Tombeau [French: 'tomb', 'tombstone'] An instrumental piece, or set of pieces, composed in memory of a deceased person.

Tombeau de Couperin, Le A suite of six piano pieces by Ravel, composed between 1914 and 1917 in homage to the French *claveciniste, François Couperin (1668–1733). The six titles are: 1 *Prélude*; 2 *Fugue*; 3 **Forlane*; 4 *Rigaudon*; 5 *Menuet*; 6 *Toccata.* In 1919, Ravel chose four of the pieces and arranged them for orchestra, now placing them in the order: *Prélude*, *Forlane*, *Menuet*, *Rigaudon.*

Tom-toms A general name applied to certain types of African, American-Indian, and Eastern drums. The tom-toms used in jazz and dance bands and pop and rock groups, in sets of two or more, are usually played with snare drum sticks. They may be single-headed (and open-ended) or double-headed, and each tom-tom may be tuned to produce a highish note of definite pitch. Other, more recent types include rock-toms, roto-toms, and timp-toms.

Ton **1** [French] A term used with several meanings, including: (a) pitch; (b) key; (c) note; (d) sound; (e) tone (e.g. *ton doux*, sweet tone); (f) the interval of a whole tone.

2 [German] Also with several meanings, including: (a) pitch; (b) key; (c) mode (major or minor); (d) note; (e) sound; (f) tone (tone-quality); (g) timbre (tone-colour); (h) music (e.g. *Tonkunst*, the art and knowledge of music).

Tonal answer See under *Fugue.

Tonality In a strict sense, the 'tonality' of a piece is its *key. However, the word is often used in a more general sense – for example, to signify the major-minor key system as a whole, or simply as a word meaning the opposite of *atonality (absence of tonality).

Tonal sequence See under *Sequence

Tondichtung [German] Tone poem. [See: *Symphonic poem]

Tone **1** An *interval of two semitones (also called a whole tone, or a major 2nd). For example: C to D, D to E, or E to F♯. **2** The particular quality of a musical sound (rich tone, harsh tone, etc.) [For the American use of the word 'tone', see under *Note]

Tone-cluster See *Note-cluster.

Tone-colour The same as *Timbre.

Tone poem See *Symphonic poem.

Tone row Same as Note row. [See under *Twelve-note technique]

Tonfarbe [German] Timbre, tone-colour.

Tonguing In playing wind instruments, giving attack or articulation to the beginning of a note by a movement of the tongue – as if pronouncing the letter 't'. In *legato* playing, only the first note of a phrase is tongued; in *staccato*, each note is tongued separately. **Double tonguing** may be called for ('t-k'); also **triple tonguing** ('t-k-t' or 't-t-k'). [See also: *Flutter-tonguing]

Tonic The first (lowest) and main note of a major or minor scale (see *degree). Also, the main note, or key-note, of the key which takes its name from that scale. And so the tonic of C major or C minor is C. The chord built upon the tonic is called the **tonic chord** or **tonic triad** (in C major: C E G; in C minor: C E♭ G). The main key of a composition – the key in which it begins and ends – is called the **tonic key**. [See also: *Key 1; *Related keys]

Tonic sol-fa A method of notating music, devised in the mid 19th century in England by John Curwen, and intended as an aid to sight-singing in schools and choral societies. The eight degrees (steps) of the major scale are called by the syllables *doh, ray, me, fah, soh, lah, te, doh'*. For example, C major:

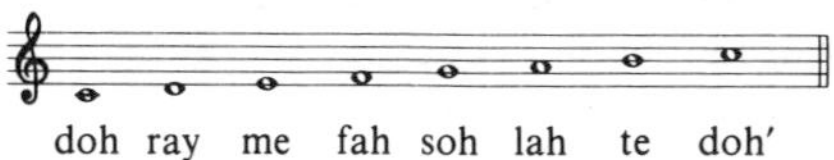

Accidentals are shown by a change of vowel sound: if a note is sharpened, the vowel sound changes to 'ee'; if a note is flattened, the vowel sound changes to 'aw'.

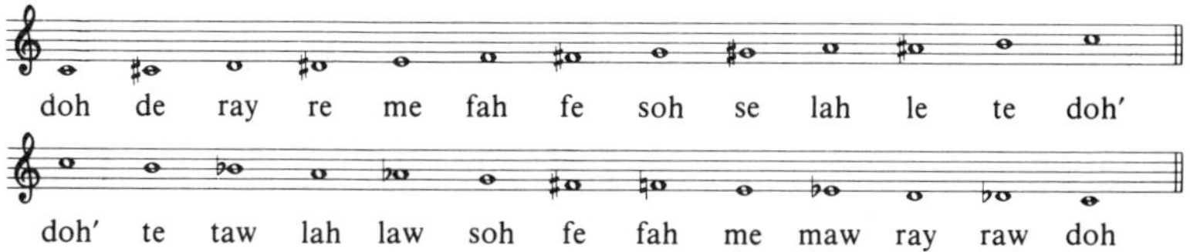

In the 'movable doh' system, when the music goes into a new key for a fair length of time, the new tonic (key-note) becomes *doh*. For example, if the music begins in C major (C = *doh*) and then modulates to G major, G then becomes *doh*, A becomes *ray*, and so on.

Any minor key is thought of in relation to its relative major (see *relative keys). And so in any minor key, the first note of the scale (the tonic, or key-note) is *lah*, the second is *te*, the third *doh*, and so on. When the sixth degree is sharpened, it is called *ba*. For instance, A minor (the relative minor of C major):

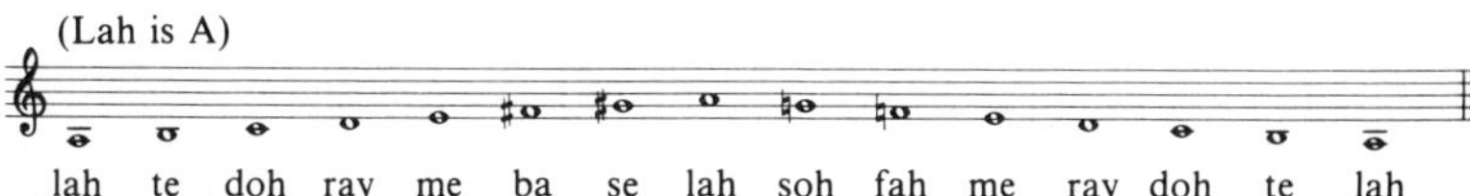

The tonic sol-fa system has been refined and altered in various details since Curwen first introduced it.

Tono [Italian] **1** Tone. **2** Key, or *mode.

Tonreihe [German] Note row or tone row. [See: *Twelve-note technique]

Tonstück (plural: *Tonstücke*) [German] A piece of music.

Tordion (tourdion) A lively 16th-century French dance often performed, as a contrast, after a **basse danse*. A well-known example occurs in Warlock's **Capriol Suite*:

Tosca Opera in three acts by Puccini, first produced in Rome in 1900 (libretto by Giacosa and Illica after a drama by Sardou). Angelotti (bass), an escaped political prisoner, stumbles into a church and finds a hiding-place prepared for him by his sister, the Marchesa Attavanti. He is protected by the artist Cavaradossi (tenor), who is working on a painting of the Madonna, and who, having seen the Marchesa at prayer, has made her his model. Floria Tosca (soprano), an opera singer and Cavaradossi's beloved, sees the face of the Marchesa on the canvas and is jealous. But Tosca is also loved by Scarpia (baritone), the dreaded police chief, who suspects Cavaradossi of helping the fugitive and has him arrested and tortured. Unable to bear his screams, Tosca reveals Angelotti's hiding-place, to the horror of Cavaradossi himself who has undergone so much to guard the secret. Scarpia persuades Tosca that, if she will be his mistress, he will arrange a mock execution for Cavaradossi. Reluctantly she agrees, but seeing Scarpia's knife on the table, she stabs him with it and he dies. Going to Cavaradossi, she tells him of the mock execution. But Scarpia has tricked her. As the shots ring out Cavaradossi falls dead. Meanwhile Scarpia's body has been discovered. As the soldiers arrive to arrest Tosca she throws herself over the battlements and plunges to her death.

Tosto [Italian] Quickly, rapidly; at once. **Che tosto**, as soon as. **Più tosto**, quicker. [See also: *Piuttosto]

'Tost' Quartets Twelve string quartets by Haydn: Op. 54 Nos. 1–3, Op. 55 Nos. 1–3, and Op. 64 Nos. 1–6. They were composed during the years 1788–90, and all dedicated to Johann Tost, a wealthy Viennese businessman who was also an excellent violinist. Two of the 'Tost' Quartets have individual nicknames; see *'Razor' Quartet, and *'Lark' Quartet.

Total serialism See under *Twelve-note technique.

Touche [French] **1** A key on a keyboard (e.g. on the piano). **2** The fingerboard of a string instrument (e.g. the violin). **Sur la touche**, indication to a string player to bow the string(s) near, or over, the end of the fingerboard, producing a rather flute-like tone-quality.

Toujours [French] Always; still; ever.

Tous; **Tout**; **Toute**; **Toutes** [French] All.

Toye Title sometimes given to a short, light-hearted piece by an Elizabethan composer (e.g. *His Toye* by Giles Farnaby, and *The Duchesse of Brunswick's Toye* by John Bull).

Toy Symphony A light-hearted symphony once credited to Haydn, but now thought to have been composed either by his brother, Michael, or by Mozart's father, Leopold. The orchestra includes 'toy' instruments such as toy trumpet and drum, rattle, and triangle; and instruments providing bird-sounds: cuckoo, quail, and nightingale.

tr Abbreviation of 'trill'. [See: *Ornaments]

Traditional jazz (trad jazz) A term introduced in the late 1930s and applied to the style of New Orleans jazz of the 1920s, to distinguish it from the *swing style of the 1930s. However, it may also be used with two other meanings: to refer to (1) the music, from 1940 onwards, of older jazzmen playing in the New Orleans style, or (2) the music of white musicians, from 1940 onwards, deliberately imitating that style (e.g. Chris Barber).

Traduction [French]; **Traduzione** [Italian] Arrangement.

Tragic Overture Concert overture, Opus 81, composed by Brahms in 1880.

Tragic Symphony Schubert's title for his Symphony No. 4 in C minor (D417) which he composed in 1816.

Tranquille [French]; **Tranquillo** [Italian] Tranquil, calm, still.
Transcription See *Arrangement.
Transformation of themes See *Thematic transformation.
Transition **1** An abrupt *modulation. **2** Another name for the *bridge passage in a piece designed in *sonata form.
Transposing instruments Instruments whose notes are *written* at a different pitch than they actually *sound* when they are played. These include, among orchestral instruments, the piccolo, double bass, double bassoon, clarinet, saxophone, cor anglais, trumpet, cornet, and horn (but trombone and tuba are non-transposing). In a brass band, all the instruments except bass trombone are treated as transposing instruments.

There is always a good reason for the transposition – though in some cases this may have had more point in the past than in the present. Usually, the purpose is to make things more straightforward for the player. For example: music for piccolo is written one octave lower than it actually sounds, music for double bass and double bassoon is written one octave higher – in each case avoiding a great many leger lines above or below the stave. Clarinets were originally made in three sizes, built 'in C', 'in B♭', and 'in A' (the clarinet in C later becoming obsolete). For the player's convenience, the music was written out in such a way that, whichever clarinet was used, the fingering was precisely the same. However, this meant that whereas notes for clarinet in C actually sounded as written, notes for clarinets in B♭ and A needed to be written higher in order to sound at the required pitch. A clarinet in B♭ (and similarly, a trumpet in B♭) *sounds* the note B♭ when C is *written*. To sound the note C, D must be written; and so on. Music for any instrument 'in B♭', therefore, is written one tone higher than it actually sounds (or, conversely, sounds a tone lower than written). A clarinet in A sounds the note A when C is written – and so the music is written a minor 3rd higher than it actually sounds (and therefore sounds a minor 3rd lower than written). The choice of which clarinet, B♭ or A, should be used in the performance of a piece is decided by the composer – according to which of the two would have fewest flats or sharps when the music is written out.

The idea of treating horns and trumpets as transposing instruments dates from the time when these instruments were 'natural' (i.e. valveless). Each player then needed a set of *crooks, any one of which could be fixed into the instrument temporarily to alter the overall length of tube and therefore provide a new set of notes. Composers would write horn and trumpet parts in the key of C, saying which crook was to be used, and the sounds then automatically came out in the correct key. For instance, horn 'in E♭' indicated that the E♭ crook was to be inserted; written C then sounded as E♭ a major 6th lower, D sounded as F, and so on. After the invention of valves (around 1820) it became most usual to write horn parts for horn 'in F' (written C sounding as F, a 5th lower) and trumpet parts for trumpet 'in B♭'. Even today, horn parts are still written without key signature and with all accidentals written in as they occur in the music.

[See also Table 14, page 395, which includes most transposing instruments]
Transposition The writing out, or the performance, of a piece of music at a different pitch from its original pitch. Unless the difference is that of an octave, the music will be transposed into a different key. A pianist, for instance, may transpose the accompaniment of a song into a higher or lower key at the request of a singer. [See also: *Transposing instruments]

Transverse flute An older name for the instrument now known simply as 'the flute', held sideways and horizontally – to distinguish it from the end-blown recorder, held vertically.

Trauer [German] Grief, mourning, sorrow. **Trauermarsch**, funeral march. **Trauermusik**, funeral music.

Trauersymphonie See *'Mourning' Symphony.

Traum [German] Dream. **Träumend**, dreaming. **Träumerei**, dreaming or reverie. **Träumerisch**, dreamy, dreaming.

Traurig [German] Sad, mournful, sorrowful.

Traversa; **Traverso** [Italian]; **Traversière** [French] Older names for the flute (the 'transverse flute', held sideways and horizontally) in order to distinguish it from the end-blown recorder, held vertically. [See also: *Flauto and *Flûte]

Traviata, La (The erring woman) Opera in three acts by Verdi, first produced in Venice in 1853 (libretto by Piave after the drama 'La Dame aux camélias' by the younger Dumas). A young Parisian, Alfredo Germont (tenor), has fallen in love with a beautiful courtesan, Violetta Valéry, the Lady of the Camelias. Violetta (soprano), having at last found her true love, abandons her dissolute life-style and goes to live with him in the country. She does not disclose to him that she is dying of consumption. Alfredo's father, Giorgio Vermont (bass), fearing that Violetta's reputation for loose living will damage his son's career, begs her to break off the association. Sorrowfully she agrees; for Alfredo's sake she will make the sacrifice. At a party given by Flora Bervoix, a long-standing friend, she appears with a new escort, Baron Douphol (bass). Alfredo taunts and insults him, is challenged to a duel, and the Baron is wounded. By now Violetta is on her death-bed, and when Alfredo, hearing of her sacrifice, comes to ask her forgiveness she dies in his arms.

Tre [Italian] Three. **A tre** (*a 3*), for three voices or instruments; or, in three instrumental parts or voice-parts. **Sonata a tre**, trio sonata (see under *Sonata).

Treble **1** The highest, 'unbroken', boy's *voice. **2** The sequence of notes making up the highest part or voice in a piece of music (the lowest being referred to as the bass).

Treble C The note C which lies one octave above middle C, and is written in the third space up on the treble clef.

Treble clef See *Clef.

Tre corde See *t.c.

Tremolando [Italian] Trembling, quivering. [See also: *Tremolo]

Tremolo (abbrev.: **trem.**) **1** The rapid reiteration of a single note – especially on bowed string instruments by making swift up-and-down movements of the bow, producing an agitated, dramatic effect. This is called 'bowed tremolo', and is notated, for example, as: 𝅗𝅥 or ♩ **2** The rapid alternation of two notes at least a 3rd apart (if only a 2nd apart, the effect is called a trill). In the playing of bowed string instruments this is called 'fingered tremolo' since the alternation is accomplished by movement of the fingers. Each group of notes is taken with a single stroke of the bow. The same effect can also be produced on other instruments (e.g. wind instruments, and the piano). Examples of ways in which fingered tremolo may be notated are:

[See also sections (2) and (3) of Table 11 on pages 392–393]

Trepak A lively Russian Cossack dance in fast duple time. The most famous example occurs in Tchaikovsky's Suite from his ballet *The *Nutcracker*.

Très [French] Very.

Triad [from Greek, meaning 'three'] A chord of three notes, built upon a main note called the root, together with the notes forming a 3rd and a 5th above it (see Example 1, below). There are four kinds of triad. The two main kinds are called *major* (Ex. 2) and *minor* (Ex. 3). Each is named according to the kind of 3rd it contains; both contain the *interval of a perfect 5th.

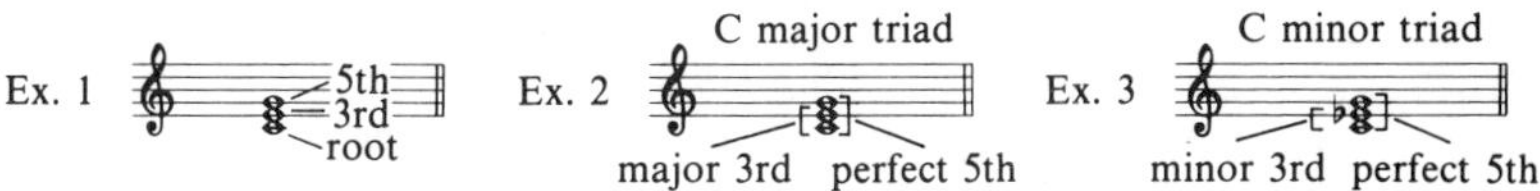

The other two kinds of triad are called *augmented* and *diminished*, and each is named according to the kind of 5th it contains (see below). An augmented triad contains a major 3rd and an augmented 5th. A diminished triad contains a minor 3rd and a diminished 5th.

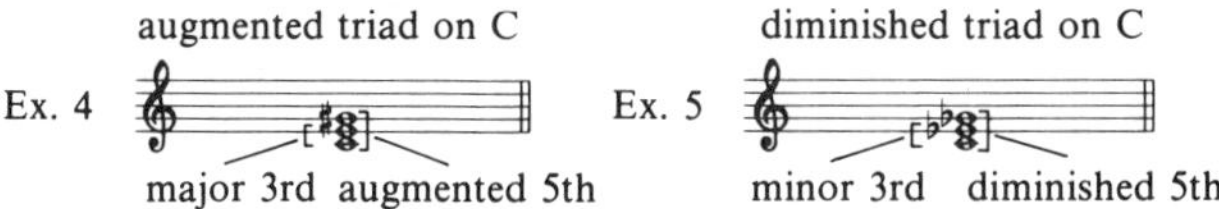

[See also: *Primary triads; and under *Chord]

Triangel [German] Triangle.

Triangle A percussion instrument, dating back at least to the 10th century. The modern orchestral triangle consists of a narrow steel rod bent into triangular shape but with one corner left open. The instrument is suspended, and struck with a metal beater (or, occasionally, with a drumstick). The player may be required to make single strokes, or to play a trill by rattling the beater inside either the upper or the lower closed corner. The sound of the triangle is high, clear ('tinkling') and penetrating, but of indefinite pitch. Triangles are made in various sizes.

triangle

The sound of the triangle can be heard in the third movement of Brahms's Fourth Symphony, and in the *Tartars' Dance* from Borodin's 'Polovtsian Dances' (from his opera *Prince Igor*). Liszt gives the triangle a particularly important part in the *Scherzando* section of his Piano Concerto No. 1 in E flat.

Triangolo [Italian] Triangle.

Trill See *Ornaments.

Trillo del Diavolo, Il See *'Devil's Trill' Sonata.

Trio [Italian: 'set of three'] **1** Music composed for three solo voices or instruments; also **2** a group which performs such a composition (see *String trio; *Piano trio, and also under *Chamber music). **3** The contrasting middle section in a minuet or scherzo structured in *minuet and trio form; also, a contrasting section in a *march. [For Trio sonata, see under *Sonata]

Triole [German]; **Triolet** [French] *Triplet.

Trionfale [Italian] Triumphal.

Trio sonata See under *Sonata.

Triple concerto A *concerto which features three solo instruments pitted against an orchestra. Examples include: Bach's Concertos for three harpsichords and strings, and his Concerto in A minor for flute, violin, harpsichord, and strings; Beethoven's Triple Concerto for piano, violin, cello, and orchestra; and the Triple Concerto (1979) for violin, viola, cello, and orchestra by Michael Tippett.

Triple counterpoint See under *Invertible counterpoint.

Triple fugue A *fugue based on three subjects, treated first separately and then in combination. [See also: *Double fugue; *Quadruple fugue]

Triple stop; **Triple stopping** See *Stopping, 1.

Triplet A group of three notes played or sung evenly in the time of two notes of the same kind.

Triple time (triple metre) Any kind of *time (or metre) which has three beats to each bar. The beat may be a plain note (such as ♪, ♩ or 𝅗𝅥) or it may be a dotted note (such as ♪. or ♩. or 𝅗𝅥.). [See the entries for *Time and *Time signature, and also the table of Time signatures on page 389]

Triple tonguing See *Tonguing.

Triple woodwind See under *Woodwind instruments.

Triplum In a medieval polyphonic piece, the third part lying above the tenor *cantus firmus* (the tenor itself being counted as the first part). [See: *Tenor, 3; also *Duplum and *Quadruplum]

Tristan and Isolde Opera in three acts by Wagner, first produced in Munich in 1865 (text by the composer after an ancient saga). Tristan (tenor) and his servant Kurwenal are at sea, taking the Irish princess Isolde (soprano) to Cornwall to marry Tristan's uncle, King Mark. Although Tristan has earlier killed Isolde's fiancé they are secretly in love, and realizing that they have no future together, Isolde orders her attendant, Brangäne (mezzo-soprano), to prepare a poison for them to drink. Appalled, Brangäne produces instead a love potion which draws them irresistibly together. Ashore in Cornwall they arrange to meet when King Mark is away hunting, but a suspicious courtier, Melot (tenor), alerts the King and they discover them together. The King (bass) is distraught and Melot, in a fit of rage, wounds Tristan with his sword. Back in Tristan's castle Kurwenal (baritone) nurses his master and awaits Isolde, who has magic powers to heal him. She arrives to find Tristan delirious. He rips off his bandage and dies in her arms. Soon King Mark, having learnt of the love potion, comes with his men to offer his pardon. Kurwenal mistakes their intentions. He mounts a defence of the castle and in the ensuing combat both Melot and he are killed. Isolde, racked with anguish, dies of a broken heart. The Prelude and an orchestral version of Isolde's final *Liebestod* (love-death) are sometimes played, as two linked items, at concerts.

Triste [French and Italian] Sad, mournful, sorrowful.

Tritone See *Diabolus in musica.

Triumphes of Oriana, The A collection of English madrigals written by various Elizabethan composers in honour of Elizabeth I, who was often called 'Oriana' in poetry. Each madrigal ends with the words:

Then sang the shepherds and nymphs of Diana:
'Long live fair Oriana!'

The collection was edited by Thomas Morley, who took the idea from a collection of Italian madrigals entitled *Il trionfo di Dori* (1592). Morley assembled the madrigals during the late 1590s, and published the collection in 1601. Among the composers represented are Weelkes, Wilbye, Farmer, Bennet, Tomkins, and Morley himself.

Trois [French] Three. **À trois**, for three voices or instruments; or, in three instrumental parts or voice-parts.

Tromba (plural: *trombe*) [Italian] Trumpet. *Tromba da tirarsi* refers to the slide trumpet; *tromba cromatica, a macchina, ventile*, all refer to the modern valve trumpet.

Trombone [from Italian, meaning 'big trumpet'] A *brass instrument, which in its early form, evolving around 1460, was known in Britain as the *sackbut. The trombone has a deep cup-shaped mouthpiece; the tube is cylindrical for much of its length, and then expands into a moderately-flared bell. Instead of valves, the trombone has a movable *slide* – a U-shaped length of tubing which can be pushed away from or drawn towards the player, so lengthening or shortening the sounding length of the tube. There are seven positions for the slide, based on seven fundamental notes (see *Harmonic series). The first position is with the slide fully drawn in. As the slide is pushed out, extending the total length of the tube, each successive position lowers the pitch of the harmonic series by one semitone. The player selects notes from the harmonic series offered by adjusting the tension of the lips.

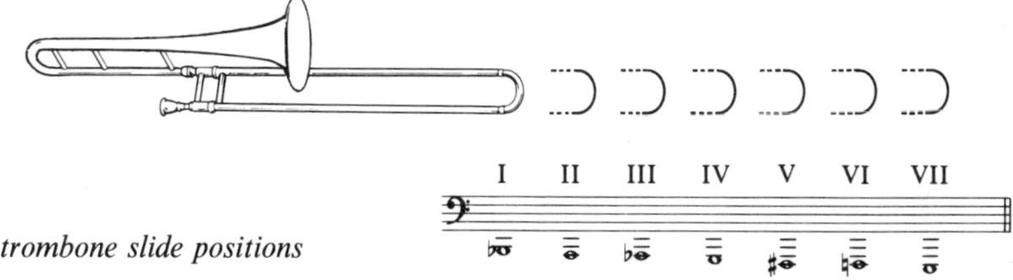

trombone slide positions

The trombone is an important member of the brass section of the modern orchestra. Composers usually write for three trombones – two tenors and one bass. They are non-transposing instruments, their notes being written at the pitch they sound. The tenor trombone, pitched in B♭ (tube length, with slide drawn in, about 2.75 metres), has the following range:

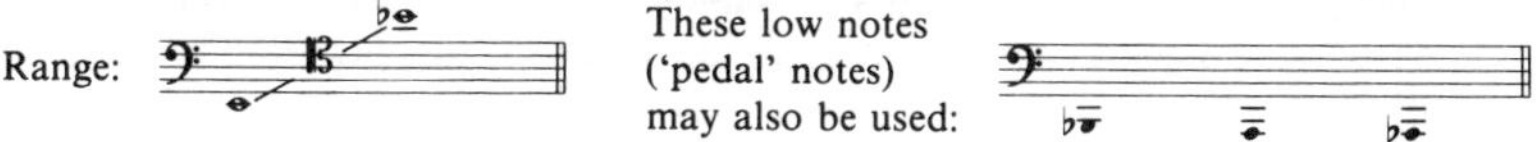

Lower notes are now written in the bass clef; higher notes are written in the tenor clef. The bass trombone, usually pitched in G, has a range lying a 4th below that of the tenor trombone. Nowadays, however, the bass trombone is usually replaced by the tenor-bass trombone (or B♭/F trombone). Basically this is the same size as the tenor trombone, though with a wider bore, and there is an F attachment – an extra coil of tubing which can be switched in by the left thumb, instantly lowering the possible pitch. (There may be an additional switch to transpose the pitch into E, E♭, or D.) The tenor-bass trombone can therefore cover the ranges of both tenor trombone and bass trombone.

Also occasionally used are the contrabass (or double-bass) trombone, pitched an octave below the B♭ tenor trombone, and the alto trombone, pitched a fourth higher than the tenor. However, parts for alto trombone printed in many 19th-century scores are often now played on the tenor trombone.

Although the trombone was frequently used in church music and operas, it did not find a regular place in the orchestra until the early 19th century.

Trombone tone-quality can be most impressive; the sound may be round, solemn and dignified – yet, when played forcefully, the tone can blaze aggressively, dominating the rest of the orchestra. The slide mechanism makes possible the use of *glissando. A mute may be fixed into the bell of the trombone, giving the tone a rather sinister quality.

The experiment has been tried of providing the trombone with valves, but this has not proved generally popular due to the alteration to the tone-quality which results.

The trombone is also a regular member of the brass band, military band, and symphonic band, and is extensively used in dance bands and jazz bands (notable jazz trombonists include Edward 'Kid' Ory, Jack Teagarden, Tommy Dorsey, and 'J. J.' Johnson).

Orchestral solos for trombone occur at the beginning of the ballet music from *The Perfect Fool* and also *The Hymn of Jesus*, both by Gustav Holst, in the *Tuba mirum* from Mozart's Requiem, in the *Vivo* (a humorous duet with double bass) from Stravinsky's ballet *Pulcinella*, and during Malcolm Arnold's Overture *Tam o'Shanter*. Good examples of the sound of three trombones (two tenors, one bass) occur in Wagner's Overture to *Tannhäuser* (bar 37 onwards), Berlioz's Overture *Le Carnaval romain* (bar 315 to the end), Rossini's Overture to *William Tell* (the Storm section, and the Coda), and, together with tuba, the last movement of Tchaikovsky's *Pathétique Symphony* (the quiet, solemn passage fairly near the end). The weight, depth, and power of bass trombone tone can be heard in Stravinsky's *Octet (especially the second movement). Muted trombone tone can be heard at the end of the slow movement of Vaughan Williams's Fourth Symphony, and in *Satan's Dance of Triumph* from his ballet *Job*. Compositions for solo trombone and orchestra include Rimsky-Korsakov's Concerto in B♭ (originally with military band), Milhaud's *Concertino d'hiver*, and Frank Martin's *Ballade*. Hindemith wrote a Sonata for trombone and piano, and Poulenc composed a Sonata for horn, trumpet, and trombone. Berio's *Sequenza V* is for solo (unaccompanied) trombone.

Trommel [German] Drum. **Grosse Trommel**, bass drum; **kleine Trommel**, snare (side) drum; **Rührtrommel**, tenor drum; **Schellentrommel**, tambourine. [See also: *Pauken]

Trompete (plural: *Trompeten*) [German]; **Trompette** [French] Trumpet.

Trope Writing 'tropes' was a favourite technique of Medieval composers from the 9th century to the 13th. **Troping** meant taking an existing plainsong melody, or its text, and adding or inserting either new words, or perhaps new music, or even both.

Troper A book containing a collection of *tropes, the most important example being the Winchester Troper (compiled from *c*990 to *c*1050).

Troppo [Italian] Too much; too. Used in phrases such as *Allegro, ma non troppo*, meaning 'quick, but not too much'.

Troubadours During the 12th and 13th centuries a great many songs were written by the *troubadours* – poet-musicians, often of noble birth, who lived in southern France (Provence) – and by the **trouvères*, their counterparts in the north. Both names are connected with the modern French word *trouver* meaning 'to find', and so a troubadour or trouvère was the 'finder', or inventor, of both the words and the melody of a song. The troubadours wrote their poems in Provençal (the 'langue d'oc') whereas the trouvères wrote in French (the 'langue d'oil'). Many troubadour poems are concerned with courtly love and the idealization of woman. About 2,500 troubadour poems survive, but less than 300 melodies.

The melodies of these songs present problems for present-day performance. They are written, usually, in the same square-shaped *neumes as those used for plainsong; this means that the pitch is clearly indicated – but not the rhythm. Another problem is that although the music of each song consists of melody only, it is almost certain that in performance there would have been some kind of instrumental accompaniment – perhaps also an instrumental introduction, postlude, and even interludes between the verses. A composer might accompany himself as he sang, or employ a *minstrel to provide an accompaniment.

Among the troubadours whose songs survive are Guillaume IX, Duke of Aquitaine and Count of Poitiers (1071–1127); Marcabru, a commoner (flourished 1128–1150); Bernart de Ventadorn (*c*1135–*c*1195); Giraut de Bornelh (*c*1140–*c*1200) called by his contemporaries *maestre del trobadors*, 'master of the troubadours'; Raimbaut de Vaqueiras (*c*1155–1207); Guiraut Riquier (*c*1230–*c*1300) known as 'the last of the troubadours'. [See also: *Minnesinger]

'Trout' Quintet (*Forellenquintett*) Nickname of Schubert's Quintet in A major (Op. 114; D667) for piano, violin, viola, cello, and double bass; composed in 1819. There are five movements: 1 *Allegro vivace*; 2 *Andante*; 3 Scherzo: *Presto*; 4 *Andantino* (theme and variations); 5 Finale: *Allegro giusto*. The theme which forms the basis for the variations of the fourth movement is the melody of Schubert's song 'The Trout' (*Die Forelle*), composed around 1817.

Trouvères [French] Poet-musicians of the 12th and 13th centuries – the northern French counterparts of the *troubadours. More than 2,000 trouvère poems have survived, at least two-thirds of them with melodies – though none of them give any clue as to how the songs might have been accompanied. The trouvères included both noblemen and commoners. Among the best known were Blondel de Nesle (flourished 1180–1200), who was a favourite of King Richard the Lionheart; Thibaut IV of Champagne, later King of Navarre (1201–1253); and Adam de la Halle [de la Hale] (*c*1245–*c*1290), a commoner.

Trovatore, Il (The troubadour) Opera in four acts by Verdi, first produced in Rome in 1853 (libretto by Cammarano after the drama by Gutiérrez). Ferrando (bass), Captain of the Guard to the Count di Luna, tells how, long ago, the Count's baby brother was bewitched by a gypsy woman, who was caught and burned at the stake. Her daughter Azucena (mezzo-soprano), stole the baby intending to burn it as revenge, but in error killed her own child. Now Leonora (soprano) has fallen in love with Manrico, a troubadour (tenor) who serenades her nightly. The Count (baritone), also in love with Leonora, challenges Manrico to a duel. Azucena urges Manrico to avenge her mother's death, but unwittingly reveals to him that he is not her son. The Count plans to elope with Leonora, but Manrico foils the attempt. Ferrando identifies Azucena as the killer of the baby, and the Count condemns her to death. Hurrying off to rescue her, Manrico is arrested by the Count's men, and when Leonora pleads for his release the Count agrees to spare him only in return for Leonora's love. Leonora consents but in desperation poisons herself, and having told Manrico of this tragic act she dies in his arms. Furious at having being tricked, the Count orders Manrico's execution and compels Azucena to watch. But Azucena has the final word. Triumphantly she confronts the Count with the ghastly news: he has killed his own brother. The old gypsy woman is avenged.

Trumpet A *brass instrument, of narrow bore, and played with a shallow cup-shaped mouthpiece. The tube is cylindrical for (usually) two-thirds of its length, and then expands into a moderately-flared bell.

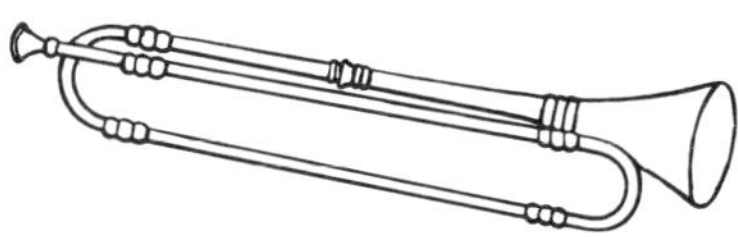

'natural' trumpet (17th century)

In Medieval times, the trumpet was long and straight. It was a 'natural' instrument – consisting of a simple tube, with no extra mechanism of any kind – and so was only able to produce the 'natural' notes of the *harmonic series corresponding to the length of its tube. Around 1400, instrument makers began to fashion trumpets into a squashed s-shape; then, soon afterwards, into a long and narrow oval-shape.

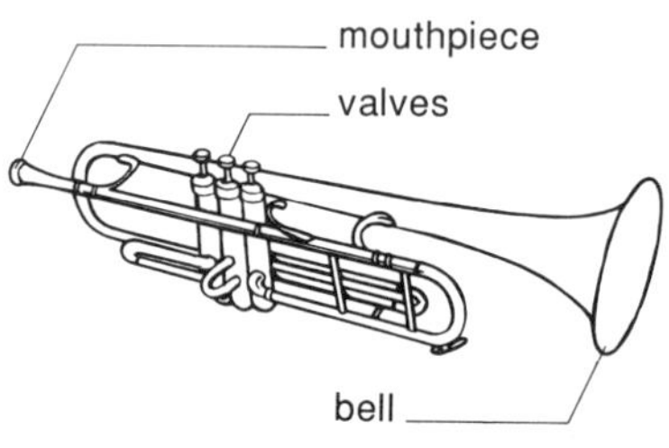

modern valve trumpet

In this basic shape, in the early 17th century, the 'natural' trumpet joined the orchestra, first being used mainly in operas and church music. By the end of the century, trumpeters were developing the skill of playing in the high *clarino* register – where the notes of the harmonic series fall more closely together. Composers (e.g. Bach, Handel) were able to give the trumpet high-pitched, elaborate tunes to play, rather than the mere fanfares it had been accustomed to. However, by the time of Haydn and Mozart, the art of *clarino*-playing had almost died out. And this meant that composers were again limited in the range of notes they could write for 'natural' trumpet.

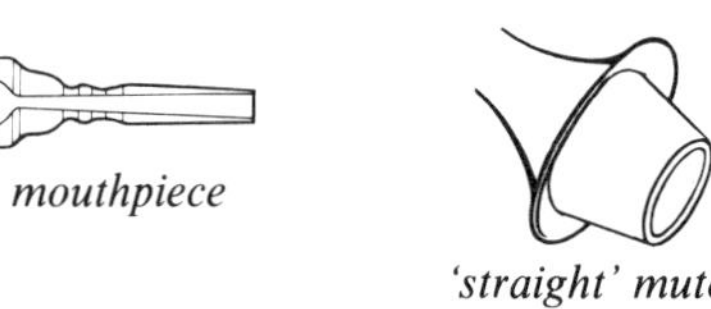

mouthpiece

'straight' mute

Various attempts were made to provide the trumpet with more notes – such as the use of *crooks, and the introduction of the 'keyed' trumpet and the 'slide' trumpet (see under *Brass instruments). But the problem was not satisfactorily solved until around 1815 when valves were invented (see *Valve system). The three valves fitted to the trumpet make it fully chromatic throughout its range, and also enable it to rival woodwind instruments in agility.

The trumpets most often now used in the orchestra are the trumpet in B♭ and the trumpet in C. The trumpet in B♭ (tube-length about 130 cm) is a *transposing instrument, its music written one tone higher than it actually sounds. The trumpet in C, which is non-transposing, is pitched a tone higher than the trumpet in B♭.

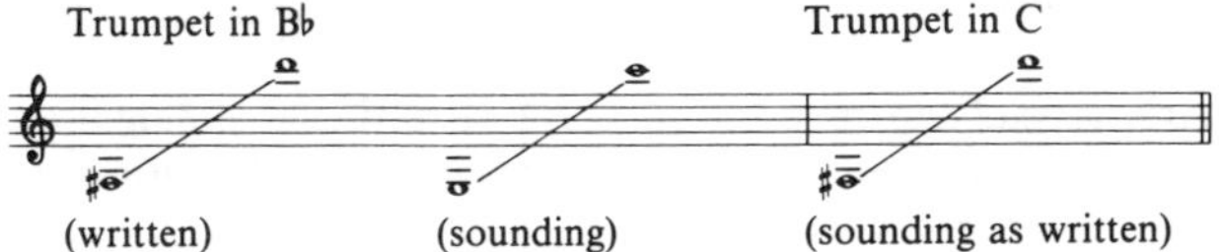

The trumpet is also used in the military band, and is an important instrument in jazz – notable jazz trumpeters include Louis Armstrong ('Satchmo'), Bix Beiderbecke, Dizzy Gillespie, and Miles Davis. (Many jazz trumpeters can achieve pitches up to a 5th or even an octave higher than the normal orchestral range shown above.)

The trumpet's sound can be brilliant and penetrating. Various types of mute can be used to alter the tone-quality. A 'straight' mute softens the tone in quiet playing, giving the effect of coming mysteriously from the distance; blown forcefully, the sound can become harsh and sinister. Other types of mute, used especially in jazz and pop music, include cup, plunger, and wow-wow (or wa-wah).

Other types of trumpet sometimes used include the bass trumpet, with wide bore and large mouthpiece, and usually pitched in C an octave below the normal trumpet in C. And also several smaller sizes of trumpet – for example, in D and E♭, and the piccolo trumpet in B♭ (usually with four valves) pitched an octave higher than the normal trumpet in B♭. Any of these smaller, high-pitched trumpets may be referred to as a 'Bach trumpet'. They are used for playing *clarino* parts in scores by Baroque composers such as Bach, and also parts in certain modern scores (e.g. trumpet in D is included by Stravinsky in *Petrushka* and *The Rite of Spring* and by Britten in *Peter Grimes*).

Among the many orchestral works featuring solo trumpet (or with important parts for one or more trumpets) are: the trumpet concertos by Haydn and Hummel (both written for 'keyed' trumpet); Bach's Brandenburg Concerto No. 2 (*clarino* register) and the Gloria and the Osanna (each including three trumpets) from his B minor Mass; the *Trumpet Voluntary* by Jeremiah Clarke (arranged by Sir Henry Wood); 'The Trumpet shall sound' from Handel's *Messiah*; the *Grand March* from Verdi's opera *Aida*; Shostakovich's Concerto (Op. 35) for piano, trumpet, and strings; Copland's *Quiet City*; 'Vision 1' from Panufnik's *Sinfonia sacra* (four trumpets positioned at the four 'corners' of the orchestra); and Harrison Birtwistle's *Endless Parade* (1987). Janáček, in his *Sinfonietta*, in addition to an already large orchestra, features an extra brass group of nine trumpets, two tenor tubas, and two bass trumpets (first movement, and end of the last movement). Muted trumpet tone can be heard in *Samuel Goldenberg and Schmuyle* from Ravel's orchestration of Musorgsky's *Pictures at an Exhibition*, in the middle section of *Fêtes* from Debussy's *Nocturnes* (three muted trumpets), in the second movement (at bar 90) of Bartók's Concerto for Orchestra, and also in Gould's *Pavane* and Scott's *Toy Trumpet*. Among chamber works which include trumpet are Saint-Saëns' Septet for piano, trumpet, string quartet, and double bass, Poulenc's Sonata for horn, trumpet, and trombone, and Hindemith's Sonata for trumpet and piano.

Trumpet Voluntary The title given by the conductor, Sir Henry Wood, to his arrangement for solo trumpet and orchestra of a harpsichord piece called *The Prince of Denmark's March* by Jeremiah Clarke (*c*1674–1707).

t.s. Abbreviation of **tasto solo.*

Tsigane See *Tzigane.

Tsuridaiko A large type of Japanese *drum, barrel-shaped, and double-headed. It is suspended in a frame and only one drumhead is struck with leather-covered beaters.

Tuba A large *brass instrument (introduced in the 1830s) with a wide conical bore, deep cup-shaped mouthpiece, widely flaring bell, and with three to six valves. Tubas exist in a wide variety of shapes, sizes, and pitches, and some members of the family commonly go by other names, such as euphonium, bombardon, sousaphone, and helicon.

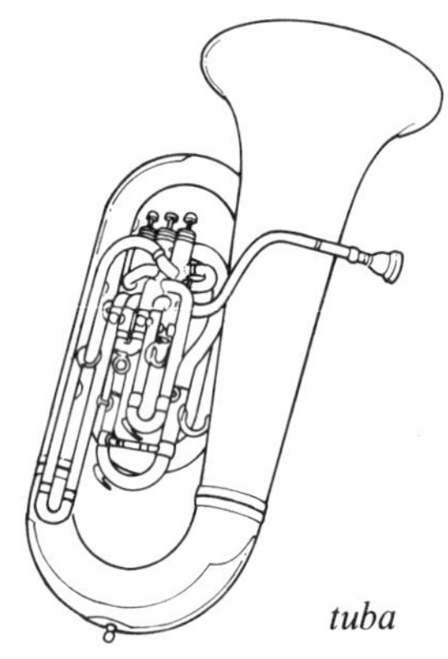
tuba

In the orchestra, the tuba provides a solid foundation for the brass section. Three sizes of orchestral tuba are commonly used – the player selecting whichever is most appropriate to the type and range of the music to be played. These are: the tenor tuba in B♭, the bass tuba in F, and the contrabass (or double-bass) tuba in C (also called 'double C' or CC tuba). Each has a range of three octaves, and the notes are written in the bass clef (orchestral tubas are non-transposing instruments – their notes sound at the written pitch).

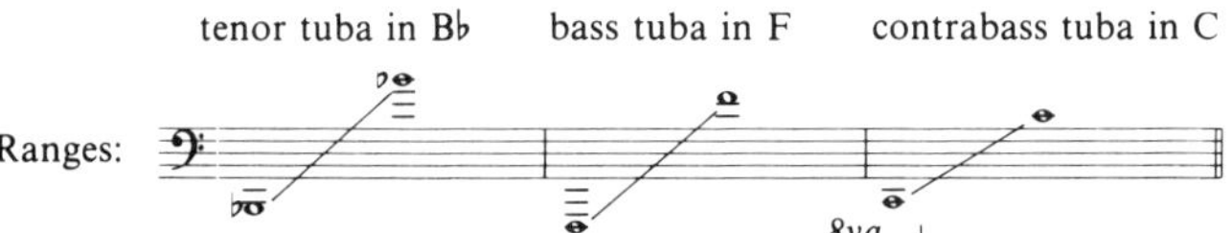

Due to the wide conical bore, the deep cup-shaped mouthpiece, and the widely flaring bell, the tone-quality of the tuba is smooth, rich, round, and full. Despite its size, however, it can be extremely agile. Like the other orchestral brass, the tuba is sometimes muted. Usually, a straight mute (often of cardboard) is used, though recently a metal mute has been devised which can be adjusted to affect the tone-quality in various ways.

Famous orchestral solos for tuba occur in *Bydlo* from Ravel's orchestration of Musorgsky's *Pictures at an Exhibition* (tenor tuba), and at bar 158 of Wagner's Overture to *The Mastersingers* (bass tuba). Hindemith wrote a Sonata for bass tuba and piano, and Vaughan Williams composed a Concerto in F minor for bass tuba and orchestra.

[See also: *Wagner tuba]

Tubular bells (orchestral chimes) An orchestral percussion instrument consisting of about eighteen metal tubes, graded in length to provide a chromatic range. The tubes are suspended from a frame in two ranks (resembling the arrangement of black and white notes on a keyboard) and the player strikes them near the top with a mallet. Their sounds are used for colourful and dramatic effects, especially to give the impression of tolling church bells.

Normal range: 

Occasionally, the range is extended downwards by the addition of extra, longer tubes.

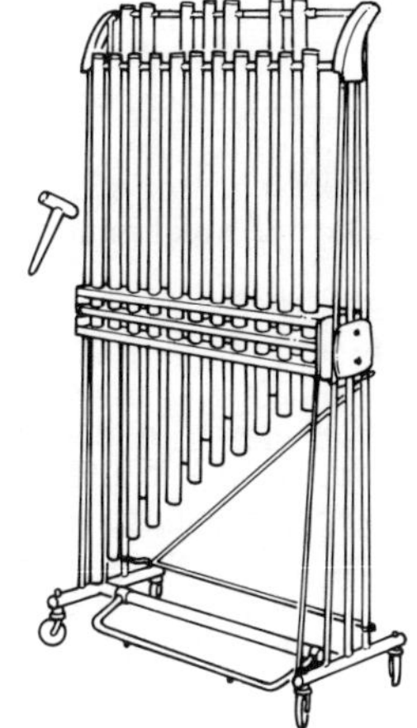

tubular bells

The sound of tubular bells may be heard in Malcolm Arnold's English Dance No. 7, in the final movement of Vaughan Williams's Eighth Symphony, and, especially, in Act 2 Scene 2 ('The Bells') of Britten's opera *The Turn of the Screw*.

Tune **1** The word is often used to mean the same as melody – especially one which is fairly simple, clear-cut, easily remembered. **2** When used as a verb, the word means to make adjustments to an instrument (e.g. tightening or slackening the strings of a violin, or piano) so that the sounds will be at the proper, accepted pitch. (Hence: 'in tune' – having the correct pitch; 'out of tune' – not having the correct pitch, producing a sound or sounds not true in pitch.)

Tuono [Italian] Same as **tono*.

Turba [Latin: 'crowd'] In settings of the *Passion, the passages to be sung by a choir or a group of singers representing, for example, the disciples, soldiers, and, especially, the crowd around the Cross. [See also: *Testo]

Turca; **Turco** [Italian] Turkish. **Alla turca**, an 18th-century term for music composed in imitation of Turkish *Janissary music.

Turkish crescent See under *Janissary music.

Turkish music; **Turkish style** See under *Janissary music.

Turn See *Ornaments.

Tutta; **Tutto**; **Tutte** [Italian] All. **Tutta forza**, with all force, with maximum strength and power. [See also: *Tutti]

Tutte le corde See *t.c.

Tutti [Italian] All. In orchestral music, the term *tutti* describes a passage in which all the instruments play – especially in a *concerto, where it refers to passages played by the whole orchestra as distinct from those which feature the soloist.

Twelfth See under *Intervals.

Twelve-note technique (twelve-note composition; serialism) A method or technique of composing devised by Arnold Schoenberg around 1920. Having abandoned key and mode in writing *atonal music, Schoenberg came to realize that an entirely new principle was needed to take the place of tonality – a new procedure in composing which would bring shape and structure, unity and coherence, to an atonal composition. His solution was 'twelve-note composition' or 'serialism'.

In a twelve-note, or serial, composition all twelve notes of the chromatic scale become of equal importance:

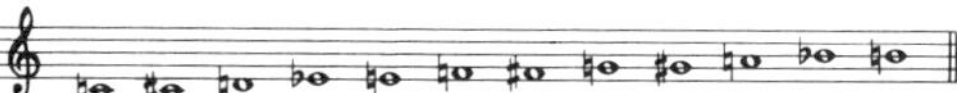

(Pitches may appear in different guises – for example, C♯ may appear as D♭, E♭ may appear as D♯, and so on.)

The composer first arranges the twelve notes in any order he or she chooses. This becomes the **note row**, the **basic series**, or **basic set**, on which the entire composition will be based. (Example (a), below, shows the basic series Schoenberg chose for his String Quartet No. 4, Op. 37, composed in 1936.) During the composing of the music, since all twelve notes are of equal importance, none of them should appear 'out of turn'. However, occasionally a note may be *immediately* repeated. And any note of the series may be used at any octave – higher, or lower.

Besides using the series or note row in its *original* form, the composer may use the notes in reverse order. This 'backwards' form of the series is called **retrograde* (compare (b) with (a)). The series may be turned upside down – called *inversion* (compare (c) with (a)). Or it may be used backwards and upside down at the same time – called *retrograde inversion* (d).

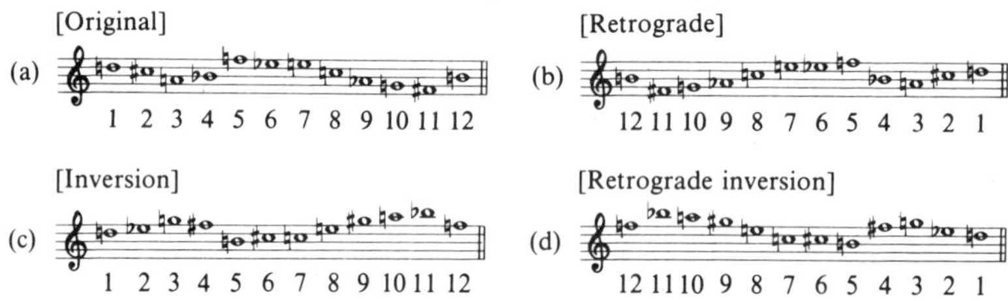

Any of these four forms of the basic series may be transposed (raised or lowered in pitch) to begin on any one of the twelve pitches of the chromatic scale. This gives a total of 48 (4 × 12) possible versions of the basic series. Any of these version may be used:

horizontally, to form melodies – two or more of which may weave along together in counterpoint; or,

vertically, with the notes stacked one on top of another, making chords to serve as supporting harmonies.

In any of its forms, however, the series merely offers a composer *basic* musical material – a *series* of notes. He must show his skill and imagination in using it to shape melodies and construct harmonies, in the rhythms he devises to bring life to the music, in the instrumental timbres he chooses, and the musical textures he creates.

The earliest work to be composed entirely in serial style was Schoenberg's six-movement Piano Suite, Op. 25 (the Prelude and the beginning of the Intermezzo were composed in July 1921; the rest in February and March of 1923). Among the finest of his later serial compositions are the Variations for

Orchestra (1928), the Violin Concerto (1936), and the opera *Moses und Aron* (1930–32; Schoenberg completed only the first two of its projected three acts, but these have been performed with great success).

Schoenberg's pupils Berg and Webern also took up serialism but in very different ways. Webern used Schoenberg's rules in the strictest possible way, e.g. in his Symphony, Op. 21 (1928), and his Concerto for nine instruments, Op. 24 (1931–4). Berg, however, was considerably freer in his approach – using notes of the basic series out of turn, and often bringing in extra musical material not drawn from the series. Sometimes he arranges the notes in a basic series to imply recognizable chords in the major-minor system. His Violin Concerto (1935) is based on a series (printed below) in which notes 1–9 rise a 3rd at a time. Notes 1–3 form a chord of G minor, while 5–7 make A minor; 3–5 offer D major, and 7–9 give E major. Notes 9–12 form part of the whole-tone scale, and this four-note motive in fact matches the opening of a chorale-melody used by Bach in his Cantata No. 60. Berg introduces this chorale in the final movement of his Violin Concerto, weaving his atonal music around it with deeply moving effect.

In the late 1940s, certain composers began to extend Schoenberg's original ideas. In 1949, Messiaen composed a piano piece called *Mode de valeurs et d'intensités* (Mode of durations and intensities) which he based upon scales, not only of pitch, but also of duration (note-values), dynamics, and attack (touch or articulation). This led to experiments by Messiaen and his two pupils, Boulez and Stockhausen, in '**total serialism**' – in which twelve-element series of pitches, durations, dynamics, and attack were all totally controlled by Schoenberg's principles of serialism. Boulez was first to use total serialism in his *Structures I* for two pianos (1951–2). Stockhausen's *Gruppen* (Groups) for three orchestras (1955–7) also makes serial use of a 'scale' of twelve tempos (speeds).

Twentieth-century music Whereas various 'labels' have been generally accepted to describe the style of other periods in the *history of Western music, no *overall* label has yet been coined to describe music composed since 1900.

Some composers continued, after 1900, to pursue the style of 19th-century *Romanticism, mainly using traditional musical techniques and perhaps national idioms (see *Nationalism). Others strongly reacted to what they now considered to be the excessive and over-ripe style of Romanticism, and chose to strike out in new directions. And so the main story of 20th-century music is one of exciting exploration and experiment – leading to a fascinating variety of new sounds and materials, new trends, and new techniques.

The first indication of an 'anti-Romantic' reaction was the style of *Impressionism closely associated with Debussy. (The French conductor and composer, Pierre Boulez, has in fact suggested that "modern music awakes with Debussy's **Prélude à 'L' Après-midi d'un Faune*".)

For details and explanation of other important styles, materials, trends, and techniques in 20th-century music, see: *Whole-tone scale; *Polytonality; *Expressionism; *Atonality; *Pointillism; *Klangfarbenmelodie; *Linear counterpoint; *Note-cluster; *Polyrhythm; *Polymetre 2; *Twelve-note technique (serialism); The *New Music; *Neoclassicism; *Microtonality; *Musique concrète; *Electronic music; *Aleatory music; *Indeterminacy; *Open form; *Graphic score; *Prepared piano; *Multimedia.

In addition to the new musical materials and totally new (and unlimited) sounds made possible by the use and manipulation of magnetic tape and electronic apparatus, many 20th-century composers have also keenly investigated and exploited various new sounds and colouristic effects from conventional musical instruments (see under *Orchestral devices). Several composers (among them, Ravel, Stravinsky, Milhaud) have used ingredients from American *jazz in some of their compositions. And the influence of music of non-Western cultures has become increasingly significant.

Prominent 20th-century composers include: Debussy, Sibelius, Vaughan Williams, Ives, Schoenberg, Bartók, Stravinsky, Webern, Berg, Hindemith, Copland, Tippett, Shostakovich, Messiaen, Cage, Britten, Boulez, Berio, Stockhausen, and Penderecki. [See the time-chart of composers on pages 398–413]

Twilight of the Gods See *Der *Ring des Nibelungen.*

Two-foot See *Foot.

Tympani A misspelling of the Italian word *timpani.*

Tzigane (*tsigane*) [French] **1** Hungarian gypsy. **2** Music written in Hungarian gypsy style (e.g. Ravel's *Tzigane* for violin and piano).

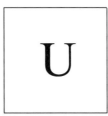

Über [German] Above, over.

u.c. Abbreviation of **una corda*.

'Ūd [Arabic: 'wood'] The Arabic short-necked, plucked lute (the ancestor of the European *lute) which dates back possibly as far as the 7th century and is still in use today. The present-day 'ūd has from eight to twelve gut strings arranged in double courses (i.e. in pairs, each pair tuned in unison). Some instruments have frets; others are fretless. In all Arabic-speaking countries, the 'ūd has been considered 'the queen of instruments' for at least 1,000 years.

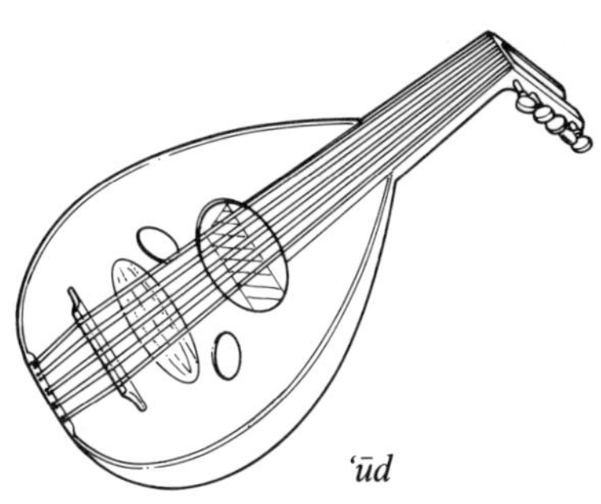
'ūd

Ukelele (ukulele) [from Hawaiian, meaning 'leaping flea'] A small Hawaiian guitar with four strings, usually tuned either to G–C–E–A, or to A–D–F♯–B:

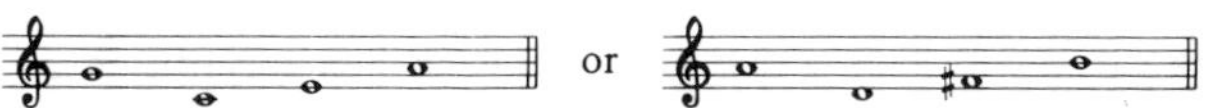

The strings may be plucked with the fingers, or with a plectrum. The ukelele developed from the Portuguese guitar, and became very popular around 1920 in the USA.

Umfang [German] Compass or range (of an instrument or a voice).

Umore [Italian] Humour.

Una corda (abbrev.: **u.c.**) [Italian: 'one string'] Indication in piano music to depress the left ('soft') pedal. [See under *Piano; also *t.c.]

Und [German] And.

Unequal temperament Any system of tuning in which intervals are kept 'pure' or 'just' in some keys, but at the expense of making other, remote keys unusable. An example is the system of tuning known as mean-tone temperament. [See: *Temperament]

Unequal voices See under *Mixed voices.

Unessential note Same as *Non-harmonic note.

'Unfinished' Symphony Nickname of Schubert's Symphony No. 8 in B minor (D759), composed in 1822. It consist of two movements only: 1 *Allegro moderato* (in sonata form), and 2 *Andante con moto* (in *abridged sonata form). However, sketches Schubert made for the third movement have survived. No one knows why Schubert decided to leave the symphony unfinished. [But see also: *Rosamunde]

Ungarisch [German] Hungarian.

Ungharese [Italian] Same as *Ongarese.

Unis [French]; **Unisono** (abbrev.: **unis.**) [Italian] Indication (meaning 'united') that all the instruments of a group, e.g. first violins, are now to play the same notes (in *unison) after a passage in which they have been divided. [See: *Divisés, Divisi]

Unison [Latin: 'one sound'] The sounding of the same note by two or more voices or instruments. The phrase **in unison** is also used to describe the effect when all the voices in a mixed choir of men and women join in singing the same melody – even though the voices may be one or more octaves apart. [See also: *Intervals]

Un poco [Italian] A little. (For example: *un poco più lento*, a little more slowly.)

Unruhig [German] Restless, troubled, uneasy.

Unter [German] Below, under.

Unterwerk [German] Choir organ. [See under *Organ]

Upbeat The last beat or impulse in a bar of music, immediately before the bar-line, as would be marked by the upward movement of the conductor's baton in preparation for the downbeat on the strong first beat of the next bar. [See also: *Anacrusis]

Up-bow See *Bowing.

Upper mordent See *Ornaments.

Upper partials See *Harmonic series.

Upper pedal Term sometimes used to mean *Inverted pedal.

Upright See under *Piano.

Urtext [German: 'original text'] Over the years, a piece of music may be printed in a great many editions, with each editor making alterations and additions to the composer's original ideas – often with later editors copying and compounding the faults of earlier editions. An Urtext edition of a piece of music aims to avoid these corruptions and to present what the composer actually wrote by basing the edition upon the composer's original manuscript (or, if this no longer survives, upon the earliest printing of the music).

Ut [French] The note C.

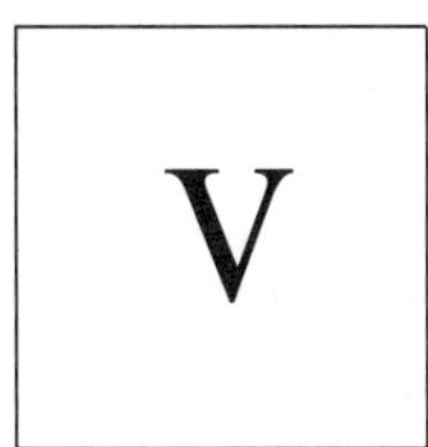

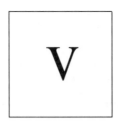

V Abbreviation standing for: **1** violin; **2** voice; **3** *voci* [Italian] 'voices' (e.g. *3 v*, for three voices); **4** verse (e.g. in certain plainchant melodies, and usually then printed with a slanting line: ℣).

Valkyrie, The See *Der *Ring des Nibelungen*.

Valse [French] *Waltz.

Valse, La A 'choreographic poem' (dance poem) for orchestra composed by Ravel in 1919–20. The music parodies the Viennese waltz, and is often used as a ballet score.

Valse triste An orchestral waltz by Sibelius. The music was originally composed, in 1903, as part of the incidental music, for string orchestra, to a play called *Kuolema* (Death). A year later, Sibelius made a version of the piece for full orchestra.

Valve horn; Valve trumpet Terms sometimes used to describe the modern horn and trumpet with valves, to distinguish them from the earlier natural horn and natural trumpet which were without valves.

Valve system A mechanical device, invented around 1815, enabling *brass instruments to be fully chromatic (able to play all semitones) throughout their respective ranges. Pressing down a valve (or piston) diverts the air along an extra piece of tubing, so increasing the total length of the tube (as shown in the simplified drawings of the trumpet, below). There are usually three valves and they may be used singly or in differing combinations, altering the tube to different lengths and offering a choice of seven fundamental notes, each with its own *harmonic series. For example: pressing down valve 2 brings in enough extra tubing to lower the harmonic series by one semitone; pressing down valve 1 lowers the series by a whole tone.

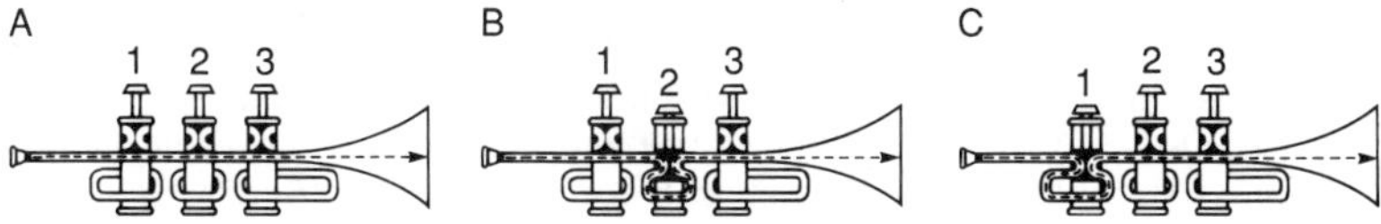

The player uses the valves as necessary, singly or in combination, and by adjusting the tension of the lips, selects the required note from the harmonic series offered. The notes possible from all seven harmonic series overlap, so offering a complete chromatic range.

The horn's valves are usually of the 'rotary' type in which, by pressing a lever, the path leading the air into the extra length of tube revolves into position – rather than being lowered, as in the case of the 'piston' valves of the trumpet.

The valve system is now used on all the main brass instruments except, usually, the trombone in which the tube is altered by moving a telescopic slide (the experiment of providing the trombone with valves has been tried, but has not proved generally popular due to the inferior tone-quality which results).

Variata [Italian] Varied. **Aria variata**, air with *variations. **Tema variata**, theme and *variations.

Variations (theme and variations, variation form) One of the earliest musical *forms, first becoming popular in the 16th century (though earlier examples exist). A melody (the **theme** – sometimes called 'air') is first presented in a fairly straightforward way, and is then repeated as many times as the composer likes but each time *varied* – altered, or disguised – in one or more different ways.

The theme itself may be in *binary or *ternary form. There are countless ways in which it may be varied – really limited only by the extent of the composer's imagination – but the most important include:

1 decorating the theme with ornaments and other extra notes;
2 presenting it in the opposite mode (a change from the major key to the parallel minor key, or vice versa);
3 presenting it with a change of harmony, rhythm, metre (number of beats to a bar), or tempo (speed);
4 'hiding' the theme by putting it down into the bass, or in an inner part;
5 treating the theme, or part of it, by *imitation, *canon, *inversion, *augmentation, *diminution;
6 the theme itself may actually disappear, but the harmonies and/or the rhythm kept so that there is a strong reminder of the theme;
7 a counter-melody may be added above or below the theme, or a new melody take its place against the original harmonies;
8 if the music is for orchestra – a noticeable change of orchestration.

A *coda may be added to the final variation to round off the whole piece, or the final variation may itself serve as a coda. Sometimes a set of variations ends with something more elaborate such as a *fugue, or the composer may simply choose to restate the theme in exactly the same way as when it was first heard. Variations composed before the 19th century consist mainly of decorating the theme in various ways. Later composers (Beethoven and Brahms in particular) often probe deeper by *developing* the theme – building up the music by searching out and exploring the various melodic, harmonic, and rhythmic possibilities of the theme (see *Development). In this way, an entire variation may be developed from a single important musical idea taken from the theme – perhaps a melodic fragment, or a distinctive snatch of rhythm.

[See also: *Ground bass; *Chaconne and Passacaglia; *Division; *Double; *Folía. Also: Byrd: *The *Carmans Whistle*; Bull: *The *King's Hunt*; Bach: *'Goldberg' Variations; Handel: 'The *Harmonious Blacksmith'; Haydn: *'Emperor' Quartet, *'Surprise' Symphony; Beethoven: *'Diabelli' Variations, **Eroica Symphony*, *'Eroica' Variations; Schumann: **Abegg Variations*; Brahms: **Variations on a Theme by Haydn*; Elgar: *'Enigma' Variations; Richard Strauss: **Don Quixote*; Rachmaninov: **Rhapsody on a Theme of Paganini*; Dohnányi: **Variations on a Nursery Tune*; Britten: *The *Young Person's Guide to the Orchestra*]

Variations and Fugue on a Theme of Purcell See *The *Young Person's Guide to the Orchestra.*

Variations on a Nursery Tune A work for solo piano and orchestra, Opus 25, composed by Dohnányi in 1914, and consisting of a solemn and weighty introduction, theme, eleven variations, and a *finale fugato*. The theme is the French tune called *Ah, vous dirai-je, Maman* (otherwise known as *Twinkle, twinkle, little star.*)

Variations on a Theme by Haydn A set of orchestral variations, Opus 56a, composed by Brahms in 1873; and arranged by him for two pianos as Opus 56b. There are eight variations, followed by a finale structured on a *ground bass. Brahms borrowed the theme from Haydn's *Feldpartita No. 1 in B flat, believing that Haydn had composed the melody himself. However, it has now been discovered that Haydn had also borrowed the melody, now identified as the 'St Anthony Chorale', and so Brahms's composition is now sometimes called *St Anthony Variations.*

Variazione [Italian] Variation. **Tema con variazioni**, theme and *variations.

Varié [French] Varied. **Air varié**, air with *variations. **Thème varié**, theme and *variations.

Veena See *Vīṇā.

Vellutato [Italian]; **Velouté** [French] Velvety, smooth.

Veloce [Italian] Quick, swift, rapid – but implying smoothness of performance as well as speed. **Velocissimo**, very swiftly. **Velocità**, velocity, speed, quickness, swiftness.

Vent [French] Wind. **Instruments à vent**, or **les vents**, wind instruments.

Ventil [German] Valve. **Ventilhorn**, valve horn.

Ventile [Italian] Valve. **Corno a ventile**, valve horn.

Vents [French] See under *Vent.

Veränderung [German] Variation. **Veränderungen**, *variations.

Verbunkos [Hungarian] A 'recruiting dance'. During the late 18th and early 19th centuries, when the Hungarian army wanted to attract new recruits, evenings of merry-making were organized in villages. The *verbunkos* was a dance performed by Hungarian soldiers, in full uniform with spurs and swords, with the aim of enticing new recruits. The dance began with a slow introduction (called *lassan* or *lassu*) followed by a swift, wild dance (called a *friska* or *friss*). The 19th-century Hungarian dance called the *csárdás was a descendant of the verbunkos.

Vergnügt [German] Cheerful, joyous, light-hearted.

Verismo [Italian: 'realism'] A term used to describe an Italian operatic movement, originating in the late 19th century. The composers avoided heroic, historical, and mythological subjects, and instead based their operas on characters and events from everyday life, vividly and realistically portrayed in the music. The plots of such operas tend to be sordid, often with a good deal of violence and murder. Examples are **Cavalleria rusticana* by Mascagni, and **Pagliacci* by Leoncavallo. Puccini, too, was strongly influenced by this trend towards realism, particularly in **Tosca.*

Verkaufte Braut, Die See *The *Bartered Bride.*

Verklärte Nacht (Transfigured night) A single-movement composition, Opus 4, by Schoenberg, inspired by a poem by Richard Dehmel telling of a man and woman walking through a moonlit wood in winter. The music was originally composed, in 1899, for string sextet (two violins, two violas, two cellos).

Schoenberg made an arrangement for string orchestra in 1917, and a second version in 1943.

Verklingend [German] Fading away, dying away.

Verklingen lassen [German] A term found in piano music and in certain percussion parts (e.g. cymbals, gong or tam-tam, tubular bells) meaning 'allow (the sound) to die away' (therefore, do not damp).

Verlöschend [German] Dying away, fading away.

Vers [French] Verse.

Verschiebung [German: 'shift'] Left pedal on the piano. [See: *Una corda]

Verschwindend [German: 'vanishing'] Fading away.

Verse anthem See *Anthem.

Vespers The seventh of the eight services of the day (the Divine *Office, Canonical Hours, Daily Hours) of the Roman Catholic Church, usually taking place at the hour of sunset. Also known as Evensong. Elaborate settings of the Vespers were composed by Monteverdi (Vespers of 1610), and by Mozart – two settings for four voices, orchestra, and organ, K321 (1779) and K339 (1780).

Via [Italian] Away. **Via sordini**, mutes away (i.e. remove the mutes).

Vibrante [Italian] Vibrant, resonant.

Vibraphone (vibes) A percussion instrument, similar in appearance to the xylophone but with bars of metal instead of wood. Below each bar is a resonating tube at the top of which is a flat metal disc, made to revolve by electricity so that the top end of the tube is repeatedly opening and closing. This gives the vibraphone its characteristic *vibrato* – a pulsating sound, rich and sweet in tone. Normally the player uses soft-headed or rubber-tipped beaters, held one in each hand (occasionally two in each hand). Notes linger on for a considerable time after the bars are struck, and so a foot-pedal is provided to enable the player to damp the sound if required. The vibraphone is much used by jazz musicians and in dance bands, when it is familiarly referred to as 'vibes'.

Normal range: 

The vibraphone can be heard at the beginning of Vaughan Williams's Eighth Symphony, halfway through the *Habanera* from *The Carmen Ballet* by Shchedrin, and during *Le Marteau sans maître* by Boulez; also, on jazz records featuring Lionel Hampton playing the 'vibes'.

Vibrare [Italian] To vibrate. The term **lasciare vibrare**, meaning 'leave to vibrate' (therefore, do not damp, but allow to continue to sound or resonate), is found in piano music and in certain percussion parts, e.g. cymbals, gong or tam-tam, tubular bells.

Vibrato [Italian: 'quivering', 'shaking'] The effect of tiny and rapid fluctuations in the pitch of notes, used mainly by string players and singers, to bring life, warmth, and expression to the tone. The effect is also possible, if required, on brass and woodwind instruments. The *Bebung* effect used in *clavichord playing is a vibrato.

Vibrer [French] To vibrate. The term *laissez vibrer* means the same as the Italian *lasciare *vibrare*.

Vide [French] Empty. **Corde à vide**, open string.

Viel [German] Much; a great deal.

Vielle (viėle) [French] Name for the *medieval fiddle; later on, however, the name *vielle* (properly, *vielle à roue*) was applied to the *hurdy-gurdy.

Viennese School A general term used to describe the composers who lived and worked in Vienna during the second part of the 18th century and the early part of the 19th. They include Haydn, Mozart, Beethoven, and Schubert. The 'Second Viennese School' refers to a group of composers working in Vienna during the early part of the 20th century – notably Schoenberg, and two of his pupils: Berg and Webern.

Vier [German] Four. **Vierhändig** (literally: 'four-handed'), for four hands.

Vier ernste Gesänge (Four Serious Songs) A song-cycle, Opus 121, for low voice and piano, composed by Brahms in 1896. The four songs are settings of texts from Luther's translation of the Bible: 1 *Denn es gehet dem Menschen* (For that which befalleth the sons of men); 2 *Ich wandte mich* (So I returned); 3 *O Tod, wie bitter bist du* (O death, how bitter); 4 *Wenn ich mit Menschen- und Engelzungen redete* (Though I speak with the tongues of men and of angels).

Vier letzte Lieder (Four Last Songs) The title given by the publisher to Richard Strauss's last works, composed in 1948: four songs for soprano (or tenor) and orchestra, setting poems by Hesse and Eichendorff. (An intended fifth song remained unfinished.) The titles of the songs are *Beim Schlafengehen* (Going to sleep), *September, Frühling* (Spring), and *Im Abendrot* (In the sunset).

Viertel; Viertelnote [German] Crotchet, or quarter-note.

Vif; Vive [French] Alive, lively, brisk, eager.

Vigoroso [Italian] Vigorous, forceful, strong.

Vigueur [French] Vigour, energy, force, strength.

Vihuela (vihuela da mano) A plucked string instrument very popular in Spain during the 16th century. It was similar in size to the guitar, but its sound was more like that of the lute, and its twelve gut strings, arranged in pairs, were plucked with the fingers. The vihuela was used as a solo instrument, and also to accompany the voice.

Villancico [Spanish, from *villano*: 'peasant'] **1** A type of Spanish song of the 15th and 16th centuries, for three or four voices, or for solo voice with *vihuela accompaniment. A villancico consists of several verses (called *coplas*) linked by a recurring refrain (*estribillo*). **2** After 1600, the name villancico was used to describe a cantata or anthem for solo voices, chorus, and orchestra, often on a Christmas theme. **3** The modern meaning of villancico is simply 'Christmas carol'.

Villanella; Villanesca [Italian: 'country girl'; 'rustic'] **1** A 16th-century type of partsong, originating in Naples (and so sometimes called *villanella alla napolitana*). The music, written in a simple and popular style, is usually in three voice-parts, making frequent use of parallel 5ths. **2** Some 19th- and 20th-century composers have used the titles *villanella, villanesca*, and *villanelle* [French] for instrumental pieces in the style of a country song or dance (e.g. *Villanelle* for horn and piano by Dukas).

Vīṇā (veena) A name given to several varieties of Indian plucked string instruments (including stick zithers and arched harps) but now referring in particular to a south Indian type of long-necked plucked lute with a deep bowl-shaped wooden body and a gourd resona-

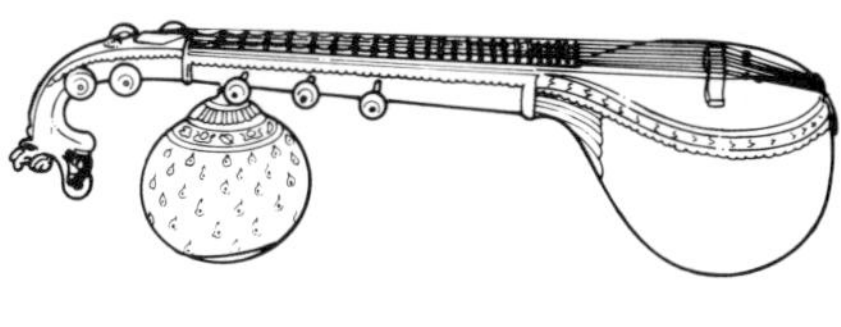

viṇa

tor below the end of the fretted fingerboard. There are seven strings, which are plucked with a wire plectrum. Four of these are melody strings, stretched above the twenty-four fixed metal frets. The remaining three strings, at the side, are used as drone strings and also to accent the rhythms. The vīṇa is associated with Saraswati, goddess of music and wisdom.

Viol [French: *viole*; German: *Gambe*; Italian: *viola, viola da gamba*] A bowed string instrument, originating towards the end of the 15th century and becoming one of the most popular instruments of the Renaissance and Baroque periods. The members of the viol family were quite distinct from those of the violin family. Viols had sloping shoulders, deep sides, and flat backs. There were six strings, less tightly strung than those of the violin; the bridge was flatter, and the soundholes were C-shaped rather than *f*-shaped. Around the fingerboard were tied pieces of gut called frets, indicating where to press down the fingers to find the different notes. A viol was held upright in front of the player rather than tucked under the chin, and the end of the outward-curving bow was held above the palm of the hand. The tone was softer, more veiled and 'reedy', less brilliant than that of the violin family.

viol

Viols were made in various sizes, the most common being treble, tenor, and bass (see *chest of viols; also *consort and *fancy). The treble viol was tuned to the notes D and G on the bass clef, middle C, and A and D on the treble clef. The tenor viol was tuned a 4th lower than the treble, and the bass viol was tuned an octave below the treble. Other sizes of viol included the 'division viol' which was rather smaller than the bass viol (see *division), and the double-bass viol (now referred to as **violone*) tuned an octave lower than the bass viol. [See also: *Viola da gamba; *Viola da braccio]

Viola [Italian] A bowed string instrument which is the second largest member of the *violin family. Like the violin, the viola is tucked under the chin to be played. It is a seventh larger than the violin, and its four strings are tuned a 5th lower:

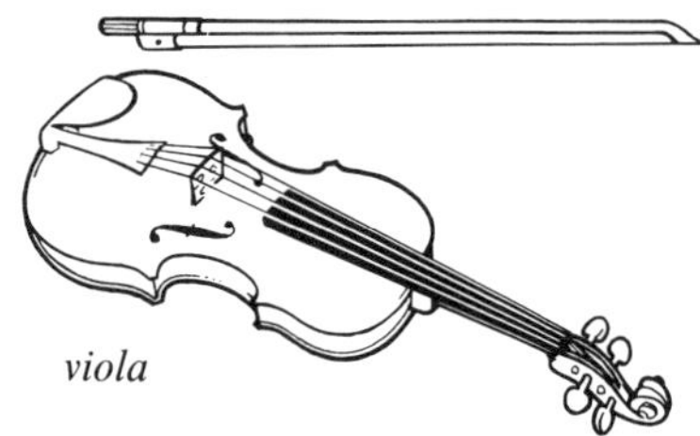

viola

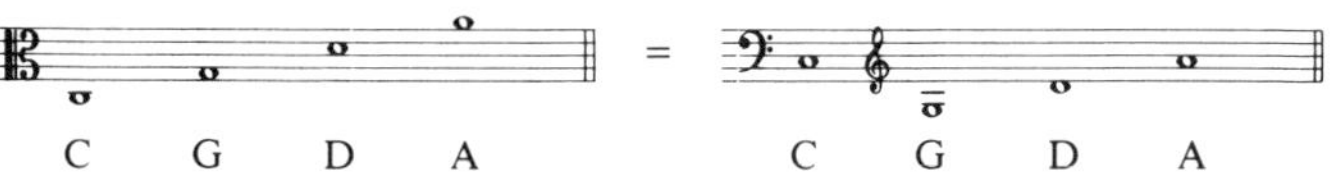

Even though the viola's strings are slightly longer and thicker than the violin's, its pitch is deeper than one might expect from its size. The tone-quality is darker, more veiled and less brilliant than that of the violin. Higher notes tend to sound rather reedy or nasal; but notes in the lower and middle parts of the viola's range are mellow, warm, and rich.

Normal range: 

Most notes played by the viola fit conveniently onto the alto C *clef (also called the viola clef); higher notes, to avoid too many leger lines, are written in the treble clef.

The viola is a standard member of the string quartet (along with first violin, second violin, and cello); the orchestra includes a section of violas (often ten or more). Melodies for the viola section can be heard at the beginning of the third movement of Rimsky-Korsakov's suite *Le Coq d'or*, and (accompanied by harps and kettle drums) in the fourth movement of Bartók's Concerto for Orchestra. The sounds of solo viola contrasted with solo violin can be heard in Mozart's *Sinfonia Concertante* (K364) for violin, viola, and orchestra. Berlioz features solo viola in **Harold in Italy*; and there are viola concertos by Telemann, Stamitz, Dittersdorf (who also wrote a *Sinfonia Concertante* for viola, double bass, and orchestra), Walton, and Hindemith (who was himself a fine viola player). Brahms adapted his two clarinet sonatas for viola. Among other chamber works with an important part for viola are Mozart's Trio in E♭ for piano, clarinet, and viola, and Debussy's Sonata for flute, viola, and harp. Berio's *Sequenza VI* is for solo (unaccompanied) viola.

Viola da braccio [Italian; *braccio*: 'arm'] Originally (16th and 17th centuries) a general term for all bowed string instruments which when played were held 'on the arm' (against the shoulder or under the chin) as distinct from those held 'on the leg' (see *Viola da gamba). This included all the members of the violin family, even though the bass violin (later the cello) was held between the knees. Later, the name *viola da braccio* became identified with the viola.

Viola da gamba [Italian: 'leg viol'] A 16th-century term originally referring to all bowed string instruments which when played were held 'on the leg' (on or between the knees) and therefore all the members of the *viol family. From about 1650, however, the name *viola da gamba*, or simply *gamba*, was applied exclusively to the bass viol, which was often used to play the bass-line in *continuo parts in conjunction with harpsichord or organ. [See also: *Viola da braccio]

Viola d'amore [Italian; *amore*: 'love'] A bowed string instrument popular during the late 17th and 18th centuries. It was about the size of a viola, but had sloping shoulders and a flat back like a viol. There were usually seven strings to be played by the bow and, stretched beneath these and running below the fingerboard, another seven sympathetic strings made of thin wire (see *Sympathetic vibrations). Vivaldi and Carl Stamitz each wrote concertos for viola d'amore; Telemann composed a Concerto for flute, oboe d'amore, viola d'amore, and strings. Hindemith's *Kammermusik* No. 6 is for viola d'amore and chamber orchestra, and he also composed a *Kleine Sonate* for viola d'amore and piano.

Violin A bowed string instrument, which is the smallest and highest-sounding member of the *violin family that is in common use. The violin has been described as one of the most perfect, expressive, and versatile of all musical instruments. Among its important ancestors are the medieval fiddle, the rebec, and the lira da braccio. The violin itself emerged, in Italy, at some time during the first half of the 16th century (the exact date is not known).

The violin basically consists of a hollow, waisted, wooden body, and a wooden neck to which is attached the fingerboard (the total length of the violin is 59.4 cm). The four strings, made of gut or metal, are fixed to the tail-piece, then stretched across the bridge and fastened around the tuning-pegs. The four strings are tuned, a 5th apart, to these notes:

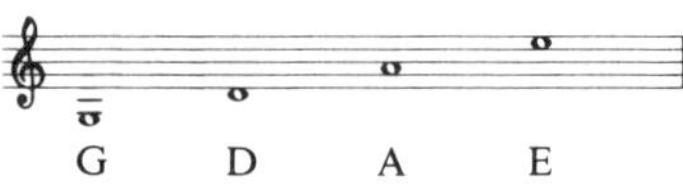

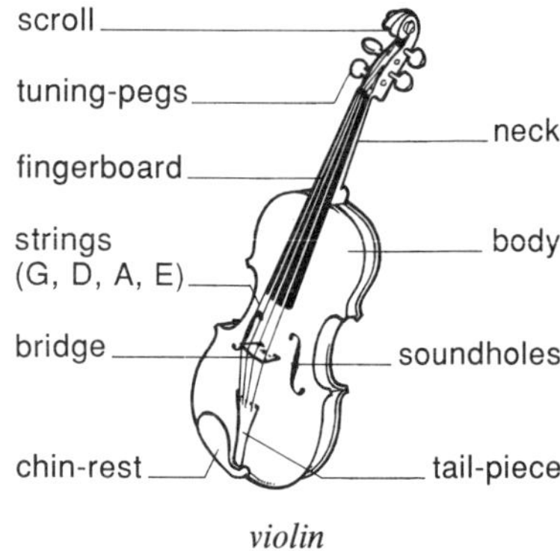

violin

All four strings are of the same length, but they produce notes of different pitch since they vary in thickness and also in tension (tightness). A thinner string will vibrate more quickly than a thicker string, and so produce a higher note. The string tuned to the note E is the thinnest string; that tuned to G is the thickest. The player tunes the strings by adjusting (turning) the tuning-pegs. The tighter a string is made, the higher the pitch will be.

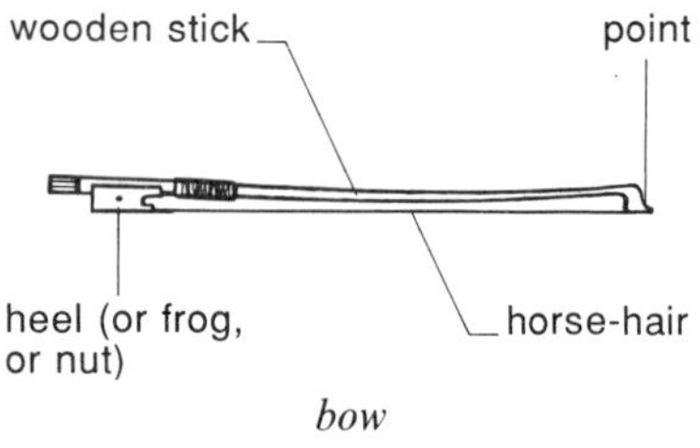

bow

In normal playing, the violinist tucks the violin between the shoulder and the left side of the chin, and, holding the *bow with the right hand, draws the horse-hair across a string, making it vibrate and so produce a note. The vibrations of the string are transmitted by the bridge into the hollow body, and this itself vibrates, amplifying and enriching the sound before it flows out through the *f*-shaped soundholes on each side of the bridge.

violin: playing position

An 'open' string will produce the note to which it is tuned. To sound notes of other pitch, the player must shorten the strings by 'stopping' them. To 'stop' a string means to press it down onto the fingerboard with a finger of the left hand. This shortens the vibrating length of the string – only the length from the bridge to the stopped point will vibrate. The shorter the vibrating length, the higher the note will be. The normal range of notes on the violin covers more than three and a half octaves, and this can be extended still higher by the use of harmonics (see *Harmonic 2).

Normal range: 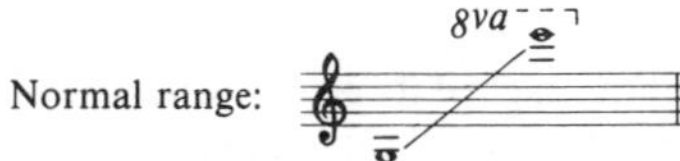

While stopping a note, the player normally uses *vibrato* – a rocking to and fro of the left hand as a finger stops a string. This causes tiny and rapid fluctuations in the pitch of the note, bringing life, warmth, and expression to the tone. Two notes may be bowed at the same time on two adjacent strings. This is called 'double stopping'. Sometimes the player is required to play three notes at once (triple stopping) – or even four (quadruple stopping) but in this case, although the four notes may be written to be played simultaneously, the player bows the lower two strings first then quickly rocks onto the higher two, since the curve of the bridge prevents the bow from being able to touch all four strings at once.

The violin is capable of an extremely wide range of expression. Dynamics and tone-colour may be varied by the way the bow is used, the way in which it attacks or leaves the strings, its pressure on the strings, or its precise positioning on the strings – close to the bridge, near or on the fingerboard, or (as is most usual) at a point midway between the two. (Some of the important ways of using the bow are listed under *bowing.) The tone-colour may also be altered by the use of a mute – a small, comb-like device, which is clipped onto the bridge. This dampens the vibrations, reducing the volume (loudness) and bringing a hushed, silvery quality to the tone. Sometimes, instead of bowing the strings, the player plucks them with the fingertips, an effect known as *pizzicato*.

Almost every work composed for orchestra includes parts for violin. In the modern orchestra there are often thirty or more violins (more than any other instrument) and they are divided into two groups: first violins, and second violins – the first violins generally playing higher notes than the seconds. In scores, the parts are often indicated, in the singular, as Violino I and Violino II (or Vl. I and Vl. 2). The violin is also extensively used in many types of chamber ensemble (see under *Chamber music, and also under *Sonata). Among the numerous concertos written for the violin are those by Vivaldi, Bach, Mozart, Beethoven, Paganini, Mendelssohn, Brahms, Bruch, Tchaikovsky, Sibelius, Schoenberg, Bartók, Berg, Prokofiev, Walton, and Penderecki. (See also: *Double concerto, *Triple concerto.)

The following are a few examples illustrating the varied tone-colours and expressive qualities of the violin. Rich, low register: the main theme from the last movement of Brahms's First Symphony (at bar 62). High register: the first Sea Interlude, *Dawn* from Britten's opera *Peter Grimes*. Full range, bowed *tremolo playing: *Moto perpetuo* from Britten's 'Variations on a Theme of Frank Bridge'. Pizzicato: third movement of Tchaikovsky's Fourth Symphony. With mute: slow movement of Tchaikovsky's Violin Concerto, and *The Death of Åse* from Grieg's incidental music to *Peer Gynt*. Col *legno: the beginning of *Mars* from Holst's *The Planets*. Harmonics: the opening of Mahler's First Symphony, and of Borodin's *In the Steppes of Central Asia*. Bowed *tremolo, played sul *ponticello: the opening of Falla's *Nights in the Gardens of Spain*. Double stoppings: Kreisler's *Caprice viennois* (from about a quarter of the way through the piece). Double, triple, and quadruple stoppings: the Chaconne from Bach's Partita No. 2 in D minor for unaccompanied violin.

Although, over the years, slight alterations have been made to the violin (and also to the bow) it has in fact changed very little since the 16th century. Superb craftsmanship in the making of violins reached its peak during the 17th century in Cremona. In this town in northern Italy lived three families of violin makers of the very highest class: the Amati, Guarneri, and Stradivari families. Any of their violins are highly prized today, but most especially those by Antonio Stradivari. In March 1988, one of his violins was sold at Sotheby's in London for £473,000 – a world record price, at that date, for a musical instrument.

Violine (plural: *Violinen*) [German]; **Violino** (plural: *violini*) [Italian] *Violin.

Violin family The main members of this family of bowed *string instruments are the violin itself, the viola, and the cello. Some authorities also count the double bass (therefore including all the bowed string instruments of the orchestra), but others maintain that this instrument is more closely related to the *viol family. Characteristically, members of the violin family have four strings and an unfretted fingerboard, and *f*-shaped soundholes. The shoulders are rounded, and the back is slightly convex.

Among other members of the family are the violino piccolo, tenor violin, and kit violin; forerunners of the family include the medieval fiddle, rebec, and lira da braccio.

Violino piccolo [Italian] A small violin, used in the 17th and 18th centuries, tuned either a 4th or a minor 3rd higher than the ordinary violin. Bach included a violino piccolo in the first of his *Brandenburg Concertos.

Violon [French] Violin.

Violoncello [Italian]; **Violoncell** [German]; **Violoncelle** [French] *Cello.

Violone [Italian: 'large viol'] A term which has been used with a variety of meanings, e.g. to mean any kind of viol, or a large viol, or even the cello. In scores by German Baroque composers (e.g. J. S. Bach) it refers to the double bass. Nowadays the word is usually taken to mean double-bass viol – the viol similar in size and range to the modern double bass, of which it was the direct ancestor.

Virelai [French] One of the three main forms of poetry and music (along with the *ballade and the *rondeau) used by French composers from the 13th century to the 15th (e.g. Guillaume de Machaut, *c*1300–1377). The music for a virelai consisted of two phrases, **A** and **B**, heard in the order:

Subsequent verses (there were usually three in all) followed exactly the same pattern, with the refrain sung both before and after each verse. An example is Machaut's virelai *Douce dame jolie*. [See also: *Ballata]

Virginal (virginals) A plucked string keyboard instrument, most often oblong in shape; really a simple type of harpsichord with one set of strings (running more or less parallel with the keyboard) and with one string per note over a range of four octaves. Sometimes the instrument was supplied with legs, but was often a mere box to be placed on a table. The first mention of the virginals (the word was often used in the plural, like 'scissors') dates from the late 15th century. During the 16th century, the virginals became particularly popular in England. Almost all Tudor composers wrote music for the virginals. They soon discovered a style very well suited to the keyboard: swift scales and brilliant running passages, spread chords, broken chord patterns, and crisp decorations. Some pieces they wrote, such as fantasias, were in contrapuntal style. Others were arrangements of popular songs of the day, or based on pieces of church music. A few were programmatic, and many were dances: almans, corantos, pavans, and galliards. Many of these pieces were constructed from three 'strains' or sections, and to make a short piece more interesting a Tudor composer would often write a decorated repeat, or variation, to follow each section. Sometimes a quite lengthy piece would be built up by writing a whole string of variations upon a chosen melody. Among the most important Tudor composers of music for virginals were William Byrd, John Bull, Orlando Gibbons, and Giles Farnaby. [See also: *Dompe; *Parthenia; *Fitzwilliam Virginal Book; *The *King's Hunt*]

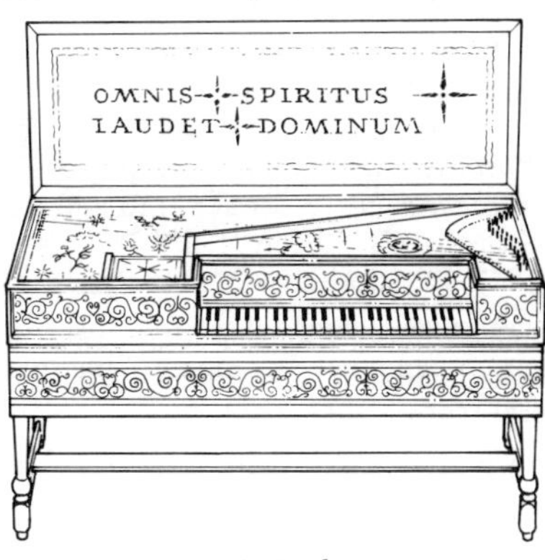

virginals

Virtuoso [Italian] A term used to describe any musician who displays extraordinary technical skill. The performance should also display sensitivity and musicianship – though, unfortunately, this is not always the case.

Visage An *electronic work for two-track tape, composed by Luciano Berio in 1961. It is based on the voice, sometimes electronically transformed, of Cathy Berberian (who was married to Berio 1950–66). The title is a French word meaning 'countenance' or 'face'. Berio described the work as 'a sound-track for a drama that was never written'. Vocal 'events', which range from inarticulate to articulate speech, from laughter to crying, and eventually to singing, are related to and combined with electronically produced sounds.

Vite [French] Quick, rapid, swift. **Vitement**, quickly.

Vivace [Italian] Lively, brisk. **Vivacissimo**, very lively.

Vivacità [Italian] Vivacity.

Vivamente [Italian] In a lively manner.

Vive See *Vif.

Vivement [French] Quickly, briskly, eagerly, in a lively manner.

Vivo [Italian] Lively, brisk, eager, quick.

Vltava See **Má vlast*.

V° Abbreviation for *violino* [Italian], violin.

Vocalise [French] A wordless vocal composition, or section of a composition, which is sung to a vowel sound (e.g. 'Ah'). Examples are Rachmaninov's *Vocalise* for soprano and piano (1912), the first movement of *Bachianas brasileiras* No. 5 for soprano and eight cellos (1938–45) by Villa-Lobos, and Stravinsky's *Pastorale* (1907) for soprano and piano (which he arranged, in 1923, for soprano, oboe, cor anglais, clarinet, and bassoon).

Vocal music Any music for voice or voices, with or without instrumental accompaniment. [Compare: *Instrumental music]

Vocal score See *Score.

Voce (plural: *voci*) [Italian] Voice. Also *part or voice-part. **A due (tre, quattro) voci**, for two (three, four) voices. **Colla voce**, 'with the voice' – warning accompanists to follow the voice closely in a passage performed in freer style.

Voice **1** A general term for the sound uttered through the human mouth, particularly in speaking and singing. In singing, air expelled from the lungs causes the vocal cords (two strips of cartilage stretched across the larynx at the back of the throat) to vibrate like reeds, and so produce a note. To sing a higher note, the vocal cords are tightened; to sing a lower note they are slackened. The various cavities of throat, mouth, and nose serve as resonators to amplify and enrich the sounds. The following table gives the names which are used to describe the range, and also the timbre, of different types of voices. For each voice, the average range is given – trained solo singers would be expected to exceed these limits.

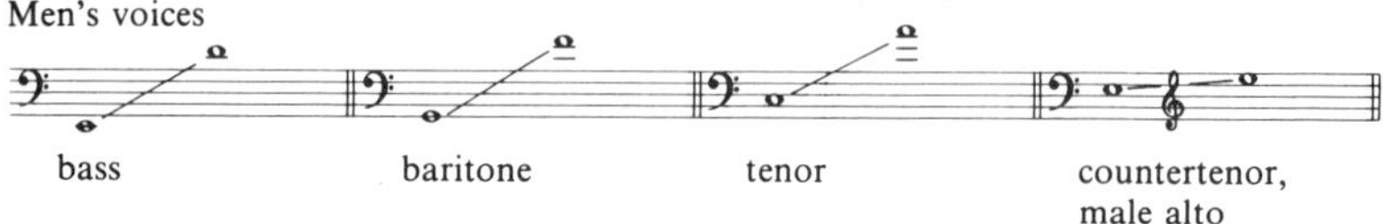

A boy's voice before it changes or 'breaks' (meaning that the vocal cords thicken, causing the pitch to become lower) is described as either treble (high range) or alto (lower range). Girls' voices are similar in range, but tend to be rather gentler in tone. [See also: *Chest voice; *Head voice; and see also under *Clef]

2 The term **voice** is also used to describe any of the individual parts or melodic strands in a contrapuntal composition (especially a *fugue) – even when the music is instrumental rather than vocal.

Voice-exchange A musical device (often found, for example, in 13th-century English music) whereby scraps of melody, or whole phrases, are exchanged between voice-parts. For example, while one voice sings **A–B**, another voice, at the same time, is singing **B–A**:

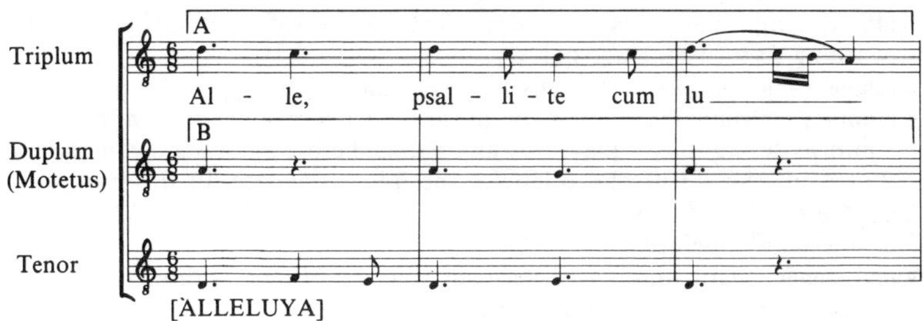

Voice-leading American term for *part-writing.

Voice-parts The individual parts or lines of music in a composition which includes solo voices or choir. A choral piece will often be written in four voice-parts, named (from highest to lowest) soprano, alto (or contralto), tenor, bass.

Voilé [French] Veiled, in tone-quality; muffled.

Voix [French] Voice, voices. Also *part or voice-part.

Volante [Italian: 'flying'] Swiftly and lightly.

Volkslied [German] Folk-song. **Volksliedchen**, a short folk-song.

Voll [German] Full, complete, whole. **Volles Werk**, *full organ.

Volta [Italian] **1** Time. **Prima volta**, first time (often abbreviated simply to 1.) and **Seconda volta**, second time (often abbreviated simply to 2.) refer to the two different endings which may be found at the end of a repeated section of music. Brackets above the music indicate the affected bars:

The first time, the performer plays the bar(s) indicated by the first bracket. In the repeat, the performer omits the music beneath the 'first time' bracket and skips straight to the music indicated by the 'second time' bracket.

2 Volta (plural: *volte*) or **Lavolta**, was the name of an energetic dance in triple time, popular at the end of the 16th century and the beginning of the 17th. It included swift leaps and turns, and at certain points the man was required to swing his partner high in the air. Queen Elizabeth I much enjoyed dancing the volta, but it was later banned at the French court as being too unseemly.

Volti [Italian] Turn (over the page). **Volti subito** (often abbreviated to **V.S.**), warning to turn the page quickly.

Volume The loudness, or intensity, of a sound.

Voluntary Originally, a piece of music which a player was called upon to *improvise, e.g. pieces played by an organist before and after a church service. Later on, pieces with this title were specially composed for this purpose.

Von [German] Of, from.

Vor [German] Before.

Vorzutragen [German] To be performed, to be played. (For example: *singbar vorzutragen*, to be played in a singing style.)

Vox [Latin] Voice.

V.S. Abbreviation of *volti subito.

Vuoto [Italian: 'empty'] A term used to mean **1** a note in string music which is to be played on an open string (*corda vuota*), or **2** an empty bar (*misura vuota*).

Vyšehrad See **Má vlast*.

Wachet auf ('Sleepers, wake!') J. S. Bach's Cantata No. 140, composed in 1731, for soprano, tenor, and bass soloists, chorus, and orchestra. It is in seven movements, and the three choral movements (1, 4, and 7) are based on a Lutheran chorale of the same title:

Bach later arranged the fourth movement of the Cantata as a chorale prelude for organ – the first of the six *Schübler Chorales.

Wagner tuba This is a special type of tuba, designed by Wagner for use in his cycle *Der *Ring des Nibelungen*. The tube, which has a steadily expanding conical bore, is coiled into an oval shape and ends in a bell which is only moderately flared. The mouthpiece is funnel-shaped liked that of the horn. Wagner scored for four of these instruments: two tenors in B♭ and two basses in F. The contrabass tuba which he combined with the group was the normal double-bass tuba. Other composers who have used the Wagner tubas are Bruckner in his last three symphonies, Richard Strauss in his opera *Elektra*, Schoenberg in **Gurrelieder*, and Stravinsky in *The *Rite of Spring*.

Wait (wayte) **1** Another name for the medieval *shawm (also called 'wayte-pipe'). **2** In Medieval times, waits were night watchmen at the gates of castles or towns who marked certain hours of the night by sounding a musical instrument (usually a wind instrument). In the 15th and 16th centuries municipal waits, besides fulfilling their watch-keeping duties, formed bands to provide music for important occasions, e.g. music for special entertainments or to accompany a play, or ceremonial music to welcome a royal visitor.

Waldhorn [German: 'woodland horn'] A handhorn; a 'natural' *horn, without valves.

'Waldstein' Sonata Nickname of Beethoven's Piano Sonata No. 21 in C, Op. 53, composed in 1803–4 and dedicated to his patron Count Ferdinand von

Waldstein. The sonata is in two movements only: 1 *Allegro con brio* (in sonata form); 2 *Introduzione* (*Adagio molto*) leading into a Rondo: *Allegretto moderato* (simple rondo form).

Walking bass A purposefully moving bass-line (e.g. played *pizzicato* on double bass), pressing forward steadily and continuously, often in notes of equal value (e.g. crotchets).

Walküre, Die (The Valkyrie) See *Der *Ring des Nibelungen.*

Waltz [German: *Walzer*; French: *valse*] A dance with three beats to a bar, usually with a lilting *dum*–dah–dah rhythm, and with the bass part often playing the root of the chord on the strong first beat of each bar. The waltz originated in Germany and Austria towards the end of the 18th century, developing from the Austrian peasant dance called the *Ländler. When the waltz was first danced in the elegant ballrooms of Vienna, some people were shocked – this was one of the first dances in which the partners held each other closely. But most were captivated by the gaiety and lightness of its whirling movements, and the 'waltz craze' soon swept right across Europe.

The most famous waltz composers were members of the Strauss family, particularly Johann Strauss the Elder (1804–1849) and his second son, Johann Strauss the Younger (1825–1899), nicknamed 'The Waltz King', whose many waltzes include *The *Blue Danube*, **Tales from the Vienna Woods*, *Voices of Spring*, and *The Emperor Waltz*.

A great many other composers have written waltzes, including Beethoven, Weber (*Invitation to the Dance*), Schubert (sets of *Walzer* for piano solo), Berlioz (the second movement, *Un Bal*, from *Symphonie fantastique*), Chopin (nineteen *Valses* for piano), Brahms (*Walzer* for piano solo and for piano duet; also **Liebeslieder-Walzer*), Tchaikovsky in his ballets (**Swan Lake*, *The *Sleeping Beauty*, *The *Nutcracker*) and also as the third movement, *Valse*, of his Fifth Symphony, Richard Strauss (in his opera *Der Rosenkavalier*), Ravel (*Valses nobles et sentimentales* and *La *Valse*), and Sibelius (**Valse triste*).

Walzer [German] *Waltz, waltzes.

Wand of Youth, The Two orchestral suites by Elgar, Opus 1a (1907) and 1b (1908), consisting of arrangements and orchestrations of tunes he had originally composed for a family play in 1869 when he was twelve years old.

War Requiem Choral work, Opus 66, by Benjamin Britten, composed in 1961 for performance the following year at the consecration of the new Coventry Cathedral (the former Cathedral having been destroyed by bombs during the Second World War). Britten sets sections of the Latin words of the *Requiem Mass, interwoven with settings of poems by Wilfred Owen who died in battle, aged 25, one week before the end of the First World War. The *War Requiem* is scored for soprano, tenor, and baritone soloists, mixed chorus, boys' choir, organ, chamber orchestra (made up of twelve players), and large orchestra with a particularly varied percussion section. At the first performance of the work, conducted by the composer, soloists were brought together from three nations: Galina Vishnevskaya (Russia), Peter Pears (Great Britain), and Dietrich Fischer-Dieskau (Germany).

Wasps, The Incidental music composed by Vaughan Williams in 1909 for a production of a comedy of the same name by Aristophanes, a Greek playwright of the 5th century BC. The best-known piece, often performed as a separate concert work, is the Overture. Other pieces include two *entr'actes and a comic *March-past of the Kitchen Utensils.*

Water Music Three suites – in F major, D major, and G major – by Handel. It is thought that the first two (for oboes, bassoons, trumpets, horns, and strings) were performed during a royal barge procession on the River Thames from Whitehall to Chelsea on July 17, 1717. And that the third (for recorder, flute, and strings) was played as an accompaniment to the royal supper at Chelsea. There used to be a story that Handel composed this music especially to regain favour with King George I, whose employment he had left (when the king was the Elector of Hanover) in order to settle in England. But it is now believed that the king had already forgiven Handel for deserting him.

Six of the twenty pieces from the *Water Music* are often played as a suite orchestrated by Sir Hamilton Harty. These are: 1 Allegro; 2 Air; 3 Bourrée; 4 Hornpipe; 5 Andante espressivo; 6 Allegro deciso. [See also: **Fireworks Music*]

Wayte See *Wait.

Wedding Day at Troldhaugen See **Lyric Pieces.*

Wehmuth [German] Sadness, melancholy. **Wehmütig, wehmutsvoll,** sad, sorrowful, melancholy.

Weich [German] Soft, smooth.

Weihnachts Oratorium See *Christmas Oratorio.

Weise [German] Manner, style, way.

Welcome Song A composition for solo voices, chorus, and orchestra by English composers of the Restoration period (1661–*c*1700), celebrating the return to London of the king or other members of the royal family. An example is Purcell's *What, what shall be done*?, composed in 1682 as a 'welcome song for the Duke of York' (afterwards James II).

Well-Tempered Clavier, The [German: *Das Wohltemperirte Clavier*] Famous collection of forty-eight compositions for keyboard by J. S. Bach, each consisting of a prelude followed by a fugue, and published in two sets (Book 1, 1722; Book 2, 1744). Each set contains twenty-four preludes and fugues – one for each of the major and minor keys, presented in the order: C major, C minor, C♯ major, C♯ minor, D major, D minor, and so on. The entire work is often referred to simply as 'The Forty-Eight'. The use of the word 'well-tempered' in Bach's title indicates his aim was to demonstrate the advantage of the new system of tuning keyboard instruments in equal *temperament. The title is sometimes translated as 'The Well-Tempered Clavichord', but in Bach's day the word *Clavier* was used to refer to any kind of instrument with a keyboard.

Wenig [German] A little, slightly. **Weniger**, less.

West Side Story Musical by Bernstein, staged in New York in 1957 (book by Laurents, lyrics by Sondheim). Though updated and set in the West Side of New York City, the story is loosely based on the *Romeo and Juliet idea. Shakespeare's warring families, the Montagues and the Capulets, are replaced by rival gangs, the Jets (Americans) and the Sharks (Puerto Ricans). Tony, a Jet, falls in love with Maria, the sister of Bernardo, leader of the Sharks. Bernardo is furious. In a gang fight (the Rumble) he taunts Tony, is knifed by him, and dies. Bernardo's girl, Anita, tries to put Maria off Tony, but, grieved as she is, Maria stands by him. Anita agrees to warn Tony that Chino, a Shark, is seeking to avenge Bernardo's death. The Jets taunt Anita, and she lies to them that Chino has killed Maria. Devastated, Tony is roaming the streets, when Maria steps out of the dark. At the very moment of joyful recognition, Chino appears, and shoots Tony dead.

When I am laid in earth Dido's Lament, from Purcell's opera **Dido and Aeneas*.

Whip (slapstick) A percussion instrument consisting of two hinged pieces of flat hardwood which, when slapped smartly together, produce a loud 'crack' resembling the sound of a whip. It can be heard in Malcolm Arnold's Overture *Tam o'Shanter* (about three and a half minutes from the start), and at the beginning of Penderecki's Symphony (1973).

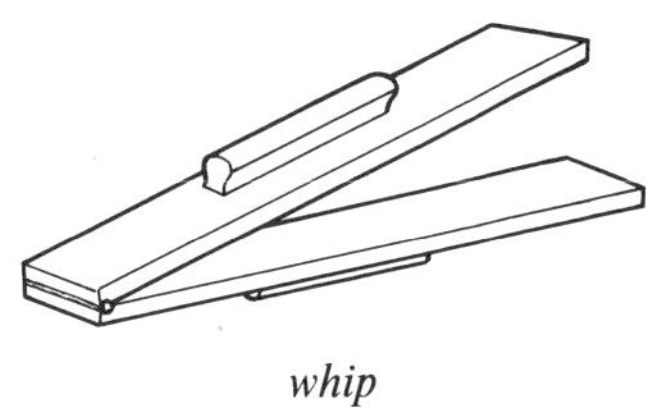

whip

Whistle flute See *Fipple flute.

Whole consort See *Consort.

Whole note *Semibreve. The term **whole rest** is sometimes used to mean a semibreve rest.

Whole step American term for a tone or *whole tone.

Whole tone An interval of two semitones. For example C to D, D to E, or E to F♯. (E to F♮, however, is a semitone.)

Whole-tone scale A scale containing no semitones, but built entirely from notes a whole tone apart. Only two whole-tone scales are possible:

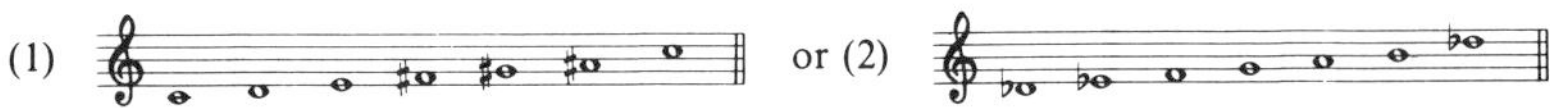

(Pitches may appear, for convenience, in different guises – for example, F♯ may appear as G♭, A♯ may appear as B♭, and so on.)

The whole-tone scale can be used to build melodies and harmonies, but since this scale lacks the *interval of a perfect 5th (and also that of a perfect 4th) no common chord, such as C–E–G, can be built from its notes. Among the composers who have used the whole-tone scale in their music are Glinka, Vaughan Williams, and, particularly, Debussy. The effect of the whole-tone scale can be clearly heard at the beginning of Debussy's second piano Prélude: *Voiles* (which may mean 'Sails', or 'Veils'):

Wie [German] As; as if; like. **Wie am Anfang**, as at the beginning. **Wie aus der Ferne**, as if from the distance. **Wie oben**, as above, as before.

Wieder [German] Again, once more.

Wiegenlied [German] A cradle-song or lullaby, usually with the accompaniment imitating the gentle rocking of the cradle. There are fine songs with this title by Brahms, Wolf, and Richard Strauss. [See also: *Berceuse]

William Tell (*Guillaume Tell*) Opera in three (originally four) acts by Rossini, first produced in Paris in 1829 (libretto by de Jouy and Bis, after a play by Schiller). Tell (baritone), a Swiss patriot, rallies his countrymen against the oppression of Austrian rule and secures their independence by killing the tyrant Gessler (bass). The opera is now remembered mainly for its famous overture and for a ballet suite which is sometimes played.

Wind band A band made up of a mixture of wind instruments (both woodwind and brass) with or without percussion. A *military band is sometimes referred to as a wind band (as distinct from a *brass band, which contains brass but not woodwind instruments). [See also: *Symphonic band]

Wind instruments All those instruments which, when blown by the performer, produce their sounds by the vibrations of a column of air enclosed in a tube (the body of the instrument). The two main types of wind instruments are ***brass instruments** – in which the air column is set in vibration by the player's lips vibrating against a metal mouthpiece; and ***woodwind instruments** – which have holes bored along the length of their tubes, and in which the air column may be made to vibrate by means of a mouth-hole (flute, piccolo), single reed (clarinet), or double reed (oboe, bassoon). The organ is also sometimes classed as a wind instrument, but more often as a *keyboard instrument. [See also: *Aerophone]

Wind machine A device used in certain compositions to imitate the sound of wind. It consists of a barrel framework covered with cloth (often silk). When rotated by a handle, friction of the cloth brushing against cardboard or thin wood simulates the sound of wind – the pitch and intensity of the sound rising the faster the handle is turned. Works in which the effect is used include Richard Strauss's **Don Quixote* and *Alpine Symphony*, and Vaughan Williams's **Sinfonia antartica.*

Wind quintet **1** An ensemble consisting of five solo wind instruments – usually, flute, oboe, clarinet, horn, and bassoon. **2** *Chamber music written for such an ensemble – for example: Nielsen's Wind Quintet (1922), Hindemith's *Kleine Kammermusik* (Little Chamber Music) Op. 24 No. 2 (1922), Schoenberg's Wind Quintet (1923–4), and Milhaud's Suite: *La Cheminée du roi René* (1939).

Wind sextet *Chamber music for six wind instruments. The most likely combinations are two oboes, two horns, two bassoons (e.g. Mozart's Divertimento No. 14 in B♭, K270; 1777) or two clarinets, two horns, two bassoons (e.g. Beethoven's Wind Sextet in E♭, Op. 71; *c*1795). [See also **Mládí*]

Winterreise (Winter journey) Schubert's most important *song-cycle, D911, for male voice and piano. It was composed in 1827, and is in two parts, each part consisting of twelve songs setting poems by the German poet, Wilhelm Müller. The titles of the songs are: 1 *Gute Nacht* (Good night); 2 *Die Wetterfahne* (The weathercock); 3 *Gefror'ne Tränen* (Frozen tears); 4 *Erstarrung* (Numbness); 5 *Der Lindenbaum* (The lime tree); 6 *Wasserflut* (Flood); 7 *Auf dem Flusse* (At the stream); 8 *Rückblick* (Retrospect); 9 *Irrlicht* (Will-o'-the-wisp); 10 *Rast* (Rest); 11 *Frühlingstraum* (Dream of Springtime); 12 *Einsamkeit* (Loneliness). 13 *Die Post* (The post); 14 *Der greise Kopf* (The hoary head); 15 *Die Krähe* (The crow); 16 *Letzte Hoffnung* (Last hope); 17 *Im Dorfe* (In the village); 18 *Der stürmische Morgen* (Stormy morning); 19 *Täuschung* (Illusion); 20 *Der Wegweiser* (The signpost); 21 *Das Wirtshaus* (The inn); 22 *Mut* (Courage); 23 *Die Nebensonnen* (The mock suns); 24 *Der Leiermann* (The organ-grinder).

'Winter Wind' Study Nickname of Chopin's Study (Étude) No. 11 in A minor (1834) from his second set of Twelve Studies for piano, Op. 25. A slow and quiet four-bar introduction hints at the theme, which is then played by the left hand beneath boisterous, whirling semiquavers, falling and rising in the right-hand part.

Winter Words A *song-cycle, Opus 52, for soprano or tenor and piano, composed by Benjamin Britten in 1953. The title is taken from Thomas Hardy's last book of poetry (1928) from which Britten sets eight poems: 1 At day-close in November; 2 Midnight on the Great Western (or The journeying boy); 3 Wagtail and Baby; 4 The little old table; 5 The choir-master's burial (or The tenor man's story); 6 Proud songsters (thrushes, finches and nightingales); 7 At the railway station, Upwey (or The convict and boy with the violin); 8 Before life and after.

Wohltemperirte Clavier, Das See *The *Well-Tempered Clavier.*

Wolf (wolf note) A disagreeable sound occasionally occurring from a bowed string instrument when the wooden body of the instrument produces unwanted resonances to a particular note in the instrument's range. Expert players are able to minimize this unpleasant effect. The term 'wolf' is also used in connection with keyboard instruments (particularly the organ) to describe any unpleasant effect due to imperfect tuning.

WoO Abbreviation of the German phrase *Werke ohne Opuszahl* (works without *opus number), and used to identify such works by Beethoven.

Woodblocks Wooden percussion instruments, of which two main types are sometimes used in the orchestra or in bands. **1 Chinese block** (Chinese woodblock): a rectangular hardwood block, hollowed out and with one, sometimes two, slots. Struck with a beater such as a drumstick or xylophone mallet it produces a hollow but resonant sound, often of indefinite pitch. (Also sometimes called 'clog box' or 'tap box'.) **2 Temple block** (Chinese temple block, Korean temple block): a hollowed-out block of hardwood, often pear-shaped, and with a wide slot. Temple blocks are made in different sizes, and often used in sets of five or more. When struck with a beater (e.g. a drumstick) each block gives a note of definite pitch; the sounds are lower and more mellow than those of the Chinese block. The sound of the Chinese block can be heard in the dance from Copland's *Rodeo* called *Hoe-Down* (with piano, just after the start). Temple blocks can be heard in the first *Intermezzo* from *The Carmen Ballet* by Shchedrin, and in *Old Sir Faulk* from Walton's *Façade* Suite No. 2.

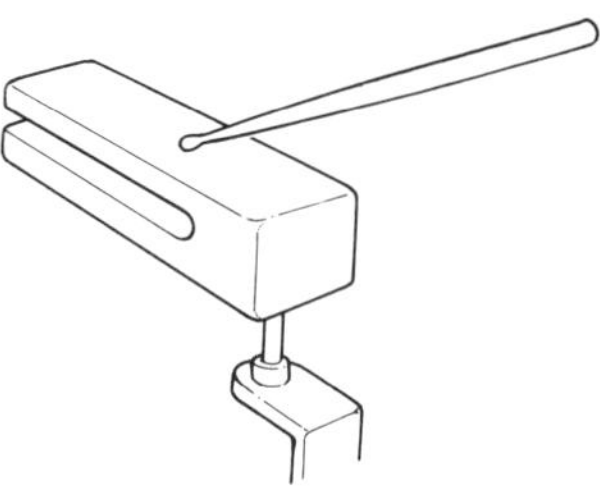

Chinese block

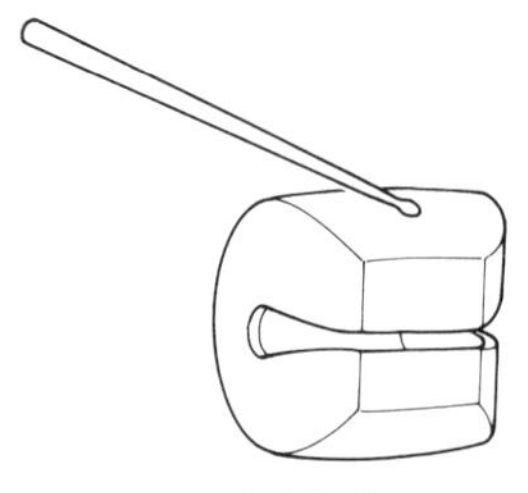

temple block

Woodwind instruments A name given to *wind instruments which were originally (and in some cases still may be) made of wood, and in which the air column is made to vibrate by means of a blow-hole (flute, piccolo), or a single reed (clarinet), or a double reed (oboe, bassoon). Saxophones (single reed) are also counted as woodwind instruments.

Cut into the tube of a woodwind instrument are various finger-holes which, when opened or closed (either by the player's fingers alone, or by means of a system of keys and levers operated by the fingers), produce the various pitches as the instrument is blown. By opening and closing finger-holes, the player shortens or lengthens the vibrating column of air inside the instrument. The shorter the air column, the higher the note; the longer the air column, the lower the note. (See also: *Overblowing.)

In the **woodwind section** of the orchestra, the four main instruments are the *flute, *oboe, *clarinet, and *bassoon. There may also be included any of the 'extras' or 'near relations' of these four standard woodwinds: *piccolo, *cor anglais, *bass clarinet, and *double bassoon.

In describing a composer's scoring for orchestra, *double woodwind* means that the woodwind section for that work consists of two flutes, two oboes, two clarinets, two bassoons. (This is the usual woodwind section of the 'Classical orchestra', as found in Haydn's last symphonies and the early symphonies of Beethoven and Schubert.) *Triple woodwind* implies that three of each of the four main woodwinds are included, usually with at least one player switching when necessary to an 'extra' instrument – for example, third flute interchanging with piccolo, third oboe interchanging with cor anglais, etc. A work for very large orchestra may include *quadruple woodwind*, meaning that four of each of the main woodwinds are required, with at least one 'extra' of each type.

Word-painting A term used to describe instances in vocal compositions when the composer uses vivid effects in the music to bring out the special meaning of certain words in the text. Word-painting was a favourite technique of 16th-century composers, especially in *madrigals. The word 'death', for instance, might be expressed in the music by a harsh discord; a phrase such as 'one by one came tripping down' might have the voices, one by one, tripping lightly down a scale.

The same technique is also often found in vocal compositions by Baroque composers – there are many examples, for instance, in the cantatas of J. S. Bach.

The effect of word-painting may be apparent in the instrumental accompaniment as well as (or instead of) the vocal part of the music.

Working out Term sometimes used to mean the development section of a piece designed in *sonata form.

Work-song A song sung by a group of workers, often based on a call-and-response pattern (soloist answered by group). The purpose of the song is to ease the monotony of a communal task performed with regular actions, and also to synchronize the efforts of the workers. Examples are the sea *shanty, and the black American slave work-songs, many of which had originated in Africa. A work-song has a steady beat, with emphasis on a syllable (often simply '*Huh*') at the moment of greatest effort – for example, at the fall of the hammer, axe, or pick:

> Take this hammer – *huh!* An' carry it to the captain – *huh!* [3 times]
> You tell him I'm gone – *huh!* [twice]

Wort [German] Word. **Lieder ohne Worte**, *Songs without Words.

Wozzeck Opera in three acts by Berg, first produced in Berlin in 1925 (libretto by the composer after a drama by Büchner). Marie (soprano), mistress of the poor, demented soldier Wozzeck, has had by him a baby son. Wozzeck (baritone) is scolded by his Captain, who disapproves. With another soldier, Andres (tenor), he goes to a field at sunset to cut sticks, but is tormented with wild visions, and his lunatic ravings alarm his companion. A Doctor (bass), himself half mad, experiments on Wozzeck in the hope of becoming famous. Meanwhile Marie surrenders to the advances of a Drum Major (tenor), but Wozzeck grows suspicious, and when the Drum Major bursts into his barrack-room at night boasting of his success and shouting insults, Wozzeck falls upon him and beats him furiously. Reading the Bible, Marie is overcome with feelings of guilt. By a pond in a wood she and Wozzeck recall their first meeting, but Wozzeck is again struck with madness and impulsively stabs her to death. Returning later to search for the knife, he wades into the pond and is drowned. Their child, playing in the street, is told that his mother is dead. He does not understand, and continues to play.

Wq Abbreviation standing for Wotquenne (Alfred Wotquenne), a Belgian musical scholar who in 1905 published a *thematic catalogue of the works of Carl Philipp Emanuel Bach (the second son of J. S. Bach), arranging them according to date of composition. Linked to the title of any work by C. P. E. Bach, **Wq** followed by a number indicates that piece's numbered entry in Wotquenne's catalogue.

Wuchtig [German] Heavy, powerful, weighty.

Würde [German] Dignity, majesty. **Würdig**, dignified, stately.

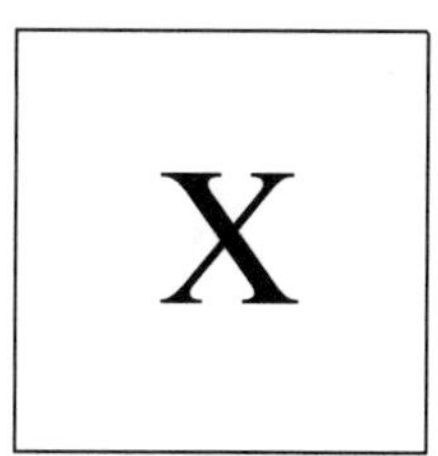

Xilofono [Italian] Xylophone.

Xylophone [from Greek: 'sounds from wood'] A percussion instrument, dating back at least to the 14th century. The modern orchestral xylophone has a series of bars of hard wood set out in an arrangement similar to that of a piano keyboard. The bars are graded in length, and therefore in pitch. Beneath each bar is a metal tube resonator which helps to enrich and sustain the sound when the bar is struck. Normally the player uses hard-headed beaters, producing a hard, bright sound which can be very penetrating; the use of softer beaters produces a mellower sound. Music for xylophone is usually written an octave lower than it actually sounds.

xylophone

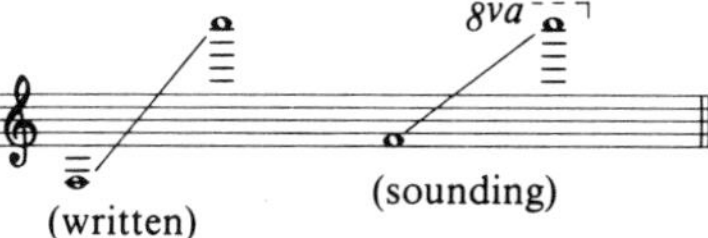

Saint-Saëns gives the xylophone an important part in his **Danse macabre*, and also in *Fossils* from *The *Carnival of Animals*. Shostakovich features the xylophone in the *Polka* from his ballet *The Golden Age*.

[See also: *Marimba: *Vibraphone]

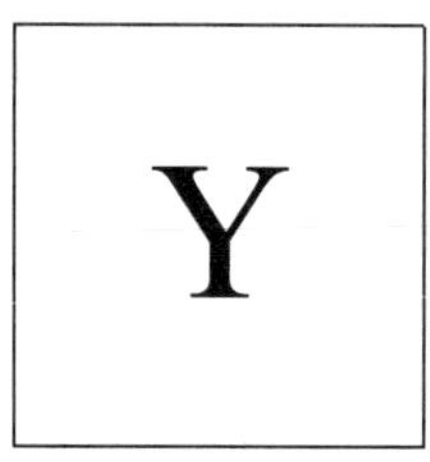

Y

Years of Pilgrimage See **Années de pèlerinage.*

Yodel See *Jodel.

Young Person's Guide to the Orchestra, The (Variations and Fugue on a Theme of Purcell) Music composed by Benjamin Britten in 1946 for a documentary film (script by Eric Crozier) demonstrating the characteristic tone-qualities and technical capabilities of the instruments of the orchestra. Britten based his variations upon a theme from Purcell's incidental music to a play called *Abdelazar* (1695). The theme is presented six times before the variations really begin (full orchestra, woodwind, brass, strings, percussion, full orchestra). Then follow variations on the theme for the instruments of each section of the orchestra, in the order: woodwind (piccolo and flutes, oboes, clarinets, bassoons); strings (violins, violas, cellos, double basses, harp); brass (horns, trumpets, trombones and tuba); and percussion. The work concludes with a Fugue (the instruments entering in the same order as above); at the end, Purcell's tune returns slowly and majestically on the brass, while strings and woodwind continue to play Britten's lively fugue tune.

Youth's Magic Horn See *Des *Knaben Wunderhorn.*

Yüeh-ch'in A Chinese four-stringed plucked lute ('moon lute' or 'moon guitar'), with short neck and flat back.

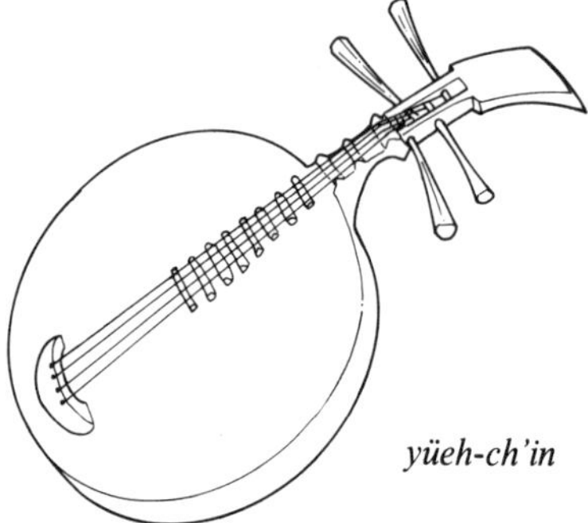

yüeh-ch'in

Yün-lo An instrument used in Chinese music since at least the early 14th century, and consisting of ten gongs, all of different sizes and pitches, hung from a wooden frame. The name means 'cloud gong'.

Z

Z Abbreviation standing for Zimmerman (Franklin Bershir Zimmerman) who in 1963 published a thematic catalogue of the works of Henry Purcell (1659–1695). Linked to the title of any composition by Purcell, **Z** followed by a number indicates that piece's numbered entry in Zimmerman's catalogue (e.g. *Dido and Aeneas*, z626; *Chacony in G minor*, z730).

Zadok the Priest The first of four anthems composed by Handel for the coronation of George II in 1727. It has been performed at every coronation since. The music is scored for seven-part choir (SSAATBB), two oboes, three trumpets, kettle drums, strings, and continuo. [See also: *Coronation Anthems]

Zampogna [Italian] Bagpipe.

Zapateado A Spanish dance in fast triple time in which the rhythms are marked by heel-tapping, often in syncopation or cross-rhythms against the accompaniment.

Zart [German] Delicate, soft, tender. **Zärtlich**, delicately, softly, tenderly.

Zarzuela A type of Spanish opera, often comic but sometimes serious and dramatic, consisting of singing and dancing interspersed with spoken dialogue. The composer often allows for certain passages to be improvised, sometimes including audience participation.

Zauberflöte, Die See *The *Magic Flute*.

Zeit [German] Time, beat. **Zeitmass**, speed, pace, tempo.

Ziemlich [German] Fairly, rather.

Zigeuner [German] Gypsy. **Zigeunerlied**, gypsy song. **Zigeunertanz**, gypsy dance. **Zigeunerweisen**, gypsy melodies (also the title of a piece for violin and orchestra composed in 1878 by the Spanish violinist, Pablo Sarasate).

Zilafone [Italian] Xylophone.

Zingara; Zingaro [Italian] Gypsy.

Zingaresca Gypsy music. **Alla zingarese**, in the style of gypsy music.

Zither A plucked string instrument, of ancient origin, and existing in many forms. The most familiar type, popular in Austria and Bavaria, consists of a flat soundbox over which are stretched thirty or more strings. Melodies are played on the five strings nearest the player, by 'stopping' them against the fretted fingerboard with the left

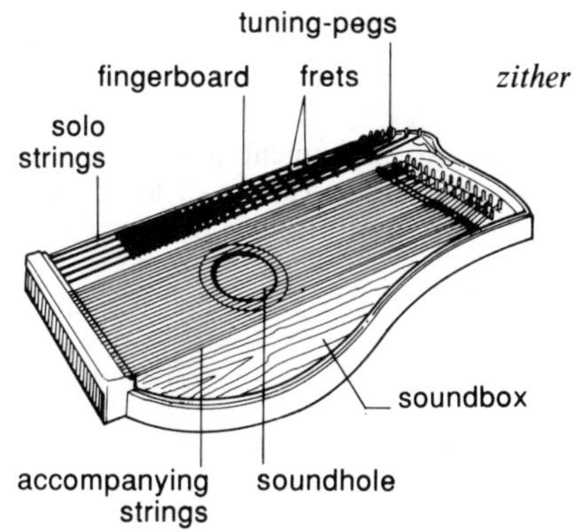

zither

thumb and first three fingers, and plucking them with a plectrum worn on the right thumb. The accompaniment is played on the other strings by plucking them with fingers of the right hand.

[See also: *Cheng; *Ch'in; *Koto; *Qānūn]

Zögernd [German] Hesitating, hesitant.

Zoppa, Alla [Italian: 'in a halting or limping manner'] A 'reversed' dotted rhythm (same as *Lombard rhythm or 'Scotch snap'). The term is also sometimes used to indicate a syncopated rhythm in $\frac{2}{4}$ time in which the second quaver of each bar is strongly accented.

Zu [German] To, for; too. **Zum**, to the, for the. **Zu 2** (*zu zwei*) carries the same meaning as the Italian **A due*.

Zug [German] **1** Slide, of a trombone (**Zugposaune**, slide trombone). **2** A stop on the organ or harpischord.

Zurückhaltend [German] Held back. (Same as Italian: *ritenuto*.)

Zusammen [German: 'together'] An instruction that all instruments of a group, e.g. first violins, are now to play the same notes (in unison) after a passage in which they have been divided (*geteilt*).

Zwei [German] Two. **Zweimal**, twice. **Zweit, zweite**, second. **Das zweite Mal**, the second time. **Zweihändig**, for (with) two hands.

Zwischenspiel [German] Interlude.

Zyklus (Cycle) Piece by Stockhausen for solo percussionist, composed in 1959. The performer may begin on any page of the score, which is spirally bound and may be read clockwise, anticlockwise, or even upside down. The player then follows the pages in order, ending with the first stroke of the page which was chosen as the starting-point.

Tables

Table 1 **Notes and rests**

Name		*Note*	*Rest*
semibreve	(whole note)		
minim	(half-note)		
crotchet	(quarter-note)		or
quaver	(eighth-note)		
semiquaver	(sixteenth-note)		
demisemiquaver	(thirty-second-note)		
hemidemisemi-quaver	(sixty-fourth-note)		

Rests may be dotted or double-dotted in the same way as notes (see *Dot). A whole bar rest is always shown as a semibreve rest – regardless of the actual time-value of the bar or the metre of the music (which may be $\frac{3}{4}$, $\frac{6}{8}$, etc., rather than $\frac{4}{4}$). A rest or silence lasting for several bars (e.g. in an orchestral part) is usually shown as:

5 or 5 (=5 bars rest)

[See also: *Breve; and *Semihemidemisemiquaver]

Table 2 **Time-values of notes in relation to the semibreve**

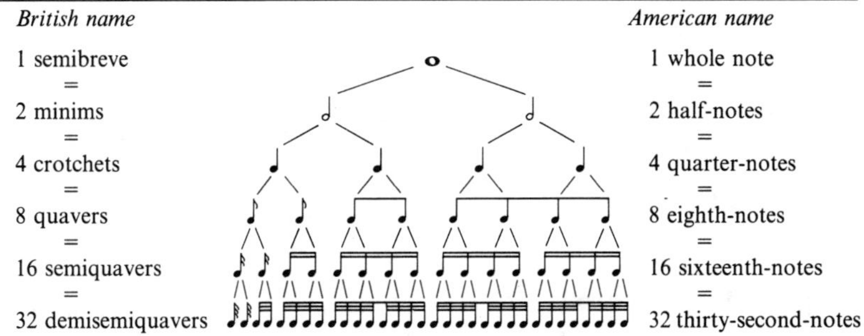

Next in order comes the hemidemisemiquaver ( ) or sixty-fourth-note, of which there are sixty-four to a semibreve. And then (used only occasionally) the *semihemidemisemiquaver.

Table 3 **Musical signs and symbols**

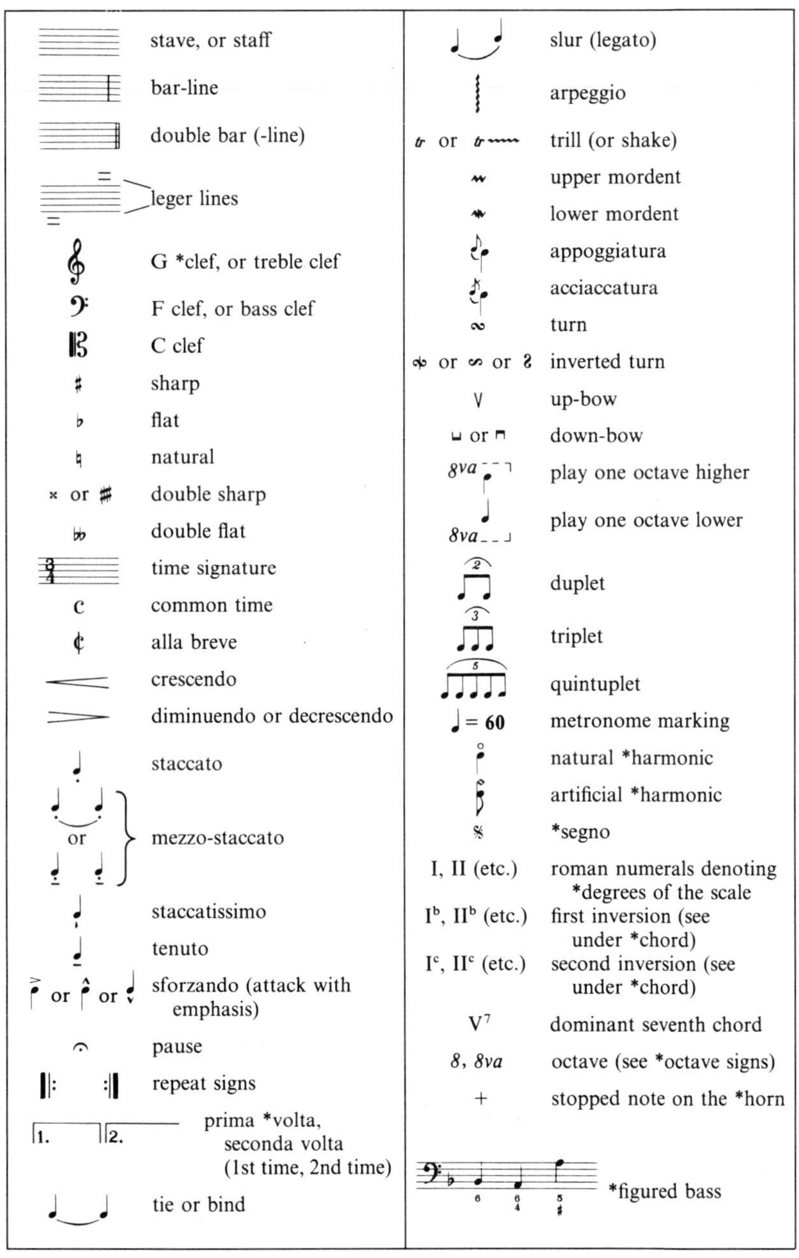

	stave, or staff
	bar-line
	double bar (-line)
	leger lines
𝄞	G *clef, or treble clef
𝄢	F clef, or bass clef
𝄡	C clef
♯	sharp
♭	flat
♮	natural
× or 𝄪	double sharp
𝄫	double flat
	time signature
C	common time
¢	alla breve
	crescendo
	diminuendo or decrescendo
	staccato
or	mezzo-staccato
	staccatissimo
	tenuto
or or	sforzando (attack with emphasis)
𝄐	pause
𝄆 𝄇	repeat signs
1. 2.	prima *volta, seconda volta (1st time, 2nd time)
	tie or bind
	slur (legato)
	arpeggio
tr or *tr*~~~	trill (or shake)
	upper mordent
	lower mordent
	appoggiatura
	acciaccatura
∾	turn
or or	inverted turn
V	up-bow
or	down-bow
8va	play one octave higher
8va	play one octave lower
2	duplet
3	triplet
5	quintuplet
♩ = 60	metronome marking
	natural *harmonic
	artificial *harmonic
𝄋	*segno
I, II (etc.)	roman numerals denoting *degrees of the scale
I^b, II^b (etc.)	first inversion (see under *chord)
I^c, II^c (etc.)	second inversion (see under *chord)
V^7	dominant seventh chord
8, *8va*	octave (see *octave signs)
+	stopped note on the *horn
6 6/4 5/♯	*figured bass

[See also, Tables 1, 4, 5, 6, 10, and 11]

Table 4 **Time signatures**

Simple time				**Compound time**		
Note-value of each beat			*Number of beats to each bar*	*Note-value of each beat*		
𝅗𝅥	♩	♪		𝅗𝅥.	♩.	♪.
2/2 or ¢	2/4	2/8	2	6/4	6/8	6/16
3/2	3/4	3/8	3	9/4	9/8	9/16
4/2	4/4 or C	4/8	4	12/4	12/8	12/16

Table 5 **Key signatures**

In each example the white note shows the tonic of the major key, and the black note shows the tonic of its relative minor key – the minor key which shares the same key signature. The leading-note of each minor key is shown in brackets. (This is 'extra' to the key signature and, where necessary, is written in the music as an accidental.)

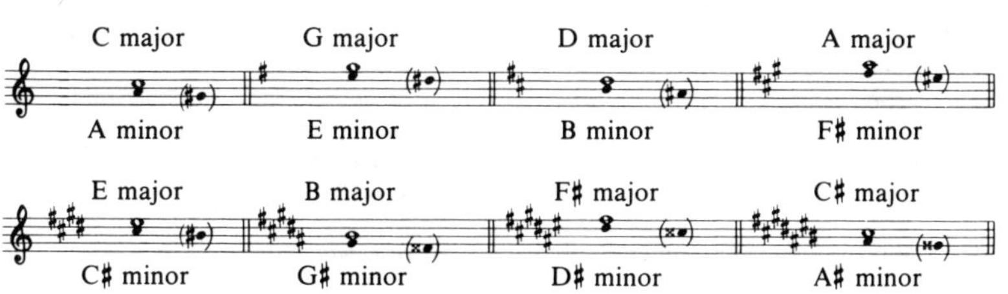

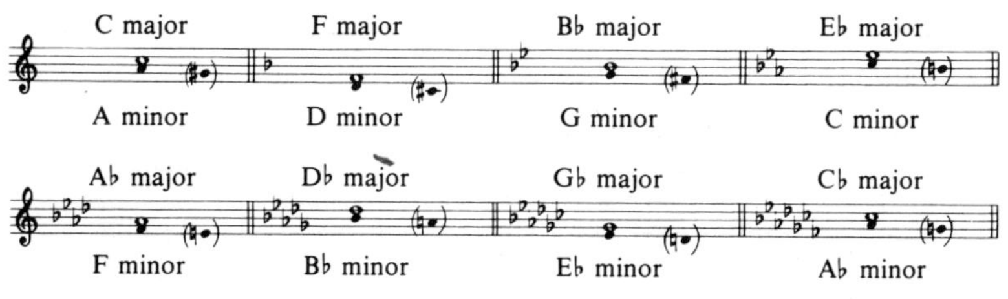

Table 6 **Dynamic markings** (markings of intensity)

Italian term	*Abbreviation*	*Meaning*
piano	***p***	soft
pianissimo	***pp***	very soft
mezzo piano	***mp***	moderately soft
mezzo forte	***mf***	moderately loud
forte	***f***	loud
fortissimo	***ff***	very loud
crescendo	*cresc.*	becoming gradually louder
diminuendo	*dim.* or *dimin.*	becoming gradually softer
decrescendo	*decresc.*	becoming gradually softer
forte-piano	***fp***	loud, suddenly followed by soft
forzato	***fz***	forcing the tone, accenting the note
sforzando	***sf*** or ***sfz***	forcing the tone, accenting the note
sforzando-piano	***sfp***	accent, suddenly followed by *piano*

A composer may increase the number of 'f's or 'p's – e.g. ***fff***, extremely loud. At one point in his *Pathétique Symphony*, Tchaikovsky asks the bassoon to play ***pppppp***.

To many of the above markings, other words may be added such as:

più	more	(e.g. *più piano*, more softly)
meno	less	(e.g. *meno forte*, less loud)
molto	much, very	(e.g. *crescendo molto*, getting very much louder)
non troppo	not too much	(e.g. *non troppo forte*, not too loud)
subito	suddenly	(e.g. *subito pianissimo*, suddenly very soft)
poco a poco	little by little	(e.g. *poco a poco diminuendo*, getting softer little by little)

The following signs are frequently used to mean *crescendo* and *diminuendo* respectively:

Table 7 **Note-names in different languages**

	British	*American*	*French*	*German*	*Italian*
𝅝	semibreve	whole note	ronde	Ganze (-Note)	semibreve
𝅗𝅥	minim	half-note	blanche	Halbe (-Note)	bianca
♩	crotchet	quarter-note	noire	Viertel (-Note)	nera
♪	quaver	eighth-note	croche	Achtel (-Note)	croma
𝅘𝅥𝅯	semiquaver	sixteenth-note	double-croche	Sechzehntel (-Note)	semicroma
𝅘𝅥𝅰	demisemi-quaver	thirty-second-note	triple-croche	Zweiunddreis-sigstel (-Note)	biscroma
𝅘𝅥𝅱	hemidemi-semiquaver	sixty-fourth-note	quadruple-croche	Vierundsech-zigstel (-Note)	semibis-croma

Table 8 **Major and Minor**

English	*Italian*	*French*	*German*
major minor	maggiore minore	majeur mineur	dur moll

Table 9 **Pitch-names (i)**

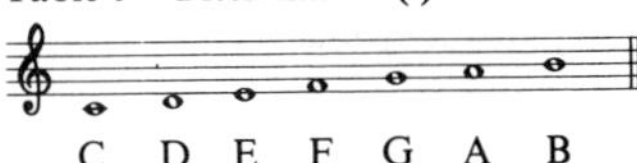

C D E F G A B

	English	*Italian*	*French*	*German*
	C D E F G A B	do re mi fa sol la si	ut ré mi fa sol la si	C D E F G A H (in German usage, B represents B *flat*)
♯	sharp	diesis	dièse	'is' is added to the letter-name (e.g. C sharp = *Cis*, F sharp = *Fis*)
♭	flat	bemolle	bémol	'es' is added to C, D, F or G (e.g. D flat = *Des*), but B flat = *B*, E flat = *Es*, A flat = *As*
× or 𝄪	double sharp	doppio diesis	double-dièse	'isis' is added to the letter-name (e.g. C double sharp = *Cisis*)
𝄫	double flat	doppio bemolle	double-bémol	'eses' is added to C, D, F or G (e.g. C double flat = *Ceses*), but B double flat = *Bes*, E double flat = *Eses*, A double flat = *Ases*

Table 10 **Pitch-names (ii)**

There are several ways of indicating the pitch of a note according to the octave in which it lies. The following shows the method most commonly used:

Table 11 **Abbreviations for repetition of notes**

When writing out music, composers often use certain abbreviations for notes or bars which are to be repeated – a kind of 'musical shorthand' which saves time and trouble, and also expense when the music comes to be engraved. This table shows various examples of this type of abbreviation, and how they are performed.

(1) **Repetition of a bar, or part of a bar** Shown by a slash, usually with a dot on each side, or by a double slash.

Ex. 1

Ex. 2

(2) **Repetition of a note** The note-head indicates the duration of the repetition (the time-value which is to be filled). The number of slashes above or below a note, or through the stem of a note, indicates the unit of repetition (/ = ♪ // = 𝅘𝅥𝅯 etc.). In example 7, the beam joining the notes together *also* counts as a slash. In example 9, the number of dots equals the number of notes to be played.

(3) **Alternation between two notes** In examples 10–13 the time-value to be filled is equal to just *one* note-head of a pair. However, in example 14 the time-value is equal to *both* notes of a pair. The unit of repetition is indicated either by the number of beams joining notes together (examples 10–12) or by the number of slashes shown (examples 13 and 14). In example 14 the beam joining a pair of notes together *also* counts as a slash.

Ex. 13

(4) **Repetition of a musical idea or pattern, but with changing pitches**

Ex. 15 *segue* ('follow')

[See also the article on *Repeat signs]

Table 12 **Intervals**

In each example, the figure in brackets indicates the number of semitones the interval contains.

perfect unison (0)	augmented unison (1)	major 2nd (2)	minor 2nd (1)	augmented 2nd (3)
diminished 2nd (0)	major 3rd (4)	minor 3rd (3)	augmented 3rd (5)	diminished 3rd (2)
perfect 4th (5)	augmented 4th (6)	diminished 4th (4)	perfect 5th (7)	augmented 5th (8)
diminished 5th (6)	major 6th (9)	minor 6th (8)	augmented 6th (10)	
diminished 6th (7)	major 7th (11)	minor 7th (10)	augmented 7th (12)	
diminished 7th (9)	perfect octave (12)	diminished octave (11)	augmented octave (13)	

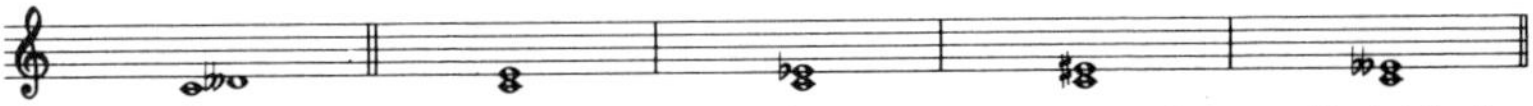

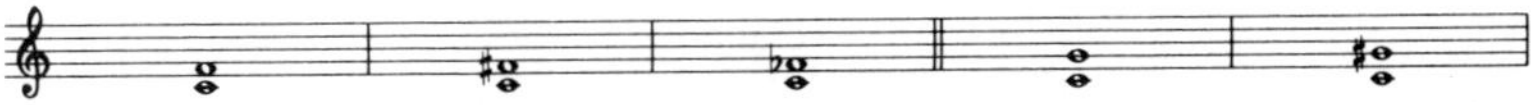

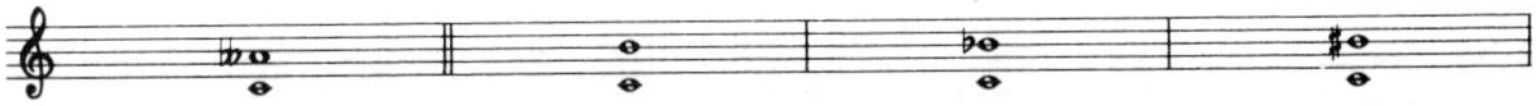

Table 13 **Ranges of voices and instruments**

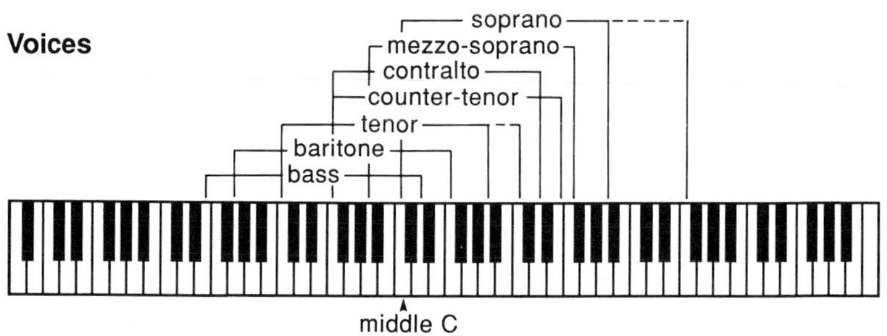

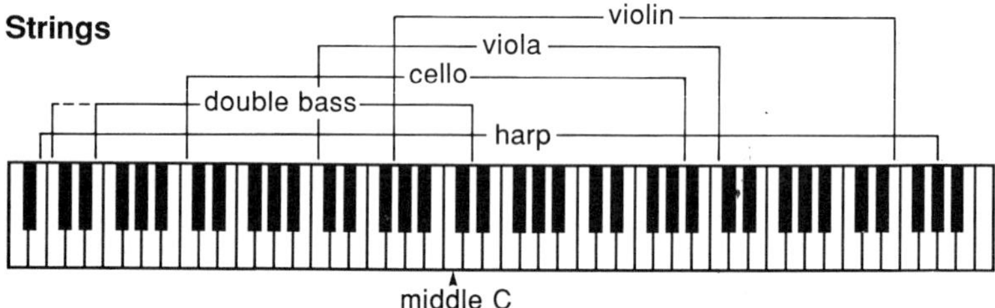

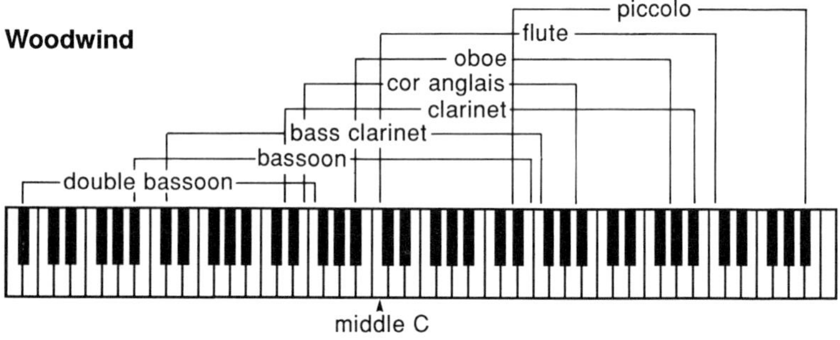

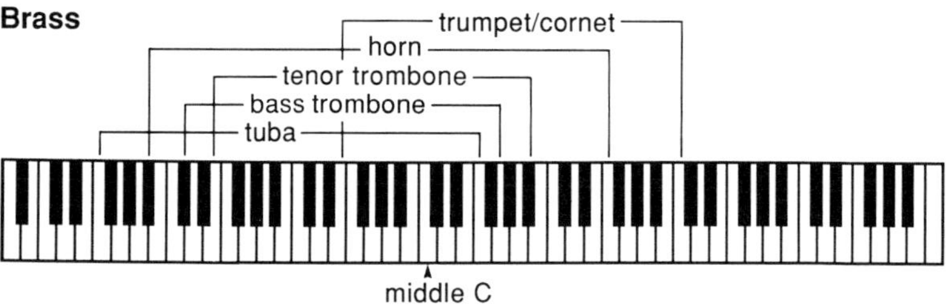

Table 14 **Transposing instruments**

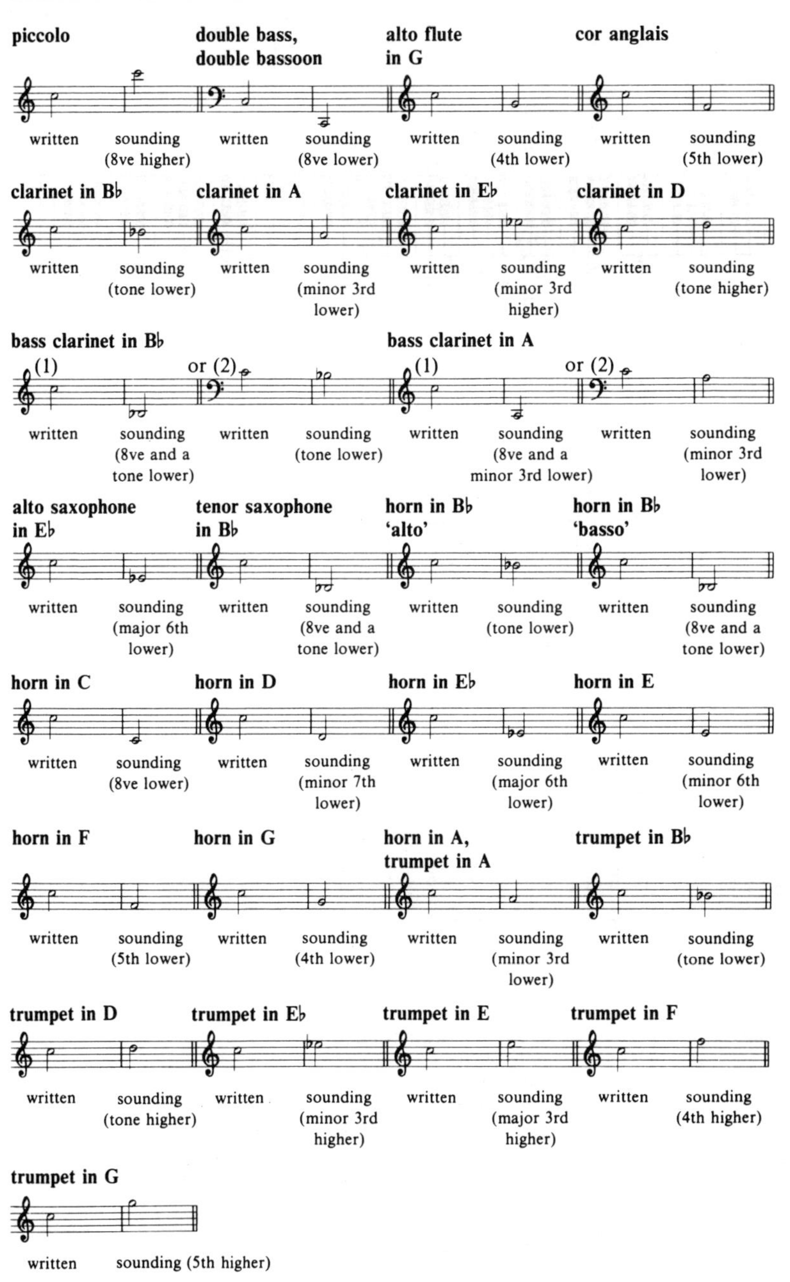

Table 15 **Foreign names for instruments** (with abbreviations)

The following table gives the names of the main instruments together with the abbreviations most often found in musical scores.

English	*Italian*	*French*	*German*
Piccolo [Picc.]	Flauto piccolo [Fl.picc.] or Ottavino [Ott.]	Petite flûte [Pte.Fl.]	Kleine Flöte [Kl.Fl.]
Flute [Fl.]	Flauto [Fl.] or Flauto grande [Fl.gr.]	Flûte [Fl.] or Grande Flûte [Gde.Fl.]	Flöte [Fl.] or Grosse Flöte [Gr.Fl.]
Oboe [Ob.]	Oboe [Ob.]	Hautbois [Hb., Htb.]	Hoboe [Hb.]
Cor anglais [C.A.] or English horn [E.H.]	Corno inglese [C.i., Cor.ingl.]	Cor anglais [C.A.]	Englisches Horn [E.H., Engl.Hr.]
Clarinet [C., Cl., Clt.]	Clarinetto [Cl., Clar.]	Clarinette [Cl.]	Klarinette [Kl., Klar.]
Bass clarinet [B.Cl.]	Clarinetto basso [Cl.b.]	Clarinette basse [Cl.b]	Bassklarinette [Bkl.]
Saxophone [Sax.]	Sassofono [Sass.] or Saxofono [Sax.]	Saxophone [Sax.]	Saxophon [Sax.]
Bassoon [Bsn.]	Fagotto [Fg., Fag.]	Basson [Bn., Bon., Bssn.]	Fagott [Fg., Fag.]
Double bassoon [D.Bsn.] or Contrabassoon [C.Bsn.]	Controfagotto [Cfg., C.Fag.]	Contrebasson [Cbn., C.bon., C.bssn.]	Kontrafagott [Kfg., K.Fag.]
Horn [Hn., Hr.]	Corno [Cor.]	Cor	Horn [Hr., Hrn.]
Trumpet [Tpt., Trpt.]	Tromba [Tr., Tbe.]	Trompette [Tromp., Trp.]	Trompete [Tr., Trmp.]
Cornet [Cnt., Cor., Cort.,]	Cornetta [Cnta.] or Cornetto [Corn., Ctto.]	Cornet à pistons [C.à.p., Cor.à.pist., Pist.]	Cornett, Kornett
Trombone [Tbn., Trb., Trom.]	Trombone [Tbn., Tbni., Trb., Trbn.]	Trombone [Trb., Trom.]	Posaune [Pos., Ps.]
Tuba [Tb., Tba.]	Tuba [Tb., Tba.]	Tuba [Tb.]	Tuba [Tb.]

Kettle drums [K.D.]	Timpani [Timp.]	Timbales [Timb.]	Pauken [Pk.]
Triangle [Trgl., Tri.]	Triangolo [Trg.]	Triangle [Trgl.]	Triangel [Trg., Trigl.]
Cymbals [Cym.]	Piatti [P., Piat., Ptti.]	Cymbales [Cymb.]	Becken [Bck., Beck.]
Bass drum [B.D.]	Gran cassa [G.C., Gr.c.]	Grosse caisse [G.C., Gr.c.]	Grosse Trommel [Gr.Tr.]
Snare (side) drum [S.D.]	Tamburo piccolo [T.picc., Tb.p.] or Tamburo militare [T.m., T.mil.]	Tambour (militaire) [Tamb.] or Caisse claire [Cl.cl., Csse Cl.]	Kleine Trommel [Kl.Tr.]
Tenor drum [T.D.]	Cassa rullante [C.rul.]	Caisse roulante [C.roul.]	Rührtrommel [Rührtr.]
Tambourine [Tamb.]	Tamburo basco [Tb.b.] or Tamburino [Tamb.]	Tambour de Basque [T.de B.]	Tamburin [Tambr.] or Schellentrommel
Castanets [Cast.]	Castagnette [Ca., Cast.]	Castagnettes [Cast.]	Kastagnetten [Kast.]
Tam-tam [T-t.]	Tam-tam [T-t.]	Tam-Tam [T-T, Tamt.]	Tamtam [Tt.]
Tubular bells [T.B.]	Campane or Campanelle [Camp.]	Cloches	Glocken [Glck.]
Glockenspiel [Glock., Gl.]	Campanette or Campanelli [Cmpli.]	Carillon [Car.] or Jeu de timbres [J.de T]	Glockenspiel [Glcksp., Glsp.]
Xylophone [Xyl.]	Silofono [Sil.] or Xilofono [Xil.] or Zilafone [Zil.]	Xylophone [Xylo., Xylop.] or Claquebois	Xylophon [Xylo.] or Holzharmonika
Celesta [Cel.]	Celesta [Cel.]	Céleste or Célesta [Cél.]	Celesta [Cel.]
Organ [Org.]	Organo [Org.]	Orgue [Org.]	Orgel [Org.]
Piano [Pno.]	Pianoforte [Pf., Pft., Pfte.]	Piano	Klavier [Klav.]
Harpsichord [Hpschd.]	Cembalo [Cemb.] or Clavicembalo	Clavecin [Clav.]	Cembalo [Cemb.]
Guitar [Guit.]	Chitarra [Chit.]	Guitare [Guit.]	Gitarre [Git.]
Harp [Hp., Hrp.]	Arpa [A., Arp.]	Harpe [Hp.]	Harfe [Hrf., Hf.]
Violin [Vln.]	Violino [V., Vl., Vln., Vni.]	Violon (Vln., Vns., Vons.]	Violine [V., Vl., Vln.]
Viola [Vla.]	Viola [Va., Vla., Vle.]	Alto [A.]	Bratsche [Br.]
Cello [Vc., Vcl.]	Violoncello [Vc., Vcl., Vlc.]	Violoncelle [Vc., Velles.]	Violoncell [Vc., Vlc.]
Double bass [D.B., D.Bs.]	Contrabasso [Cb., C.B.] or Basso [B.] (which may also include cellos)	Contrebasse [Cb., C.B.]	Kontrabass [Kb.]

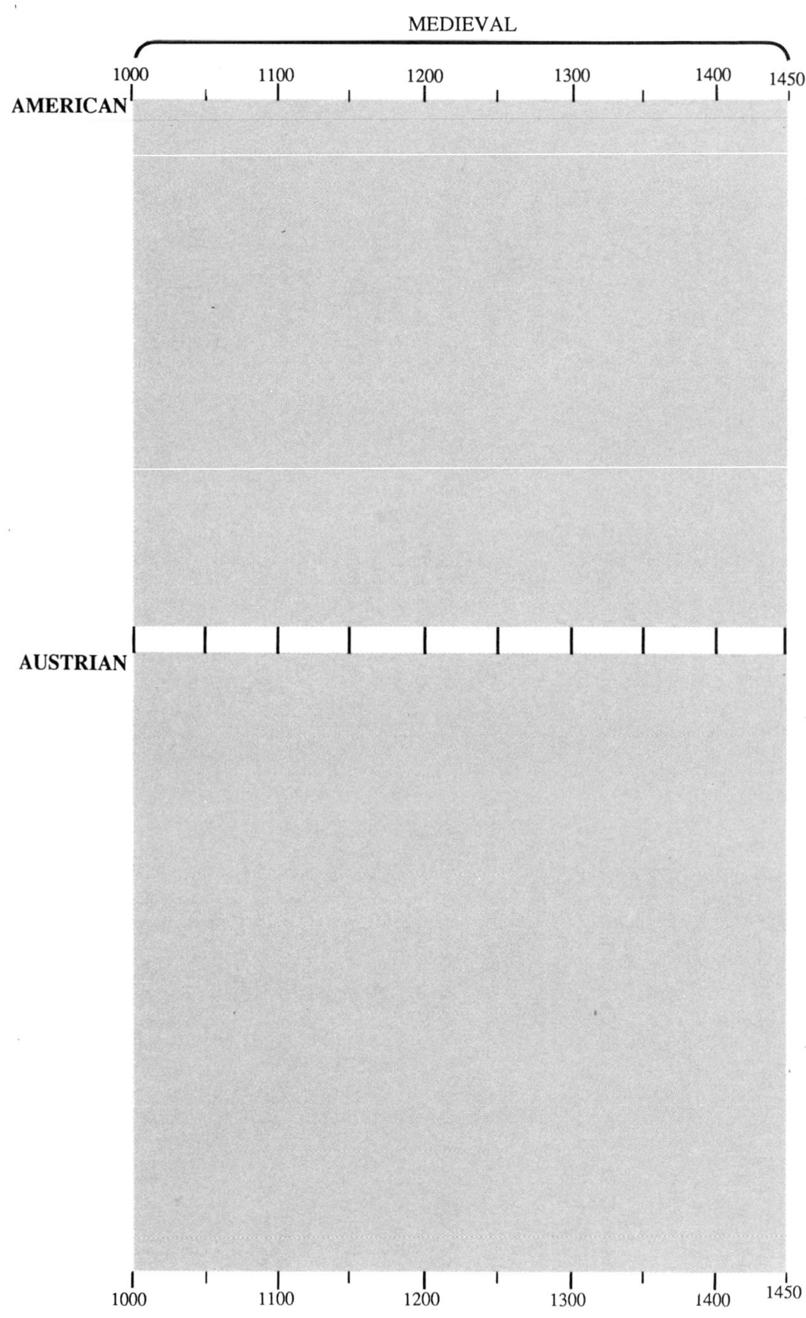
MEDIEVAL
1000
1100
1200
1300
1400
1450
AMERICAN
AUSTRIAN
1000
1100
1200
1300
1400
1450

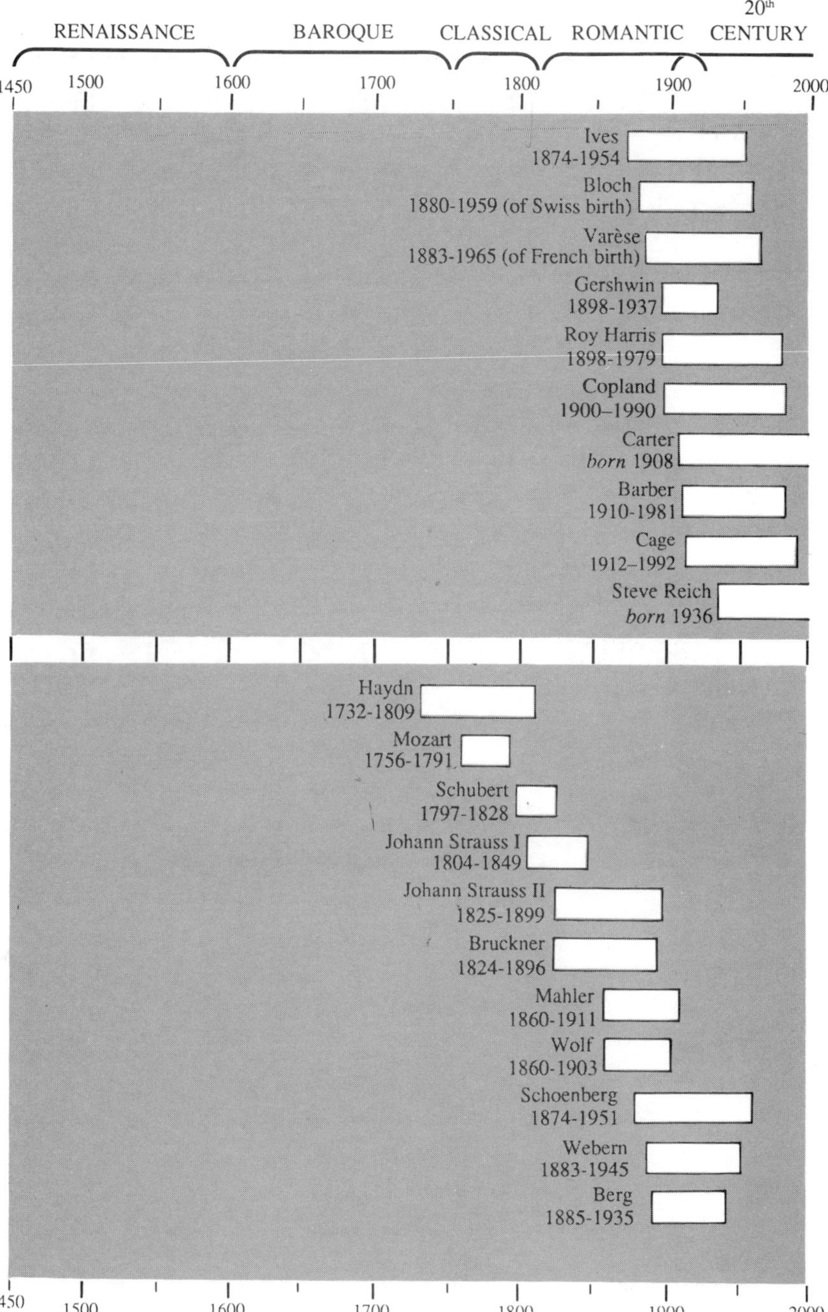

RENAISSANCE
BAROQUE
CLASSICAL
ROMANTIC
20th CENTURY
1450
1500
1600
1700
1800
1900
2000
Ives
1874-1954
Bloch
1880-1959 (of Swiss birth)
Varèse
1883-1965 (of French birth)
Gershwin
1898-1937
Roy Harris
1898-1979
Copland
1900–1990
Carter
born 1908
Barber
1910-1981
Cage
1912–1992
Steve Reich
born 1936
Haydn
1732-1809
Mozart
1756-1791
Schubert
1797-1828
Johann Strauss I
1804-1849
Johann Strauss II
1825-1899
Bruckner
1824-1896
Mahler
1860-1911
Wolf
1860-1903
Schoenberg
1874-1951
Webern
1883-1945
Berg
1885-1935
1450
1500
1600
1700
1800
1900
2000

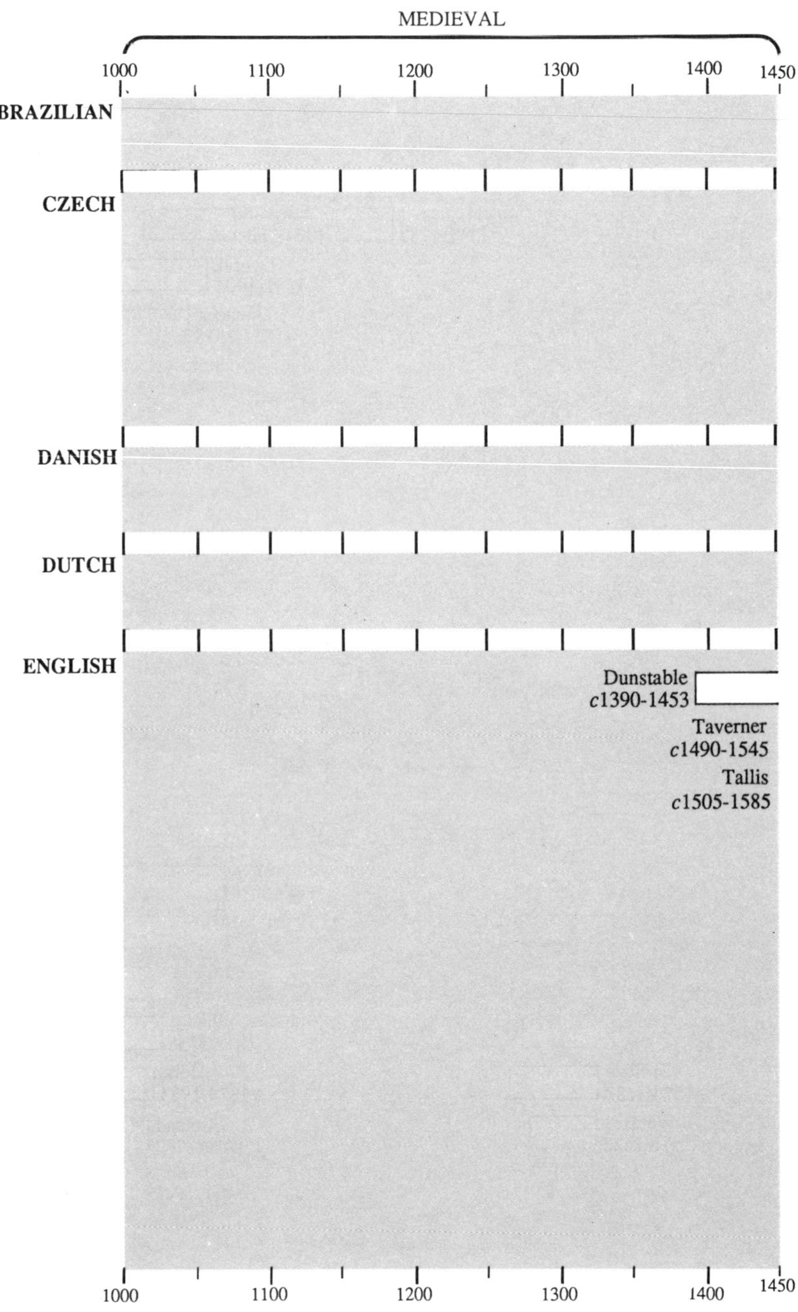
MEDIEVAL
1000
1100
1200
1300
1400
1450
BRAZILIAN
CZECH
DANISH
DUTCH
ENGLISH
Dunstable
c1390-1453
Taverner
c1490-1545
Tallis
c1505-1585
1000
1100
1200
1300
1400
1450

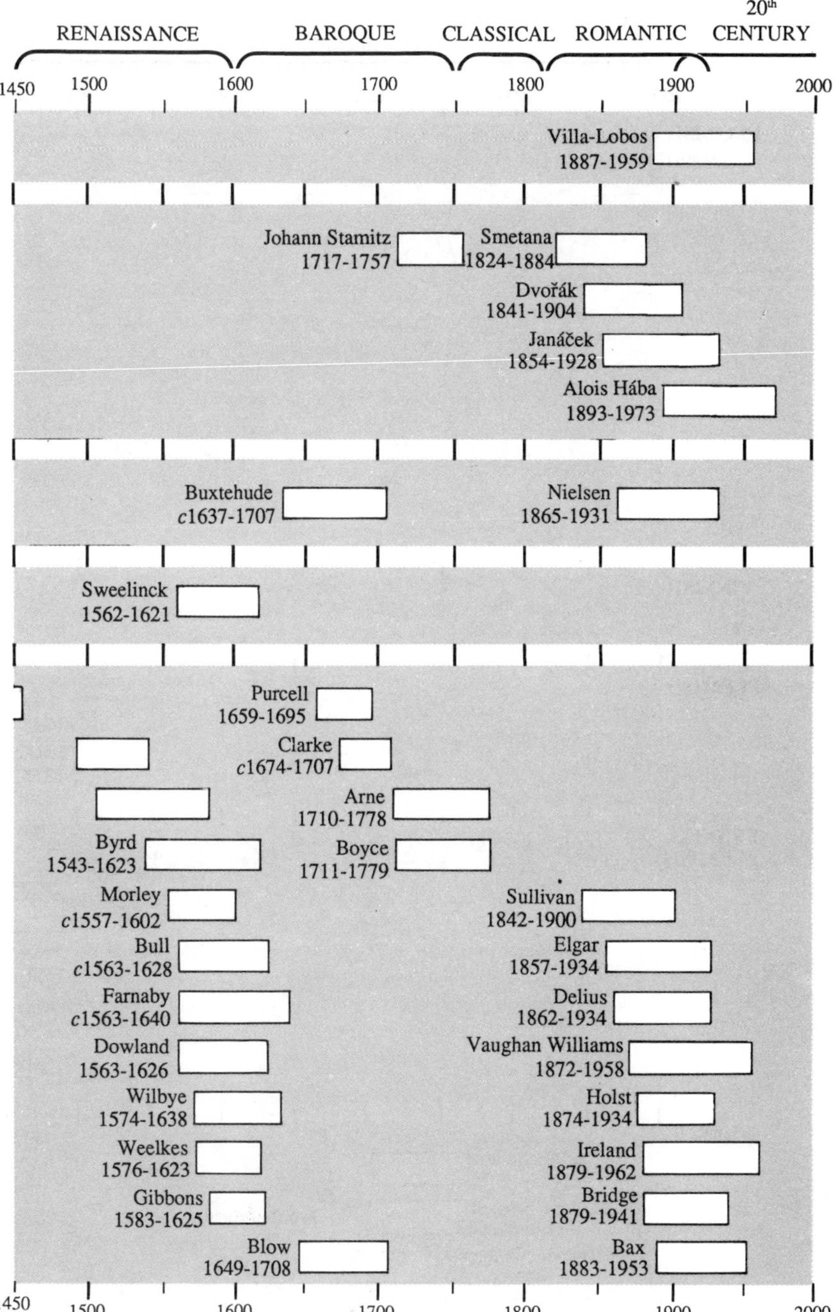

20th
RENAISSANCE
BAROQUE
CLASSICAL
ROMANTIC
CENTURY
1450
1500
1600
1700
1800
1900
2000
Villa-Lobos
1887-1959
Johann Stamitz
1717-1757
Smetana
1824-1884
Dvořák
1841-1904
Janáček
1854-1928
Alois Hába
1893-1973
Buxtehude
c1637-1707
Nielsen
1865-1931
Sweelinck
1562-1621
Purcell
1659-1695
Clarke
c1674-1707
Arne
1710-1778
Byrd
1543-1623
Boyce
1711-1779
Morley
c1557-1602
Sullivan
1842-1900
Bull
c1563-1628
Elgar
1857-1934
Farnaby
c1563-1640
Delius
1862-1934
Dowland
1563-1626
Vaughan Williams
1872-1958
Wilbye
1574-1638
Holst
1874-1934
Weelkes
1576-1623
Ireland
1879-1962
Gibbons
1583-1625
Bridge
1879-1941
Blow
1649-1708
Bax
1883-1953
1450
1500
1600
1700
1800
1900
2000

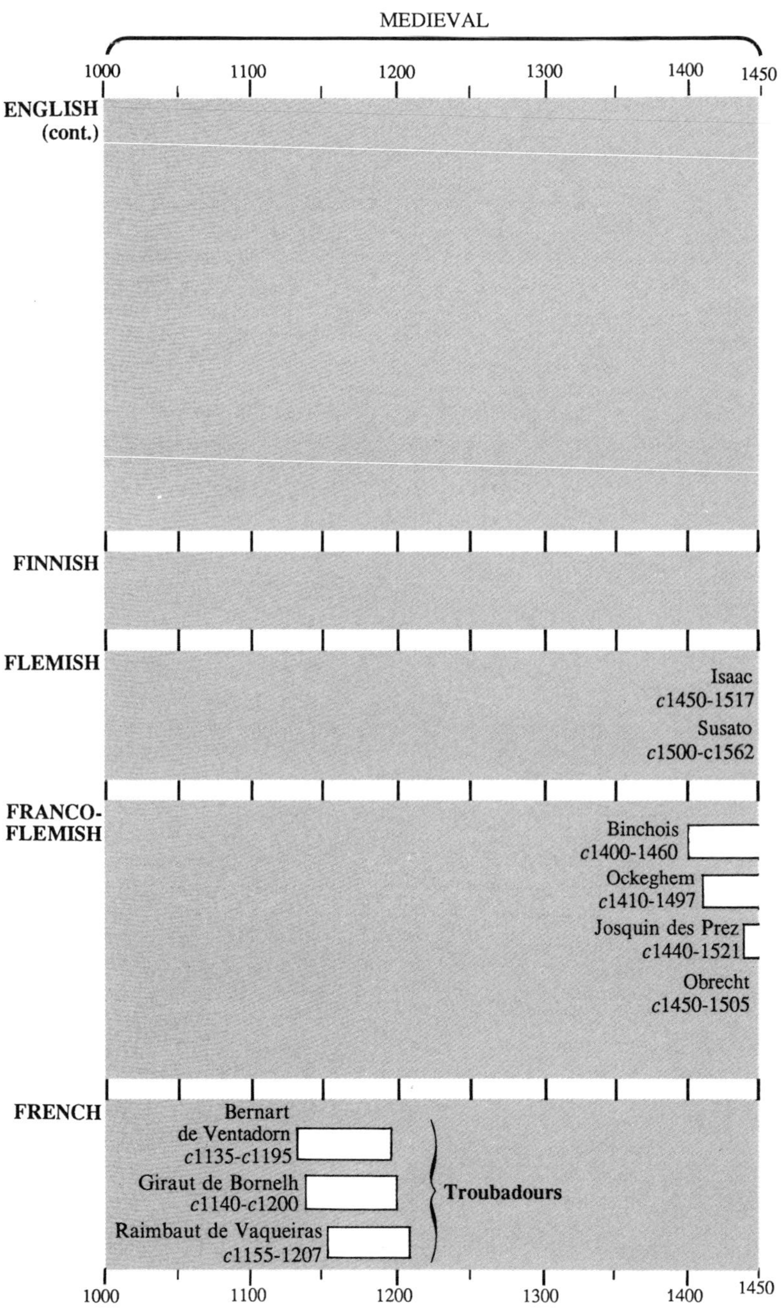
MEDIEVAL
1000
1100
1200
1300
1400
1450
ENGLISH (cont.)
FINNISH
FLEMISH
Isaac c1450-1517
Susato c1500-c1562
FRANCO-FLEMISH
Binchois c1400-1460
Ockeghem c1410-1497
Josquin des Prez c1440-1521
Obrecht c1450-1505
FRENCH
Bernart de Ventadorn c1135-c1195
Giraut de Bornelh c1140-c1200
Raimbaut de Vaqueiras c1155-1207
Troubadours

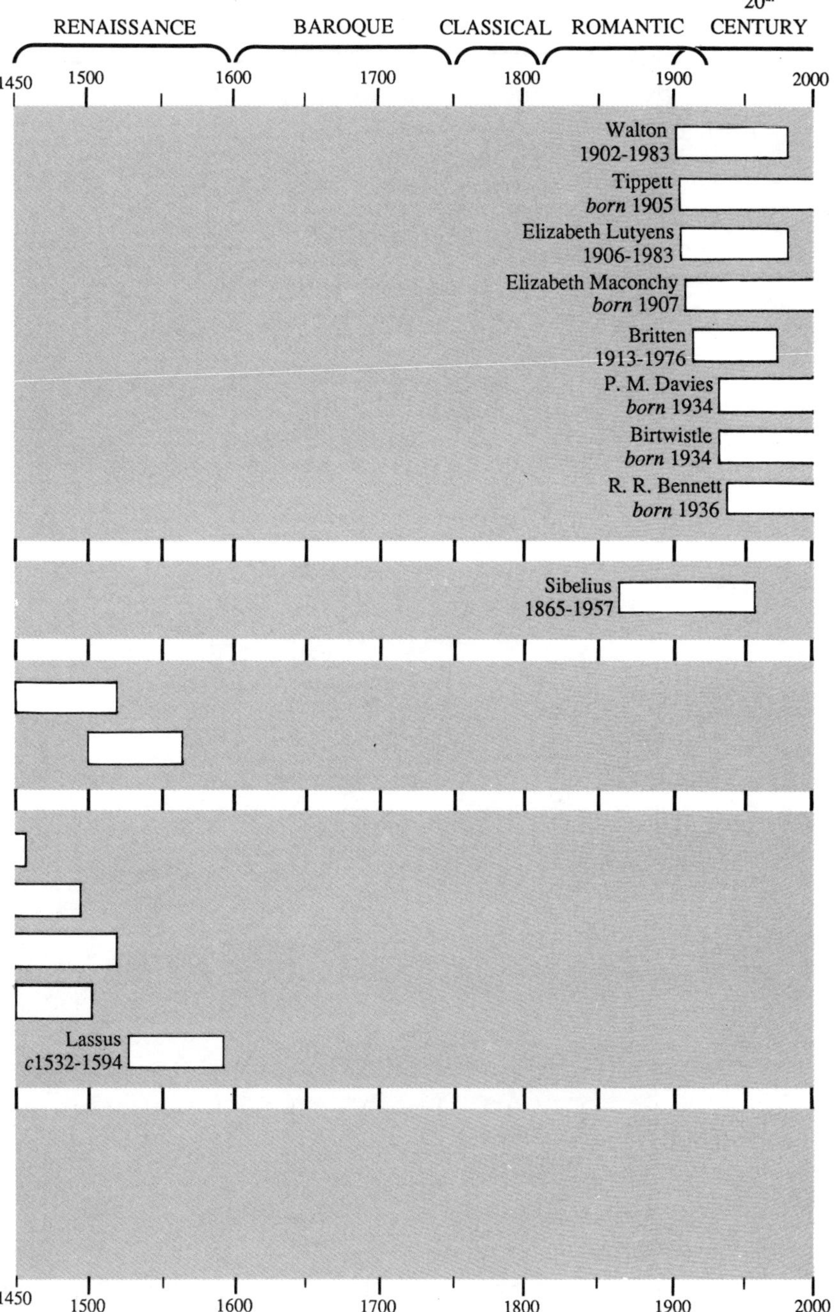
20th
RENAISSANCE
BAROQUE
CLASSICAL
ROMANTIC
CENTURY
1450
1500
1600
1700
1800
1900
2000
Walton
1902-1983
Tippett
born 1905
Elizabeth Lutyens
1906-1983
Elizabeth Maconchy
born 1907
Britten
1913-1976
P. M. Davies
born 1934
Birtwistle
born 1934
R. R. Bennett
born 1936
Sibelius
1865-1957
Lassus
c1532-1594
1450
1500
1600
1700
1800
1900
2000

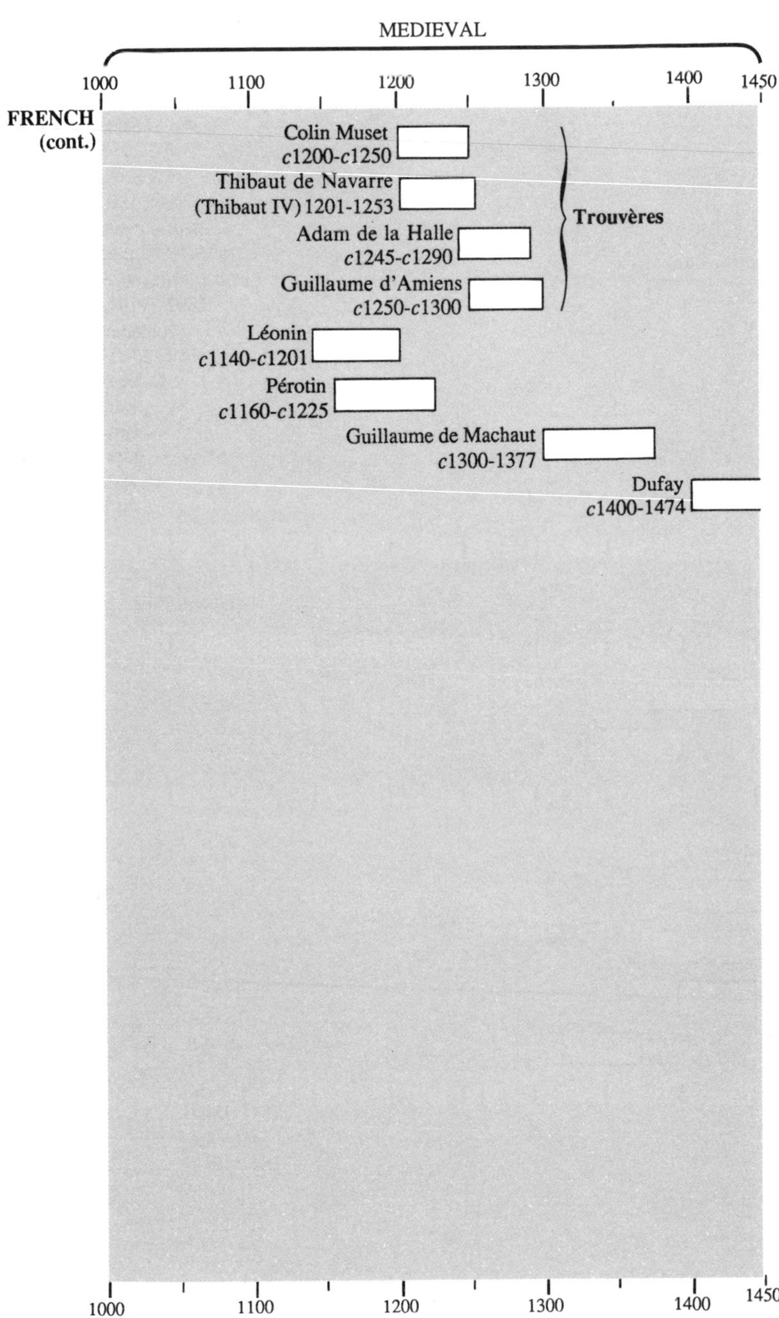
MEDIEVAL
1000
1100
1200
1300
1400
1450
FRENCH (cont.)
Colin Muset c1200-c1250
Thibaut de Navarre (Thibaut IV) 1201-1253
Adam de la Halle c1245-c1290
Guillaume d'Amiens c1250-c1300
Trouvères
Léonin c1140-c1201
Pérotin c1160-c1225
Guillaume de Machaut c1300-1377
Dufay c1400-1474
1000
1100
1200
1300
1400
1450

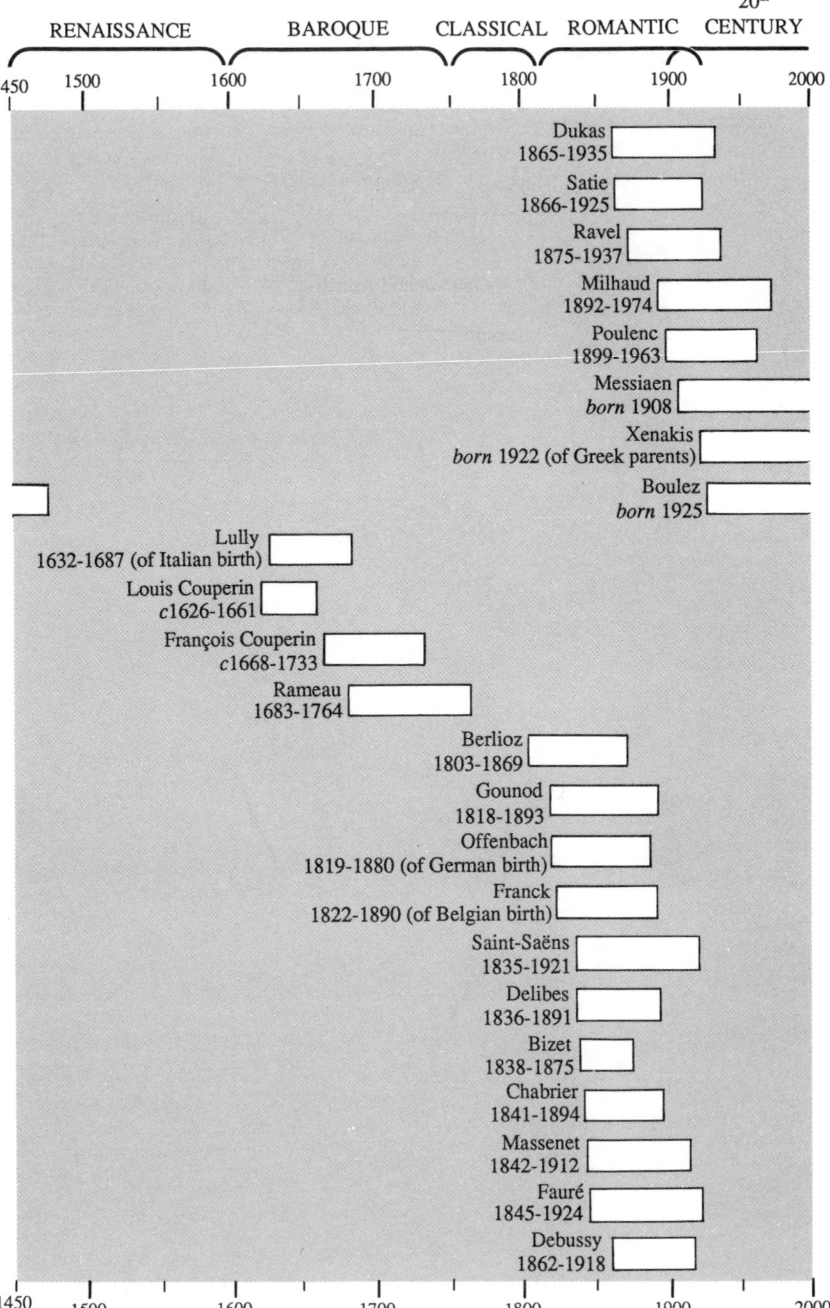
20th CENTURY
RENAISSANCE
BAROQUE
CLASSICAL
ROMANTIC
1450
1500
1600
1700
1800
1900
2000
Dukas 1865-1935
Satie 1866-1925
Ravel 1875-1937
Milhaud 1892-1974
Poulenc 1899-1963
Messiaen *born* 1908
Xenakis *born* 1922 (of Greek parents)
Boulez *born* 1925
Lully 1632-1687 (of Italian birth)
Louis Couperin *c*1626-1661
François Couperin *c*1668-1733
Rameau 1683-1764
Berlioz 1803-1869
Gounod 1818-1893
Offenbach 1819-1880 (of German birth)
Franck 1822-1890 (of Belgian birth)
Saint-Saëns 1835-1921
Delibes 1836-1891
Bizet 1838-1875
Chabrier 1841-1894
Massenet 1842-1912
Fauré 1845-1924
Debussy 1862-1918

MEDIEVAL
1000
1100
1200
1300
1400
1450
GERMAN
Walther
von der Vogelweide
c1170-c1230
Neidhart von Reuental
c1180-c1240
Minnesingers
Paumann
c1410-1473
HUNGARIAN
1000
1100
1200
1300
1400
1450

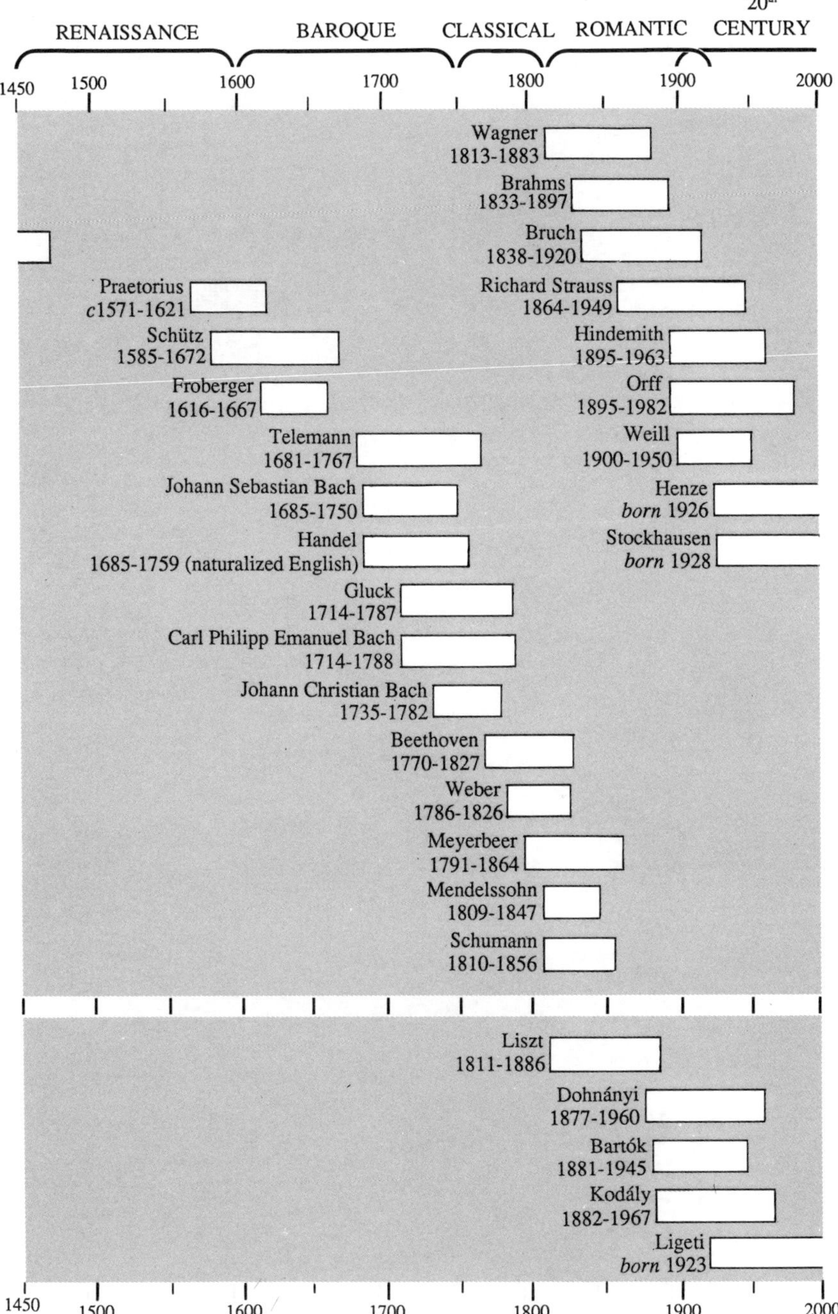
20th
RENAISSANCE
BAROQUE
CLASSICAL
ROMANTIC
CENTURY
1450
1500
1600
1700
1800
1900
2000
Wagner
1813-1883
Brahms
1833-1897
Bruch
1838-1920
Praetorius
c1571-1621
Richard Strauss
1864-1949
Schütz
1585-1672
Hindemith
1895-1963
Froberger
1616-1667
Orff
1895-1982
Telemann
1681-1767
Weill
1900-1950
Johann Sebastian Bach
1685-1750
Henze
born 1926
Handel
1685-1759 (naturalized English)
Stockhausen
born 1928
Gluck
1714-1787
Carl Philipp Emanuel Bach
1714-1788
Johann Christian Bach
1735-1782
Beethoven
1770-1827
Weber
1786-1826
Meyerbeer
1791-1864
Mendelssohn
1809-1847
Schumann
1810-1856
Liszt
1811-1886
Dohnányi
1877-1960
Bartók
1881-1945
Kodály
1882-1967
Ligeti
born 1923
1450
1500
1600
1700
1800
1900
2000

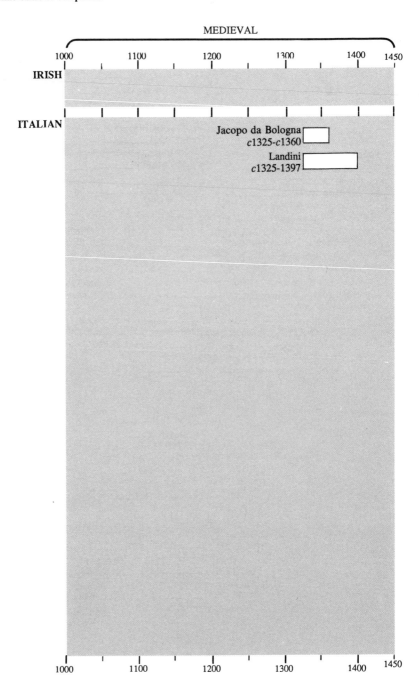
MEDIEVAL
1000
1100
1200
1300
1400
1450
IRISH
ITALIAN
Jacopo da Bologna
c1325-c1360
Landini
c1325-1397
1000
1100
1200
1300
1400
1450

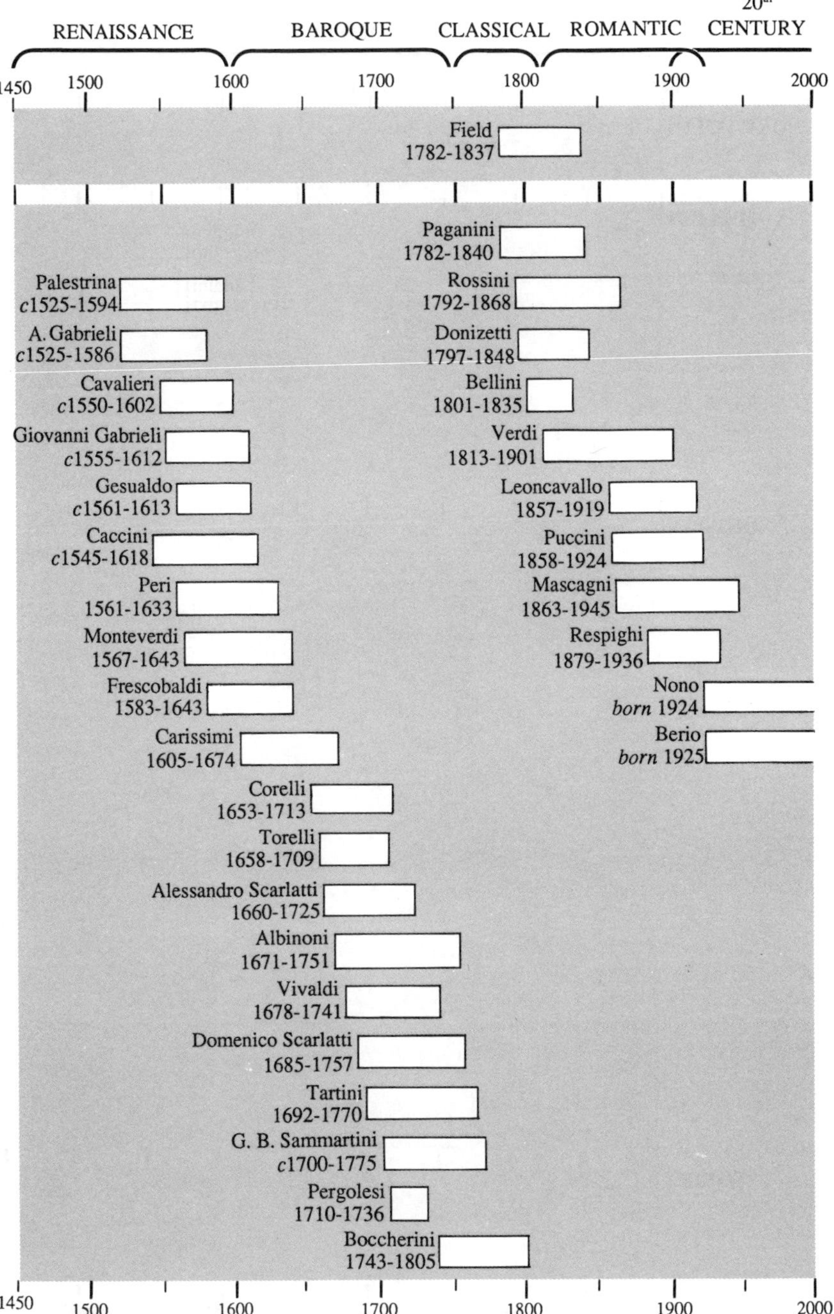

RENAISSANCE
BAROQUE
CLASSICAL
ROMANTIC
20th CENTURY
1450
1500
1600
1700
1800
1900
2000
Field 1782-1837
Paganini 1782-1840
Palestrina c1525-1594
Rossini 1792-1868
A. Gabrieli c1525-1586
Donizetti 1797-1848
Cavalieri c1550-1602
Bellini 1801-1835
Giovanni Gabrieli c1555-1612
Verdi 1813-1901
Gesualdo c1561-1613
Leoncavallo 1857-1919
Caccini c1545-1618
Puccini 1858-1924
Peri 1561-1633
Mascagni 1863-1945
Monteverdi 1567-1643
Respighi 1879-1936
Frescobaldi 1583-1643
Nono born 1924
Carissimi 1605-1674
Berio born 1925
Corelli 1653-1713
Torelli 1658-1709
Alessandro Scarlatti 1660-1725
Albinoni 1671-1751
Vivaldi 1678-1741
Domenico Scarlatti 1685-1757
Tartini 1692-1770
G. B. Sammartini c1700-1775
Pergolesi 1710-1736
Boccherini 1743-1805
1450
1500
1600
1700
1800
1900
2000

MEDIEVAL
1000
1100
1200
1300
1400
1450
NORWEGIAN
POLISH
RUSSIAN
SOVIET
1000
1100
1200
1300
1400
1450

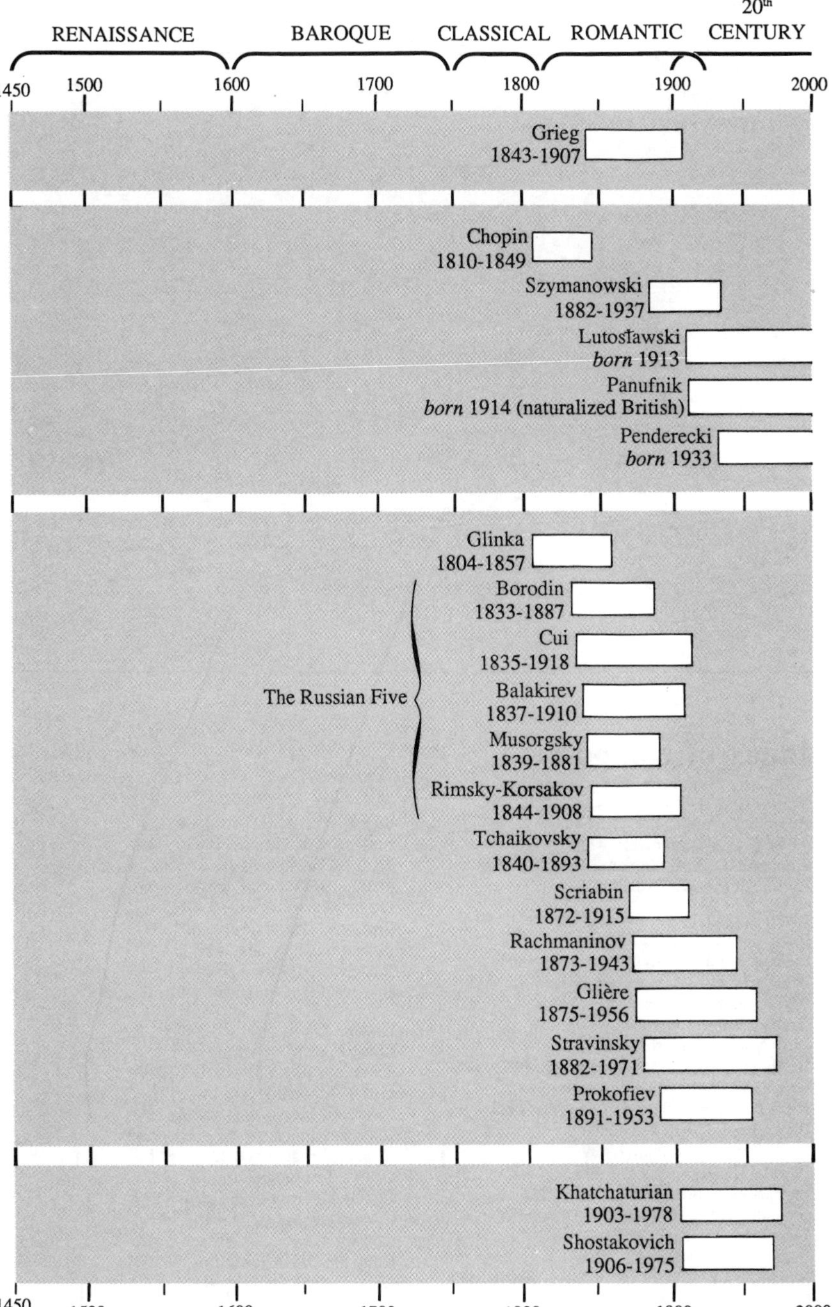
RENAISSANCE
BAROQUE
CLASSICAL
ROMANTIC
20th CENTURY
1450
1500
1600
1700
1800
1900
2000
Grieg 1843-1907
Chopin 1810-1849
Szymanowski 1882-1937
Lutosławski *born* 1913
Panufnik *born* 1914 (naturalized British)
Penderecki *born* 1933
Glinka 1804-1857
The Russian Five
Borodin 1833-1887
Cui 1835-1918
Balakirev 1837-1910
Musorgsky 1839-1881
Rimsky-Korsakov 1844-1908
Tchaikovsky 1840-1893
Scriabin 1872-1915
Rachmaninov 1873-1943
Glière 1875-1956
Stravinsky 1882-1971
Prokofiev 1891-1953
Khatchaturian 1903-1978
Shostakovich 1906-1975

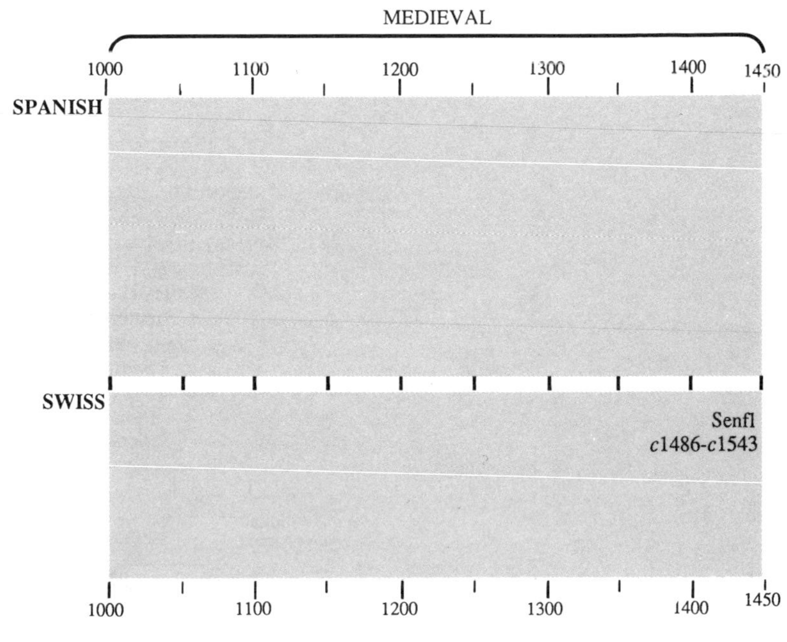

Index of composers

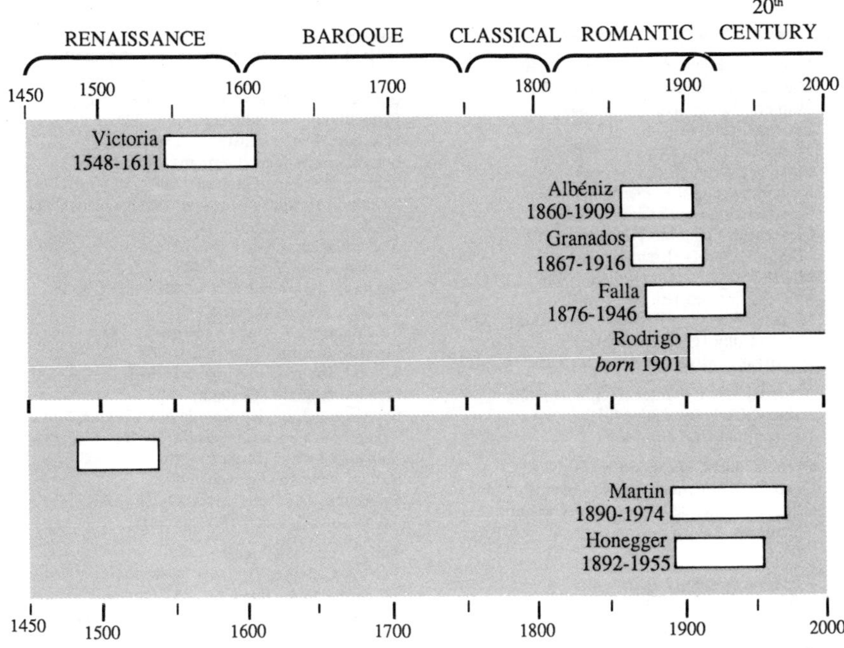

RENAISSANCE
BAROQUE
CLASSICAL
ROMANTIC
20th CENTURY
1450
1500
1600
1700
1800
1900
2000
Victoria 1548-1611
Albéniz 1860-1909
Granados 1867-1916
Falla 1876-1946
Rodrigo born 1901
Martin 1890-1974
Honegger 1892-1955
1450
1500
1600
1700
1800
1900
2000